History of the Hellenic World

PREHISTORY
AND
PROTOHISTORY

History of the Hellenic World

PREHISTORY AND PROTOHISTORY (to 1100 B.C.)

IN PREPARATION

THE ARCHAIC PERIOD (1100 B.C.-479 B.C.)
THE CLASSICAL ERA (in two volumes) (479 B.C.-336 B.C.)
ALEXANDER THE GREAT AND THE HELLENISTIC PERIOD (part I) (336 B.C.-201 B.C.)
THE HELLENISTIC PERIOD (part II) (201 B.C.-30 B.C.)
HELLENISM AND ROME (30 B.C.-A.D. 324)

Further volumes will follow on the Byzantine and modern periods.

History of the Hellenic World

PREHISTORY AND PROTOHISTORY

EKDOTIKE ATHENON S.A., Athens
HEINEMANN, London

Heinemann Educational Books Ltd
LONDON EDINBURGH MELBOURNE AUCKLAND TORONTO
HONG KONG SINGAPORE KUALA LUMPUR
IBADAN NAIROBI JOHANNESBURG
NEW DELHI LUSAKA

ISBN O 435 36600 9

LIBRARY OF CONGRESS CATALOG CARD NUMBER 73-79236

Published in Great Britain by
HEINEMANN EDUCATIONAL BOOKS LTD
48 Charles Street, London WIX 8AH

Printed and Bound in Greece
by
EKDOTIKE HELLADOS S.A.
Athens

PREHISTORY AND PROTOHISTORY

GEORGE A. CHRISTOPOULOS *Publisher & Editor-in-Chief*

JOHN C. BASTIAS *Publisher & Managing Editor*

SUPERVISING COMMITTEE

JOHN N. THEODORAKOPOULOS *Member of the Academy of Athens*

CONSTANTINE D. TSATSOS *Member of the Academy of Athens*

GEORGE E. MYLONAS *Member of the Academy of Athens*

APOSTOLOS E. VACALOPOULOS *Professor of Greek History*

COSTIS J. BASTIAS (1901 - 1972) *Writer*

English translation directed by PHILIP SHERRARD
Editor of the English Edition GEORGE PHYLACTOPOULOS

CONTRIBUTORS

STYLIANOS E. ALEXIOU *Director of the Herakleion Museum*

CHRISTOS G. DOUMAS *Curator of Antiquities*

GEORGE C. HOURMOUZIADES *Curator of Antiquities*

SPYRIDON E. IAKOVIDES *Professor of Prehistoric Archaeology, University of Athens*

VASSOS KARAGEORGHIS *Director of Antiquities, Cyprus*

SPYRIDON N. MARINATOS *Member of the Academy of Athens, General Inspector of Antiquities*

JOHN K. MELENTIS *Professor of Geology and Paleontology, University of Thessalonike*

GEORGE E. MYLONAS *Member of the Academy of Athens, Professor Emeritus, Washington University (St. Louis)*

NICHOLAS E. PLATON *Professor of Prehistoric Archaeology, University of Thessalonike*

JOHN A. SAKELLARAKIS *Curator of Prehistoric Collections, National Archaeological Museum, Athens*

MICHAEL B. SAKELLARIOU *Professor of Greek History, Université de Lyon II*

DEMETRIOS R. THEOCHARIS *Inspector of Antiquities, Thessaly*

MARIA D. THEOCHARIS *Archaeologist*

PREFACE

Greek history, it can be reasonably asserted, represents a rich and venerable capital on which western civilization has drawn generously; furthermore, it embodies many of the generative principles of contemporary culture. Greek antiquity has entered the blood-stream of western civilization and set its seal upon it. It is precisely for these reasons that the western world, steeped in classical tradition and conscious of its origins, has arduously pursued the study of Greek history, producing works monumental in their scope. Yet, Greek history does not end with the classical era. In subsequent centuries the Greeks moulded into the ancient tradition the fermenting ideals of Christianity, and created a new civilization, the Byzantine. The latter evolved in parallel with western civilization, clashed with it during the Crusades, influenced it and in turn was influenced by it. Finally, it made a decisive contribution to the renascence of the ancient tradition in the West, when Byzantium as a political entity was coming to an end. In the following centuries, and despite foreign rule, the Greeks kept alive their separate identity, and based their bid for independent political existence on a synthesis of the ancient and Byzantine traditions, as well as on western ideals. In this instance, the Greeks made a great contribution to the vindication of the principle of nationality.

The aim of the present work is to present all the phases and periods of the history of the Hellenic world and all that this world stands for. Conscious of the great difficulties in store for them, the Greek publishers and scholars that are collaborating in the present venture believe that a work of such a scope is possible; a difficult task and quite taxing, indeed, but all the more rewarding for that. A single work, emcompassing the whole course of Greek history from ancient times to the present day: this is the ambitious aim of the present work. The centuries of Prehistory, the Archaic period, Classical times, the world of Alexander the Great, Hellenistic and Roman times, the world of Byzantium, the centuries of Latin and Ottoman rule, and finally Modern Greece will be treated in their true perspective and significance; yet, the guide will be the striking continuity that pervades all these chronological periods. The strong conviction of the men that undertook this great task is that the tremendous corpus of source material accumulated through the labours of scholars of all times will bear out this continuity. It must be said here that the debt owed to foreign scholarship is not mere mention of acknowledgement; the Greek scholars collabo-

6

rating in this work are only glad to stress that, in their efforts to present an accurate and lively picture of the Hellenic world, they have drawn generously on the vast reservoir of knowledge built up by the generations of both Greek and foreign scholars, adding at the same time their own information and interpretations, the result of years of rigorous study. The fact only that such an array of Greek scholars have been brought together in a collective effort of such a scope is by itself a remarkable achievement.

At this point, a brief explanation is needed with respect to the methods followed in the preparation and presentation of this work. A venture of such a scope, covering a wide range of subjects and drawing upon a vast body of sources, could not have been possibly written by one man alone, and had necessarily to be a collective effort. Greek specialists in every subject and period were brought together to contribute their particular knowledge, while a committee of Academicians and University Professors was set up to coordinate and unite the various contributions into a single whole, filling gaps and eliminating overlaps, and presenting an integrated and free-flowing text to the reader.

The publishers also, in their conviction that Greek history is of interest not only to scholars, have attempted to make this work accessible to the widest possible reading public, without however lowering the stringent standards of scholarship. Moreover, prolific use was made of meticulously chosen illustrations, photographs and reproductions, which supplement the text. Pictures of important sites, inscriptions, monuments, works of art from museums all over the world, many of which have never before been accessible to the wider public, enliven the written word and bring it into sharper focus. In addition, relevant maps, most of them original, elucidate the historical narrative, especially the military operations described. Finally, it must be added that the *History of the Hellenic World* is made up of self-contained units — Prehistory and Protohistory, the Archaic Period, the Classical Era, Alexander the Great and the Hellenistic Period, etc. — which can be acquired and read independently from one another. Each unit does not only relate the political events of the respective period, but presents at the same time an exhaustive account of the contemporary life and culture, such as religion, philosophy, literature, art, science, etc., in special chapters.

TABLE OF CONTENTS

THE STONE AGE IN GREECE

THE BRONZE AGE IN GREECE

THE PEAK
OF MINOAN CIVILIZATION

THE MYCENAEAN CIVILIZATION

NOTE ON TRANSLITERATION

I. Ancient Greek

In this volume, Greek proper names are rendered in English by a standard letter-for-letter system according to the following table:

α = a (Argos)
β = b (Brauron)
γ = g (Gela)
δ = d (Dionysos)
ε = e (Epidauros)
ζ = z (Zakynthos)
η = e (Epeiros)
θ = th (Theseus)
ι = i (Ionia)
κ = k (Karpathos)
λ = l (Lesbos)
μ = m (Melos)
ν = n (Nemea)
ξ = x (Xenophon)
ο = o (Olympos)
π = p (Pentele)
ῥ initial = rh (Rhegion)
ρ medial = r (Paros)
ῤῥ = rrh (Antirrhion)
σ,ς = s (Skopelos); not doubled unless it is double in Greek
τ = t (Taras)
υ after a consonant = y (Πύλος = Pylos)
υ after a vowel = u (Εὔβοια = Euboia)
φ = ph (Phoinike)
χ = ch (Chalkis)
ψ = ps (Psara)
ω = o (Orion)

δασεῖα(ʽ): rough breathing = h (Ἄδης = Hades)

In retaining the Greek spelling, no distinction is made between the *epsilon* and the *eta*, the *omicron* and the *omega*. The *gamma* presents the following peculiarities:

γγ = ng (ἄγγελος = angelos)
γκ = nk (Ἀγκὼν = Ankon)
γχ = nch (Ἀγχίαλος = Anchialos)
γξ = nx (φόρμιγξ = phorminx)

Since the way Greek was pronounced in antiquity is a matter of dispute, this correspondence of letters to sounds may at best be regarded only as an assumed phonetic equivalence. But it does have the merit of consistency and seems to be in line with the usage adopted nowadays by many prominent classical philologists and archaeologists.

A major exception to this practice has been made for patronymics and toponymics which have become established in English in their latinized forms or their anglicized versions.

There are many such words: *Aegean, Aristotle, Athens, Helen, Hesiod*, and *Homer*, to mention only a few; also, *Oedipus, Meander, Phoenix*, and the like, since these too have infiltrated into English under a variety of metaphorical meanings. The following list contains most of the proper names which appear in this volume under their naturalized forms:

Achaian
Achilles
Acropolis
Aegean
Ambracian Gulf
Anatolia
Apollo
Argive
Argolid
Argonaut
Aristotle
Arrian
Asia Minor
Athens
Attica
Atreid
Black Sea (also as Euxine)
Caucasus
Centaur
Cilicia
Constantine
Constantinople
Corfu (also as Korkyra, Kerkyra)
Corinth, but Korinthia
Crete
Cyclades
Cyclop
Cyprus
Danaan
Delphi
Demeter
Dodecanese
Dodona
Dorian
Europa
Euxine
George
Greece
Hebros (also as Evros)
Helen
Hellespont
Heptanese (also as Ionian Islands)
Hermionid
Hesiod
Homer
Ida
Iliad

Ionian
Isthmus
Ithaca (also as Ithake)
John (also as Ioannes)
Libya
Lipari
Luvian
Macedonia
Marmara, Sea of (also as Propontis)
Meander
Megarid
Minyan
Mycenae
Nereid
Nicosia
Nile
Odyssey
Patras
Phoenicia (also as Phoinike)
Pindar
Plato
Plutarch

Priam
Rhodes
Samothrace
Sardica
Sicily
Smyrna
Strabo
Suda
Syracuse
Tarsus (also as Tarsos)
Thebes
Thessaly
Thrace
Thucydides
Troad, Troy, Trojan

Proper names and place-names of the ancient Greek world which have changed form in the course of centuries have on the whole been retained under their original Greek forms rather than under their Roman or later equivalents. Thus, *Akragas, Odysseus, Naupaktos, Halikarnassos* instead of *Agrigentum, Ulysses, Lepanto, Bodrum.*

II. Modern Greek

The application of the letter-for-letter principle to modern Greek presents serious difficulties. ·This is because the orthography of modern Greek has remained virtually unchanged, while its pronunciation has undergone considerable change in the course of time, so that the adoption of the letter-for-letter system would no longer fit the phonetic substance of the modern language.

On the other hand, in a volume such as this, which deals entirely with the ancient world, an attempt to reproduce the sounds of modern Greek in designating ancient localities would disfigure the visual image of the word and obscure its meaning for the classical reader, often beyond recognition.

The adoption of a dual system of transliteration, involving one set of rules for ancient place-names and another set for modern localities, (many of which have retained their ancient names) would be equally unsatisfactory, for it would lead to needless confusion and justified irritation for the reader, who would be constantly called upon to realize that *Imitos* is his familiar *Hymettos, Ipiros* is *Epeiros, Vraona* is

Brauron, Festos is *Phaistos, Evia* is *Euboia,* and that the *Boiotian* Lakes lie in fact in *Viotia.*

For these reasons, modern proper names which have retained their ancient spelling as well as those which are derived from classical stems have been transcribed in this volume in accordance with the orthographic rule adopted for ancient Greek. A concession has been made only in transcribing certain archaeological sites: *Enkomi, Erimi, Franchthi,* and *Saliagos* are the main exceptions.

Even so, since it is impossible to avoid a certain degree of inconsistency, some names in this and subsequent volumes appear under a double spelling. Thus, it is the *Hebros* River in references to the ancient world but the *Evros* in contexts dealing with events in medieval and modern times. Cross references in the Index would eliminate any confusion which the double spellings might cause.

The monistic system of transliteration, adopted for use in this volume, in no way commits the publishers to its continuation in subsequent volumes.

INTRODUCTION

It is a little less than a century ago that the speculations and astonishing discoveries of Heinrich Schliemann opened the way for archaeological research into the prehistorical era of Greek civilization. Today, on the basis of both direct and indirect evidence, we are in a position to form an image of the remotest past: of a world that once belonged to the sphere of mythology. Research and excavations carried out through an area extending from Thrace and Macedonia to Cyprus and Crete have produced a prodigious quantity of objects dated to the Stone and Bronge Ages. The limits that once circumscribed Greek prehistory have thus been enormously extended and, crossing the threshold of our age, it is now possible to enter the vanished world of the Pleistocene. Light has been cast on ages formerly obscure, on unknown periods and phases of time, and the true depths of the prehistory of the country have been revealed.

It is generally accepted that every civilization, even such a brilliant one as that of the Classical era in Greece, must first be regarded as the outcome of tradition. The study of this tradition, without preconceived limits, is therefore imperative. Where Greece is concerned, it is even more imperative. As Carl Blegen, one of the most distinguished scholars in the field of prehistoric Greece, has pointed out, the "Greek-ness" of the Mycenaeans is not without consequence. "The definite recognition of the Mycenaeans as Greeks," he says, "calls for something more than mere passing mention. Let it be an early stage in the history of that race, perhaps before Hellenic speech had yet been fully evolved. Nonetheless it demonstrates the inherent strength of the Greek people and their astonishing power of survival: they still exist and flourish today, retaining their distinctive character, their language, their exclusiveness along with their cohesiveness, despite intense individualism. Apart possibly from the Chinese, there are few, if any, other comparable peoples in their tenacity to endure. In their long history they have at least three times blossomed out into world leadership in culture: in the Late Mycenaean Age, in the Classical period, and in the heyday of the Byzantine Empire."

The decisive argument in favour of this view was the great achievement of Michael Ventris's decipherment of the linear B script. There can be little doubt now that the tablets, with their Greek language, have become almost historical documents thanks to his effort, and offer a definitive basis for the identification of the Hellenic character of the Mycenaean civilization.

The exceptional duration and continuity of the tradition of Greek civilization means we have to go back in time as far as possible in order to discern its roots. Thus, the first part of this volume, under the heading "The Natural Setting", attempts to present the physical and geographical background of the Helladic area, the successive geological transformations and climatic changes, and the place of Greece in the Mediterranean and Near Eastern world. The second part deals with the Stone Age in Greece, the epic and moving story of man fighting an endless struggle for survival in an inhospitable and hostile world. It is the experiences and achievements of man whose only weapon and tool was the stone, of man the hunter

and food-gatherer, and later the timid cultivator of land. From the first Palaeolithic settlements in Thessaly to the Neolithic "Cultures" of Sesklo, Saliagos, and Dimeni, man in Greece had traversed the long and painful distance in time, actually measured in tens of thousands of years, from the state of insecure existence to civilization. Already, the first stirrings of thought had taken shape in the form of organized communal life, a crude understanding of the cycles of life, bewildering as the latter might have been, and artistic expression. Man had in fact surpassed the limitations imposed on him by the natural world and was on the way to mastery of this world and to higher forms of civilization.

In the third part, the initial periods of the Bronze Age are treated. The experiences and achievements of men in mainland Greece, the Cyclades, and Crete are seen both in their characteristic differences and the common features, the local developments and the possible foreign influences. A deserved place is devoted here to the activities and charming world of the Cycladic mariners who furrowed the then known seas in their swift ships, venturing even farther afield, thirsty for adventure and the fruits of commerce. Also treated are contemporary and later developments in Crete such as the first palaces, Minoan writing and art.

The Minoan and Mycenaean civilizations, chronologically the last stages of the Bronze Age in Crete and mainland Greece respectively, follow as the fourth and fifth parts of the volume. This is the dazzling world of New-Palace Crete and Golden Mycenae; of the great palaces of Knosos and Phaistos, to name but the best known; of that highly perfected and wisely balanced politico-religious organization and system of government; of predominance in the sea; and of the various and stupendous manifestations of artistic expression. Also included in the fourth part is the civilization of prehistoric Thera, in fact an open book whose pages are still in the process of being turned by archaeologists to the wonder of modern man. Finally, ample space is devoted to the Mycenaean civilization: the birth of Mycenaean power and the various theories with respect to this controversial topic; the Mycenaean script, whose decipherment established the close links of the Mycenaeans with their successors in the Greek lands; the centuries of Achaian supremacy and expansion; religion and art, and finally the presence and influence of the Mycenaeans in Crete and Cyprus, which irrevocably linked the latter to the fate and experiences of mainland Greece for ages to come.

The closing part is devoted to the linguistic and ethnic groups that settled and evolved in the Greek lands from the dawn of prehistory onwards. It is in fact the theme which, along with the overpowering Mycenaean experience, linked the prehistoric part with historical times. The Greeks of the Archaic Period —the subject of the next volume in the series—would search for their heroes and gods in the dim past, and were to use the tongues and dialects that had evolved in prehistoric times. As a whole, and in view of later developments in the Greek lands, Greek Prehistory and Protohistory is the necessary starting point for the study and understanding of subsequent Greek history.

The Natural Setting

THE SEA AND THE LAND

The purpose of this work is to relate the dramatic history of man in the Hellenic world from prehistoric times to the present day. But no drama can be enacted without a stage. In this case, the stage is Greece and its environment, and it is these that have mainly affected the course of events on the historical plane. Hence this narration must start with a description of the land and its environment—of the physical and geographical framework—before going on to speak of man and his historical development.

The Birth of the Aegean Land Mass

Hundreds of millions of years ago, Greece lay submerged under the sea. Its geological forms have undergone—and will indeed continue to undergo—numerous transformations in accordance with the laws of immutable change: for "everything flows", as Herakleitos once said.

The sea-bed, which extended across the whole of what is now Greece, from the Ionian Sea to Asia Minor, presented a strange aspect: where the massif of the Pindos range now rises there was a deep underwater channel, the "Pindos ditch". West of it extended another channel, the "Ionian ditch". The two channels were separated by a high barrier, the "hump of Gabrovo".

The sea-bed had acquired these forms by the beginning of the Mesozoic Era, that is to say, over 180 million years ago. It was to retain this aspect for another 150 million years—until the Oligocene. During this unimaginably long period, the two channels of the sea-bed were filled with deposits formed either by a process of erosion of distant land masses or by the accumulation of sea shells and husks of small living organisms which, when they died, fell in a continuous shower on the sea-bed and settled there.

In the meantime, at the beginning of the Cretaceous Period, 140 million years ago, a gigantic mountain-building convulsion thrust the so-called Pelagonian chain above the surface of the sea. The range consisted of a narrow strip of land which included the northernmost part of Macedonia (Pelagonia), Mt. Olympos, eastern Thessaly, and northern Euboia. The so-called "Attic-Cycladic" mass, namely Attica, southern Euboia, and most of the Cyclades, is believed to be an extention of this mountain chain.

About 35 million years ago, when the Pindos channel was filled with deposits, further cosmogonic disturbances occurred in the interior of the earth. As a result of a very strong upward thrust, the composition of the channel assumed the shape of a series of folds which rose above the sea, forming the great Pindos range. This period corresponds to that of the formation of the alpine seams and of the emergence of the world's highest massifs, including the Himalayas, the Alps, and the Pyrenees.

After many million years, the "Ionian ditch", like the Pindos channel before it, was silted up with materials formed in the course of geological upheavals, which accompanied the disintegration of the Gabrovo mountain chain. At the beginning of the Miocene, a further tectonic disturbance caused the sea-bed to rise. Furrowed with seams, it emerged above the sea level, forming the largest section of western Greece. The once submerged *Aigaiis* (Aegean land mass) had now acquired the form of an unbroken uniform mass of land, corresponding approximately to the present extent of Greek territory between the Ionian Sea and Asia Minor and Crete. Amidst successive geological upheavals and the endless struggle between land and sea, life had meanwhile appeared in this restless world. Thirteen million years ago, vertebrate monsters roamed the slopes of the Aigaiis, now covered with vegetation.

The Submersion

Geological upheavals, however, did not come to an end with the formation of the Aigaiis. Another period of change in the geological evolution of the country, a very important phase lasting several million years, set in. It was during this phase that the continental mass of the Aigaiis began to be broken up, the Mediterranean Sea advancing into the interior of the land and submerging large sections of it.

The Aigaiis naturally did not constitute a uniform land mass. About 18 million years ago, during the Middle Miocene, it included high mountain ranges, but also deep hollow troughs and inland lakes. A large lake extended across central Thessaly, the Northern Sporades, and north-east Euboia. Other lakes lay east of Skyros and, to the south, between Andros and Chios.

The sea advanced slowly but relentlessly into the interior of the land. Following a number of tectonic breaches, the Mediterranean penetrated into the region between Crete and the Dodecanese. The southern and eastern parts of Crete had not yet surfaced; and sea covered Corfu, the west coast of Epeiros, Leukas, and the western parts of Kephallenia and Zakynthos.

After another six million years, the penetration of the Mediterranean into the hinterland of the Aigaiis was still in progress. At the beginning of the Pliocene, about 12 million years ago, the Ionian Islands broke off from the land mass and thrust their rocky summits above a sea which covered the western part of Elis, western Achaia as far as Patras,

the plain of Achaia, and the Lakonian Gulf.

Later, corrosion created the valleys of the Hellespont and the Bosporos. Through these two valleys the waters of the Caspian-Pontic and Propontic basins (i.e. the Caspian and the Black Seas and the Sea of Marmara) made their way to form one large central river, the Aigaios River, into which its tributaries, the Axios, the Strymon, the Evros (Hebros), etc., also poured their waters.

At the end of the Pliocene, about two million years ago, an arm of the Mediterranean advanced from east of Crete towards the Propontis; another arm rushed into the gap between Crete and the Peloponnesos (an area corresponding roughly to the present Myrtoan Sea), reached the periphery of Athens, and thence advanced through the southernmost part of Attica and Euboia to the Northern Sporades and the Thermaic Gulf. These maritime inroads into the land mass constitute the beginning of the formation of the Aegean Sea.

The Period of the Lakes

During the Pliocene, 12 million to 2 million years ago, large lakes extended across the hollows of the Aigaiis. The largest was that which we now call the Cretan Sea, north of the island itself. Smaller lakes began to form north and east of the Sporades and east of Euboia. The banks of some of these lakes, including the Corinthian, Megarean, and Elean, as well as the Argolic, were not solid. They consequently filled with sea and became saline. On the other hand, the inland lakes, whose banks were firmer and did not suffer from the erosion caused by the endless friction of waves, contained fresh water for a greater length of time. Hinterland lakes of this kind included the valley of the Eurotas, the plains of Megalopolis and Lokris, and the whole of Thessaly (before the land barrier was breached by the Vale of Tempe).

Meanwhile geological disturbances continued. Parts of the Aigaiis were carved up, others inundated; many tracts of land disappeared into the sea, others rose above the water level. The Mediterranean advanced into the Corinthian lake from the Rhion-Antirrhion narrows and formed the present gulf. The isthmus of Corinth emerged, the north side of the Corinthian lake subsided, and the abrupt coastline of Boiotia and Phokis thrust upwards. The northern part of the Peloponnesos rose above the sea, the coasts of the Argolic peninsula were submerged, and Aigina was separated from the mainland. The sea in the Ionian receded, the islands grew larger, and the land areas of Elis, Messenia, and Lakonia solidified. In the east part of the Aigaiis, a vast lake was formed between Euboia and Asia Minor; in the midst of it, Skyros and Lesbos could be distinguished. By the end

19

of the Pliocene, the outlines of the relief were apparent, and the general configuration of the country had been formed.

The Island World

The definitive shape of the land masses did not, however, become wholly apparent until the Pleistocene. Further geological changes and geographical displacements, now on a relatively small scale, accompanied by a repeated rise and fall in the level of the sea and by periods of sharp fluctuation in temperature, characterized this age, which lasted hundreds of millennia (between 2 million and 10,000 years). This is the Glacial Age. More important, it is the period in which man first appears on the stage of world history.

Several inland lakes disappeared entirely during the Pleistocene: namely, those of Megalopolis, the Eurotas, central Greece, and Thessaly. On the other hand, some of the lakes extending across the area between the Cyclades and the northern Aegean united into a single lake, although this did not yet link up with the Cretan Sea.

Successive submersions occurred in the eastern section of the Aigaiis. At first, the sea penetrated the narrow breach between Kythera and Crete and later poured through the wider one between Crete and the Dodecanese and the gap between Andros and the promontory of Kaphereus. Advancing north-east, it flooded the valleys of the Hellespont and the Bosporos, as well as the Black Sea basin. The northern and southern Aegean basins were thus formed. An underwater chain, whose peaks were ultimately to emerge as the numerous islands of the Cyclades, extended between the two basins.

With the stabilization of the land masses, the formation of Greece can be said to have been definitely completed. Nevertheless, the sea level continued to undergo numerous fluctuations, which affected the configuration of the coastline. In the course of a period of extreme cold during one of the Glacial Ages, the Aegean and Ionian Seas were deprived of immense bodies of water, and the level of the sea fell by 100 to 200 metres. Fluctuations in the sea level had important repercussions. Almost all the Cyclades emerged from the sea in the form of a uniform land mass. Crete and the Peloponnesos were probably linked by a natural causeway passing through Kythera and Antikythera. The Northern Sporades were joined to Thessaly. The Thermaic Gulf was hardly formed, while Thasos and Chios were united with the mainland. The Pagasitic and Ambracian Gulfs and the Euboian Channel had not yet been formed. Corfu was joined to Epeiros, Euboia to Attica.

As one millennium succeeded another, the transformation of the land continued. The disintegration of mountain masses as a result of wind and rain, accompanied by changes in temperature and humidity, affected the general configuration. The level of the mountain ranges was lowered, and the deposits created by disintegration were carried down by rivers and torrents to the sea and into enclosed basins and valleys, such as those of Thessaly and Boiotia. This process led to the creation of a fertile soil which ultimately provided suitable land for the settlement of the first man. Loam, clay, sand, conglomerate, sandstone, the familiar reddish-brown soil, and numerous sedimentary rocks were thus formed.

Earthquakes and volcanic action also contributed to the definitive shape of the land. Alone among Mediterranean countries, Greece and Italy are subject to volcanic action, mainly along the coasts and in the islands. As a result of the fissures caused by tectonic disturbances, the earth's crust failed to solidify in these areas. Magma fluids were consequently spewed up from the bowels of the earth. The most important Greek volcanoes—those of Aigina, Methana, Poros, Melos, Kimolos, Polyaigos, Pholegandros, Thera, Nisyros, and Kos—formed a crescent of volcanic activity around the southern base of submerged land. Deep fissures in the northern Aegean led to the emergence of the volcanoes of the Troad, of Lesbos, and probably of Chios, all of which were situated within the same volcanic belt. Another volcanic crescent, similar to that of the southern Aegean, extended farther north. It included the volcanoes of Oxylithos (Kyme), Lemnos, Imbros, Samothrace, and Thracian Pherai. All these volcanoes provided a valuable supply of minerals which have been of service to man since prehistoric times.

From a historical point of view the most important volcano in Greece is that of Thera (Santorini). It is also probably the most interesting volcanic complex in the world. The present configuration of the island is the result of geological changes which began at a very early period. Following the carving up of the Aigaiis and the submergence of large tracts of land, a rocky islet, whose situation corresponded roughly to that of the present Mt. Prophetes Elias and Pyrgos, was all that remained of Thera. The first eruption

THE AGE OF THE EARTH AND OF MAN

TIME	GEOLOGICAL PERIOD	TEMPERATURE	CULTURAL PERIOD	MAN
×1000 yrs 10.5	HOLOCENE		BRONZE AGE NEOLITHIC MESOLITHIC	HOMO SAPIENS
12 35 75 100	UPPER PLEISTOCENE	IV 3 2 1	LATE PALAEOLITHIC — MIDDLE PALAEOLITHIC	NEANDERTHAL
120 200 300 320 400	MIDDLE PLEISTOCENE	III 2 1 B	EARLY PALAEOLITHIC	HOMO ERECTUS
500 600 1000	LOWER PLEISTOCENE	II 2 1 A 2 1		HOMO HABILIS

The geological and climatological development of the earth and the evolution of man and his progress towards civilization from the Lower Pleistocene, one million years ago, to the present day. The blue sections of the curved line indicate the peak periods of the Glacial Ages, the red ones the intervals of warm weather. Man first appeared in Greece during the last Inter-Glacial Period.

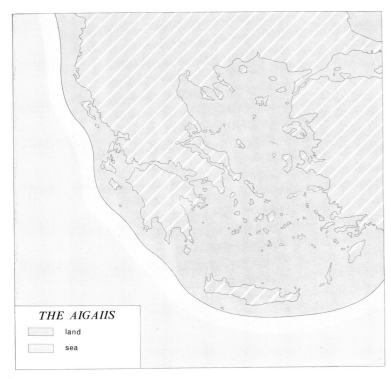

THE AIGAIIS

- land
- sea

GREEK LANDS DURING THE PLIOCENE

- sea
- land
- lakes

The Greek lands rose from the sea about 30 million years ago. The Aigaiis (left) consisted of a solid mass of land extending from the Ionian Sea to Asia Minor and the southern coast of Crete. Five million years ago, large tracts of land subsided, emerging again in different forms (right); the Mediterranean poured into the breaches, and inland lakes were formed. Below: Greece 400,000 years ago, when the level of the sea was 200 m. lower than it is today.

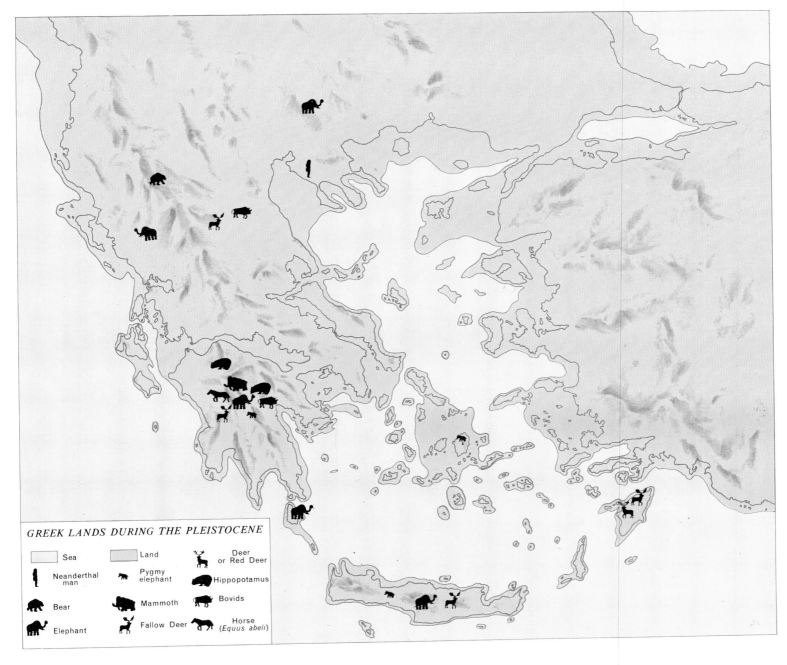

GREEK LANDS DURING THE PLEISTOCENE

- Sea
- Land
- Neanderthal man
- Pygmy elephant
- Bear
- Mammoth
- Elephant
- Fallow Deer
- Deer or Red Deer
- Hippopotamus
- Bovids
- Horse (*Equus abeli*)

on this island is dated to the period beginning about 26 million years ago and ending 13 million years ago.

The materials thrown up in the course of eruptions by the volcanic centres of Thera, Peristeria, Semanteri, Skaros, and Therasia formed a new island, Strongyle. Imagination alone can conjure up the scene: an imposing volcanic cone, one thousand metres high, with a crater on the summit and smaller ones at the sides; lava discharged intermittently from the craters flowing in a molten stream down to the sea. Basing their deductions on volcanic material settled on the sea-bed of the eastern basin of the Mediterranean, scientists believe that the first major eruption took place about 25,000 years ago, that is, towards the end of the Pleistocene. It was followed by further destructive eruptions. In c. 1500 B.C. practically the whole island was blown sky-high, and volcanic ashes rained down on places as far away as Crete and Sicily.

The Pine-Woods of the Aigaiis

Sparse vegetation covered the hills of the Aigaiis. Impressions left by leaves and specimens of fossils and polliniferous fruits found in the lignite deposits of Kyme in Euboia have enabled scientists to identify vestiges of an extremely ancient flora, which is for the most part assigned to the Miocene, a period 26 to 13 million years ago.

The vegetation consisted of trees and shrubs of a South African and Australasian type: conifers, acorn-bearing shrubs, as well as laurels, myrtles, mulberries, heather, and roses. None of these, however, possessed features similar to those of their present day equivalents. Nor is there any trace of the existence of grasses or ferns.

The sparse forests, extending over a hilly sun-drenched countryside with a dry soil, unbroken by gulleys or rivers, characterized the Aigaiis of that period. According to the evidence of the lignite deposits of Kyme, conifers—pines in particular—must have prevailed throughout the country during the Pleistocene, between 2 million and 10,000 years ago. Scarcely any other trace of the ancient flora of the country has been found. A methodical study of Greek flora of the Pleistocene began only a few years ago; detailed documentation of results so far obtained is consequently still somewhat limited. But there is no doubt that the plants that grew on Greek soil during this period were similar to the flora of other countries in the same geographical latitude. Since climate partially determines the nature of the flora of a country, it may be assumed that the flora of Greece consisted of tropical vegetation during the warm seasons of the Pleistocene, of steppe and tundra-like vegetation during cold periods.

The Pikermian Fauna

Dinotheres (gigantic animals of a height of four metres), mastodons (progenitors of elephants), rhinoceros, sabretooths (*Machairodus*), lions, giraffes, hyenas, apes, antelopes, dogs, deer, pigs, birds, and tortoises existed in Greece 13 million years ago, a period prior to the emergence of man.

An accumulation of fossilized remains of various members of this animal kingdom was discovered in the most extraordinary circumstances in the region of Pikermi, Attica, a few kilometres north-east of Athens. In 1838, a Bavarian soldier, crossing the gulley of the Megalo Rema,

which winds down to the Euboian Gulf near Raphena, happened to come across a fossilized bone, the hollow of which was filled with glistening crystals. Believing these to be diamonds, he hastened to remove his "treasure" to Germany. There he was informed by experts that the crystals were valueless calcite, formed in the fossilized lower jaw of an ape which had lived about 13 million years ago. The discovery was one of incalculable value to scientists.

Between 1839 and 1912 the gulley was excavated to a depth of between three and nine metres. A series of investigations was undertaken, and a vast quantity of skeletons of vertebrate animals was discovered: The finds, now exhibited in various palaeontological museums (including that of Athens University), brought to light the wonderful so-called *Pikermian fauna*, which provides us with a picture of the Greek animal world of 13 million years ago.

A number of questions was inevitably raised. Why should such a large quantity of animal remains (estimated to derive from fifty-three different species) be concentrated in a narrow gulley at Pikermi? Did they live in entirely different regions? Why should herbivorous and carnivorous beasts, proboscidiferous animals and forest antelopes, ostriches, and giraffes of the wide open spaces and cave-dwelling carnivora and rodents, all be found in the same place? Many conjectures have been made and theories advanced, some of a completely non-scientific nature, in order to elucidate the mystery.

Some scientists believe that a terrifying prehistoric cataclysm of a highly dramatic nature took place at Pikermi as a result of cosmogenetic disturbances in the Aigaiis. This is thought to have caused a subsidence of the land and a consequent inrush of the sea, forcing the panic-stricken

beasts to assemble in certain specific areas, such as Attica. Here they were destroyed, and their corpses were borne by floods to the Megalo Rema, in which they were buried under several layers of light red clay. Others support the theory that the catastrophe was neither sudden nor localized. The skeletons or corpses, they maintain, were swept across long distances and concentrated in what was a river bed, or the bottom of a lake, or a shallow bay. There they remained until they were fossilized. Yet others argue that the mass destruction of the animals was brought about by lack of fodder and water, resulting from radical changes, such as the drying up of lakes and the disappearance of vegetation.

The view held by O. Abel, an Austrian professor and one of the leading excavators at Pikermi, is a different and indeed a more acceptable one. He believes that a sudden fire, catastrophic in its proportions, caused either by lightning or as a result of a prolonged drought, broke out on the slopes of Mt. Pentele, where these herds of animals roamed. The fire spread across the whole of Attica, leaving nothing but desolation in its wake. Choked by clouds of smoke, scorched by flames fanned by winds, the panic-stricken animals stampeded across the country and fell headlong over the precipice at Pikermi. Abel bases his theory on the fact that the bones of the extremities of many of the animals, in particular of those that belonged to herds, reveal fractures, as though the beasts had fallen from a considerable height.

The most common and characteristic beast of the Pikermian fauna is the small pony, both the so-called Mediterranean *hipparion* and the "short-legged" pony, which had three-toed feet and whose height was 1.30 m. Steppe-country is the usual habitat of the Pikermi animals which, according to zoologists, were of Asiatic provenance. Similar remains of skeletons have been found in Samos, in the Halmyropotamos stream in Euboia, in Thessaly, and around Thessalonike. Farther north, their traces extend through Serbia to places as distant as England and Spain.

The Elephants of Megalopolis

The most comprehensive picture of the Greek animal world of a much later age is provided by the fossilized bones of elephants and other animals which dwelt in the Megalopolis basin during the Pleistocene, which began two million years ago.

In 1902 a woodcutter of Isioma, which is situated on the foothills of Mt. Lykaion at the south-west end of the plain of Megalopolis, descended a steep neighbouring ravine in search of an axe he had lost. In the course of his search, he observed some enormous bones, not unlike the roots of plane trees, in the torrent bed. This chance event led to the discovery of the extraordinary *Pleistocene fauna of Megalopolis*. Within a few months Professor Skoufos began excavating, and five tons of fossilized skeletons, representing a mine of scientific material, were removed to the Palaeontological Museum of Athens University.

Hundreds of thousands of years ago, the Megalopolis basin was a shallow lake bordered by luxuriant vegetation, among which roamed herbivorous animals. Later, the waters forced an outlet towards the sea through the gorge of Karytaina, the lake was drained, and the animals perished. In time the Alpheios and its tributaries caused considerable erosion of the soil—a geological process that was to render the ultimate discovery of the fossilized skeletons possible.

Thirteen million years ago, Pikermi in Attica was the haunt of gigantic dinotheres, lions, and rhinoceros; 200,000 years ago, hippopotami and elephants dwelt in the Megalopolis basin. Left: excavations carried out in the ravine of Pikermi in 1912. The three strata at which the bones of animals were discovered are clearly visible. Right: the enormous fossilized elephant tusk discovered at Isioma near Megalopolis in the course of excavations in 1902. (Photograph by Professor Skoufos)

The discovery of Palaeolithic tools, together with fossilized bones of animals on the banks of the Peneios River, indicates *that there must have been some form of cohabitation of men and animals.*

The fossilized bones had indeed fired the imagination of the peoples of antiquity. Their immense size aroused popular curiosity and provided material for the fabrication of numerous myths. Pausanias, for instance, in his description of Arkadia, says: "Here are also kept bones, too big for those of a human being, about which the story ran that they were those of one of the giants mustered by Hopladamos to fight for Rhea..." In attempting to explain the phenomenon of these prodigious skeletons, popular imagination was naturally haunted—not only here, but in Thessaly too—by ancient legends about giants.

Research into the origins of fossilized skeletons revealed that two different species of mammals inhabited the banks of the lake of Megalopolis: one consisted of animals (elephants, deer, forest-dwelling rhinoceros, hippopotami, horses) which dwelt in a warm climate amid luxuriant vegetation;

the other, of animals (mammoths, bison, and woolly rhinoceros) accustomed to cold temperatures and even ice-covered stretches, where the vegetation resembled that of steppe and tundra countries.

The fact that the two categories of skeletons were found at different strata would seem to indicate that the mammals dwelt in the same locality, but at different periods and under different climatic conditions. The discovery of the skeletons of the Megalopolis basin, therefore, proved that the climate of southern Greece underwent many changes during the Pleistocene. Scientists have in fact identified four Glacial Ages and three Inter-Glacial Periods. Because of the ice-drifts down to southern regions, the vegetation was sparse and stunted during the Glacial Ages. The types of animals capable of existing in such low temperatures were naturally restricted. On the other hand, the rich vegetation which flourished in a warm humid climate during the Inter-Glacial Periods favoured the existence of a greater variety of animals.

Careful study has been devoted to the animal kingdom of Megalopolis. The different species of beasts have been classified, the most common of these being the elephant, of which the earliest specimen was the "southern elephant" (*Archidiscodon meridionalis*), a monster of African origin, four metres in height, with very strong, somewhat curved, tusks two and a half metres long. This animal lived at the beginning of the Pleistocene in the Mediterranean area. After this, is the "ancient elephant" (*Palaeoloxodon antiquus*); its height was the same, but it had straighter and thinner tusks about three metres long. Then comes the mammoth, the primeval elephant (*Mammonteus primigenius*), a creature of the last Glacial Period, which began 70,000 years ago at Megalopolis and elsewhere, notably Thessaly.

Only one species of hippopotamus was found at Megalopolis: the *Hippopotamus antiquus*. The rhinoceros, however, is represented by three species. The first two were forest-dwellers and almost hairless. Megalopolis is the southernmost point in the world in which the existence of the woolly rhinoceros has been identified. Other specimens of this animal have been found in ice-bound Siberia and Poland, where they were in such a remarkable state of preservation that even their skin and hair were retained. The Megalopolis basin was also the home of the "progenitor ox" (*Bos primigenius*), a kind of bull encountered in Minoan Crete, and the fallow deer (*Dama*), a species of small-bodied deer with wide antlers, which survives to this day in Rhodes. A species of large-bodied horse, 1.80 m. in height, anatomically not altogether dissimilar to its modern counterpart, also dwelt around Megalopolis during the last Inter-Glacial Period, about 100,000 years ago. The only carnivorous animal was the hyena. Fossilized bones of pigs, beavers, reptiles, and birds were also discovered.

Thessaly : 100,000 Years Ago

The animal world found in the Megalopolis basin has also been identified in more northerly areas of Greece—in the Kozane and Grevena basins, at Drama—and, to the south, even in Crete. Moreover, numerous fossilized bones of animals, mainly mammals, were discovered in Thessaly on the banks of the Peneios, near Larisa. The latter are, however, of a later date and should be assigned to the last Inter-Glacial and the beginning of the last Glacial Age, about 100,000 to 70,000 years ago. No animals that thrive in a cold climate were found in Thessaly. It can therefore be assumed that the animals of the Peneios valley dwelt in a warm climate and that the environment included wooded areas and tracts of steppes covered with low scrub.

The fossilized remains in the Peneios valley were discovered either together with palaeolithic flints or at strata of the same general age as the palaeolithic implements. This is an important point, for it confirms the theory that there was some form of cohabitation between men and animals in the Thessalian basin one hundred thousand years ago. Some of the fossilized remains in Thessaly reveal traces of having been worked by human hands. It is possible that they served as tools or weapons, such as clubs and points.

A state of mutual interdependence and interchange of influences between men and animals in the valley of the Peneios is thus verified. If human activities influenced animals, man too was influenced by the activity of animals, on whose existence he remained directly dependent. Remains of the so-called cave bear (*Ursus spelaeus*) found in a cave of Agrapha, south of Thessaly, suggest that this animal probably played an important part in the survival of man in Thessaly. In winter, he would have hunted the bear fearlessly in caves, when the animal was hibernating, and would have provided himself with a rich supply of food.

The Cave of the First Man

The fossilized remains of animals discovered in the cave of Petralona in the Chalkidike Peninsula have attracted much attention, for among them was the only skull of a palaeolithic man of the Neanderthal type identified in Greece. There were few animal bones, and these appear to belong to the same type of beasts as those which roamed the Thessalian basin over 120,000 to 50,000 years ago during the last Inter-Glacial and the beginning of the last Glacial Age. No elephants, of course, dwelt here, but the presence of a certain kind of woolly rhinoceros (*Rhinoceros antiquitatis*) points to a warm climate, confirmed by remains of other animals, including the *Equus caballus*, the *Cervus elaphus*, and the fallow deer (*Dama*). On the other hand, the wild mule of the steppes and the alpine dog (*Canis alpinus*) indicate a somewhat colder climate. Here again we are confronted with evidence that animals accustomed to a warm climate co-existed with certain types that adapt easily to a cold one. And as the animals do not appear to have been unconnected with the Neanderthal skull, the remains of the Petralona cave may be dated to a period of 75,000 to 70,000 years ago, although more recent research may tend to alter this conclusion.

Important zoological remains of the Upper Pleistocene have been identified in other caves: bones of rhinoceros, bears, and members of the deer family at the lower strata of the cave or rock shelter of Asprochaliko in the Louros valley in Epeiros; bones of animals common to the end of the Pleistocene at the higher strata of the same cave, as well as in the rock shelter of Kastritsa, in caves of Seidi in Boiotia and Franchthi in the north-east Peloponnesos. The proportion of various species of the deer family in these caves is a large one. Here, for the first time, we find the wild goat (*Capra aegagrus*), which likes a cold climate, besides the more familiar bovidae, bear, mule, and deer.

Scientists have discerned many points of similarity between these animals and those of the same period discovered in the Romanelli cave in Apulia, Southern Italy. It is consequently assumed that climatic conditions in Italy and Greece were roughly identical during the Upper Pleistocene, since both countries, together with the Southern Balkans, were situated in the same geographical latitude, that is to say, in the relatively favourable Periglacial Zone. More important is the fact that both regions possessed characteristics of a typical Mediterranean milieu. It must therefore be assumed that migratory animals found ideal winter quarters in Greece. A north-south movement to the more temperate Greek lands seems very probable. There is no doubt that the migration of animals to southern areas had an effect on human existence at that time.

GREECE IN THE MEDITERRANEAN
The Geographical Basis

Europe meets Asia at the point where the south-east tip of the Balkans advances towards the western projection of the Anatolian peninsula. This point of junction is one of the most important geographical linch-pins in the world. The features which unite the two continents are more apparent than those which separate them geographically, such as the Bosporos, the Propontis, the Hellespont, and the Aegean Sea with its bridge of islands stretching from shore to shore.

Organically united, the Greek peninsula and Asia Minor belong to the same wider geographical unit of the Middle East. From a geophysical point of view, this wider area is considered to be the most favourable area of the ancient world. The deep inroads made by the sea into the land mass, the various forms assumed by the coastline and, above all, the unparalleled variety of geographical and climatic features and conditions contribute to provide this part of the world, where the continents of Europe, Asia and Africa meet, with a particularly distinctive character.

In a unique synthesis of contrasts, every kind of geographical and climatic feature is represented in an area extending from the Eastern Mediterranean across the Propontis and the Black Sea to the Caspian, the Persian Gulf, and the Red Sea: from frozen steppes to scorching deserts, from the melancholy banks of the Caspian to the sun-drenched islands of Greece, from Alpine massifs and lowlands to large plains and small enclosed valleys. The warm temperate climate of the Mediterranean and an impressively variegated rainfall, vegetation, and fauna prevail throughout the greater part. But the most important aspect of the Near and Middle East, in so far as their history and geography are concerned, is the fact that they were the cradle of the most brilliant civilizations of antiquity. Consequently, from the point of view of its impact on civilization, the Mediterranean may well be considered the most important sea in the world. This womb-like basin, formed by the contours of three continents, can be compared to a vast oasis. Its influence on the climate of peripheral lands has been great; its role in blending diverging cross-currents, in moderating the violence of contrasts, in creating new entities, is of even greater significance.

Although it is not a rich region, its mildness and beauty were to exert their attraction on man. The ideal climate, which tends to make life so agreeable throughout the Mediterranean area, compensates for the somewhat restricted physical resources. Nowhere in the world is the climate more genial than along the narrow band of continuous coastline, easily identified by the growth of that most venerable and typically Mediterranean of trees, the olive. The influence of the sea is not, however, confined to the coastal areas. It penetrates deep inland, more in the peninsulas than in the large solid tracts of land. And it is in Greece that the variety and synthesis of contrast, so characteristic of the Mediterranean, are most evident. The western and the eastern basins of the Mediterranean present two very different pictures. The Iberian peninsula is a compact land mass, the Italian a long slender projection, the Greek a configuration of exceptional variety. Beyond the eastern basin extends the vast continent of Asia; beyond the western, only the ocean.

Greece is situated at the point where the central and eastern basins of the Mediterranean unite. Geographically, the country joins Europe with Asia; climatically, it lies midway between Mesopotamia and Italy. It possesses Mediterranean and European features but no Asiatic ones. The striking contrast between Western Asia and the rest of the continent seems to produce an effect of thrusting the Near East westward across the Mediterranean towards Europe. Western Asia Minor and, in particular, the coastal fringe extending from the Bosporos to the foothills of the Tauros do not in the least differ, either geophysically or climatically, from Greece. The coastline is almost equally indented, accented by the string of islands of the eastern shore of the Aegean; the oreographical distribution is almost identical, with slightly lower altitudes and numerous narrow valleys

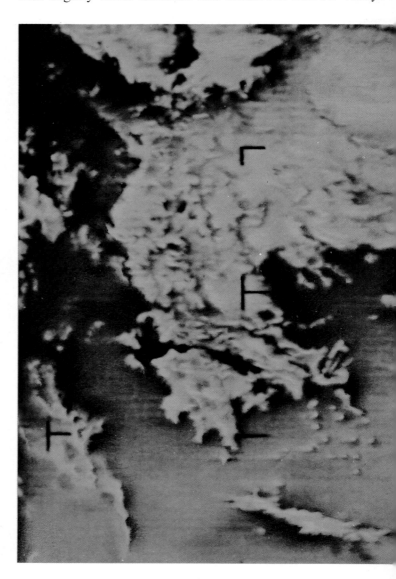

The Greek lands as represented in a photograph taken by the American satellite Nimbus *in 1964. Situated at the point of junction between Europe and Asia, Greece combines all the typical features of this region of the Mediterranean, the most important sea in*

terminating in gulfs. The valleys of the Hermos and the Meander, destined to develop into important highways to the Aegean, emphasize the contrast between the coastal areas and the interior plateaus where an altogether different way of life developed. Research has revealed the southern part of the Asia Minor plateau to have been one of the most important centres of early civilization and a rich source of creative energy and human resources. It was therefore natural that this, as it were geographical, centrifugal force should influence developments in the Aigaiis from the dawn of prehistory.

To the north, the Greek lands extend from the Akrokeraunia to Constantinople. They include the west coast of Asia Minor, the Ionian and Aegean Islands, Crete, Rhodes, and Cyprus. Although no longer possessing any relation to the frontiers of the Greek State of today, this area nevertheless constitutes the wide framework within which Hellenism was able to develop and to extend farther afield: across the Mediterranean, the Black Sea, and to the East.

The centre of these lands consisted of Central Greece, the Peloponnesos, the islands of the Aegean, and Crete. It is therefore appropriate to review more comprehensively the geographical elements of this particular part of the Greek lands. It has always possessed a typically highland character, from the time when the alpine seams were originally formed and the Pindos range—a veritable spinal column occupying the whole of the north-west side of the area in question—first raised its peaks above the country. The range continues through the Peloponnesian mountains, Crete, and Rhodes towards Asia Minor, where it terminates in the Tauros and the Antitauros mountains.

The fact that four fifths of the country are, in effect, mountainous or semi-mountainous played a decisive part in determining the distribution of the population: not unnaturally it concentrated in the plains and coastal regions. But although the mountain ranges traverse the country in parallel lines, mainly in a NW-SE axis, they sometimes intersect each other, curve round tablelands and enclose hollow basins, form and isolate numerous small valleys and cut up narrow bands of level ground and hilly coastal areas. They thus provide the relief with a restless and variform aspect not encountered in any other part of the Mediterranean. Countless little plateaux and valleys, bays and gulfs of varying size, innumerable islands dotted about the Aegean, a few plains and many hills, cultivated slopes and abrupt or dentillated coastlines, deep ravines and gentle declivities of olive groves and vineyards—all these compose the astonishingly beautiful picture of the Greek landscape.

Constant change and variety of form constitute its most distinctive features. There are also some striking contrasts. Nothing could be more different than the western from the eastern part of the mainland, than Attica from Akarnania, than the Thessalian plain from the Arkadian highlands, than the parched Argolid from verdant Messenia, than the maze-like Chalkidike from Aegean Thrace. Two elements predominate throughout: mountains and sea. The height of at least twenty mountains exceeds 2000 metres, above which extends the snow belt. Mt. Olympos (2915 metres), majestic and "radiant", home of the ancient Greek gods, forms part of the main continental mass, thrusting its peaks skywards at a distance of only twenty kilometres from the coast. In the Southern Peloponnesos, the summit of the imposing Taygetos range (2409 m.) is no more than thirteen kilometres from the sea. From the Rhodope range (2923 m.) in the far north, where the winds, according to Homer, go "back again to betake them home over the Thracian main", to the Cretan Mt. Ida (2457 m.), "many-fountained... mother of wild beasts", as the poet describes it in the *Iliad*, mountains tower above the cloudless horizon, as though set in some magical stage design. There is not a mountain from which the sea is not visible. At no point is the land more than 100 kilometres from the coast; in Central Greece this distance is reduced to 60 kilometres, in the Peloponnesos to 50. This interplay between mountains and sea gives the Greek landscape a very special quality.

The confined nature of the land, the disjointed forms of the mountain ranges, and the sudden torrential rain-showers do not contribute to the formation of great rivers. The sources of the few large waterways lie in remote regions beyond the confines of Greece. At the extreme north-east, the Hebros, the great river of ancient Thrace, was probably navigable as far as Didymoteichon in antiquity. There are

the world as regards its impact on civilization. The area extending from the Ionian Islands and the Akrokeraunia Mountains to the Black Sea, Asia Minor, Cyprus, and Crete forms the framework within which Hellenic civilization initially flourished.

27

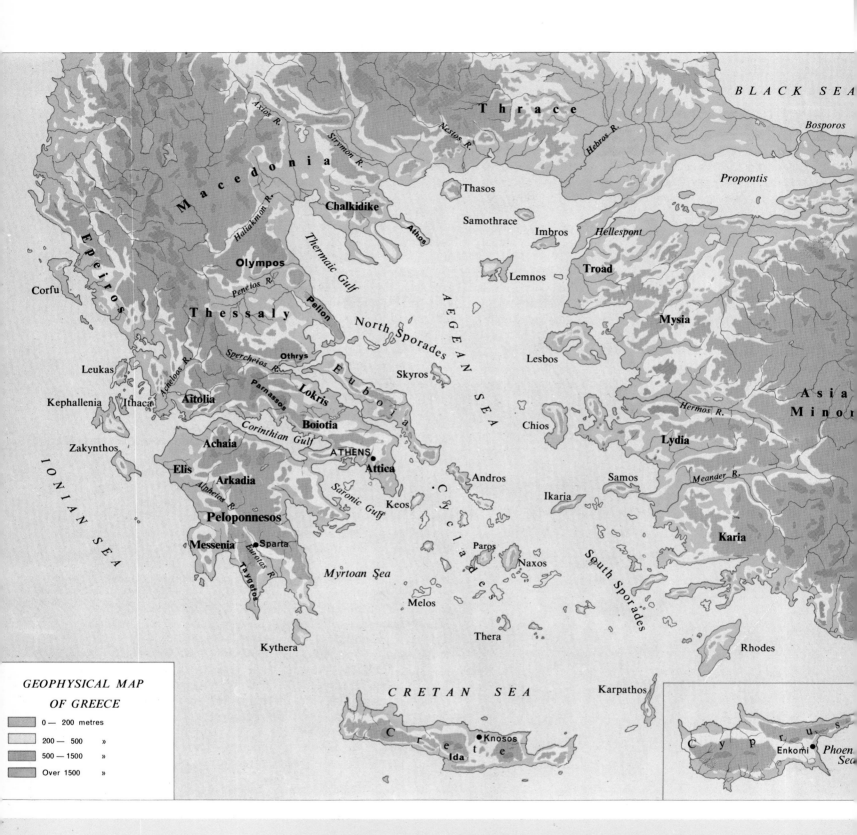

GEOPHYSICAL MAP
OF GREECE

	0 — 200 metres
	200 — 500 »
	500 — 1500 »
	Over 1500 »

Although mountains predominate over four fifths of the Greek lands, there is no part of the country that is not exposed to sea breezes. No point in the interior is further than 100 kilometres from the coast. The relief is rugged and broken, the coastline deeply indented. Between the mountain ranges lie numerous basins and plateaux. The coast is penetrated by numerous gulfs; large and small islands are scattered across the Aegean. Rivers flow in a series of tortuous windings, and their waters irrigate fertile interior plains, riparian valleys, and coastal belts. From prehistoric times the river valleys provided means of communication between different regions. The sea around the peninsula penetrates the land through calm windless channels, providing a persistent inducement to navigators from earliest times. Within this physical framework men created one of the great civilizations of antiquity.

no other navigable rivers. The importance of most of the streams as means of communication was, however, always considerable. The principal roads followed the river valleys. From prehistoric times the Strymon seems to have been a natural means of communication with the Central Balkans and the Danubian lands. The same applies to the Axios, the great river of Macedonia—"broad-flowing", Homer calls it—which flows southward, irrigating ancient Paionia, and pours into the Thermaic Gulf in Southern Macedonia. The Hebros too determined the course of the important road which ran from north-west Asia Minor to the plateau of Sardica, in the heart of the Balkan peninsula, and from the coast of Aegean Thrace to the Thermaic Gulf.

Greek rivers were therefore never of any considerable size. But they served as carriers of the precious element of water and were consequently regarded as sacred. Moreover, owing to the complicated topographical configuration of the land, the streams flow in many extraordinary ways between strangely formed banks; when they descend from limestone mountains, their waters are turbulent and crystal-clear, as in Epeiros; others—the Nestos, for instance—wind sinuously through fantastically formed defiles; elsewhere, cloudy waters—"smooth as oil", says Homer of the Peneios—meander across plains, narrowing as they pass through gorges bordered, as at Tempe, with venerable plane trees; still others, like the Eurotas, irrigate rich and beautiful valleys. But the typical Greek river is waterless in summer, and so becomes known as the *xeropotamos* (the dry stream).

The disposition of the mountain ranges and the fragmentation of the land as a result of its irregular configuration, the little rivers, and the broken coastline have always made it difficult to build large interior roads. Communications were never good between Western Greece and the more fertile eastern part of the country, the main axis of which was crossed by a wide road roughly following the same course as the present national highway. This great arterial road ran southward from Macedonia and the Thermaic Gulf (where another road beginning in the Propontis ended) through the Vale of Tempe or some other mountain defile into the Thessalian plain, crossed the foothills of the Othrys range into the Spercheios valley, penetrated the pass of Thermopylai (or crossed the heights of Mt. Oite) and led through Phokis, Boiotia, Attica, and the Megarid, terminating at the isthmus of Corinth, which served as the junction of all the most important strategic and commercial roads and maritime routes in the country. Communications in Western Greece presented a far more difficult problem. However, it was possible to penetrate inland from the north-west part of the country along the course of certain valleys, like that of the Aoos. Moreover, something resembling a precursor of the great Via Egnatia was probably already in existence. Another road ran from the Ambracian Gulf across Aitolia to the coast of the Corinthian Gulf and the west shore of the Peloponnesos. But there was nothing in the nature of a complete road network. Roads with a good surface of any considerable length were unknown. Pack animals were used for transport. In fact, they provided the chief means of land transport until the 19th century.

On the other hand, the possibilities of communication by sea were unlimited. The penetration of large and small gulfs into the interior of the land, the island archipelagoes, the expanse of sea fringing the bold contours of the coastline, the absence of tides, the regularity of the winds, and the clarity of the atmosphere made conditions ideal for seafaring. The numerous gulfs, even more than the islands and peninsulas, provided the impetus for the development of maritime life. Of these gulfs, the Corinthian, penetrating deep into the centre of the country in a west-east direction, was by far the most important. Its eastern counterpart, the Saronic, completed the separation of the Peloponnesos from the mainland and, bounded by the coasts of Attica and the Argolid, formed a replica in miniature of the Aegean. The Thessalian land basin would have been wholly deprived of a maritime outlet but for the Pagasitic Gulf, whence the Argonauts set sail. The Chalkidike and the Peloponnesos would have been unbroken land masses had they not been penetrated by sea, the former by two deep inroads, the latter by the Argolic, Lakonian, and Messenian Gulfs. The same applies to Epeiros, where the coastline is broken by the Ambracian Gulf. Winding channels and deep penetrations of sea separate Euboia from the mainland, provide the Spercheios valley with an outlet, and Macedonia with a maritime exit and gateway to the south and east in the Thermaic Gulf. Even Arkadia is not very far from the sea. There is not, in fact, a single region of the country which is not freshened by cool sea breezes.

The cradle of Greek seamanship is the Aegean, popularly referred to now as "the White Sea". Like the Mediterranean, which constituted a vital element in the heart of the ancient world, the Aegean, placed in the centre of the Greek lands, provided what the mainland was unable to supply. From the Thracian coast and the Hellespont as far as Crete and Rhodes, it is studded with archipelagoes of islands of varying size—a unique geographical feature in the Mediterranean basin. The most typical groups are the central and southern Cyclades. Scattered like stepping-stones across the sea, they extend from Attica and Euboia to the off-shore islands of Asia Minor, forming a kind of bridge spanning the two shores of the Aegean. The Northern Sporades constitute an eastward prolongation of the elbow-shaped headland of Magnesia, and Thasos and Samothrace guard the Thracian coast like sentinels. Farther north, Lemnos and Imbros complete the bridge of islands leading to the Troad and the Hellespont.

The island-bridge is even more apparent when we look at the large off-shore islands of Asia Minor—Lesbos, Chios, Samos, and even Rhodes. Neither prolongations of Asia nor even of Asia Minor, they form rather the wedge of the eastward geophysical thrust of the Greek lands towards the opposite coast. The Ionian Islands, a western extension of the Peloponnesos and the mainland, look to the north and west; and Italy is visible from Corfu. Like a great breakwater to the south, Crete, birthplace of the earliest European civilization, links Greece with the most important part of the Mediterranean, joining the Aegean with Cyprus and the Syrian and North African coasts. Finally, Cyprus, isolated in the south-east, is destined from late prehistoric times to become a junction between East and West and to remain from then on the most extreme projection of the Hellenic world into the Eastern Mediterranean basin.

The Greek islands are not only a geographical feature of the land. They correspond to the division of the mainland into small territorial units from which the city states were to develop. Almost every Greek island was once a state in its own right; even today each one of them remains something of a microcosm in itself.

The Climate and Greek History

Greek history was decisively influenced by numerous geographical divisions, the broken configuration of the land, the forms of the coastline, and the existence of an island world. The Greek soil was never rich, nor its yield abundant. From the earliest times the population relied on minor cultivation and stockbreeding for its basic nourishment. Thanks to the olive, the numerous fruit-bearing trees, and fishing, it was possible to maintain an adequate food supply, although not without hard labour. The climate compensated for what the soil was unable to provide. But difficulties on land, hazards at sea, the struggle for the limited supply of water, the battle with winds and waves produced in the inhabitants their stubborn character. At the same time, geographical fragmentation fostered the growth of a distinctly regional patriotism, and the sea encouraged a quest for adventure.

In the final analysis, historical development is partially determined by a land's potential productivity. Greece was not an ideal country for the cultivation of cereals. The production of pulses and barley (Homer refers to the "fruitful corn-land") provided better prospects. In addition, in coastal and southern areas, the olive and fig made a valuable contribution to the food supply. A combined agricultural and stockbreeding economy, complemented by the development of fisheries in the coastal areas, formed the basis of existence.

Basic metals existed in small quantities: copper in Euboia and the Cyclades, lead in Lesbos, silver at Laurion, gold on Mt. Pangaion and in the Macedonian river-beds, iron in many localities. Marble, on the other hand, was extensively quarried, and there were considerable quantities of different kinds of clay and various volcanic materials: obsidian, a kind of volcanic glass used by man of the Stone Age for making blades, points, and other implements; grindstone for millstones; sulphur; iron alum, used for leather tanning; a bright coloured pigment (*Melinum pigmentium*); potter's clay; chalk; and a number of semi-precious stones, including jasper, opal, and chalcedony. Mountain forests, of which there were more extensive tracts in antiquity than today, supplied the timber essential for shipbuilding.

To the relative paucity of their physical resources the Greeks opposed great powers of endurance, ingenuity, innate frugality, and commercial and nautical dexterity. But the struggle for existence would have been even more arduous had they been denied one vital natural element: the Mediterranean climate, the so-called "climate of the olive tree". Geographically, the country lies in the temperate zone, and, from a thermometrical point of view, can be divided into three distinct zones: (a) the northern, bounded to the north by a line running from the Akrokeraunia to Constantinople, with a mean temperature of 16°-14° centigrade; (b) the central, with a mean temperature of 18°-16° centigrade; (c) the southern, with a mean temperature of 20°-18° centigrade. This range of temperature is approximately similar to that of the Iberian peninsula, of Italy (south of the Po), and of Asia Minor.

In this area, the climate is profoundly affected by the geographical configuration and the distribution of land and sea. The higher mountain belt differs climatically from the lowlands and coastal areas. The rainfall is not the same at both levels. Variety in vegetation distinguishes the different localities. Consequently, averages do not always lead to cor-

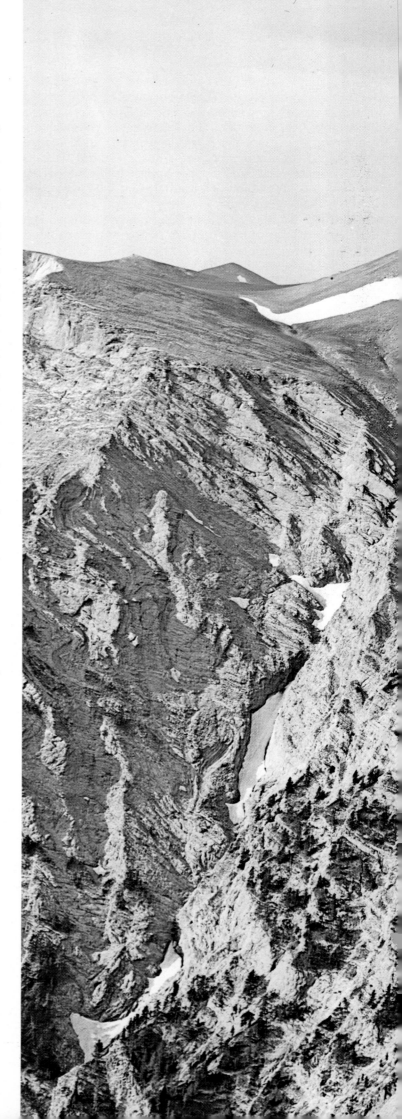

Mountains dominate
the Greek landscape.
But the sea is never
far away.
The majestic
snow-capped
peaks of Olympos in
Central Greece rise
only twenty kilometres
from the coast
of the Northern
Aegean. The interplay
between sea
and mountain
had a decisive
influence on the
course of Greek
history.

31

rect conclusions, and the general picture does not provide a true assessment. Essentially, the Greek climate consists of a synthesis of numerous regional climates. A typically Mediterranean vegetation (olives, figs, and, in the south, citrus fruits) prevails along the coasts and in the islands. The forests are not extensive and, for the most part, consist of conifers. On the whole, Mediterranean vegetation predominates up to an altitude of 600 m. in Southern Greece, of 400 m. in the North.

A different picture, more "European" in character, is presented by the mountainous and northern areas. In the northwest, where the physical connection with Europe is at its closest, the annual rainfall averages between 1000 and 1500 mm. The highest average, 1520 mm., is registered at Metsovo. At the south-east end of Crete, however, the figure is as low as 200-300 mm. (six times lower). Throughout Greece, the highest rainfall is registered between November and February, while the period of total drought lasts for months on end. Generally speaking, the rainfall is much heavier in the north and west than in the south and east.

The climate is characterized by a short spring, a hot summer, a mellow autumn (the most beautiful season of the year, with an average temperature slightly higher than that of spring) and a relatively mild winter. In spite of regional variations, it is, by and large, the most agreeable climate in the Mediterranean. In the interior of Thrace, for instance, the winter is almost Central European, whereas in the south-eastern peninsulas, such as Attica, the Argolid,

The countless bays, the quiet beaches, and the winding channels were important factors in the growth of seafaring and strong stimulation for quest, adventure, and expansion (photograph: below left). Enclosed fertile valleys, rivers, and steep-sided defiles formed the small territorial units within which the Greek city states were to develop. Tempe, through which the Peneios winds at the foot

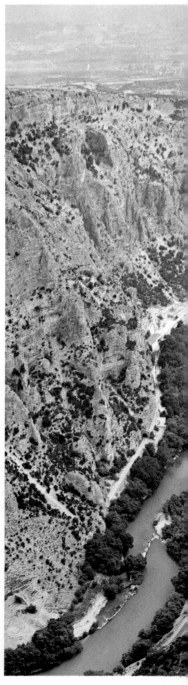

and the southern Aegean, it is very mild—and even more mild in the lowlands of Crete. In the Aegean and the coastal regions, the heat in summer is tempered by sea breezes and the north-east Etesian winds (the *meltemia*). In the interior of Thessaly, temperatures run high, but the neighbouring mountains provide ideal summer quarters for sheep and goats and also for human beings. There is a great deal of sunshine in the southern areas, and cloudy days are rare. The contours of mountains and islands, drenched in sunshine and the "delicate ether", are sharply outlined in an atmosphere which is generally clear and diaphanous. All these factors contribute to the special character of the Greek climate, which has exerted a considerable influence on the inhabitants and, perhaps indirectly, on their evolution.

Climatic conditions are not, however, solely responsible for the development of an advanced civilization in the Greek lands. Nor, of course, is the privileged climate the prime factor in the development of Greek history. Consequently, to ask whether the climate has undergone any decisive change since antiquity is not important. Generally speaking, man, possessing immense powers of adjustment, reacts dynamically, not passively, to his environment; he is consequently able to dwell in all latitudes and under all climatic conditions, from the polar regions to the equator.

It is in fact now established that the main features of the Greek climate have not altered radically since the earliest millennia of the Holocene—that is to say, for at least eight thousand years. All the theories, past and present,

of Mt. Olympos, was the gateway guarding the highly populated Thessalian plain (aerial photograph: centre). The sea is dotted with small islands which formed bridges between the opposite coasts

from the most ancient times. It was in the Cyclades and the Sporades that the earliest inhabitants of the mainland first settled in the course of their seaward expansion (aerial photograph: right).

regarding sudden and catastrophic changes have been proved groundless. At one time, for instance, it was believed that a major change in climate had been caused by deforestation (destruction of woods and decrease in vegetation), by increasing scarcity of water, and impoverishment of the soil. On what grounds are these views based? True, the extent of forest land has been considerably reduced throughout the country. But the same applies to the Middle East and the whole of Europe. The influences exercised by climatic changes were therefore of a more widespread nature, and the adverse effects did not concern Greece alone. Scarcity of water was admittedly a hardship which had to be endured by the inhabitants of the greater part of the country from the earliest times.

Homer called the plain of Argos "thirsty". The epithet is still apt. In antiquity, small streams were worshipped as deities, and every spring was sacred, devoted to the Nymphs. Then as now, peasants awaited the first rains with anguish in order to sow the land. Prayers were addressed to Zeus for rain ("Rain, rain, o dear Zeus..."). Aristotle affirms that periods of drought alternated with years when the rainfall was adequate. It is certain that in Athens there was a shortage of water, and Plato describes the famous Athenian streams of the Kephisos and the Ilisos, as "streamlets". The Kephisos, like the Ilisos, was, according to Strabo, "a torrential stream most of the time, although in summer it decreases and almost dries up".

Has the soil undergone any radical change since then? Erosion, added to the destruction wrought by wild goats in shrub-lands, has undoubtedly had disastrous effects. But there is nothing new in this process. Plato refers to it in the *Kritias*. On the whole, Greece has always been stony. Ancient writers from the time of Homer refer to the poverty of the soil. The "thin soil" of Attica was a byword. Research into the growth of the palm tree has revealed that the temperature has not undergone the slightest change. The beginning

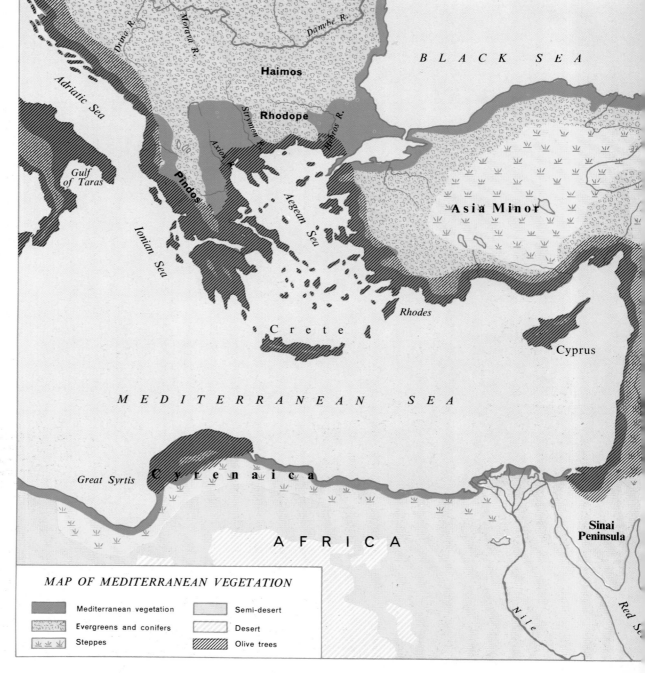

The vegetation is varied, with fruit orchards and small holdings. On the whole, the land is poor. An agricultural and stockbreeding economy, together with fisheries, provided the basic necessities of life. The climate, the innate frugality of the people, together with their commercial and maritime abilities, compensated for the lack of material resources.

MAP OF MEDITERRANEAN VEGETATION

Mediterranean vegetation Semi-desert
Evergreens and conifers Desert
Steppes Olive trees

and end of the seasons of the year have remained stable, and the periods of sowing and harvesting are the same today as they were in the time of Hesiod. The climate, the relief, and general configuration therefore remain unaltered. Certain minor fluctuations—such as that of the sea level—are virtually imperceptible or at least have not had any general repercussions.

The climate, the physical framework as a whole, in conjunction with numerous other factors, undoubtedly influenced the course of events. But they did not create Hellenic civilization. The poor soil did not prevent the development of the inhabitants. It was the qualities of endurance shown by the people, who had to wage a ceaseless struggle against a barren soil, that Thucydides had in mind when he proudly referred to the immense courage of the Greeks who, with poverty as their "everlasting companion" and so few natural resources at their disposal, created one of the great civilizations of antiquity.

SOURCES OF PREHISTORY

Archaeology

The moment man begins to make tools, that is to say, the moment when physical objects invented for specific purposes are added to the attributes with which nature has endowed him, Man the Maker (*Homo Faber*) becomes an object of historical study. An initial difficulty is that of saying when precisely this important development took place. It is generally believed that it occurred about a million years ago, perhaps much earlier. A second, more serious difficulty lies in the lack of sufficient evidence upon which to base an account beginning so far back in time. Therefore, the starting-point usually taken is the period to which the first stone-made tools of certain types, together with the corresponding anthropological remains found in different parts of the ancient world, can be dated. This would be about 600,000 years ago. This vast period, covering the whole of man's existence on earth up to the time of the first written records, is known as prehistory, and the science related to it as prehistoric archaeology.

Nowadays it is generally believed that prehistory constitutes an essential part of the history of man, and that no difference or line of demarcation exists between them. Both prehistory and history are concerned with the same subject: the study of human activity on earth. Admittedly, we know far less about the prehistorical than about the historical period. Consequently, in order to form a historical perspective of prehistory we have to rely exclusively on such man-made objects as have been brought to light in the course of excavations; in fact, on whatever is disclosed by prehistoric archaeology, which is the basic source of all knowledge in the prehistoric field. Does not history itself, even when abundant written records exist, require archaeological confirmation of the conclusions reached? What would we really know about art and religion, about life in general in Classical times were it not for the monuments and objects brought to light by archaeological excavations?

The most serious obstacle encountered in the study of prehistory is the absence of any direct information about man's mental attitudes or the social life of human groups. For the most part, there is no trace of any written records, but this does not mean that there are no other ways by means of which we may arrive at a tolerably fair appraisal of human evolution. Just as it is impossible to cast doubt on the very existence of our prehistoric forefathers, simply because we possess no concrete picture of them, in the same way it is not logical to question the historicity of prehistory, simply because there are no written records. Even without these, human activity may be accorded a rightful place in the annals of history if supported by direct archaeological evidence, that is to say, by actual finds made by archaeologists. Scholars have laboured hard to record and date events and to shed some light on the obscurity of at least half a million years of prehistory, even when fully conscious that the picture that emerges from their deductions can represent no more than a skeleton framework of historical evolution. The obstacles they have encountered would appear to have been insuperable. The chronological span covered by prehistory is at least a hundred times greater than that of the whole of history proper. A study of man's most primitive creations had to be carried out in the obscurity of a remote and limitless past, unsupported by any kind of chronological verification.

Throughout the greater part of prehistory, particularly the remotest prehistorical period, namely the Stone Age, man was so closely associated with his environment, so directly dependent on natural elements, that his development seemed to conform exactly with the course of nature itself. Scholars have therefore had to consider his natural environment as much as the tools he used and such other vestigial remains as may have survived. In examining the various phases in the evolution of the genus man, palaeo-anthropologists were aided by the discoveries of geology and archaeology. But in order to trace the development of human civilization, archaeologists were in turn obliged to find a corresponding point of departure in the affiliated sciences, by means of which the natural framework and environment of man (climate, flora and fauna, geological stratification, etc.) during the Pleistocene could be studied and a means established for determining chronology. In coordinating these various branches of research, scholars have recently formulated a new field called environmental archaeology. Partial deductions are scrutinized, comparisons drawn, and findings are in the end incorporated in prehistoric archaeology, which is now also environmental archaeology. Thus, in order to describe the activities of man during the prehistoric "preliterate" period, not only archaeological finds, such as tools, monuments, and works of art, but also environmental features, and anthropological remains—anything in fact which might bear, directly or indirectly, on man and his activities—must now be examined in conjunction with each other.

The influence exercised by nature on man and his destiny seems to have been of the utmost importance during the early period in prehistoric times. But as man evolved, he began to react against the forces of nature and the difficulties of the environment by the exercise of his own free will and the impetus supplied by his creative imagination. It was this ability of man to react actively, rather than the differences which distinguish him from all other beings, that contributed more than anything else to his increasing independence of natural forces.

The part played by environmental archaeology decreases as we approach higher levels of civilization. There, the evidence provided by its study is not in itself sufficient to create an historical image. At best, it may provide a skeleton framework of man's evolution, a shadowy picture of the material side of life. The other aspect of life, that which concerns man's ideas, fears, hopes, and beliefs, remains more or less shrouded in obscurity. The question then arises as to whether it is possible to illumine this obscurity. Can the naked skeleton be given flesh and blood? Is it possible to revivify an utterly lost world?

Before answering this question, we must make use of every means at our disposal. Prehistoric archaeology alone will not suffice. Other affiliated sciences, principally ethnology and sociology, must also make their contribution. Contemporary "primitive peoples" have been studied with great patience in the belief that, since basically human nature remains unchanged, such a study might help us to understand the "thought-world" of prehistoric man. Some scholars have even gone so far as to create a theoretical reconstruction of prehistoric society by trying to standardize motive phenomena and to formulate something approximating to natural laws, and all this in a field where in fact everything was unique and in a state of constant flux. Today, all are in agreement as to the limited possibilities for the reconstruction of a credible image of the prehistorical period. The lack of basic material cannot be made good by sociology, ethnology, or environmental archaeology, whose contribution merely complements archaeological indications. Life in its various aspects cannot be expressed in figures or statistics, nor is it possible for formulae to make good the lack of substance. Archaeological material is therefore the main source of knowledge; nothing else can replace it. It is to archaeology too that we must turn for any evidence that would allow us to form a picture of man's mental processes. It is only for confirmation that we turn to other sciences.

Problems of Interpretation

Another fundamental problem is how to interpret the material clues provided by archaeology, and in what way this material should be sifted in order to make an historical reconstruction possible. It is easy, of course, to talk of the need for objectivity, critical elaboration, and the adoption of accurate formulae. But it may not always be so easy to avoid the siren call of theories which explain everything *a priori*. It is also difficult for us to accept the idea that the investigation of causes is not always possible, just as it is not always easy to know what is hidden behind the facts. Of necessity, every reconstruction of prehistory must be subjective and temporary; and every judgement must be tempered with the statement, "so far as is known", or "according to the evidence so far available". Above all, it must be understood that the past, and above all the very remote past, cannot be interpreted in terms of contemporary criteria. Nor can it be explained by means of one-sided theories which either interpret historic evolution in terms of economic factors or place race and environment among the fundamental motive forces. Something much more complex than the sum total of all the partial inferences, something much more vital than any single theory, is evidently necessary.

Linguistics and Philology

Linguistics and philology rank second only to archaeology in their contribution to the study and reconstruction of the prehistoric and proto-historical scene. In particular, Greek prehistory and protohistory are illuminated by certain facts which emerge from a comparative study of:

1. the Indo-European languages, one of which is Greek,
2. the Greek dialects, and
3. survivals of Indo-European languages identified in Greece and other Mediterranean countries.

Similarities and differences revealed by comparative study allow conclusions about the origin and development of languages, their relation to other languages, both affiliated and foreign, their fragmentation into dialects, and the process of gradual differentiation that occurred in their structure.

The history of a language or dialect constitutes a distinct aspect of the history, particularly the intellectual history, of an ethnic group the members of which spoke or speak that language or dialect. It also reflects past historical events, such as the origins of the ethnic group, the assimilation of foreign ethnic elements, contacts with other peoples, remote religious beliefs, and ancient forms of social organization.

No texts in common Greek survive, that is to say, in the Greek language before it broke up into various dialects. All Greek texts are written in dialect. The earliest, dated to c. 1400 B.C., are confined to short memoranda in Mycenaean dialect and are composed of symbols, many of which do not reproduce Greek sounds accurately. These are followed by the Homeric epics written in the 8th century B.C. in Ionic with interpolations from other Greek dialects. Students of linguistics resort to texts of even the post- Classical period as the only available source for the study of certain dialects.

Can this linguistic material be considered a source for early Greek history and, consequently, for drawing pertinent conclusions? The answer is in the affirmative, for the ancient Greek language in general, and the dialects in particular, have not only preserved features from the past, but have also developed in accordance with well-established linguistic laws. If we take these laws as a starting-point, we can proceed backwards, either directly or in stages, from the dialects to a language common to all Greeks, and from the latter to the Indo-European language.

Some Greek words, while apparently of an Indo-European origin, do not in fact follow the laws of Greek. These are residues from other Indo-European languages assimilated into the Greek tongue. It is not easy to examine the character of these words and to find out the laws they have obeyed, because they are survivals of completely vanished languages. Even greater are the problems which arise from the study of non-Indo-European languages.

It is not within the province of comparative philology, as in the case of archaeology, to trace the evolution of man from the most remote prehistorical times. The light it casts on the prehistory of the Hellenic race does not reach farther back, at the very most, than the 4th millennium B.C. Nevertheless, it should not be forgotten that it is this light which has made it possible to record and deduce events which would have otherwise remained shrouded in obscurity and that because of it we may hope to distinguish further facts in the future.

Traditions and Legends

It is from ancient texts that we learn about the genealogy of the heroes and their exploits, about the wars and migrations of ethnic groups which, according to the established system of chronology, must have occured more or less prior to 1000 B.C. Some modern scholars have little patience with these accounts; others, on the contrary, believe that all of them contain the germ of historical truth. The negative attitude adopted towards the earliest Greek traditions, which prevailed during the second half of the 19th and the first quarter of the 20th century, rejected as untrustworthy almost all genealogies and narratives about events prior to the sixth century B.C. Conversely, during recent decades, the tendency has been to accept accounts of events and personalities of remote periods without reserve, and even to stress, somewhat dogmatically, that on the whole these accounts reflect true facts. This tendency goes too far in the opposite direction, to the extent that it rejects all criticism. For, how is it possible, on the one hand, to question the veracity of the writings of Herodotos and Thucydides, who were eyewitnesses of events and actually heard with their own ears the words they quote, and, on the other, to accept unreservedly whatever the chroniclers and epitomists of the Alexandrian and Roman periods recount about events and personages of the 2nd millennium B.C.?

Both tendencies are harmful. The first rejects, along with what are undoubtedly legendary narrations, the echoes of genuine historical traditions which they contain; the second accepts as facts stories which cannot stand up to even the most elementary criticism.

The Earliest Scripts

The invention and use of writing constitute one of the most important stages in the evolution of civilization. It was by means of writing that man was able to record his thoughts, to bequeath his experience to future generations, and to contribute to the organization of life. And it was chiefly on writing that historians have based their reconstruction of the past. Material remains, language, and tradition have always been complementary factors.

In Greece writing was in use from the earliest years of the Bronze Age. It continued in use almost uninterruptedly until the establishment of a new alphabetical system based on the Phoenician alphabet. Archaeology has brought to light fragments of many kinds of inscribed objects: seal-rings, tablets, utensils, tools, effigies, etc. These proved to be extremely useful in providing information about contemporary conditions: about public life, bureaucratic organization, state control, religious ceremonies, economic affairs, and so on.

Ideographs, namely pictorial signs which speak for themselves, were frequently used in prehistoric writings. It was thus possible to obtain some information from—even to hazard a guess at the subject matter of—these writings before their actual decipherment. The earliest specimens of writing in Greece consist of a few isolated symbols inscribed on seals and utensils of Cycladic and Cretan provenance dated to the Early Bronze Age. These can hardly be described as written texts in the proper sense of the word. The first real inscriptions are found on Cretan seals.

The excavations undertaken by Sir Arthur Evans at Knosos, the most important centre of Minoan civilization, brought to light seals inscribed with the oldest writing in the Helladic world, namely hieroglyphics. Archaeological research also revealed that other methods of writing were evolving at the same time as hieroglyphics. These methods developed into linear script, a system by means of which linear designs instead of pictures were used by scribes. This new kind of writing, known as Linear A and Linear B, combined two methods, consisting of the use of both ideographs and syllabic signs. Only a few dozen clay tablets inscribed in Linear A, belonging to palace archives, were found. On the other hand, tablets inscribed in Linear B survive in thousands (mostly in the palaces at Knosos and Pylos). Writing in Crete, and later in the Mycenaean area, developed uninfluenced by, and almost independently of, corresponding developments in Egypt and the near East. It is not of course impossible that the Cretans adopted the basic idea and the main form of the writing after coming into contact with the highly civilized countries of these areas. Nevertheless, the independent evolution of the Creto-Mycenean script is now accepted as an established fact.

Many attempts have been made to decipher these scripts. Success has been achieved only in the case of the Linear B tablets, which are inscribed with letters belonging to an archaic Greek tongue. Linear A, however, still remains undeciphered. In spite of continuous research, there seems to be little hope of a decipherment. There is even less hope of a speedy decipherment of the hieroglyphic system. The deciphered material in the Creto-Mycenaean script has proved to be a valuable historical source, both for archaeology and linguistics. In the first place, it has supplemented, or made possible the reappraisal of, earlier theories. Even more important has been its contribution to our knowledge of contemporary political, social, economic, religious, and private life, although this contribution is less than might have been desired. The different stages in the development of the scripts will be described in later chapters.

There remains the problem of the degree of accuracy achieved in the interpretation of the texts. The spelling presents many difficulties, which render the transcription uncertain and the meaning ambiguous. As a result, many scholars are doubtful whether in fact the Creto-Mycenaean script has been deciphered. Conclusions based on it should be treated with great critical caution and regarded as scientific hypotheses that have still to be verified. Attempts to decipher and interpret the texts continue. Only the discovery of new archives and epigraphical material will provide a more solid foundation on which positive historical analysis may be based.

THE STONE AGE

The Palaeolithic and Mesolithic Periods

PALAEOLITHIC GREECE

Three major landmarks distinguish the history of man. The first is the so-called Food-producing Revolution, as a result of which agriculture and stockbreeding governed man's existence for the first time. The revolution started in the Near East and is dated to about 10,000 years ago. The second, the so-called Literate Civilization, associated with the Urban Revolution, began about 5,000 years ago, also in the Near East. The third, of much more recent date, namely the Industrial Revolution, is of Western European origin; from it developed the present Scientific Revolution, better known as the Atomic Age.

From the outset it is essential to bear in mind that the Food-producing Revolution, the first landmark which radically altered man's destiny and the course of the human race and was the genesis of all future developments, began during the Stone Age. This was the most critical moment in the history of mankind, mid-way between the two geological periods of the Pleistocene and the Holocene, about 12,000 to 10,000 years ago. Consequently, the Stone Age, which historians were once reluctant to investigate, is the starting-point of man's cultural development. Any account of the entire historical span of this development must therefore begin with the Stone Age.

Over the history of civilization and the achievements of the Food-producing Revolution and behind whatever facts can be recorded, stands the figure of man himself. For man alone was the maker of history and the chief protagonist during that immense period of time associated with the Pleistocene, which lasted for one, perhaps two, million years— a hundred times longer, in fact, than the actual period of the history of cilization.

Only geology and physical anthropology are capable of throwing any light on the physical evolution of the genus *man* during the greater part of this period. About halfway through it, when quantities of tools fashioned into specific shapes begin to be identified in different parts of the world, archaeology steps in. From that moment, estimated at about 600,000 years ago, begins the Palaeolithic Period, the oldest and longest phase of the Stone Age. The story of the Palaeolithic Period is therefore the history of mankind during the Pleistocene. In the following pages it will be seen how far back it is necessary to go into this distant past. Because even in the case of Hellenic civilization, any version of the human story must begin with the Pleistocene if a complete picture is to be formed. We now know that it was the man of the Pleistocene who created revolutionary changes which sparked off the development of civilization and laid the initial foundations on which all subsequent civilizations of an advanced nature could be solidly based. Furthermore, it was during the Pleistocene that *Homo Sapiens* or Modern Man ("that thinking animal, man", Aristotle calls him) first acquired his present physical traits. From him developed directly all human races of historical times. Man's psychological make-up was also laid in that misty past of the Palaeolithic Period. There, if it were possible, we would have to look for the motivational elements that govern civilized man's existence.

These then are the elements that lend a kind of glamour, a spirit of human grandeur to the dawn of prehistory. It is here that may be found the only common source of all humanity and all civilizations, the fountain-head of a world from which all the various races and nations of the future were eventually to spring. Consequently, modern historians not only recognize, but actually stress the fact that by far the major part (as much as 99%) of the history of man's existence on earth is built on foundations laid during that period. Shrouded in obscurity as this remote past may be, it can no longer be dismissed as a myth. It is the protracted prelude to history itself.

The First Stone Tools

The term *palaeolithic* (like *mesolithic* and *neolithic*) may not mean very much to the average modern reader. It refers to the period during which stone was the basic raw material for the making of tools; flint or some similar kind of hard stone which offers resistance to impact and has sharp edges. Although it is now thought that man's most ancient tools were made of wood, we know hardly anything about them, as only very rare specimens, and these of a much later date, survive. The same applies to tools made of other materials, of which no trace remains. Since stone implements possess almost limitless powers of endurance, and their shapes do not change, they have acquired a special significance in the study of primitive man's inventory of tools.

The stone implements of the Palaeolithic Period were hammered into shape, never polished, as was the case in the Neolithic Period. The oldest extant examples had no definite or standard shape or design; they were simply stones which served man's daily needs, and it is only when they are found in conjunction with anthropological remains that we may go so far as to describe them as tools. Later, large pebbles or water-worn rounded stones, suitable for

the human hand, were picked out of streams; after being slightly hammered on the circumference, they acquired the form of tools. These so-called pebble tools belong to the oldest known inventory of Palaeolithic implements. By means of the hammered technique—the actual degree of hammering often varied—the first flints were fashioned. These underwent a gradual process of elaboration until they acquired the form, first of core or bifacial implements (hand-axes), then of flake tools (sharp splints). The uses to which all these implements were put were of a purely practical nature, corresponding to man's direct needs and intended to ensure his survival. As always, however, trial and error, allied to experimentation, were indispensable factors in the creation of even the simplest object. All these artifacts, as well as their subsequent more elaborate forms, the workmanship of which showed signs of progressive ingenuity, were not the creation of a single man in a single day. They reflect the progress achieved by thousands of generations of men. The application of the lessons learned as a result of experience would never have taken place had not man been a social being. Individuals came and went, but the experience they gained survived through the group until it acquired an almost indestructible quality. Thus the creation of tools is the privilege of man alone—that is to say, of the pre-eminently social being. This basic quality which distinguishes him from the animal groups enabled him to establish his dominance over them. Through the tool he first acquired a sense of his freedom. And since a tool is the product of reason, it is perhaps not too far-fetched to regard it, however imperfect in form, as the first scientific invention.

For all that, this important creation, the tool, remains an external factor, a technical achievement. And it is truly disappointing that we have to base any reconstruction of cultural development during the dawn of prehistory on it. Of the mental side of man's life during that period we know nothing; not a scrap of direct evidence survives.

On the other hand, the progress made in the evolution of shapes, particularly of tools of the earliest times, was so slow, so barely perceptible, that it is not difficult to imagine the countless difficulties which man must have encountered in these early stages of his evolution. From present-day Germany to the southernmost extremity of Africa, the stone hand-axe was man's primary tool and weapon for hundreds of thousands of years. This static uniformity may mean much in terms of the original homogeneity of the human race. But the extremely slow rate of progress registered in the fashioning of implements provides evidence of the silent drama of the palaeolithic man, ceaselessly striving, within a hostile

The existence of settlements
of the Middle
Palaeolithic Period,
i.e. 100,000-40,000
years ago, has been disclosed
in a series
of astonishing
archaeological
discoveries
made during
the last fifteen
years. Tools found in Thessaly,
Epeiros,
the Ionian Islands,
the Peloponnesos,
and the
Northern Sporades
indicate the presence
and activity of
Neanderthal man
throughout
the greater part of what were
to become
the Greek lands.
Sites of
palaeolithic and
and mesolithic
remains are
indicated on the map.
Man was still
then a cave-dweller
and a hunter.

and ever changing environment, to ensure his survival and secure his nourishment by means of hunting and tracking down migratory animals. To meet the appalling climatic upheavals of the Pleistocene, everything had to be changed—tools, shelters, hunting methods, group organizations—if this frail creature was to survive the intense cold of the Glacial Age and the torrid humidity of intervening periods of intense heat. Moreover, he was obliged to keep a close watch on the habits of animals in order to achieve success in hunting. He had to take into account local raw materials, the potentialities of stone, the availability of fire and water, the changes in vegetation, and the signs of the weather.

For at least several hundred millennia, this desperate struggle for survival, the struggle for the achievement of a more satisfactory adjustment to the physical environment and a more effective exploitation of its potentialities, did

not leave time for anything else. It was only much later that palaeolithic man was able to confront the mystery of life and death.

Culturally, the Palaeolithic Period is divisible into two unequal but distinct parts. The Lower and Middle Palaeolithic, which lasted for about 95% of the entire time, are characterized by a static quality. Evolution was very slow, activity imperceptible, progress hardly noticeable. The second period, Upper Palaeolithic, which occupied the remaining 5% of the period, was more dynamic. Progress was now rapid and no longer confined to technical matters. It extended to intellectual concerns with the first appearance of the art found in caves and dwellings. The period is moreover distinguished by the most significant of all anthropological transformations: the disappearance of primitive man and the emergence of modern man, *Homo Sapiens*. The dramatic story of man the hunter thus reached a climax in the Upper Palaeolithic Period, when radical changes in his material equipment coincided with this anthropological development and the first manifestation of what may be called the intellectual aspect of life.

The Earliest Inhabitants of Greece

It is not known when man first appeared on the Greek scene. Recent research in Roumania and Hungary has brought to light primitive tools and fragments of skeletons of *Homo Erectus* which, in the opinion of anthropologists, may be dated to a period of 300,000 or even 500,000 years ago. In theory, therefore, man probably first appeared in Greece during the Middle Pleistocene. But there is not yet any certain evidence, and some pebble tools found in the bed of the Xerias torrent near Volos in Thessaly have not been dated geologically.

So far the most conclusive evidence of a settlement in Greece during the Lower Palaeolithic Period is a single object: a stone hand-axe found in 1963 at Palaiokastro, south of Siatista, in Macedonia. This implement (15.3 × 10 cm.), fashioned out of a rough greenish stone, amygdaloid in shape, with an unworked base and only a few dents, resembles the hand-axes of the Acheulean type (so-called from the site of Saint-Acheul in France). Although typologically it would appear to be early palaeolithic, it cannot be dated with any certainty. It is believed to be about 100,000 years old. Furthermore, according to F. Lenorman, an eminent French archaeologist, a stone hand-axe of the Acheulean type, found at Megalopolis together with the fossilized bones of animals (the Pleistocene fauna of Megalopolis) was, in 1867, in the possession of a doctor at Argos. Finally, some years ago, a stone implement of an early palaeolithic type was observed by H. Breuil in the Manchester Museum. It came from the Thessalonike area. Consequently, the existence of settlements of the Lower Palaeolithic in Greece would appear to be confirmed by the fact that their traces are not totally lacking and by the discovery of similar remains in the countries on the periphery of Greece, including the Balkans, Italy, and Asia Minor. The earliest indications of a primitive palaeolithic settlement in Greece have, significantly enough, been identified in Macedonia. It was in this part of the country that the only important anthropological relic of the Pleistocene, namely, the skull of a Neanderthal man, was found in the cave at Petralona.

The first tools of the Middle Palaeolithic Period in Greece were identified in 1958, when a German archaeological team under V. Milojčič brought to light various kinds of tools and fossilized zoological remains, which could be dated to the early phase of the Upper Pleistocene, 100,000 to 50,000 years ago. They were found on the banks of the Peneios, near Larisa in Thessaly. This discovery encouraged further research in other parts of the country, which soon seemed to confirm the existence of settlements in Greece during the Middle Palaeolithic (c. 100,000 to 40,000 years ago).

As the Peneios winds sinuously across the plain around Larisa, carving through strata of the Pleistocene, it uncovers layers of earth on which palaeolithic men had once settled.

The amygdaloid bifacial stone hand-axe of Palaiokastro, near Siatista, the oldest palaeolithic implement found in Greece, about 100,000 years old, now in the Veroia Museum. Composed of rough greenish stone, it is 15.3 × 10 cm. Above: the manner in which this primitive implement was handled. It was used by man for flaying and carving animals; sometimes too it served as a missile.

The cave of Kokkines Petres (The Red Stones) at Petralona in Chalkidike, where the fossilized skull of a Neanderthal man was found in 1960. The length of the cave, composed of chambers and galleries filled with stalactites, is 1500 metres.

44

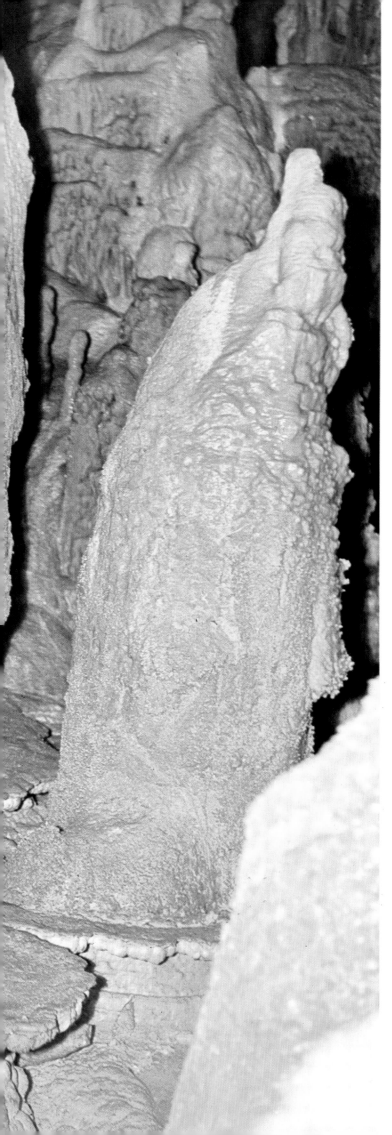

Here were found relatively large numbers of palaeolithic implements, chiefly scrapers of different types, plain flakes, and occasionally bifacial leaf-shaped points with fine retouche. The large number of scrapers indicates that palaeolithic man worked the hides of animals, which he may subsequently have worn to protect him from the cold. The localities where the stone tools were found would appear to have been camp sites (perhaps purely temporary ones), since the flakes have not been swept away by water, as is shown by their cut edges. Here the hunters probably assembled before and after the hunt; they may even have stayed for quite a while. The relatively large number of these sites permits us to conjecture that the plains were fairly densely populated. This was only natural, because the herds of animals hunted by palaeolithic man gathered here for a variety of reasons, including plentiful supplies of water and food.

Tools of the Middle Palaeolithic Period have also been located at sites farther inland (at Krannon "Theopetra", near Kalambaka, for instance), often at the edge of a stream or a bog, or in an important pass, and generally in places where animals gathered or through which they moved. There is also evidence for the contemporary occupation of caves or shelters under rocks.

The Louros Valley

The largest number of significant remains of the Middle Palaeolithic Period in Greece have been located in Epeiros,

Anthropologists believe the Chalkidike skull (below) to be that of a woman who lived between 75,000 and 50,000 years ago. This is the oldest evidence of the presence of palaeolithic man in Greece. The skull is now at the University of Thessalonike. 40,000 to 35,000 years ago Neanderthal man was succeeded by Homo Sapiens, destined to lead mankind along the road to civilization.

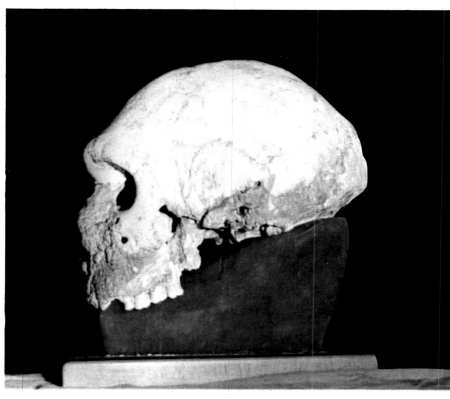

the most mountainous region in the country. Important observations have also been made there about the climate, the flora, and the fauna of the Upper Pleistocene.

In 1962 a British team from Cambridge, led by E.S. Higgs, carried out preliminary investigations in Northern Greece and succeeded in identifying a number of palaeolithic sites in Epeiros. The following year systematic excavations of camp sites and caves began. The largest number of remains were found in the valley of the Louros river, the ancient Inachos. The most important site is in the locality of Kokkinopelos, about 50 kilometres from Ioannina, to the right of the national road in the direction of Preveza and opposite the village of Hagios Georgios, known for its springs, the waters of which flow into the Louros. 800 implements and limestone flakes were found in a layer of *terra rossa* (red earth) which, it is believed, was formed during a warm oscillation of the last Glacial Age, about 50,000 to 35,000 years ago. They were chiefly scrapers, flakes, and points, both plain and worked, and a few bifacial leaf-shaped points. Similar tools were found in fifteen other sites in Epeiros, in valleys, or high upland basins, always in layers of red earth. It was thus confirmed that this terra rossa was the soil upon which man operated in this area during the Middle Palaeolithic.

The spacious cave of Asprochaliko (3½ kilometres from Kokkinopelos in the direction of Ioannina, to the left of the road from Preveza to Ioannina) rises 15 metres above the bed of the Louros. An admirable refuge in winter — shepherds take shelter in it to this day — it faces south, commanding a magnificent prospect of the southern reaches of the valley. It occupies a strategic position above an important pass, which had always been used by migrating animals.

Large quantities of tools were found in the deep accumulation of the cave. A specimen of charcoal from one of the layers, examined radiochronologically, revealed the date to be 37,900 B.C. This is the earliest date so far ascribed to any landmark in the evolution of civilization in Greece, a date moreover which coincides with the closing stages of man's activity during the Middle Palaeolithic in Greece. Other valuable knowledge was obtained as a result of the work carried out by the British team. The animal bones in the lower strata at Asprochaliko belonged to bears, different species of deer, rhinoceros, and other animals hunted by man.

Augustus Sordinas, the Greek scholar, discovered artifacts of palaeolithic man in the Ionian Islands also, principally in Corfu. Several sites of red earth contained palaeolithic tools. During a glacial period, when the sea level was at least 100 metres lower than it is now, Corfu was joined to the mainland of Epeiros; thus, the men of Asprochaliko could reach Corfu in the course of hunting forays without any difficulty. Palaeolithic traces have also been identified in Kephallenia. Fossilized bones of large mammals of the Pleistocene indicate that this island too was linked with the mainland.

The Peloponnesos

The incredible palaeolithic finds of Megalopolis furnish an impressive picture of the animal world of the Pleistocene.

Evidence for the existence of tools of the same period leave little room for doubt that man the hunter co-existed with the enormous mammals, the colossal elephants, and all the other beasts.

In 1960, Jean Servais discovered Middle Palaeolithic tools among various geological layers at a site slightly east of Kastro Chlemoutsi, at the westernmost point of the Peloponnesos. The fact that the Peloponnesos was inhabited by man during the Upper Pleistocene was thus established. From 1962 onwards, a French team under Professor A. Leroi-Gourhan carried out a series of explorations along the coast of western Elis and Achaia, where from Lakkopetra in the north to Katakolo in the south hundreds of tools and flakes of the Middle Palaeolithic were found.

Another French team also discovered tools of the Middle Palaeolithic in the interior of the peninsula, in particular at Lykouresi, a site near the village of Vasilaki along the Olympia-Tripolis road near the Erymanthos valley in eastern Elis. Man had therefore penetrated inland. The site is 22 kilometres from the sea, and this thrust into the interior of the land confirms the theory that the diffusion of Middle Palaeolithic man was a wide one, probably extending throughout the whole of the Peloponnesos.

The Sporades

Recent excavations (1969 – 70) carried out by a Greek team under D. R. Theocharis have brought to light reliably dated remains of the Middle Palaeolithic in the Aegean islands. The most important site was on the island of Liadromia, officially Halonnesos, and undoubtedly the ancient Ikos. Many tools and flakes of limestone that had undergone transformations resembled both in appearance and in regard to material those identified at Kokkinopelos in Epeiros. They were discovered in a layer of terra rossa on an islet no more than 150 metres long, off the southwest coast of Halonnesos, opposite the headland of Kokkinokastro, which is the site of the ancient city of Ikos. Fossilized bones of large and small mammals, attributed to the period of the Pikermian fauna, including rhinoceros, deer, members of the horse family, and other specimens whose identity has not yet been established, were found in the deeper layers. The site may have been an assembly-point during the Middle Palaeolithic, but, millions of years before that, it must have been a place where animals of the Pikermian fauna period roamed.

The palaeolithic finds of Halonnesos are the most ancient surviving relics of man's existence in the Aegean and of his activities in that area. There is no doubt that during the ice periods of the Pleistocene, when the sea sank to a low level, most of the islands of the Northern Sporades were joined to the opposite coast of Magnesia. They formed a part of the Aigaiis, a peninsula in fact, easily reached by large mammals and herds of various animals. The Pagasitic Gulf was then a level basin, and the Channel of Halonnesos, on the coast of which the palaeolithic sites have now been identified, was a valley. Further research to be followed by systematically conducted excavations in these

GREEK PREHISTORY

	AGE	CHRONOLOGY (B.C.)
BRONZE AGE	Late Bronze Age	1,580—1,100
	Middle Bronze Age	2,000/1,900—1,580
	Early Bronze Age	2,800/2,700—2,000/1,900
NEOLITHIC	Upper Neolithic	4,000—2,800/2,700
	Middle Neolithic	5,000—4,000
	Lower Neolithic	6,000—5,000
	Preceramic Neolithic	7,000—6,000
	MESOLITHIC	8,000—7,000
PALAEOLITHIC	Upper Palaeolithic	33,000—8,000
	Middle Palaeolithic	100,000—33,000
	Lower Palaeolithic	600,000 (?) — 100,000

(HOLOCENE spans the Bronze Age and Neolithic; PLEISTOCENE spans the Palaeolithic.)

The successive ages of Greek prehistory and their corresponding approximate chronology, from the earliest Palaeolithic Period to the end of the Bronze Age, which coincides with the dawn of archaic Greece (1100 B.C.).

islands is bound to furnish fresh evidence of the way of life of that primitive being who probably lived to see the submersion of the Aigaiis.

The Age of Neanderthal Man in Greece

The question arises as to who was the creator of the tools of the Middle Palaeolithic. A definite anthropological type predominated in Europe, Asia, and Africa throughout this age. This creature is known as Neanderthal man, because it was in the locality of Neanderthal near Düsseldorf in Germany that skeletal remains of *Homo Neanderthalensis* were first identified.

Neanderthal man possessed the distinctive features of primitive man, such as exaggeratedly developed brows, unequal cranial volumes, a very short neck, and a peculiar skeletal structure with a correspondingly awkward gait. But his brain was considerably larger than that of his predecessor: in fact, almost equal in size to that of modern man. Moreover, the stone tools he fashioned were more elaborate than those invented by his predecessors.

A skull, of which only the jaw is missing, belonging to this Neanderthal-type creature was discovered in Greece a few years ago. On 16 September 1960, a group of visitors who had entered through an artificial opening into the cave of Kokkines Petres (The Red Stones) at the foot of a limestone hill called Katsika (642 metres high), near the village of Petralona in the Chalkidike (75 kilometres southeast of Thessalonike by road, about 40 as the crow flies), came upon the skull by chance. The cave, which is filled with stalactites, is very large, the total length of the galleries and chambers exceeding 1,500 metres. The fossilized skull, partly covered with limestone deposits, was found near the entrance. It is now at the University of Thessalonike.

Anthropologists believe the skull to be that of a Neanderthaloid man. A number of conflicting morphological features nevertheless distinguish it from that of the so-called "classical" Neanderthal type. Unusually oblong, it is less broad than the ordinary type. The capacity of the cranial capsule is small (only 1,220 cubic centimetres) as opposed to the usual 1,650, common to Neanderthal skulls. Other features, however, provide conclusive evidence that it belongs to the type of Neanderthal man who lived in Europe, Asia, and Africa. Although both the age and sex to which the creature belonged are difficult to determine, the skull is thought to be that of a woman about 25 years old (rather old for that time). Since Neanderthal man dwelt in the early part of the Upper Pleistocene, it is not difficult to date this important anthropological discovery, the only one of its kind in Greece. Moreover, zoological remains found in the cave—those at least that can be associated with the skull—date to the last Interglacial or the beginning of the next Glacial Period, that is to say, to between 75,000 and 50,000 years ago. This is clearly the earliest direct evidence for the existence of an "ancient" man in Greece. Indirect evidence in the form of an abundance of tools of the Middle Palaeolithic Period, excavated by archaeologists in recent years in different parts of the country, furnishes further proof of his existence.

Material remains would therefore appear to confirm the

fact of man's existence and activities (from the end of the third Interglacial Period or the beginning of the last Glacial Period) over a much larger area of Greek territory than had been hitherto imagined. Remains of tools used by man of the Middle Palaeolithic, who, judging from the Petralona skull, belonged to a Neanderthaloid type, have been identified all over Greece, from the extreme end of Greek Thrace, Epeiros, and Thessaly, to the Ionian Islands, the Northern Sporades, and the Peloponnesos. In itself, however, the Petralona skull may not be regarded as sufficient evidence for determining the physical type of the inhabitants of Greece during the Middle Palaeolithic Period. A type of creature closer to early modern man (*Praesapiens*) lived in Europe and southwest Asia both before and partly at the same time as the Neanderthal man. So far, however, no trace of this creature has been found in Greece.

The different skills practised in the Middle Palaeolithic in Greece and the variety of types of tools that go with these skills contribute to the overall picture. The many scrapers, the flake tools, plain or worked, the points, and the leaf-shaped bifacial tips, which were probably attached to lance heads, indicate some degree of technical progress. Man of the Middle Palaeolithic was not unskilled in fashioning tools. The numerous bones of animals found in his camp sites indicate that he was also an expert hunter.

Weapons, on the other hand, were confined to wooden javelins. The larger animals, such as the mammoth and the rhinoceros, as well as the more swift-footed wild horse and reindeer, were probably caught in traps since the bow was as yet unknown. The excellent condition of the teeth of surviving skulls indicates that man was pre-eminently carnivorous, and that his diet consisted mainly of the meat of the animals he hunted. He would cut up the animals where he killed them and carry back to the settlement only certain choice parts, including the head for the brain, and the pelt.

During cold periods, cave-dwelling was not without advantages. But in order to gain possession of the caves, man had first to contend with the bears, hyenas, and other animals that inhabited them. Fire, man's most ancient weapon, was the means used to drive out the beasts. Many hearths have been identified in the caves, as well as a number of rather carefully made graves.

The end of this type of man was both sudden and general. The social and technological changes that accompanied the predominance of *Homo Sapiens* throughout the world are a most important landmark in the history of prehistoric man. The Neanderthal man was irrevocably doomed. His place on the world stage was now taken by a much more vital creature, one that was destined to lead humanity along the path of progress and civilization.

Homo Sapiens in Greece

It is generally believed among specialists that after the first peak period of the last Glacial Age, some 40,000 years ago, Neanderthal man became wholly extinct. His place was taken by Modern Man (*Homo Sapiens Diluvialis*) of the Pleistocene. His advent was accompanied by a remarkable technological revolution, which emphasizes the dra-

An anthropomorphic 'earring' (or 'earplug') found in a cave on Mt. Pelion. It is conjectured that the 'earring' was the first attempt made by palaeolithic man in Greece to represent the human body. (Volos Museum)

matic nature of the change from one type of human species to another. The extinction of the older primitive man must have been total, since no traces are left of the way in which he disappeared, not even in the material sphere. Almost in the same way as the animal kingdom, where animals unable to adapt themselves to new conditions are doomed to extinction, so here a species of man disappeared totally.

Modern man is not thought to be indigenous to Europe. He probably came from the southeast. Without actually going so far as to pin-point his birthplace, most anthropologists believe that his formation must have taken place in Western Asia and its periphery, and that he probably developed in more than one particular locality, perhaps in a wider area of the Middle East, which might even have included parts of the Balkans and Africa. Southwest Asia in particular has provided evidence of early anthropological remains of modern man (who is an earlier type than, or partly contemporary with, Neanderthal man) and of fragments of tools which could be described as prototypes of those associated with later palaeolithic times. The problem, however, has not yet been wholly solved.

It was undoubtedly somewhere in the Near East, and probably not very far from the shores of the Mediterranean, that modern man, after a period of gestation and formation, began to consolidate his way over the whole of the then known world and ultimately to extend his dominion over remote regions of the earth, as yet unknown to the human race.

Greece, situated at a point where Europe meets Asia, and therefore in close proximity to both Asia Minor and North Africa, probably played some part in the dissemination of *Homo Sapiens* and in his passage from one continent to another, and may have even contributed to his actual development. This would have applied particularly to periods when the sea level of the Aegean sank, rendering communications easier between the Balkan peninsula and the opposite coast. Moreover, since the presence of this species of man is accompanied by revolutionary changes in technology, there ought to exist, in theory at least, implements of the Upper Palaeolithic Age in Greece. Recent research, even if still in an embryonic stage, tends in fact to point in this direction.

What then were the physical characteristics of this man who was from now on to prevail throughout the entire world and become the progenitor of all the races known to history? What was the structure and general appearance of this man, whose physical traits have remained unchanged during the last 50,000 years? The most cursory comparison between skeletons of Neanderthal man and those of early modern man reveals striking differences. The erect position of the skeleton is not yet wholly formed in Neanderthal man: the femur is somewhat curved. In modern man, the stance is erect, the body on the whole slender. The animal-like prognathism of the earlier species, the disproportionately large skull on a short neck, the low forehead, the hypertrophic brows, are all absent in the later species. Almost from the outset *Homo Sapiens* appears differentiated into distinct physical branches, which were ultimately to develop into the principal races of mankind.

Do anthropological remains which can be attributed to the human type of the Pleistocene exist in Greece? Unfortunately, the rare finds attributed to the Upper Pleistocene are questionable. So far as is known at present, none comes from a systematic excavation or any other scientific investigation; not one can be dated with any degree of certainty.

The Technique of Blade-making

As already observed, the emergence of modern man on the world scene was followed by the invention of a new technique in the production of flint flakes, which brought about revolutionary changes in the inventory of man's implements, accompanied by new methods in their use. It was the last great technological turning-point in the history of the human race destined to influence man's subsequent evolution up to the time of the Bronze Age.

The new method is called the technique of blade-making. The blades were in fact nothing more than oblong flakes with parallel sides, very much like the plates of a double-edged knife. In the preparatory process, a flint core, usually oblong, cone- or prism-shaped, was used. An entire series of by-products, consisting of implements of different types in standard forms to serve specific purposes, was fashioned on the basis of the original blade. The range and number of objects were thus considerably enlarged as they grew smaller in size, while less labour and a far smaller quantity of raw material were required to produce them. This ingenious innovation introduced by *Homo Sapiens* in the technical field had incalculable consequences. In the first place, it had an influence on man's hunting equipment. Whereas Neanderthal man's armoury consisted virtually of a wooden spear, modern man, equipped with blades as a basic tool, found no difficulty in fashioning arrow-heads with blades backed on one side and fastened to a wooden shaft or to the extremity of an arrow. He also cut notches and worked with bone, making sharp points. He invented a valuable tool, the burin, with which he worked on wood, bone, and horn to open oblong slits in which blades and flakes could be fixed. With these new tools at his disposal, he was able to fashion bows, bone splint throwers, toothed harpoons, and other tools and weapons, and to hunt nimbler and swifter-footed small animals. Progress in hunting methods proved so efficacious that man was now assured a plentiful food supply. Apart from the increase in population, the foundations were thus laid for the development of art, which makes its first appearance during the Upper Palaeolithic from 30,000 B.C. onwards.

This seemingly simple change in technique exemplified by the production of blades had an immense impact on man's life in general, on his intellectual progress, and even on his social evolution. It seems essential to stress the importance of details which might otherwise be dismissed as trivial or irrelevant to the story of the human race in the Palaeolithic Period.

Equipped with special tools for work on other materials, man was now able to produce bone and horn objects. Even needles with eyes were used for stitching hides, and garments began to assume recognizable shapes. As the range of workmanship grew wider, progress in the art of decoration became more rapid. Bone implements and weapons were now ornamented with attractive designs, and necklaces were strung with beads fashioned out of bone, animals' teeth, and perforated sea-shells. More important, small female idol figurines, some of which possessed an extraordinarily vital and expressive quality, were fashioned out of bone,

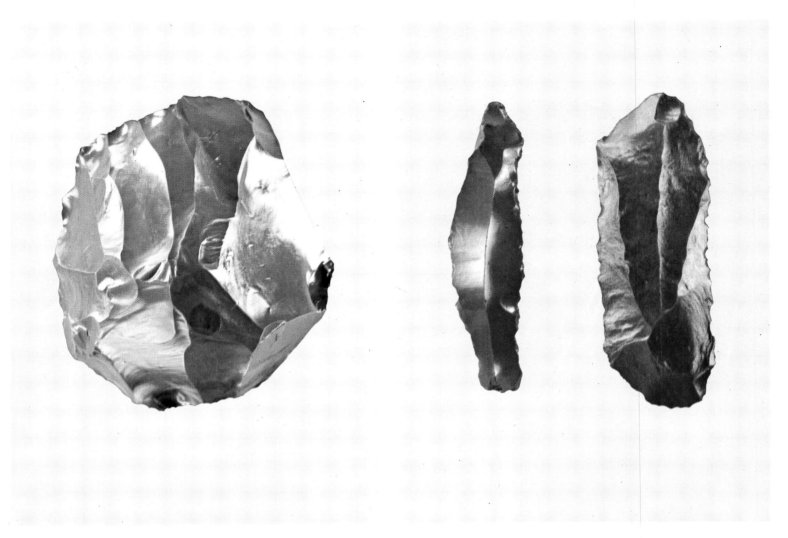

During tens of thousands of years, blades and flint flakes were the main types of tools used by palaeolithic man in Thessaly. Left: large flint-core with indications of some working. Right: *two blades of the Upper Palaeolithic from a site on the banks of the Peneios. The use of blades continued until an advanced stage of the Bronze Age. (Volos Museum)*

ivory, and stone. The walls of caves were chiselled, and the sombre chambers and galleries filled with remarkable representations in outline of animals, often accompanied by paintings.

The art of the Upper Palaeolithic, which included carved and engraved ornaments and other portable objects, is regarded as the greatest early aesthetic achievement of the human race. This astonishing phenomenon, extending over an area two thousand kilometres long, from the banks of the Don to the foothills of the Pyrenees, assumed worldwide proportions. It was the first human expression without immediate connection with practical needs, a major manifestation of the creative spirit which, in terms of its geographical context, may be characterized as "European". Whatever interpretation is given to this form of artistic expression, whether it is called "magical" or "symbolical", it is an expression of the soul in response to the basic problems which occupy man's mind, an attempt to give an answer to the enigmas of life. Considering the relatively short time it took palaeolithic man to attain these heights and how rapidly he advanced from the condition of static barbarism of his predecessors to an intellectual level which may almost be called "modern", palaeolithic art must appear as little short of miraculous.

If there is any single period in which the first glimmer-

ings of religious faith are discernible, it is surely the Upper Palaeolithic. Men's graves bear witness to this spiritual awakening. The meticulous way in which the corpses were placed in pits within caves might well be a legacy of Neanderthal man. But in several instances during the Upper Palaeolithic we find corpses buried fully clothed with their ornaments beside them (especially in the case of men and children), and always laid out in the same flexed position, which endured throughout almost the whole of the prehistorical age.

That some kind of articulate speech, a "language", existed, must be regarded as certain. If the anatomical characteristicts of Neanderthal man (the large cranial volume, the shape of his jaw and the cavity of his mouth) indicate that this creature probably possessed the power of some form of speech, there can be no doubt whatsoever that palaeolithic man, endowed with the physical traits of modern man, was able to speak. Indeed, the existence of a language, however imperfectly developed, would up to a point explain the rapidity of man's evolution and the accelerated rhythm of his progress.

The number of objects and implements used by "modern man" of the Pleictocene so far discovered in Greece is neither great nor impressive. Research is still in the preliminary stage. Nevertheless, some important remains of the Upper

51

Palaeolithic have been identified in the same general areas where Middle Palaeolithic remains were discovered. The reason is that so far methodical excavation has been undertaken in only two caves; in a third the work is not yet at an advanced stage.

The first serious attempt to excavate an Upper Palaeolithic site was made in 1941, during the days of the enemy occupation of Greece, at the small cave of Seidi, near Haliartos, in the Kopais basin. The stone-industry is believed to be terminal palaeolithic and may be dated to c. 12,000 B.C. or slightly later. Excavations undertaken by German and Greek teams on the banks of the Peneios, near Larisa, have also revealed late palaeolithic tools, such as blades, burins, and end-scrapers. On the whole, however, types of implements belonging to the Upper Palaeolithic are rare. Manifestly, late palaeolithic objects must be sought in caves rather than in open country.

On the other hand, several important discoveries in Thessaly (in the Pelion area in particular) indicate that palaeolithic art had spread to Greece. The outlines of a wild horse incised on a piece of hard stone in the shape of a point, found outside a small cave above the village of Lechonia on Mt. Pelion, although not precisely dated, would appear to be of palaeolithic origin. The outline is firm and vivid, the image definite and plain without details.

Epeiros has yielded the largest quantity of remains of the Upper Palaeolithic. A stone-industry of small backed blades was found in a layer of red earth at Kokkinopelos. It may be about 35,000 years old—the oldest of its kind in Greece, if not in Europe. It resembles flints discovered in North-Eastern Europe and at the Romanelli cave in Apulia. It is in fact believed that these "eastern" sites are earlier than the corresponding ones in Western Europe. Kokkinopelos might have been a station on the road followed by men at the beginning of the Upper Palaeolithic in the course of their westward migrations.

The finds of Kokkinopelos and the caves of Asprochaliko and Kastritsa constitute the main source from which it is possible to form some idea of life in Greece during the Upper Palaeolithic Period. From the point of view of technique, particular importance must be attached to the very early appearance of backed blades (Kokkinopelos) and to the great length of time during which they were in use (Asprochaliko and Kastritsa), in fact, from the beginning to almost the end of the Upper Palaeolithic. This continuity in stone-work indicates that the men who produced it did not change radically throughout the Upper Palaeolithic Period.

From the Pleistocene to the Holocene

Remains of the Upper Palaeolithic so far identified in Greece appear to have been distributed throughout the same area as those of the early Middle Palaeolithic. The techniques of stone-work are however entirely different from those of the earlier period. Their relatively distinctive character is reminiscent of cultures of Eastern Europe and Italy, and possibly of certain areas of the Balkans.

For at least part of the year men dwelt mostly in caves. The open sites are more likely to have been camps where they assembled before and after the hunt. E. S. Higgs estimates the number of cave-dwellers at Kastritsa at approximately twenty-five during the summer months. In winter, snow-falls must have caused the deer and other animals to descend to the lowlands, where men would necessarily have followed them. Thus caves like the one at Asprochaliko, or Corfu and the coastal belt, probably provided the hunters with winter quarters. To ensure his food supply, man of the Upper Palaeolithic was therefore probably nomadic, not wholly unlike the modern Sarakatsans who descend in winter from the mountains of Zagori to the southern lowlands and coastal areas.

Little is known about climatic conditions in Greece during the Upper Palaeolithic and the closing stages of the Pleistocene. Some indications of a similarity of climate between Greece and other Mediterranean countries, particularly Southern Italy, have been noted. Although the climate was on the whole more temperate than in the rest of Europe, there must have been a period of extreme cold between about 25,000 and 10,000 years ago. As elsewhere, man in Greece must also have had to face all the difficulties resulting from a hostile and changing climate. About 8,500 B.C., however, a temperate climate, not very different from the present one, appears definitely to have set in throughout the country. This is the beginning of the Holocene, which marks the end of the Palaeolithic Period.

In the absence of any anthropological remains, next to nothing is known of the physical traits of man of the Upper Palaeolithic in Greece. But there can be little doubt that physically he belonged to the same type of man as the one who disseminated his species throughout a large part of Europe and the Near East from the beginning of the Upper Palaeolithic and who took the leading part in subsequent

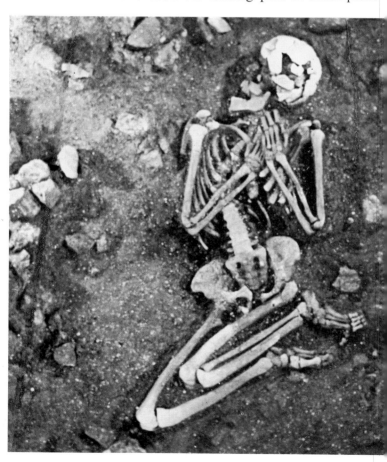

In the cave of Franchthi (right), near Hermione, an American archaeological team has brought to light numerous remains from

developments, leaving indelible traces of his activities in this part of the Old World, which was later to become the cradle of civilization. This type did not of course disappear with the end of the Pleistocene, nor did he vanish from the world, as Neanderthal man did. He did not just go through Greece, which was a most favourable land from the geographical and climatic points of view. He remained there and probably formed the basic stock from which sprang those tribes which, after the brief transitional phase of the Mesolithic, proceeded to the productive stage.

THE MESOLITHIC PERIOD

Changes in Climatic Conditions

The significance and main features of the Mesolithic Period and its relation to previous and subsequent phases raise questions which demand answers before any examination of the surviving traces of Mesolithic times in Greece can be carried out. The term itself implies that it was a transitional phase between two completely different stages, between a period when man's occupation was confined to hunting animals and another when he actually began to produce food. It constituted, in fact, a bridge between the old hunting and food-gathering economy and an economy based on agriculture and stockbreeding.

In techniques, the Mesolithic Period is an extension of the end of the Palaeolithic. As regards the economy, however, it belongs to the pre-productive phase. Although hunting still played a decisive role, the economy is more of the food-gathering kind. Fishing and the gathering of wild fruits, vegetables, and crustaceans increased, and the first animal, the dog, was tamed.

Culturally, the Mesolithic Period resembles the terminal Palaeolithic, adapted to the new environmental conditions of the Holocene. Why was it necessary for man to readjust and change his way of life? The answer lies in the fact that a great global change in climatic conditions had occurred towards the end of the Pleistocene during the ninth millenium B.C., following the final withdrawal of the ice-floes towards the polar regions and the subsequent prevalence of a warmer and drier climate not unlike that of today. Particularly in the Periglacial zones, which were more directly affected by glaciers and heavy rainfall, the abrupt change in climatic conditions caused a greater upheaval. The equilibrium of life at the end of the Palaeolithic was profoundly disturbed, man's cultural development was disrupted, and all living creatures were directly affected. The large animals, such as mammoths, hairy rhinoceros, and reindeer, which had succeeded in adjusting to the cold climate and corresponding vegetation and which had provided man with his means of nourishment, migrated to the extreme north, and the largest species soon became extinct. Smaller and more nimble animals appeared on the scene. Consequently, the entire technique of hunting, as well as the weapons and tools

the Mesolithic (c. 8th millennium B.C.), a hitherto unknown phase of the Stone Age in Greece. Also Mesolithic is the skeleton (left), which was found in the cave in a contracted position, covered with stones.

associated with it, had to undergo a radical readjustment. Stone implements had to be adapted to the hunting of smaller animals which now roamed the forests.

The Mesolithic Period did not end at the same time everywhere. In Europe it lasted until 4000 B.C., whereas the earliest Neolithic phase began in the East in the 8th millennium B.C. The Mesolithic is not a chronological but a cultural period, and its duration differed from one area to another, always beginning with the close of the Palaeolithic Period and ending with the opening of the Neolithic.

We may now examine the subject more closely and review the Mesolithic remains so far discovered in Greece. The most important of these were identified in successive Palaeolithic and Mesolithic strata in the cave of Franchthi near the village of Koilada, not far from Porto Cheli, in the Hermionid. The Mesolithic layer was 4 m. deep. This large cave in the limestone hillside, about 10 m. above sea level, is 150 m. long; the entrance, which faces NW, is 30 m. wide. The bones of animals found in the various strata indicate that the game hunted by the cave-dwellers consisted largely of deer. In fact, 75 to 85% of the bones identified belong to this species. The ox and bison are represented in smaller quantities; wild boar, fox, hare, dog, and wild goat in even smaller ones. Remains of bones of large fish grow in quantity in the layers of a later date. We may therefore conclude that man initially depended on game, and especially deer, for his nourishment, and that fishing appeared only at a later date. The life led by the cave-dwellers would appear to have been extremely simple. The stone tools were very simple, and there were only a very few bone tools; there is nothing to suggest any distinctive or elaborate workmanship. An attempt at some rudimentary decoration may only just be discerned, and the cultural level appears to have been low. During the latter part of the Mesolithic, the use of obsidian, believed to be of Melian provenance, may suggest some kind of maritime activity, or at least the possibility of some form of bartering of goods.

The Earliest Skeleton of the Aigaiis

The scanty human remains found in the Mesolithic layers of the cave of Franchthi belonged, according to anthropologist J.L. Angel, to men and women of short stature; the height of the men was 1.56m., that of the women 1.35—1.39m. In some instances, the skeletons were affected by anaemia and arthritic deformities. One extremely well preserved grave of the earliest Mesolithic phase contained remains of great importance; namely, the skeleton of a man, about twenty-five years old, 1.58 m. in height, who had died as a result of a crushing blow on the head. The grave, situated in a shallow recess, showed signs of improvization. The legs of the corpse were flexed, and the hands were placed symmetrically across the chest. The grave contained no personal belongings; but there were traces of fire. For reasons as yet unknown, stones were placed around, and partly on top of, the skeleton. The grave, the earliest complete one of a man so far found in the Aigaiis, has been dated to 7,592 B.C.

The Mesolithic men who inhabited the cave apparently buried their dead without ceremonial rites or adornments in shallow ground close to where they dwelt. The attitude of contraction of the legs does not seem to possess any partic-

ular significance; it may have been due to the desire to save space. The traces of fire have no connection with the burial. The placing of stones on corpses has been observed in several other instances, both during the Palaeolithic and later ages.

The excavation of this cave, which has not yet gone beyond the preliminary stages, may not in itself present an altogether clear image of the Mesolithic Period in Greece; but it does allow us to establish the existence of this period in Greece and to perceive how the Palaeolithic ended and how the Mesolithic succeeded it. So far as we now know, the transition from one period to the other was the result of changes in environmental conditions and in the fauna. A sudden change in the size, and partly in the species, of animals is in fact confirmed by scientific research. The change was natural, for the animals of the Palaeolithic Period belonged to the Pleistocene, while those of the Mesolithic to the Holocene.

The stratigraphic evidence in the Franchthi cave during the Mesolithic also appears to have followed quite a normal course. Whereas the remains of deer in the earlier (deeper) strata indicate the hunting character of the earlier phase, fishing begins to acquire greater importance in the later period and even more so in the earliest Neolithic phase. The materials used for fashioning tools indicate the same normal development and transition. Obsidian appears again in the second half of the Mesolithic, and its use grows in the Early Neolithic Period, until later it becomes general. The Mesolithic Period was obviously a transitional one, serving as a bridge between two different stages.

Blanks in our knowledge of the progressive stages of development in the remote prehistorical period of Greece, between the Palaeolithic and the Neolithic Periods, have, for the first time, been partially filled in by the discovery of remains in stratified deposits. The significance of this discovery is enhanced when we recall that the most important role of Mesolithic peoples was that they were the means whereby the food-producing revolution of the succeeding period spread throughout the world. In the beginning of the chapter on the Neolithic Period, it will be observed that the men responsible for the great Neolithic revolution in the central area of the Near East were its Mesolithic inhabitants. It follows that those who accepted the idea of change in a wider area adjacent to the central Near East and who actually increased its scope were also mesolithics.

It is too early as yet to reach any definite conclusions as regards Greece and the Aigaiis in this context. Further research will have to be undertaken before we can judge whether the Mesolithic Period was a follow-up of the final phases of the Palaeolithic in so far as tools and the economy are concerned. So far the evidence offers no grounds for supposing that there was any kind of colonization of the country during this transitional period; consequently, the indigenous character of the mesolithic population may be considered to derive from palaeolithic times.

Opposite page: pebble on both sides of which a human form is incised in a strongly contracted position. The striking position of the human form, the details, and the 'abstract' style in general are reminiscent of the art of the last phase of the Palaeolithic, or the Mesolithic, rather than the Neolithic, from which it actually dates. The pebble comes from the Neolithic settlement of Magoula Karamurlar, northwest of Volos. (Volos Museum)

The Neolithic Period

A NEW WAY OF LIFE

Greece played a minor role, purely regional in character, throughout the various stages of man's evolution as a migratory hunter. But with the opening of the food-producing era, its role in Europe became prominent. As far as the continent of Europe is concerned, it is only here that important evidence has come to light of an early agricultural and stockbreeding way of life dated to the 7th millennium B.C.

This sudden transformation is not unrelated to the country's geographical position and its proximity to the Middle East, where revolutionary changes altered the future of the human race. The basic features of this new economic and cultural phase—the Neolithic or food-producing phase—are of the greatest importance. Looking back on the world we are about to leave, one is struck by the significance of certain comparisons. The Palaeolithic Period, together with the brief transitional Mesolithic—in fact, the whole of the time when man was a migratory hunter—lasted sixty times longer than the food-producing age. The Lower and Middle Palaeolithic Periods, which correspond to the age of primitive man, lasted for 95% of the time in relation to the Upper Palaeolithic and the Mesolithic, when modern man enters upon the scene. Moreover, the Upper Palaeolithic was at least nine times longer than the Mesolithic. Development and progress acquired a new momentum, further accelerated by the emergence of *Homo Sapiens* from about 35,000 B.C. There has been no important anthropological change in man since then.

The new epoch cannot therefore be wholly separated from the earlier one. As already indicated, certain phenomena associated with the closing stages of the late Palaeolithic and Mesolithic Periods prove that latent forces, which radically altered the economy and the general way of life, were already at work when man was still a hunter. The introduction of agriculture and stockbreeding and the emergence of permanent settlements constitute the two bases on which the new economy was founded. Dwelling places, or at least seasonal shelters, were not unknown in the Upper Palaeolithic. The consistency shown by certain late Palaeolithic and Mesolithic tribes in hunting specific animals indicates the existence of some form of cohabitation between hunters and hunted, some kind of closer relationship between man and the most useful animal species. It also portends the ultimate domestication of animals. If man had not been thoroughly acquainted with animals in their untamed stage, he would hardly have been capable of domesticating them at a later stage. He had to be acquainted with various preparatory processes, including the selection of the species that would prove most useful to him; he had to be aware of the different varieties of fruits and of the kind of soil on which they would flourish. He had, moreover, to make these observations at a time when he was still only a fruit-gatherer during Upper Palaeolithic and Mesolithic times.

Finally, in man's inventory of tools, the transition from the Late Palaeolithic to the Mesolithic stage and from it again to the beginning of the food producing stage may be regarded as a normal development, a readaptation rather than a replacement of equipment. The only new element is the polishing of stone implements.

The transformation from one economy to another took place not abruptly but gradually. Some features of the hunting period, particularly where game, fishing, and fruit-collecting are concerned, survived into the food-producing era and probably later. But now man was no longer wholly dependent on these sources of nourishment. The transition from a hunting economy to a food-producing one can hardly be described by the popular term "revolution", especially with regard to events in the Near East. The revolutionary aspect of the change has in fact been over-emphasized. The change was revolutionary in the sense that it was so in its consequences. Throughout the period when man depended on hunting for his livelihood, he was little more than a parasite, living on the flesh of animals, on anything he found ready to hand. He was the prisoner of his physical environment, utterly dependent on the forces of nature.

With the emergence of the new food-producing economy, this total dependence on the environment virtually came to an end. For the first time man was able to live on the stockbreeding and agricultural foodstuffs which he himself produced. He was now in a position to exercise increasing control over his environment, a kind of dominance over nature itself.

The consequences of this new way of life, based on the settled community and an agricultural and stockbreeding economy, were tremendous. The fact that man was now master of the main sources of his livelihood radically altered the further course of mankind. In this respect, it was indeed one of the greatest revolutions in the history of mankind. Actually, the largest proportion of the world's population continues to this day to obtain its food from agriculture and stockbreeding, and people continue to live in villages which do not differ substantially from Neolithic settlements. A modern city, however great in extent, is virtually no more than an enlarged version of such a settlement. The difference is quantitative rather than qualitative.

The consequences of this revolutionary transformation were not however confined to the material sphere. They exercized an enormous influence on social organization and culture, and this new way of life continued virtually unchanged until the Industrial Revolution. The Neolithic Period can no longer be described, as it once was, as "the polished stone period". Even the term *neolithic* has been questioned by some scholars.

The association of the primarily economic and cultural Neolithic Period with the polished stone axe and hand-made pottery is of secondary importance. These are merely additional characteristics of an age essentially based on agriculture, stockbreeding, and the settled community. Only where there is archaeological evidence of the threefold existence of agriculture, stockbreeding, and the settled community (accompanied by a corresponding absence of metals) are we entitled to refer to a food-producing or neolithic period. The stone axe and pottery are not among its essential attributes. In other words, the basic elements of the Neolithic Period, especially during its early phases, must not be sought in man's inventory of implements and household goods.

Progress in the Near East

An important question now arises. Where did this new stage first become apparent and how did its main features spread to other areas? Apart from its general significance, the question directly affects later developments in Greece, since it is linked with the time when the Neolithic stage started in Greek lands.

What then was the basic reason for this great change? Man would surely not have altered his whole way of life, if game, supplemented by food-gathering, had continued to provide him with adequate means of livelihood. The great climatic upheaval at the end of the Pleistocene as the result of a final withdrawal of the glaciers and of a general rise in the world's temperature is believed to have been one of the principal causes. According to the findings of scholars working in the Middle East, the onset of the new age is dated from about 10,000 to 7,000 B.C., and this period actually corresponds to the change of climate from the end of the Pleistocene to the beginning of the Holocene. As already noted, the change in climatic conditions was more pronounced in the Glacial Zone and its periphery. Consequently, the results were more destructive in that particular area and, with the disappearance of the large animals, the old economy perished too. It was not there, however, nor was it in the Periglacial Zone, that the food-producing stage began; it was in the Near East. Although the climatic change was an almost world-wide phenomenon, the corresponding cultural change was circumscribed to a particular, admittedly wide, region. If the passive element in the change was the altered climate ("the challenge of the environment" Arnold Toynbee would say), the active one was man's response to the challenge. Henceforward the cultural history of man is no longer an extension of natural history, in which the blind forces of nature play the principal part. Man is now the chief protagonist.

Systematic exploration for a generation in the Near East has demonstrated the early appearance of the food-producing stage in that area. In the tenth millennium B.C., when Europe was still Palaeolithic in character, the Near East had already passed into the Mesolithic Period. This

was soon followed, in the ninth millennium B.C., by the emergence of settlements, now described as Protoneolithic throughout the central zone of this area; this is the so-called Fertile Crescent, which extends westward from the foot of the Zagros Mountains in Iraq and the sources of the Tigris and the Euphrates in the north to Palestine. A mixed economy, no longer Mesolithic nor yet Neolithic, prevailed. In one settlement, dated to just after 9,000 B.C., the existence of domesticated sheep has been confirmed; in others the gathering of some primitive cereals, or fruits and generally vegetable products, is strongly indicated by the presence of sickles, knives for reaping, blades for scythes, millstones, mortars, and graters.

At the same time, the Natufian civilization, which was formerly ascribed to the Mesolithic Period, flourished in Jordan and Palestine. Centred apparently in the valley of the Jordan River, the Natufians settled, long before 9,000

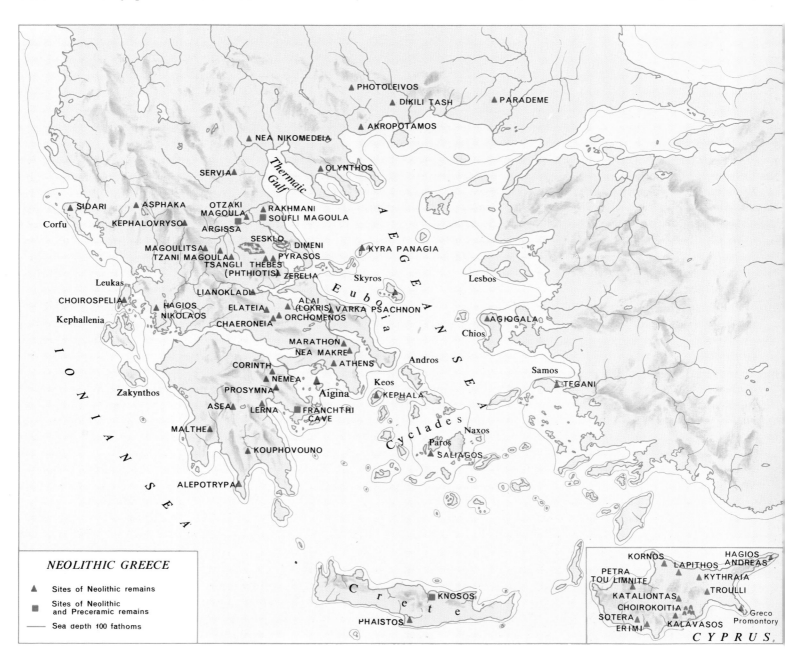

The Neolithic sites which have been established through the excavations of recent decades cover almost the entire area of Greece, including Crete. Shown on the map are only a few of the excavated settlements and geographically important sites. Separately marked are some of the principal sites which have been archaeologically ascertained as Preceramic.

B.C., at the oasis of Jericho (230 metres below sea level). and even established a sanctuary there. Three successive villages were discovered at the settlement of Eynan, where remains of round dwellings with stone foundations were identified. The village, extending over an area of 2,000 square metres, consisted of at least fifty houses, corresponding to a population of about 300. Numerous graves provided valuable information regarding burial customs, such as the use of red ochre and the burial with the dead of his favourite possessions. The inhabitants, who belonged to the Eurafrican race, had oblong heads, and were over 1.50 m. in height. It may be assumed from the graves that the general artistic standard was relatively high for the period. Although probably derivative of some as yet unknown early palaeolithic stage, Natufian art appears to have been in the main tradition of European Palaeolithic. During the succeeding millennium, the eighth B.C., which belongs to the second part of the Protoneolithic Period in the central Middle East area, the settlement at Jericho developed into a town of two thousand inhabitants with impressive architectural structures, that is, strong fortification walls.

The Neolithic proper, which began in the Middle East in about 7,000 B.C., was distinguished by the emergence of numerous communities still at an *aceramic* or *preceramic* level. There is fully confirmed evidence of the cultivation of cereals and the domestication of animals, but the use of clay pottery had not yet been introduced. Similar features apply to the earliest known Neolithic phase (Preceramic Neolithic) in Greece. Clearly, the Neolithic Revolution therefore took place in the so-called nuclear area of the Near East: in the valleys at the foot of the Zagros Mountains, in the semi-mountainous region of Northern Mesopotamia, and the Jordan valley. Here then, even before the end of the Pleistocene, appear the beginnings of that second major cultural phase in the history of man, the food-producing phase, and it is this centre that was to generate the motive power for further development and for the dissemination of the new economy throughout the ancient world.

The lead taken by the Near East in new developments is often attributed to the presence in that area, in a wild condition, of the basic plants cultivated, and animals domesticated by man at the start of the Neolithic Period. Such plants and animals exist in that area in their wild condition even today. Wheat, both einkorn and emmer, barley and, on a lower level, pulses, are plants of a medium height. The same is true of the most important animals: goats and sheep, and, later, oxen and swine. The cultivation of these plants and the domestication of these animals would clearly take place more rapidly in their natural habitat, where they had existed in a wild state, under pressures resulting from the need to adapt to the new conditions of life, which were in part imposed by the changed climate of the early Holocene. But the change did not take place suddenly, nor was the new economy a purely environmental accident. It was man that provided the dynamic element for the change. Man tamed the animals and cultivated the land; man set the direction of the course.

The question now arises: when and in what way did these new conditions spread from the centre to the periphery, to Greece, and to the whole of Europe? A rapid increase in population was one of the major consequences of the new economy, which for the first time provided man with abundant nourishment. Possibilities for the absorption of the growing numbers of inhabitants were limitless. The diffusion of the new way of life must have occurred after it had first been firmly established in territories propitious for further physical and ecological development: primarily in the wider area of the Near East, which is surrounded by the south-eastern basin of the Mediterranean, the Aegean, the Black Sea, the Caspian, the Persian Gulf, and the Red Sea. It probably originated from movements of small groups of settlers or colonizers, as well as from the exchange of goods, ideas, and technical methods, for the new economy was above all a progressive one, and progress, *ipso facto*, cannot be static.

THE PRECERAMIC NEOLITHIC IN GREECE

Sites in Thessaly

Greece, in which Neolithic settlements of the seventh millennium B.C. have recently been identified, lies within the confines of the first zone of diffusion—the Middle East area. Remains of the earliest known Preceramic Neolithic settlements in Greece were revealed for the first time on European soil by Vladimir Milojčič at Argissa in 1956 and later by D.R. Theoharis at Sesklo in Thessaly. This earliest Neolithic phase has been termed Preceramic Neolithic. Preliminary excavations carried out at other Thessalian sites (Achilleion near Pharsala, Soufli Magoula, Yediki near Larisa) have revealed preceramic remains in the lowest layers. Later, excavations carried out by John D. Evans revealed the earliest Neolithic settlements at Knosos in Crete to be Aceramic. Thomas Jacobsen, working in the cave at Franchthi in the Hermionid, identified a stratum

about one metre deep as Late Aceramic. The method of dating strata by radiocarbon provided the absolute date to be 5,844 (or 6,078) B.C. for the preceramic stratum at Franchthi and 6,100 (or 6,341) B.C. for the one at Knosos. The Preceramic Neolithic phase can therefore be dated to the seventh millennium B.C.

Relatively little is known as yet of the Preceramic Neolithic phase in Greece. Few sites have been thoroughly excavated, and nowhere have the strata been examined horizontally so as to reveal the outlines of a settlement. Scanty as the remains may be, they are important in that they can be dated to the earliest Neolithic phase. Three sites in Thessaly have been rather satisfactorily studied: (a) Argissa (Magoula Gremos, 4.5 km. west of Larisa, on the left bank of the Peneios); (b) Sesklo (the acropolis of Kastraki, approximately 8 km. west of Volos); (c) Soufli Magoula (a knoll 5 km. north-east of Larisa on the right bank of the Peneios). Excavation of preceramic layers in the other sites (Achilleion near Pharsala, Yediki near Larisa) has been quite limited.

Dwellings and Tools

The settlement at Argissa was of considerable extent (80 metres in length). As only a very small part of the site has been excavated, the disposition of the dwellings remains unknown. Six small shallow pits appear to have been dug into hard soil to a depth of from 0.30 to 0.60 m. The holes found there were probably intended for the insertion of posts and may have belonged to huts. There are no vestiges of houses or walls above ground. The largest pit, oval in shape like the others, is about 4 m. long by 2.20 m. wide. It could therefore have served as a habitation or dug floor. Hearths and pebble floors were found in some of the pits.

Carbonized grains of cereals found in Early Neolithic strata in Thessaly provide direct evidence of the agricultural character of Early Neolithic civilization in the Thessalian plain (Volos Museum). Indirect evidence exists in the abundance of graters, millstones, etc. The carbonized grains constitute the earliest extant proof of the cultivation of cereals in Europe. Superior civilizations flourished only in areas in which the cultivation of wheat had been assured.

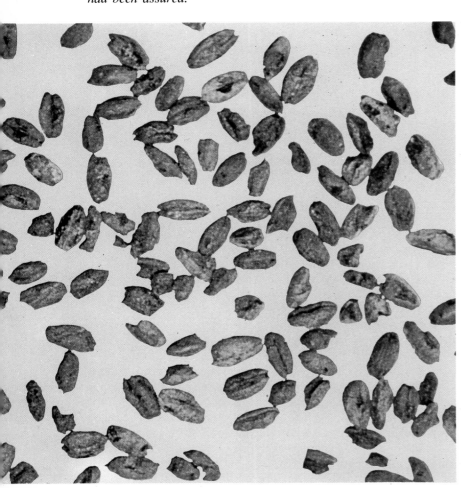

One very small pit smeared with clay, may have served for storage. There are several indications of the existence of some form of permanent habitation. The walls and roof were probably made of branches, reeds, and rushes.

A comparison of these scanty remains with those found elsewhere reveals that floors of huts dug in the soil are similar to those of the Upper Palaeolithic in Central and Eastern Europe, while floors of oval or other shape are also found during the Mesolithic. The dwellings of the Natufian settlements in the Orient of the eighth millennium B.C. were also either round or oval. On the other hand, no comparison can be made between the scanty remains at Argissa and the contemporary Near East structures. In the seventh millennium B.C., Jericho was a real town with fortification walls, four-sided houses built of mud bricks, plastered floors often dyed red and polished, and sanctuaries, the ground plan of one of which is in the form of a megaron. At Hacılar in Asia Minor, where preceramic culture is believed to have been of a simpler character, there are rectangular houses, built of mud bricks on stone foundations, with plastered floors sometimes painted with designs.

The preceramic structural remains at Sesklo are similar to those at Argissa. Here too pits dug in the hard soil and apparently belonging to huts, sometimes four-sided, with walls probably made of branches, are the prevalent dwelling types.

The humble dwellings of preceramic Thessaly seem very primitive and backward in comparison with the corresponding ones in the East. On the other hand, their layout suggests a continuing Mesolithic of European origin, although in Greece this has not yet been archaeologically established. However wretched these preceramic constructions in Thessaly may have been, they give an idea of the first attempts made by the earliest farmers and stockbreeders of Europe to settle in a specific place.

Preceramic man's inventory of tools does not appear to have been a large one. For the most part, his basic implements must have consisted of small pieces of flint-stone or obsidian mounted in wooden or bone hafts. The most common implement is the small flint or obsidian blade, the length of which seldom exceeded 2 cm. Blades which must have been attached to sickles and knives, one side of which acquired a polish from the continuous reaping of cereals, have also been found. Progressive trends were observed in the carefully polished stone objects, the most important of which were the small pick-axes and the chisels, which appear for the first time. These tools were obviously used for woodcarving. The skill required in making them may account for their rarity.

Another interesting object of the preceramic period is the so-called "earplug". Usually of stone, more rarely of clay, it is distinguished by a notch similar to that of a button. It has been alternatively suggested that these objects served as stoppers for goat-skin bags, hair ornaments, or buttons. The former is unlikely, as stoppers are even today made of wood in Greek villages. The finish of some of these "earplugs" and the fact that some were made of clay indicate that they were not intended for any practical use and suggest that their significance may have been symbolical. They appear to be attempts of late Palaeolithic origin to represent the human body. Other ornaments consisted of very small patens of steatite, bored in the centre so that they may have been strung on a necklace, pieces of worked steatite of different shapes, and sea-shells, the upper parts of which were pierced.

Bone implements of the Preceramic Period are plentiful: they are largely points, usually made from the extremities of goats and sheep which are often polished; chisels; and spatulae made from ribs of animals. Two small biconical sling bullets made of baked clay were found at Argissa and at Soufli Magoula. Such bullets (encountered again during the Ceramic Neolithic), and not only round pebbles or other suitable stones, were apparently also used in slings, though rarely.

Preceramic Economy

Animal bones and carbonized grains and seeds are more important than tool remains in any reconstruction of Preceramic economy. Most animal bones are of goats and sheep. At Argissa, the proportion is estimated at 85%. Although statistical data are not yet available from the other sites, bones of goats and sheep clearly predominate. The proportion of bones of oxen is much smaller (approximately 10%), and that of swine even smaller (approximately 5%). Conversely, the proportion of wild animals, such as deer, roebuck, hare, and birds (geese) is almost negligible.

Hunting apparently ceased to be a major preoccupation as soon as man began to obtain his principal means of nourishment from stockbreeding and the cultivation of cereals. The remains of charred cereals and pulses found in all the excavated sites indicate the importance of agriculture in the life of a Preceramic community. The cultivation of two kinds of wheat and two kinds of barley, as well as millet, peas, lentils, and vetch has been verified. Some acorns, which may have been edible, have also been identified.

It is generally agreed among specialists that the cereals correspond more closely to those of our day than to their wild forms. They must therefore have been cultivated over a long period of time or have been introduced from elsewhere in their cultivated form. Emmer wheat and barley are believed to have been imported from Western Asia. Other cereals, such as einkorn wheat and pulses, not wholly dissimilar to those that grow wild in the Southern Balkans, Western Asia, and the Mediterranean area, appear to have been cultivated from the original wild varieties or at least to derive from indigenous species. On the whole, the animals that were tamed and the plants that were cultivated in Greece during the Early Neolithic are identical to those in Asia Minor and the Middle East. The existence of the dog at Argissa in Thessaly has been verified, and the identification of fish-bones at Sesklo indicates that fishing was not unknown. Abundant sea-shells have also been identified in the riparian sites. Snails were common to all the settle-

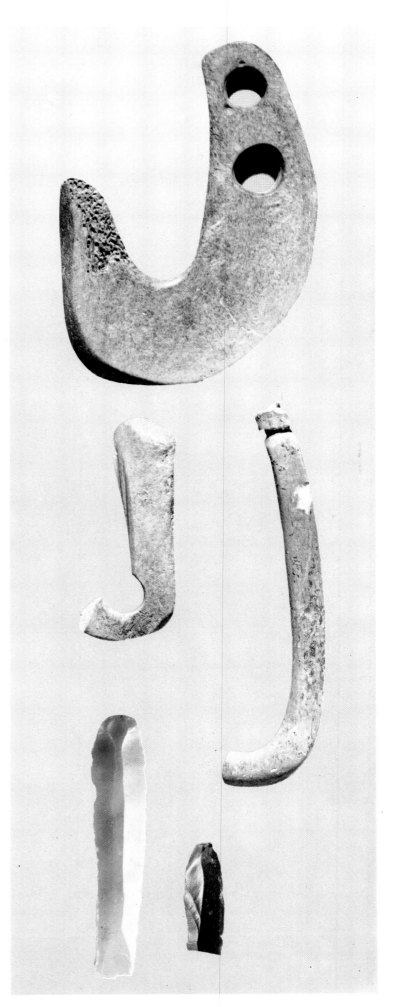

Objects of daily use in the Preceramic Period. Above and centre: hooks or buckles from Sesklo and Soufli Magoula (Volos Museum). Experimental attempts to fasten by means of grooves or double holes in the Early Neolithic phase. Below: large and small blades of flint-stone. The large one served as a knife; the small one was attached to a bone or wooden haft and used for reaping cereals. Obsidian from Melos, as well as flint-stone, was used by man of the Preceramic Period for fashioning tools.

ments. No Preceramic graves have so far been identified in Thessaly; at Knosos, however, children's graves without funerary offerings have been excavated. The few facts emerging from archaeological finds confirm that the economy of the Preceramic Period was based on agriculture and stockbreeding. Agriculture of course presupposes a settled community, and, although the architectural vestiges discovered in Greece are so humble as to suggest only improvized huts, they are sufficient to prove permanency of settlement.

A reconstruction of the physical environment of the period is out of the question. But since the flora and fauna were more or less identical to those that prevail today, the environment cannot have been very different from the present one.

The Preceramic Period in Greece, as in Asia Minor, seems, in most respects, to be a prelude to the Neolithic, in which indigenous features, whether of Mesolithic or Lower Palaeolithic origin, still prevailed. The vestigial architectural remains, the form of idols, and the burial customs neither prove nor disprove that this civilization came from Anatolia. On the other hand, all the main elements of the economy are the same, and probably some varieties of cultivated cereals and domesticated animals were imported from the Asia Minor coast. The likelihood of an early form of communication with culturally more advanced Anatolia, perhaps even a kind of primitive navigation, cannot be ruled out. The wide use of obsidian from Melos throughout mainland Greece adds force to the argument. The various dates, whether verified or arrived at by comparative methods, indicate that the seventh millennium B.C. was the chronological framework to which the preceramic cultural phase, herald of the food-producing stage in Greece, should be assigned.

THE EARLY NEOLITHIC PERIOD

Permanent Dwellings

The Neolithic Period is, above all, an economic and cultural phase, the main features of which are agriculture and stockbreeding. In this respect, the Preceramic can be classified as Early Neolithic. If the term *preceramic* is retained, it is only in order to distinguish it from the ensuing period, which is Ceramic Neolithic. The term *ceramics* refers to the art of pottery. The role played by pottery as a distinctive feature of the Neolithic Period cannot be ignored, however far-fetched it may appear to attach major importance to the relatively minor art of the potter. Nevertheless, the craft of fashioning vessels of baked clay is regarded as a distinctive feature of a period that lasted in Greece for three millennia, if not longer, until the use of metals became general. If pottery plays such an important part, it is because there is nothing so humble and yet so unalterably stable as a piece of a broken clay vessel. Being of no use to anybody, it attracts no attention, but remains wherever it happened to be abandoned. Some new use can always be found for a stone-wrought tool, a stone axe or a chisel. Not so with sherds, that is, fragments of such broken vessels. They are the only intact remains we have, and they are found in large quantities at every site that was inhabited by man throughout antiquity from 6,000 B.C. onwards. All other portable finds are either very rare or badly damaged. Wooden, leather, cloth, and wicker-work objects are subject to the ravages of time; metal ones, generally more rare, were frequently remoulded, are prone to rust and, if they possessed any value, were subject to the attentions of plunderers. Archaeologists have consequently devoted more exhaustive study to pottery than to any other prehistoric relic. A great many categories, divisions, and styles of pottery have thus been distinguished. Entire phases or periods, even "civilizations", have been classified on the basis of potsherds. Pottery has become the standard of comparison by which late prehistory is assessed just as flint is the standard for early prehistory.

The food-producing age is not necessarily linked with pottery. In the central zone of the Middle East, the potter's art did not appear for at least a thousand years after the beginning of the food-producing period. The same probably applies to Greece. On the other hand, the discovery of large quantities of clay pots proves stability and permanence of habitation. Household goods made of clay cannot be associated with a nomadic or semi-nomadic way of life. And since the period of the permanent dwelling corresponds, in Greece at least, to the emergence of pottery, ceramics would appear to be a distinctive feature of the Neolithic Period.

The Neolithic may be divided into periods, and its principal phases may be dated. After the preceramic phase, the remainder and major part of the Neolithic is subdivided into three periods: Early, Middle, and Late. This division merely facilitates historical narration and the classification of material. It is not intended to correspond to an exact sequence of events or to possess the same validity in all localities. The very nature of prehistory precludes precise clear-cut divisions. The chronology of the Neolithic is therefore hypothetical. Certainty may be claimed only to the extent that something in a particular locality is said to be earlier or later in relation to something else in the same locality. Beyond that, everything is uncertain. The development of carbon-14 dating may eventually enable scientists to compile a definitive chronology. For practical purposes, the Early Neolithic is dated to the sixth millennium B.C., the Middle Neolithic to the fifth, and the Late Neolithic to the fourth. The close of the Neolithic Period in Greece should be dated after 3,000 B.C., since the Bronze Age does not begin until a few centuries later.

The Settlements of Thessaly

Any attempt to reconstruct a picture of the Early Neolithic Period on the Greek mainland would have to depend mainly on the discoveries made in Thessaly. In a wider sense, these discoveries also shed light on the whole Neolithic Period. Facts of unique significance emerge as one stage succeeds another, particularly at the sites of Sesklo and Dimeni, the two well-known Neolithic acropolises near Volos, with their remarkable architectural remains, and in the excavations in depth at Otzaki Magoula and Tzani Magoula. Nevertheless, Thessaly is not the original cradle of Neolithic civilization in Greece, nor the only area where significant vestiges of the earliest phases of the Neolithic Period have been identified. But, for the time being at least, it is only here that the existence of Preceramic settlements has been archaeologically ascertained, so that any continuity between the Preceramic Neolithic and the Ceramic, represented in thick strata, may more easily be traced. Even so, in Greece, there are also other, equally rich and possibly more promising, localities.

In spite of the enclosed configuration of the land and the economic self-sufficiency that prevailed during the agricultural stage, Thessaly was never completely cut off from the rest of the world. From the earliest times, it seems to have been a vital centre of communications and cultural evo-

lution. The existence of an Early Neolithic civilization has been verified throughout an area extending from the Gulf of Volos in the south-east to Trikala in the west, from the foothills of Mt. Ossa in the north to Domokos in the south. The most important excavations are those undertaken at Sesklo, Argissa, Otzaki Magoula, Nessonis I, Pyrasos and Prodromos and Magoulitsa near Karditsa. Continuity of habitation is proven at all five sites where excavations identified Preceramic strata by the discovery in their higher levels of Early Neolithic remains, particularly of the earliest phase of monochrome pottery. No Preceramic site had been wholly abandoned, and the types of Early Neolithic dwellings are identical with those of the Preceramic. There are low settlements at riparian, lake-side, and level sites in the plain and higher settlements situated on ridges, invariably beside a stream or spring, or on hilly but soft ground.

More light has been shed on the economy and the material culture of this period than on those of the Preceramic. Agriculture and stockbreeding provided the livelihood of small communities and larger groups. Direct evidence of cultivation is found in charred grains of cereals and pulses, evidence of the domestication of animals in

These heads of Neolithic clay figurines were unearthed in the settlement of Hagios Petros (Kyra Panagia) on the island of Halonnesos. As on many similar figurines found at Hacilar, the artist's attempt to suggest the hair by means of incisions is evi-

dent; yet these Aegean specimens of Neolithic modelling are plainly different from those found in Asia Minor, being on the whole rather closer to corresponding ones in the Helladic area. (Volos Museum)

the bones of sheep, oxen (tamed in Greece at a very early stage), and pigs. Indirect evidence is supplied by the large quantities of millstones, mortars, and hammer stones, as well as by the scarcity of wild game. This primitive economy, basically agricultural, was virtually a self-sufficient one. But self-sufficiency does not imply isolation. Evidence of a system of communications and exchange of goods, if not of some kind of commerce between neighbouring communities, or even between distant settlements, is not lacking. The interchange of pottery between neighbouring communities points towards some form of communal cooperation. Moreover, obsidian, unless obtained from an as yet unknown mainland source, must have been imported from Melos, obviously by some indirect route.

Architecture and Tools

Astonishing advances were made in food production and the distribution of labour during the Early Neolithic in comparison with the earlier—what one might call experimental—stage. The multiplication of small hamlets, virtual nuclei of future expansion, indicates the degree of progress. The Thessalian settlements, numerous in the fertile regions, were still small, each with 20 or 30 houses on the average and a population of about 150 inhabitants. Nothing is known of their general layout, road system, or fortifications. Details regarding contemporary architecture are scanty. The earliest houses of the Early Ceramic Period differed little from those of the Preceramic. They were huts, sometimes four-sided, with a superstructure of branches and reeds or some other perishable material. One such hut at Argissa is 5 m. × 4 m.; it had a hearth in the interior and storage pits, and wooden posts supporting the roof. A kind of small clay furnace, something between a hearth and an oven, discovered on a floor at Soufli Magoula, probably indicates bread making. At Sesklo, there were, already at the beginning of the period, huts with floors dug on firm soil, as well as four-sided dwellings with superstructures of wattle and daub. During the second phase of the period, both at Sesklo and elsewhere, structures with walls of mud bricks seem to have been raised beside post huts made of rods interlaced with twigs and coated with clay. But a remarkable structure with a stone foundation, assigned to a date prior to the end of the period, has been identified at Megale Vryse (otherwise Hagia Anna) near Tirnavos in northern Thessaly. On the other hand, in the settlements of the plain around Larisa, where stone is rare, mud brick structures continued to be raised until the Middle Neolithic.

Progress in architecture was accompanied by increased ingenuity in the fashioning of tools. At first, stone-work differed little from that of the Preceramic, flint and obsidian being used as before, although blades of large size were now more numerous. Stone axes, although not of standard types, become more plentiful, as also do bullets used in slings. Blades with worked edges seem to have been fastened to reaping knives and sickles. Spindle whorls, generally made of potsherds, imply the existence of a weaving industry. Quantities of needles and other bone implements, clearly similar to earlier types, have been found in all the settlements.

64

Pottery

From a historical point of view, Early Neolithic man's most important creation—pottery—possesses a special significance; and its universal use raises the question of its provenance. Palaeolithic clay figurines (miniature representations of human and animal forms) bear testimony to the fact that the modelling and baking of clay objects is a Pre-Neolithic invention. But the fashioning of clay vessels for storing liquids, foodstuffs, and other materials was a Neolithic innovation, indicating the existence not only of permanent domicile but also of the needs satisfied by pottery. Although the moulding of clay is not a difficult process, the fashioning of baked vessels of high quality requires specialized experience as well as careful preparation, such as cleaning of the clay, removal of fatty substances, drying of the vessel before baking, and an overall temperature of over 600°C. while baking. It was, in fact, the work of a somewhat specialized artisan who had been relieved of the task of cultivating the soil and producing food. The potter's art—man's first "industrial" effort—could thus have developed only in areas where the Neolithic economy had reached an advanced stage. In this sense, it is not a primary, but a secondary, attribute of the economy, at least in areas which pioneered in Neolithic developments.

Nowhere, except perhaps at Sesklo, is there any evidence of the initial attempts and accompanying failures made by man in fashioning clay vessels. The assumption is that the process took place outside the periphery of the settlement, beyond the reach of inflammable objects. The oldest and rarest potsherds of the Late Preceramic and Early Ceramic periods were found at Sesklo. They belong mostly to small vessels. Fragments of clay pots, usually hemispherical in shape, thick-walled, and made of impure clay, are sometimes so fragile as to dissolve in water. Occassionally, the shapes have been distorted in the course of very strong firing. Sometimes clean clay was used, and the pots were either left to dry in the sun or to bake slowly beside the hearth. There is some similarity between the shapes of these pots and the oldest pottery found in the cave at Beldibi and the settlement of Çatal Hüyük in Asia Minor. One tiny vessel of this period resembles a plaited object like a basket. On the whole, the shapes of these primitive vessels lack clay-modelling fluidity.

The monochrome pottery of this first phase of the Early Neolithic is relatively advanced technically, but the shapes and some of the details appear quite primitive. Dark coloured—usually dark brown, rarely light brown—they have neither distinctive bases nor handles. The production of these dark brown bowls continued into the second more

Samples of Early Neolithic modelling. On this page: clay figurine of a woman in standing position from Nea Nikomedeia: a mere suggestion of a face with slit "coffee-bean" eyes, no chin, long neck, arms bent, and hands characteristically placed below the breasts—an idealized figure of woman the mother (Veroia Museum). Below left: frog modelled in greenstone from Nea Nicomedeia. It is natural for the frogs around the large marsh at Yannitsa, which was probably a beach in Neolithic times, to have served as part of the repertory of representational themes (Veroia Museum). Above left: two Neolithic seals. The large one is from Tzani Magoula, the smaller from Nea Anchialos. (Volos Museum)

mature phase, but soon the surface took on a variety of hues ranging from black to white, the clay was cleaned with greater care, and the texture became finer. Signs of the first "archaic" painted decoration also appeared on a small scale: generally red or brown on light-coloured clay or over a whitish varnished coating; more rarely, white on a light or dark brown background. The decoration is usually linear: parallel lines, zig-zags, triangles, etc. The designs appear to have been borrowed from woven or plaited fabrics, possibly blankets. On the whole, however, painted pots are rare, and the monochrome variety predominates. On the other hand, the shapes become more elegant, and there is an increasing predominance of the graceful *phiale*, a bowl whose circumference at the belly is wider than that at the lip, resting on a ring base—a characteristically Helladic shape.

In the third phase of the Early Neolithic, coarse vessels with impressed or incised decoration made their appearance in the plain around Larisa and in western Thessaly, while painted pottery decreased appreciably. The incised pots resembled those found at Nea Nikomedeia in Macedonia and other more northern localities but also those found in Epeiros, Corfu, and Leukas. It is probable that this pottery was introduced into Thessaly as a distinct style. It is also claimed that this deterioration during the third phase of the Early Neolithic is associated with arrivals of new groups from the North or the West. Other parts of the country, and particularly the Sesklo region in the south-east, were unaffected by this supposed migration. At Sesklo, as in many other localities in southern Thessaly, the tradition of the painted vase continued unbroken to appear with greater vigour at the beginning of the following phase, known as the Middle Neolithic. Impressed pottery continued to be produced in the Middle Neolithic, when a mixed incised-painted style emerged—an indication that the native style prevailed and assimilated the alien one, if indeed there had been any penetration by new population groups.

Figurines

Almost the only art objects of the Early Neolithic in Thessaly are the figurines, which should not, however, be dated, as was once believed, to the beginning of the period. Here again we have an instance of development by stages. Admittedly, a few clay objects, which might be described as figurines, dated to the very beginning of the Ceramic, were found at Sesklo and other settlements. Probably intended to be stylized representations of the human body, they certainly derive from the Preceramic, if not from some older, tradition. The production of the Preceramic "earplug", whether of clay or stone, continued uninterrupted. With only a few exceptions, figurines first appear during the mature phase of the period, when they tend to be naturalistic in style. The trunk of a female body found at Otzaki Magoula north of Larisa, is a piece remarkable for its vigour and symmetry and shows at what an early stage the spirit of disciplined naturalism had been established in Greece. Most figurines have female forms. The male ones, fewer in number, are often enthroned from the end of the period;

this type continues into the Middle Neolithic. The man is formally seated on a throne, his hands usually placed on his thighs. The fact that no corresponding type of female form has been identified so far is an argument against the theory of Neolithic matriarchy.

Although some form of "worhip" may not be entirely excluded, no shrines have been discovered. The figurines were usually found in houses, never in graves. As yet, little is known about burial practices. There were no grave ornaments or offerings in a child's grave found at Argissa; the skeleton lay in a shallow cut pit. Similarly, no grave goods were found beside the skeleton of an adult uncovered at Kephalovryso west of Trikala. Graves were seldom situated within the area of the settlement, and no separate cemeteries have so far been identified.

Important Clues and Indications

Emphasis has been laid on the Early Neolithic Period in Thessaly, because it is there that a direct continuity between the Preceramic and the Ceramic Neolithic may be established. It is in the initial phases of the Neolithic civilization of Thessaly, therefore, that one must seek those indigenous elements which in their pure form would point to the possible origin and subsequent course of Early Neolithic civilization. All indications so far point to the fact that this civilization did not come ready-made from elsewhere, whether from the North or from the East, but that it probably evolved naturally from the older, Preceramic civilization, passing through successive stages essentially unaffected by alien influences. The obvious indigenous character of the architecture alone precludes the possibility of outside provenance. The same applies to pottery. The discovery of primitive pottery at Sesklo would tend to refute the theory of its introduction from the East. Here, as on the southern Anatolian plateau, pottery passed through similar evolutionary stages. Some general evolutionary similarities may be ascribed to a common origin, most probably Pre-Neolithic. Nor is it necessary to assume that decorated pottery, particularly painted pottery was brought from the East by a wave of newcomers. All pottery shapes of the "archaic phase" of painted decoration descent from those of the older monochrome stage, while, in the earliest decoration too, there is an emphasis on the tectonic features of the vessel (lip, base, lugs). It is true that the clay figurines display great "ideological" affinity with those of the opposite shore, undoubtedly betraying a source common to both sides of the Aegean, but the differences already apparent from the start give the Helladic specimens a distinct character.

From Central Macedonia to the southern Peloponnesos, from Skyros in the central Aegean to Leukas in the Ionian, the basic features of what little is known of Early Neolithic civilization appear to possess a characteristic uniformity and are similar to those prevailing in Thessaly. Regional peculiarities, sometimes very pronounced, do exist, however, and in some localities they are so obvious as to necessitate their being probably ascribed to preexisting traditions or special local circumstances. Since these peculiarities apply chiefly to pottery, they may be without special historical significance. On the other hand, the diffusion of Early Neolithic civilization as far as Nea Nikomedeia near Veroia in Macedonia is worth noting. Pottery found there indicates that this remarkable settlement must be dated to an advanced phase of the Early Neolithic. Excavations have brought to light important facts regarding the architecture and disposition of houses. These were built on a framework of beams and branches which supported clay walls. The ground plan is square, and the measurements, varying from 8×8 metres to 12×12 metres, suggest spacious dwellings. From the remains of interior posts it may be surmised that the roofs were inclined. The economy was basically an agricultural and stockbreeding one. The cultivation of cereals has been fully verified. Bones of domesticated sheep, cattle,

and pigs, as well as of fish, were found in large quantities. A considerable number of Early Neolithic burials were also identified at Nea Nikomedeia. As a rule, the dead were buried, without any special preparation, in shallow pits without grave offerings. The position of most of the skeletons was the typical flexed one. Especially interesting is the burial of a woman with two children, all three in the same pit.

Early Neolithic remains exist in Epeiros; in Corfu and Leukas in the Ionian Islands; at Hagios Petros on the islet of Kyra Panagia in the Northern Sporades; on Skyros; at Hagia Marina, Chaironeia, and Elateia in Phokis; at Orchomenos in Boiotia; in Athens and Nea Makre in Attica; at Old Corinth, Gonia, Lerna, and the caves of Nemea and Franchthi in the Peloponnesos. The general economic

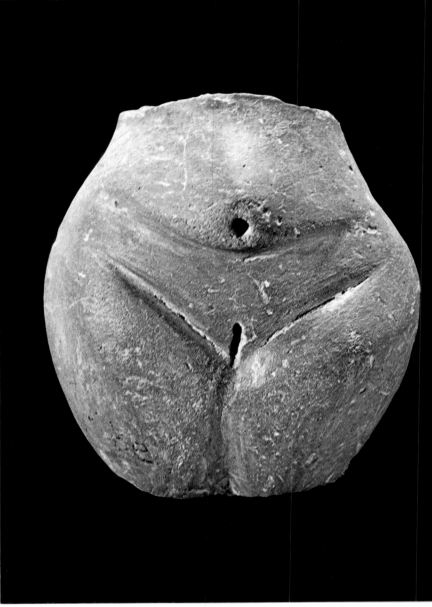

Left: head of male figurine of the Neolithic Period with characteristically shaped mouth and chin; the eyes and mouth are depicted by means of deep incisions (Volos Museum). Right: trunk of female clay figurine of the mid-sixth millennium B.C.

from Otzaki Magoula. The harmonious disposition of volumes and the remarkable rendering of anatomical features make this figurine an admirable example of the naturalistic art of the Early Neolithic Period. (Volos Museum)

67

and cultural level seems to have been uniform throughout the country. Two important early settlements have been partially excavated in Attica: Early Neolithic traces have been identified at the Agora below the Athenian Acropolis and also at the site of the ancient Academy and at Glyphada. There is also a large settlement at Nea Makre at the end of the Marathon plain, where excavated pottery has presented interesting variations already from the start.

THE MIDDLE NEOLITHIC PERIOD

Transition and Evolution

No sudden break in continuity marked the transition from the Early to the Middle Neolithic. The foundations of civilization remained the same; yet man advanced considerably, especially in the pottery industry, as well as in architecture and the disposition of houses in settlements. The distinguishing characteristics of this period are particularly evident in Thessaly, where the so-called Sesklo culture flourished. Since in Thessalian prehistory more is known about this period than any other, any review of the Middle Neolithic in Greece consequently pivots on the Thessalian sites and on the succession of evolutionary phases in this area, where the chronological framework is more clearly defined and the characteristic features of the period more obvious. Particularly outstanding is the painted pottery (linear designs in red on a whitish background) which, allowing for regional variations, occurs throughout an area extending from the Macedonian plain to southern Peloponnesos, a kind of *koine* in the evolution of the material culture of the Stone Age in Greece. Settlements now began to acquire the aspect of small fortified "towns" which, for the first time on the continent of Europe, were founded according to a predetermined town-planning design.

Judging from the thickness of the Thessalian accumulations, we may conclude that the Middle Neolithic must have lasted a very long time—probably the whole of the 5th millennium B.C. The period can be subdivided into phases, which have little historical significance, since they are exclusively confined to pottery styles. The purely or largely agricultural character of the period, at least in the fertile Thessalian and Macedonian plains and the valleys of mainland Greece, is attested by the material remains and other direct evidence.

There was also stockbreeding, and fishing in the coastal regions. The increasing use of obsidian from Melos shows improved maritime communications with the islands and a new emphasis on the exchange of goods. But on the whole, there seems to be no important change in the general course of man's activities in relation to the Early Neolithic. On the contrary, everything points to a continuity and normal development of the old ideas.

Such knowledge as we possess of the Neolithic Period in Greece is derived mainly from pottery. The theory has consequently been advanced that "a profound and sudden change in cultural development" occurred at the beginning of this period, which would imply that there are indications of a break between this period and the earlier one, possibly due to the arrival of immigrants from the East. But there is no evidence to support the hypothesis of an incursion of new cultural elements at the beginning of the period. On the other hand, towards the end of it, intense regional differentiation attests to some general disturbance, which was to herald the Late Neolithic Period.

The Sesklo Culture

The excavations undertaken by Chrestos Tsountas on the acropolis of Sesklo and the lucid presentation of his findings in Αἱ Προϊστορικαὶ Ἀκροπόλεις Διμηνίου καὶ Σέσκλου (Athens, 1908), provide a complete picture of the Middle Neolithic, a picture complemented by excavations carried out by Vladimir Milojčič at Otzaki Magoula near Larisa and by a recent re-examination of the Sesklo acropolis by D.R. Theocharis.

After a phase of retrogression, which was probably due to the infiltration of incised ware into Thessaly, and the suspended use of the painted pottery of the earlier period, a new phase set in, during which richly decorated pottery was progressively produced with fresh vitality. The new decorative themes indicate: first, that this painted pottery represents a normal development from the early or "archaic" painted pottery of the Early Neolithic; second, that the new styles were formulated in southern Thessaly, from where they spread throughout the country after assimilating the foreign elements which had somehow penetrated into the northern and western areas; and, finally, that almost from the outset there were regional variations both in decoration and in the shapes of the vessels. The period is one of greater maturity than the previous one, but it is a more advanced phase of the same civilization.

The acropolis of Sesklo projects steeply like a headland between two streams. A long process of erosion has reduced its area to almost half the size of the original acropolis. Situated at the foot of mountains in undulating country, it can hardly be described as a "typical" Thessalian Neolithic site; it is not a *magoula*, a small knoll in the midst of level, plain country like one of the many sites to be found in the area between Larisa and Pherai (Velestino), which are more numerous in fact than the modern villages of the plain.

Sesklo, the first and so far most thoroughly excavated Neolithic site in Greece, provides the best picture of a Middle Neolithic settlement. From the beginning of the period, houses were built on a stone socle (foundation and base) reaching a height of about 1 metre from the floor, while the upper part of the walls consisted of mud bricks. The houses, four-sided and rectangular, belong to various architectural phases. The prevailing type is the one-room house, almost square or somewhat elongated; the dimensions are small on account of space limitations on the acropolis. There are also two-room houses, rectangular or square, of larger dimensions, occasionally with interior buttresses. In addition, there is the megaron or megaroid house, which will be examined later. Close observation shows that the outline of the houses remained unchanged throughout the various architectural phases and that property limits seem to have been strictly defined. Narrow roads ran in parallel lines between houses, and the general disposition conformed to a definite plan. This impression is corroborated by the identification of a square or common court between every four or five houses and of fortifications on the more accessible, western side of the acropolis. Here Tsountas identified walls of considerable thickness (over 1 m. wide), running parallel to others which were not related to the houses as well as retaining walls on the south-western side. It is quite likely that the fortifications extended to the other sides. Fortification walls have also been identified by Kimon Grundmann at Magoula Hatzimissiotike, another Thessalian site on Lake Boibeis. At two other settlements situated on river banks—at Soufli Magoula and Servia—fortification trenches were found by W.A. Heurtley. It thus appears that the original impression that the earliest settlements were pacific in character is not correct, and that, contrary to prevailing opinion, these settlements, whether situated on high or low ground, were in fact fortified. The defence system of Sesklo probably included towers. The acropolis was entered through doorways placed in very narrow passages flanked by walls. It also appears that dwellings extended beyond the acropolis. Remains of houses of the Middle Neolithic have been unearthed hundreds of metres to the west of the acropolis. Moreover, there are strong indications that dwellings did exist within a wide area beyond the acropolis even during the Early Neolithic. This would tend to alter the old impression of Sesklo as an isolated spot to one of a fortified acropolis surrounded by a large village.

Reconstruction of the Neolithic acropolis of Sesklo, one of the oldest settlements in Europe, situated on the hill of Kastraki, near the road leading from the Pagasitic Gulf into the interior of Thessaly. The reconstruction is based on the findings of both early and recent excavations. It gives a picture of the settlement during the Middle Neolithic, a period now commonly referred to as the Sesklo culture. Walls and terracings were splayed across the least easily defended side, whence the ascent began. The houses were built of mud bricks on stone foundations. Huts and isolated houses have been identified in the vicinity of the acropolis. The reconstruction is the work of Markellos Galanos on lines suggested by archaeologist D.R. Theocharis.

It is estimated that on the original acropolis there were at least fifty houses, with about three hundred inhabitants. In times of danger, the population increased considerably by the influx of the people of the village who would take refuge within the walls.

One of the most important buildings at Sesklo is a megaron, probably dated to the middle of this period which seems to have been the central edifice on the acropolis. It had an open tiled court in front of the main room and was made secure at the back by an interior court. House walls as well as roads, wherever the configuration of the ground permitted, are in the same direction as this central megaron. It may therefore be assumed that it was the seat of the community or the chief's residence.

In another house, three small interior buttresses were coated, like the walls, with clay (Tsountas' "potter's workshop"); plastering of interior walls has also been observed at Tsangli. The buttresses may have supported a gallery. This house was destroyed by a tremendous fire, perhaps as a result of an earthquake, before the end of the Middle Neolithic, and it appears that the settlement at Sesklo had since been deserted for many centuries. Neither the latest phase of the Middle Neolithic nor the early part of the Late Neolithic is represented at Sesklo. Similar signs of destruction and devastation by fire have been observed at Tsangli, although there, unlike Sesklo, life went on and the settlement was not abandoned.

The settlement at Otzaki Magoula has been well known ever since Milojčič carried out systematic excavations of Early Neolithic strata there for the first time. But, there, equally important were the Middle Neolithic remains belonging to eight different architectural phases. The houses, huddled together, were as a rule four-sided; the roads were narrow (0.60-1.45 m. wide) or consisted of rudimentary passages enclosed between small side walls. The structures here were made of clay, stone being scarce in the middle of the plain. Ground plans show the houses to have been small, more or less square, with one or more interior buttresses, very much like the Tsangli type; but alongside these houses, there were also houses of the megaron type. The fact that houses were repaired or repeatedly rebuilt on the same spot and according to the same plan points to the existence of a definite town-planning scheme and rather well defined ownership limits. The density of houses in the excavated sectors conjures up a picture of something like a small town in an embryonic state. Therefore, on the whole, here too we have the same housing arrangements as those at Sesklo.

The Middle Neolithic settlement named after the neighbouring village of Tsangli, near ancient Eretria, excavated by A.J.B. Wace and other archaeologists, is situated on a large knoll (approximately 200 × 200 metres) with thick accumulations. Besides a large quantity of pottery, which forms the most impressive collection in Thessaly, the site revealed important architectural remains of the period. By coincidence, all the houses were of the square type, with two interior buttresses on each side, stone foundations and socles, and, in one instance, an interior row of posts, which divided the house in two. The interior buttresses strengthened the walls at the points where the beams supporting the roof crossed.

Small plain one-room houses, square or oblong, as well as megara were also common throughout Thessaly. The latter were with or without front or back porches; sometimes, there was a spacious front porch flanked by posts. It is likely that both the square house with the interior buttresses and the megaron served different, though as yet unknown, needs. Nor is it established that these architectural types were introduced by immigrants from the East; they may represent parallel and independent developments serving similar needs.

It must be pointed out here that the Middle Neolithic is well represented by settlements, acropolises, fortifications, and megaroid houses. This fact makes less plausible the theories once held that the Dimeni fortifications derive from Trojan models (which are of a later date) and that the megaron was introduced by "invaders" from the north. We now have evidence of the early character of these developments, which may have been introduced from the culturally more advanced Anatolia but which may also have been of independent origin.

Figurines are an important aspect of creative activity during this period, continuing the tradition of the Early Neolithic without important changes. Clay female figurines continue to be plentiful, but already from the beginning of the period there appear representations of enthroned male figures. Most of them are naturalistic in style and some are painted. The *kourotrophos* type, depicting a mother holding a child in her arms, appears at the same time. Figurines of animals are relatively scarce. Stone seals are plentiful, the designs being usually meandroid or cross-shaped. Symbols, representing ownership rights or the stamp of the workshop, are sometimes found on the base of vessels.

The economy was always based mainly on agriculture and stockbreeding, and to a lesser degree, on fishing in the coastal regions. With the foundations of new settlements the cultivation of the land must have extended to new areas, and the organization of the economy must have been quite successful, since we now have the first indications of the appearance of specialized potters whose standards were sufficiently high for their products to be exported to distant localities. The wider distribution of obsidian and the established fact that it was locally worked suggest improvements in commerce.

Judging by the shapes of vessels at the end of the period, one may even conjecture that copper was not entirely unknown. Many of these shapes, chiefly at Tsangli and Sesklo, seem to be influenced by copper models, the colour of the pots imitating the colour of copper, while the barely evident scraped decoration resembles the shades of this metal. The thinness of the walls, which at times are less than 2 mm., may also support the theory of the influence of metal models. Although there is no confirmation of the use of copper in Greece at this period, at least in the pottery industry, specialized potters in Thessaly may have had some idea of the potentialities of this new material, which in the more ad-

---

Opposite page: clay figurine of a fleshy woman (restored), found in the vicinity of Pharsala. The figurine dates from the Middle Neolithic Period. In contrast to contemporary male figurines, which are represented seated on a high stool, this figure is shown in a low sitting posture, which seems to have been appropriate to her sex, and actually rather similar to the sitting posture assumed by women in Thessalian villages to this day. (Volos Museum)

vanced East had been known for a long time. In Southern
Greece, the glaze associated with Neolithic Urfirnis ware is
clearly influenced by metal work, although this new technique
owes its origins to the earlier method of coating the surface
of vessels with a "slip".

The Sesklo culture in Thessaly did not come to an end
in the same way or at the same time everywhere. At some
settlements, such as those at Sesklo and Tsangli, there is
definite evidence of destruction by fire as the result of an
earthquake rather than of hostile action, and this is confirmed
at Tsangli, which was not abandoned. Elsewhere the
transition between the Middle and Late Neolithic periods
occurred somewhat later, in stages, and without violent
changes. Sesklo, at any rate, was abandoned for centuries
and not reinhabited until an advanced phase of the Late
Neolithic. Irrespective of the manner in which the end came,
Middle Neolithic civilization died a natural death. Decline
was evident in the last stages, although new features were
by then already apparent.

Summary

The Middle Neolithic Period, chiefly associated with
Thessaly but not without similar features in more southern
sites, followed directly on the Early Neolithic without any
sudden or radical change at the beginning. In Thessaly the
cultural level rose. Progress in town-planning and the fortification of acropolises continued into later periods. In the
absence of anthropological remains, it is reasonable to assume that the creators of this culture belonged to the indigenous tribes of the Early Neolithic.

Progress in commerce and barter, as well as the emergence,
towards the end of the period, if not earlier, of Thessalian
pottery influenced by metal ware, together with the application of new techniques, seem to indicate contact between
Neolithic Greece and the East. Metal must have somehow
become known in Greece together with the new inventions
and technical achievements of the more advanced East.
But neither the cultural level nor the social framework were
as yet conducive to the application of metallurgical techniques. Only later, in the Late Neolithic, are a few metal objects encountered as rare and rather exotic things.

Towards the end of the Middle Neolithic, new elements,
which would ultimately alter the whole aspect of civilization,
point the way to the Late Neolithic. In Thessaly, the transformation occurred rather late, because the old ways of life
were more firmly rooted and the agricultural character of
the economy did not favour innovations. But in the south
the changes appear earlier, at least in pottery, and in the
Peloponnesos perhaps at an even earlier date. It is doubtful
whether some burials which are ascribed to the end of the
period and betray new customs, such as the jar burials,
can be of such an early date. In the "ideological" sphere
there seems to have been little change. Despite opinions to
the contrary, certain as yet uninterpreted phenomena cannot be ascribed to the existence of a cult; there is not a single
trace of a shrine or communal cult place. Nor is there any
evidence that certain objects, such as "tables of offerings",
phallic symbols, and figurines, all of which occur in the
Sesklo culture, served any religious purpose. The same may

apply to the "votive pits" at Otzaki Magoula and Elateia and to the multiform human figurines.

A certain amount of cultural differentiation during the second half of the period indicates an atmosphere of disquiet and disturbance, which was eventually to erupt into more violent manifestations. Towards the end of the Middle Neolithic, many of the Thessalian settlements were simultaneously destroyed. Sesklo was abandoned. Elsewhere, however, Seskloid features survived the catastrophe and were blended with the new ones. Lack of anthropological remains does not encourage the formulation of a plausible hypothesis of incursions by new racial elements. Changes in pottery cannot in themselves prove the advent of foreign colonizers. In general, there is so far nothing to prove that the Middle Neolithic was not a purely local development.

Undoubtedly, the most important achievement of this period was the organization of small rudimentary townships. The hamlet, with narrow streets between closely packed houses within an enclosure, was not of course inhabited by a single family or clan, but by a larger social group, a community. This way of life continued practically unchanged in Greece almost until Mycenaean times. This organized hamlet or *polis* (the term may be permitted here only because there have already been references to "acropolises", but it is used without any implications of urbanization), was the nucleus of all future developments. Within the framework of this hamlet, technical advances, though neither impressive nor very different in substance from those made during the Early Neolithic, were not negligible. Judging by the rich decoration of ceramics, we may assume a corresponding advance in other important industries, such as weaving and knitting. The high technical standard achieved in pottery indicates also that this art, among others, was now in the hands of skilled artisans, and not the work of women, who helped the economy of the household by fashioning clay utensils for daily use. Certain pottery types were now fine creations, often made for export to distant areas. The elegant pottery of Tzani Magoula was to be found all over Thessaly.

Specialization and barter, however, presuppose the existence of some kind of social organization and a communal authority, which supervises distribution of labour, general security, the safeguarding of the seed for sowing, protection of property, and provision of imports. It does not, therefore, seem altogether unreasonable to hazard a guess that life was already organized on the basis of the small town, fundamentally agricultural in character, which remained unchanged throughout the country for thousands of years.

Left-hand page: head of a Middle Neolithic female figurine from Pyrasos (Nea Anchialos). The slanting eyes, the large nose, the oblong face, and the long neck are typical characteristics of many contemporary figurine heads. The hair is indicated by small disks painted, like the cheeks, a vivid red (Volos Museum). This page, top: upper part of a Neolithic clay figurine from the settlement of Megale Vryse (Hagia Anna, Tirnavos). The prominent hair, bird-like face, long neck, and full breasts contribute a sense of strength to the figure (Volos Museum). Bottom: marble female figurine of the Late Neolithic, from Dendraki, near Dimeni, The lack of plasticity and the conventionality of form must be attributed to a general trend toward standardization rather than to any proclivity towards a Cycladic technique, which in fact makes its appearance much later. (Volos Museum)

THE LATE NEOLITHIC

Changes in Pottery

The phases of man's evolution are not as clearly separated from one another as are the successive strata in the earthbanks of a prehistoric settlement. The last period of the Stone Age in Greece, known as the Late Neolithic, is now thought to be closely linked with the preceding period, even though its more advanced phases are characterized by a very different type of culture. Only a few decades ago, it was believed that the Late Neolithic civilization of Greece —called the Dimeni culture after the best known site of this period—was completely different from its immediate predecessor, the Sesklo culture. There were indeed great differences and a marked discontinuity between the Sesklo and the Dimeni cultures, particularly in pottery: the one type was painted in a bright reddish monochrome with strictly linear motifs; the other was an orgy of decoration, of combinations of painted or incised meanders and spirals. Tsountas had in fact discovered at Sesklo, above a layer of destruction, remains of the Dimeni culture. However, as has already been noted, recent excavations have shown that the acropolis of Sesklo was abandoned after a fire before the end of the Middle Neolithic Period and remained uninhabited for several centuries, perhaps for as long as 500 years.

The blank which formerly seemed to separate these two cultures has now been carefully studied, and more recent findings prove the Dimeni culture to have been an advanced phase of the Late Neolithic, restricted to eastern Thessaly. It was a regional culture whose importance had earlier been overestimated—not without justification since Dimeni represents a peak both in pottery and architecture. Now, however, we are in a position to study the pre-Dimeni phases of the early part of the Late Neolithic Period not only in Thessaly but almost throughout the Greek mainland and, even more important, to examine the cultural manifestations of this period as a whole over wide areas.

The results of recent excavations indicate that the Late Neolithic lasted for a very long time, perhaps even a whole millennium. It divides into several phases and presents, despite certain common features, such markedly different regional variations as to allow us to accept now, for the first time so far, the arrival of new population elements or a sudden expansion in trade exchanges and communications between distant regions. Thus the epilogue of the Stone Age, although of relatively short duration (less than half that of its predecessors: the Middle and Early Neolithic Periods together) was a period of brisk movement and dramatic changes. Its last phases may even mark the prologue of a new age characterized by a retrograde movement of tendencies and influences in the Aigaiis. The earlier, basically homogeneous, culture, whose homogeneity testifies to a normal process of development during the Early and the Middle Neolithic periods, now became diversified, at least as far as pottery was concerned; and pottery is one of the most important sources of our knowledge.

At one time, students of this period sought for parallels and comparisons in the North and in the Balkan-Danubian area. This tendency reached extravagant dimensions: by applying the "selection of evidence" method, they had no difficulty in finding numerous "northern" elements in everything from the type of the megaron to the most insignificant detail in vase decoration. Whole "cultures" were explained on the basis of supposed invasions from Hungary or South Russia, Transylvania, or even the Caucasus. In recent years, the source of these "invasions" has been moved to another quarter: it is now generally believed to be Asia Minor, where important recent excavations have revealed a Late Chalcolithic civilization in some of its regions. The site of Beycesultan in particular has excited as much interest as once did the Troad. We shall examine these various suppositions, which derive mainly from similarities in pottery, whenever they are not based exclusively on it.

One of the chief difficulties is to determine how this period began in Greece, and even more important, how it ended. As was noted above, we have to rely chiefly on pottery for a rough reconstruction of developments during this period. The question is to determine what may have been inherited from an earlier indigenous tradition and what may be due to foreign influences or to migrations. At present, we have only very fragmentary knowledge of the various aspects of Late Neolithic culture in Greece. In some regions, whole phases of the architecture and organization of settlements are missing. Elsewhere, there are only pottery remains, and these are stratigraphically of uncertain dating. Information from many of the Aegean islands is lacking entirely.

It was precisely during this period, however, that the Aegean Islands became important for the first time. Some elements, now considered to be "eastern", may have originated in the islands, or they may have come to the Greek mainland from the East via these islands. It is equally probable that they may have originated on the western coast of Asia Minor; but for the most part this area has not been systematically excavated yet.

The "northern" theory faces the same difficulty. Northern Greece, particularly Epeiros, north-west Macedonia, and the Hebros (Evros) region, has scarcely been excavated at all, and it is therefore difficult, if not completely impossible, to form a clear idea of the source or direction of these influences, or the manner in which they spread. A proper awareness of the great gaps in our knowledge of this period must

Opposite page: marble figurine, of a corpulent female in a standing position, from the Sparta area. Although there are similar Middle Neolithic figurines from mainland Greece in clay, this exquisite piece is considered remarkable by reason of the artist's skill in transferring to hard stone the forms achieved in clay and in imparting a monumental tone to the contemporary concept of ideal womanhood. This is the completest and most significant Neolithic stone specimen found anywhere in Greece; the few other specimens, which come mostly from Thessaly, have some of their parts missing. This type of figurine dates back to the Early Neolithic. (National Archaeological Museum, Athens)

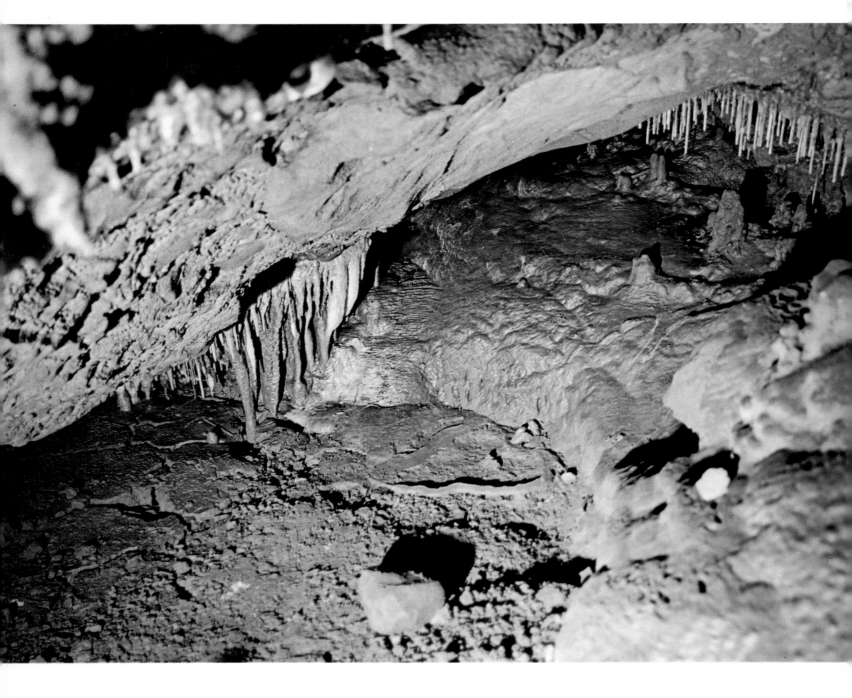

Grave pit in the Alepotrypa cave at Pyrgos Dirou in Mane (Peloponnesos), which is now in the process of excavation. On *top of the stalactite formations are bones from Neolithic burials.*

make us sceptical of most of the theories which seek to explain the diversity of late Neolithic culture by postulating influx of populations either from the North or the East.

Since pottery is the single most important diagnostic element of this period, it is to pottery that we must of necessity turn in our search for the general characteristics of the change. The distinguishing characteristic of the Late Neolithic is thought to be the introduction of dark or black colour in pottery decoration, matt-painted at first, a technique which was employed for some time. Quite soon, however, black burnished (black on red background) as well as polychrome wares began to appear. The latter technique is another characteristic feature of the Late Neolithic over a wide area of Greece. The repertory of subjects now also included curvilinear decoration (not altogether unknown even earlier) and,

at a later stage, spiraliform and meandroid designs. There were other innovations, perhaps even more important, e.g. monochrome grey, black, and blackish-brown vases, sometimes decorated with white linear designs, or with incised or glazed patterns.

A completely new technique, employed in Aegean Thrace and eastern Macedonia during the Late Neolithic was graphite decoration. This technique predominated in the North, where the so-called "Gumelniţa culture" evolved, and appeared sporadically as far south as Thessaly. Still another new technique was the use of a thick crust-like layer of ochre on the so-called crusted ware, which again is to be found chiefly in northern civilizations but also in the Thessalian Chalcolithic "Rakhmani culture" and, sporadically and independently, further south as far as Crete.

The Saliagos Culture

In the Aegean islands, it has not been possible so far to trace an unbroken succession of the Early, Middle, and Late Neolithic, though some progress in this direction has recently been made in the Cyclades (Saliagos), on Chios (Emporio), on Samos (Tegani-Kastro), and in the Northern Sporades.

The islands naturally had closer links with the East than did the Greek mainland, and the most easterly ones (Lesbos, Chios, Samos) may be regarded as an extension of the western coast of Asia Minor. However, as far as we can judge on the basis of the available evidence, even on these islands strongly individual elements were present. Particularly marked was the special character of the Saliagos culture. (Saliagos is a very small island close to Antiparos in the Cyclades). Here we have a Cycladic version of the early part of the Late Neolithic. The predominant pottery type is a dark-coloured vase with white, severely linear, designs. The shapes and the thematic repertory are reminiscent of mainland pottery, while some of the details, such as the horn-shaped handles, have parallels both in Sterea Hellas and in the easterly islands (Samos) or even in Macedonia and Thrace (Parademe). In general, everything points to the conclusion that this settlement should be dated to a much earlier period than the beginning of the Cycladic civilization of the Early Bronze Age.

Although chronologically there is a gap between the end of the Saliagos culture and the beginning of Early Cycladic, there are indications that the latter did in fact grow out of the former. The Saliagos settlement was fortified with the same simple type of enclosure as in later Cycladic and Early Bronze Age coastal settlements. Furthermore, the great number of arrow-heads shows that the bow was in general use, and its use has also been confirmed in mainland Greece during the Late Neolithic and the subsequent Early Bronze Age.

Stone tools of the Neolithic Period in Thessaly: adzes and celts made of hard, highly polished stone, always of small dimensions.

The Dimeni Culture

In Thessaly, three sub-divisions of the Late Neolithic may be distinguished: (a) the early phase (referred to as Tsangli and Arape after two typical settlements), which may also be called the Pre-Dimeni phase; (b) the Dimeni culture in the restricted geographical sense of the term; and (c) the ultimate phases, which finally merge into the Chalcolithic "Rakhmani culture".

The most obvious mark of Dimeni pottery is the liberal use of combinations of spiraliform and meandroid subjects. The meander first appeared in Europe in the Late Palaeolithic, as did the spiral in France. These subjects also appeared sporadically in the East at an early date, meandroid patterns appearing as early as the Preceramic. Meanders and spirals on pottery were scarcely known in the period corresponding to the Sesklo civilization, and they are totally absent in Thessaly. Because the decoration of Dimeni ware appears to be completely different from that of Sesklo, there has been an altogether natural temptation to attribute its introduction to a wave of invaders from northern lands. There are indeed some striking similarities, which perhaps cannot be explained simply by the theory of parallel development or external influence. So far, however, no single fragment of pottery has been found which can definitely be shown to have been introduced from the Danubian region. Nor is there any evidence at all for the theory that this style of pottery decoration was introduced into eastern Thessaly by invaders from the north. There are at present no traces either of the former homeland of such invaders in the Balkans, or of the route by which they are supposed to have descended into Greece. It is, of course, always possible that new evidence may come to light which will reverse this position.

It must be admitted in any case that there must have been some penetration by more northerly Balkan peoples into Thessaly during this period, even if it cannot be shown

They appear to have been used for work on wood, after being fastened to a handle or inserted into a haft. (Volos Museum)

whence and how they came. They probably came peacefully in small groups and were easily absorbed into the existing population. All the other features of the Dimeni civilization may be interpreted as natural developments out of pre-existing ones in Thessaly and the surrounding regions. With the exception of pottery, there is some evident continuity from the early part of Late Neolithic in every other field.

The acropolis of Dimeni, situated on a low hill called Toumba near the village of Dimeni, four kilometres west of Volos, was excavated at the beginning of this century by Valerios Staes and Chrestos Tsountas. The chief feature of its architecture is the series of six successive circuit fortification walls, each built within the other, in an area little more than 100 metres long. The innermost and thickest wall enclosed a central courtyard and formed, along part of its length, the back wall of an almost typical megaron which jutted out into the courtyard. The position of the megaron dominated the plan of the entire complex; the main entrance of the complex, built like a sort of propylon, was on the same axis as the megaron. There were other buildings within the fortified area, but they were evidently of secondary importance. The settlement itself must have lain outside the acropolis; this alone can explain the existence of a second entrance next to the megaron.

That the walls were built for purposes of fortification emerges clearly from the manner of their construction. The concentric circular areas between the walls are broken up by transversal walls to make penetration of the fortress more difficult, and the doors are competently distributed at different points in each wall so that the centre can be reached only by a zig-zag route. The purpose of the megaron is less obvious. The building is fairly large: it has a length of approximately 11 metres and an interior width of approximately 6 metres. The open court with two columns at the front, the hearths and pillars in the main room, and the completely enclosed room at the back combine to present us with a perfect example (except for the unusual shape of the room) of a Neolithic megaron. Its size and central position in the inner courtyard facing the main entrance suggest that it was the dwelling of the chief of the settlement. We have no means of telling whether the remains of the hearth found in the central court formed part of an altar, as has been suggested. In any case, it is natural to suppose that if the settlement had a religious centre, it would be located within this innermost courtyard.

That the megaron was of the usual type and occupied the usual position in the inner courtyard and in the acropolis generally is shown by a comparison with the contemporary architectural remains on the acropolis of Sesklo. These were discovered several years ago but have recently been studied

Reconstruction of the Neolithic acropolis at Dimeni, in the region of Volos. In the Late Neolithic, the period otherwise known as the Dimeni culture, such low elevations would be fortified with multiple circuit walls. In the stone walls, there were gateways leading to the centre, but a series of transverse walls broke up the narrow circular areas so that attackers could not easily storm the acropolis. The fortifications at Dimeni were constructed with amazing skill, foreshadowing Mycenaean acropolises. This reconstruction is a modified version of an original sketch by V. Zesis drawn on the basis of a plan by archaeologist Nicholas Papahatzis.

79

Top, left: the famous clay 'Krannon Hut', being the earliest known model of a house in Greece and, more generally, in Europe; it belongs to the Sesklo culture, beginning of the 5th millennium

B.C. (Volos Museum). Right: Middle Neolithic clay cup, from the settlement of Dzani Magoula (Sophades), in the so-called 'solid style'; dark red clay coated with a white slip and deep

again. Here, the megaron belonging to the Dimeni phase is much bigger (length, including the back porch: over 20 metres; interior width: over 8 metres), but it has the same interior distribution of spaces: two columns are conjectured in the forecourt, and there are three surrounding the hearth in the main room. Recent excavations have revealed the existence of an inner circuit wall around the megaron, remains of a second wall with a gateway behind the megaron room, and probably traces of a third wall, to which the sections of the thick wall unearthed by Tsountas on the western side also belong. This goes to prove then, that, on the acropolis of Sesklo too, the megaron was enclosed by a series of at least four walls, which, very likely, were built very much like those at Dimeni. The fortifications of Dimeni are no longer unique. Its circuit walls must be attributed to normal custom rather than to lack of natural tenability on that particular site.

The megaron of Sesklo is generally regarded as the most imposing Neolithic building in Greece. However, a third and much larger megaron was discovered in 1941 at the Neolithic settlement of Magoula Visvike, close to Velestino, about 14 kilometres northwest of Dimeni. For this period, it is a building of astonishing dimensions, clearly megaroid, though not very typical. Its total length is almost 30 metres, i.e. it is longer than any of the megara of the Mycenaean palaces of Mycenae, Tiryns, or Pylos. As well as the usual

features, such as an open stoa at the front with two columns between the door-jambs, there is an extra room divided into two by a wall built on the same axis as the length of the megaron, and a large hearth in the main room (the *domos* of a Mycenaean megaron) surrounded by four wooden columns, exactly as in a typical Mycenaean megaron.

It is quite possible that these amazing architectural achievements of the Dimeni culture were the earliest precursors of Mycenaean acropolises and megara. Megaroid buildings and fortified acropolises must have been built in subsequent periods right down to Mycenaean times. Any existing gap must be due to insufficient excavating rather than to actual blanks. It should also be noted here that the back porch of the last Neolithic megaron described above (really a rudimentary stoa formed by extending the walls) as well as the side doors are elements which will appear later in Greek architecture.

Our knowledge of the other aspects of life at Dimeni is incomplete. As has already been mentioned, its pottery had exceptionally rich decoration, which was without parallel in prehistoric Greece. Figurines, though rarer now and often stylized, retained some of the naturalism of Sesklo. Typical examples, both from Sesklo, are a clay figurine of a seated *kourotrophos* and another clay female figurine with fine rendering of anatomical detail. But it is not only the figurines that belie the old dogmatic simplifications. Equally

red paint (Volos Museum). Right-hand page: two fine specimens of Late Neolithic decorative art; Left: polychrome clay amphora from Dimeni; the severe dark brown decoration is diversified by isolated spirals and interspersed red patterns (National Archaeological Museum, Athens): cross-shaped marble figurine from a Thessalian settlement. (Volos Museum)

mistaken is the view that phallic symbols appeared for the first time during this period allegedly signifying a reversal of the earlier "matriarchal" conception of the deity. Phalli, both painted and monochrome, are known at Sesklo and cannot be regarded as an innovation. Similarly, the arrowheads and spear-heads that are probably of this date had much earlier predecessors in central and southern Greece (Elateia, Saliagos) and continued in use in the Bronze Age.

The Dimeni culture, representing a real peak, was localized in the most fertile region of Thessaly. With the exception of vase decoration, which betrays obvious northern influence, most aspects of this culture may be traced back to an earlier indigenous tradition. Recent excavations have shown that choice Dimeni vases were exported to the Thermaic Gulf and Chalkidike, so that there must have been regular contact with Macedonia. The abundance of obsidian, along with other indications, shows that there was also exchange of goods with the Cyclades and more generally with the South. Without such contacts, Dimeni in isolation could not have attained such a high level of civilization. The achievements of Dimeni in organizing settlements and developing the megaron were not without consequences. From that period onwards, throughout the Bronze Age, fortified "cities" appeared in almost every part of the Aegean, until the megaron finally reached its ultimate form on the Mycenaean acropolises.

Summary

The Late Neolithic Period as a whole seems to have been a critical one. It grew out of the earlier period, the Middle Neolithic, but the transition took place at different times and in different ways in different regions. Wherever there were previously strong Seskloid traces, the change was less abrupt. Dark-coloured pottery existed side by side with the new painted pottery, which in its early phases seems to have followed the trends inherited from the earlier tradition. This is not the case, however, in Aegean Thrace or in some other northern regions. Almost from the beginning, there was strong differentiation, testifying to unrest and some cross-fertilization of outside influences. Development was slow in central and southern Greece in contrast to Thessaly and Macedonia, where there was greater restlessness. Phases like the Dimeni culture or the marvellous flowering of painted pottery in eastern Macedonia (Photoleivos II) have no parallels in the South. Neither can they be interpreted as intrusive episodes or as products of northern invasions. A decoration that blossoms forth after some change is usually a sign of vigour, not of upheaval. It is more reasonable to suppose that an invasion would be attended by perturbation and retardation rather than progress. All the main features of the Dimeni culture can be linked to the earlier tradition. The new element is the style of decoration; but this too could well be due to outside influence and not necessarily to the arrival of a new population. The Dimeni culture certainly had no connection with the East or with the Cyclades in the South. Any influences which may have affected its development must have come from the north-east. The same applies to the Rakhmani culture (the Chalcolithic period in Thessaly), which may more aptly be characterized as Thracian or proto-Thracian.

The eastern and southern islands of the Aegean followed another path of development. There, although eastern elements seem to dominate, there was also such strong individuality as to preclude their being cursorily assigned to a Late Chalcolithic Asia Minor culture. Perhaps the links between the two will become clearer when the western coast of Asia Minor, particularly its southern section, will have been investigated.

NEOLITHIC CRETE

To form an integral picture of the Neolithic Period in the Aigaiis, it is necessary to extend our survey geographically to include the Greek islands, particularly Crete and Cyprus. These two islands were to be important centres of development during the subsequent period; on both there is clear evidence of continuity and normal transition from the Neolithic to the Bronze Age.

We do not know when Crete was first inhabited. Excavations of strata which can be dated with any certainty have so far failed to produce any palaeolithic material. The first signs of human activity on this island appear somewhat abruptly at Knosos. In 1900, Sir Arthur Evans, the indefatigable excavator of Minoan Crete, unearthed a whole Neolithic settlement, a real "town", below the courtyards of the Minoan palace. Recent excavations by John D. Evans and others on the same site have provided additional information.

There was, first, an early Preceramic settlement, dated at the end of the seventh millennium B.C. It was a sort of semi-permanent settlement, though probably not exactly a camp site. There is evidence for the cultivation of cereals, structures made of perishable materials, burials without grave goods, and coarse but characteristic stonework with abundant use of Melian obsidian. In general, the level of civilization seems to have been similar to that of Preceramic Greece. All this goes to show that Crete had been inhabited at the dawn of Neolithic times and the beginning of the food-producing era.

Next follows the so-called Early Neolithic Period of Knosos, which may be said to have begun in the middle of the fifth millennium B.C., or a little earlier, and to have ended about 3500 B.C. The distinguishing marks of this period in pottery are the prevalence of dark tones, ranging from black to brown or with variations to red, incised and plastic decoration, and forked handles. The use of fired bricks in the construction of the buildings has no parallel in the rest of the Mediterranean. Figurines were generally of clay, somewhat stylized and more or less standardized; an exceptionally fine male figurine of white marble has also come to light in recent excavations.

There was considerable progress but no change in tradition during the Middle Neolithic, which is represented not only at Knosos but at several other sites, such as Gortys and Katsambas. The buildings, which again are of clay on stone socles, are larger, with more rooms and a court, sometimes with clay-covered interiors. In pottery, there was standardization and improvement of the incision technique; a new type of rippled decoration also appeared, which consisted in pleating the surface of the bowl.

The most important architectural remains from this period are the structures found by Sir Arthur Evans in the southern section of the central court of the palace of Knosos. It is a multi-roomed complex with the rooms arranged irregularly, interspersed with pebble-covered courtyards and annexes. The structures are again of clay built on stone foundations, the floors are covered with clay, and there are permanent built hearths. The pottery seems simplified and less carefully made; rippled decoration has disappeared, but incised decoration survives, and glazed decoration (a technique in wide use at the end of the Neolithic elsewhere in Greece) appears for the first time along with some new shapes, which almost presage later Minoan ones. A copper axe and fragments of Egyptian stone bowls, which are believed to date from the beginning of the dynastic period, testify to contacts between Crete and the surrounding world: the East, the South, and also the Cyclades. These contacts brought Crete closer to the new cultural developments during this period of transition to the Bronze Age.

The transition to the Pre-Palace Minoan period was smooth with no abrupt changes. Crete gradually emerged from the relative isolation in which she had remained throughout the Neolithic Period. This isolation was due partly to the very nature of neolithic economy and partly to the self-sufficiency and geographical position of Crete itself. Throughout the Neolithic Period, which must have lasted for more than two millennia, the cultural level does not appear to have been high, and progress came only very gradually. The general impression is one of monotony and stagnation. We do not know where the Neolithic inhabitants of Crete came from, although the Aegean world would seem to be the most likely area of their origin. But wherever they came from, they were the people who formed the nucleus of the population from which sprang the Minoans, who are known to have belonged to the Mediterranean branch. Naturally, this does not exclude the possibility that related population elements arrived later and strengthened the original population, especially in eastern Crete. But whereas this is only a probability, there is certainty in the fact that the Neolithic inhabitants of Crete did not disappear.

We may, therefore, conclude that the Neolithic tradition survived in Crete, at least as a static force, even if later developments had their origins not in it but in a new creative urge, which eventually led to the birth of Minoan civilization on the island.

This 14.5 cm. high clay figurine from Kato Hierapetra is a most important piece of Neolithic sculpture from Crete. Of particular interest is the position of the legs in the typical "oriental" manner. Yet, a similar position is to be seen in some Thessalian figurines. (Herakleion Museum, Yamalakis Collection)

This 21 cm. high stone male figurine from the Neolithic settlement of Choirokoitia in Cyprus dates from the beginning of the 6th millennium B.C. Simplification of the shape of the human body is a characteristic feature of Choirokoitia figurines. There are no corresponding Anatolian or Egyptian specimens. (Cyprus Museum, Nicosia)

NEOLITHIC CYPRUS

Like Crete but on a different scale, Cyprus remained isolated throughout the Neolithic Period. Cyprus provides a most striking example of insularity, combined with a closed and self-sufficient Neolithic economy. The whole cultural development of the island during the Stone Age had such peculiarly local character as to indicate that the island remained entirely uninfluenced by its geographical position. Yet, after the development of metallurgy in the East, this geographical location was to prove singularly important.

Geologically, Cyprus was once part of Asia Minor and it was also connected with the Syrian coast. Geographically, it is almost equidistant from the shores of southern Asia Minor and of Syria. And yet, during the Stone Age, Cyprus followed a course of its own and, despite evidence of contacts and trade exchanges with the continent of Asia, its civilization was not associated with the cultures of either Asia Minor or the Syro-Palestinian region. Nor does it seem to have had much affinity with developments in the Aigaiis. Must we ascribe then, this independent course merely to insular isolation or assume the pre-existence of some strong pre-Neolithic tradition?

There has been little excavating of caves on the island; even so, no palaeolithic or mesolithic remains have been identified anywhere. The Early Neolithic civilization of Cyprus makes its appearance suddenly and mysteriously without any identifiable previous stages. It is known as the culture of Choirokoitia after the best known site of this period (6020-5850 or 5800 B.C.). This as well as several other Neolithic and Bronze Age sites were excavated by Porphyrios Dikaios.

The Choirokoitia settlement, named after a nearby village, was founded on a hill encircled by the Maroni River, not far from the south coast of the island, between Lemesos and Larnax. Culturally, it belongs to a Preceramic Neolithic, but a definitely distinct version of it. The houses, estimated to have numbered about one thousand, were densely built, close to one another, and covered the whole area of the hill, which was 250 metres long. In fact, it was more than just a settlement; it was a small town of four to five thousand inhabitants. On either side of a paved central road (185 m. long × 1.50 to 2.50 m. wide), which ran down through the settlement was a compact agglomeration of round vaulted houses built of mud bricks or clay on stone foundations. Preserved traces of corbel vaulting show the houses to have had dome-like roofs. The diameter of most of the domes did not exceed six metres, but in some of the larger ones it was as much as ten. In all, 47 domed houses have been unearthed and three building phases recognized in the settlement. From the first phase there are only scant architectural remains, but the domed houses appeared immediately afterwards. Inside some of the larger ones were stout pillars, which are believed to have supported some kind of gallery or loft, from which a staircase led down to the floor, which was generally covered with clay. Hearths were found in all the buildings, and there were indications of small windows in the walls. The entrances were narrow with high thresholds to prevent flooding of the interior. Often an inclined pebble path led down to the central road. Some buildings had cobble courtyards and annexes.

Although carbonized cereals have not been found, the discovery of millstones and sickle blades provide indirect evidence that agriculture was practised. Some animals, such as the sheep, and probably also the goat and the pig, had been domesticated. Hunting, however, must have still been important, and this is indicated by the many flint points. There is evidence of great progress and skill in the working of hard stones, especially the volcanic variety, like the grey-green andesite, which abounds in this region. From this and similar materials (diabase, basalt, diorite), fine stone utensils were made: mainly shallow basins, circular, oval or quadrilateral in shape, often with a spout, though rarely with handles; and also shallow trays. Sometimes the stone vessels were decorated with incised lines or relief bands. More than two hundred of these have been found in the excavations. It appears that during the first phase of the settlement there were unsuccessful attempts to make clay vases; the only pottery found from the first Choirokoitia period are a few fragments of badly fired grey vessels. This civilization remained aceramic to the end, but the attempt to make clay vessels is instructive. First, it shows that the Choirokoitia culture was contemporary with the Early Ceramic Neolithic Period of the East. Second, it proves that the use of poterry was not essential to the attainment of a Neolithic level of civilization. Even then stone vessels were rare; ordinary utensils were made of wood, straw, or leather, and often stone vessels seem to be imitations of these more perishable prototypes. Curiously enough, stone vessels suggestive both in shape and decoration of those at Choirokoitia have been found in the Neolithic settlement at Nea Makre, in Attica. Another vessel, clearly Cypriot, has been found in a very early settlement in Syria (c. 6000 B.C.). Nowhere else, however, has anything similar been found. Thus, stone vessels are the distinguishing characteristic of the Early Neolithic

Stone vessel from Choirokoitia in Cyprus (30 cm. in length, 10 cm. in height) dated to the beginning of the 6th millennium B.C. A fine example of the skilful stone-cutting work of the early Neolithic inhabitants of Cyprus. (Cyprus Museum, Nicosia)

Period in Cyprus, though they are not unknown in much later phases on the island.

There is evidence of weaving at Choirokoitia during this period, and it may be safely assumed that garments were made, probably of wool. The finds include bone pins and needles, which were obviously used for sewing, and a few pieces of jewellery, such as necklace beads of carnelian and other stones or of sea shells. Of particular interest are the schematized human figurines with no indication of the sex characteristics, usually made of the same hard stone and, exceptionally, of unbaked clay (e.g. a woman's head on which the hair is shown). This technique and type of figurine continued in later periods.

There were many burials in the vaulted houses belonging to 138 individuals: infants (25% in one group, indicating a high infant mortality rate), children, men, and women. The bodies were buried immediately after death in roughly dug pits inside the houses. The bodies were laid in a strongly contracted position, evidently with their clothes on, as suggested by indications of the existence of clothing. A few grave goods were left by their side, usually stone vessels and jewellery. Towards the end of the period, a woman and child were sometimes buried together. In one case, a human sacrifice is conjectured in honour of some eminent person who had died. The average life span seems rather long for such an early period: about 35 years for the men and 33.5 for the women. The skulls are brachycephalic to such a surprising degree that Cyprus is considered the centre of brachycephalism in the Mediterranean. It seems clear from certain finds, however, that to some extent this characteristic was due to the artificial reshaping of the skull by means of some kind of swaddling band which was wrapped around the infant's head. Specialists are divided over this question of brachycephalism as well as over the interpretation of paedomorphism and some other physical characteristics peculiar to the island. Some believe that it was Cyprus's geographical isolation which is responsible for the development of brachycephalism; others maintain that the original "colonists" who settled on Cyprus came from the Balkans or perhaps from regions like Macedonia and Thessaly, or that some elements in the population of the island probably arrived from Cilicia or Armenia. Obviously, the latter theories all attempt to explain distinctive local phenomena by means of the all-too-familiar formula of migrations, but they do not seem to explain the facts adequately.

The Preceramic Period here ended as mysteriously as it had begun. The large centre at Choirokoitia was abandoned, and after a break of unknown duration, a new ceramic civilization appeared. At Troulli, another settlement on the north coast, close to Hagios Epiktetos, Dikaios discovered clay vessels of excellent quality; they are red and glazed, and a few are decorated with negative ornaments.

The following important period in prehistoric Cyprus is called Neolithic II. The chief settlement of this period is the Tepes hill at Sotera; hence this period is also referred to as the culture of Sotera. The settlement is located close to Episkope, west of Lemesos in the south-western part of the island. A thousand or more years separate Preceramic Choirokoitia from the Ceramic culture of Sotera. The structures are now made of clay; they are square, four-sided with rounded corners, oval, or circular. As in the upper stratum at Choirokoitia, there are monochrome red glazed vessels side by side with painted pottery with combed decoration. In this

Reconstruction of the Neolithic settlement of Choirokoitia in Cyprus, built on the Maroni hill close to the south coast of the island, between Larnax and Lemesos. It shows the settlement at the beginning of the 6th millennium, i.e. in the Preceramic Period, otherwise known as the Choirokoitia civilization. Choirokoitia was a township of perhaps 5,000 inhabitants with round vaulted dwellings (tholoi), 6 to 10 metres in diameter, built of unbaked bricks on stone socles. A cobbled road, 185 metres long, ran through the middle of the settlement, flanked by the domes.

technique, the light-coloured clay of the vessel was first covered with a dark red or reddish-brown coating, and then scraped with a comb-like instrument, probably of wood or sea-shell which, in the process of being drawn, dragged the slip producing patterns of wavy parallel lines. A similar technique was used on the opposite continent, but this particular type of combed vessel is a Cypriot peculiarity of this period.

About the end of the fourth millennium B.C., there was another change in the culture. The phase which followed, the culture of Erimi, so called after a typical site of this period close to Sotera, is considered Chalcolithic. The combed decoration, still used at the beginning of this phase, disappeared, monochrome glazed pottery prevailed, and new styles of painted decoration emerged. The most im-

portant innovation, however, was the appearance of copper.

The first Chalcolithic phase was brought to an abrupt end when all the settlements of the Erimi culture were abandoned, probably after an earthquake or some other natural cause, some time before the middle of the third millennium B.C. The second Chalcolithic phase which followed, represented chiefly by the site at Ampelikou in the region of ancient Soloi, was but the prelude to the Bronze Age, which by then had already begun on the opposite continent. Culturally, the island, as part of the rapidly developing Bronze Age world, was soon to become a bridge between East and West. With characteristic island stubbornness, however, it was to retain its own distinctively Cypriot cultural elements, which distinguish prehistoric Cyprus from the Asian continent.

THE NEOLITHIC INHABITANTS OF GREECE

Early Questionings

For the Helladic lands, like the rest of the Neolithic world, the Neolithic Period was one of radical changes in Palaeolithic tradition and of dramatic adjustments, especially with regard to living conditions. Under the pressure of new external factors, the first human community made its appearance. Though "productive" in character from the beginning, this community was now fast developing into an institution based on man's new awareness as a farmer and determined by the new means of production.

With the discovery of new techniques of tool-making came new methods of domestic organization. Permanent dwelling areas were now essential so that there could be proper supervision of the various types of production (farming, stockbreeding, fishing). This new conception of the dwelling area, associated as it was with the allotment of land for farming, led to the first form of property ownership. The seals which were made and used in Neolithic times were probably intended to establish rights of ownership to a certain plot of land or group of objects. This right originally belonged to the clan, but it was gradually claimed by smaller and smaller groups and finally by individuals. These external changes in the way of life of the community must have been accompanied by even more profound changes in man's ideas and attitudes. For the first time in history, the Neolithic farmer was ready to turn his mind away from his daily practical concerns and to speculate about the world around him and, more particularly, about his own role in it. Man had already taken the first great step forward in his mental development when he distinguished the cycle of his own personal life from that of his physical environment. The second great step consisted in the recognition on his part of individual capacities. The discovery of new ways of making things with his hands revealed man's distinctive ability for creativity. The more he possessed this ability, the more he stood out as an individual in his group. Means of production, too, were distributed on the basis of ability, and this distribution led, in its turn, to a primitive social structure developing within the framework of a cenobitic community.

Under pressure from external changes there also followed an inward transformation which expressed itself in the new preoccupation of prehistoric man with theoretical, and at times metaphysical, problems. He felt the need to explain certain phenomena and to explore some of the inherited beliefs that he carried deep in his primitive consciousness. The cultural life of the Neolithic farmer is in fact the aggregate of his confused attempts to grapple with these problems. This impressive development was not of course restricted to Greece. It occurred in every part of the Neolithic world, and its extent and quality depended, on the one hand, on the degree of tenacity of the old Palaeolithic traditions, and, on the other hand, on the speed with which man could make a successful adjustment to a new way of life. In the Aegean area, the spiritual development of Neolithic man may be traced through a study of the archaeological evidence for two aspects of his life: his religion and his art.

By religion, we mean those first seeds of religious speculation which were noted in the Late Palaeolithic Period; but now these had grown into a sort of "proto-religion". It is conjectured that there was now some attempt to clarify the relation between the individual and his environment, and there is clear archaeological evidence that special care was accorded the dead as well as the female figure. This care reflects to some degree the attitude of Neolithic man to the important and inexplicable facts of birth and death.

The agricultural character of the Neolithic settlements of the Aegean area implies that man was in direct contact and collaboration with earth and nature. This collaboration is a dominant characteristic of the Neolithic culture. All other activities were subsidiary. It was, therefore, natural that Neolithic man should come to believe that the fact of life was dependent on the harmonious collaboration of animate man with impersonal but ever-present nature. Man relied on nature to provide him with the basic necessities of his existence but, on the other hand, nature could not be properly exploited without his own intelligent intervention. Without his participation, nature would be but an inert landscape.

It was still too early, however, for man to have developed any aesthetic appreciation of his surroundings. Perhaps this explains why his decorative art in the Aegean area was geometric rather than naturalistic.

About the important relation between man and nature it may be said that the Palaeolithic belief that success in hunting or stockbreeding depended on magic was now on the way to being abandoned. The new "wizards" of the community were now the ablest farmer, the most skilful potter, the best stockbreeder, and the most fertile woman. It is they who manipulated and to some degree "shaped" nature. Creation depended on them. Production had the form and character that bore the mark of his own genius. Everything seemed to depend on his power, and yet this power was itself subject to the laws of decay and the agony of dissolution. Alas, destruction comes inevitably, often unexpectedly. Death and other disasters wipe out whole communities. Old age renders farmers helpless, women barren, and bodies useless. Must there not be, then, some power, higher than any in man's mortal existence which determines rights to duration and immortality? It was the need to find an answer to this disquieting question, dramatic in its very simplicity, which drove Neolithic man to formulate his religious ideas.

Man's religious consciousness depended on his ability for contemplation and the existence of a mythology. Reflection helped him to draw close to the two poles of human life, birth and death, and to try to interpret them. Mythology helped him to formulate and typify these interpretations through the allegorical use of everyday concepts. But since the Neolithic farmer of the Aegean could not write or, perhaps, even express his philosophical and mythological ideas in synthetic language, he had to resort to some practical means of expressing his religious beliefs.

Burial of the Dead

Religion, then, in this context, means a certain series of simple activities which are neither of a productive nor a biological nature. It includes burial customs and the use of cult areas and objects. Burial customs in Neolithic Greece were simple. The body was interred in a simple pit, and occasionally a few simple grave goods were left beside it. Fragments of vessels often found in and around the grave may have been deliberately broken during the burial. There is evidence for a similar custom in earlier periods. Both Neanderthal man and the hunters of the Late Palaeolithic Period used to break and scatter human or animal bones around graves. The Neolithic graves of Greece contain no traces of any red colour (symbolizing life and death) painted on the dead. This was the practice in Palaeolithic times elsewhere and, in some parts of the world, also during the Neolithic Period.

Both animal bones and ash have been found in Neolithic

Left: the upper section of a female clay figurine from the prehistoric settlement of Otzaki Magoula in Thessaly. Despite the coarse effect, this is evidently an attempt to model the face naturalistically: the moulded eyes and the prominent nose are *obviously meant to stress the chief features of the face (Volos Museum). Right: seated male figurine found at Sesklo (Thessaly). The figurine dates from the Middle Neolithic Period. (Volos Museum)*

Ithyphallic clay figurine of large dimensions (height 48 cm.) from the vicinity of Larisa, probably belonging to the last phase of the Neolithic or the Chalcolithic of Thessaly. Despite its crudity, it is considered one of the most impressive products of prehistoric modelling. (National Archaeological Museum, Athens)

graves in Greece, but it is not clear that they were associated with any particular funerary custom. They may be simply due to an accidental destruction of the settlement. Human sacrifice was evidently not among the funerary customs. Since the prosperity of a Neolithic community depended on its productive capacity and the amount of manpower available, human sacrifice would have been a senseless waste.

The grave goods were rough hand-made vessels, which were laid beside the dead during the burial. Being of no special character so as to suggest that they were intended specially for funerary use, they must have been the vessels which the dead man used in his everyday life. The depositing of grave goods close to the dead was a very old practice which went back to earliest Palaeolithic times after surviving countless changes. It is to be thought of as an expression of the bond of affection that united hunter and farmer with their fellows and enabled them to form their first small communities and to protect their few material possessions. To the Neolithic farmer, the earth was the source of life; from the earth came bread, water, wood for fires and tools, clay for pottery and house-building, grass for animal fodder. Perhaps man too came from the earth, and thither he must return after death. His link with the earth was direct and substantial. The Neolithic farmers of Greece did not place their dead in coffins, as was the practice in later times, but buried them in a shallow pit, in "the bosom of the earth". At most, the dead body was placed in a jar, but, then, this too was made of earth and water. The jar was too small to hold a full-grown body, so that the dead man had to be squashed inside it. The same was true of bodies buried in shallow pits, because the pits were evidently dug hastily and without any special preparation. This accounts for the strongly contracted position of most of the bodies found from this period.

Neolithic man in Greece could have hardly formed the idea of an "underworld". His awareness of inexplicable phenomena, his vague notions of a supernatural world perhaps inhabited by strange and invincible powers, all were associated with the heavens. Clouds, rain, sun, stars, and the night, these made up the unattainable "world above". The earth was something familiar, a kindred element. When buried in it, he was not out of reach of his intimate world. He was protected, surrounded by his treasured possessions. Often too he was safe within his own settlement, close to his own straw or mud-brick hut.

Cave burials can be interpreted in the same way. For the man of those times, caves offered protection; they were his dwelling-places. They were not related with any "other world". It has been claimed that the adornment of the dead and the care taken over their burial shows Neolithic man's belief in, and fear of, an after-life; that he did not consider death to be the end, but believed that, in some strange and indefinable way, he would continue to exist after death and that he must be prepared for this continued existence. It is difficult to know exactly what the Neolithic farmer in Greece did believe. From the archaeological evidence (the coarse grave goods, the scanty burial spots, the variety of forms of burials, the lack of a typical orientation in the position in which the dead were laid), it may be inferred that although Neolithic man considered death to be an event of considerable importance, he had not yet developed any particular mode of behaviour in respect of it, nor had he evolved any definite funerary customs.

Cult Places

It is difficult to know whether the primitive religious notions of Neolithic man prompted him to organize communal worship and, consequently, to mark off special cult areas as public sanctuaries. By the Middle Neolithic, the first communities which had been formed during the Early Neolithic Period were living in organized permanent settlements presumably built on a definite plan. The central structure probably belonged to the chief, who would be responsible for the communal behaviour of the inhabitants and the progress of the process of production. Under the guidance of this central authority, Neolithic man must have participated in collective action to meet the problems of survival. May we then suppose that his religious life too was organized on a collectivist basis? A communal discharging of religious duties by the inhabitants of a settlement would have necessitated the founding of public sanctuaries or open-air altars. Archaeologists have found no traces of either. In the Neolithic sites which have so far been excavated in Greece, the structures are ordinary houses of the usual dimensions with no special features in their construction. Buildings like the megara at Dimeni and Sesklo, which are exceptional both for their size and the interior arrangement of spaces, are thought to be the dwellings of chiefs. Only at Nea Nikomedeia and Chaironeia have any buildings been found which could possibly be cult areas. At Nikomedeia a large building contained many female figurines, two large stone spades, and some minute vessels. At Chaironeia, remains of a court-yard were found, which probably enclosed an open-air altar. But all this is entirely speculative: there is no definite evidence. It seems more logical to suppose that the dearth of archaeological evidence for cult areas indicates that there were no public sanctuaries in Neolithic Greece. There may, of course, have been house shrines, i.e. special areas inside the house of the Neolithic farmer dedicated to some form of primitive cult. This could have been simply a shelf or a corner of a room which held the objects which may, with some reluctance, be regarded as being associated with some rudimentary form of cult. Similar ikon stands are very common in Greek houses today. House shrines are also known to have existed in the East. The figurines which are thought to have a religious character were not found, except in one or two obviously chance cases, gathered together in one place, which might suggest a sacred space, but were scattered, along with fragments of broken vessels, among the remains of Neolithic houses, evidently in the places where they fell when the houses collapsed. There is, therefore, no evidence at all to suggest that Neolithic man built communal sanctuaries. It was evidently not in his nature, or he thought it unnecessary to worship in public places. For his simple rituals he preferred his own home. He was later to create his gods on the same familiar level.

Artistic Expression

Art is the second field in which the cultural life of Neolithic man may be studied. The term is used here in its widest sense and includes both its religious manifestations which, in the absence of any written or synthetic spoken language, were the chief vehicle of his religious expression, and its ordinary everyday manifestations, which constituted his means for artistic expression.

A work of art, in a prehistoric and especially a Stone Age context, may be defined as any simple or composite product of man's handiwork which serves no direct or indirect practical purpose. A geometric pattern painted on an ordinary vessel of everyday use or a simple design incised on the surface of a bone implement are by this definition works of art. The decoration does not increase the efficacy of the object; it simply enhances and enlivens its appearance; it gives it an aesthetic value.

Decorative Art

Neolithic art may be divided into decorative art, i.e. painting and engraving, and plastic art. Decoration had been important in Palaeolithic tradition and continued to evolve during the Neolithic Period, reflecting in concrete or symbolic fashion man's most profound, and sometimes most sacred, thoughts. The notion of writing in fact derives from decorative art. The symbols too which man used to express, often with terse simplicity, his innermost thoughts and deepest beliefs about the universe are derived from decorative motifs, which at first were no more than simple designs.

The decoration, both painted and incised, consisted basically of various combinations of straight lines. To the primitive artist, a landscape, man-made objects, the human body itself were a pattern of lines. He was not yet capable of analyzing things or finding their causes; consequently, his drawing was generally restricted to patterns.

Among the objects decorated by Neolithic man are the figurines, which he fashioned with amazing skill and charming simplicity, bone and stone tools, and various clay and stone objects in everyday use. Most of all, though, he decorated his vessels, painting them red, brown, or black, or incising them with a sharp-pointed instrument. He discovered a method of perfecting the surface texture and of giving his vessels a white, off-white, or tile-colour. Then he added the decorative subjects, not haphazardly, but skilfully in a definite pattern, achieving harmony of surface and decoration. Sometimes he was not satisfied to employ a single technique, but engraved his patterns on a vessel and then filled the incised part with white paint. As a result of the use of these various decorative techniques, certain distinctive styles have evolved, which characterize whole periods and make dating possible. A very characteristic example is the close style, i.e. densely packed decoration, of the Middle Neolithic Ceramic phase in Thessaly, which covered a period of approximately a thousand years.

The decorative art of Neolithic man, however, was not restricted to pottery, sculpture, his scant everyday tools, and simple jewellery. It may be assumed that long before pottery was invented, he knew how to weave and to make straw mats and baskets. His first attempts at decoration must have been on these. Later, he must have used colours, firing techniques, sharp instruments, and plastic decoration on pottery.

The only likeness we have of a Neolithic house is a small model from Krannon, which shows constructional details with exceptional realism. The four sides and the roof are decorated in a manner similar to the close style of Neolithic pottery. It is possible, therefore, that the Neolithic inhabitants of Greece decorated the exterior, and probably also the interior, of their houses.

Plastic Art

Plastic art in the Neolithic Period was confined to the fashioning of figurines up to 0.10 m. in height, representing women, men, and animals. They were generally made of clay, though sometimes of marble or stone. There were doubtless wooden figurines too, but these have not survived. The anatomical details of the figures were either incised or moulded separately, and the figures were always naked.

Female figures are by far the most numerous. They are always shown as unnaturally fleshy with particularly prominent genital area. Indeed, some figures seem to have been made simply to show these areas, since the features of the face are entirely absent, and sometimes even the arms and legs are missing.

The male figure is always shown seated on an imposing chair or "throne". The front legs of the chair and the legs of the figure merge into one another, producing a surrealistic effect and making it difficult to understand the group at first glance.

Animal figurines are rare. They are of dogs and pigs and sometimes other animals, which seem to bear little resemblance to anything that exists in the real world. Perhaps they are imaginary creatures invented by man to express his awe and wonder at curious specimens of the animal kingdom. Perhaps, too, these fantastic creatures represent man's first timid attempts to frame a mythology.

House Worship

These figurines present an extremely thorny problem: how should they be interpreted? They have been found in great numbers, both by chance and in the course of excavations; they are of many different types; specimens having the same schematic shapes have been found in widely separated periods. Faced with this puzzling evidence, scholars find it difficult to come to any firm conclusion about the purpose of these small clay and marble figurines, which in many cases present a perfectly satisfying aesthetic effect. The general opinion is that these Neolithic sculptured figurines were associated with the religious life of prehistoric man, while the great number of female figurines which have been found suggests that these were connected with the cult of the Mother Goddess.

It seems that these figurines of the Mother Goddess should be regarded as a material expression of Neolithic man's general feeling of awe and wonder in the face of the mysterious facts of birth and the natural world rather than as symbolic representations of a particular deity, embodying clearly conceived religious ideas. If one takes into ac-

Neolithic clay figurine of a pregnant woman sitting cross-legged, and with her arms resting on her extended abdomen. The figurine was found at Magoula Karamurlar (Thessaly), and dates from the Neolithic Period. (Volos Museum)

count the unprecedented conservatism of an art which produced the same type of figurine throughout a period of 30,000 years, one is bound to admit that, from the Late Palaeolithic Period onwards, man felt the spiritual need to give material form to birth, this supreme act of creation. Prehistoric man, aware of the special role of woman in this act, believed her to conceal within her some secret inexplicable power. As the power of the earth produced fruit and crops every year and provided man with nourishment, so the power of the female ensured the propagation of the race. This being his explanation of woman's life-giving powers, he gave expression to them in his plastic art by fashioning female figurines that stressed woman's sexual attributes and genital area.

In the Late Palaeolithic Period, the role of the male in the act of creation was not clearly understood, and the male figure was absent in its representations. In Neolithic times, however, it was begun to be realized that man too was essential to procreation, that he too held within him a part of the power which secured the propagation of the species, so that in the art of the Neolithic Period the male figure was now represented along with the female. The male figurines indeed have a far more monumental appearance and are shown seated on a "throne". The erect phallus of many of the figures shows that the male is now proud of his role as the master, through his strength and intelligence, of the earth, and perhaps also of the female, since these were two closely identified concepts in prehistoric times. It was the recognition of the importance of the male role which caused the Neolithic farmer of the Aigaiis to construct a monumental type of male figure, which had no parallel in other regions at that early date. This conception sprang from his desire to give a realistic and honest explanation of his surroundings rather than to resort to supernatural explanations, which in other regions of the world often attributed the secrets of life to some unfathomable transcendent realm ruled by strange and uncomprehended powers. Mystic feeling of this sort is entirely absent from the sculpture of Neolithic Greece. The shapes, even when some of the basic features are missing, still remain obviously human.

Figurines are not the only objects associated with a possible form of rudimentary house worship. Many figurines of utensils and of pieces of furniture (including a large number of small three and four-legged tables) may have been associated with prehistoric man's tendency to isolate his own creations and to link them with his own personal life rather than to any urge to offer them to invisible and demanding powers. It was this same attitude which led him to organize his religious life around the familiar house shrine and to prefer small-scale representations of human figures, animals, vessels, furniture, and buildings. In this way, he gave greater prominence to his own strength and presence and to his mastery over everything concerned with his own life and that indefinable mysterious "something" which gave him the power to conquer it.

A Late Neolithic clay figurine of a kourotrophos, i.e. of a woman with a child in her arms, from Sesklo. The woman is seated on a stool. (National Archaeological Museum, Athens)

THE BRONZE AGE

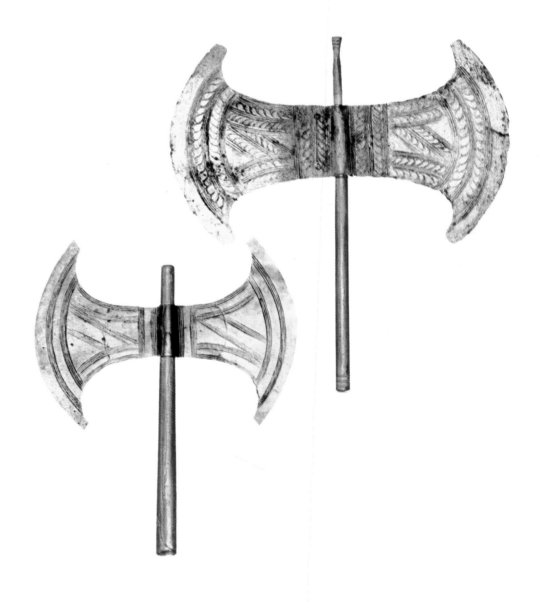

The Early Bronze Age

THE EARLY HELLADIC PERIOD

After the long duration of the Neolithic Period, now estimated to have lasted approximately three millennia, the Aegean world seems to have entered upon a new age shortly after the beginning of the third millennium B.C., when metals were introduced and gradually came into general use. Of course, the Late Neolithic culture, which had reached its culmination in the preceding period, did not disappear overnight. At the dawn of the Bronze Age, the Helladic world still clung to the old Neolithic traditions and agricultural economy, and these persisted in some isolated regions right down to historical times.

It should be emphasized that the new age, at least in its initial stages, was not marked by any revolution in the economy either of Greece or of the surrounding area. Metallurgy was of secondary importance to the economy, since all metals came from the East. If in the last period of the second city at Troy, life "was clearly based on an agricultural economy", we can imagine what the situation must have been in less important centres and in the numerous small settlements in the Aigaiis in the Early Bronze Age. The real "action" was taking place in far distant regions. While the Aegean world was still passing through the final stages of Neolithic culture, the second great revolution in men's history was taking place in the East. About 3,000 B.C., the first powerful city states grew up, first in Mesopotamia, then in the Nile valley, and high-level *literate* civilizations developed in both these regions.

Another thousand or fifteen hundred years were to pass before the Aegean world attained this level. The supremacy of the Eastern cultures was evident throughout the Early Bronze Age; they were the source of all new ideas, inspirations, techniques, and developments. Copper ore was known in the East from early Neolithic times. It began to be smelted and cast, after a lengthy Chalcolithic period, as early as the fifth millennium B.C., but it did not come into general use until much later, when irrigation of the great river valleys brought new and increased possibilities of production. In Mesopotamia, where this new economy first appeared, the great increase in production created the conditions in which a more advanced and broadly-based culture could evolve. Large-scale public works could not be undertaken unless there was a strong central administrative authority, a new social and political structure. It was necessary to found "cities" to house large numbers of work people and skilled craftsmen, to build secure storehouses, and to be able to guard the wealth which was accumulating. The old closed Neolithic and Chalcolithic agricultural economy and primitive farming methods were gradually abandoned. More advanced techniques of production were now employed in the newly-irrigated plains, a barter economy was established and goods were exchanged with distant regions, metallurgy began to be practised, dynasties and priesthoods were established, large palaces and even larger temples were built. Finally, clear class distinctions emerged, and art took on a monumental character which expressed the new ideology.

This was the second great revolution in man's history, and it marked the beginning of the historical period in the central belt, i.e. in the area which stretched from Asia Minor to Mesopotamia and Egypt. The new Age of Metal, therefore, did not represent merely a technological advance—the use of a new basic raw material in the making of weapons and utensils; it was a much more radical change in the course of man's development. The new culture naturally began to expand, first to the Nile valley, where all the conditions necessary to its development were present, and much later to the Indus valley, with important local variations in both regions. Later, it expanded northwards and westwards to Asia Minor, an area rich in ores but also in old traditions. The Aigaiis, and particularly Greece, were remote from the springs of the new culture, but they came into contact with it indirectly along the western coast of Asia Minor, which geographically is an integral part of the Aigaiis.

The Aegean Islands (especially the Cyclades) and Crete played the chief role in transmitting the ideas, inspirations, and technical advances of the East to Greece. It was natural, therefore, that the new way of life should take on a maritime character. Indeed, the comparative ease of sea communication between the coasts and the islands of the Aegean made up for the lack of other prerequisites for the development of the new civilization. It was not by chance, therefore, that the important centres of the Early Bronze Age grew up on the coasts and islands. Even small islands, which in the past had not presented any possibilities for development, now became more densely inhabited. On Lemnos, the settlement at Poliochne grew into a town almost twice the size of Troy, the most famous Early Bronze Age settlement in the Aigaiis.

The Bronze Age civilization of the Aegean developed a highly individual character. It did not sweep uniformly over a continuous area, as in the East, but was anchored to a number of separate islands. Islanders have a different mentality from mainland dwellers and are more sharply separated into small and scattered units.

Even Asia Minor, in spite of its rich ore deposits, lagged behind its eastern neighbours and developed along its own lines. Writing did not appear in this region until the beginning of the second millennium B.C., when it was introduced by merchant-colonists from Assyria. Progress was even more delayed in the Aigaiis, especially in Greece, where there was to be a sharper change in cultural direction. Professor John

L. Caskey has rightly remarked that the power of the Greek land to make everything that touched it Greek was already in evidence in the Early Bronze Age. This power had indeed already been at work in the Neolithic Period, when a previous wave of ideas and goods came to Greece from Asia Minor. It is difficult to follow this earlier movement with any accuracy, but it is clear that in neither case was an oriental civilization simply transplanted in its original form to Greek soil.

Although Greece lay on the fringe of the Bronze Age world, the developments which took place there were of great historical significance, and had far-reaching consequences over a much wider area. Greece was the south-eastern outpost of Europe through which civilization was to be brought to that "barbarian" continent. Further, it seems probable that towards the end of the Early Bronze Age, the Greek "nation" first took shape and perhaps even spoke a common language. In Crete, at approximately the same period, the first really advanced civilization of Europe began to develop. This was the famous Minoan civilization, which was later to culminate in the New-Palace Period on Crete and to exercise an important influence on the younger Mycenaean civilization, which was developing in Helladic Greece. The Creto-Mycenaean civilization with its unrivalled achievements in the field of art did not make a sudden "miraculous" appearance in the Late Bronze Age, but had a gradual development through the Early and Middle Bronze ages. In its culminating phase, it may be described as a European version of an Eastern civilization in a Mediterranean environment. This is evident in the sense of humanity which informs the art and the ideology of this civilization—the absence of any "inhuman" or "superhuman" elements. Oriental despotism and theocracy could not take root in Greek soil. This important change in outlook was decisive in shaping the future course of Greek, and indirectly European, civilization. It is clear that the history of Greece no longer begins with the Dorians. The early chapters are now devoted to the Bronze Age, the period during which the Greek race began to take shape.

The Bronze Age in Greece lasted over one and a half millennia (2800 or 2700 to 1100 B.C. approximately). It is divided into three periods: Early, Middle, and Late. The Early Bronze Age, which covers about a half of the total period (2800-1900 B.C.), is horizontally subdivided in this volume into three separate parts: first, the Early Helladic civilization, i.e. the Early Bronze Age civilization which developed in mainland Greece, stretching from Aegean Thrace to the Peloponnesos; second, the Early Cycladic civilization; and third, the Early Minoan or Pre-Palace civilization on Crete.

Deep clay sauce-boat (phiale) with spout, from the Early Helladic acropolis of Asketario, Raphena. A fine example of Early *Helladic pottery (2800 or 2700-1900 B.C.). The precise purpose of this vessel is unknown.(National Archaeological Museum , Athens)*

It is obvious that these three areas did not form the whole framework of the Early Bronze Age civilization in the Aigaiis. Evolution on the Greek lands at this period was directly influenced and inspired by ideas which came chiefly from the western coast of Asia Minor. There may even have been minor population movements. For a complete picture of Bronze Age civilization in the Aigaiis, it would be necessary to examine developments in Anatolia as a whole, since it is difficult to take the western coast of Asia Minor in isolation. But this would be beyond the scope of this work.

If we look for a moment at north-western Asia Minor, we see that the so-called Trojan civilization, which was then passing through its final Chalcolithic phase, extended to many of the large Greek islands, like Lesbos (settlement at Therme) and Lemnos (Poliochne) and influenced development in Thrace (Michalitsi) and, more indirectly, in eastern Macedonia (Photoleivos V) and Chalkidike (Kritsana), though some scholars see enough evidence of direct influence here to support a colonization theory. We should remember, however, that northern Greece was part of the Balkan area and though its Bronze Age culture was originally of Eastern inspiration, it was also open to influences from the north throughout the course of its development.

Recent important excavations in south-west Asia Minor (at Iasos in Karia, and particularly at the large centre of Beycesultan) have shown that this was a flourishing region in the Early Bronze Age. So far, however, there is not sufficient evidence to confirm the old theory that the Helladic civilization of this period had its origins in south-west Asia Minor. A careful study and comparison of the cultures of these two regions (Helladic Greece and Asia Minor) has shown that in spite of noteworthy similarities in their development—natural in two regions which border on the Aegean and are linked ecologically—the Early Bronze Age civilization in Greece seems to have followed a clearly local line of development and not to have been directly derived from Asia Minor.

Although it is still too early to form any definite conclusions about this period, recent discoveries have enabled us to revise some of our former mistaken theories. It used to be thought that there was no Neolithic civilization in the Cyclades, and that these islands suddenly became inhabited at the beginning of the Bronze Age. It seemed natural to suppose that this was the result of colonization from Asia Minor. Later, however, when the Saliagos settlement on the small island of Antiparos was excavated, it became evident that the Cycladic civilization had its origins in a long Neolithic tradition with a special Cycladic character of its own. Another mistaken notion was that, whereas Early Helladic settlements were founded on the coast, Neolithic settlements had always been located in the interior, and so it was inferred that there was a radical change in the location of settlements at the beginning of the Bronze Age. We know now that many Neolithic settlements were in fact situated right by the sea as for instance, the settlement of Nea Makre on the east coast of Attica, and that the increased population of the islands and coasts in the Bronze Age was the result of adaptation to the new conditions of this age rather than due to any radical change.

It should be emphasised too that the early phases of the Early Helladic civilization (the period called Early Helladic I, of which little is yet known) seem to have a clearly sub-Neolithic character. It is obvious that in its critical early stages, the Early Helladic civilization assimilated a good deal from the preceding Neolithic culture. Although the development of the Early Helladic civilization was affected by influences from the East (whence too came copper, the chief metal in use in the new age, and the technique of working it), the civilization remained basically Aegean in character.

The question of dating is important if we want to compare the Early Helladic with other contemporary civilizations, estimate their mutual influences, and indeed trace the origins of this prehistoric civilization, which has left no written records. Both the relative and absolute chronology of this period still present problems; but it seems clear that the Early Helladic civilization is more or less contemporary with the Early Cycladic as well as with the Early Minoan. It must have some general correspondence too with the Early Bronze Age of Asia Minor. The beginning of the Early Bronze Age in the Aigaiis may perhaps be dated between 3000 and 2800 B.C. Its end can be dated with more certainty around 1900 B.C. Its subdivisions depend on the determination of this chronology, but, roughly, it may be subdivided into three phases: Early (c. 2800 or 2700-2500 B.C.), Middle (c. 2500-2100 B.C.) and Late (c. 2100-1900 B.C.).

We shall begin our account of the development of the Early Bronze Age civilization by describing the chief sites so far excavated in Greece; we shall then consider the cultural achievements of this civilization so far as we can judge them on the meagre evidence at present available.

The civilization of northern Greece, i.e. the modern regions of Thrace, Macedonia, Epeiros and Thessaly, is best described as "Early Bronze Age", since the term "Early Helladic" seems appropriate only for the civilization of southern Greece. The north-eastern part of Greece seems to have been directly influenced by developments in the northern Aegean where, at that period, a "para-Trojan" civilization was flourishing. The islands of the north Aegean (Lemnos, Lesbos) are so closely linked with the Troad that the civilizations at Poliochne on Lemnos and at Therme on Lesbos are generally considered to be local variations of the Early Bronze Age civilization of north-west Asia Minor.

How did this para-Trojan civilization reach the shores of Aegean Thrace, eastern Macedonia and Chalkidike? Was it transmitted via Thrace, or, to some extent via islands like Lemnos, and perhaps also Thasos and Samothrace? Were these islands, like the Cyclades in the south, instrumental in spreading Eastern culture in the north Aegean? And what exactly was the nature of this process?

It is generally agreed that there are clear Trojan elements in the Early Bronze Age civilization of this region. Some scholars believe that these were the result of colonization.

Remarkably naturalistic silhouette of a dog incised on the surface of a large clay jar (pithos) *found in the main room of an Early Helladic house at Asketario, Raphena.* (*National Archaeological Museum, Athens*)

Excavations at Dikili Tash, and particularly at Photoleivos, have shown that para-Trojan elements also predominate in Eastern Macedonia, from the Nestos to the Strymon and the Langadas basin. An Early Bronze Age civilization has been found at Thasos too. It seems probable that it was through the islands off the Thracian coast that Eastern ideas and skills came to the interior.

The Chalkidike Peninsula juts out so far from the mainland that it can almost be regarded as an island. Perhaps the existence of this peninsula accounts for the Aegean character of the civilization in Macedonia and for the fact that, from the dawn of prehistory, the fortunes of this region were closely bound up with developments in Greece. With the spread of the Bronze Age civilization came greater contact between this peninsula and the East, no doubt through Lemnos. From the remains at Kritsana, the most important Early Bronze Age site (on the shores of the Thermaic Gulf close to Epanome), one gets the impression of direct contact with the East.

In central Macedonia, bones of horses have been found by W.A. Heurtley, which are thought to date from the Early Bronze Age. If this is confirmed by future evidence, we would have to revise our present theories which attribute the introduction of the horse into Greece to northern tribes who moved southwards from the distant steppes during the Middle Bronze Age. The Axios valley was the chief communication channel to the northern parts of Macedonia and an important passage through which Aegean culture spread northwards. In western Macedonia, the most important settlement is at Armenochori, close to Florina.

In Thessaly, an enormous amount of Bronze Age material came to light during earlier excavations by Chrestos Tsountas and by A.J.B. Wace and M.S. Thompson at Sesklo, Dimeni, Rakhmani, Tzani Magoula, Zerelia, and elsewhere. The most important recent campaign has been by Vladimir Milojčič at the site of ancient Argissa, close to Larisa, where many Macedonian or, more accurately, western Macedonian elements of the last phase of the Early Bronze Age were found. In pottery, shapes and techniques seem to be the forerunners of characteristics of the Middle Bronze Age. Perhaps we may assume a population movement from the north to Thessaly some time before the close of this period.

The islands of the northern Aegean, as can be seen from a glance at the map, formed a bridge which linked the Troad with Aegean Thrace and eastern Macedonia. The excavations undertaken by the Italian Archaeological School of Athens at Poliochne on Lemnos, the only island in this group where prehistoric sites have been systematically excavated, have brought to light the imposing remains of a civilization of distinctly individual character. Although the first settlement at Poliochne seems to have been no more than a village, the second appears to have developed swiftly into a fortified city twice as large as the contemporary city at Troy, while the fifth contained treasures to equal Schliemann's finds at Troy.

Of course, the long narrow megara at Poliochne (and at Therme on Lesbos) are not as advanced architecturally as the buildings of the second city at Troy. There is no doubt, however, that a rich civilization flourished on Lemnos in the Early Bronze Age, and its appearance can only be interpreted as the result of a sudden swift development of mercantile activity at the very beginning of the new age. It is instructive to examine this "beginning" at the Poliochne settlement. It was not marked by any invasion or colonization; the Bronze Age civilization there developed naturally out of the previous sub-Neolithic stage, retaining many elements of the earlier tradition while introducing new forms at the same time. It is clear that no "migration" was necessary to bring about these cultural changes. They were simply the result of pressures normally exerted by new ideas. The developments that we can trace on Lemnos, a Greek island which is closer to Chalkidike than to the Troad, must have taken place also on Euboia and Naxos, which are much closer to the central body of Greece. As in the north, where Poliochne was the most important representative of Trojan civilization, so in the south development came more swiftly to the islands than to the mainland. It is, of course, possible that some important sites have been submerged as a result of corrosion and a rise in the sea level. Corrosion has been observed both at Poliochne and at Therme on Lesbos. The greater part of the latter settlement (also considered to be para-Trojan) has been submerged, but enough remains to show that it was built on lines similar to those at Poliochne.

We turn now to southern Greece to examine the Early Helladic civilization which developed chiefly in the eastern Sterea Hellas and the Peloponnesos (from the Island of Leukas and the northern tip of Euboia down to the southernmost point of the Peloponnesos).

n the eastern Sterea Hellas, the most important sites so
excavated are: Hagia Marina, Orchomenos, Thebes, the
ement and cemetery at Lithares, and Kirrha; in Attica:
ia Kokkinia, Hagios Kosmas by George E. Mylonas,
hena and Asketario by D.R. Theocharis; in Euboia:
opolis-Leukanti; in Aigina: Kolona. The site at which
lopment is most fully attested, however, is at Eutresis in
tia (H. Goldman).

he settlement at Eutresis in the late phases of the Early
adic Period consisted of a group of small houses. They
built on a rectilinear ground plan and had stone socles
foundations. There was a marked improvement in the
ity of the pottery, and many new shapes appeared.
e is no doubt that this phase was both long (c. 2500-
B.C.) and flourishing. The beginning of the subse-
t Early Helladic phase is not marked by any destruc-
or change in the style of architecture, but there is a
change in the appearance of the pottery (new shapes,
ted decoration), in which the wheel is used for the first
. One house appears to be megaroid (long and narrow
a large main room, a brick column in the centre, and a
ler room at the back). The thick layer of ash and burnt
rial which covers the inside of this house and almost
vhole of the rest of the settlement shows that there was
olent destruction at the end of Early Helladic times,
aps a little after 2000 B.C.

The Civilization of Lerna

The clearest picture of the Early Helladic Period is given
by the finds which have come to light in the Argolid and in
the Corinth region. These fertile and geographically hospi-
table regions were densely populated during the Bronze Age.
The preliminary excavations by Carl W. Blegen at Korakou
and later at Zygouries opened up new horizons in archaeology. And in recent years, the large-scale systematic excavation of Lerna by John L. Caskey enriched our knowledge
of Greek prehistory with findings of great value.

The site lies at a favourable point on the Gulf of Argos,
close to the perennial spring of Lerna. At approximately the
beginning of the late phase of the Early Helladic Period,
the area (inhabited from Late Neolithic times) was artificially levelled, and a city was built. From the first, the city
was enclosed by a fortification wall. This was later repaired
many times and extended until eventually it became a double wall with many small inner compartments and projecting horseshoe-shaped towers. The buildings of the settlement are four-sided and spacious, and are evidently arranged around a large central building, which had thick
walls, large rooms, and surrounding corridors. In the last
phase, after a destruction, this large central building was
rebuilt in a more monumental form. It now covered a total
area of 25 × 12 m. and consisted of two large rooms sur-

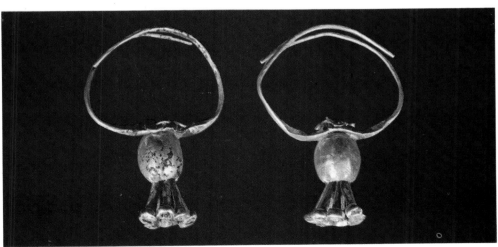

*Typical art specimens
of the particular civilization
which developed at Poliochne
on the island of Lemnos during
the Early Bronze Age
(3rd millennium B.C.),
when decorative metal-work
was flourishing.
Left page: gold pin with birds.
This page, left above:
gold jewellery from Poliochne;
similar finds were made
by Schliemann at Troy.
Below: simple,
beautifully-designed jewellery
from Poliochne, suggestive of
Archaic Greek work. (National
Archaeological Museum, Athens)*

rounded by corridors. The plan bears no relation to that of the megaroid type of building; indeed, the whole conception is completely different and considerably more advanced. The thickness of the walls and the presence of a stair-well show that there was an upper storey. There was a large main entrance at the front, and a secondary one at the back, as well as smaller openings along the two long sides. A great number of roof tiles have been found (hence the building is called the "House of the Tiles") as well as schist stones, so it seems that the building was covered by a sloping tile-covered roof, like other buildings at that period, such as the *tholos* at Tiryns.

Certain features in the architecture—the polished surfaces of the floors and interior walls, the benches which run along the length of the walls, and the wooden covers of the doorways—reveal the amazingly high level of technical skill which had been attained at this early period. Although the building contained nothing of value, since it had been looted probably by those who destroyed it, the many clay seal markings found there are alone ample evidence of the wealth which had been accumulated at Lerna. The organized trade of the region was evidently controlled by this "palace". The whole arrangement of the settlement— buildings distributed around a focal point and enclosed by fortifications—reveals a greater degree of civic organization than anything found in earlier periods.

Before the rebuilding of the "House of the Tiles" could be completed, this building along with almost the whole settlement was destroyed by fire, and the last phase of the civilization of Lerna came to an end.

The precise date of the destruction of the "House of the Tiles" and Lerna III is not known. Of the various dates suggested, the most probable is 2100 B.C. Nor is it clear whether the destruction was part of a more general pattern of destruction in the north-west Peloponnesos or more generally in Greece at that period, or an isolated occurence. It is probable that it was one of the many "destructions" and successive upheavals which marked the transition from the Early to the Middle Bronze Age in Greece around 2000 B.C. (perhaps from 2200 to 1900 B.C.), making it a period of constant unrest during the critical final phase.

Life and Art

The Early Bronze Age is regarded as one of the most critical periods in Greece's history. In its final phases about 2000 B.C., certain movements and changes took place which heralded the formation of an identifiable Greek race. These changes must have taken effect during Early Helladic times chiefly on the mainland of Greece, where emerged a cultural rather than an ethnic, *koine*, which may be associated with the ascendancy in Greece of Greek-speaking peoples. Our account of the Early Helladic civilization would be incomplete without a discussion of the problems concerning the origins and mutual relations of the tribes which were to make up the Greek "nation" in the Early Bronze Age.

Culturally, the Early Helladic is similar to the roughly contemporary Early Cycladic and Early Minoan civilizations. It is linked too with the Early Bronze Age culture of northern Greece, which is examined here, along with the Early Helladic civilization proper, not only because it too occurred on Greek soil, but because these two civilizations had much in common. In mainand Greece, as in the Cycla-

des and Crete, there was an earlier Chalcolithic tradition, variously manifested in different regions, which formed the base of a common Aegean culture.

This base was already well-established when, around 3000 B.C. (earlier in some places, later in others), the Bronze Age began to emerge. This explains why the earlier phases of the Early Helladic civilization have a clearly sub-Neolithic character. During this early phase of the Early Helladic Period (2800 or 2700-2500 B.C.), development was slow and the cultural level low, especially in comparison with the achievements of the Cycladic civilization. The old Neolithic sites were still inhabited, and although new ones were founded at this period, changes came about only gradually. There is evidence of some early contact with the Cyclades, but in general the economy seems to have remained a closed agricultural one. Copper had made its appearance in a few places, and the new techniques of metal-work brought about changes clearly observable during the last phase of Early Helladic.

In the late phases of Early Helladic (c. 2500-2100 B.C.), development suddenly speeded up, and rapid progress was made in every field. There is little evidence of any preparation for this in the previous period. The change is particularly striking, since it was evidently not the result of any upheaval. Most of the sites of the earlier phases continued to be inhabited, a few were abandoned, and some new ones founded. The change was evidently a purely cultural one and not necessarily the result of colonization or migration, although quite possibly some people from the islands or the East established themselves in Greece in a peaceful manner at this period. Clearly apparent in this period are the changes brought about by the spread of metal-work and the gradual establishment via the Aegean Islands of a maritime barter economy. Metal was now regarded as a necessity. It began to be worked not only on the coast but at inland sites; moulds have been found even in settlements in Thessaly. The smelting of metal, however, was not a simple process, which could easily be handled by individual craftsmen. It was now necessary to collect together groups of workmen, to provide storage space, and to organize the economy on completely different lines. It is difficult to find archaeological evidence for this change since few metal objects have survived from this period. (At the beginning, they were often melted down into new shapes). There is no doubt, however, that before long the basic tools were made on the spot and not imported from the Cyclades or other advanced regions.

In pottery, too, a change is evident. An enormous number of new shapes appear, and a primitive kind of tinning technique begins to be used. Many of the new shapes seem to be of Eastern origin; others show Cycladic influence. At the same time, some clearly Helladic shapes are created, and there is an attempt to revive earlier Neolithic styles. From a systematic study of the pottery it would clearly emerge that the Early Helladic style could not have been derived from any prototype in Asia Minor. Equally evident is the independent character of Early Helladic civilization during its middle and late phases.

In architecture, there are various minor local variations, but the houses are all constructed basically in the same manner; they have a stone socle and brick walls resting on stone foundations. In this respect, they differ very little from houses of the Neolithic Period. They are built on a quadrilateral ground-plan and consist usually of two rooms and a front

The development of metal-work techniques in the Early Helladic Period went hand in hand with important cultural changes. Metallurgy could not have been practised locally had there been no technological progress, collective activity, stocks of materials, and organized trade. Above: one of the rare masterpieces of Early Helladic metal work, a gold phiale with a spout (Israel Museum, Jerusalem). Below: silver vessel of the Early Helladic Period from Euboia. (Benaki Museum, Athens)

A superb example of Early Helladic metal-work, a gold vessel from Euboia (Benaki Museum, Athens). The characteristic linear decoration is reminiscent of the Cycladic style. Few specimens remain of the original types of these vessels since, like all metal objects, they were melted down into new shapes according to progress in techniques and the needs of the moment.

courtyard. The houses and other auxiliary buildings are huddled close together, with narrow passageways running between them, often in small neighbourhoods. Usually an open hearth is built at the centre of the settlement. A few buildings are reminiscent of the earlier megaroid type of building, common in the north Aegean (Troy, Therme, Poliochne). The settlements are usually unfortified, but some coastal settlements (Manika, Raphena, Asketario) have circuit walls, and larger centres (Aigina, Lerna) are enclosed within fortifications with towers. Fortification moats, perhaps of a much earlier date, are known in Thessaly and the central mainland. This new development, however, represents more than a simple improvement in methods of fortification. Lerna has the appearance of an organized "city"; a monumental building stands at the heart of the settlement. And it seems probable that the settlement at Aigina was built on a similar plan. The prototypes of these organized and centre-orientated cities must surely have been the Sesklo and Dimeni settlements, the first examples we have of settlements in which the buildings were arranged around a central focal point. The central megaron of these fortified acropolises in Thessaly, like the "House of the Tiles" at Lerna, may be regarded, as the dwelling of the ruler of the community, i.e. his "palace".

There is no doubt that the amazing organization and the prosperity of Lerna (and perhaps of Aigina and other settlements of the Sterea Hellas, which have not yet been excavated) was due to the successful way in which new ideas and trends were combined with the long experience gained during an agricultural and stockbreeding economy. In spite of the development of maritime activity, which was particularly rapid on the islands, and of a barter system of trade, agriculture still remained the basic method of securing the necessities of life. Fishing too must have been important in coastal areas. Thus, towards the end of the last phase of the Early Helladic Period, several important centres, comparable to those of eastern Crete and the Cyclades, had grown up and seemed set to develop even further.

From the scant archaeological evidence available, it is difficult to form any clear idea of the beliefs of the people. Certainly their religious ideas must have been extremely rudimentary. Not a single Helladic "shrine" has been unearthed anywhere in Greece. This absence of religious architecture and other related indications show the difference in orientation between Early Helladic and Eastern civilizations, for, in the latter, sacred buildings and shrines appear at a much earlier date.

The plastic art of this period is restricted to animal figures which, with the exception of a few Neolithic survivals in Thessaly, are almost aniconic. Cycladic figurines found in tombs, chiefly in Attica, and imported marble figurines from the islands, or local imitations of them, are no more than evidence of cultural affinity. The Early Bronze Age ithyphallic figurine from Zerelia, which may be explained as a product of Thessalian tradition, is an exception. Even in the Middle Helladic Period, figurines are rare. That naturalism still survived in art, however, is shown by various finds and an Early Helladic jar from Asketario, on which the figure of a dog has been boldly engraved.

Few Early Helladic cemeteries have been found. The most important is at Hagios Kosmas, where there are Cycladic graves and some Cycladic grave goods.

A great number of seals and seal markings have survived from the late phase of the Early Helladic Period. Seals were not a new invention; they had been used even in Neolithic times. The seal markings of Lerna, however, reflect the development of the new and flourishing barter economy, which was taking on as yet unprecedented dimensions. Greece was not to reach this level again until Mycenaean times when, at the dawn of the Late Bronze Age, "treasures" of valuable royal vessels, made of gold or silver, suddenly appeared in the shaft graves of the Peloponnesos.

The Last Phase of Early Helladic

The destruction of Lerna around 2100 B.C. may have been an isolated incident, but it was a typical consequence of the emergence during this period of new factors, which were to have a steadily increasing effect on developments and which were to lead eventually to the disintegration of the Early Helladic civilization and the establishment of a Middle Bronze Age culture.

Despite indications that there was a smooth and gradual transition between the Early and the Middle Bronze Ages in some parts of Greece, such as Thessaly and the Cyclades, it is now thought that there was some break between the Early Helladic and the Middle Helladic periods. Some settlements were destroyed at an early date, others later. Some were never rebuilt. At the same time, new racial groups established themselves by peaceful infiltration or violent means in southern Greece. We have no sure knowledge of their origins, but it is clear that the period around 2000 B.C. was one of general upheaval. Tsountas's theory, based chiefly on finds from the Middle Bronze Age, that the creators of the Bronze Age civilization in Thessaly were Greeks, "the first true Greeks to tread the soil of this country" has been confirmed by recent excavations. There is no evidence for the descent of Thessalian tribes into central Greece before the end of the Early Helladic Period. If tribes of Thessalian origin, perhaps pushed southwards by Macedonian tribes, settled in southern Greece around the end of the third millennium B.C., it is they perhaps who introduced the horse, which makes its first appearance at Lerna at the beginning of the Middle Helladic. It was certainly these "northerners" who may also be considered responsible for the new retrogressive trends in culture and for the return to the closed agricultural economy, which characterizes the early phases of Middle Helladic. These less advanced "northern" tribes were still at the Early Bronze Age level of civilization, but were not altogether unrelated to the tribes they encountered when they moved down south of the valley of the Spercheios River.

During the same period, small groups of eastern tribes may also have arrived in Greece, while in the periphery of developments, there were yet other backward tribes from the north-west who advanced southwards as far as western Messenia. These population movements may have been the result of a more general upheaval in the Balkans and Asia Minor which had repercussions in the Helladic world. In any case, the gradual penetration, peaceful or otherwise, and establishment of northern Helladic and, to a lesser degree, eastern tribes into southern Greece resulted in the change from the Early to the Middle Bronze Age, from Early Helladic to Middle Helladic civilization.

THE EARLY CYCLADIC PERIOD

Aegean Mariners

The mild climate of the Cyclades favoured the establishment of settlements there at an early date, and the strategic position of these islands in the Aegean helped them to develop one of the oldest civilizations in Europe. They were from the earliest times a cultural bridge between Europe and Asia. A sailing boat leaving the eastern shores of the Greek peninsula in the morning could, given a favourable wind, reach the shores of Asia Minor on the same evening. Distances between the islands were short, and the sea was regarded not as a hostile element, but as the familiar back-cloth of all activity, movement, and adventure. The early inhabitants of the Cyclades were not slow to make the acquaintance of their neighbours. At first, they attempted only small sailing expeditions to nearby islands; later, they undertook hazardous voyages to distant coasts. In the Bronze Age, Cycladic ships sailed to every corner of the Aegean.

The earliest traces of human habitation which have so far been discovered in the Cyclades are dated to the end of the 5th millennium B.C. A Neolithic settlement, evidently at an advanced phase of development, has been found on the small island of Saliagos. There was a natural transition between the Neolithic Period and the Early Bronze Age (Civilization of Kephala, Keos, c. 3200 B.C.). The period which followed saw the development of a new civilization with a strongly individual character—the so-called Early Cycladic civilization. It lasted for the whole of the third millennium B.C. and had a parallel development with the Early Minoan civilization in Crete and the Early Helladic civilization in mainland Greece. Although geographically restricted to the Cyclades, it was in close contact with other regions bordering on the Aegean, and there is evidence of mutual influence in their cultures.

In almost all the Cycladic islands, even the smallest, excavations have revealed traces of Early Bronze Age settlements. There were no large centres, partly because the islands were of limited area and partly because there was no arable land to encourage the development of an agricultural economy under some central control. There was simply a group of small autonomous settlements, each made up of several related families. Life was closely bound up with the sea, and, despite all external influences, the civilization which evolved under these conditions retained its basically island character.

The civilization of the Cyclades began to be studied in the last decades of the 19th century when collectors of the art treasures of the ancient world turned their attention to the Aegean, hoping to enrich their collections. The first excavations, therefore, were little more than amateur treasure hunts.

The first systematic study of the civilization of the Cyclades was carried out by the eminent Greek archaeologist.

Cylindrical and spherical pyxides (cosmetic boxes) and stone utensils are the chief products of the art of the Early Cycladic Period (roughly 3000 – 2000 B.C.). Left: stone pyxis decorated with relief spiral motifs; perhaps it is an imitation of the shape of a house. Centre: clay cylindrical pyxis with symmetrical incised decoration. Right: typical clay utensil from the second phase of the Early Cycladic Period, perhaps the back of a mirror; among the spiral motifs at the bottom is the stylized outline of a boat. (National Archaeological Museum, Athens)

Chrestos Tsountas. In his excavations in 1898 and 1899, he unearthed settlements and hundreds of graves on Syros, Paros, Antiparos, Siphnos, Amorgos, and other smaller islands. It was Tsountas who first noted that the civilization of the Cyclades was distinct from that of other areas of the Aigaiis.

The Early Cycladic civilization has three main phases: the first covers roughly the period from 3200 or 3100 to 2800 B.C., the second from 2800 to 2200 B.C., and the third from 2200 to 2000 B.C. Each phase presents a different type of culture. Characteristic finds from the first phase have been found at Pelos on Melos and at Lakkoudes on Naxos; from the second phase, on the islands of Keros and Syros; and from the last phase, at the City I at Phylakope on Melos.

Since there are no written records of the Early Bronze Age, the historian has to rely solely on archaeological evidence in his attempt to reconstruct its history. There is no evidence to support Thucydides' statement that the islanders were Karians or Leleges. All we know is that the people who evolved the Early Cycladic civilization were small in stature and belonged to the Mediterranean physical type.

Settlements

Most of the settlements of the third millennium B.C. in the Cyclades were situated on the coast; they were generally founded on the slopes of low hills, where they were protected from natural disasters like flooding and from enemy attack. In the earliest phase of the Early Cycladic Period, the settlements were unfortified. The inhabitants of Pelós and Lakkoudes, for example, felt it unnecessary to build any special fortifications, and their houses were scattered over a relatively wide area. The Cycladic islanders were skilled and bold seafarers. In their small boats they sailed all the surrounding seas and distinguished themselves as pirates. No-one dared approach their island bases. Around the middle of the third millennium, however, the Early Cycladic settlements were threatened by foreign attack. As a consequence, settlements began to be founded inland at points where it was easier to guarantee the safety of the inhabitants in the event of an attack. The usual site was a high hill with at least one steep and unscaleable side. The houses were built close together on the peak, with narrow passageways between them. A wall with towers enclosed the settlement on the sides of the hill where the slope was gradual; a second, less formidable, wall was built in front of the first to act as an initial obstacle in the path of attackers. Settlements of this type have been unearthed on Syros, Naxos, and Delos. Clearly, the islanders now felt less secure and were forced to fortify their cities against attack, perhaps from neighbouring islands, perhaps from further afield.

The Cyclades were in fact no longer the leading sea power in the Aegean. It was at this period that Minoan Crete began to extend its commercial links with other Mediterranean countries like Egypt, Syria, and Asia Minor. Minoan ships must have suffered constant harassment from Cycladic pirates, and it seems that Crete retaliated by trying to wipe out piracy, since safe sea communication was vital to her

own commercial development. In the face of this new danger, the Cycladic islanders were forced to fortify their settlements. However, this provided no check on the expansion of Minoan sea power, and when Crete became the undisputed master of the Aegean, fortifications could no longer serve any useful purpose. Thus, later settlements, of the so-called Phylakope I civilization, on Melos, Paros, Amorgos, and Thera (in the third phase of Early Cycladic) were again founded on the coast without fortification walls or towers. In all these settlements, there are clearly marked Cretan elements in the culture. Obviously, the coastal settlements of this last phase, such as those of Phylakope I on Melos, were no longer pirate bases, but harbours and trading stations controlled by Crete. Thucydides may have been referring to this period when he said in the first book of his *History* that it was Minos, king of Crete, who first rid the sea of pirates and gained control of the Cyclades.

Architecture

The houses of the earliest inhabitants of the Cyclades were built of perishable materials and have naturally disappeared without trace. We can perhaps get some idea of them from the small porous stone model of a house which was found on Melos and from two stone *pyxides* (jewellery boxes), one from Melos, the other from Amorgos.

In the period between c. 2800 and 2200 B.C. (the second phase of Early Cycladic, known as the Keros-Syros civiliza-

tion), the houses were built on a simple plan with one or, at the most, two rooms. They were either rectilinear or curved, depending on the space available within the walled settlement. In the third phase of Early Cycladic, the houses were built on a more regular plan and always with straight walls. The building materials were rough slabs of stone and mud without straw. The thinness of the walls—always less than 0.50 m.—shows that the roof, whether flat or sloping, was made of some light material: wood, branches, or reeds, daubed with a layer of beaten clay. The interior walls of the houses were given a coat of plaster, at least in the later settlements. The floors were covered with beaten earth, or with small slabs, or both. There were no hearths in Early Cycladic houses; there was little firewood on the island, and in any case the mild climate made hearths unnecessary.

The fortifications around the settlements were built in the same way as the houses, though the walls were much thicker (up to 1.60 m.). It is noteworthy that the herring-bone building technique is entirely absent from Cycladic architecture, although, in the second phase of the Early Bronze Age, it is found throughout almost the whole of the Mediterranean, from Troy to the Iberian peninsula.

Burial Places

Early Cycladic cemeteries are always situated very close to the settlements, usually on the gentle slopes of low hills.

The graves of the first two phases (Civilizations of Pelós-Lakkoudes and of Keros-Syros) are generally cist graves of trapezoidal plan. In cist graves, three sides of the pit were lined with upright slabs, while the fourth, on the shortest side, was blocked up with dry walling after the interment. In tombs of the first phase, the fourth side too was closed with a slab. The graves on Syros, however, were built of small flat stones with corbel vaulting (i.e. the sides converged towards the roof), leaving only a small opening at the top which could be covered with one small slab. The graves were quadrilateral or circular and had a false entrance, an imitation of a house door. The dead person was lowered into the pit through the opening in the roof. Whereas the cist graves were very small (at the most 1 m. in length × 0.20-0.30 m. in breadth), the Syros graves were relatively spacious, often with a diameter of 1 ½ metres. A third type of grave, found only on Melos, was the chamber tomb cut into soft rock.

Where the cemeteries are built on a slope, the entrance of each grave faces down towards the plain, but where the cemetery is on level ground, no definite plan is observed. Sometimes the graves are separated into small clusters. Large well-built graves containing rich grave goods are found in the most prominent parts of the cemetery and at a fair distance from one another, while smaller and poorer graves are huddled close together in one of the corners.

In the first phase, each grave usually contained one body, but in the cemeteries of the second phase, there were often multiple burials in the same two- or three-storied graves. The bottom section of this type of grave was used as an ossuary so that the upper sections were left free for new interments, though, characteristically, care was taken that the skulls should not be moved from their original position.

The dead person was laid in the tomb in a contracted position with his arms covering his face and his legs drawn up so far that his knees touched his chin. The body must have been forcibly flexed into this position and was perhaps bound soon after the occurrence of death. In some cases, the body was covered with stones inside the grave. Grave goods were placed in front of the face or around the body. They consisted of objects in everyday use: clay or marble vessels, marble figurines, amulets, necklaces, bronze tools or weapons, or small objects used for embellishment or tattooing, such as needles, pins, tweezers, and obsidian blades. In the Syros cemeteries the grave goods were often placed in special niches in the walls of the grave.

After the interment, the entrance to the grave was blocked with dry walling or an upright slab. A bigger slab sealed off the roof opening, and on top of this a small wall was built with its façade facing down the slope. This served as a marker and also held the roof slab in place. Wherever the cemetery was on level ground and not on a slope, the position of the grave was marked with a layer of white pebbles. The small paved areas found close to the cemeteries were evidently connected with some funeral ceremony.

Religion

Since there are no written sources to give us information about the religious beliefs of the Cycladic people in the Early Bronze Age, the historian must base his conclusions solely on a study of the funerary customs. The great care that was taken over the burial of the dead suggests that there was a belief in afterlife. Personal belongings were placed in the grave of the dead person perhaps not so much that he might use them in the next world as to prevent him from returning to the settlement in order to claim them. Perhaps this same fear accounts for the practice of burying the dead in a strongly flexed position and in a space too narrow to allow movement. At the same time, there were established ceremonies, perhaps involving the group, which aimed at the exorcism or propitiation of the dead. From all this, the conclusion may be drawn that Cycladic religion in the Early Bronze Age was a mixture of superstition and magic.

Economy

The Cycladic islanders could never hope to achieve economic self-sufficiency. There was little arable land, poor hunting, and even fishing produced a low yield. The sur-

Three examples of the last phase of Early Cycladic art. Left: clay triple lamp with three stems, decorated with painted geometric motifs. Centre: clay kernos (ceremonial vessel in which various offerings were placed). Right: clay Cycladic vessel in the shape of a bear holding a basin in its forelegs. The figure of the animal is rendered in a remarkably naturalistic fashion. (National Archaeological Museum, Athens)

vival of the Early Cycladic settlements depended on a type of mixed economy. From the excavations and from the works of art which have been found, it appears that farming, stockbreeding, hunting, and fishing were the chief occupations of the islanders, but commerce too was important from a very early date. From the Neolithic Period onwards, Melos exported obsidian to Crete, the other Aegean islands, mainland Greece, and Asia Minor. In the first Early Cycladic phase, there was only limited contact with the extra-Cycladic world, somewhat more with Crete, but in the second phase, goods began to be exchanged over a wide area, evidently as the result of the rapid spread of metal. The Cyclades had trade links with the coasts of Attica (Hagios Kosmas, Palaia Kokkinia, Brauron, Raphena, Marathon); with Boiotia, Euboia, the Argolid, and Korinthia. In the East, traces of Cycladic civilization have been found in Karia, Samos, Lemnos, and Troy. There are indications that trade links were also forged with the Danubian region and the Sea of Azov as well as with the islet of Hvar in the Adriatic. Mercantile activity, which was now of first importance, was organised in a more systematic way in the third Early Cycladic phase, though by then trade was coming more and more under Cretan control. Perhaps it was mercantile rivalry that prompted the islanders to undertake their daring voyages to the Western Mediterranean. Vases dating from this last phase have been found as far away as the Balearic Islands. There was naturally an exchange of goods between the Cycladic islands themselves. The guilds of potters and marble-workers evidently channelled their products through certain centres. Their workshops produced clay vessels, marble figurines, and many kinds of bronze objects.

Social Organization

In Minoan Crete, the very architecture of the buildings shows that everything was subordinate to one central authority, but in the Early Cycladic settlements there is not a single house which might be regarded as the dwelling of a ruler. And since none of the islands or settlements presents any features that might be associated with a political centre or capital of the entire Cycladic world, it can only be concluded that every settlement was a sort of autonomous village, which had to find its own means of providing the necessities of life. The existence of fortifications shows that there was some communal activity, but this was organized by persons who could assert themselves in the community without being its chiefs. It was no doubt these prominent individuals who were buried in the larger graves which contained more valuable grave goods than the ordinary graves. A study of the cemeteries also reveals that an Early Cycladic community was divided up into clans or tribes. The difference in wealth between person and person and between family and family, a natural consequence of the increase in trade and piracy, was reflected in the funerary architecture.

The chief weapons used by the Cycladic peoples in the Early Bronze Age were the bronze spear and dagger, the bow, and the sling. Arrow points were made of obsidian, and small sea pebbles were used as sling bullets. The excavations at Kastri on Syros and at Panormos on Naxos showed that

sea pebbles had been used in attacks against fortified settlements.

Art

There was no monumental art in the Cyclades in the Early Bronze Age. All that remains to testify to the artistic activity of the Early Cycladic people are small works—pottery, marble vessels, figurines, and miniature work.

In the early phases of the Early Cycladic civilization, all the vessels were hand made; the potter's wheel was not used. There were two main types of vessels: cylindrical and spherical *pyxides* (jewellery boxes), often decorated with engraved herringbone patterns. Both shape and decoration were inspired by the natural world and everyday activities. The cylindrical *pyxis* is reminiscent of wood-carving work, while the spherical, with its slightly compressed shape, of the plucked shell of a sea urchin. The addition of a low neck, or a leg, or both to the pyxis produced the stemmed pyxis with no neck and the *kraterisk* (small *krater* with or without a foot). These vessels, pyxides and kraterisks, often had polished surfaces and were found chiefly in the sites of the Pelós-Lakkoudes phase. More refined versions of the same vessels were found at sites of the Keros-Syros phase as well as a host of new shapes either of local inspiration or imported from other regions. Typical vessels of this phase, are the "frying pans", the beak-spouted jugs with handle, the "sauce-boats", the stemmed cups with or without a handle, the deep or shallow bowls, and animal-shaped vases. There is now both incised and impressed decoration—usually concentric circles and spirals, the first curvilinear motifs in the Early Cycladic repertoire. The incision lines are usually cut very deep and filled with some white substance. Sometimes the entire surface of the vessel is given a coat of light colouring. In the second phase, the use of a primitive kind of varnish (the Urfirnis technique) is introduced, painted decoration is further improved through the technique of colour, and the potter's wheel begins to be used. Linear geometric motifs painted in white on the dark-coloured surface of the vase are replaced by black painted decoration, applied in later phases over a light-coloured coating. Perhaps the painting of the white motifs is a development of the technique of filling incised lines with a white substance. Bright colours are used on early vessels in this phase; later, darker tones prevail. In the last Early Cycladic phase, some earlier types of vessels continue to be produced, some new ones appear, and others vanish completely. The cylindrical pyxis, for example, is replaced by the broad-based conical pyxis, the beak-spouted jug develops into a type with the neck tilted backwards, and the footed kraterisk disappears altogether. New vessels of this phase are the *askos* (clay jug for water or wine), the *kernos* (ceremonial vessel with two

The abundance of white marble on the islands encouraged the development of artistic activity from the earliest phase of the Early Cycladic civilization. Left-hand page, above: small marble k r a t e r, one of the most typical vessels produced by the Cycladic workshops: the same type of vessel was also fashioned in clay. Below: fiddle-shaped figurine in a stylized rendering of the human figure, reminiscent of Neolithic sculpture. Right: marble figurine of a woman, a fine example of the distinctive art of the Cyclades. (National Archaeological Museum, Athens)

handles) and a large variety of moulded vessels in animal shapes. Incision is still used as a means of decoration, but it becomes gradually less frequent and eventually disappears. Painted decoration, on the other hand, is used more and more and replaces incision after the introduction of curvilinear motifs.

Towards the end of the first Early Cycladic phase, white island marble is used for making vessels and utensils. Among the earliest specimens are a small rectangular palette (a small box with compartments in which the various paints were placed) and a deep cylindrical cup. From a slightly later phase come the small *phiale* and the kraterisk with a conical foot and high neck, probably an imitation in marble of a clay prototype. After a while, when the craftsmen gained more experience, they began to experiment with more ambitious shapes. In the second phase, they produced small

stemmed cups, stemmed *kylikes* with a spout goblets), vessels moulded into animal shapes, e materials besides marble were now used: grey schi large rectangular palettes and querns (a type of m better variety of schist was also used to make mor vessels, which were decorated with incised, chie linear, motifs and a bright red stone to make de walled cups. Stone vessels were not much made i stone-cutting was a laborious and unrewarding t Stone eventually came to be used only for delicate art and household utensils like mortars.

The art of the Early Cycladic civilization is ch resented by figurines. The abundance of raw mate able locally encouraged prolific production and be imentation. Few works of the prehistoric period, those worked in a hard material like marble, have

Marble figurines were produced in particularly large numbers in the early phases of the Early Cycladic Period, but disappeared in the subsequent Middle Cycladic. Right: a rather unusual type of marble figurine — a pregnant female figure (National Archeological Museum, Athens) Right-hand page: male figure, perhaps a warrior or hunter. (Goulandris Collection, Athens)

fully moulded proportions as the Cycladic figurines. At the beginning of the first phase, before metals were introduced, the craftsmen could not use delicate resistant tools on their intractable material, and so the figurines have wholly stylized shapes and can hardly be distinguished from small slab-like pebbles of an indefinite form.

Stylized figurines were produced up to the end of the Early Cycladic Period, but there is obviously a difference in the attitude of the craftsman in the later phases. The earlier figurines were inspired by his determination to master his material and give it a definite shape. The later ones were an attempt to imitate and reproduce a traditional type. But now the craftsman uses metal tools and can experiment with new ideas of his own inspiration. The small so-called fiddle-shaped figurines have greater anatomical detail and develop from stylized into naturalistic figures in the latter part of

the first phase. There are female figures with almond-shaped heads, on which eyes, ears, nose, and mouth are shown in relief. The breasts, and often the navel, abdominal muscles, pubic triangle, knees, and toes are moulded onto the figures. These are the only Cycladic figurines whose feet stand horizontally on the ground and whose arms meet on the chest without touching each other.

In the second Early Cycladic phase, a new type of figurine appears: the head is usually lyre-shaped and tilted slightly backwards, the arms are crossed below the breast with the left forearm resting as a rule on the right, the knees are slightly bent, and the feet are slanted, giving the impression that the figure is standing on tip-toe. The figurines usually show women, but generally with less pronounced anatomical detail. Eyes, ears, and particularly the mouth, are rarely shown. The toes are usually moulded, but rarely the fingers. One large group of figurines shows women in an advanced stage of pregnancy. Figurines of this general type, with minor local variations, were produced throughout the second and third Early Cycladic phases; they are the commonest and best known products of Cycladic art.

Strict frontality is a basic characteristic of Cycladic figurines. They have the appearance of two-dimensional paintings and were intended to be viewed from the front, not the side, although the back is often carefully moulded. In the second Early Cycladic phase, the modelling of the figures became more ambitious as the artists tried to free themselves from the limitations of their material. These attempts to escape frontality and give a third dimension to the figures produced figurines like the flute-player and the seated harpists from Keros (National Archaeological Museum, Athens), and a host of others, now in museums and private collections. There were also groups of several figures together. The musicians, the famous toast-master (holding out his right hand to propose a toast and resting his left hand on his chest), hunters, and warriors are all male figures.

We are still not sure how to interpret these figures. At various times they have been held to be goddesses, concubines, nymphs, heroes, children's toys, magic amulets, and so on. But there is nothing to indicate their purpose. The fact that they were used as grave goods does not help to solve the riddle, since many other types of objects were also used as grave goods. Many of the figurines had been repaired before being deposited in the grave, many had pieces missing from them. Figurines were also found in the settlements, which suggests that they were objects in everyday use.

In our discussion of Cycladic art, we must not omit miniature work in the form of jewellery, which was often placed in graves. There were necklaces made of coloured stone beads, often in the shape of animals or some other strange object, and sea-shell necklaces. Also among the grave goods were small stone amulets, silver pins, silver diadems, bronze needles, tweezers, and obsidian shaving blades. Small bone tubes, often with engraved decoration, were used to hold colouring matter, which was probably used in tattooing.

Rock and plaque carvings found recently on the islands would place the Cyclades in the group of countries of prehistoric Europe where rock art was practised. One group of incised stones (Apeiranthos Museum, Naxos) shows everyday scenes: dancing, hunting, various animals, ships. Elsewhere, there are spirals, soles of human feet, and other less clearly recognizable designs.

3908

*Masterpiece of Early
Cycladic sculpture.
Left: seated marble male
figure playing the harp.
The artist here has
overcome
the limitations of matter
and functions
in a spatial world.
Right: marble figurine
of a rare type:
a male figure playing
a double flute.
(National
Archaeological Museum,
Athens)*

THE PRE-PALACE MINOAN PERIOD

Early Excavations and Chronology

At about the time when Schliemann was excavating "golden" Mycenae and making his first amazing discoveries there, chance finds and makeshift digs in Crete (where in 1878 the Sultan had conceded certain rights and a measure of autonomy) were beginning to bring to light the relics of a very ancient civilization that was clearly related to the Mycenaean.

In the year in which the concessions were granted, two events occurred to fan the flames of archaeological enthusiasm. The first was that a Cretan from Herakleion, Minos Kalokairinos, made a rough excavation on the hill of Kephala at Knosos, which was the property of a Turkish aga, and uncovered some magazines full of *pithoi* (storage jars). These magazines, the first of many to be discovered, were part of a large building, which he immediately identified as the palace of Minos. The second event of the year was the foundation in Herakleion of the Educational Society (*Philekpaideutikos Syllogos*). Its principal objectives, finally settled on thanks to the strong advocacy of two members of its governing board, Joseph Hatzidakis and Stephanos Xanthoudides, were to be archaeological research and the preservation of antiquities. In the twenty years that elapsed before the start of the first large-scale excavations (made possible by the achievement of Cretan autonomy in 1899), an enormous number of ancient monuments and small finds came to light. They testified to the existence of a very ancient civilization and aroused immense interest among scholars everywhere. Schliemann himself entered into negotiations with the owners of the land on Kephala with the aim of starting on systematic excavations at Knosos. However, what with the rumours of buried treasure, the clash between the landowners' demands and Schliemann's excessive flair for business dealings, the talks came to nothing. In 1898, Arthur Evans appeared on the scene. It is doubtful, though, whether the great English archaeologist's investigations would have yielded what they did without the enthusiastic support of Joseph Hatzidakis and the timely improvement of the situation brought about by the declaration of Cretan autonomy.

In 1900 excavations started on a large scale, not only at Knosos under Evans but at a number of sites in central and eastern Crete under other archaeologists, such as the Italians L. Pernier and F. Halbherr at Phaistos and Hagia Triada, the Americans H. Boyd, H.R. Hall, and R.B. Seager on the isthmus of Hierapetra, the Englishmen D.G. Hogarth, R.C. Bosanquet, and R.M. Dawkins at Zakros and Palaikastro, and the Cretan pioneers Xanthoudides and Hatzidakis in the Messara plain and in a few sacred caves.

From the outset, Evans and the other excavators were convinced that the civilization that was coming to light was similar in its main features to the Mycenaean. It soon became apparent that the palaces and other centres of habitation had passed through an earlier period of great accomplishment. The pottery of this earlier period was a brilliant polychrome ware, reminiscent of the specimens found in the cave at Kamares. The resemblance led archaeologists to describe this period as the pre-Mycenaean or Kamares period. Beneath the ruins of the palaces at Knosos and Phaistos the remains of still earlier palaces were found, which meant that there was an early palace period too. Then, when Evans came to examine the stratification and to compare the different forms of the civilization found in different parts of the island, he soon came to the conclusion, with the help of his personal assistant, D. Mackenzie, that this civilization had undergone a long period of development even before the earliest palaces were built. The different strata could be distinguished from one another by observation of the changing pottery styles. This makes it quite clear why Evans based his whole system of dating on the development of pottery. By studying the stylistic variations, he divided the civilization into three main periods, each of which he later subdivided neatly into three sub-periods. This nonary system seemed to fit in very well with the tradition that Minos "commenced his reign anew every ninth year". And so, on the strength of the tradition of Minos' power and maritime supremacy, Evans used the name *Minoan* to describe the civilization that had come to light.

This term, though arbitrary, was convenient, and it came to be generally accepted by scholars. All, unhesitatingly, recognized Evans as the leading authority on the subject: for it was he who cast the first rays of light upon a new chapter in the history of civilization. The same term is still in general use today, even though modern scholars are aware

that it is not an entirely accurate description, since the supremacy of the kings of Knosos was limited both in time and in extent. It would probably be more appropriate to use a broader, more neutral term comparable with *Cycladic* and *Helladic*, used to describe the parallel forms of the civilization found on the islands and in mainland Greece: something like "Cretan" or "Early Cretan". Later, the term *Creto-Mycenaean* came to be used to describe Cretan civilization together with its continuation in Mycenaean Greece. Another term that was to find currency, side by side with the others, was the general name *Aegean* civilization, which covered the whole family of related civilizations that flourished in the Aigaiis in prehistoric times, namely, the Minoan, the Cycladic, the Helladic, and the Trojan.

Despite the general acceptance of Evans' system of chronology, many voices were raised in protest against its conventionality and its apparent incompatibility with the historical periods demarcated by the various great disasters: these formed dividing lines, marked by real changes in the way of life and in artistic style. Because of this, a new dating system was proposed at the Eighth International Congress on Prehistory at Hamburg in 1958. It was to be based on the chronological divisions created by the successive disasters that struck the earlier and later palace centres, from which civilization had radiated outwards over almost all of Crete. The divisions thus determined were called the Pre-Palace, the Old-Palace, the New-Palace, and the Post-Palace periods, each of which was subdivided on the basis of minor disasters into sub-periods or phases.

Evans pioneered the absolute dating of the various periods and sub-periods of Minoan civilization. With masterly skill he succeeded in drawing parallels between these and the corresponding dynastic periods in Egypt and the East, working from the reciprocal evidence of Minoan objects found in Egyptian or eastern deposits of known date and of Egyptian articles found in deposits of Minoan pottery of stratigraphically established dating. His correlations were confirmed by other evidence, so that today there are many dates which are regarded as definitive datum points and thus help to establish an entire system of absolute dates. The importance of this work to the study of history was demonstrated when the Cretan dating system was used as the basis for the determination of the chronology of the other branches of the civilization of the Aigaiis and also of the other prehistoric civilizations of the Balkans and of Europe generally.

In broad terms, the Pre-Palace Period of the Minoan civilization covers the years from 2600 to 1900 B.C., the Old-Palace Period from 1900 to 1700 B.C., the New-Palace Period from 1700 to 1450 B.C., and the Post-Palace from 1450 to 1150 B.C.

From Neolithic to Early Bronze Age

So remarkable an impression did the Minoan civilization make with its many unique features, even in the initial stages of the Old-Palace Period, that it was long thought that its birth was a miracle out of the blue, which coincided with the settlement of totally new racial elements and radi-

Two fine examples of works of art from the earliest phase of the pre-Palace civilization on Crete (2600 – 2400 B.C.). Facing page: bi-conical cup from a grave in the region of Pyrgos of Anopolis, obviously an imitation of a wooden vessel. The artist has rendered the veins of the prototype on the outer surface (Herakleion Museum). This page: vessel in the shape of a teapot made from polychrome stalactite; it was found in a grave at the settlement of Mochlos. (Herakleion Museum)

117

cally altered the aspect of Neolithic culture. It was thought that the arrival of the new settlers and the first use of copper and precious metals had inaugurated a new way of life, which quickly led to the formation of an original and highly-developed style of art. The only problem was to discover where the migrants to Crete had come from, considering that at exactly the same period other peoples, clearly related to these, had given birth to the Cycladic and Helladic cultures of the Early Bronze Age.

We now know that the change, important though it was, was not as sudden as was once thought; nor was it quite so radical, since a number of features of the earlier Neolithic culture were retained and continued to develop. The first phase, then, is one of transition from Neolithic to Minoan and may be aptly termed "Sub-Neolithic".

It would hardly be reasonable to believe that the Neolithic population of Crete, which was fairly numerous, to judge by the density of the Neolithic settlements all over the island, was annihilated by the relatively small bands of settlers who established themselves in the central and eastern parts of the island around 2600 B.C. The first penetration must have been a matter of sporadic landings at odd points on the Cretan seabord from the middle of the south coast eastward round to the middle of the north coast; at any rate, it is in these parts that the earliest finds bearing the marks of the new culture have been found. The immigrants would have arrived in small boats of primitive construction, and the local inhabitants would easily have been able to drive them back into the sea when they first attempted to establish themselves. The fact that they were not driven out indicates that these first arrivals were on an insignificant scale and that the native Cretans preferred to take advantage of the intellectual and technical accomplishments which the immigrants, whose culture was in every respect more advanced, were ready to share with them.

What can we learn from the anthropological evidence? Unfortunately, there is little to go on, which makes it difficult to draw positive conclusions. But, at least, it has established the presence of a new racial type on the island. This type, known as the Mediterranean type, coexisted with another which differed in no way from the earlier Neolithic. The coexistence of these two racial elements explains why the Cretan civilization took the form that it did during this transitional period. Unfortunately, experts disagree over the origins of the new race. Evans suggested that there were two main streams of immigrants to Crete: (1) Proto-Libyans driven out from the Nile Delta when the Egyptians established the Old Kingdom. This explains, in his view, the similarities between features of Cretan life and those of the Proto-Libyans, such as the vaulted chamber, the loincloth with codpiece worn by the men, the men's soigné, long-plaited hair style, a propensity for megalithic constructions, and stylized stone figurines. (2) A different anthropological type from Asia Minor. Migration of this Anatolian race to Crete, in Evan's view, accounts for the similarities between the two areas in racial features, linguistic peculiarities, religious beliefs, pottery styles, and some other features. During the first (transitional) phase, the Neolithic element remained dominant over the two groups of immigrants, as attested

Stone figurine of a man from either the last phase of the Pre-Palace Period or the beginning of the Old-Palace Period; it was found in a tholos tomb at Porti in the plain of Mesara. (Herakleion Museum)

by the innumerable sub-Neolithic features of life and art. Living habits remained essentially unchanged: a troglodytic existence in small caves or primitive huts. Although the inhabitants had started to use metal (chiefly pure copper), stone work and earthenware utensils of sub-Neolithic type formed the basis of their everyday life. Imitative tendencies, apparent in pottery from time immemorial, manifested in attempts to reproduce in clay familiar objects of less durable material, such as leather, wood, and wicker-work. These continued, though now in highly-developed imitative styles.

The same tendencies are apparent in the shapes of the vessels: some are spherical or gourd-shaped with a cylindrical neck and a well-fitting lid; others imitate the shapes of vessels made of skin, of wood (round-bottomed), of wicker-work (decorated with a variety of patterns of angular and intersecting lines), and of metal. It seems that the Cretan potters must have come across metal vessels from Anatolia, cradle of an Early Chalcolithic civilization, and used those as their models, for metal was scarce in Crete, and the islanders had not yet started importing it on a systematic basis. The few implements and weapons of pure copper that have been discovered are small and crudely made. The triangular-bladed daggers were almost all distorted when they were found, because pure copper is not very resistant. With weapons such as these the native Neolithic inhabitants would have been hard put to it to repel the invaders, but in any case it seems that they did not in fact offer any resistance.

It is evident that the Neolithic natives were soon assimilated by the new settlers, for hardly any Neolithic remains from the second Pre-Palace phase have been found. The rapidity with which the immigrants' civilization developed along independent lines indicates that from the very outset it had a totally different orientation from the preceding culture, making full use of the island's plentiful resources and searching out other raw materials from elsewhere, initially from nearby lands, later on from more distant ones. It would seem that an important factor in this respect was frequent communication with the Cyclades, where the Early Cycladic civilization was beginning to evolve at the same time. This at least is indicated by the evidence of early imports from the islands: earthenware vessels, perhaps mostly from Melos, marble vases, and figurines.

The proven resemblance between Cretan pottery of the first Pre-Palace phase and the pottery of South-western Anatolia suggests, quite possibly, not merely common origins but also a continuance of close contacts between Crete and the region that later comprised Karia and Lykia. Relations with the Cyclades were even closer, a fact which hints at the existence of a common racial stock, one branch of which settled along the northern and eastern shores of Crete.

The Brilliant Second Phase

According to Sir Arthur Evans, the Early Minoan or Pre-Palace Period was divided into three successive phases. Excavations have confirmed this ternary sub-division and, most important of all, have proved that the three phases exactly correspond to the three stages in the development of the Early Cycladic and the Early Helladic civilizations.

The first (transitional) phase of the Pre-Palace Period was followed by a sudden cultural blossoming and important changes in the way of life in Crete. The same rapid advance is also to be observed in the other two branches of the civilization of the Aigaiis, the Cycladic and the Helladic, as well as in the Troad and on Lemnos, as witnessed by the treasures of Priam and of Poliochne. It appears that during this period there was cultural reinforcement of the Mediterranean stock from Anatolia.

Our sources of information about the brilliant second Pre-Palace phase, which lasted for about 300 years (2400 – 2100 B.C.), are the excavations at Vasilike and at Myrtos near Hierapetra. Vasilike commands the isthmus, where Crete is at its narrowest and there is an easy route for the transportation of goods overland from the Libyan Sea to the north coast for distribution to central and eastern Crete.

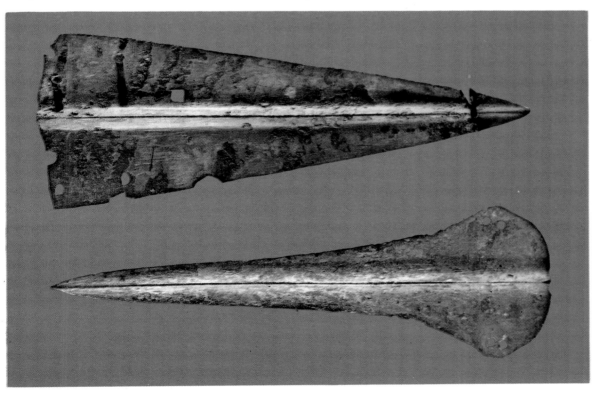

Metallurgy made rapid progress in the second phase of the Pre-Palace Minoan civilization (2400 – 2100 B.C.). Utensils, tools, weapons, and ornaments were made from copper, silver, or gold. Left: two silver daggers from the tholos tomb at Koumasa in the plain of Mesara. (Herakleion Museum)

The "law of the isthmuses", formulated by the Homeric scholar Victor Bérard, applied in times when sea voyages were a difficult undertaking. Sailors, who naturally avoided the hazardous circumnavigation of the island, would disembark passengers and cargo and send them from one coast to the other across the narrowest neck of land, which at this point, is only just over 12 kilometres across. A large building stood at Vasilike. It was L-shaped, with a paved courtyard, corridors, apartments, workshops, and store chambers. The walls were solidly built, with upper courses of large bricks resting on a high basic structure of stone, faced with a hard plaster painted bright red. It seems to have been the mansion of a local squire, as the other buildings round about were much smaller and of less careful construction.

The discovery of the settlement at Myrtos gives a general picture of the architecture of the village communities in this period. Two principal complexes of stone and brick apartments cling to the slopes of a hill overlooking the sea. The architectural design of these constructions is irregular, and there is nothing remotely resembling town-planning, though there are some alleyways, usually dead ends, intersecting the main building complexes. Nowhere is there any sign of a real village square or any meeting-place for community life. The only communal building is a peak sanctuary at the top of the hill, built in the last years of the settlement's existence. All in all, the makeshift construction and the way the houses cascade down the hillside are reminiscent of many Cretan mountain villages today. Its situation, facing the Libyan Sea, indicates the great importance of the south coast of Crete in those days for communication with Egypt. Egyptian influence is to be observed in all branches of the arts, as well as in finished articles imported from the Nile Delta.

The finds yielded by excavations of burial grounds, isolated tombs, and funerary enclosures assist the historian to reconstruct a fair picture of the way of life and to draw conclusions regarding social structure, economy, private life, and religion. We can see a consistent line of development entirely different from those of the great contemporary civilizations of Egypt and the East.

During the transitional phase of the Pre-Palace Period the dead were buried in small vaulted "beehive" tombs (*tholos* tombs) with small doorways. They were built entirely of stone. Tombs of this type are to be found in the little bays on the south coast of Crete and in the narrow defiles of the Asterousia range (the modern Kophinas), which run down to the precipitous coast of the Libyan Sea—a possible evidence of Proto-Libyan origin. Occasionally, one finds clusters of two or three *tholoi* together, as at Lebena.

In the second Pre-Palace phase, these vaulted chambers developed into structures of monumental dimensions, with much thicker walls and fine doorways, which were often formed of three very large stones. These are early precursors of the later tholos tombs found both in Crete and, later still, in Mycenaean Greece. One of the best preserved of them, in fact, near the Hodegetria Monastery, still retains its tall trilithic doorway surmounted by a rudimentary relieving triangle, a device which saved the lintel from succumbing under the thrust of the vault above. There are very few tholos tombs to be found in north central Crete (around Krasi), and it is only towards the end of the Pre-Palace Period that they appear in eastern Crete (at Galana Chara-

kia, near Myrsine, in the Seteia region). Much commoner in these parts of the island are rectangular enclosures, divided by parallel partition walls into a number of narrower chambers. Elsewhere, as for example on the island of Mochlos, which was then a peninsula joined to the mainland, the dead were buried in smaller graves, which usually consisted of a vestibule and a main chamber, tucked away at the foot of a precipitous cliff, or else in small caves or rock shelters. Sometimes the bodies were contained in narrow elliptical or rectangular sarcophagi or in narrow jars. In some of the late tholos tombs of the Pre-Palace Period, a mixed system of burial in clay sarcophagi or jars was used. Most of these tombs were used for multiple burials. Large numbers of bodies were deposited even in the enclosures. It is clear that the tombs were cleared from time to time to make room for new burials, with only the skull and leg bones of the old occupants being retained.

In some parts of the island, larger groups of vaulted chambers have been found. A likely explanation of this is that they were the tombs of entire castes, which would lead to the conclusion that the social structure of the period was based on the unit of the caste or *genos*. This view is supported

There was rapid progress in pottery-making. The potters produced some bold shapes, even though the wheel was not yet in use. Below: jug in the mottled style from the Pre-Palace settlement at Vasilike on the isthmus of Hierapetra. (Herakleion Museum)

Stone pyxis (cosmetic-box),
a fine specimen of
Cycladic art, from a tomb
in the Gorge of the Dead
at Zakros
on the eastern coast of Crete.
A reclining dog
forms the handle;
the whole vessel is decorated
by incised lines in
triangular patterns.
(Herakleion Museum)

by other similar indications. What is certain is that the reins of power had not yet been gathered into the hands of kings; hence, the absence of palaces. In the wealthier districts, where some kind of centralized control was necessary, it is probable that communal leaders were appointed, selected from the headmen of the bigger kins. It would have been one of these leaders that lived in the mansion at Vasilike, and probably another in the main building complex of the hilltop settlement at Myrtos.

The structure of Cretan society began to grow more complex as soon as metal started to predominate in the manufacture of arms, tools, and luxury utensils. It then became necessary to look abroad for the raw materials. Cyprus had plentiful deposits of copper, and teams of miners had to be sent to extract it, or else merchants to barter Cretan finished goods for the much-needed metal. Then, the metal-workers needed tin to mix with the soft copper in order to produce the harder bronze alloys; this had to be brought from the heart of Asia Minor. This marked the beginning of Crete's international trade, which in turn called for a fleet of ships of improved design to stand up to the buffeting of the often stormy seas. It was immediately apparent how much there was to be gained from the barter method of trade, and so the production of local commodities and the processing of raw materials, particularly metals, needed to be properly organized on a sound footing. Specialization now became the order of the day, and the various categories of specialized artisans formed the basis of the whole social structure, together with the farmers and graziers, the merchants and the seamen. As they got to know the civilized outer world better, so their own knowledge and ideas broadened too. Cultural development proceeded at a quickening pace.

Prosperity was ascribed to the intervention of supernatural powers, and it was felt that gratitude was due to them for their aid. So, it was only natural that a form of religion and religious ritual should develop, which no doubt led to the establishment of a priestly class. On the other hand,

wealth brought dangers with it and needed to be guarded, so the next step was to form military units. They were small at first, as the ships were quite capable, with the necessary modifications, of keeping the island safe against foreign intervention.

As the way of life changed and a social class structure gradually took shape, many of the settlements started to evolve into towns, and the need for administrative organization began to be felt. The caste headmen with the greatest authority acquired more and more power, no doubt with the consent of the populace, and attained the status of communal leaders. This, at any rate, is roughly how scholars see the process of change that set in with the second phase of the Pre-Palace Period. Similar developments, of course, took place at about the same time on the islands and in mainland Greece.

Art and Metalwork in the Second Phase

We have already discussed the principal forms used in domestic and funerary architecture. For the first time we find an extensive, complex building which, with its two wings and the courtyard in between them, seems to be the forerunner of the later palaces. The basic feature of the design is the spatial and positional proportion of the rooms.

The walls were of solid construction, and the internal timbering gave the structure flexibility. Special attention was paid to the interior finish of the walls, which were coated with a glossy-surfaced red plaster. The huge vault that was a feature of the funerary monuments, carrying on an old tradition, was a useful way of roofing over a large floor area without using internal supports, and it also created the illusion of standing under the vault of the sky. Proportion was very carefully studied.

Remarkable progress was made in the crafts of stone-carving, pottery, and metalwork. This provided unlimited opportunities for the manufacture of utensils which were not only excellent for their functional purpose but at the same time works of art of peerless quality.

Craftsmen selected and carved with wonderful artistry pieces of stone of every imaginable kind: variegated, veined, and flecked marble, multicoloured stalactites, cobbles, basalt, different varieties of alabaster. They devised all manner of original shapes, elaborate or simple and elegant: vessels with small handles, beautifully made spouts and beaks, turned bases, and slightly flaring rims. The veins in the stone were skilfully used to obtain the maximum effect in emphasizing the vigorous shape of the vase, bringing out its formal balance or highlighting the features that revealed its purpose. There was a tendency towards whirling patterns full of swirls and convolutions, which the craftsmen achieved by cutting their vases with the veining of the stone at an oblique angle. Any collection of these vases is a display of elegance and grace and gives proof of the early beginnings of the stylistic trends that were later to dominate all Minoan art; and every one of these vessels on its own is a masterpiece. Each is apparently unique of its kind even though some of them are modelled on Egyptian originals. In the variety and grace of their products, the Cretan practitioners of this difficult craft seem to have surpassed even the Egyptians themselves, in spite of the centuries of experience which the Egyptians had behind them in the manufacture of stone vessels that were to live for ever. No less to be admired is the technical method used in the making of these superb artefacts: first, the stone core was blocked out with tubular reed drills worked by means of a leather thong and extracted with the help of sand and water, and then the surface was finished off with emery.

The best stone vases of this period come from the burial places of the small settlement on the island of Mochlos, near Seteia (excavated by Seager), which was then a peninsula with twin harbours, one on each side of the isthmus joining it to the mainland. Numerous similar vessels were also found in the tholos tombs of the Mesara plain.

The incised decorations found on schist vases are reminiscent of Early Cycladic designs: friezes of tight spirals, incised hatching arranged in triangles, and so on. Some of the shapes are also Cycladic, so that one wonders whether in fact they were imported from the Cyclades. Other features, however, are quite clearly Cretan: for example, on two *pyxis* lids, one from Mochlos and one from Zakros, the handle takes the form of a Cretan dog lying at full stretch —a marvellous combination of naturalism, abstract convention, and functional utility.

The potters of the period, working with their more malleable material, developed their styles with deftness and grace. The development was rapid, despite the fact that the potter's wheel had only just come into use. The Hagios Onouphrios style, with its dark intersecting linear motifs on a light-coloured ground, gave way to the Koumasa style with

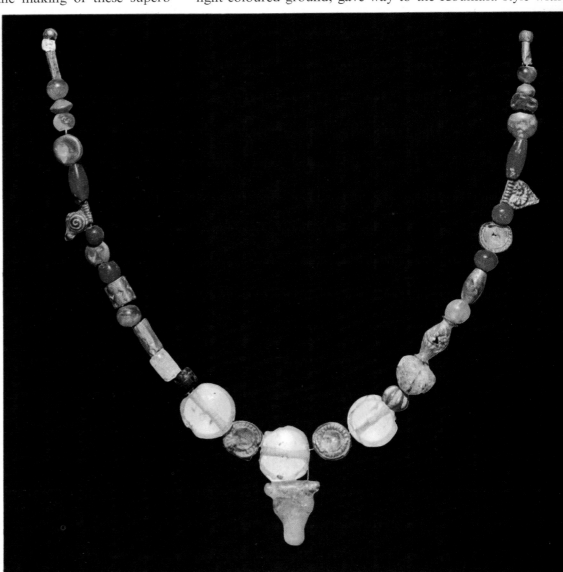

A fine example of Minoan jewellery of the Pre-Palace Period, from a grave in the Mochlos settlement in eastern Crete; a necklace composed of beads of various shapes worked in gold, rock crystal, amethyst, and sard. One of the beads is in the shape of a bull's head. The delicate working of the materials and the polychrome composition are characteristically Minoan. (Herakleion Museum)

An example of miniature carving
from the Old-Palace Period:
an ivory seal from the tholos tomb
at Marathokephalo
in the plain of Mesara.
(Herakleion Museum)

its dense cross-hatchings, elongated linear triangles, and a greater variety of shapes. In the Hagios Nikolaos style, the shapes become more angular, and the surface is decorated with incised close-hatched triangles and rows of semicircles, showing Cycladic influence. The old technique of oxidation produced by the firing developed into the extremely fine style of the Vasilike ware; here the firing was regulated by some as yet unknown method so as to give a mottled effect with snaky patches, stippling, or regularly spaced spots of colour. The Vasilike style saw the introduction of much bolder shapes, such as "teapots" with elongated spouts, ewers with tall beaks, jugs with bridged spouts, and stemmed goblets. Out of vessels such as these the people drank the various concoctions of fragrant herbs that are still drunk in Crete today.

It is in this period that we first find vessels in the form of a bust of the Mother Goddess or in the shape of the sacred bull. A particularly interesting specimen, from the peak sanctuary at the top of the hill settlement at Myrtos, is a jug in the shape of the goddess decorated in the same way as jugs used in everyday life.

It is beyond doubt that vessels were also made of metal (copper, silver, or gold), since many skilful ceramic copies have been found. Unfortunately, not one such vessel has survived. The rapid progress in metalwork as a specialized craft is to be observed rather in the development of weapon and tool manufacturing, as well as in jewellery, where precious metals were used in combination with a variety of semiprecious and precious stones. The very short triangular daggers of pure copper were succeeded by stronger ones of bronze made of alloys containing arsenic and tin; these were bigger and often reinforced with a medial rib. Many kinds of tools were made, and it is clear from a classification of them that professional specialization had already begun: there are stonecutters' tools, carpenters' tools, builders' tools, and so on.

The goldsmith's craft, which was almost exclusively devoted to the manufacture of jewellery, made rapid and great progress. Proof of this is provided by the collections of jewellery that have been found, notably in the Mochlos necropolis and in most of the tholos tombs of the Mesara. Funerary pieces they may be, but they are evidence of the state of technical development, the artists' exquisite taste, and the contemporary fashions in adornment for men and women. Remarkable progress was made in all branches of the goldsmith's technique: in beating out the gold into foil, in riveting and soldering, in cutting-out into elaborate shapes, in filigree, and in granulation. The range of artefacts included diadems, hairpins shaped like flowers, gold braid for the hems of dresses, bracelets and rings, necklaces and other accessories, all in a wide variety of designs. Many of the necklaces were composed of alternating beads of gold, amethyst, sard, agate, and other stones—another example of the leaning towards polychrome compositions.

The flair for miniature art forms is even more clearly evident in miniature sculpture, that is, in the carving of figurines and in seal-engraving. The figurines are somewhat stylized in form and usually carved out of relatively soft materials, such as steatite and ivory, though sometimes of harder stones such as marble. Seals were carved from the very beginning of the period; they were made of soft materials in a variety of shapes: cylindrical, hemi-spherical, button-like, and discoid. The designs on the seal faces were simple geometrical ones at the beginning, similar to the decoration on ceramic vases, developing later into complex curvilinear compositions. We also find representational designs used for the first time, though these were still very schematic. Though the seal-engravers of this period certainly developed styles of their own, they were much influenced by the seal-engraving of neighbouring lands, particularly Anatolia.

Further Development in the Third Phase

Many scholars hold that there was no break at all in the continuity of the Minoan civilization between the second and third phases of the Pre-Palace Period. It is undeniable, however, that a number of settlements that were developing and prospering were suddenly destroyed and were then rebuilt much more crudely, while others were completely abandoned, and others again were rebuilt somewhat differently. This certainly suggests that some kind of disruption occurred between the two phases. The same signs are visible at the end of the second phase of the Early Cycladic and the Early Helladic civilizations. In the latter case, indeed, the settlements appear to have been destroyed by fire on such a large scale that it is reasonable to believe that they were overwhelmed by invaders. In Crete, evidence does not indicate such extreme violence, and there is no question of a change of culture, since the existing culture continued to develop along the same lines.

Some differences are, however, apparent in the third phase: it was the period of transition leading up to the Palace Civilization, and it lasted for about two hundred years, roughly from 2100 to 1900 B.C. At Vasilike, the large mansion was destroyed, and a number of hovels were built among the ruins. A pit-well was used as a dump for broken pots. Later, Vasilike was rebuilt. The slope of the hill was covered with sizeable new buildings comprising a number of service rooms in addition to the principal quarters. Shallow flights of steps served as narrow alleyways, with level lanes branching from them. Polychrome ceramic pots were found in the later buildings; this ware is the forerunner of the Kamares polychrome style of eastern Crete.

The settlement at Myrtos was razed to the ground and never rebuilt. The settlements around the Mesara plain, however, were reoccupied and reconstructed on the old system of a closely-packed jumble of houses in large irregular clusters. Unfortunately, we know very little about these settlements although excavations have been carried out at Koumasa, at Apesokari, and in the bay of Leben.

It is even more difficult to form any clear picture of the

In the last Pre-Palace phase (2100-1900 B.C.), Cretan pottery began to be adapted to new styles of decoration. A considerable number of the vessels were given unusual shapes, evidently because they were intended for ritualistic purposes. Below: a clay rhyton, from the tholos tomb at Koumasa in the plain of Mesara, in the shape of a bull with small figures of bull jumpers (athletes of the Minoan bull sports) clinging on to the animal's horns. (Herakleion Museum)

settlements of this period on the sites where the first palaces were later to be built. What we do know is that the houses of the settlements at Knosos and Phaistos were clustered down the slopes of the hills. The only ones of which any remains have survived are those that stood outside the area where the ground was levelled for the construction of the palaces. At Malia, where the palace is sited on flat ground, the remains of the Pre-Palace houses extend over a wide area beneath the courtyards and under the foundations of the palace buildings themselves. All these Pre-Palace houses were sizeable complexes containing a large number of small, cramped rooms jostling each other so closely that it is difficult to tell where one house ends and the next begins.

Art in the Third Transitional Phase

At first sight there does not appear to be any monumental architectural form in existence heralding the highly complex, superbly constructed first palaces. The distance forebears of

the palaces came earlier on, at the beginning of the second Pre-Palace phase (2400-2100 B.C.). The new buildings of the third phase, whether houses or tombs, were simpler in form than their predecessors. Many of the old tholos tombs remained in use, with only some external additions in the form of enclosures for further burials or for votive offerings to the dead. Nevertheless, many features of constructional technique show some improvement, and undeniable progress was made in town planning. The large burial enclosures of the type found at Chrysolakkos, Malia, and Hellenika (Palaikastro) were succeeded by smaller ones of a more regular design (e.g. at Zakros, Palaikastro, Archanes). Two very strange constructions hewn out of the solid rock, like gigantic beehives, with descending spiral tunnels, were investigated by Evans in the course of excavations at the edge of the palace of Knosos. These so-called *hypogaiai* have now been filled in, and no one can satisfactorily explain what they were used for. The first peak sanctuary buildings were constructed during this period. The huge oval edifice on a high peak near Hamaizi, with its plan of radial partition walls around a central courtyard, was presumably a peak

Below: clay rhyton in the form of a bust of the Mother Goddess squeezing the life-giving milk from her breasts, from the Pre-Palace settlement at Mochlos in eastern Crete (Herakleion Museum). Right: bridge-spouted vessel in an advanced *technique with decorative designs, an example of the early Kamares style of central Crete (2000-1900 B.C.), from the Pre-Palace settlement on the Kephala hill at Knosos. (Herakleion Museum)*

sanctuary, in fact the first properly planned religious building in Crete.

The grave goods found in the tholos tombs of the Mesara belong to this transitional period, and they are of considerable use in helping to reconstruct the course of development in the way of life and in the arts. Advances were made in the techniques of stone-working, which produced attractive small vases that served mainly as burial offerings. Examples of this progress are the plastic rendering of decorative themes on the surface, the inlaying of a variety of coloured materials in the stone, and the output of composite vessels (*kernos*) with two or more containers. On the other hand, the uniformity of burial customs gave rise to a measure of standardization. The vases from the Mochlos burial ground display a noticeable variety in comparison with the deposits found in the tholos tombs. Innumerable burial offerings have been found, all in the same standard shapes, known as "birds' nests" and "salt and pepper" vases.

Pottery styles display ever-increasing variety. The most typical decorative styles of the period herald the arrival of the brilliant polychrome Kamares ware, which was to make its appearance in the palace centres of the Old-Palace Period. In eastern Crete, the mottled Vasilike ware gave way to a new Vasilike style characterized by light-on-dark decoration. The forms remain much the same as before: "teapots", jugs, cups, and ewers all rather more restrained in shape. The decoration consists of curvilinear motifs with great emphasis on swirls and convolutions, spirals and hanging loops. In the last stage of this phase, the creamy white of the decoration becomes pure white, and the dark background is more highly burnished. At this time, too, red paint in various shades makes its appearance, often alternating with the white, and to the abstract curvilinear designs are now added a few animal and plant motifs, decorative in style and always schematic. Along with these, the dark-on-light type of decoration continues to develop, especially on the bigger vessels.

The pattern of development was much the same in central Crete, though there the polychrome decoration leads more rapidly to the central Cretan Kamares style. The technical standard reached is quite remarkable: we find very delicate ware that points to the coming of the later "eggshell" pottery. Another feature is the appearance of a highly lustrous deep black varnish. Most of the pottery was still hand-made, even though a slow-turning form of potter's wheel had started to be used by the end of the second phase (c. 2100 B.C.), as the excavations at Myrtos have proved.

Many of the vessels assumed plastic forms decorated in accordance with the new styles. Some were vessels used for ritual purposes, which explains their peculiar shapes: representations of the goddess squeezing her breasts with her hands to express the life-giving milk; *rhyta* (libation vessels) in the form of a bull, sometimes (e.g. the Koumasa and Porti bull rhyta) with bull-leapers clinging to the animal's horns in a manner suggestive of the Minoan bull-games; and rhyta in the shape of other animals, usually ducks or pigeons. The most advanced form of pottery work, however,

Seal engraving made amazingly rapid progress in the final phase of the Pre-Palace Period. This page: unique ivory seal with 14 seal surfaces, from Archanes. Facing page, above: ivory seal in the form of a dove covering its young with its wings, from Koumasa. Below: ivory seal in the shape of a seated ape, from the tholos tomb at Platanos. (Herakleion Museum)

126

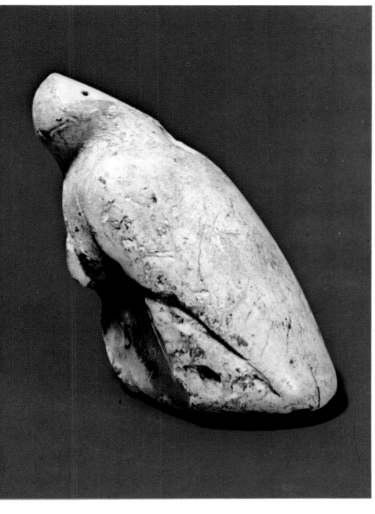

is to be seen in the purely sculptural pieces—the innumerable terracotta figurines representing men, women, or animals and the tiny models of human limbs—all of which were placed as votive offerings in the sanctuaries on the mountain peaks by votaries who wished to express their thanks for a recovery or to ask for a cure. Some of the figurines are most interesting for their sensitive rendering of the attitude of worship and for their polychrome representation of dresses and loincloths, which tells us a great deal about contemporary costume.

Progress in metalwork during this phase was more a matter of technical improvement and increased sensitivity of execution than of any research leading to the discovery of completely new methods or forms. The daggers become longer and stronger; in particular, the medial rib is strengthened, and the handle more securely attached with extra rivets. Double axes make their appearance, now, both in tool form, stoutly cast in moulds, and as symbols made of beaten sheet metal. Chisels, cutters, gravers, saws, fire-tongs, and all sorts of other implements testify of specialization in tool making to cater for the various specialized craftsmen.

Developments in goldwork are best illustrated by the jewellery found in the Mesara tholos tombs. We now find frequent use made of delicate filigree and granulation of fantastic precision. Filigree work often graces necklace beads and cylindrical pendants; the finds include a small gold bead in the shape of a toad. What makes this latter technique so exacting is the difficulty of soldering the microscopic grains of gold. It was only a few years ago that an English expert rediscovered the lost secret of the technique used by the Minoans in their granulation work and later bequeathed by them to the Ionians and the Etruscans.

Even greater progress was made in seal-engraving. Still using the same rather soft materials, the seal-engravers devised a great variety of shapes for their seal-stones and further developed the designs on them, both representational and purely decorative. These designs were the personal identification marks of their owners, who used them to ensure that nobody tampered with their property. They thus served as a kind of picture-writing; the designs became a way of giving visual expression to personal ideas, in other words, ideograms, and this was the first decisive step in the evolution of an ideographic script which rapidly developed into hieroglyphics. It was on these seals that the first experiments were made with the complex decorative compositions of flowing curvilinear motifs which were later taken over by the Kamares style of pottery decoration. It was also on these seals that we find the first efforts at pictorial composition, at first with groups of animals and, later, with scenes connected with the occupation of the owner of the seal or with religion and ritual. The commonest shape was the cylinder, with designs engraved on the flat ends, not on the curved surface as was the practice in the East. Then, as it became necessary to fit in several ideograms together, many-sided seals were introduced, generally simplified into three- and four-sided prisms. But one seal from the burial enclosure at Archanes has no less than fourteen sealing faces! Again, the idea of providing seals with handles to facilitate the taking of a clear impression led to the introduction of button-seals and seals with a rounded shaft. Another interesting variation was to make the handle a miniature animal sculpture of some kind, sometimes a whole animal sitting or lying down, sometimes a head or a hoofed foot, sometimes a bird. Among these are a dove protecting her chicks under her wings, a lion over his felled human victim, and the humorous little apes sitting on flat or round-bottomed seals.

Public and Private Life

We have already mentioned the principal changes in the social structure and general way of life brought about by the introduction of metal; on the other hand, the study of the development of the arts has led to a description of some of the material aspects of life. It remains to outline certain other evidence that would help us to form a fair idea of the social, political, economic, religious, and private aspects of life. There are of course no historical records of events, so our reconstruction of the Minoan way of life has to be based on such relics and remains as have survived.

Anthropological evidence has established that the driving force behind the new civilization was a race of the Mediterranean type. Fortunately, we are familiar with this racial type, since it has survived to the present day in some parts of the Mediterranean. Its members were of smallish height, somewhat swarthy, light-boned, curly-haired, slim and wiry and full of nervous energy and drive. Odysseus was probably a good example of this race of restless men whose life was so closely bound up with the sea and adventure. They owed their ascendancy more to their wits than to success in physical conflict. Hence their pursuit of a peaceful policy which aimed at establishing overall prosperity in which everybody would have a real share. The superiority of their civilization soon enabled them to assimilate the culture of the indigenous Neolithic population, while profiting at the same time from the fruits of its long local experience.

Their social structure based on the *genos* or caste is to be deduced from the size and layout of their settlements and, even more, from the evidence of the tholos tombs and multiple burial enclosures. Some scholars who hold that the social system was founded on a second basic unit, the *phratria*, or clan, which existed side by side with the caste grouping, have tried to identify survivals of totemistic beliefs. However, it is doubtful whether the system went to the length of division into tribes, each with its own separate structure of castes and clans, for we have no evidence whatsoever for the existence of a tribal organization. Gradually the strength of the clans and castes must have declined as communities grew and villages developed into towns. Once this point was reached, a better organized administrative system was needed, and it appears that communal leaders were appointed to exercise administrative authority, possibly with the assistance of the clan and caste leaders. With the gradual accumulation of wealth the aristocracy of the old castes gave way to a more plutocratic order. Nevertheless, the lack of discrimination in burial customs indicates that the backbone of the social system was the common man.

We do not know to what extent the shape of society was influenced by religion. Certainly, religious worship and the associated ritual were by now formalized and exerted considerable influence on social life, but there is no question of a fully developed theocracy at this stage.

The communal leaders presumably exercised some form of control over the economy of their district, or so at least we can assume from the commanding positions in which their mansions were built, but there is no question of a com-

pletely centralized system of commerce. The poorer classes evidently worked for the rich and the gentry, and it is likely that the service quarters in the big mansions were occupied by people of a servant class. There is no evidence, though, of the existence of a slave class living apart from the rest in crude sheds or huts.

Pre-Palace Economy

The various craftsmen formed a middle class, whose position steadily improved with the growth of wealth. Much of their energy was directed towards the production of luxury goods, which implies that the general standard of prosperity was now well above subsistence level. Security against internal dangers was certainly always a matter of concern, though it seems that such dangers never presented a serious threat thanks to the establishment of a social equilibrium. Friendly relations were established with neighbours across the sea, not without the use of diplomacy, though this did not mean complete disregard for defence: land forces existed up to a point, and naval defences much more so. However, the few small weapons found so far do not argue for a particularly well-organized military system.

The women of Pre-Palace Crete did not enjoy the same privileged position that was to be theirs in the Minoan society of the Palace periods. It is clear that women did play an important part in religion, and we may also conjecture that much of the handicraft work was left to them, but there are no real grounds for arguing that such status as they enjoyed was derived from a matriarchal system.

The settlements were concentrated mainly in the more fertile districts of the island, which indicates that the basis of the economy was arable farming, and the number and capacity of their storage magazines proves that their agricultural production was considerable. We know that the crops cultivated were the same as in the later Palace periods: all the known varieties of cereals and pulse, several kinds of fruit, olives, and grapes. Earthenware vats used as wine presses have been found at Myrtos and implements for splitting and crushing olives in various other places.

Animal husbandry was making great strides at the same time. Meat and cheese were basic foods, but much of the rest of the animal produce served other purposes, such as wool for weaving. The Cretan mountains were covered with flocks of sheep and goats, just as they are now, and herds of pigs were kept at the settlements. In the open plains, herdsmen would graze large herds of cattle; a flock modelled in terracotta has been found intact inside a large earthenware bowl at Palaikastro. The commonest kinds of poultry were ducks and geese. The diet was supplemented by hunting but not to a large extent. As for the way in which their food was prepared, we can learn a certain amount from the kitchen utensils that have been found: tripod cooking pots, mixing bowls, ladles, strainer jars for cheese, funnels, and chafing-dishes. Undoubtedly Crete was well able to support its population on its own food resources, but only by means of a systematic cultivation of crops.

The Cretan potters' products not only catered for the home market but evidently found their way abroad, too. Many were the jars that left the island filled with oil or wine, two commodities very much in demand in certain parts of the outside world. Not only this, but the vessels themselves, at any rate the ones exemplifying the best workmanship, were exported for their own sake. This explains how Cretan stone and clay vessels have come to be found not only in the Cyclades but further afield as well. The designs on some Pre-Palace potters' seal-stones cast some light on their production techniques, such as the methods of moulding, attaching handles, drying, and firing.

The materials used for making stone vessels were carefully selected pieces of the native rocks of the island, though some of the more uncommon stones were brought from abroad. The metal for the manufacture of bronze utensils and tools was also imported, even though there are copper ore deposits on Crete, admittedly of poor quality, from Cyprus.

Organized commerce, is attested to by the position of several settlements in strategic sites—an isthmus, a bay, an offshore islet—where there was not enough room to support any other major occupation. Communications with the Cyclades were responsible for the growth of the coastal settlements along the northern seaboard, for trade between Crete and the Aegean islands was flourishing, to judge by the quantities of Cycladic products found in settlements of the Pre-Palace Period, and of Minoan vessels and tools in Early Cycladic settlements. There was an especially close link with Phylakope on Melos, because of its supply of obsidian, a

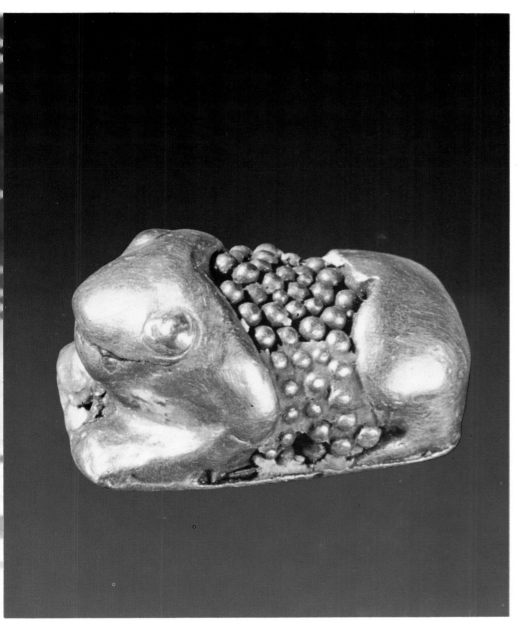

Gold-working made tremendous progress in Minoan Crete in the 20th century B.C. It is noteworthy that the secrets of the granulation technique have been rediscovered only recently. Above: two fine examples of gold working from the last phase of the Pre-Palace Period. *Left: gold bead in the shape of a frog with delicate granulation, from the tholos tomb at Koumasa. Right: small bead from a necklace with filigree spiral decoration, from a tholos tomb at Kalathiana. (Herakleion Museum).*

129

hard crystalline volcanic rock which made good knife blades. Towards the end of the Pre-Palace Period, a Minoan trading post was established at Phylakope for the exploitation of the obsidian trade, developed later into a proper Minoan colony. It seems probable that the many-oared Cycladic ships were both better equipped and faster than the Cretan ones, to judge by the pictures of the two kinds of vessels on Cycladic "frying-pans" and Minoan seal-stones, respectively. Two or three terracotta models of Minoan ships have been found in burial enclosures, obviously funerary offerings for sailors: they are simplified representations, more boat than ship, with a high prow and a low stern.

We have no information about overland communications. However, one four-wheeled cart has been found at Palaikastro, which implies that there were roads suitable for small wheeled vehicles for transporting produce from the fields to the settlements and ports.

The Cretans had to import gold and alabaster from Egypt, ivory from Syria, copper from Cyprus, and tin from Anatolia, and so it was essential that they should be able to offer high-quality products and finely-made artefacts in exchange. In Egypt, for example, timber was the commodity that was most in demand, and the Cretans were able to supply the requirements out of the ample forests covering their island.

GENERAL OUTLINE OF THE EARLY BRONZE AGE
Independent Development and Common Features

In the preceding chapters we have tried to reconstruct a picture of cultural developments in the Aegean basin from three different view-points: the Early Helladic, the Early Cycladic, and the Pre-Palace Minoan. We might have added a fourth heading dealing with the evidence from the northeastern corner of the region; there, the Trojan civilization, similar to these three, established itself in the large offshore islands of Lesbos and Lemnos and in the outlying "Greek" territories of Western Thrace and Eastern Macedonia. In fact, the overall picture of the local civilizations of the Early Bronze Age in the Aegean basin would not be complete without a review of contemporary developments in the whole of western Asia Minor. If we have confined ourselves to the three civilizations mentioned above, it is because we are chiefly concerned with them here. As one might expect, the cultures of the Aegean basin are directly related to each other, and there are remarkable parallels between them in the course of their development. Obviously, the fact that they evolved at the same time, against the same background, and in similar ecological conditions largely explains the similarities and the parallel lines of their development. At one time, these similarities were over-emphasized, so that the several local cultures were regarded as variations of a single civilization.

The first problem we have to deal with, then, is the question of the origins of these civilizations. Belief in the common descent or common root of all these local variations used once to go virtually unchallenged. The term "Aegean Civilization" attests to the prevalence of this belief, which—like many other theories and historical evaluations—was based on the evidence of pottery. As early as 1918, A.J.B. Wace and Carl W. Blegen drew a distinction between the Early Helladic, Early Cycladic, and Early Minoan civilizations on the strength of differences in pottery styles, but they stressed that these civilizations were essentially three branches of the same tree, three varieties of a single original culture. The theory was definitively formulated ten years later by Blegen and J. Haley. It rested on two hypotheses: first, that the Early Bronze Age civilization in Greece (Helladic, Cycladic, Minoan) was a homogenous one, Pre-Hellenic without a doubt, and that its origin must be sought outside Greece; secondly, that the highest concentration of Pre-Hellenic place-names with suffixes in -ssos and -nthos (which are also the suffixes of many Helladic place-names) occurs in southwestern Asia Minor. Consequently, it is there

that the source must be located. They drew further support for their theory from the fact that the archaeological and linguistic evidence was backed by literary tradition (cf. Karians, Leleges).

Today the situation is different. Grave doubts have been cast on the validity of the hypotheses on which the theory rested. Excavations are constantly being carried out and proving ever more clearly that the differences among the three local civilizations are much more marked than the overall similarity and that these civilizations are virtually independent of each other. Basically, the differentiation was due to the prior existence of distinct regional "neolithic" or "chalcolithic" traditions, and it was only natural that the differences should multiply and become more marked under the influence of local geographical conditions, such as the scale of the environment (island or mainland), the degree of isolation or ease of communications, the fertility of the soil, and so forth. In other words, the initial sub-neolithic phase of the Early Bronze Age was quite different in each of the three local civilizations. Consequently, it seems to be out of the question that these three different "beginnings" were all descended from a common root. If, on the other hand, we were to disregard the early stages and to pass on to the period when these civilizations had reached greater maturity, we would find that their autonomous character was by then even more marked. It is now difficult, therefore, to accept the simplifications of the old theory, and harder still to ascribe the origins of these three independent civilizations to any given part of Asia Minor, least of all the southwest. Since the theory was propounded, a fair amount of progress has been made through archaeological excavations in this area: the great excavation at Beycesultan and other excavations at important centres have yielded an enormous quantity of new material dating from the vital periods, i.e. the Chalcolithic and the Early Bronze Age. Nowhere has anything been found to indicate a direct link, let alone an ancestral relationship, between the culture of this area and the cultures of the Early Bronze Age in Greece. Evidence for such a relationship, if it exists, ought to be found at a level slightly earlier than the beginning of the Early Bronze Age in Greece, but the archaeological evidence available so far does not point to anything of the sort. Evidently, it is not yet possible to prove on archaeological grounds that the Early Helladic, the Early Cycladic, and the Pre-Palace Cretan civilizations are descended from southwest Asia Minor.

If one is to make a correct evaluation of the independent development of the Helladic area, one must take into account two important factors: first, the part played by the old traditions of the autochthonous peoples, and, secondly, the geography of the Helladic area, which favoured the growth of self-contained local civilizations and to a large extent ruled out, or at least hindered, unification. Under these conditions, fragmentation was inevitable; civilization never reached the level of creating a single centralized power. Indeed, in the Helladic world this stage was not reached even in Mycenaean times. Therefore, the answer that must be given to the crucial question of the origin of the Early Bronze Age civilization in Greece is this: that it is not a single culture with local variations but a number of separate independent civilizations, with connections among them and also with the Trojan and other cultures in western Asia Minor. The Early Helladic, the Early Cycladic, and the Pre-Palace Minoan civilizations evolved from mainly local elements subject to continuous influence from the East.

Although it is possible to refute the theory that the Greek Bronze Age civilizations are directly derived from a particular source in Asia Minor, it remains undisputed that the East played an important part in the formation and development of the Early Bronze Age in Greece. Throughout the third millennium B.C., the East in general, and Asia Minor in particular, exercized a constant influence in the Aegean, chiefly by spreading ideas, cultural attainments, and technical inventions.

This influence, however, had made itself felt earlier on; we have seen it in action as early as the Early Neolithic Period. Consequently, the similarities that can be observed between the more or less independent civilizations of the Aegean basin should be attributed partly to earlier contributions or contacts.

To postulate a series of "colonizations" or "migrations" or other such shifts of population is merely to advance a theoretical explanation to account for simple similarities or parallel developments due to imitation or indirect influence. At any rate, modern scholarship would be highly sceptical of such facile theories as would explain successive stages of development simply in terms of successive population shifts or conquests. The very absence of evidence precludes the possibility of an Asia Minor civilization having transplanted itself into mainland Greece at this time. The evidence does not preclude, however, the possibility of peaceful infiltration by small groups of settlers from the East. These infiltrations did not all take place at the same time, nor were all from the same locality. Nor should we assume that they had a catalytic effect on the indigenous populations. A change in culture does not necessarily imply a change of race. To prove such a change, the cultural premises should have to be supplemented by anthropological evidence, and there is so little of that to go on that one cannot safely draw conclusions from it.

Quite apart from all this, there is one other factor, a subtle one, to be considered: the "hellenizing" influence of the Greek environment and its ability to assimilate alien elements. Without this, it is difficult to explain how it was that the Helladic civilization of the Early Bronze Age followed a path of development of a completely different character from that of the contemporary civilizations of Egypt and the East. It is this independent, western orientation, that makes the Bronze Age in Greece particularly important for

the part that it was to play in future developments.

In considering the main features which the local civilizations of the Early Bronze Age in Greece had in common, it is necessary to examine the economy in its wider implications. The most important common feature was the dependence of the economy on arable farming and stockbreeding wherever the terrain allowed, as on the Greek mainland and Crete. For the Cyclades we must assume a broader-based economy, which included fishing and barter or entrepot trade, particularly in obsidian and metals. Even so, primary production formed the basis of the economy over most of Greek territory.

The second common feature was the steadily increasing importance of metallurgy, leading eventually to a gradual restructuring of the economy and of society. Metal being rarer in Greece than in the East was at first not greatly used. In Phase I of Early Helladic and Pre-Palace Minoan it was virtually non-existent, but in the Cyclades not only was metal in use at an early stage but also metallurgy was practised quite extensively. What was important during this new age was that a community should not merely be able to acquire bronze tools and weapons by barter exchange, but should be capable of manufacturing them itself and even have a sur-

BRONZE AGE CIVILIZATIONS IN GREECE

PERIODS	MAINLAND GREECE	CYCLADES	CRETE
LATE BRONZE AGE 1600 - 1100 B.C.	CRETO-MYCENAEAN		
			NEW-PALACE MINOAN 1700 - 1450 B.C.
MIDDLE BRONZE AGE 1900 - 1600 B.C.	MIDDLE HELLADIC	MIDDLE CYCLADIC	OLD-PALACE MINOAN 1900 - 1700 B.C.
EARLY BRONZE AGE 2800/2700 - 1900 B.C.	EARLY HELLADIC	EARLY CYCLADIC	PRE-PALACE MINOAN

Table showing the main chronological divisions of the Bronze Age in Greece. The Bronze Age lasted approximately 1700 years (from 2800/2700 to 1100 B.C.). Early and Middle Bronze Age civilizations evolved in mainland Greece, the Cyclades, and Crete. These were succeeded by the Creto-Mycenaean civilization in mainland Greece and Crete and a similar civilization in Cyprus, both belonging to the Late Bronze Age, and covering a relatively brief period when compared with the Early Bronze Age.

plus left with which to trade. It would appear that the people of the Cyclades were very skilled in metalwork, and it was probably through them that the craft spread to mainland Greece by way of places like Raphena. The fact that most of their weapons and tools, such as the single-edged dagger, the celt, and the double axe, were of a Helladic type and not of the kind prevalent in Asia Minor testifies to the independence of the whole region in a vital field of craftsmanship. The metallurgy of mainland Greece appears to have been of Cycladic origin, at least in the beginning. It is likely that the gold and silver vessels found (or alleged to have been found) at Helladic sites came from the same source, since other silver vessels of similar type are definitely known to be of Cycladic origin. We do not know where the islanders of the Cyclades obtained their supplies of tin, which was hard to come by. Possibly it was from very far away. But the fact that they secured and transported common and uncommon metals from far afield presupposes the existence of ships, a transport trade, and a capacity for stockpiling metals for use in bartering and manufacturing.

Metal was important not so much for its own uses as for the part it played in reorienting the economy, which now started to break out of its narrow neolithic bounds. Historically, the most important feature of the new age was the development of sea communications. With the islanders leading, the first extensive contacts were established with the further corners of the Mediterranean—the "Lebensraum" of Hellenism in historical times. Little by little, the small, manoeuverable Cycladic ships ventured out of the Aegean, to the Black Sea and the Adriatic, possibly to the Balearic Islands. Later, the Cretans were to go as far as Cyprus and North Africa. These contacts with foreign-speaking alien races, whose ideas and impulses were different, undoubtedly influenced the subsequent course of events. They marked the end of the age of static isolation; no longer could any region afford to be self-sufficient and keep itself in self-imposed confinement. Ideas and technical expertise were exchanged along with material goods, new horizons were opened up, and cultural progress through trade relations began to be an important factor in the way of life.

Community development followed more or less the same lines in all three regions. The basic unit was still the small neolithic-type settlement with houses built very close together, narrow alleys, and some kind of natural protection or walls in the coastal settlements. There are only a few cases where this basic unit developed into a larger settlement formed round a central core, but it never reached the stage of a small town. To explain the incidence of exceptional cases like Lerna, Aigina, or Vasilike, in Crete, we must suppose that the inhabitants, in addition to occupying a strategic site, were exceptionally successful in exploiting the potential of the new economy by combining agriculture and stockbreeding with barter trade and shipping. Although there were Neolithic forerunners of the type of settlement built round a central main building as at Dimeni, these cases seem to have been independent developments. The monumental "palace" at Lerna, with its outbuildings, subordinate houses, and strong turreted walls, is clearly an architectural type belonging to another period. All the same, neither here nor at Vasilike can one talk in terms of palaces and kings. Such a stage would imply a "king" excercizing sole control over trade and an urban form of social organization. Yet, during the mature phase of the Early Bronze

Age, both Crete and the Helladic region had reached a stage not far removed from such a level.

The fact that the terrain was split up into small compartments encouraged the development of small, scattered centres and hindered the concentration of wealth and power in one large main town. Accordingly, the social structure must have been very different from the centralized system prevailing in the East. Where the East had its all-powerful princedoms, here one may assume a kind of much broader-based society and more direct participation of the ordinary people in the commonweal.

The relatively independent character of the three local cultures comes out more clearly in the field of the arts and in ideology. There was no monumental art as yet in this part of the world, which means that one of the basic elements of an urbanized society was lacking. The new technique of toreutics and jewellery-making in precious metals reached an early and remarkable degree of development from Leukas to Crete, the Peloponnesos, and the Cyclades. Rapid progress was also made in stone glyptics, and real masterpieces were produced in Crete and the Cyclades. It is in the modelling of figurines more than in any other branch that local differences are most clearly apparent. In the Sterea, the old naturalistic tradition had by now departed from the styles of the Late Neolithic, and only in Thessaly were stylized representations of the human form in marble and terracotta still produced. In the Cyclades, the marble figurines represented the highest form of art of the times to be found anywhere in the Greek world. The art of the Early Helladic civilization, on the other hand (and of the Middle Helladic later on) was almost entirely non-representational, while the terracotta figurines of the "votaries" of Pre-Palace Crete testify to the difference in orientation, which is also evident in other manifestations of religion and ritual.

Crete, more eastern in its ways, progressed almost without any change of direction to the Middle Bronze Age with its palace centres and urban life. By contrast, in mainland Greece and the Cyclades, which were beyond the reach of Minoan influence, there was a general contraction of scale as the distinguishing feature of their Middle Bronze Age— a kind of gestation that was to usher in a new civilization.

The Cultural Sequence

Whether or not there were any intermediate breaks in the historical development of the Early Bronze Age is a question that is still being debated. Though it does not seem likely that there were any breaks or dividing lines with general application over the whole region, nevertheless three broad stages of development may be distinguished: an early or preliminary phase, a second phase of maturity, and a final phase which, in some parts at least, appears to have been transitional.

There is no doubt that the mature second phase of the Early Bronze Age was a period of peak development in all three regions. It was marked by a high level of creativity; the near-urban state of development which was reached in some centres and the wide expansion of cultural and commercial contacts were not to be seen again in mainland Greece until Mycenaean times. It is precisely these attainments and the whole spirit of the Greek Early Bronze Age, so definitely different from the theocratic system and the despotic centralization of the East, that lead some scholars to believe that Hellenic tribes had begun to settle in Greek territory at this early stage.

Other modern scholars believe that there was some kind of general disruption at the end of the second phase, some disturbance which led, by way of the transitional third phase, to the Middle Bronze Age. However, it is still impossible to be certain either that there was a definite break or, if so, what caused it, nor is there any conclusive archaeological evidence that its effects were felt throughout the region. Possibly undue significance has been attached to the destruction of Lerna at about this time. If it is ever proved conclusively that mainland Greece and, to a lesser extent, the Cyclades and Crete (where there is no evidence of a break in the continuity) were in fact affected by this wave of unsettlement and violence, then there will be no doubt that some event of grave importance occurred, which possibly originated outside the area. It could have been an invasion by alien tribes or a chain effect of the displacement of related tribes under pressure from invaders from beyond the periphery.

At about the same time, that is, at the end of the second phase of the Early Bronze Age, there are signs of a large-scale disaster in western and southern Asia Minor according to the excavators of sites in those areas. This catastrophe, which involved the destruction of the main centres by fire and the abandonment of other settlements, is attributed, quite hypothetically, to a movement of tribes from north-western Asia Minor or from further afield in the Balkans, but in any case via the Troad peninsula, towards the south and east. The civilization that established itself thenceforth all over that region appears to have been Trojan in character, and it remained unchanged until the end of the Bronze Age.

Greece, too, must have been directly or indirectly affected by this great movement of peoples. There is not, as yet, any evidence of a radical break before the end of the Early Bronze Age, but it is most probable that the almost universal decline that set in with the third phase of the period reflects the influence of new factors at work or new racial elements which were destined eventually to come to the fore and to lead the way to the new period which is called the Middle Bronze Age.

In Early Bronze Age Greece (2800/2700—1900 B.C.), three main civilizations developed along similar lines in southern mainland

Greece, the Cyclades and Crete. The map shows the main centres of these three independent local civilizations.

GREECE IN THE EARLY
BRONZE AGE
(2800/2700 – 1900 B.C.)

- ■ Early Helladic centres
- ● Early Cycladic centres
- ● Pre-Palace (Minoan) centres
- ● Cypriot centres
- ● Northern and northeastern centres of the Early Helladic region

133

The Middle Bronze Age

THE MIDDLE HELLADIC PERIOD

Around 1900 B.C., the founders of the Middle Bronze Age civilization, generally called Middle Helladic, settled in the southern part of mainland Greece. The dating was originally based on a study of the pottery, the architecture, and the burial customs. Subsequently, the carbon 14 method, which was applied to finds dating from the earliest years of the Middle Helladic settlement at Lerna, indicated that the beginning of the Middle Bronze Age should be dated to 1948 ± 117 B.C. The end of the period is somewhat ill-defined, since it is not marked by any widespread catastrophe or the appearance of any new cultural elements. It is generally placed at about 1600 B.C., which is the time when Helladic art had become thoroughly minoanized, when burnished colours came into use in the decoration of pottery, and when burial enclosures and shaft graves were introduced at Mycenae. As with the earlier periods, our only source of knowledge regarding the Middle Bronze Age is the archaeological excavating that has been and is being carried out all over Greece. However, the evidence that has so far been compiled is incomplete and uneven, so that it is impossible to reconstruct a full picture of the Middle Bronze Age civilization in mainland Greece; in some parts, indeed, we cannot form any kind of picture of it at all.

Very little excavating, for example, has been done in the northern part of the Helladic region. We are still completely in the dark about Thrace and Epeiros in the Middle Bronze Age, although we have a few sherds from Dodona (D. Evangelides), which suggest that there was some communication with southern Greece and support the tradition of the extreme antiquity of the oracle and of the presence of Greek tribes in the area.

In Macedonia (W. A. Heurtley) several sites have been located; these give every indication of having been extremely flourishing settlements in the Middle Bronze Age. It is thought that in Macedonia there was an unbroken continuity between the Early and the Middle Bronze Age and that the few new features that make their appearance are not enough to prove that new tribes had settled in the region at the end of the Early Bronze Age.

More is known about Thessaly. We can conjecture that the dense population of the Thessalian hinterland preserved its neolithic character even after the use of bronze had made some advance in the south of Greece, and that it was from the south that the typical features of the Middle Helladic civilization were introduced. This seems to have happened on the seaboard of the Pagasitic Gulf (Gulf of Volos), where there are remains similar to those found in southern Greece. There is also the possibility, however, that the most ancient features of the Middle Helladic civilization were developed in Thessaly and spread from there to the southern part of the mainland as Thessalian tribes migrated southwards.

There is a characteristic uniformity in the general lines of development during the Middle Helladic Period throughout the eastern part of mainland Greece, from the Spercheios valley to the capes of Malea and Tainaron. Up to now, over 120 settlements have been located, and excavations or preliminary surveys have been carried out at almost half of these. It is of interest to note that very considerable Middle Helladic and Mycenaean remains have been found in places immortalized in Greek mythology. Only quite recently, for example the pickaxe has brought to light what appears to have been the city of Tetrapolis in Attica, reputedly founded by the mythical king Xouthos.

The magnificent edifices built in historical times have completely wiped out all traces of the Middle Helladic buildings on the Acropolis of Athens. Only a few sherds found scattered over the surface of the rocky sanctuary and a tumulus on its southern slope, prove that Athens was in fact inhabited in the Middle Helladic Period. The same fate befell the prehistoric buildings at Eleusis, where the remains of the old settlements were destroyed by the builders of the sanctuaries of Demeter.

Of the thirty-seven settlements that have been located in the provinces of the Argolid and Korinthia, the two outstanding ones are at Korakou, near Lechaion (one of the ports of ancient Corinth), and the very important settlement at Lerna, five miles south of Argos. Lerna was inhabited almost without a break from Neolithic times to the end of the Bronze Age, and its stratigraphy has remained undisturbed. The Middle Helladic settlement there, in contrast to its Early Helladic predecessor, was unwalled, and the characteristic features of its earliest phase are the grey Minyan ware (see below) and the apsidal houses. Typical Middle Helladic tombs have been found at Lerna, as well as two shaft graves, possibly for royal burials, which had unfortunately been looted.

The great palace buildings that covered the hill at Mycenae in the last period of the Bronze Age (the Late Helladic Period) obliterated all traces of the Middle Helladic buildings on the site. The sparse remains of their foundations and the many sherds found scattered all over the hillsides (A. J. B. Wace, G. E. Mylonas) proved, however, that the Middle Helladic settlement covered a large area and had a fairly large population. It is possible that at the end of the Middle Helladic, or a little later, there was a royal palace at the top of the hill, since the shaft graves of Grave Circle A (Schliemann, P. Stamatakis) and Grave Circle B (J. Papademetriou, G. E. Mylonas), with their rich contents of gold, belong to

precisely this period. The finds from these graves testify to the wealth of Mycenae and its high level of attainment in this period and also to the existence of powerful and ambitious kings.

In the western Peloponnesos, the most important settlement of this period is possibly one situated on a hill in the north-western corner of the plain of Messene, near the village of Malthe. The summit of the hill is covered with the foundations of houses, protected by a fortification wall. In the earlier years of the period, the houses were relatively few in number and in separate blocks, but later there were more of them, densely packed and joined together with party walls. The increasing density of the buildings implies a gradual rise in the economic standard of the inhabitants, who not only practised agriculture and stockbreeding but also made the most of the strategic importance of their hill in local communications and the entrepot trade.

We know a fair amount about the Middle Helladic civilization over the whole area from the Spercheios valley to Gytheion and from Euboia to the Ionian Islands. A count of the sites in the region reveals that 187 have so far been located, of which 62 have been more or less fully excavated by Greek or foreign archaeologists.

Pottery, Architecture, and Burial Customs

The most typical pottery of the period is the monochrome ware of the type Schliemann christened "Minyan". Schliemann, who was both a great scholar and a lucky archaeologist, discovered the first specimens of this type of pottery at Orchomenos in Boiotia. Putting his faith in Homer, as was his practice, he attributed it to the Minyans who, according to the *Iliad*, lived in that area. This pottery is certainly much older than the Minyans, but Schliemann's name for it has become generally accepted. It is all monochrome, and the best specimens were made on the wheel. Its colour is light or dark grey, its surface is glossy, almost "soapy" to the touch, and it comes in symmetrical shapes with somewhat angular outlines. The shapes would appear to have been copied from metallic originals. The commonest are the tall-stemmed goblets decorated with annular mouldings and the low bowls (*kantharos*-shaped *skyphoi*) with two tall ribbon-like handles. A variation of this style is the black Minyan ware, known as "Argive" from the fact that it is widely found in the Argolid. In the middle of the period, yellow Minyan ware makes its appearance: it is made of yellow clay with a yellow outer surface, sometimes coated with a slip. The yellow Minyan ware, which is mostly from the latter part

135

of the period, marks a transitional stage leading to Mycenaean pottery.

Another style of pottery that is typical of the period is the so-called matt-painted ware. The vessels belonging to this style are usually hand-moulded and include large jars (e.g. *pithoi*, *stamnoi*, *prochoi*) and broad shallow bowls. The decoration, which is confined to the upper part of the vessel, is black, white, and reddish. The earliest decorative motifs are rectilinear geometrical shapes, with curvilinear designs and concentric circles being introduced later. Towards the end of the period, better-quality painted vessels, rather like the yellow Minyan ware, began to appear, including some with polychrome decoration. For all the problems they raise, Minyan and matt-painted ware are of great help in marking the different phases represented by Middle Helladic remains, and they have the additional merit of being easily recognizable.

The characteristic buildings of the Middle Helladic Period are long, narrow houses consisting of an oblong principal room preceded by an open porch or enclosed vestibule on its short side and with a smaller chamber behind, all in one long line. We may call these three compartments by their Homeric names: the *prodomos*, *domos* and *thalamos*. The domos usually contains a fixed hearth; the thalamos is sometimes elliptical or semicircular and sometimes rectangular, so that many of the houses are apsidal in form. Every house was a separate detached unit, party walls being unknown in early times. The construction rested on a low foundation or a socle of rubble and clay about 45 cm. wide and 15-20 cm. high, and the walls above that were of mudbricks. It would appear that the apsidal houses had a ridged roof, and the rectangular ones possibly a flat roof made of reeds or branches and clay, of the sort still commonly used in many Greek villages today. The settlements would appear to have been unwalled in the early part of the period, and in fact this is one of the features that distinguish them from Early Helladic settlements. Only three walled settlements of the Middle Helladic period have so far come to light: at Brauron, Aigina and Dorion, but it is not known exactly

when their walls were built. The first Middle Helladic inhabitants of Aigina and Dorion evidently repaired the older (Early Helladic) walls to protect their homes. None of the buildings excavated so far seems to have been used as a sanctuary, nor have any remains been found of any large building that might have been a palace. Some of the settlements of this period were built on top of the debris of earlier ones, which in most cases had been pillaged and burned, while others were new settlements built on coastal sites. Some Early Helladic settlements were never rebuilt after their destruction.

No sufficiently complete excavation of any Middle Helladic settlement has as yet been carried out so as to give us a clear picture of its overall plan or particulars about the density of its population. However, working on what has been brought to light, we can assume that on the whole the settlements were not large, that they were unwalled, and that at least in the early part of the period they formed small villages of detached houses, not more than fifty in number. If we assume that every house held a family with an average of six members, the population of each village would have been about 300. Obviously, there must have been smaller settlements, too, and some larger ones such as Mycenae. They were not very far apart, but certainly far enough for each village to have a sufficiently large area of farmland to feed its own population.

Large numbers of tombs have been excavated in many parts of mainland Greece, even as far afield as Thessaly, giving us a detailed picture of the burial customs of the Middle Helladic Period. Cremation was unknown. Children and adults were often buried in narrow, shallow pits dug between the walls of adjacent houses or under the floors of the rooms. Sometimes the sides of the pits were lined with mudbricks or stone slabs. Infants and smaller children were buried in *pithoi* (storage jars) under the floors or between the walls of houses. Besides these methods of burial, cemeteries were also widely used, one of which has been excavated at Eleusis. The burials are in cist graves, small box-shaped tombs (average size 90 × 55 × 50 cm.) consisting of four

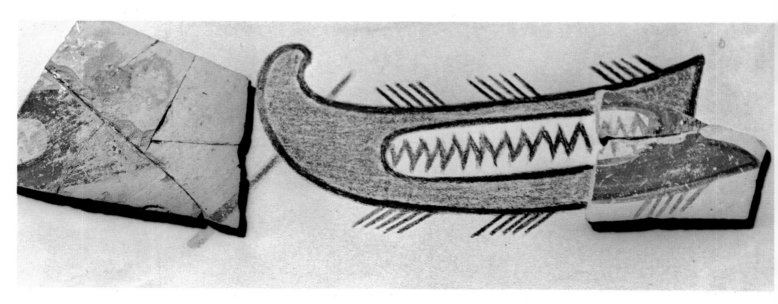

A polychrome representation of ships from a vessel of the Middle Helladic Period that was found at Iolkos. The style is characteristic of the end of Middle Helladic times or rather of the transitional phase leading to the Late Helladic or Mycenaean Period.

Specimens of this phase have been found at Mycenae, Thera, and the other islands of the Cyclades. Historically significant is the row of many-oared ships painted on the vessel. (Volos Museum)

MIDDLE HELLADIC GREECE

■ Investigated settlements

● Settlements not investigated

Map showing all known settlements, whether excavated or not,
southern mainland Greece during the Middle Helladic Period.
The three centuries of the Middle Helladic (about 1900 to 1600
B.C.) correspond to the Middle Cycladic and to the Old-Palace
Period and the early part of the New-Palace Period on Crete. The

Middle Helladic on the Greek mainland, in contrast to the Early
Helladic of the third millennium B.C., was a period of decline and
stagnation. There were many settlements (as can be seen from the
map), but no important centres. The country underwent a radical
change, and there was a return to a 'closed' economy.

137

stone slabs standing upright in the earth. A layer of pebbles was laid on the floor of the graves, and the top was covered with large stone slabs. In this cramped space the body was buried in a contracted position with the knees drawn up on to the chest and the calves of the legs folded back flat against the thighs. This burial position, attributed by many anthropologists to religious beliefs, since it is found in the burials of all primitive races, was probably simply due to the shortage of space; it would not appear to have had any special significance, at least in the Middle Helladic Period. In the early part of the period only one body was put in each grave, with no grave goods. Gradually the graves became larger, with sides formed of more than one slab or with walls, and two or more bodies were buried in the same grave in a more extended position. Here and there, grave goods start to make their appearance: a single jug or goblet to begin with, more and more as time went on, until by the end of the period large deposits of offerings to the dead are to be found, including precious jewellery. The custom of making burial offerings had been imported from abroad and evidently indicates close contact between the Middle Helladic population and the Cretans.

Even in the larger shaft graves, the floor space was not enough to accommodate two or more burials at once. This gave rise to another striking and very significant custom the bones of the first burial would be pushed aside into heap in one corner or on one side of the grave, and the ol grave goods would be carelessly thrown out to make roon for a second or even a third body. From the middle of th period onwards, a marker or *stele* was evidently placed o top of the grave, round which a funerary feast was hel after the interment.

It is worth stressing the change in attitude toward burial from the middle of the period onwards. At th interment, the dead body and the gifts accompanying i were placed in the tomb with great care and solemn respect After the body had decomposed, however, the bones wer hastily and callously shoved aside to a corner of the tomb and the grave goods, mostly vases, were smashed and throw out. This striking reversal of attitude may well shed ligh on one of the beliefs of the Middle Helladic people, namely that the soul of the deceased descended to the shades onc the flesh had dissolved and, thereafter, had no link with th living; therefore, he would no longer have any need c funerary gifts. Belief in the complete separation of the livin from the dead is further attested to by the absence of an cestor-worship and the fact that gifts and offerings ceas after burial.

Two characteristic examples of Middle Helladic pottery. This page: grey vessel, typical of Minyan pottery (so called after Minyas, the legendary king of Orchomenos). The technique of Minyan ware is strongly reminiscent of metalworking. This type of pottery is found chiefly in the eastern and southern regions of the Greek mainland. Facing page: matt-painted vessel of the last part of the Middle Helladic Period from Grave Circle B at Mycenae. (National Archaeological Museum, Athens)

Apart from the burial customs, nothing is known of the religious beliefs held by the Middle Helladic people. It may be assumed, nevertheless, that their religion was uniconic, since not one idol or figurine has so far been found in the excavated sites. Nor has any building been found that can be definitely identified as a sanctuary.

Economy

The remains of the settlements prove that, to start with, farming and stockbreeding were the sole foundations of the economy. As time went on, commercial relations with neighbouring districts were developed, and closer communication was established with the Cyclades and Crete. It was this communication that was responsible for the intellectual awakening and cultural advancement of the Middle Helladic people. At the beginning of the period, their rate of cultural progress was very slow, their attainments hardly more than rudimentary, their settlements small, and their dwellings mean. The signs of poverty are everywhere to be found. Little by little, however, the villages grew bigger and their inhabitants more prosperous, until by the end of the period wealthy towns (e.g. Mycenae) had grown up. Trade with the islands was probably not the only source of this advance-

ment; it is quite possible that piracy contributed to it and also the military needs of foreign powers that were always ready to hire mercenaries at high rates of pay. Some authorities believe that mainland Greeks served as mercenaries in Egypt, where they helped the Egyptians to shake off the yoke of the Hyksos. They would have returned to their own country bringing back not only wealth but a host of new ideas. Further proof of their dynamic energy is given by the way they carried their own attainments afield, to Thessaly and Chalkidike, during the first half of the period. Another distinguishing feature of the Middle Helladic people was their receptiveness and ability to adapt alien ideas to their own habits and ways of thinking, to transform them and develop them to an amazing degree. These are qualities that mark them out as a people endowed with imagination, intellectual ability, and artistic sensitivity.

A full anthropological study of Middle Helladic remains has yet to be made. Many of the skeletons that have survived were found at a time when there was no such thing as anthropological research. One fact is certain; the rulers buried in the shaft graves were taller than the Cretans of the Minoan period and had a stronger bone structure.

At present we are able to reconstruct some sort of picture of life in those times, but many puzzles remain unsolved and many questions unanswered. No agreement has yet been reached among the experts as to the origins of Minyan or matt-painted ware. Both styles exhibit obvious differences from the pottery of the Early Bronze Age, but whether they evolved in mainland Greece or were imported, whether they are evidence of an incursion of new tribes or simply a product of local creativity that gradually spread over the whole region—this is a question that has yet to receive a definite answer. There is a tendency for problems of this kind to be tackled by reference to a single element of culture and by formulating hypotheses and conclusions on the basis of that one feature alone. This is not sound. Answers to questions of such importance must be based not merely on one or two types of vases, in other words, on pottery alone, but also on the evidence of architecture and burial customs. The overall features of the culture as we know them today reveal differences between the Early and the Middle Helladic periods. How are these differences to be explained? Most researchers ascribe them to an incursion of new tribes that settled in mainland Greece around 1900 B.C. They point to the violent destruction by fire of the Early Helladic settlements, the abandonment of some of them, the foundation of new ones, and the signs of retrogression clearly visible in the economic life of the country and its people. Others see the differences as the result of peaceful contacts and of new ideas introduced from abroad. But it is difficult, if not impossible, to explain away all the discrepancies between the Early and Middle Helladic periods, as well as the linguistic differences dealt with in a later chapter, in terms of peaceful intercourse. The view now held by archaeologists is that the founders of the Middle Helladic civilization settled in mainland Greece around 1900 B.C., that they were Greek-speaking (using an archaic form of the language), that they belonged to the Indo-European ethnic group, and that they possessed the intellectual characteristics of the Hellenic race. From then until the end of the prehistoric era, their civilization evolved smoothly, without any abrupt changes that could be attributed to an incursion of new racial elements.

THE MIDDLE CYCLADIC PERIOD

The old theory that the Cyclades were abandoned after the Early Bronze Age is no longer tenable. Modern research and excavations have proved that the Aegean Islands continued during the Middle Bronze Age to play an important part in historical and cultural development. The civilization of the Cyclades during this period is called Middle Cycladic, to differentiate it from the Middle Helladic in mainland Greece and the Middle Minoan or Old–Palace Period in Crete. It lasted for a period approaching half a millennium, i.e. from about 2000/1900 to 1550 B.C.

The transition from the Early Cycladic to the Middle Cycladic civilization came about without any abrupt changes. The first town of Phylakope on Melos was destroyed, possibly by an earthquake, but not abandoned. The houses were immediately rebuilt in different positions but still within the limits of the same settlement. The civilization represented by the second town, that is, the Middle Cycladic one, evolved directly and naturally from Phylakope I, which represented the final phase of the Early Bronze Age.

Remains of Middle Cycladic settlements have been uncovered by excavators on many of the islands. On Melos (Phylakope), Paros (Paroikià), Keos (Hagia Eirene), Thera and Therasia, important Middle Cycladic centres have been brought to light, and over twenty more Middle Cycladic sites have been located on other islands, such as Delos, Tenos, Syros, Siphnos and Amorgos.

Nearly all the Middle Cycladic settlements are on the coast or close to it. The sites had to combine safe anchorage for seagoing ships and good fertile land for farming. It is clear from this that the economy of the Middle Cycladic settlements was based primarily on farming and the entrepot trade, which was mostly with Crete and mainland Greece. All three of the large settlements that have been excavated —Phylakope, Paroikià and Hagia Eirene—were important trading posts. They were small, well laid-out towns, with streets, a drainage system, and, at least at Phylakope and Hagia Eirene, with fortifications. Middle Cycladic houses were a mixture of Helladic and Minoan architectural elements: the simple and clear design of the Helladic megaroid house adapted to the Minoan pier for the support of the roof. As in the preceding period, the walls were made of rubble and clay without straw. Now, however, the corners of the houses and the door and window jambs were meticulously constructed of large blocks of ashlar masonry. The walls, or at least the inside walls of the rooms, were coated with plaster and decorated with frescoes of Minoan inspiration and technique.

From the archaeological evidence available, it is possible to conclude that the Middle Bronze Age inhabitants of the

Cyclades believed in a female deity, whom they worshipped in a special sanctuary within the settlement. The remains of such a sanctuary have been unearthed in the course of excavations at Hagia Eirene on Keos. Several large terracotta statues were found there, the biggest of which (about 1.50 metres tall) is presumably of the goddess, while the others may represent her female votaries.

Cemetery excavations provide considerable evidence regarding the burial customs practised in the Cyclades. Bodies of small children were deposited in large jars and interred, always within the confines of the settlement, either near the houses or actually indoors under the floor. Evidence for the use of this method in the Cyclades has been found at Phylakope and Hagia Eirene, and it would seem that it came to the islands from mainland Greece. Adults were interred outside the settlement, either in shaft graves (Hagia Eirene) or in rock-hewn chamber tombs (Phylakope). Both types of graves were already in use in the Cyclades in the Early Bronze Age. The Middle Cycladic tombs contain no grave goods as a rule, the only exception being a twelve-year-old girl's grave at Hagia Eirene, in which was found a large number of vases, a gold diadem, and a necklace made with beads of gold and semi-precious stones.

So far as the arts are concerned, almost the only contribution of the Cyclades of the Middle Bronze Age was in the field of pottery. The Early Cycladic tradition was continued, and the craftsman's repertoire of vase forms developed on the basis of those of the Phylakope I civilization. The long-beaked jug evolved into a jug with bosses (*mastoprochous*), and the shallow bowl with lips curved inwards gave way to a similar type with a short, straight, wide neck. The same evolutionary process is apparent in the style of decoration. Out of the lustrous dark-on-light decoration found in the penultimate phase of the Phylakope I civilization, there evolved a darker variation of the same style, similar to and, sometimes identical with, the matt-painted ware of mainland Greece. Both techniques, the lustrous and the matt, were in use in Phylakope II, but eventually the matt-painted style prevailed. Hand in hand with the development of the local pottery, close contact with Crete and mainland Greece led to the introduction of new vase forms and new ideas for the vase-painter's repertoire of subjects. Grey Minyan ware imported from the mainland and Kamares ware from Crete prompted the potters of the middle of the Phylakope II culture to produce local imitations, which sometimes embodied a mixture of elements from all three regional cultures. The Cycladic mastoprochous, for example, combined the matt-painted technique with the Cretan decorative motif of the crocus, and the bridge-spouted jar of Cretan form was decorated with a Helladic matt-painted bird design.

Generally speaking, the Cyclades in the Middle Bronze Age played an intermediary role. They were the crossroads where the cultures of Crete and mainland Greece met and mingled, and of this fusion, Mycenaean civilization was born.

In the Cyclades, there was some retardation in cultural development between 1900 and 1600 B.C. However, contact with Minoan Crete and maritime activity generally helped to ensure smoothness of continuity. In art, the Early Cycladic tradition continued. Facing page: part of a fresco showing a seascape with flying fish. This page, above left: birds on a clay jug. Stylization emphasizes rather than reduces liveliness. Below: crocuses on a clay jug. Right: painting of fishermen on a clay vessel. (National Archaeological Museum, Athens)

THE OLD-PALACE MINOAN PERIOD

The First Palaces

It is not known what occurred about 1900 B.C. to bring about the abrupt change of which such clear evidence is to be found in the remains of the old palace centres. The construction of great palaces in the commandingly situated Minoan centres in central and eastern Crete indicates a concentration of power in the hands of kings and a new system of government. It seems clear that the change was sudden, and that it was caused by some great events. Those events need not necessarily have taken place in Crete alone, and in fact there are indications of radical changes having affected mainland Greece, the Aegean islands, and the eastern coastlands of the Aegean. New tribes descended from the Northeast or the North and settled in Asia Minor and mainland Greece. They came in small bands at first, but after a time the influx may have swollen to the proportions of a mass migration. The rise of the Hittite civilization in Asia Minor and the Middle Helladic in central and southern mainland Greece must have been connected with these incursions of new tribes, which most authorities believe to have been branches of the Indo-European family of races. It is quite possible that the local community leaders in Crete realized that the only way of stemming the tide of migration before it overwhelmed the islands too was by instituting a centralized form of government. Archaeological

examination of the early palace centres leaves no doubt that there was a thorough redistribution of power along lines that would preclude the possibility of new-comers invading and settling in the islands, least of all Crete. Another consequence of the centralization of power and concentration of wealth was an unprecedented burst of cultural development. The palace centres themselves became the focal points of all cultural activities and ideas. It is difficult to reconstruct a complete picture of the life and civilization of the Old-Palace Period, for all we have is a jigsaw puzzle with many of the pieces missing. Nevertheless, it is quite clear from such remains as have been investigated that the political, social, economic, and religious life underwent a sweeping reorganization, and that living conditions improved.

The discovery that there was more than one palace, each one being the administrative centre of a sizeable self-supporting region of central or eastern Crete, made it clear that the kings either reigned with the active consent of the communal leaders or else had managed to overpower their fellow leaders in one or other of the economically important districts of the island. The biggest palace was in the north central plain, at Knosos, where there had been a prosperous and important settlement for centuries. In the Mesara plain

in south central Crete, where there were many flourishing settlements, right on the hill that commands the seaward approaches, stood the palace of Phaistos. The third palace, an important administrative centre, was in the coastal strip stretching along most of the northern seaboard between Knosos and the isthmus of Hierapetra. It is conjectured that there was probably a fourth administrative centre, with its own palace, in eastern Crete. To the west of the great massif of Mount Ida, near Monasteraki in the fertile plain of Amari, yet another palace—a smaller one—has come to light.

It is still not known whether any palace centres grew up in the western end of Crete, though recent excavations have produced abundant evidence of the existence of Old-Palace settlements in these parts as well. The most likely supposition is that a palace centre did spring up in the fertile coastal plain of Chania, possibly on a site quite near the modern town where Old-Palace remains have been found. A later Greek tradition—a somewhat shadowy one, it is true—has it that a city was founded by King Minos at Balchania, the modern Chania.

Right from the outset, the palaces were extremely complex buildings. They testify to the complexity of the organization behind the centralized power of the kings: a hierarchical class structure with the king at its apex, an advanced way of life largely controlled by the palace, a bureaucratic administration very closely associated with the palace sanctuaries, and sets of palace workshops for the practice of certain crafts and industries on an organized basis. It is clear that the power of Minoan Crete rested on harmonious cooperation among the several palace centres; otherwise, the fierce rivalry that would inevitably have broken out among them would have led to internal dissension and war. Up to now nothing has been found to indicate that such rivalries ever existed.

From the evidence of the pottery found in the foundations of the three main palaces, it has been established with certainty that they were all built at the same time, the end of Phase III of the Pre-Palace Period, i.e. about 1900 B.C.

Evans held the view that the very first palace grew up out of a number of isolated blocks of buildings, with rounded corners, grouped around a central courtyard with broad open passages between them. He believed that these blocks, which he called *insulae* or islands, were joined together by the process of roofing over the open spaces between them to form the first unified palatial building. To the west there was a paved courtyard, which fulfilled a double function as the principal forecourt giving access to the palace building and as an assembly place for the discussion of political and social matters. Each "island" contained deep basement rooms with no outside entrance; these rooms would obviously have been reached from above through trapdoors. In these basements, which when seen from above look like deep, sunless dungeons, were found quantities of household utensils dating from the time of the first palace. However, if the basements were so deep, while other rooms were at a higher

The first palace of Knosos was built about 1900 B.C. on a small rise on the plain which stretches between the mountain masses of Ida and Dikte. Facing page: aerial view of the remains of the west wing of the palace. Clearly visible are the paved court, the main approach to the palace, the circular deposit pits, and the causeways of rectangular slabs.
This page: detail from the west court.

The palace of Phaistos, the seat of a Minoan ruler, was built on a hill on the western side of the fertile plain of Mesara. Above: aerial photograph of the palace buildings seen from the west.

Clearly visible are the middle western court and theatral area, the early façade, and beyond that the sanctuary buildings. On the right-hand side is the old palace, built on three successive

level, this would simply mean that the general ground level grew higher later on. This was confirmed by the evidence of other sections of the west wing, where there was a long row of storage magazines, each fitted with built-in chests beneath the floor, not very different from those that were a feature of the later palace. There is good reason to believe that the western façade did not follow the same line as the façade of the later palace, as Evans thought it did. At Phaistos and Malia, it was further to the west and fronted on to the paving of the west court. At Malia, only its foundations can be seen; they join on to the foundations of rooms that occupied the whole northwestern section of the palace. At Phaistos, however, the excavations have laid bare the whole solid base of the façade with its frontage of *orthostates* (flagstones standing on edge) and a narrow *podium* (low ledge) round the bottom. Behind the façade, whole sets of rooms were unearthed: some of these were used as storerooms, some as workshops, and others for cult purposes.

Since the early palace at Phaistos was built on different

levels, with artificial terraces descending down the hillside, the broad paved courtyards in front of the western façade were staggered. The northernmost one was the highest, almost on the top of the hill, the middle one was slightly below the floor level of the later palace, and the southernmost was incredibly low down. High retaining walls were constructed to strengthen each level of terracing. In front of the northernmost retaining wall, there is a flight of very broad, shallow steps—a kind of grandstand for a theatral area—facing a courtyard which was sometimes used for ritual ceremonies. Paved processional pathways run across the courtyard, one of them leading to the tiers of theatre seats and continuing up them to a point where the royal throne may have stood. One branch of the processional way led to the main entrance of the palace, a monumental structure with a columned *propylon*. From there a corridor ran straight through to the central courtyard. Another opening in the western façade led into the set of rooms which was used as a sanctuary, easily recognizable as such by the interior design of the

rooms, the cult objects, and portable libation tables found there. Thus, one can be quite sure that sacred rites were held in the west courtyard of the palace, attended by the members of the royal court and the ordinary people. None of the ground-floor rooms immediately behind the western façade are fit to have been royal living quarters. They would presumably have been used as workshops or store-rooms, as indeed the quantities of pottery found there seem to imply. There were also some antechambers that look like vestibules or waiting rooms. The layout here was the same as in the later palace, which means that the ground-floor rooms in the west wing were used as regular storage magazines and workshops connected with the sanctuary.

The great halls for ceremonial rites must have been on the upper floors. That there were upper floors we know from the existence of staircases leading up from the ground-floor rooms, and in fact in the southeastern section of the palace at Phaistos some parts of the upper storeys have survived to this day. The excavator of the site put forward

the view that the different storeys represented different phases of the earlier palace. According to this interpretation, the lowest floor facing on to the lowest of the three fore-courts would naturally belong to the first phase. This view is very difficult to accept, since the same styles of pottery were found at all three levels, and even fragments of the same pots were found scattered in the different strata, which according to the excavator had been completely sealed off with lime mortar at the end of each phase.

When the later palace was built, the débris of the old one was covered over with a thick layer of lime mortar, as a result of which countless vases and other articles were preserved for posterity, most of them magnificent examples of palace workmanship. These finds help us to determine the purpose for which the rooms were used and to reconstruct a partial picture of life in the early palaces. Unfortunately, most of the Old-Palace finds were discovered in the section that projected beyond the line of the later palace façade, since that was the only place where the excavation could proceed unhindered and where the remains had lain undisturbed, away from the havoc wrought elsewhere by later foundation-laying. To form a more complete picture, though, we must consider the evidence from the rest of the palace as well.

The Italian excavators ascribed to the last phase of the first palace some remains that they found incorporated in the structure of the later palace and some others grouped together in the northeastern quarter that had remained covered from the end of the first palace's lifetime. Even the paved central courtyard itself, together with the porticoes that originally used to run right round it, was thought to have been the courtyard of the first palace. However, detailed examination of the features associated with the pottery of the end of Phase I of the New-Palace Period confirms that the ruins in question in fact date from then, and not earlier. Thus, we cannot form a complete picture of the first palaces from a study of Phaistos alone. The northwestern section of the palace at Malia, razed to the ground though it is, gives us an idea of some of the larger rooms with small communicating porticoes. The wooden columns of the porticoes stood on high stone bases. In none of the three major palaces can we be certain that the first central courtyard was at the same level as that of the later building; there is reason to believe that the latter were slightly higher. At Knosos, though, it is easier to see how the hillside was cut away into terraces to make room for the palace storage magazines and workshops and possibly, in the southeastern corner, the royal apartments. That corner, unfortunately, underwent drastic alterations when an even deeper cut was made in the hillside to take the royal apartments of the later palace. Nevertheless, we are fortunate to be able to identify the royal storerooms, with their gigantic *pithoi* still in place, and the workshops where the famous "eggshell" ware was made. What we can conclude with certainty on the evidence available is that the earlier palaces covered an extremely large area, possibly larger than the later palaces, that they were very methodically laid out in sections, each of which served a specific purpose, and that at least in their general plan they were not very different from the later palaces.

Three Disasters

It is estimated that the total lifetime of the early palaces was about 200 years, from 1900 to 1700 B.C. Over this period, they were destroyed three times. The third time they were flattened so completely that it was considered a hopeless task to try and rebuild them on the same plan using what remained of the old palaces; so the rubble was banked up, and the new palaces—or, at any rate, the greater part of them—were built on a slightly higher level. In the first two disasters, the palaces were not totally destroyed, and so they were rebuilt on more or less the same plan as before, with those parts that remained standing incorporated in the new structure. That is why the palace buildings of all three phases are considered as one palace, the whole of which is referred to as the "first" or "old" palace. The different phases in its history can be distinguished by the utensils found in the various strata, particularly the pottery, about which we know a great deal because of the abundance and continuity of the deposits.

Phaistos has told us more than either Knosos or Malia about the way of communication between the different floor levels and courtyards and the roads leading to the palace. Winding paved ramps led from one courtyard to the next, though possibly there was originally a staircase connecting the northern one with the middle level of the western forecourt. The main roads climbed the hillside from the south and west and led to different levels of the western court.

There is no sign of a defensive wall or any other fortifications round any of the palaces. At Knosos, it is true, there is a conspicuous enclosure wall of a kind; this is actually the retaining wall of the western forecourt. There was a gently-rising stepped ramp leading up to the top of the wall, which came out into the forecourt. Another road led up from the south; at the bottom of the ascent, it crossed a tributary of the Kairatos River on a great viaduct.

Engineering Works

The early palaces' infrastructure of public works was truly amazing. The drainage system was extremely efficient. The waste water was collected in stone gutters laid at a well-judged gradient and channelled off into a main drain, which got deeper and deeper as it went down the hill, till at the bottom it was deep enough for a man to stand upright in. It is not uncommon to find junctions with three or four gutters meeting at the same point. Elsewhere, the peripheral system was used: little channels emptied into a gently-sloping main drain which looped round collecting storm water from all the unroofed spaces. Evidently, there were downpipes draining the water from the roofs of the upper storeys.

Another feature was the organization of supply systems to provide the palaces with drinking water and water for washing and cleaning. Different systems were used in different places. The palace of Knosos had a proper aqueduct which brought water from a spring about ten kilometres away on the slopes of Mount Juktas (or Iyktos, to give it its Minoan name) in earthenware pipes that ran up hill and down dale and were carried across the gullies on narrow stone bridges. Remains of the aqueduct have been found in the precincts of the palace, in its east wing, and others on the southern slopes of the hill. The pipe sections were made with great skill, their internal structure carefully designed so as to let the water gain momentum at regular intervals and thus prevent the pipes from blocking. Each pipe section tapered to a narrow neck at one end, and this was cemented on to the next one. As an extra precaution, there were also curved clamps securing the joins. Gradients were carefully regulated so that the pipes would not break easily. It is quite clear that the Minoans were well acquainted with the principles of hydraulics. Since the spring was high up the mountain, there was no difficulty in bringing the water to the hill of Kephala, where the palace stood. Similar aqueducts have been found elsewhere, for example at Tylisos and Vathypetro. As for the other palaces, we cannot be certain what arrangements existed for the supply of drinking water, though there is evidence to suggest that there were large cisterns.

Some curious stone-lined pits resembling broad wells were found sunk in the paving of the western courtyards. At Knosos, the workmen referred to them as "kouloures", and Evans adopted that name for them himself. They were full of pots-herds and broken stone vases, and it is very likely that they were used in sacred rituals. Thus, they came to be described as *hieroi apothetai* (sacred repositories), which is probably not far off the mark when one considers

Around 1900 B.C. the Minoans built a palace on the eastern side of the long northern coastal plain which stretched up to the region of Malia. The site was at the cross-roads of communications between eastern and western Crete. In the aerial photograph above: view over the palace from the northeast. Clearly visible are the paved courts, the roads, and the northwestern section, which dates from the Old-Palace Period. Below: the royal road at the palace of Malia leading to the northern entrance, and a huge Old-Palace pithos decorated with successive rows of handles and bands that look like rope.

147

how common such circular rubbish pits are in Old-Palace centres. In the palace of Malia, eight similar "kouloures" were found, arranged in two rows of four. There, however, the walls were lined with plaster, and there were central pillars which indicate that they were roofed over. Some authorities, therefore, think that they were used as cisterns, others as granaries. The latter seems less likely, since the palace was equipped with whole sets of store-rooms, in which both grain and liquids were stored in pithoi.

Old-Palace Settlements

Outside the palaces there were various auxiliary buildings serving special purposes. One such building at Knosos, a sort of crypt with monolithic supporting pillars, may have been used for religious "mysteries". A much more interesting example is a construction near the palace at Malia. It consists of a set of intercommunicating crypts furnished with benches all along the walls; here too, there were some interior supporting pillars, and the walls and floors were covered with brightly-coloured plaster. The crypts were reached by stairs leading down from the upper floor. The upper floor looked out over a broad paved courtyard, which was obviously used for public gatherings, since it has raised tiers in some places. It would appear that the crypt building played a very important part in the life of the early palace.

Very little is known about the settlements surrounding the palaces. At Knosos, a few houses have been excavated along the roads leading up to the palace. At Phaistos, some blocks of houses on the hillside have been excavated and, at Malia, some houses to the west of the palace and around the bay that was used as an anchorage. One of the houses at Malia is of great interest. The walls and floors of the rooms are carefully plastered. Short stairways led down to other

rooms at a lower level, which are reminiscent of the lustral basins and bathrooms of later times. Excavations there have unearthed some beautifully decorated vases, many of them superior to the vessels found in the palace itself. But these few scattered ruins can hardly give us a general idea of the whole town, its street plan, its various facilities, the public works, and all the rest. Similar remains found under the ruins of later settlements, as at Palaikastro, Zakros, Gournia and elsewhere are equally sparse. We might be able to form an overall picture of the villages and small towns only if further excavations were to be carried out at those settlements in the Mesara plain which continued in existence into the Old-Palace Period, since these were not rebuilt after their destruction at the end of it. Unfortunately, only very small areas of them have been excavated so far, but nevertheless this is enough to make it reasonably certain that the houses were densely-packed and the facilities rudimentary. The settlements on the coast, which grew into flourishing ports, were more advanced, but the modern harbour towns and villages have been built on the same sites, and so all that has survived are a few fragmentary remains.

Public and Private Life

If we collect together all the scattered evidence brought to light by the excavation of Old-Palace centres, we can reconstruct some aspects of the life of their inhabitants. The resulting picture is a very fragmentary one, but the gaps are continually being filled in as excavation continues.

On the anthropological side, the scientific evidence acquired from a study of the skeletons unearthed in the burial grounds (and from comparison with representations of the human figure in the arts) makes it clear that racially there was no significant difference between this society and that of the Pre-Palace Period. The Mediterranean type reigned

Façades of Minoan houses made of faience plaques. Although scarcely three to five centimetres high, they give an idea of house *architecture at Knosos. The buildings were several storeys high and their walls were constructed of stone, layers of clay, and tim-*

supreme, and it was clearly he that guided the course of cultural development. It would appear, though, that the founding of the palace centres and large towns wrought a considerable change in the social structure. The separate social classes which had been formed were now organized into a graded hierarchical structure with an aristocracy at the top and the royal family at the apex. Striking differences can be seen between the homes of the farming communities and those in settlements whose economies were based on handicrafts or shipping and trading, and it is clear that increasing wealth and the concentration of vital commodities in the hands of a few people created considerable class distinction. But the centralized political administration, as evidenced by the arrangement of the palaces, imposed a hierarchical structure on the different classes precisely so as best to serve society as a whole. One gets the feeling that a very important part in the graded social structure was played by religion and the system of priesthood, which had the royal family at its head. The close association between the palaces and religion is revealed by the design of the palaces themselves. It has been established that, from the time of their initial foundation, a large section of the west wing was given over to the goddess and formed a kind of sanctuary area. So, it seems most likely that the political system of the first organized society was, to some extent at least, theocratic. This would mean that the kings ruled in the name of the goddess and drew their authority and power from her. The legal code must have been founded on divine law, and as such must have been respected by all. Later Greek tradition preserved the memory of the close association between Minos and the goddess in the story of his nine-yearly renewal of sovereignty—so, at any rate, some authorities interpret Homer's phrase "ἐννέωρος βασίλευε"— when Minos would retire to a high mountain or remote cave to receive the divine laws from the deity in the manner of a Moses or a Hammurabi.

One can point to certain pieces of evidence that indirectly support the hypothesis of a theocratic administration. First, it is very difficult to explain how such vast and complex palace buildings ever came to be constructed unless it was with the voluntary participation of the whole population. The only sufficiently strong motivation to account for such an outlay of both capital and labour would have been the belief that they were building a home for the goddess, in which the king would live as her representative. It seems impossible to believe that those incomparable edifices were built by an enslaved people working under a tyrant's lash. Furthermore, it is clear that Crete enjoyed good government from the Old-Palace Period onwards, and indeed the memory of it remained undimmed right through to Hellenic times. Good government of a quality to account for Crete's unique internal balance of power would have been difficult to achieve unless it rested on a theocratic organization.

If we could be more sure of the royal titles accompanying the portraits of the king and the prince in seal impressions found in the "hieroglyphics repository" in the palace of Knosos, we might find confirmation for our conjectural picture of the sanctuary-palace. Evans concluded that the hieroglyphic symbols of the title had some special religious significance, since the same symbols were used on associated royal seals in conjunction with the emblems of the throne and the sacred wild cat. The portrait impressions are of particular interest: here, for the first time, we make the personal acquaintance of the men who wielded supreme power. The king wears a diadem round his flowing tresses, and both his and the prince's features are very striking. What is clear from these seals, which undoubtedly date from the Old-Palace Period, is that the sovereign power was primarily wielded by men, though of course this does not preclude the possibility that women, too, were capable of exercising royal power while at the same time holding public office at

ber ties. Like the palaces, they have no windows at ground-floor level. The faience plaques were perhaps inlaid sections from a box which showed a town and a hunting scene. (Herakleion Museum)

Commercial and cultural links were gradually forged between Crete and the main centres of the East, and Minoan goods were exported to Mesopotamia. A Babylonian sealstone dating from the Hammurabi dynasty was found in a tholos tomb at Platanos in the plain of Mesara. One side of the seal (top) shows the goddess Ishtar, and the other side (bottom), a god or a ruler. (Herakleion Museum)

the highest level, notably as priestesses.

It is clear from the layout of the palaces that they were the seat of the central administration. The storage magazines were not there simply to hold the produce of the king's own estates; they were also used for storing the gifts or tribute offered to him, possibly in the name of the goddess, by his subjects, to be put to use for society as a whole. It is also established that there were archives in existence, in the palaces of Knosos, Phaistos, and Malia, though, unfortunately, all that have survived are the tablets used as labels for the chests that contained the actual documents. There is, therefore, no doubt that there was a bureaucratic system, which helped the business of administration.

Trade

The amazingly high standard of the products manufactured in the palaces proves the existence of workshops which not only catered for the needs of the palace itself, or even the town centred round it, but also for export. Further proof of this is provided by the innumerable articles of Cretan palace workmanship found in Egypt and the East. At Knosos and Phaistos, in fact, excavations have uncovered palace workshops for the manufacture of high-class pottery and, at Malia, a seal-engraving work-shop has been found. Tools, raw materials, half-finished articles, and scrapings had been left lying around, which indicates that the catastrophe struck suddenly while work was in progress.

Trade, then, was controlled by the palaces, and palace production was one of the main sources of supply. This explains the great determination with which manufacturing was developed until it reached a high standard. Superb Cretan-made articles were shipped abroad, packed in jars or boxes. Production was geared to the demands of foreign markets, as is illustrated by the number of Cretan products found in the major centres of Egypt and the East. A "treasure" of elaborately-wrought silver articles, of typical Minoan craftsmanship, was found in the foundations of a temple at Byblos, in Phoenicia; and at Tod, in Egypt, another hoard was unearthed, this time of silver vessels with embossed decoration that is also typically Minoan in technique. Some XIIth Dynasty tombs at Abydos were found to contain fine vessels of Kamares ware decorated with rosettes and garlands. In the town rubbish deposits of ancient work camps set up for the construction of Pharaonic pyramids, as at Kahun, Illahun and Harageh, a good many sherds of Kamares ware were turned up; they were obviously used by workers, who were possibly Cretans. From written sources found at Mari, on the middle Euphrates, we learn that the artifacts made by the "Kaptaru" (Cretans) were highly prized there. Frequent mention is made in written documents from Egypt and the East of the cedarwood timber that was shipped from Lebanon in the ships of the "Kephtin". It would seem that Cretan vessels were also engaged in the transit trade, chiefly in goods from the ports of Phoenicia. Cretan daggers and vessels of the Old-Palace Period have been found in Cyprus, indicating that Crete maintained close contacts with the island; and that is only to be expected, since it was from Cyprus that the Cretans obtained the bulk of their supply of copper. No doubt the royal courts of Crete did their best to establish friendly diplomatic relations with the other civilized lands further afield and sent delegations with precious gifts to their fellow-kings and to foreign shrines. They would also have been visited by envoys of the Pharaohs and other Eastern princes; this explains the presence in the Minoan palace centres of precious Egyptian stone vases and statuettes, scarabs, and oriental cylinder-seals. This interchange and importation of goods provided valuable help in establishing the positive dating of the Minoan periods. One such object which deserves special mention is a diorite statue of a certain User, apparently an envoy of a Pharaoh of the XIIth Dynasty, which was found beneath the paving of the central courtyard in the palace of Knosos. Another interesting one is a Babylonian haematite cylinder-seal dating from the time of King Hammurabi, which was discovered in a tholos tomb at Platanos. As regards the degree of organization of the island's foreign trade, it is significant that the Cretans constructed a harbour on the island of Pharos off the coast of the Nile delta. It was an immense work of engineering, with long piers, breakwaters, and entrances leading into a large basin and a smaller one. The first to realize that it was a prehistoric construction was the engineer Gaston Jondet, and Evans adduced powerful arguments to prove that the Pharos port installations were the work of Cretans of the Old-Palace Period. It would seem that the Egyptians lent their backing to the project in view of the enormous stimulus it would give to their country's trade with Crete and the Phoenician coast. Evans recognized the touch of experienced Minoan hands in the fit of the irregular flagstones that paved the quays.

It need hardly be said that an essential condition for large-scale development of commercial relations in the Mediterranean was the establishment of trading posts and agencies at strategic points, and there is much to indicate that such a system of commercial centres was already in existence in Old-Palace times. The trading posts about which we know most are those in the Aegean islands, such as those at Phylakope on the Island of Melos and on Kythera. Goods also had to be transported overland in Crete itself, across from one coast to the other and on a larger scale between the various palace centres. This required a system of roads suitable for wheeled vehicles. It is probable that the paved roads linking the ports on the south coast of Crete with Knosos and the north coast were constructed during the Old-Palace Period. Evans succeeded in tracing much of the course of these roads: the main arterial route ran up from the south over the foothills of Mount Ida, through the high narrow pass of Hagia Varvara (just like the modern road over from the Mesara plain) and down to the northern coastal plain. It was a major engineering feat involving a great deal of constructional work: small bridges, high retaining walls, parapets, and guardhouses. At the Knosos end, the road was carried over a stream on a huge viaduct with four great arches to let the water through. Gigantic engineering works like the port at Pharos and the Knosos viaduct show clearly that the Minoans were well acquainted with the technique of megalithic constructions.

Seafaring

Although seafaring was unquestionably very highly developed, there is unfortunately very little positive evidence available about it. Our only sources of information about the ships are a few illustrations, most of them on tiny seal-stones, where the minute space available permits only a

Clay votive figure of a worshipper with a dagger from the peak sanctuary at Petsophas in eastern Crete (end of the Pre-Palace Period or beginning of the Old-Palace Period, c. 20th century B.C.) The Minoans regarded hills and mountains as suitable places for sanctuaries of the deity. The votaries ascended to the peak carrying symbolic offerings for worship or supplication. (Herakleion Museum)

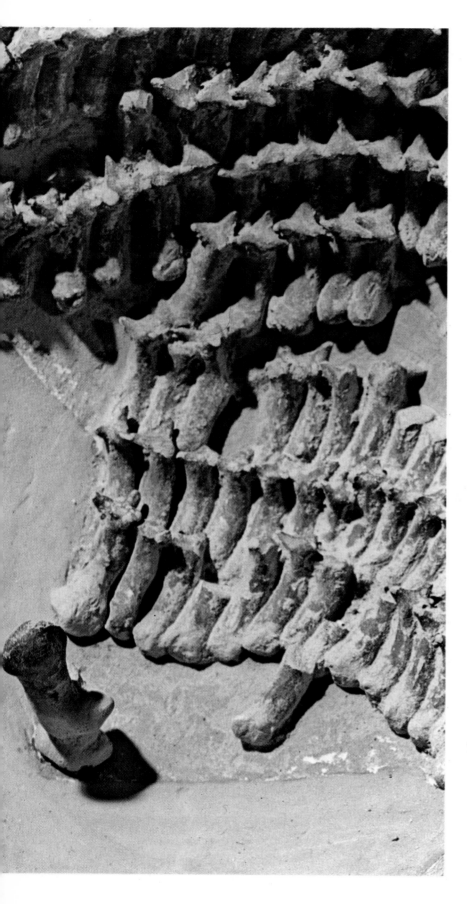

condensed and conventionalized picture; from it we can learn something only about the main features of their design. They had a high prow, which often ended in a forked prong, and a low stern, often with a ram-like spur projecting from the after end. Most of them were sailing-ships, with from one to three masts supported by stays and shrouds, and with one or two main sails and sometimes smaller auxiliary sails as well. Most of the sailing-ships also carried oars so that they could keep way on even without a favourable wind. Often the steering oars are much bigger than the others. Occasionally, one finds ships with bulwarks, raised decks or midship deckhouses. We can be sure, though, that vessels made to withstand stormy conditions would have had to be more stoutly constructed and better fitted out.

A question that arises is whether the Cretans had warships to protect their island against pirates and other invaders, considering that none of the towns were walled, not even the palace centres. Only hypothetical answers can be given, since there is no conclusive evidence on this point. In any case, the fact that in the New-Palace Period, when the Minoans were at the height of their power, we find no trace of a fighting navy makes it even less likely that there was one at the time of the early palaces. It would appear that the merchant ships were equipped with emergency armament for use in both attack and defence, like the Venetian and Genoese vessels of later times. The size of the island made it possible for forces to assemble in good time wherever they were threatened. In any case, there were no great dangers facing Crete in those days. The Egyptians seldom ventured out of the Nile and, when they did, they stuck to the coasts, since their vessels were not very suitable for the open sea. Phoenicia had not yet developed into a naval power to be reckoned with, and the great empires of the East were more or less cut off from the sea. The naval power of the Cyclades was much less than it had been in the Early Cycladic Period, and many of the islands were under Cretan control. The Middle Helladic people were farmers and strangers to the sea; it was unthinkable that they might ever be able to mount a sudden concerted attack on Crete. In the circumstances, it is easy to see how the Minoans came to enjoy the virtually unchallenged supremacy of the seas. In fact, it may well be that this was the period of Minoan thalassocracy, the memory of which lingered on into the Classical Period.

Agriculture

There was a great gulf between rural life and life in the big towns, especially the palace centres, as is apparent from the differences in housing conditions. Life in the farming and stockbreeding communities was very simple. Even so, there is no comparison between the standard of living in the rural communities of Egypt and the East and in contemporary Minoan villages, where it was much higher. This implies that in Crete there was no abuse of power by the palace centres, and that the arm of good government reached to the remotest inhabited corners of their domains. In the Old-Palace Period we find none of the country houses showing signs of local feudalism that were to make their appearance later on. The outlying districts at this stage came more directly under the control of the palace centres. There was evidently a strong link in the

Above: the shepherd and his flock. Detail from a deep clay bowl from the Minoan settlement at Palaikastro (eastern Crete). On the inside of the vessel, there is a whole herd of over two hundred sheep and a shepherd, all fully moulded. Perhaps this was a ritual vessel. It dates from the period 1900-1800 B.C. (Herakleion Museum)

common religion; participation in the communal worship of the goddess in the palaces, the sacred caves, the peak sanctuaries, and the rural shrines brought the different classes into close contact with each other.

There is good reason to believe that agricultural production was developed along systematic lines and covered a wide variety of crops. From the storage magazines we can tell that particular attention was paid to the cultivation of cereal crops, vines, and olives. Although no specialized study of agricultural production has yet been published, we can be certain that great efforts were made to effect improvements by employing new methods of cultivation. Possibly, it was this period that saw the construction of the first large-scale irrigation systems, which we will discuss later.

Life in the Palaces

We have a much clearer picture of life in the palace centres, even though our knowledge of the royal residential apartments is only fragmentary. All sorts of amenities were introduced. Even in the inferior quarters of the palaces, the interiors were beautifully furnished, with special wall linings, fine paved floors, and plastered surfaces adorned with decorative motifs or painted in bright contrasting colours; they were furnished with comfortable benches, alcoves, and wall cupboards; and in some of the rooms we find supporting columns or square piers, with double doors for easy intercommunication. There can be no doubt, then, that the royal apartments contained all these features in a more sophisticated and better-made form. The high standard of interior design is found in the bigger sections, such as those in the northwest crypts at Malia.

With regard to these quarters, their excavator, H. van Effenterre, has expressed the view that the king was advised by a large consultative body, a sort of senate or council of nobles, which limited the king's power. The popular assemblies held in the broad courtyard nearby presumably served to give the people some kind of check on royal authority, as in Homeric times. This interpretation was regarded as a very bold conjecture in dealing with such an early period, and it was felt that the design and layout of the palace at Malia did not provide sufficient grounds to justify such conclusions. Certainly, the theocratic system did involve ritual ceremonies calling for the participation of a great

Excellent plumbing and drainage systems were among the chief features of Minoan architecture. The drainage system at the palace of Knosos was the most advanced in the western world until Roman times. Stone conduits led out of the various apartments into a central cloaca, in which all the rain water collected. Above: section of the drainage system in the eastern part of the palace of Knosos. Rain water from the terraces in the main buildings was brought down vertical clay pipes into the square drain-head.

many priests; but these ceremonies provided an opportunity for the ordinary people, too, to take some part in the life of the palace. Indeed, it was with such assemblies in mind —assemblies involving all levels of society—that the outer courtyards were designed as they were. The royal family, attended by a magnificent retinue, would make its public appearances in the so-called "theatral areas", as we can infer from the paved processional ways leading to them from the palace gates. Even if the regalia (ceremonial sword and sceptre) found behind the throne room of the new palace at Malia do not, as was originally thought, belong to the time of the first palace, nevertheless they are symbolic expressions of the dual authority—religious and political— which the kings had certainly already acquired by the time of the early palaces, as we can tell from representations on royal seals of the period.

One of the symbols depicted on these seals is the throne, which was not very different in form from the thrones used in the New-Palace Period. The royal retinue was presumably composed of several different grades of dignitaries and officials, about whom nothing specific is known. The only clue is a seal impression found at Knosos, which might have belonged to the court musical director: it has two many-stringed lyres in the centre with an encircling wreath of wild cats' heads, the wild cat being both the royal and the sacred animal.

Dinner at the king's table would have involved the use of many of those magnificent polychrome vessels that were found put away in chests and cupboards in the palace storerooms. It is not too difficult to picture the scene at royal banquets, which would have also been attended by a sizeable company of foreign dignitaries. There was a fantastic variety of crockery and plate for the many courses—main dishes, sauces and condiments, entrées, fruit, and so on— and an even greater variety of vessels for the wine and other drinks: mixing bowls, wine jugs, bridge-spouted jars, goblets, cups, and many more. There can be no doubt that many of these vessels were made of precious metals, since there were so many earthenware imitations of metal forms, moulded

with incredible skill. It is particularly interesting to note that even ordinary kitchen utensils were often brilliantly decorated, and many of them were made in elaborate shapes cheese-graters, for example, that fitted firmly inside wide bowls; strainers fitted into elaborate spouts or else forming perforated trays to strain the liquid through into the lower compartment of the vessel, from which it was poured off through a separate spout running up from the base to the upper rim; not to mention the multiple egg-stands, stands for other vessels, small chafing-dishes, and so on. Then there were some very curious objects which look as if they were used as "safety lanterns" for carrying lighted lamps about out of doors; and another, even more curious, was a torpedo-like cylinder with tubular openings in its side which might have been used in the workshops to create a draught of air to fan the flames up to the melting-point of the metal.

Some of the small semi-basement rooms reached by short flights of steps look rather like the bathrooms that were installed in later buildings. However, it is impossible to be certain if this is what they were used for, since no bath tub has ever been found in any of them. In fact, we know nothing at all about the dressing rooms of this period though a great many toilet articles have been found in excavations. As far as clothes are concerned, we can see from the many statuettes of votaries that have been found (most of them in peak sanctuaries, a few in houses) that by this time the standard basic forms of dress for both men and women had been established. Differences had been visible all along since the Pre-Palace Period, but now dress styles —especially for women—began to be dictated by real fashion trends, most of which were almost certainly set by the ladies of the court. Men's loincloths, though still simple began to undergo changes of design: often they took the form of a short sash wrapped gracefully round the hips and held up in many cases by a separate tight belt which was sometimes combined with the codpiece. The most striking development in women's fashion was the dress with open breasted bodice, high collar at the back of the neck like a

Detail from an Old-Palace pithos in the Kamares style from Phaistos. On the vessel, which is 50 cm. high, is a decorative design representing a large fish caught in a net.
(Herakleion Museum)

Medici collar, full skirt resembling a crinoline, adorned with gaily-coloured flounces, and girdle with a tassel at the free-hanging end. Headgear and hairstyles were often extremely elaborate and very tall, sometimes like broad Breton hats and sometimes formed of successive coils growing wider towards the top. Obviously, there must have been a great difference between the costumes of the nobles and courtiers and those of the humble artisan and peasant classes. We can see these differences, in fact, reflected in the votive figurines dedicated by people of all ranks and classes.

THE DEVELOPMENT
OF MINOAN WRITING
Pictorial Hieroglyphs

Arthur Evans was the first person to draw serious attention to the possible existence of a prehistoric script in the Eastern Mediterranean that seemed to centre round Crete; he called this script Pre-Phoenician. He based his views principally on a series of mysterious hieroglyphic-like signs found on seals, mostly three-sided prisms. We now know that most of these were Cretan products of the Old-Palace Period and that they were indeed examples of a system of writing that could be described as Cretan hieroglyphics. It was to solve this problem that Evans started digging at Knosos, where fortune favoured him, and he found a large number of texts written in this mysterious script. The inscriptions engraved on seals were inevitably very short, even though they covered all three or four sides of the prismatic seals; and thus he felt that it was a great stroke of luck when he came across clay tablets with much longer texts, often inscribed on both sides, and clay bars inscribed on all four sides. It was soon established that the tablets and bars did not all date from the same period and that they represented different forms of writing. The earliest ones, which were found in the same context as vases of Kamares ware, were inscribed in a hieroglyphic script similar to that used on the seals but composed of linear incisions. Evans described this script as "linear hieroglyphics". The other two forms of script, which were found to date from the New-Palace Period, were named Linear A and Linear B. Only a very few texts in hieroglyphics and in Linear A script were found, but there were many hundreds of tablets inscribed in Linear B. Subsequently, more hieroglyphic tablets came to light in the palace of Malia, and in recent years others have been found in the palace of Phaistos, though it is now accepted that the system of writing on the latter is more like an early form of linear script than pure hieroglyphics. When, in 1908, L. Pernier discovered at Phaistos a clay disk with a very long inscription of hieroglyphic characters stamped in a spiral on both sides, it became apparent that this new find represented yet another form of script, quite different from the hieroglyphics found in the other palaces. This gave rise to an unending controversy over the provenance of the disk and the meaning of the inscription. As far as the dating of it was concerned, no one at that time had any doubt that it belonged to the Old-Palace Period, since it was found in a section of the buildings which the excavator then believed to be part of the first palace.

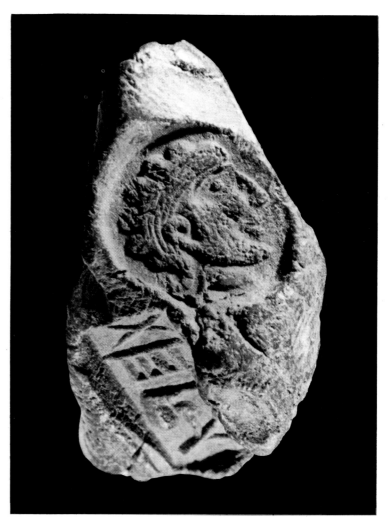

The first form of Minoan writing was ideographic, i.e. the pictorial representation of known objects on seal-stones, such as a head, a hand, a star; an arrow, and so on. The pictures were later impressed one by one on clay. Above: two sealings on clay, the first showing the profile of a king and his royal title; the second, the profile of a young prince. (Herakleion Museum)

155

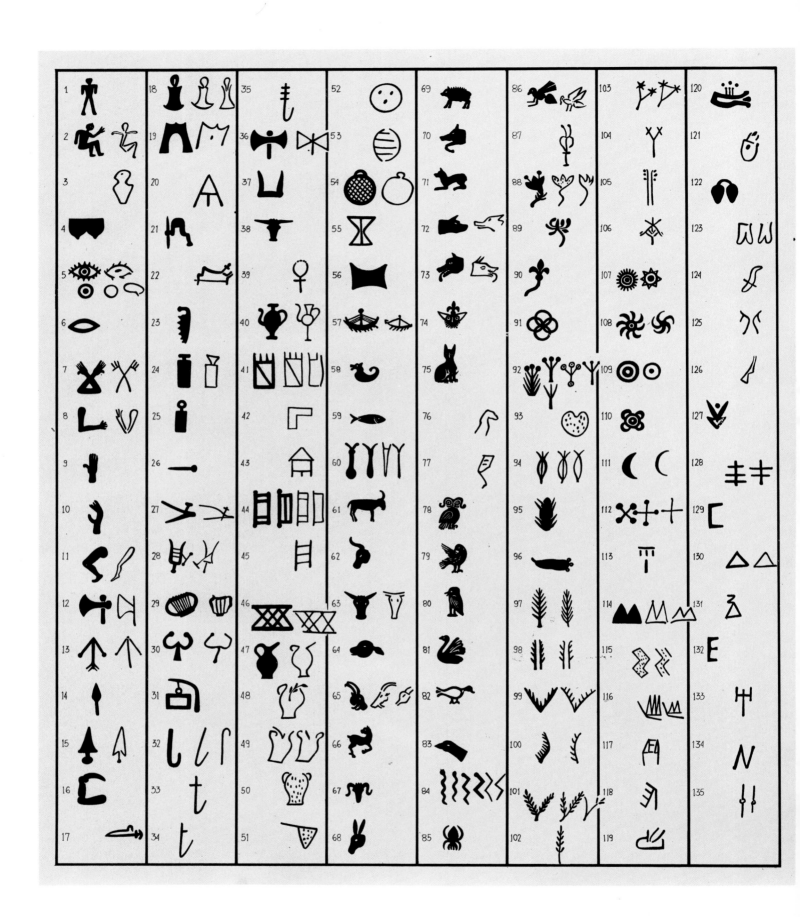

In time, the process of 'printing' or 'engraving' hieroglyphic signs became simplified, and the signs themselves became no more than outlines. In other words, the pictorial hieroglyphic script was replaced by a linear hieroglyphic script. Evans identified and classified 135 signs in both scripts. He drew up a table (above) showing in each column the pictorial hieroglyphic sign of the first script and next to it the same sign in its later simplified linear hieroglyphic form. Some signs are almost the same in both scripts, some appear only in one form, pictorial or linear. From the table of 135 hieroglyphs, 21 of the most characteristic are shown separately on the facing page. Number 5, a human eye, may signify inspection; 23 is a saw; 27, the Minoan plough, which remained substantially unchanged for millennia; 29 is the multi-stringed lyre; 31 is perhaps a winch used in Minoan building; 37 is the

Nowadays the whole matter appears in a very different light, since it has been established that the hieroglyphic archives found at Knosos and Malia and the disk of Phaistos both belong to the early part of the New-Palace Period. Moreover, hieroglyphic inscriptions have been found on other articles of proven date, such as a double axe from the Arkalochori cave and a stone that was used as an altar in the palace of Malia, proving that hieroglyphics continued to be used right up to about 1600 B.C. Even so, we know from the Old-Palace seal-stones, the Phaistos inscriptions in protolinear script, and other tablets recently discovered in Old-Palace houses at Malia that that was the peak period in the development of the hieroglyphic scripts. This, therefore, seems to be the most appropriate place to discuss all the earlier Minoan systems of writing under one heading.

The germs of a hieroglyphic script with pictorial characters that can be classified as ideographs are to be found on Pre-Palace seals of the end of the third millennium B.C. Very often these pictorial signs represent objects connected with the occupation of the owner of the seal, and so it is not always certain that they were in fact true ideographs. Nevertheless, there is one three-sided seal from Kalo Chorio on which the forms of the objects depicted are stylized in the same way as in the hieroglyphics on later seals. The exquisite polyhedral seal-stone found in the burial enclosure on Phourni hill, near Archanes, has no less than fourteen pictograms or ideographs on it. By the time of the early palaces the hieroglyphic script had been perfected, so that on most of the inscribed seals, made of precious or semi-precious stones, the signs are beautifully carved and well arranged with an eye to calligraphy. The most artistic examples are inscribed on the several faces of three-sided or four-sided prisms or, more rarely, on signet seals with a discoid sealing-face and a turned handle. The many-sided prisms were preferred, because of the desire to fit in as many characters as possible. One superb example is an octahedral prismatic seal-stone with a hieroglyphic inscription which is now in the Ashmolean Museum at Oxford. There are also a few solid gold prism seals with hieroglyphic inscriptions, one of the finest being in the Herakleion Museum.

Many of the seals are engraved with both hieroglyphic inscriptions and ideogrammatic pictures; frequently, these inscriptions appear to be titles, sometimes royal titles, since some of the ideographs are associated with royal insignia or represent the royal animal, the wild cat. We have already mentioned two of the seal impressions that fall into this category, one with a portrait of the king on one of its faces and the other showing a prince. Among the signs that appear in the royal titles are a trident, a bent leg, and a doorway, but it is hard to be sure what they each actually signified.

By the end of the Old-Palace Period it was common to find "occupational" seals engraved with symbols representative of their owners' crafts or trades. Thus, the hieroglyphic characters present us with an inventory of objects in common use in the Old-Palace Period: utensils, tools, musical instruments, sacred symbols, ships, weapons, plants, animals, and so on. Some typical examples are the single-bladed axe stoutly attached to its helve, the arrow with a double barb at the tail of its shaft, the spear with its leaf-shaped blade, the triangular dagger with a round pommel, and the sickle, forming an extension of the arm holding it. Of the many hieroglyphic symbols depicting tools and implements, one can single out the saw, the pestle, the builder's plumb-bob, the leather-knife, the awl, and the compass. Bronze specimens of these tools have been found in excavations. There are other signs, too, which may or may not represent implements. The curved stanchion with a square weight hanging from it by a ring may possibly be a winch or hoist of some sort.

Musical instruments, such as the many-stringed lyre,

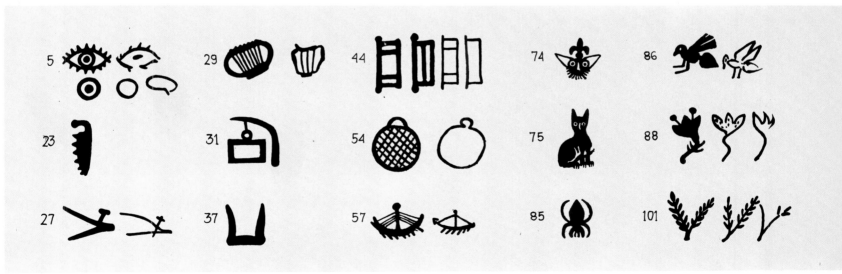

sign of the bull's horns, one of the most important Minoan religious symbols; 44 shows a house door; 54, a farming implement, perhaps a sieve of the kind still used today by Cretan peasants; 57, a many-oared ship, is a symbol which frequently appears in Minoan hieroglyphic writing. The lion and cat heads (74, 75) were royal emblems. The spider (85) is probably connected with weaving, while the bee (86) indicates that bee-keeping was widely practised in Minoan times. The crocus flower shown in 88 played an important role in Minoan industry as it provided the colour of bright yellow. Finally, the olive branch (101) shows that olive production was an important part of Minoan agriculture. These symbols have been used not only as ideographs, but also as signs with a phonetic value. The Minoan script provides a wealth of information regarding the economy of Minoan Crete and life in general.

the harp, and the sistrum (a wire rattle that was shaken to give the beat) are easily recognizable since they sometimes appear on court musicians' seals. Other symbols that are equally unmistakable are the sacred double axe, the horns of consecration, and the *boukranon* or oxhead. Others again are taken from the builder's trade: houses, fences, and doors. Among the utensils depicted on seals we can recognize some familiar shapes in metal or clay, many specimens of which have been found in Crete, in Phoenicia (Byblos), and in Egypt (Tod): amphorae, pitchers, spouted ewers, pans, and strainers.

It is quite common to find representations of ships on hieroglyphic seals, sometimes as ideographs on their own and sometimes in combination with other complementary signs. There is considerable variety to be found in the ships depicted on these seals as regards the shape of the hull, the number of oars, the masts, the shape of the prow, and the projection at the stern. Although these signs were simply intended as succinct symbolic representations, it is easy to see the love of the sea and seafaring that went into the making of them and of the other complementary hieroglyphs such as the fish, the cuttlefish, and the little sea-horse.

The animal kingdom, so familiar to the Minoans from their own domestic animals or their huntsmen's prey, was a great source of hieroglyphic signs which were full of grace and movement, even though in most cases only the head of the animal was shown. The repertoire included bulls, wild goats, deer, rams, hares, wild boars, pigs, wolves, dogs, jackals, and cats. The wild cat was an emblem of the king and is found on royal seals together with the royal throne, recognizably similar to the famous alabaster throne from the last phase of the palace that was found intact at Knosos.

Bird symbols include the eagle, the dove, the finch, the swan, and the owl. Bees, too, appear on seals as they were very important, because of the honey and wax they produced. The spider possibly symbolizes the craft of weaving and may therefore be the mark of the royal weaver.

Of the plants represented by hieroglyphic signs, the most frequently found are those that were most widely cultivated as farm crops, such as wheat and barley (sometimes the whole stalk, sometimes just the ear), the olive, and certain herbs and highly-valued plants, such as saffron and silphium. The saffron species of crocus was much in demand for the bright yellow dye it produced, as was the purple shell (*murex*), which yielded a red dye. Silphium, which is represented as a three-branched stalk with bobbles on the tips, was later to be systematically cultivated at Kyrene, where a colony was established by settlers from Thera under a Cretan leader, and it became the colony's principal export. Evans believed that this much-prized plant was first cultivated in Minoan Crete.

To round off the list of hieroglyphic characters, there are the stars, star-signs, and heavenly bodies generally, which may have had some religious symbolism, and the human figures, limbs, and other parts of the body. The anthropomorphic features evidently had some symbolic significance connected with the pose or gesture depicted. One of the human body hieroglyphs was that of woman's breasts, which possibly retained its primeval meaning as a symbol of the divine mother, the source of nourishment.

There are many similarities between the Cretan and the Egyptian hieroglyphic scripts. Very few of the signs are the same, however, and the writing did not serve the same function as in Egypt. Egyptian influence is clearly apparent, but there is no question of imitation.

UNITS	$)$ or $\mid = /$		$)))))$ or $\mid\mid\mid\mid\mid$ or $\mid\mid\mid\mid = 5$	
TENS	$\bullet = 10$		$\vdots\vdots = 40$	$\bullet\bullet\bullet\bullet\bullet = 50$
HUNDREDS	$\backslash$ or $/ = 100$		$\backslash\backslash\backslash\backslash\backslash = 500$	
THOUSANDS	$\lozenge = 1000$		$\lozenge\lozenge\lozenge\lozenge\lozenge\lozenge = 6000$	
FRACTIONS	$\vee$ perhaps $= \frac{1}{4}$		$\vee\vee = \frac{3}{4}$	
EXAMPLE		$\lozenge\lozenge\lozenge\ \backslash\backslash\backslash\backslash\backslash\backslash\ \vdots\vdots\ )))) \vee\vee\vee = 3644\frac{3}{4}$		

Linear Hieroglyphs

Parallel with this went the development of the linear variant of the hieroglyphic script, which was used for inscriptions incised on clay bars, disks, balls, and tablets. It may be that these were labels for the chests and boxes which contained the actual documents themselves. The latter were probably made of perishable material, such as parchment, papyrus, or palm leaves. They formed the first sets of systematically kept palace archives, and they were kept in chests secured with sealed lumps of clay, which explains why the "labels" were usually found in deposits containing large number of sealings or other stamped impressions.

Although most of these archive sealings date from the first phase of the New-Palace Period, the symbols on them maintain the Old-Palace tradition unchanged. The most important deposits were found in the so-called Hieroglyphic Deposit at Knosos and the archive in the palace of Malia. The signs are very similar to the hieroglyphs on seals, though more stylized. It is still easy to recognize the objects from which the symbols are derived. Some new signs have been introduced. It is not always an easy matter to distinguish the ideographs from the syllabic phonograms. The signs were incised with a pointed instrument on unbaked clay, becoming more and more cursive as time went on, and this led to the formation of a script that could be called proto-linear rather than hieroglyphic. Specimens of this script have been found at the palace of Phaistos among Old-Palace pottery. The sudden change to the "cursive" form shows on the other hand that writing was mainly with ink. Examples of this kind of writing have in fact been found at Knosos.

The relative paucity of hieroglyphic tablets discovered means that there is some uncertainty concerning the number of syllabic phonograms and the variety of ideographs. Of the first, over 90 have been counted. The direction of the writing varies. Sometimes the inscriptions read from right to left, more often from left to right, and occasionally they are written alternately in either direction, in the so-called *boustrophedon* manner. The unevenness of the lines and the untidiness of the signs —some of which are drawn back to front—show that this script was still in its infancy. Small marks, the most common being two small dashes in the form of an X appear to be determinative signs and do not occur only at the beginning, as Evans believed. Many of the tablets also included numerals. The repetition of the numeral signs between 1 and 9 indicated a decimal system (as in the Egyptian, though not the Mesopotamian, script). Units were represented by perpendicular lines or half-moons, tens by dots, hundreds by slanting lines, thousands by rhombs. This early numerical system was retained in a modified form in the later linear scripts. It is clear that the archives consisted chiefly of inventories and accounts. Some tablets contained perhaps simply lists of titles, others probably referred to property, while yet others were straightforward book-keeping records.

Since the Cretan script seems to have been only loosely related to the hieroglyphic script of Egypt and never more than superficially influenced by it, many scholars have sought the origins of the Cretan hieroglyphics in other regions. H. Hrozný and I. Gelb claimed to have traced a connection between Cretan and Hittite hieroglyphics, while H. Bossert and F. von Bissing even maintained that these two scripts had been formulated on the same basic principles. However, the differences proved far greater than the similarities, and other scholars turned their attention to southwest Anatolia,

Hieroglyphics (i.e. impressed pictures), and their linear forms are accompanied by auxiliary signs, such as lines or crosses, which indicate the beginning or the direction of the script or mark certain signs as ideographs, i.e. as symbols with a meaning but no phonetic value. Facing page, above, and this page, left: hieroglyphics in a simplified linear style on a clay tablet and on a label with a suspension hole, from the palace of Knosos (c. 1700 B.C.). This page, right: Old-Palace prism seal of green jasper with hieroglyphic script (Herakleion Museum). The hieroglyphic script included a complete numerical system (units, tens, hundreds, thousands, and even fractions). Table of the numerical signs on facing page, below.

though we have only scant knowledge of the script of this region. No plausible connection has been traced with the Proto-Elamite or Sumerian scripts, and in any case these are of too early a date to have had any direct influence on Cretan writing. The whole question has been further complicated by the discovery of hieroglyphic texts at Tataria in Transylvania (Roumania), which S. Hood claims to bear a clear relation to Cretan hieroglyphics. The Tataria texts cannot be dated with accuracy, but there is general agreement that they must be earlier than the end of the third millennium B.C. This dating makes them the most likely predecessors of the Cretan texts, but still does not solve the real problem, since both scripts must have had a common ancestor in some other region, most probably Mesopotamia.

The protolinear texts found at Phaistos show that towards the end of the Old-Palace Period writing was no longer purely hieroglyphic. The original hieroglyphic characters became gradually simplified, stylized, and transformed into linear signs, and new determinative signs were added.

The Disk of Phaistos

In spite of the appearance and development of linear systems of writing, the hieroglyphic script continued to be used for sacred texts. The co-existence of the two scripts on Crete was proved beyond doubt by the discovery of both Linear A and purely hieroglyphic texts dating from the first phase of the New-Palace Period. These texts clearly had a sacred character, and so the literal meaning of "hieroglyphics" (sacred carvings) is extremely apt here. The most important of these texts is the so-called Disk of Phaistos, discovered in 1908 by Pernier in a small compartment in the northwestern section of the palace of Phaistos. This section was in use only in the first phase of the New-Palace Period (1700-1600 B.C.), and so the disk could be dated with great accuracy. Its unique shape, the spot in which it was found, and the inferences which have been gleaned from the text inscribed on it, all suggest that it was an object of sacred and ritual character. The text was impressed in a spiral on both sides of the disk, reading from the circumference to the centre, and with many repetitions of the same signs. Each of the impressed signs was a hieroglyphic character, and in most cases it is easy to recognize what the signs depict: human figures, parts of the body, weapons, tools, utensils, various animals and plants, ships, and so on. A few signs are difficult to interpret, and there has been much controversy over them. We may confidently assert that the disk provides the first known example of printing, since printing is based exactly on this principle of impressing movable signs on a surface. Altogether 241 signs of 45 different types appear on the disk. They are divided into 31 + 30 groups divided by perpendicular lines. An engraved spiral line follows the text, dividing the coiling rows. Perhaps each group represents a word or phrase. Some combinations of these groups appear again and again, sometimes at regular intervals. And there is a similarly regular distribution of the individual signs. It also looks as if the text is rhythmically arranged, i.e., that it is in metre. If so, then the obviously sacred character of the disk itself suggests that its metrical text was in fact a hymn to the deity. Some small signs which

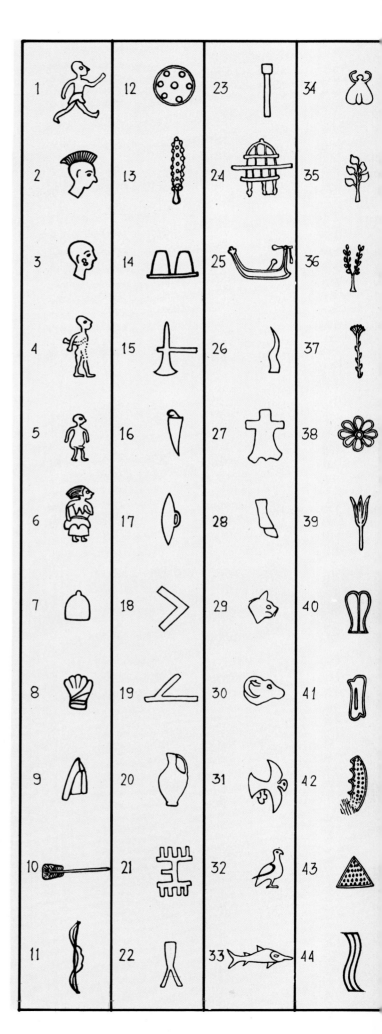

160

The most important specimen of a hieroglyphic script from Crete is on the clay Disk of Phaistos, the two sides of which are shown on this page. The signs are impressed spirally and depict men, women, children, birds, fish, insects, heads and feet of animals, plant subjects, ships, bows, mattocks, etc.

The Disk of Phaistos is the first known example of printing—the signs had been impressed one by one with seals on the surface of the clay. It has so far proved impossible to decipher the hieroglyphics and to understand the content of the text. The most commonly held view is that it is a hymn to the deity (Herakleion Museum). Facing page: table of the hieroglyphic signs impressed on the Disk of Phaistos. Most of these signs differ from the usual ones of the hieroglyphic script. Although their phonetic value is syllabic, they depict figures and objects from everyday life: men, parts of the body, tools, weapons, utensils, vaulted buildings, ships, various animals, and plants, some of which are difficult to identify. In symbol 3, the figure-of-eight mark on the face perhaps represents a tattoo or a dangling jewel. Symbol 4 is a nude man, perhaps a prisoner, since his hands are bound behind his back. Symbol 7 perhaps represents a breast; 8, a boxing glove; 9, probably a tiara; 12, a circular shield; 13, a club; 14, perhaps manacles; 16, a knife; 17, a tool for cutting leather; 18, a builder's angle; 19, a carpenter's plane; 21, a curious double comb; 23, perhaps a hammer; 25, a ship; 26, a bull's horn; 27, a skin; and 31, a bird in flight. Some symbols are still undetermined.

Bronze double axe from the sacred cave at Arkalochori in central Crete. On the centre ridge are some barely distinguishable votive hieroglyphic symbols in three columns. The script is related to the hieroglyphic script on the Disk of Phaistos, showing that the Disk is not of foreign origin. The axe is dated c. 1600 B.C. (Herakleion Museum). Right: an enlargement of the ideographs.

look like accents may have been for the benefit of the singer or reciter.

At the time of the discovery of the Phaistos disk, the hieroglyphics shown on it had no known parallel in Crete, and it was therefore believed to have been of foreign origin. The plumed head which regularly appears at the beginning of many words—never in the middle or at the end—is thought to be one of the chief determinative signs, and since it is reminiscent of the plumed head coverings worn by the Pulesata, one of the "seapeoples" who invaded Egypt, some scholars believed that the disk came from the original homeland of these peoples. However, there is an enormous difference between the date of the tablet (17th century B.C.) and the date of the invasion of the seapeoples (12th century B.C.). Another sign which resembled the façades of Lykian two-storey rock-cut tombs gave Evans the idea that the disk must have originated in southwest Asia Minor. Finally, it emerged that there was no reason to assume that the disk had been imported from abroad. Similar hieroglyphic signs were found in an inscription on a bronze double axe from Arkalochori, and related signs were found on other contemporary inscriptions. Further, it is known that spiral writing was used in Minoan Linear A inscriptions, as for example on the bezel of a gold ring from a tomb at Knosos and on the inside of "magic" cups found in the area round the palace.

There have been several ambitious attempts to decipher the Phaistos disk, or at least to determine the general subject of the text. Some of the wilder interpretations were based on a determination of phonetic values, in accordance with the acrophonetic system, which were supposed to correspond in Greek or another language to the pictographs of the text. The text which had been thus boldly "read" was then even more boldly interpreted by deducing the meanings of the words from their supposed connection with all manner of roots. One scholar declared the text to be a hymn to Athena, another that it was a stores list. The language of the text was identified variously as Greek, Semitic, Basque, Finnish, and so on. It may in fact prove impossible ever to decipher this script. The disk is evidently a unique object, written in a language we do not know and perhaps in a conventional script used for sacred texts, with signs whose phonetic values we cannot determine.

The theory that the text was a hymn to the deity seems a reasonable one, for it is based on the general arrangement and character of the signs, rather than on any over-ambitious attempt at their decipherment. We may conclude that several different scripts were used in Crete in the Old-Palace Period and that they were developed independently of each other in different regions. Some of these continued in use in the New-Palace Period for the writing of sacred texts.

FUNERARY CUSTOMS

Traditional attitudes toward death are deeply rooted in peoples and change only gradually. Consequently, we find that in the Old-Palace Period there was a continuation of the earlier methods of burial in the very ancient tholos tombs of the Mesara plain and in rectangular partitioned enclosures in the rest of Crete. However, the change which had meanwhile taken place in the social structure now made it unnecessary to build huge tholos tombs or extensive enclosures. There was an evident trend towards individual burials, both in *pithoi* (jars) and in small clay sarcophagi. Extensions were built on to the large tholos tombs, and there were still burials in beach graveyards and in wide hollows in rocks by the sea. It now became a general custom to bury the dead on the slopes of nearby hillsides wherever there were small caves or natural hollows in the rock. The caves were often enlarged by cutting out niches and recesses, and the various burial areas were connected by tunnels. Typical hillside cemeteries have been found on the hills of Prophetes Elias and Monasteriako Kephali at Knosos. These natural and artificially hollowed-out caves, comprising a chief burial area and a passage for access, were undoubtedly the prototypes of the later rock-cut tombs.

A few grave goods were left by the side of the dead person—both everyday necessities, such as toilet articles, and possessions he specially prized, like jewellery. Seals which he had used to stamp objects or documents were buried with him and have been discovered in great numbers in the cemeteries.

A vaulted tomb on the Gypsades hill at Knosos was built in an architectural style previously found mainly in southern Crete and representing the intervening stage before the development of the monumental tholos tomb of Minoan New-Palace and early Mycenaean times. It has been suggested that the tholos tomb at Kamelares close to the settlement at Hagia Triada, also dates from this period, but this is somewhat doubtful. The more conservative inhabitants of the region round the New-Palace centre at Malia continued to bury their dead in the old enclosures at Chrysolakkos.

OLD-PALACE ART
Architecture

From the incomplete and scattered remains of the old palaces, it is impossible to form a proper idea of their original appearance. We can guess at, rather than recognize, the arrangement of the various apartments. Even the little that remains, however, is enough to call forth our admiration for the Minoan architects of this period. They were the first to combine such a complex variety of forms into a completely harmonious whole which was perfectly adapted both to its own purpose and to the site on which it was built.

The ingenious use made of the different levels of the hillside is particularly noteworthy. They were formed into a series of terraces which supported the various sections of the multi-storey palace and provided space for activities connected with social, political, and religious life. Similarly impressive are the stoutly-built façades with their irregular arrangement, the well-planned links between the outer courts and the central court, the entrances whose grandeur matched that of the rest of the palace, the system of connecting corridors between different quarters of the building, the distribution of the various rooms according to their function, the decoration of the interior spaces, and the staircases running from many points on the ground floor to the upper storeys. All the basic principles of later palace architecture can be observed here. The palaces were built on a unified plan prepared by competent architects.

Considerable progress had been made in the techniques

Certain changes took place in the funerary customs in the Old-Palace Period: mass burials in huge tholos tombs were replaced by individual burials in pithoi or clay sarcophagi. Left: chest-shaped clay sarcophagus from the Old-Palace Period, found in a tholos tomb at Vorou in the Mesara region. (Herakleion Museum)

163

of interior decoration. Walls were painted in a variety of colours or covered with gypsum slabs in imitation of dadoes. Decorative fresco paintings did not appear until towards the close of this period. A few fragments showing stylized plant subjects have been found. Floors were covered with plaster, sometimes decorated with paintings. The only surviving example of a floor with all-over surface decoration (rows of square curving patterns) comes from a small ritual room at Phaistos. Other floors were covered with polished slabs of crystal gypsum brought from quarries close to Hagia Triada. Red plaster joints gave an extra touch of colour to rooms or porticoes with wooden columns on tall bases of variously coloured stone.

Pottery

The Minoan fondness for decorative painting found its best expression in pottery decoration. We can form a relatively complete picture of the progress of this art from the huge quantities of palace pottery which have been preserved in the two large palaces at Knosos and Phaistos, particularly in the latter, because the earlier strata were sealed by a layer of concrete which formed a firm basis for halls and apartments of the new palace. Most of the vessels were in the polychrome Kamares style, so called after the vessels found in the region of that name in 1884. Kamares ware is generally agreed to be the most decorative pottery found anywhere in the world.

The techniques of vase painting had reached a high degree of perfection. The background glaze (the composition of which is still a mystery to us), always dark-coloured, usually black, was particularly shiny and solid. On this glaze, delicate decoration was painted in a white colour combined or dotted with various shades of red. Occasionally, other colours, such as brown and yellow, were also used. However, a striking effect of polychromy was produced by the alternation of decorative motifs and their flexible arrangement on the vessel. The technique was often a combination of the plastic and the pictorial arts, and the style became amazingly varied; the barbotine and barnacle styles drew their inspiration from the marine world. In some cases, marine, plant, and spiral motifs were impressed on the vase; in others, relief or fully moulded plant and animal subjects were added to it. The techniques of making delicate slender-sided vessels, particularly cups and glasses, had now been completely mastered, and this type of pottery is often known as "egg-shell" ware. It was obviously an imitation of vases made from precious metals. The rapidly-rotating potter's wheel had also been perfected, and an immense variety of vase shapes was produced, including many vessels for the royal table: kraters, jugs, fruit-bowls, salad-bowls, amphorae, cups, and tumblers of many types.

Minoan pottery reached a culminating phase in the Old-Palace Period. Painted designs were combined with moulded decoration on the vases, and the polychromy technique used for the painted motifs produced a vivid effect of movement.
Facing page, first column: details from two pithoi in the Kamares style: the top one is the so-called 'racket and balls' pithos from Knosos: the lower one is a stylized rendering of palm trees (1750-1700 B.C.). Second column, top: polychrome jug in the barbotine style from a tholos tomb at Hagia Triada (1900-1820 B.C.). Below: an ornate Kamares style krater with moulded flowers. (Herakleion Museum)

Particularly admirable was the adaptation of the polychrome ornament to the skilfully moulded shapes of the vases. Decoration based on spiral and rosette patterns was very popular. Also common were decorative motifs which could be extended indefinitely in two or more directions, as for example, bands or nets of spirals, meanders, shoots, or interwined undulating lines. In general, the motifs retained a purely decorative character. Even where they developed into flexibly and naturalistically drawn pictures of plants or animals, such as palm trees, crocuses, lilies, octopuses, argonauts, and fish, the subjects were still purely decorative in manner. For example, on a small pithos from Phaistos, a fish is shown being caught in a net but the overall pattern is that of a revolving rosette. On another small pithos, this time from Knosos, two palm trees bend their trunks round the upright trunk of a central palm tree, but the leaves are rendered decoratively in a regular pattern. Even when human figures were introduced for the first time on Kamares ware, chiefly in religious scenes, they were transformed into kinetic decorative subjects. An example is the chorus of worshippers around a cult idol painted on a fruit bowl and on a basin from the palace of Phaistos.

The Kamares vessels can be divided into various categories according to their use: table ware, kitchen utensils, vessels for storing goods and vessels for transporting exports, toilet articles, etc. A most important group consisted of vessels intended for use in religious ceremonies. Among these were the moulded and conical rhyta which now acquired the shapes which were to predominate in the New-Palace Period. Some vessels found at the palace of Phaistos were shaped like the heads of bulls or feline creatures.

Other interesting pottery styles based on the "black on white" technique of decoration developed alongside the Kamares style. In order that the rounded shapes of the decorative motifs should stand out more clearly, they were often framed by white lines. Even the large storage jars were charmingly decorated with successive rows of handles, bands painted to look like ropes or medallions, or regular patterns of small protruberances. Some were of a gigantic size, like the "giant pithoi" from the palace of Knosos and an enormously tall pithos from the palace at Malia. Ridges had been constructed on the inner walls of the latter to make the inside accessible for cleaning. Often these large jars were decorated by simply squeezing sponges from which the colour "dripped down", as if the liquid which the jar held had oozed out and discoloured the vase.

Stone-work and Seal-engraving

Great progress had been made in stone working, although stone vessels had now been replaced for the most part by vessels of fine clay. However, the decoration on clay vases was strongly influenced by stone prototypes: vases of breccia with interior red veins framed in white and standing out clearly against the dark background of the stone, and also vases decorated with untidy veins and blotches. The inlay technique which had begun to be employed in the last phase of the Pre-Palace Period increased the effect of coloured variety. Beautiful examples of stone vases of this sort were found in the small shrines in the palace of Phaistos. On other stone vases, it is engraving which supplies the possibility to render not only decorative but also representational ornaments, such as birds or animals.

Stone was a suitable material for the carving of small figurines or votive animals, and yet very few stone-carved figures have been found. The moulding of figures in variously coloured clays was much more common. However, miniature stone-carving produced some wonderful examples of seal-engraving. The Minoan craftsmen became exceptionally skilled at engraving microscopic shapes on hard semiprecious or precious stones. The subjects were sometimes ideographs or hieroglyphic signs, sometimes representations of various scenes indicating the profession or the identity of the owner of the seal. The superb naturalistic scenes which first appeared on these gems were later copied in larger-scale art forms. The subjects included scenes from the marine world, from the world of insects and small land creatures, idyllic scenes of wild animals resting among rocks, and exciting scenes of fights between animals, sometimes rendered in a humorous way. On one beautiful sealstone a dog barks helplessly at a wild goat which has taken refuge, after the chase, on a high cliff, from where it looks mockingly down at its pursuer. These scenes show that the art of seal-engraving had already reached a peak in the Old-Palace Period. More evidence of this comes from the wonderful carving of certain seals to resemble flower buds or moulded stalks. The seal-stones were made in an immense variety of shapes, chiefly prisms, seals with stems, and double convex disks. The latter often had skilfully worked tectonic subjects with meshes of delicate lines framed by thicker lines. Towards the end of the period, the com-

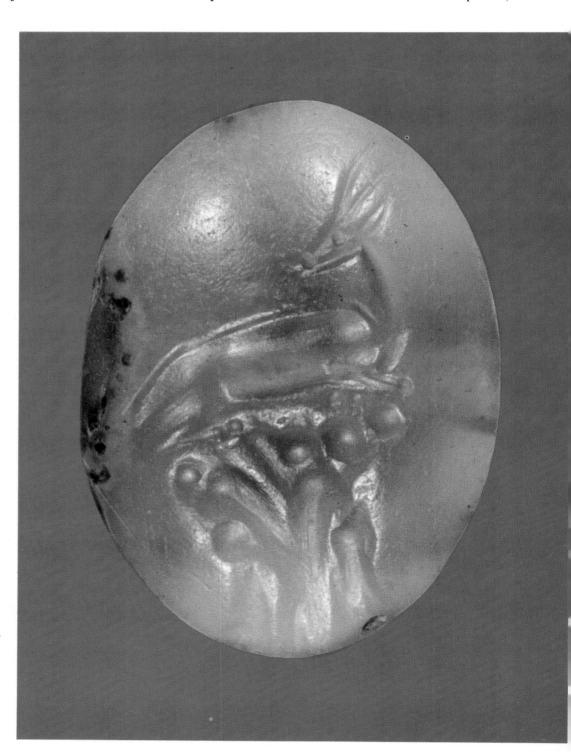

The technique of engraving seal-stones had reached a high degree of excellence in the Old-Palace Period. Whole scenes with microscopic figures of humans and animals were engraved on stone. Right: chalcedony seal-stone showing a wild goat lying on a rock—a fine example of early naturalistic work. (Herakleion Museum, Yamalakis Collection)

pressed cylinder began to be used, and this provided an excellent surface for the engraving of representational subjects. Of the precious stones used, the most popular were chalcedony, amethyst, rock crystal, haematite, and jasper. There were also many royal seals carved on precious stones. We can see the great variety and amazing technique of the seal-engravings not only from the seals which have been preserved but from many seal impressions on clay.

Metal-work

The fact that very few examples of metal-work have been found in Crete does not mean that this art had a restricted development. Judging from the egg-shell ware imitations of metal vessels, the latter must have been superbly made with exceptionally fine repoussé decoration. This is confirmed by the finds of treasures of Cretan origin in the Syro-Palestinian town of Byblos and at Tod in Egypt. The superb metal vessels found in the Mycenaean tombs had obviously developed from Cretan prototypes. There must have been a parallel development in the art of gold jewellery-making, judging at least from the few pieces of jewellery which have escaped the notice of pillagers in the palaces and the royal tombs. The treasury of gold ornaments from Chrysolakkos at Malia and the Aigina treasury (which R. Higgins has shown to be of contemporary Cretan origin) are both dated by most scholars to the Old-Palace Period. Even if this superb jewellery is of a slightly later date, as some believe, it certainly represents a continuation of the Old-Palace tradition. The technique of making gold ornaments had evidently been perfected in the Old-Palace Period, for great quantities of Pre-Palace jewellery have been found in tombs at Mochlos and in the tholos tombs of the Mesara plain.

There was a similar development too in the making of weapons and tools. From the few which have been preserved we can see that metal implements were now both better made and more pleasingly designed. Daggers had a strong shape, and their hilts were safely secured by a row of gold nails. It was perhaps towards the end of this period that the type of long sword with an ivory and gold-plated wooden guard and ornate handle was first introduced. At this time, too, a kind of ceremonial sword made its appearance. A superb example of such a sword has been found in the palace at Malia along with a sceptre head in the shape of a leopard combined with an axe. Excavations in an Old-Palace building west of the main palace unearthed a superbly wrought dagger with its hilt covered by an open-work pattern of intertwining four-leafed plants. This shows beyond doubt that there was great progress in the techniques of making metal weapons during the Old-Palace Period.

HISTORICAL SUMMARY

The simultaneous founding of three palaces in three separate important areas of Crete evidently came about as the result of conditions created by migratory movements of peoples into Helladic Greece and Asia Minor, and perhaps also as a result of an agreement among the local rulers in central and eastern Crete. A similar type of planned development was organized in each of the three palace regions. Perhaps a union of kings was agreed upon, in which the king of Knosos was recognized as *primus inter pares*. This would explain the harmonious development of the three kingdoms, their close and peaceful relations, and the general state of law and order which prevailed on the island. Although we have no specific knowledge of the character or achievements of the kings, it is evident that they reigned wisely and leniently without any abuse of power.

There is no information about any historical events which took place in the Old-Palace Period, except for the successive destructions which occurred simultaneously at all the Old-Palace centres. These destructions, which were accompanied by extensive fires, can only have been due to geological causes, more specifically to terrible earthquakes. Crete had always been subject to such disasters, because the greater part of the island lay over an extension of the fault under the sea-bed which caused most of the geological upheavals in the Eastern Mediterranean. In the Minoan period, the southern part of the Aegean was passing through a particularly turbulent phase, and earthquakes were both frequent and violent. The Cretan settlements were destroyed and rebuilt from scratch many times. The damage caused by the first two earthquakes, which took place c. 1820 and 1750 B.C., was serious but not irreparable. The Old-Palace centres rose from the ruins, the buildings were repaired or rebuilt wherever necessary. However, the final earthquake, which is dated to about 1700 B.C., completely destroyed all the Old-Palace centres. The inhabitants either abandoned their previous homes for good, or built completely new settlements on the site of the old ones, after the remains of these had been covered over with a thick layer of earth. Three new palaces were erected in this way, and so this new period, called the New-Palace Period, marked the beginning of a new stage of development.

Some scholars believe that some of the destructions mentioned above were due to surprise invasion and attack by foreign peoples. They claim that the Luvians crossed from the region of Beycesultan in southwest Anatolia to the Aegean region, destroying the old palaces on Crete and creating the New-Palace civilization. The chief evidence put forward by the proponent of this theory, L. Palmer, is linguistic; it is based on similarities between the Luvian and Linear A scripts and between place-names in Crete and the Luvian homeland. Palmer also pointed out some common elements in Luvian and Cretan palace architecture and religion. These arguments are unconvincing, since the Minoan language and script did not change after the destruction of the old palaces, and Cretan religious beliefs and customs had deep roots on the island. Other scholars have proposed that the invaders were the Hyksos who, after conquering Egypt and consolidating their power in that country, began to look acquisitively towards Crete. The only piece of evidence for this theory is an alabaster lid inscribed with the name of the king of the Hyksos, which was found in a stratum at Knosos of the beginning of the New-Palace Period. However, this vessel merely proves that the kings of Knosos resumed their contacts with Egypt as soon as they had recovered from the immediate effects of the disaster. It is certain that such widespread destruction, occurring simultaneously in all the regions of Crete, could not have been caused by foreign invasion, and in any case there is no real evidence of such an invasion.

GENERAL OUTLINE OF THE MIDDLE BRONZE AGE

A detailed examination of the three chief Aegean civilizations of the Early Bronze Age—the Early Helladic, the Early Cycladic, and the Early (or Pre-Palace) Minoan—shows that all three developed along similar lines and reached approximately the same level.

In the subsequent period, however, this uniformity of development was broken. The chief characteristic of the Middle Bronze Age was the noticeable difference in the rate of development in different regions. The level of the Old-Palace civilization in Crete was far higher than that of the simpler Middle Helladic in southern mainland Greece. In this period, the Minoans were systematically extending their trade contacts throughout the Eastern Mediterranean and attaining an unprecedented high level of civilization on Crete, while, in mainland Greece, an almost "neolithic" level of culture had reappeared; development was restricted and slow, sometimes even retrogressive. The sudden emergence of the southern region of the Aigaiis as the main centre of activity and the simultaneous sinking into isolation of the Helladic region are historical events of great importance which require interpretation.

It is clear that the causes of these events must have had particularly drastic effects on the Helladic region, since it is here that there was a great slowing up of development.

The seeds of uneasiness were already present in Helladic Greece at the end of the Early Bronze Age. Even more dramatic were the events that were taking place in the lands bordering on the Aigaiis, while in Asia Minor the transition from the second to the third phase of the Early Bronze Age was marked by a series of destructions on an unprecedented scale, stretching over a wide area right down to the Syrian border. There is no evidence of such general and widespread destruction in Greece, although at Lerna the central building of the settlement was sacked at some date before the end of the Early Helladic Period. Towards the end of this period (i.e. in the 20th century B.C.), there was a great upheaval both in Asia Minor and in Greece, marked by the simultaneous appearance in these regions, respectively, of the Hittite and the Middle Helladic civilizations. The general opinion among scholars is that this upheaval and the destructions which accompanied it were caused by successive waves of Indo-European invaders. Many believe that it was during this period that the first "Greeks" or Greek-speaking peoples arrived in Greece.

1. The archaeological material relating to Middle Helladic has been described above. The three centuries which make up this period (1900-1600 B.C.) represent the Helladic Middle Bronze Age. It should be noted that, in Crete, the corresponding period ended earlier (1700 B.C.) and that its end was marked by the total destruction of the old palaces. Thus, there is a difference not only in the cultural level but also in the duration of the Middle Bronze Age in the two regions. In Helladic Greece, there was no destruction or break in culture to mark the transition from Middle to Late Helladic (Mycenaean). Despite the great difference in the cultural, social, and political levels of the two periods

and the changes which took place in art, the Middle Helladic Period is regarded as the forerunner of the Mycenaean. Middle Helladic culture was once thought to be confined to the region of southern Greece below the Vale of the Spercheios, not including the western coast, but these limits now appear too narrow. If we do not include Thessaly (where the Middle Bronze Age can be regarded as a local variant of Middle Helladic), we risk leaving out the region where many of the elements of Middle Helladic originated. The same argument applies in the case of Macedonia, since the original pressures which brought about the change in culture must have been felt first in this region. A survey of the Middle Bronze Age cannot really be complete, therefore, without an examination of the developments which took place in the whole of mainland Greece, including the regions north of the Spercheios. We are obliged to confine ourselves, however, to a survey of Middle Helladic culture in the southern part of the Greek mainland, which is regarded as the "traditional" Middle Helladic region.

It was in this region that, in Early Helladic, an "urban" kind of civilization was about to make its appearance in such settlements as Lerna and Aigina. There were similar settlements on Crete (Vasilike), but while Crete swiftly progressed to a higher stage of development, the Helladic world passed into a period of stagnation. The archaeological evidence shows the level of civilization at this period to be low. The Middle Helladic villages were not much different from Neolithic; there were no "towns" other than a few simple survivals (Malthe, Aigina), and there was certainly no progress beyond the Early Helladic level of culture. This was a period of contraction and isolation rather than of progress, and it may be supposed that contacts became restricted, and there was a return to the old closed agricultural economy. These facts, in combination with the developments that took place in art, undoubtedly suggest some radical change. It was originally thought that at least some of the changes in pottery were due to a revival of indigenous neolithic styles. But the overall change in culture is now usually attributed to the arrival of a new racial element, the Indo-European tribes, whom most scholars agree in identifying as the first "Greeks" or Greek-speakers. This identification is necessarily hypothetical to a large extent, since there were no written records at this early date (inscribed texts did not appear until after the middle of the second millennium B.C.), and there is no way of establishing the identity of these tribes archaeologically or of isolating the elements of culture which should be attributed to "Arians" or "Greeks". On the other hand, the decipherment of the Linear B tablets has strengthened the belief that the creators of the Middle Helladic culture were Greeks.

From the positive evidence at our disposal, it emerges that the earlier phases of Middle Helladic (1900-1750/1700 B.C.) were periods of stagnation, while towards the end of the period there was some progressive development (also attested to by the widespread use of Minyan pottery). It would be difficult to interpret this difference during the

Middle Helladic Period without assuming the arrival of a new racial element. But beyond this assumption, we can go no further in reconstructing the events of this period. Nothing is known of the internal history of the Middle Helladic region or the role now taken by the indigenous population, which certainly survived the upheaval.

It is extremely difficult to find any sign or indication that might be held to presage the sudden appearance of the magnificent royal tombs at Mycenae at the end of this period. However, since this phenomenon cannot be attributed to any racial change or foreign occupation, we can only assume that towards the end of the period the conditions which made the change possible were already present. Present at least was the amazing receptiveness which the Helladic elements were to display in the following period, and which in fact became a distinguishing characteristic of Mycenaean civilization.

It seems, therefore, that although the Middle Helladic Period may be poor and insignificant from the cultural or archaeological point of view, it was in fact important as a period of preparation for a new world and perhaps of racial unification. Perhaps this is why it gives the impression of stagnation. The situation may be described in a simplified way by saying that since the development in Helladic Greece was so different from that of Minoan Crete, some new factor which did not affect Crete must have been responsible for the cultural difference; and since the newly arrived peoples, who were the new factor, caused a sharp break in the cultural development of the Helladic region, they must have been extremely backward, if not barbaric, in comparison with the population of the Aegean islands and Minoan Crete.

2. The Cyclades played only a limited intermediary role during this period. The first tidal-wave development of Early Cycladic had subsided, but there was still steady progress, despite all the changes.

The southern islands, which were more directly influenced by Crete, became progressively "minoanized", while the northern islands were affected to some extent by the uneasy situation in the Helladic mainland and assimilated some elements of that region. However, all the islands of the Aegean as well as some of the southern coasts of Greece were affected directly or indirectly by Minoan thalassocracy, the founding of Cretan trading stations, and the suppression of piracy. The Cycladic fleet now appears to have been used only for transporting goods to and from agricultural mainland Greece, and there was a consequent limiting of the activities of the Cycladic islanders.

For the mainland, however, the Cyclades were always a stepping stone over which from time to time the refreshing influences of other, more advanced, cultures were received. Perhaps the role of the Cyclades in the "awakening" of the Greek mainland of the end of the Middle Helladic Period was more important than is usually realized.

3. The amazing achievements in Crete in the period 1900-1700 B.C. and the sudden emergence of an advanced "urban" civilization there were due basically to the unbroken course of development on the island and partly to external factors. Old-Palace civilization was a natural development of the Pre-Palace Period under the influence of eastern cultures. But it would be a mistake to think of the Old-Palace civilization as substantially eastern in character. With the "urbanization" of life and a radical change

in the system of government, Crete naturally adopted some cultural elements long present in the East but until then unknown in the Aegean. But, in Crete, the concentration of power in the hands of kings seems to have been balanced by popular participation in the management of public affairs, while the conception of theocratic kingship was not predominant as in the East. There were no large temples, and no place for a powerful hierarchy of priests; the deity was worshipped in small shrines as a familiar, benevolent, almost a household figure. The Greek legend concerning the admirable state of law and order on Crete and the sense of justice of her rulers may not quite refer to this early period, but it seems certain that the Cretans of the Old-Palace Period were a free, independent people with a keen taste for the joys of living. Eastern currents underwent a process of refinement under the influence of the Mediterranean spirit, so that Cretan culture evolved in a Western rather than an Eastern direction. Thus, since Crete was ever a part of the Aegean world, when the moment came for the Helladic people to rouse themselves from their state of stagnation (probably after some equilibrum had been attained between the newly arrived Greek-speakers and the indigenous population), the influence of Minoan culture on the Greek mainland was so fruitful that, in art at least, there was a wholesale transplantation of the Minoan spirit. Without some latent affinity between the two cultures, this could not have occurred.

4. The appearance of the Hittites in Asia Minor after the 20th century B.C., at approximately the same period as the Middle Helladic took shape in Greece, is not the only historical event to be taken into account. Modern scholars hold the Indo-Europeans responsible for the destruction of the first city of Troy (c. 2800, at the earliest, or 2600-2500 B.C., at the latest). More important, they believe that it was Indo-European tribes, crossing from the Pontic steppes, that caused the widespread destructions which occurred between the second and third phases of the Early Bronze Age (c. 2300 B.C.). These destructions, which were accompanied by fires at many large centres (Troy II, Poliochne V, Beycesultan XIIIA, Kusura, Tarsos, Polatlı I, etc.), and the abandoning of others, are associated with the arrival of the Luvians in southwestern Asia Minor. Their arrival is thought to mark the beginning of a new cultural era in which newly arrived Indo-European tribes predominated on the Asia Minor peninsula and founded the kingdoms of the latter part of the second millennium B.C. After this break, there was no other abrupt change on the peninsula until the Late Bronze Age.

The details of the theories about these population movements need not be discussed here except in so far as they concern developments in Helladic Greece. According to some theories, the Greek-speaking newcomers who brought the "Minyan" pottery to Greece came "by sea" from Asia Minor; according to others, they were Luvians from Asia Minor, who invaded Greece (c. 1900 B.C.) and, later, Crete.

However, neither of these theories satisfactorily fit the facts. The first is completely implausible, as we shall see below, while the second, which has Luvians invading Crete at the beginning of the New-Palace Period, is totally untenable.

5. Cultural developments in the Early Bronze Age can throw little light on the problem of identifying the Indo-European tribes that began to filter into Greece from the

Early Bronze Age onwards. To begin with, the Indo-Europeans were a linguistic group, not a race. They spread throughout Greece in a series of migratory movements over a long period of time, which cannot be determined with any accuracy but which probably began before the end of the third millennium B.C. It is possible that Indo-European tribes came to Greece before the arrival of Greek speakers, (if indeed the latter settled in southern Greece c. 1900 B.C.). So far as we know at present, there was no widespread destruction in Greece similar to, or contemporary with, the one which caused the mass invasion of Asia Minor by such tribes c. 2300 B.C. It is by no means certain that the "violent destruction" which some excavators see around 2100 B.C. was a general phenomenon or one that could be associated with developments in Asia Minor or the Balkans. On the other hand, we cannot exclude the possibility that Indo-European tribes had already arrived in Macedonia and Thessaly from the North in the Early Bronze Age. There is no way of proving that Middle Helladic was Indo-European, while Early Helladic was non-Indo-European.

As for the break between Early and Middle Helladic, we have already seen that there was a similar upheaval in Asia Minor when the Hittites settled there a little before 1900 B.C., but there is no indication of any connection between these population movements and the "invasion" of southern Greece by the bearers of Middle Helladic culture.

6. We are chiefly concerned here with the problem of Middle Helladic origins. Summarizing the most widely-held view, John Caskey speaks of a new people who came to central Greece in the 20th century B.C. from the North or the East or from both directions. The origin of this people is a problem of paramount importance if we are properly to appreciate subsequent developments.

The theory that the Middle Helladic population or the Greeks along with Minyan pottery came to Greece "by sea" from northwestern Asia Minor cannot easily be accepted, first, because it links two unconnected elements (the Greeks and Minyan pottery), and, second, because it does not take into account the agricultural character of Middle Helladic Greece, though this was in fact its distinguishing characteristic. If the invaders came "by sea", they must have been experienced sailors and must have possessed a tremendously large fleet considering that they settled in Greece in such large numbers that their language eventually prevailed. They would also have been required to turn themselves overnight from sailors to farmers, to make up the bulk of the population, and to spread swiftly throughout the southern part of the Greek mainland. Such a large-scale sea operation would naturally be expected to affect the Cyclades as well, but there is no trace of it in the islands. As regards Minyan pottery, it should have normally appeared at Troy earlier than in Greece, but there is no evidence for this. On the contrary, excavations (at Lerna, Leukanti) have revealed the existence of very early, or rather primitive, "Minyan" pottery there. The evidence from Minyan pottery, therefore, is not in itself sufficient to show that Middle Helladic culture (and the Greeks) came originally from northwest Asia Minor.

Before examining the possibility that Middle Helladic culture was brought into Greece from the North, we must examine some other questions. The old theory that there was a radical difference between Early Helladic and Middle Helladic has now considerably weakened. Despite changes in burial customs, the general style of architecture can now be seen to have changed very little. Apsidal buildings have been found at several sites of the late Early Helladic phase, and there are even earlier ones in Thessaly. The "megaron" did not make its appearance during the Middle Helladic; it had a long earlier history both in the Helladic region and in the northern islands (Lemnos). Pottery was affected by many mutually opposed influences of various origins. The tradition represented by Minyan ware, for example, is completely different in technique from that represented by the matt-painted ware. So, we may assume a combination of different traditions, including perhaps tribal ones, rather than one new tradition unrelated to everything that had gone on before.

7. The Middle Helladic Period may be regarded as a local variant of the Helladic Middle Bronze Age, confined to the area in the eastern Greek mainland from the Vale of the Spercheios to Malea and Tainaron. This is almost exactly the area in which Early Helladic had evolved, and since it is difficult to imagine that the earlier inhabitants simply melted away before the advancing "invaders", we must assume that the older population made some contribution to the development of the new culture. What exactly this contribution was is not easy to determine.

Geographically, the narrow Middle Helladic region is directly in contact with a much wider hinterland which stretches away chiefly towards the North. It is here that we must now turn in our quest for Middle Helladic origins, since the North-East has been discounted, and the South-East is out of the question.

Leaving aside earlier attempts to trace the path of the "invaders" from the Danube region or from Central Europe, we shall confine ourselves to the more immediate area, Thessaly in particular. Recent excavations have shown that the pottery dating from the beginning of the Middle Bronze Age in the interior of Thessaly (Argissa) seems to be similar to the pottery from the same period in Boiotia (Eutresis). The similarity extends to other features, including tectonic style. However, Minyan pottery, which appeared in Boiotia towards the end of the Middle Bronze Age, is unknown in Thessaly. On the shores of the Pagasitic Gulf, on the other hand, (Iolkos, Neleia, etc.) Minyan ware appeared at an early date. In spite of the changes which mark the new (Middle Helladic) period, the continuation of Early Bronze Age, including some "Macedonian" influences, is clearly established at Argissa.

It seems reasonable to suppose, therefore, that Thessalian tribes, evidently under pressure from other more northerly tribes, descended southwards (Lianokladi) and finally reached Boiotia (Eutresis) and other more southerly sites in the 20th century B.C. This movement (Tsountas would have referred to it as "infiltration"), which may have taken place in successive stages, sometimes peacefully, sometimes not, resulted in the establishment in southern Greece of a large and compact agricultural population, which can in no way be associated with Minyan pottery (itself not a northern technique). This brought about a return to the closed economy which came to characterize the first phase of Middle Helladic. These mainland, agricultural, and backward tribes may have been not only Indo-European but also Greek-speaking. This mass descent of Greek-speakers does not preclude the possibility that there were other, less important, migratory movements from other directions, especially from the East.

Naturally, this is only a theory, but it does seem to fit the known facts. It also assigns Thessaly its traditional role as the cradle of Hellenism and as the area that nurtured Greek cosmogony and theogony. And indeed there could have been no better region to rear an emergent people than the fertile Thessalian plain.

A similar southward movement of backward Greek border tribes in the 12th century B.C. was to bring about the destruction of Mycenaean civilization and to plunge Greece into the Dark Ages.

8. The theory that Greeks or Greek-speakers were present in Greece in the Middle Helladic Period had found wide acceptance even before the decipherment of Linear B proved that the Mycenaean language was Greek. The chief arguments rested on the obviously Greek character of Mycenaean civilization and on the archaeological evidence of an uninterrupted development from Middle to Late Helladic. These arguments still remain sound, although it would be an anachronism to refer to the Middle Helladic population as "Greeks" in the sense that this term took on in historical times. They are, therefore, usually called Greek-speakers or Proto-Greeks.

However, this makes no substantial difference to the argument. It is clear that the Greeks cannot be identified with the Dorians. The Indo-Europeans swamped vast areas of Europe and the East, but nowhere else did they succeed in developing as advanced a civilization as in Greece. Without the cultural traditions of the Mediterranean, particularly the Minoan, and without the blending of antithetical elements and trends in the special melting-pot of the Aegean, Creto-Mycenaean civilization could never have come into being.

GREECE IN THE MIDDLE
BRONZE AGE (1900 – 1600 B.C.)

- Middle Helladic centres
- Middle Cycladic centres
- Old Palace (Minoan) centres
- Cypriot centres

Map of Greece in the Middle Bronze Age, which is the period of the Middle Helladic, Middle Cycladic, and Old-Palace Minoan civilizations. In Helladic Greece and the Cyclades, the Middle Bronze Age was a period of arrested development, while in Crete the Minoan civilization was beginning to flourish, to reach its peak in the Late Bronze Age.

THE PEAK OF MIN

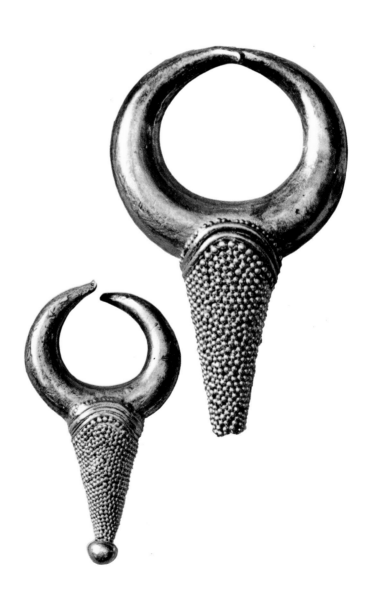

New-Palace Crete

THE NEW-PALACE MINOAN PERIOD

After the destruction of the Minoan centres on Crete around 1700 B.C., the whole civilization of the island was created anew in the following period. There is no evidence, however, of any substantial change at this time either in the composition of the population or in the character of the culture, and we may therefore reject the theories which attribute the destruction to foreign invasion. As has been shown above, the destruction was in fact due to some geological cause, probably an earthquake.

Immediately after the disaster, the native rulers set about the tremendous task of reconstruction, and their concerted efforts eventually brought about the renewal and reorganization of life and culture on the island. Their main effort was directed towards the rebuilding of the great palaces. These were the centres of the island's life and civilization, and it was these which had suffered the most extensive damage. The actual rebuilding must have taken some considerable time, perhaps as long as three decades, because the new palaces seem still to have been incomplete by the middle of the 17th century B.C. The economic life of the palace centres, however, was reorganized without delay; for smooth and efficient working in this sector was essential to a more general recovery. There was, too, a strong revival of religious life. Splendid palace sanctuaries were built, and a multitude of objects dedicated to the deity, the giver of protection and inspiration. Evans was right to emphasize the important influence of religion on every aspect of life in the new era.

From the wealth of material which has come to light in excavations, chiefly at the palace centres (wherever these can be clearly distinguished from later constructions), we can build up a relatively complete picture of the new civilization, though it is not always easy to distinguish its precise phases. There has been endless controversy concerning the dating of the various finds and the significance of the changes which took place during this period. Many scholars regard the distinctive character of this culture in its culminating phase as evidence that the changes that preceded it were both radical and abrupt. In particular, they point to new trends in the architecture of the palaces and other buildings and to important changes in the pottery styles. However, if we examine the initial stages of these developments, we shall see that, despite the innovations, there was no real break in the continuity of the civilization, and that all the main elements of the earlier tradition were retained. In pottery, decorative multi-coloured vases were eventually replaced by monochrome vases with naturalistic motifs, but the change came about by gradual stages and through a long process of experimentation. Changes in architecture and in the decoration of buildings were similarly gradual.

Since the palaces were repeatedly damaged by earthquakes, there were many opportunities to introduce modifications and improvements. We do not know precisely how many times the new palaces were damaged by earthquakes before their final destruction. Often there was but slight damage, and only minor repairs were necessary. On two occasions, however, the first c. 1600 B.C., the second c. 1500 B.C., there were major destructions with important historical consequences. The first coincided with the founding of the great Mycenaean centres, the second with the colonial expansion to the Eastern, and probably the Western, Mediterranean and the accompanying spread of Minoan civilization. There were important repercussions in Crete too, for the seat of power seems to have been shifted to Knosos at this period. Finally, there is no doubt that political and commercial relations with the more advanced countries of the East and Egypt must have been affected by the growth of the Mycenaean centres.

Three Brilliant Centuries

The New-Palace Period on Crete may be divided into three main phases: (1) 1700-1600 B.C., the period of renewal and reconstruction; (2) 1600-1500 B.C., the culminating period; and (3) 1500-1450 B.C., the period of expansion. Together these three phases make up the long Golden Age of Minoan civilization. This civilization was capable of exercising a powerful influence on the development of less advanced peoples, as is attested by the growth of Mycenaean civilization, and, at the same time, of penetrating and assimilating highly advanced cultures, such as that of the Cyclades. In the culminating period, there was a great flourishing in every sphere of Minoan life—political, social, economic, and artistic. The Minoans had developed mental and spiritual qualities which, combined with their material prosperity, enabled them to raise their civilization to a very high level. This was the culmination of a development which had been in progress throughout the earlier Pre-Palace and Old-Palace periods. The successive disasters that afflicted the island did not act as a brake on progress but rather as a spur to it, and the combination of internal peace and good political and cultural relations with the outside world produced a stable framework in which development could proceed without hindrance. From the very beginning of this development, the Minoans had been led by their general outlook on life to feel a strong sense of closeness between man and nature. Their lives were closely bound up with the natural world, and it was in the natural world that they felt the presence of divine powers. The naturalistic spirit reigned supreme, and life was organized that man might live, carefree and happy, in the embrace of sanctified nature.

Social organization had now reached a degree of perfection. The necessary equilibrium between the classes had been established, and there was lasting internal peace. The political organization, while retaining its theocratic base, had accomplished a real feat in establishing a proper legislative and judiciary system, which was to exert an important influence many centuries after the destruction of the palace centres which had created it. The Minoans extended their beneficial rule to the outside world; they controlled the surrounding seas and guarded the sea routes between Crete and neighbouring countries. The natural result was an increase in trade and political communication with the islands and coasts of the Eastern Mediterranean and, further afield, with the highly advanced countries of Egypt and the East. Minoan penetration, whether close to home or further afield, was always peaceful and beneficial. It was not confined simply to the establishment of trading stations, but took on the character of proper colonization. When the great Mycenaean centres were first founded, they no doubt made their contribution to Minoan prosperity; but, later, these same centres were to become the dangerous rivals and challengers of Minoan supremacy. In the meantime, great wealth was being amassed in the Cretan palace centres, and the island enjoyed a high degree of material prosperity, happily divorced in this case from the ills of decadence or abuse of power which often accompany it.

In the New-Palace Period, the architectural style of the buildings, especially the palaces, was not only eminently suited to the climate of the island but also perfectly fitted for the dual task of preserving man's contact with the natural world while at the same time catering to the manifold and complex needs of his highly developed life. Religious life flourished, but did not exert a tyrannical influence on other spheres of life. Despite the rapid development of towns, no corresponding decline occurred in the many smaller settlements. Indeed, the country districts became more prosperous now than ever before.

The sense of kinship with nature found clear expression in Minoan art. Not only did the artists draw inspiration from the animal and plant kingdom; they also brought the mysterious pulse of life which beat there into their own work by their skilful adaptation of decorative motifs to the various art forms: painting, carving, sculpture, metallurgy, and jewellery-making. The feeling of affection which had come to characterize man's attitude towards nature developed into a special sort of sensitivity, a leaning towards whatever was gentle in life, whatever was motive

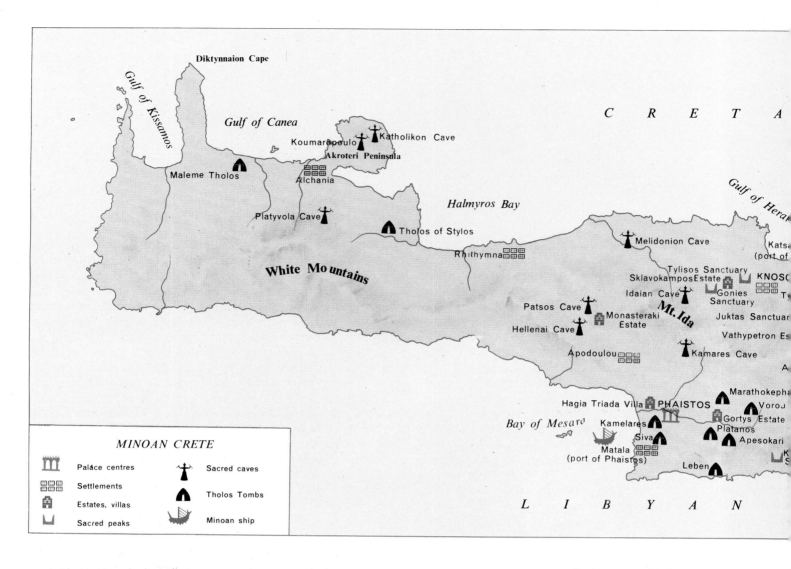

and flexible, varied and picturesque. In such a world, there was no sense of pressure, no nagging anxiety; there was simply a great outpouring of *joie de vivre* on every side. Art was basically religious in character, since the natural world from which it drew its inspiration was regarded as a divine gift. One of the chief purposes of art was to extol the sacred gift of nature, and motifs were often taken from religious ritual. A large proportion of the works of art were intended for use in religious ceremonies or as votive offerings at shrines.

Although religion and life were more closely bound up together in the Minoan civilization than in many others, overt religious coercion was almost entirely absent. Many scholars, misled by this, have failed to realize that religious expression was the chief function and purpose of Minoan art.

Even in the culminating period, Minoan Crete was influenced to a considerable extent by the advanced cultures of the East and Egypt, from which she had many valuable lessons to learn. Elements of foreign cultures were quickly assimilated, sometimes in a Minoanized form. But in her culminating phase, Crete herself exercised an important influence on the surrounding world, and elements of her culture were assimilated by many other peoples. Minoan works of art were in great demand and widely admired. It was generally recognized, too, that Crete was the leading sea power in the Eastern Mediterranean, and since her benevolent suzerainty was in the general interest, her supremacy

was accepted more with relief than resentment by the surrounding countries. By pursuing a foreign policy of "good neighbourliness" towards the rest of the world, Crete became recognized as one of the great powers of the age and won the respect and admiration of other big empires. In her immediate region of the Eastern Mediterranean, her dominance was almost absolute, but her penetration of neighbouring cultures was always both peaceful and beneficial and was, therefore, readily accepted and turned to advantage by less advanced peoples.

According to one theory, the great wealth accumulated on Crete at this period tempted the poorer inhabitants of Helladic Greece to make a surprise attack on Knosos, the chief Minoan centre. This resulted in an abrupt change which, according to this theory, eventually led to the creation of the great Mycenaean centres.

THE PALACE CENTRES

Although the earthquake of about 1700 B.C. caused serious and extensive damage on Crete, it could call no more than a temporary halt to development and progress.

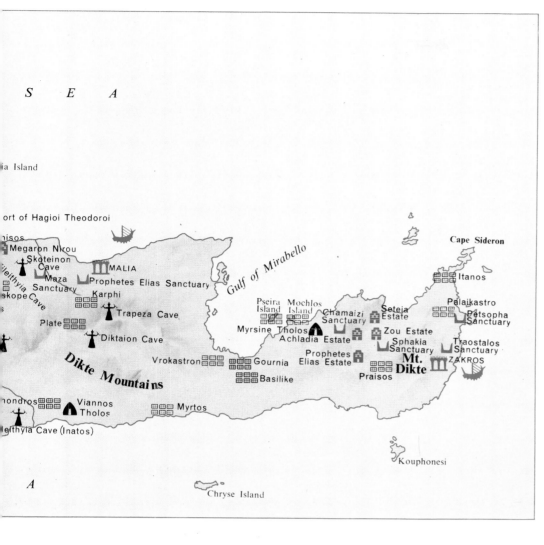

The map shows various sites across Crete including:

S E A

a Island

ort of Hagioi Theodoroi

nisos
Megaron Nirou
Skoteinon Cave
MALIA
eithyia Maza Sanctuary Prophetes Elias Sanctuary
skope Cave Sanctuary Karphi
Plate Trapeza Cave
Diktaion Cave
Dikte Mountains
Vrokastron Gournia Prophetes Elias Estate
Basilike
nondros Viannos Tholos Myrtos
eithyia Cave (Inatos)

Gulf of Mirabello

Pseira Mochlos Island Island Chamaizi Sanctuary
Myrsine Tholos Achladia Estate
Seteia Estate
Zou Estate
Sphakia Sanctuary
Mt. Dikte
Praisos

Cape Sideron
Itanos
Palaikastro
Petsopha Sanctuary
Traostalos Sanctuary
ZAKROS

Kouphonesi

A
Chryse Island

The golden age of Minoan civilization lasted for approximately three centuries, from 1700 to 1450 B.C. During this period, the peace and prosperity that prevailed in central and eastern Crete made it possible for large settlements to grow up around the palace centres. Marked on the map are the main sites on the island where excavations have unearthed remains of the first advanced civilization in Europe. These remains have enabled archaeologists to reconstruct the history of the New-Palace Period of Crete.

The palaces and sacred buildings were rebuilt swiftly and on an even grander scale. No effort was spared, no means neglected to achieve this end. The architects were able to draw on the immense experience gained in the Old-Palace Period and, at the same time, to introduce whatever modifications seemed appropriate to meet changing conditions, both actual and potential. An examination of the remains leaves us in no doubt that the new palaces were built according to a properly worked out plan designed to serve preconceived purposes, and today we still marvel at the thorough and excellent manner of its execution.

The new palace at Knosos was bigger and grander than anything which had been built before. It covered an area of 22,000 square metres, compared with 900 square metres for the palaces of Phaistos and Malia and 7000-8000 square metres for Zakros. The palace of Knosos had also more storeys—three on the west side, four, or perhaps five, in the eastern section containing the royal apartments. On the most modest estimate, the number of rooms exceeded 1500. These included the living quarters of members of the court, official reception rooms, store-rooms, workshops, and auxiliary spaces, like staircases and corridors. So cunning and complex was the overall design that the "labyrinth of Knosos" became a legend in later times. It was indeed easy to lose one's way in that maze of rooms and corridors. The meaning of the name *labyrinth* given to the palace at Knosos was explained, long before any excavations took place, by philologists like P. Kretschmer. It was the place of the

labrys, the double axe. However, it was not until after the excavations that the connection between palace and labyrinth was properly understood. It was seen, then, that the palace was indeed the "House of the Double Axes", the chief sanctuary of the Minoan deity, and its connection with the mythical labyrinth became clear.

All the new palaces were built on the same basic plan: the buildings were grouped around a central court that communicated with all the surrounding sections. From the court, the buildings were extended outwards on every side, but the main axis ran from north to south, leaving two wings, on the western and eastern sides. The anisometric arrangement of the various quarters explains why the façade, especially on the western side of the palace, is broken up into an irregular series of projections. Nothing could have been better calculated to appeal to the Minoan taste for the picturesque than this touch of variety in the palace architecture. The uneven façades produced a pleasing alternation of light and shadow on the colourful surfaces of the whole, and further variety was added by the use of timber ties in the construction of the walls. Smaller projections and recesses in the façades mark the position of the large double windows, through which light from the western court entered the upper storeys. The various sections of the wings seem to have been of unequal height, and this must have added to the overall effect of variety presented by the façades.

The central and western courts both had important functions. The central court acted as a lung to the densely packed buildings in the main body of the palace. It provided ventilation for the large apartments and easy communication with all the various sections of the wings. The western court served as the chief approach to the palace. Both courts were filled with people on feast days and holidays. Most of the festivals were evidently religious in character, since altars, sacrificial pits, sacred deposits, and sacred symbols have been found in the courts.

On every side, passages and porches led off to the various sections of the palace; their entrances were given whatever shape and position were appropriate to their importance and function. The various apartments were arranged on a similar principle, but their distribution differed from palace to palace. Only the sacred area occupied the same position in all the palaces. It was always placed in the west wing, no doubt for some special religious reason. Special care was taken to ensure that the royal apartments were located in the best possible position from the point of view of ventilation, view, and easy communication. Store-room systems were built wherever they were most convenient: the sanctuary store-room close to the sacred area, the palace magazines close to the workshops, the equipment stores close to the service area.

In spite of these similarities, each palace had a distinctive character and must be considered separately if its role in the life of Minoan Crete is to be properly understood.

THE PALACE OF KNOSOS
The New Palace Complex

We owe our knowledge and understanding of the huge and complex palace at Knosos chiefly to the tremendous work of excavation, interpretation, and restoration carried out by Arthur Evans. Unfortunately, some of Evans's theories have led to misconceptions which still confuse the study of prehistoric Crete.

Evans has been criticized chiefly for his bold reconstruction of whole sections of the palace at Knosos with the aid of reinforced concrete and for his restoration of entire upper storeys, timber sections, and fresco decoration. While some restoration was necessary in order to preserve the palace, it must be admitted that Evans overdid it. At the other palaces, the excavators avoided large scale reconstruction and confined themselves to the necessary work of consolidation and preservation.

At the palace of Knosos, the gently sloping ramp which formed the chief approach to the western court was not much altered. The paved surface at the court was repaired, and one section of it renewed. The old circular "kouloures" (deposit pits) had fallen into disuse; only one was kept open for a while in the first phase of the New-Palace Period.

The hill of Knosos and the remains of the Minoan palace. Spread around the palace-complex, which lies four kilometres away from the sea, was an unfortified town large enough to hold 80,000 inhabitants. Together with the inhabitants of the port area, the total population must have exceeded 100,000. This was the largest town on the European continent at this period. The picture shows the central court of the palace and the two reconstructed wings, on the west and east sides.

The raised walks or causeways built of rectangular flags had been preserved and, by dint of a little alteration, they were now linked up with the new southwest porch and the space known as the theatral area. The latter was created by building a second flight of steps at right angles to the original wide stairway leading to the north royal road, so that an enclosed rectangular space was formed. Evans called this the Theatre of Knosos, and though this term may be misleading, there are indications that suggest that it was in this area that the Court and the royal guests congregated to watch various spectacles, probably of a religious nature. The massive square structure (*podium*), arranged like an open room at the juncture of the two sets of steps, may have been the royal box. In its foundations and beyond the steps of the first staircase, two deposits were found. Both contained bell-shaped sacred objects dating from the Old-Palace Period, a fact which suggests that this area had long been regarded as sacred. Further evidence for this was provided by the discovery, close to the theatral area, of a partly preserved huge pair of horns made of gypsum. There is a similar theatral area dating from the Old-Palace Period at the palace of Phaistos. Evans was probably right, therefore, in thinking that these were primitive theatres, and it is certainly tempting to believe his theory that the theatral area at Knosos was the dancing place that Daidalos built for fairtressed Ariadne.

Religious rituals were evidently performed in the western court too, for the bases of two sacrificial stepped altars have been unearthed there. One lies not far from the theatral area, the second close to the façade of the new palace. This had been built further back than the original façade, and perhaps its purpose was to demonstrate the sanctity of the newly released court space. The western façade of the palace rested on a base built of a double row of huge gypsum *orthostatai* (flagstones standing upright). The space between the two facings was filled with a rubble core, and the structure was strengthened by placing crossbars of wood between the stone blocks. From the sherds found among the filling material, we can tell that the façade was built shortly after 1700 B.C.

The four entrances to the palace were each of a different plan. The official entrance was the west porch, a sort of propylon of an antichamber with one column between two enormous doorjambs, opening into the west court. This led into a long corridor which ran first southwards, then eastwards round the propylaia and along the length of the southern veranda, and finally turned northwards into the central court. After each destruction, this whole section was rebuilt on a more grandiose scale than before; the porch was widened and deepened, the corridor was enlarged, and the whole was adorned with even more splendid mural decoration. In the last phase, the corridor was decorated with a long fresco of a procession ascending towards the propylaia. The propylaia eventually developed into a monumental structure which may be regarded as the prototype of the propylaia of Mycenaean and Classical times. Two propyla, each with two columns, protected either side of the central gate.

The northern gate led out onto the harbour road. Goods arriving by sea were brought from the harbour to this gate to be checked and distributed to the appropriate storerooms. Evans called this area the Customs House, and it is abundantly clear that it was a control post of some kind.

Beyond the entrance with its specially constructed double door and guard posts, was a room with large square piers where goods could be temporarily deposited. An upward sloping entrance passage, which ran between a double row of small towers, all topped by balconies with beautiful fresco decoration, led to the central court. The third gate, at the eastern end of the south portico, was very simply constructed and was evidently a service entrance. It gave easy access to the south wing and the southeast section of the palace and, by a staircase, to the central court. Another entrance of monumental proportions, at the southwestern end of the southern portico, ceased to be in use after the end of the first phase of the New-Palace Period, when an earthquake destroyed the winding stepped portico which led from the road bridge to the southwest corner of the palace. The fourth surviving entrance to the palace was the small "side-door" on the eastern side, where a small staircase ran down the interior wall of the East Bastion. This entrance led out towards the River Kairatos and the royal gardens where the royal villa was situated.

The Sanctuary of the Deity

From the arrangement of the west wing, it is clear that the sanctuary and its auxiliary apartments were the main elements of the palace. This shows that the political organization at Knosos still retained the theocratic basis which had been so evident in the Old-Palace Period. The sanctuary stood in the centre of the west wing, facing the central court. Its pillared façade was divided into three parts; the middle one, higher than the other two, was crowned with pairs of horns. Only the base of the façade remains today, but its original appearance is known to us from palace frescoes. The sanctuary comprised the priests' vestibule; pillar crypts with engravings of sacred axes on the pillars and special arrangements for the reception of votive offerings; the three-columned sanctuary of the divinity on the upper floor, above the pillar crypts; the archive rooms; the temple repositories, which contained valuable ritual vessels and cult objects stored carefully away in special containers and fine faience figurines of the various deities; the "sacristy", where there were shallow basins used in preparations for the sacrificial ceremony; and the long row of 21 magazines, linked by a corridor. The latter were equipped with special underground cists and vats to hold various offerings and contained rows of jars in which produce of every kind was stored, for the Minoans offered their deity the first fruits of each harvest. The upper storeys of the sanctuary were reached by the wide stairway of the propylaia, which was enclosed by columned wings, and the central staircase which led directly to the sanctuary rooms from the central court. These rooms stretched northwards beyond the staircase, but we can see them now only in the form they finally took in the last phase of the New-Palace Period. They centred then around the throne room, which was easily reached from the central court through a multi-doored vestibule. Benches ran along the length of the walls and flanked the throne of the priest-king. They were evidently intended for the members of the priesthood who took part

Top: the 'Royal Road' on the northern side of the palace of Knosos leading to the stepped stand of the 'theatre'. Originally, this road linked the small palace, which lay to the west, with the northern gate of the main palace. The paved section in the centre of the road was used for ceremonial processions and visits by official personages.

Below: looking south from the large propylaia at the palace of Knosos; the sacred horns standing on a special socle decorated an opening in the wall of the processional corridor, which led along the length of the southern side of the building and into the central court.

181

in the sacred rituals. The same room contained a columned lustral basin with a staircase leading down to an inner area. No doubt this basin was connected with some aspect of religious ritual. The sacred throne, a gypsum imitation of a wooden throne, was flanked by painted representations of sacred griffins: supernatural creatures with the body of a lion, the head of an eagle, and a snake-like tail. Beyond the throne room, there was another smaller room with a high ledge, which evidently held figurines and cult objects. Other small interior rooms, used for various ritual purposes, contained altars of various types and other special features.

It is difficult to form any proper idea of the large ceremonial rooms that lay above the group of magazines on the western side. Evans was probably correct in thinking that they comprised a row of square rooms, each with two interior columns to support the roof, and one larger room divided into three sections by two rows of three columns apiece. There was another large ritual chamber above the rooms of the northwest section. That all these formed part of the sanctuary is shown by their fresco decoration which portrays exclusively religious subjects: libation scenes, the three-columned sanctuary, the sacred grove, and so on. A large exterior staircase, splendidly decorated with stone friezes in relief led up to these magnificent rooms directly

from the western court.

The complex group of rooms which made up the sanctuary covered the entire western wing of the palace and had a separate entrance close to the harbour gate. The reason for the building of a special entrance so close to the monumental northern gate becomes clear when we remember that the sanctuary was regarded as a separate entity of a closed character within the palace. This accounts, too, for the unusual construction of the sanctuary entrance. Next to the door and the two-columned porch, was an open-air enclosure containing a lustral basin similar to the one in the throne room. Evans called this open space the initiatory area and proposed the theory that the lustral basin was used for the purification of the votaries who wished to enter the sanctuary.

The Throne Room and the Royal Apartments

If the west wing was the seat of the king's religious authority, the east wing was the seat of his political power. The large and imposing throne room, known as the Great East Hall, lay exactly at the centre of the east wing and

The northern gate of the palace of Knosos seen from the northeast. The harbour road terminated at this gate, where goods which had been imported by sea were brought in. That this entrance was a control post is shown by its peculiar construction—there *were double gates, guard posts, and a room where goods could be stored temporarily. The picture also shows the hypostyle room and the 'bastion' topped by a veranda with a fresco relief of a bull.*

was reached by a wide staircase, which led up from the central court to a pillared landing. Few remains of this hall survived, but Evans succeeded in restoring a plan of its main elements and in persuading his fellow scholars to accept his view of its general arrangement: from the pillared landing, which also acted as a vestibule, tall doors led into the main hall, which had a central peristyle supporting a kind of light-well with side openings resting on the columns of the peristyle. The splendid relief decoration from the walls of this hall (sections of it were found lying in the rooms below) showed griffins tied antithetically to finely-wrought columns and also various athletic scenes.

The royal apartments were built four or five storeys high in order that they might have an uninterrupted view over the lush valley below, and, to this end, a deep section was cut in the hillside at the confluence of the Kairatos River and its tributary, the modern Vlychia Stream. Access to the royal apartments was by the impressive Grand Staircase from the central court to the upper storeys past a series of verandas with beautiful fresco decoration. The staircase received its light from a vertical central light-well, from which light was shed sideways into each storey. Guard posts on each level controlled the entrances to the apartments, the royal store-rooms, and the royal workshops. The fresco decoration in this section appropriately showed figure-of-eight shields hanging on the wall.

The royal apartments were admirably designed. In each storey, the king occupied a suite of spacious rooms, each consisting of two sections linked by a polythyron, a series of doors which served as a partition. Each apartment could, therefore, be easily converted into two smaller rooms. A vertical light-well, separated from one room by a line of columns and from the other by an outside portico (in the upper storeys the porticoes became pillared verandas) ensured adequate ventilation and direct contact with the open air. This ingenious system, which was eminently suitable for the semi-tropical climate of Crete both in winter and summer, was employed in the construction not only of palaces but also of more humble buildings. The apartments of the queen and the princesses were similarly arranged, though they were slightly smaller and more isolated. They were linked to the king's rooms by small winding passages and to the upper storeys by a private staircase. The subjects of the fresco decoration here were specially chosen to appeal to women's tastes: dancing girls whirling in the openings of partition windows or a seascape with dolphins and other fish. From the queen's megaron a porticoed entrance led into the queen's bathroom. The clay bathtub, which was discovered lying in pieces in the area outside the bathroom, has been reassembled and replaced in its original position. Another passage, dark enough to need artificial lighting by lamps, led to the queen's specially constructed dressing room, which received water from a cistern built behind the wall; a small dais for toilet articles and a closet with running water completed the arrangement. The room was lighted by a small interior light-well, called the Court of the Distaffs because of certain masons' marks found on the walls. Also in this section were the royal archive room on the ground floor and the treasury on the upper floor, reached from the same encircling passage.

It is clear, even from the surviving remains of these two lower storeys, that the royal apartments comprised a whole maze of rooms and passages, and yet they formed only a small part of the eastern wing of the palace. There was a host of other buildings: the rooms which made up the various parts of the royal chapel, the workshops, and the magazines. The chapel, in which the king and his family offered their own private worship to the deity, was similar to the other sanctuaries and contained the usual lustral basin, repository for ritual vessels, etc.

The Royal Workshops

From the Old-Palace Period onwards the palaces administered and controlled the productive and commercial life of the surrounding regions. The new palace at Knosos incorporated a whole section in the northeast corner that was entirely given over to this purpose. Workshops producing many different types of goods were distributed on various levels and linked by a stairway to the main approach passage to the royal apartments, so that the king himself could easily direct and supervise production. When the stone-cutter's workshop was unearthed, it was found to contain various types of stone, chiefly Spartan polychrome basalt. Half-finished stone utensils and abandoned tools were mute witnesses of the sudden catastrophe which had overtaken the palace. Next door was the potter's workshop, where mortars and enormous amounts of clay were found heaped up close to basins. A workshop of the seal-engraver lay in the southern part of this section close to the end of the long processional corridor at the point where it led into the central court. It was at this point that the priest-king fresco, known as the Prince of the Lilies, was found. A furnace with a special system of air conduction to keep the fire blazing was found just outside the palace, close to the southeastern house.

On the ground floor of the palace, below the Great East Hall, lay the royal magazines. They contained many large pithoi decorated with medallions with white rosettes, as well as special types of cooking utensils. These magazines, which were in use only in the early phases, succeeded the Old-Palace store-rooms with the giant pithoi. Another group of magazines, more to the north, served the staff quarters. Little is left of this section because it was quarried for stone by the Venetians when they built the walls of the Megalo Kastro, the Herakleion of today. The one building that has escaped destruction seems to have been an enclosure for small domestic animals.

The Decoration of the Palace

The palace of Knosos was splendidly decorated, both within and without. From certain fresco representations of the buildings, it is clear that the outer façade of the palace must have presented a striking effect of varied colour. The timber sections were covered with decoration; cornices were filled with discs in various colours intended to represent

Reconstruction of the south approach to the palace of Knosos. To reach the south gate, visitors crossed a viaduct and ascended the steps of a winding porticoed passage. The portico was ornamented with a large number of Minoan columns and terminated at the south gate. (Drawing by Thomas Phanourakis)

the ends of the wooden beams of the original roof; many of the façades were crowned with sacred double horns, and this added to the picturesque effect of the whole. In the interior of the palace, the floors and walls were covered with slabs of gypsum, its crystalline whiteness producing an impression of great splendour. To give some variety to the colour of the corridor floors, the edges of the gypsum slabs were framed with a line of green schist stone held in place by red plaster. The large halls of the palace were a-dorned with frescoes both decorative and representational, sometimes arranged in friezes round the walls, sometimes in large frames covering the whole wall surface. On the of-ficial entrance doors, friezes and jambs were of variously coloured stones and bore relief decoration of rosettes, run-ning spirals, etc. The ceilings, too, in many rooms were covered with fresco decoration in endlessly intertwining pat-terns.

Life in the Palace

From this general description of the lay-out and con-struction of the palace of Knosos, we can form some idea not only of the appearance but also of the life of the palaces in the New-Palace Period. But in order fully to understand the function of the new palaces, we must supplement the evidence of the remains with whatever other material we are able to gather about Minoan life, even though such material is not easy either to collect or to interpret.

It is clear that the palace at Knosos was an extremely busy centre. There was constant movement of traffic along the paved roads from the harbour to the north entrance and from the south to the stepped porticoes and ramps that led to the western court. Goods arriving by sea were brought to the north entrance and placed initially in the hall with the massive square piers (called the Customs House by Evans). Here they were recorded on clay tablets by palace scribes and sorted for distribution to the appropriate maga-zines. The royal guard controlled entrance to the palace, and the double north door contained two guard posts. Those who wished to enter the sanctuary in the west wing had to pass through a separate door and to submit to a special purification ceremony. Offerings to the deity—figurines, artistic goods, or produce of various kinds—were all handed to the temple superintendents. Detailed records of these offerings were drawn up and kept for a while in special boxes in various sections of the archives before being finally hand-ed over to the palace magazines for safe storage. The magazine keepers had developed special methods for storing valu-able objects. Sometimes they concealed them in pits be-neath removable flags in the floor, sometimes in hidden recesses behind the wall facings. Other goods, such as wine, oil, corn, pulse, and herbs, were stored in jars. The door of the magazine keepers' room was fitted with stout bolts on the inside.

Although it is difficult to form a clear idea of the rituals that took place in the pillar crypts with the sacred symbols, it seems certain that the chief part of the ceremony was the offering of both sanguinary and bloodless sacrifices. Pre-liminary preparations for the ritual were carried out in the various auxiliary rooms which contained special tables of offering, basins, and various utensils. The priests and priestess-es wore a special garment, usually an animal skin which covered the lower part of the body. Presumably, mysteries included a ceremony of holy communion in which special chalices were used. Blood from the sacrificed bull was dripped into these chalices through a rhyton shaped like the head of a sacred animal, usually a bull or a lion. Very few persons were present at these ceremonies, perhaps only the royal household and its immediate circle. One of the most important ceremonies took place in the red-painted throne room of the sanctuary in the presence of the king, in his capacity as high priest, and of the whole council of his priests and priestesses. The lustral basin in this room was used in the necessary purification ceremony, and the ritual included anointing with sacred oil. Cult figurines were placed on the sacred ledge at the back of the room, and ritual vessels—libation rhyta, sacred cups, alabastra for holding oil, ceremonial jugs, etc.,—were taken from their underground storage places in the temple treasuries. The details of the ceremony are obscure. Did the priest-king wear a bull mask during the ritual or did the priestess-queen play the most important role? Was the throne room used as a court room where supreme justice was dispensed in the name of the deity from whom the divine laws emanated? It is, alas, unlikely

that these questions will ever be answered.

On the days when religious ceremonies took place, crowds of people flocked to the two main courts of the palace. A festival was regarded as an important social occasion, and the ladies of the court, colourfully and elegantly dressed and coiffured appeared on every balcony and veranda, anxious "to see and to be seen". The theatre filled up with royal guests, and finally the royal family, amidst the acclamations of the people, took their places in the royal box. The sacred procession followed the Royal Road, which linked the small and large palaces, passed the theatral area, and approached the west gate along a special paved causeway. From there it proceeded along the Corridor of the Procession as far as the propylaia. Then, the main section of the procession ascended the steps of the propylaia to the three-columned shrine. Here the sacred *peplos* and the various votive offerings were dedicated to the divinity, prayers were offered, and thanksgiving hymns sung. The three-columned shrine was evidently open to all-comers, even envoys from other lands who came to pay honorary tribute to the Minoan deity, for many objects of Eastern and Egyptian origin were dedicated there. The propylaia

Reconstructional drawing of the west wing of the palace of Knosos overlooking the central court. In the centre of the columned two-storey façade was the tripartite sanctuary, each wing of which was crowned with horns of consecration. The staircase on

the right led to the upper storey, where the ceremonial rooms were situated. Today, only a few traces of the grandiose façade of the palace survive, but its appearance is known from frescoes, which formed the basis of this drawing by Thomas Phanourakis.

In the culminating period of Minoan Crete, grave architecture acquired a monumental character, and imposing tholos tombs of hewn stones were constructed. The 'temple-tomb' shown above has been found to the south of the palace of Knosos. The paved entrance led into a sort of interior court, beyond which was a hypostyle cult crypt. The grave chamber had been cut deep into the rock close to the crypt, and its roof was supported by a square pillar.

served as the official reception area for important visitors, native or foreign, to the Minoan court. The spacious rooms on the upper floor of the west wing with their splendid fresco decoration of religious themes, their valuable utensils, and large flower vases, were evidently used for ceremonies attended not only by the court but also by many other official guests at the palace.

The Great East Hall in the east wing was spacious, exceptionally well lighted by an interior peristyle, and splendidly decorated with fresco reliefs. On the assumption that political authority was separated from religion, this throne room was evidently the seat of the king's political power, and yet even here the fresco decoration had a markedly religious character. The royal apartments, too, contained private shrines and all the usual auxiliary rooms with tables of offering, lustral basins, repositories, treasuries, and priests' rooms.

Passing through the restored sections of the grand staircase and the royal apartments with their light-wells, polythyra, and porticoes, we can sense, even today, the atmosphere in the Minoan Court, the life of which is so vividly represented on Minoan frescoes, seal-stones, seal impressions, and gold rings. We can picture the svelte and lively court ladies attired in colourful dresses, designed to leave the bosom bare, and the slender men in their light kilts mounting and descending the staircases, passing through the dim passageways, assembling in the spacious halls, emerging onto the balconies and verandas of the upper storeys to breathe the fresh air and to relax during the cool evening hours, or strolling through the royal gardens that surrounded the palace in a series of terraces. The members of the royal family—men, women, and children alike—were accorded all the privileges due to personages of royal blood and, doubtless, of divine lineage. They lived a pleasant, comfortable, carefree, and peaceful life, sometimes gathering together in the communal rooms, sometimes retiring each to his own apartments. These apartments, distributed over several floors, were exceptionally well designed and appointed, and blended harmoniously with the surrounding landscapes. They were decorated with frescoes in beautiful colours and adorned with works of art of all kinds. The living quarters were conveniently close to the auxiliary rooms: bathrooms, toilet rooms, recreation rooms, etc. The king and his household evidently amused themselves by playing draughts, for a draughtboard was found in a corridor close to one of the verandas.

In order that the palace staff might perform their duties efficiently and without too much intrusion into the private life of the royal family, a special service staircase was constructed, and the staff quarters were built close to the royal apartments but in a separate block. The dense system of passages and stairways linking the two areas suggests that the palace staff must have been exceptionally numerous.

The artists and craftsmen employed by the palace were housed in special workshops, not far from the royal apartments, so that the king could exercise personal supervision over production. He was on the spot to issue instructions and to give encouragement. However, trade secrets were jealously kept by craftsmen. The legends about Daidalos and his refusal to confide the secrets of his art even to Minos echo the relatively independent status of the craftsmen who worked under the auspices of the palace.

We should like to have much more information about the various practical aspects of daily life in the palace: the preparation of food, the keeping of domestic animals, the making and washing of clothes, the cultivation of the decorative plants that filled the gardens and the flower vases. Unfortunately, the theories which Evans has put forward about such matters are rather the product of a vivid imagination than of sober appraisal of the archaeological evidence. There can be no doubt, however, that the life in the palace of Knosos, in that labyrinth of fifteen hundred rooms, was sophisticated and varied, and yet at the same time closely bound up with the simplicity and freedom of the natural world.

THE PALACE OF PHAISTOS

To complete our picture of Minoan life in the New-Palace Period, we must examine certain unusual features of the smaller palaces, especially where these illustrate aspects of palace life which are not observable at Knosos.

At the palace of Phaistos, a substantial part of the reconstruction work was the raising of the level of the west wing and the western court, which stretched in front of it. A firm ground surface in this section was obtained by covering over the remains of the old palace with a thick layer of concrete. The court itself was enlarged by moving the western face of the new building eastward about seven metres. The overall result was a more splendid approach to the palace and a better link between the successive levels of the hillside. The broad steps in the western court —the theatral area— and two splendid staircases formed part of the magnificent approach through a very high double doorway to the chief hall of the propylaia, which was probably used as a throne room. Twin doors opened into a wide passage which led directly to the central court, in which the flagstones, like those in the central court at Knosos, were arranged in the early phase of the New-Palace Period in an irregular rectangular pattern. The splendour of the interiors of the halls and corridors was due not so much to the fresco decoration, which was relatively meagre at Phaistos, as to the facing of the floors and walls with slabs of fine-grained gleaming white gypsum. The palace at Phaistos

might aptly be called the "White House".

Here, too, the sanctuary was built in the west wing. It seems to have incorporated the group of western magazines that lay immediately to the north of the entrance passage. The magazines were arranged on either side of a central corridor. One of them contained a special system for collecting liquids, perhaps oil; the liquid was poured out of pithoi into special containers sunk into the ground. (An improved and enlarged version of this system was in use both at Malia and Zakros.) Pillared crypts and lustral basins close to the main rooms of the sanctuary contained ledges, on which figurines and cult objects were placed. As at Knosos, there were spacious ceremonial rooms on the upper storey of the west wing, but we have no clear idea of their arrangement or appearance.

From the central court, a splendid entrance way, flanked by half-columns and recesses in the walls serving as guard posts, opened into a corridor and a gently sloping passageway which led up past an interior court to the royal apartments. These were similar in most respects to the royal apartments at Knosos, though here they were located at the edge of the north wing of the palace, so that their porticoes and verandas would look across to the peaks of Mount Ida. The sacred Kamares cave, below one of these peaks, was visible from the palace. The bathroom was specially constructed so that attendants could shower the bathers with water from above. Immediately to the west of the royal apartments and on a higher level was a large reception room with the same polythyron (pier-and-door) system employed at Knosos. It was lighted by an ante-room with an interior peristyle and had a paved floor of rhomboid slabs. In the east wing, there was another group of apartments, smaller and less luxurious, for the use of the princes. From the first New-Palace phase some remains have survived of beautiful hypostyle halls with alternating columns and pillars. Many of these elements were incorporated in the walls of rooms built in later phases. However, one whole section has been discovered which was in use only in the first New-Palace phase and which was later covered by an embankment of earth, and it is, therefore, possible to form some idea of the early New-Palace buildings. The famous Phaistos disk with its hieroglyphic inscription was found in one of the deposits in this group of buildings.

The workshops were centered around a court on the eastern edge of the palace. Very little has survived of their contents, and it is, therefore difficult to determine their precise use in most cases. In the centre of the court, however, one horse-shoe shaped building has been unearthed which contained layers of molten metal. It was evidently some type of furnace for smelting copper ore, and so furnishes evidence for metallurgy within the palace.

THE PALACE OF MALIA

In comparison with the palaces at Knosos and Phaistos, the palace of Malia must have seemed decidedly provincial. It was built of inferior materials, all of local origin, with the exception of the ironstone which was used chiefly for thresholds. Only in extent did it rival the palace at Phaistos. It has now been established that the remains that have been preserved date from the New-Palace Period, and we can, therefore, form a fairly clear picture of the new palace centre at Malia with its distinctly local character. The outer façades and the more important interior walls were constructed of huge ashlar of hewn sandstone. A coloured coat of plaster on the walls and, occasionally, on the floors was substituted for the splendid wall facings and floor coverings used in the other palaces. Gypsum was almost entirely absent, and the door jambs were, therefore, often made of wood and sunk deep into the floors. This made it difficult to recognize the pier-and-door system used in the royal apartments in the north section of the palace. A further difficulty facing

the first excavators was that even the ground floor rooms had been largely built of mud bricks and, when these were baked in the conflagration which destroyed the palace, they were formed into a series of unusually solid strata. The sanctuary was sited in the west wing and contained the usual pillar crypts, priests' rooms, and groups of magazines flanking a long corridor. The position occupied by the throne room at Knosos was here taken up by a small elevated room, a sort of loggia, linked by a staircase to the central court. The throne stood in the centre of the back wall, in front of a columned balustrade through which one could enter the room which contained various symbols of power: a sceptre-head in the form of a hatchet at one end and a panther at the other and a ceremonial sword with a crystal pommel

and ivory hilt. Wide staircases led up from the central court to the upper storeys; the steps of the widest of them could have been used as seats for onlookers when spectacles were held in the central court. On this staircase was a niche with a specially built bench where a circular *kernos* was discovered. This vessel, which was used for multiple offerings of cereals and fruit to the deity, had 34 small hollows round the rim and a larger hollow in the centre to hold oil. So, in the palace of Malia, as in all the other palaces, the sanctuary area occupied almost the whole of the west wing. The royal magazines in the eastern section offered the best example of a liquid storage system. Royal treasuries were found at various points; one which had particularly thick walls was named "the Dungeon" by the excavators. One apartment of the palace was set aside for official banquets. The porticoed banqueting room lay on the upper storey, and there was an auxiliary room with pillars underneath. A special service staircase linked the kitchens with the upper storeys. Apart from the central court, there were other large interior courts distributed between the various auxiliary rooms, workshops, and store-rooms. One of these, with a porticoed stoa along two sides, was linked up with the northern gate. This was the main entrance to the palace, directly connected with the wide and beautiful paved road leading to the harbour. The southern entrance was in the form of a double porch with a long covered paved passage, which acted as a guard room. From the eastern entrance, paved roads led off to various parts of the city.

Masterly frescoes showing religious subjects decorated the rooms of the palace at Knosos. Facing page, left: fragment from the 'libation offerings' fresco showing a priestess, the famous 'La Parisienne' of Knosos. Facing page, right: the rhyton-bearer, a fragment from a fresco showing a religious procession, from Knosos (1500-1450 B.C.). This page: dancing girl, a fragment from a fresco in the queen's apartments. (Herakleion Museum)

189

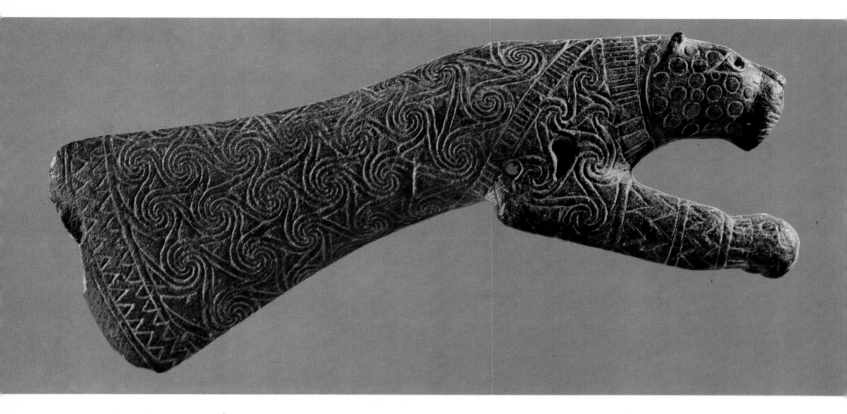

In the palace at Malia, the sacred throne room lay in front of a columned balustrade. Its nature was indicated by the discovery of various emblems of royal authority in the adjacent room. Among these was a royal sceptre-head (above) made of schist stones, and terminating in the figure of a panther and an axe. It dates from the 17th century B.C. (Herakleion Museum)

THE PALACE OF ZAKROS

The presence of three palace centres in the chief regions of central Crete suggested that there should be at least one palace centre in the eastern part of the island. The most likely sites were the fertile valleys of the Praisos River or one of the protected gulfs of the eastern coast, from which there would be swift and direct communication with Egypt and the East. Knosos would certainly have favoured the building of a palace on this coast, since it would provide a conveniently located base from which to exercise her control of the seas. These arguments were strong enough to encourage a search for a fourth in the eastern part of the island, and this was eventually discovered on the gulf of Kato Zakros, opposite the shores of the Syro-Phoenician region, Cyprus, and the Nile Delta. It is the only Creto-Mycenaean palace which is being excavated by Greek archaeologists. Its position, in a narrow valley between two hills, was revealed by the presence in that area of large amounts of hewn porous stone and great piles of stones, from which one properly constructed corner projected. Excavations revealed that this palace was the only one which was left substantially unpillaged and undisturbed after its final and sudden destruction. Compared with the other palaces, Zakros was small in extent, not more than 8000 square metres, including the annexes (the central court was but a third of the size of the one at Knosos); but as a whole, it presented a particularly pleasing appearance. Certain special features in the construction took account of local conditions and the particular purpose for which this palace was built.

The plan was in general the same as that of the other palaces with some slight differences in the distribution of the rooms. The sanctuary occupied the west wing, the royal apartments the east, the service quarters the north, and the workshops the south. The sanctuary included a shrine with a bench and a ledge in a recess to hold figurines; a lustral basin; a treasury containing wonderfully wrought ritual vessels and cult objects which the excavators discovered intact in specially made cists; archives containing Linear A tablets carefully "filed" in cupboards; a large ceremonial room (with a polythyron, a light-well, and an interior colonnade); a banqueting room in which wine amphorae and *oinochoai* have been found in various recesses or cupboards; a room beautifully decorated with a frieze of relief spirals immediately below the roof; and finally a multiple system of store-rooms: some on the upper storey containing carefully stored raw materials, such as copper talents and elephant tusks, and also a great variety of four-handled amphorae, some on the ground floor or semi-basement, containing jars placed in rows along the walls and a host of other utensils of all kinds, the majority of them superbly decorated.

The arrangement of the royal apartments in the east wing is somewhat obscure, since this section of the palace has been badly damaged by subsequent cultivation of the land. However, we can still make out the apartments of the king and the queen, built close together with the usual multiple doors (polythyra), light wells, and side porticoes facing the central court and supporting the verandas of the upper storeys. The bathroom, which lay at the end of a corridor, was adorned with high benches on slender columns and frescoes of altars crowned with horns. It was presumably used both as a royal bathroom and as a ritual purification chamber. The throne room may perhaps be identified with the large quadrilateral room next to the royal apartments, which contained a central circular basin with gushing water, surrounded by a parapet and columns supporting the roof. This is the first example we have found of a specially constructed water installation inside an official room of a palace. The water came from a spring which bubbled up into a basement room below the floor of the throne room, close to the staircase that led up to the royal apartments (perhaps the sleeping quarters). The water from the spring was channelled into a semi-underground building, from where it could be drawn by the inhabitants of the palace. The fountain itself was reached by a special stairway. All these installations have, fortunately, been very well preserved. A similar well-spring was built in a room on the south corner of the central court. Many offerings were made to the deity at this well-spring during the terrible hours of the final destruction of the palace.

The service rooms in the north wing were carefully designed. They included: a large kitchen-dining room with six piers, over which the main royal banqueting hall was built; the auxiliary rooms to the kitchen, which were discovered full of remains of provisions and of utensils needed for the preparation of food, especially meat; and a staircase which led from the portico in the northern section of the central court to the upper banqueting halls and neighbouring rooms.

The southern section of the palace contained various workshops, and, from the utensils and materials found there, it appears that perfume-making and the manufacture of stone, crystal, ivory, and faience objects were among the chief industries of the palace. This group of buildings was surrounded by corridors that converged from three directions into a single corridor leading to the central court.

An upward-sloping paved court in front of the western façade of the palace was later split up into separate levels, perhaps linked by steps, and a paved and, at some points, stepped road led up the north western side of the hill past the various palace annexes. These annexes, which perhaps housed palace officials, were arranged in several groups and connected to each other and to the main arterial roads by a network of lanes. The most important road was the one which connected the harbour with the large north-eastern gate. From this gate a stepped ramp led down to the first outer court of the east wing. There were doubtless gates in the other exterior façades of the palace too, since various passages led from these to the central court. There were two main building phases, from 1600 B.C. to 1500 B.C. and from 1500 to 1450 B.C., when the palace was destroyed along with all the other New-Palace centres. After the earlier destruction around 1500 B.C., certain sections, chiefly on the north side, ceased to be used, and these have given us a good deal of information about the architecture and contents of the earlier palace.

On a special dais close to the large staircase in the palace of Malia, a circular altar (kernos) was found. It was used for the offering of the first fruits of the year to the deity; it has 34 small hollows round the rim and a large hollow in the centre for oil. It comes from the period between 1500 and 1450 B.C.

THE LITTLE PALACES

Several small palaces have been unearthed in the same or neighbouring regions as the main palace centres. Their purpose is not clear, though it seems probable that some of them were intended to be summer villas for the royal family. This would indicate a high standard of living for the noble classes in Minoan Crete. A huge building, which appears to have been a palace of this sort, has recently begun to be excavated in the region of Archanes (Minoan Acharna), behind the sacred mountain of Juktas (Minoan Iyktos), ten kilometres from the palace of Knosos. The site of the building and its proximity to the larger centre at Knosos suggest that it may have been used as a summer palace. This would explain the presence of the royal tholos tombs found in the neighbouring region on the Phourni hill. The construction of the building was similar, if not superior, to that of the palace at Knosos.

A similar extensive villa has been unearthed on the hill of Hagia Triada, three kilometres from the palace of Phaistos.

The fourth Cretan palace was found on the eastern coast of Crete, at the small bay of Zakros. The Minoan settlement stretched over two small hills at the end of a narrow valley with olive trees and fruit orchards. Excavations showed that Zakros was an

The site—close to the green banks of the Geropotamos River (ancient Lethaios)—was certainly ideal for a summer villa. The building was in fact a miniature palace. In plan, it formed an irregular L-shape, and the open area enclosed by the L lay on the crest of a ridge into whose slopes the ground floor rooms were terraced. The villa contained miniature versions of all the various types of rooms found in the larger palaces: halls with multiple doors (*polythyra*) and light-wells, sanctuary rooms, groups of magazines, treasuries, and workshops. The main rooms had superb fresco decoration with subjects suited to the character of a summer palace. Royal treasures were found both in the palace itself and in the neighbouring tombs: steatite vessels with relief decoration, skilfully fashioned objects of liparite, alabaster and veined marble, and fine gold jewellery. There was also a large collection of imported copper talents. The discovery of extensive archives of Linear A tablets and a huge number and variety of clay sealings provided evidence of a well-ordered palace bureaucracy, no doubt connected with the larger palace at Phaistos. The villa was linked to Phaistos and to the harbour by carefully planned roads.

important Minoan naval base and had established close commercial relations with Egypt and the East. Ships discharged raw materials at this harbour, and Cretan products destined for export to foreign markets were loaded here.

In the villa itself, staircases, porticoes, courts, terraces, and balconies were skilfully arranged and combined to create a most pleasing and harmonious effect.

The two buildings known as the "Little Palaces" of Knosos and Malia have a completely different character. They are too close to their mother palaces to be regarded as summer villas and, in any case, neither their position nor their design is appropriate. Evans thought that the small palace at Knosos was an expiatory shrine to the divinity, built after the destruction of the palace by the earthquake c. 1600 B.C. His evidence for this theory was the large number of sacred rooms contained in this one small building, especially the crypts with pillars and the small sacrificial basins. Evidence of similar shrines has been unearthed in the small palace at Malia. However, both these buildings contained all the usual types of ordinary apartments as well, and so a more probable explanation is that they were intended for the use of important members of the royal household or of the Minoan hierarchy.

It seems probable that each palace harbour would have contained a special royal residence, since the king, in his capacity as controller of the commercial life of his region, must have been a frequent visitor there. At Amnisos, the port of Knosos, for instance, the Villa of the Lilies, with its magnificent fresco decoration, could well have been used as a residence for the king of Knosos. Unfortunately, we have no evidence of such buildings in any of the other palace harbours on Crete.

The name "palaces" is sometimes given to large buildings excavated in Minoan towns, such as Gournia, or in isolated districts, such as the settlement at Plate in Lasithi; but these should more properly be regarded as the dwellings of local rulers.

DWELLINGS OF PROVINCIAL GOVERNORS

Extensive buildings, which appear to have been farmsteads or villas, have been unearthed at widely scattered

Left: a rhyton of dark-coloured chlorite in the shape of a bull's head, found in the ceremonial hall of the palace of Zakros. The eyes of inlaid crystal and the gilded horns were missing and have been restored. In the same room, a stone rhyton with a represen- *tation of a peak sanctuary has been discovered. Right: detail from the relief on this rhyton: on the lintel of the sanctuary doorway, two pairs of wild goats sit facing each other on either side of an aniconic idol of the deity. (Herakleion Museum)*

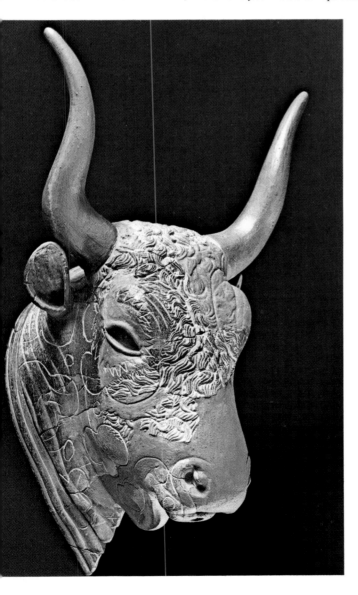

sites in central and eastern Crete. All are situated in favourable positions and at most date from the second or third New-Palace phase. They remained in use for only 100 to 150 years. Their sudden appearance at the end of the first phase of the New-Palace Period suggests that the social and political system underwent some changes at this time resulting in a greater degree of feudalism and the creation of a class of regional chiefs or provincial governors dependent on the favour and the support of the kings. Among dwellings of this sort so far excavated are, in central Crete: the villas at Sklavokampos and Nirou Hani and the large farmsteads at Vathypetro, Vitsilia in the region of Lykastos, Metropolis in Gortys, and Plate in Lasithi; in eastern Crete: the farmsteads at Seteia, Zou, Achladia, Prophetes Elias in the region of Praisos, Hagios Konstantinos in the same region, and Epano Zakros. Most of these buildings contained sanctuary rooms and, in many cases, apartments quite similar to those of the palaces. They were almost all at least two storeys high and must, therefore, have contained at least thirty and, in some cases, more than fifty rooms. The farmsteads were equipped with special agricultural "machinery": wine presses with both fixed and movable components, including large vats for the treading of the grapes, special vessels for collecting the must, and a drainage or waste disposal system. The most interesting installations of

this type have been found at Vathypetro and Epano Zakros. Olive presses were rarer, but there were other workshops with grinding stones, graters, mortars, pestles, and hand-mills. An interesting pottery workshop discovered at Zou in Seteia contained specially built troughs for the kneading of the clay, spaces where small vessels could be fired, pottery kilns, and areas where the unbaked vessels were laid out ready for firing. Domestic animals were kept in special pens, and in nearly all the farmsteads there were extensive systems of magazines for the storage of produce. Weaving was evidently a popular occupation with women, for most of the villas and farmsteads contained great numbers of loom weights; in some cases, there were also specially constructed basins for the dyeing of materials.

Special care was taken in the building of the farmsteads to make them pleasant as well as functional. There were beautiful sitting rooms with seats set at right angles to large low windows. Balconies and verandas on the upper floors and small porticoes on the ground floor looked out over the green valleys below. At the megaron at Seteia, which was built near the bed of a river, two long and narrow stairways, one on either side of the building, led down to a jetty, where small boats could tie up. Today the river follows a different course, but its original bed is still marked by a thick deposit of sand in front of the jetty. The villa at Nirou

At Vathypetro in central Crete, close to Archanes, on a delightful hill opposite Juktas, the smart farmstead of a Minoan "baron" has been discovered. The manor, which is like a small *palace, was built sometime after 1600 B.C. It contained various types of agricultural installations, such as a wine press, an olive press, remains of a pottery kiln, and subterranean store-rooms.*

Left: a complete wine press with its various accessories found in the service quarters of the farmstead at Vathypetro. This is the first Minoan wine press to be discovered in such a good state *of preservation. The grapes were pressed in a clay bowl, and the juice ran out into a large clay bucket. Right: olives from the New-Palace Period, found at the palace of Zakros in 1964.*

Hani lay close to a small creek, which had boat anchorages cut into its sides. The villa contained a huge hoard of ritual vessels, mainly low tripod altars for offerings, and Evans put forward the theory that it was the residence of an important religious official whose duty it was to supervise the export of ritual vessels, for purposes of religious propaganda, from this creek at Hagioi Theodoroi to the Mycenaean region. This theory is more plausible than it might first appear, since nothing less than an organized propaganda campaign could account for the widespread influence of Minoan religion in the Mycenaean world.

NEW-PALACE SETTLEMENTS

A more rewarding study for the historian is the development of the Minoan settlements in the New-Palace Period. They were all destroyed and rebuilt twice before their final destruction at dates coinciding in every case with the dates of the destructions and reconstructions of the palace centres. This shows that the destructions of the settlements were not due to local uprisings or upheavals, or to any isolated instances of foreign invasion, but to natural disasters (chiefly in the form of earthquakes) which overtook a great part of the island. Evans's arguments for attributing the destructions to earthquakes are entirely convincing and were in fact formulated after his own experience of a Cretan earthquake in 1926. He realized then that the fate of the palaces had been closely bound up with the constant geological upheavals which must have taken place in Minoan times.

Among the ruins of a Minoan house outside the palace, he found enormous blocks of stone which had been hurled several metres from the southeastern corner of the palace. He christened this building the "House of the Fallen Blocks". A neighbouring building he called "The House of the Sacrificed Oxen" because, after its destruction in the same earthquake around 1600 B.C., oxen were sacrificed there, and their remains were left in one of the collapsed rooms.

Very little of the actual town of Knosos has been excavated because attention has been concentrated chiefly on the palace. However, a few houses, which evidently belonged to important officials, have been unearthed in the surrounding zone. In some cases, sections of the palace had been sacrificed in order to make way for these buildings, and Evans has suggested that there were religious reasons for this. Two houses, known as the House of the High Priest and the House of the Chancel Screen, which cut into the palace in this way, were certainly of a religious character, for they contained many ceremonial rooms and great quantities of ritual vessels. Behind a columned balustrade in the House of the Chancel Screen, there was evidently a throne or sacred table of offering placed on a low dais. Better examples of such installations can be seen in two other buildings: the Royal Villa and the House of the Priest of the Royal Tomb (so-called because it lies close to the royal tomb to the south of the palace). These altars are similar in many respects to the sacred altars in later Christian churches. All in all, it seems probable that these houses were the dwellings of important members of the priesthood and were used for religious ceremonies.

Many other houses have been unearthed close to the palace of Knosos and are known today by the names which

Above: a royal villa, built around 1550 B.C. at Hagia Triada, three kilometres from Phaistos, on the verdant banks of the Lethaios River, an ideal site for a summer residence of the royal family at Phaistos. The wonderful decoration inside the villa, the frescoes, and the rest of the art work, all date from the culminating period of Minoan civilization. Below: aerial view of Tylisos, one of the most important Minoan towns in central Crete. It lies on the road which linked the eastern palace centres with western Crete. Excavations at Tylisos at the beginning of this century unearthed three dwellings of regional leaders.

196

Evans gave to them. More interesting, however, are the buildings flanking the paved road which linked the large and small palaces. One of these is called the House of the Frescoes, for it had beautiful fresco decoration showing royal gardens filled with exotic creatures, such as birds and blue monkeys. Some of these buildings must have been palace annexes; one which contained quantities of arrows and tablets speaking of arms and chariots is known as the Arsenal. The famous "Town Mosaic" of faience tiles gives us a picture of the façades of houses in a Minoan town.

Evans's estimate of the size of the town of Knosos was based on a study of surface sherds, the remains of the buildings, and the position and size of the cemeteries. The population is thought to have been over 80,000—an exceptionally large figure for that period. It seems, too, that Knosos, like other cities which have been more extensively excavated, was built in a series of blocks of buildings, and that the houses were linked closely together. The city was not confined to the level area, but stretched up the slopes of the surrounding hills.

We know very little about the lay-out of the two ports of Knosos, referred to in Homer as "difficult harbours": Poros-Katsambas in the region of modern Herakleion and Amnisos. The site of the first has been covered for the most part by the suburbs of modern Herakleion, where a few Minoan houses have been discovered below the foundations of modern buildings. When the sea is calm, it is possible to see from the nearby beach the remains of submerged houses with columns. A huge artificially pierced rock, known today as the Trypeto Charaki, perhaps served to protect ships drawn up on the shore. At Amnisos, the chief port of Minoan Knosos, some interesting buildings have been unearthed. We have already mentioned the Villa of the Lilies. A high polygonal stone base may have formed part of a signalling tower, on which fires or torches were kept burning. Light from these fires at night, and smoke in the daytime, would have provided a landmark for mariners.

The palace towns of Phaistos, Malia, and Zakros have been only partially excavated. At Phaistos, there are extensive remains of various quarters of the town on the hillside at Chalara and Hagia Photeine, sites which had been inhabited since the Old-Palace Period. More interesting is Malia, where whole sectors of the town have been unearthed. The houses were grouped in square blocks linked by a crisscross network of main and subsidiary roads. At Zakros, there were many large and well constructed buildings with numerous rooms (over thirty in some cases) and a variety of installations. Small pathways and stairways ran up the slopes of the hillside.

The clearest picture of Minoan towns, both large and small, is provided by certain New-Palace centres which have been more systematically excavated in eastern Crete: Gournia, Pseira, and Palaikastro. The Minoan name for Gournia is unknown. The town took its present name from the small stone basins, "gournakia" in Greek, which were found in great quantities in this region by the local inhabitants. Excavations directed by the American archaeologist H. Boyd, revealed the Minoan town with its Lilliputian houses and its small hilltop palace. Several pathways encircled the palace, while other small paths and stairways radiated out down the hillside. This palace centre dominated and controlled the Gulf of Hierapetra, the passage between the two Cretan seas. The houses were constructed on two levels,

with the roof of the ground floor serving as a balcony for the upper storey (a common type of architecture today in Cretan mountain villages). Some of the houses, doubtless those of the wealthier inhabitants, were built on a larger scale than the rest. Several workshops were established along the roads which encircled the hill; when these were excavated, various "tools of the trade" were found still in situ. A public shrine dating from this period came into use again later in Post-Palace times. Unfortunately, very little remains of the small, and evidently typical, palace which stood on the peak of the hill. The hilltop had been levelled to form a small "square" in which palace ceremonies could be carried out. This was evidently a Minoan palace in miniature, for it contained all the usual features and installations familiar to us from the larger palaces: the ascending levels of the propylon, interior porticoes, magazines, and a residential quarter.

On the small island of Pseira in the wide gulf of Mirabello, a flourishing commercial town and port grew up on the slopes of a tongue of land which formed a protected harbour. The houses were simply constructed and huddled close together along the pathways which ran up the hillside. The houses of the rich merchants were decorated with frescoes in relief, which equalled those of Knosos in artistry. The wealth of household equipment found in these buildings shows that the inhabitants of this remote settlement enjoyed a comfortable existence and a high standard of living. Even more prosperous and splendidly built was the harbour settlement at Palaikastro. It was laid out according to a carefully conceived plan with extensive blocks of buildings separated by wide or narrow paved roads. Many of the houses were spacious and comfortable, with interior open porticoed courts and large rooms, deposits containing ritual vessels, and many magazines. Ashlar masonry was lavishly used on the frontal façades. The intervening roads consisted of a central pavement with gutters running along the edges. One quarter of the town was evidently particularly sacred because, in Classical times, it became the site of the famous Diktaian sanctuary, where the celebrated Hymn of the Curetes was discovered.

In the New-Palace Period, the network of roads built in the earlier period was extended and improved, and guard-posts and guest houses were constructed at various points. The most important improvements were made at the terminating point of the chief arterial road close to the palace of Knosos. The old viaduct at this spot was linked to the palace by a winding stepped portico. In front of the bridge was a guest house, which Evans called the Caravanserai. It comprised an open dining room, decorated with a fresco frieze of partridges, and sleeping quarters on the upper floor. There were installations to provide warm baths and cold foot-baths, and special watering troughs for animals. In a neighbouring spring chamber, there was a small shrine with a niche and a bench for idols and cult objects.

TOMB ARCHITECTURE AND FUNERARY CUSTOMS

There was no substantial change in the burial customs at the beginning of the New-Palace Period. The dead were still interred in natural caves or in chambers artificially carved out of hillsides; in coastal settlements, they were placed in upturned jars or small clay sarcophagi and buried under the sand of the beach. During this same period, however, tomb architecture took on a marked monumental character. More care was taken over the selection and preparation of building materials with the result that the old type of tholos tomb now acquired an imposing and grandiose appearance and a far more solid construction. The tholos tombs at Kamelares in the region of Phaistos were built at the beginning of the first New-Palace phase. One of these was very spacious, with exceptionally thick walls and an imposing entrance. The space between the monolithic door jambs was closed by a single slab of stone. Of a slightly later date are the tholos tombs which have been found in the region between Knosos and Herakleion, at Tekes, and Kephala. Here, greater care had been taken with the cutting of the wall blocks, and there were deep, properly-constructed entrance passages and exterior recesses for the cult of the dead. All these tombs had a circular main chamber. A different type of tholos tomb, also constructed in this period, had a square or rectangular main chamber and a keel-formed vaulted roof. An example is the huge royal tomb at Isopata. Here, besides the niches of the antichamber, there were in the chamber itself an artificial door for the communication of the dead with the terrestrial world and a grave pit dug into the floor.

Many valuable grave goods which had evidently escaped the notice of pillagers, were found intact in this royal tomb: vessels and utensils of alabaster and basalt, and jewellery made of gold or precious stones. Evans and many other scholars believe that the monumental royal tombs of the Mycenaeans had their prototypes in Crete, where the tholos tomb had a long history of development. Tholos tombs dating from the last New-Palace phase have been found in the region of Archanes, close to the summer palaces of the kings of Knosos. One tomb had a smaller side chamber similar to the secondary burial chambers in the famous treasuries of Atreus and Minyas, at Mycenae and Orchomenos, respectively.

An unusual type of royal tomb, found on the hillside south of the palace, was called by Evans the Temple Tomb. The sepulchral chamber (a crypt with a square pillar supporting the beams of the blue-painted roof) was cut deep into the soft rock and had an interior facing of large gypsum slabs. Outside this chamber was the pillared crypt for cult purposes. An ante-room led into the shrine, which was on the upper storey. The memorial cult for the dead kings apparently took place in the small court in front of the entrance, for numerous "holy communion" cups have been discovered there in situ. The shape of the tomb corresponds in many respects to the description preserved in legend of

From the summer palace at Hagia Triada comes this famous rhyton of black steatite in the shape of an ostrich egg. It is decorated with a complex relief group of harvesters and winnowers.

The artist succeeded in compressing the line of marchers into a band scarcely 7.5 centimetres high (1500-1450 B.C.). Below: three details from the festival procession.

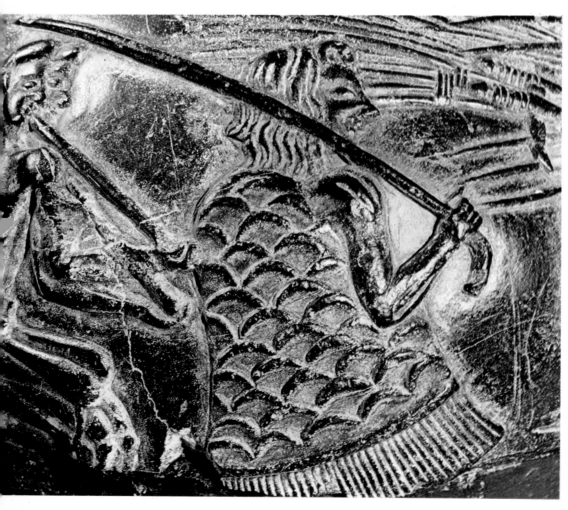

the tomb of Minos. According to the legend, the king of Knosos was murdered by the daughter of King Kokalos at Kamikos in Sicily during his expedition to that island and was later buried in a double tomb, of which the upper section was a shrine dedicated to Aphrodite.

Rock-cut tombs had a parallel development with tholos tombs. In these, the main chamber could be circular, elliptical, horseshoe-shaped, square, or polygonal. The entrance was a descending passage (*dromos*), short or long, cut into the rock of a hillside. Undoubtedly, these had their origins in the earlier cave burial chambers, which had themselves often been artificially widened at various points. The technique used in building these rock-cut chambers influenced the building of tholos tombs so that, from being free-standing structures on more or less level ground, the tholoi became underground chambers cut into the rock with interior stone wall-facings and a long entrance passage. All these techniques of sepulchral architecture were later adopted in the Mycenaean region, where both rock-cut and tholos tombs were even further developed and improved.

The chief cemeteries of rock-cut tombs in Crete have been discovered close to Knosos and to Phaistos. Although most of these tombs had been pillaged, large numbers of grave goods, which had evidently been overlooked, or discarded as useless, by the looters, were found in situ inside the tombs or scattered about in the surrounding area. Fortunately, several tombs have been found intact, and these tell us a great deal about the funerary customs of this period. The dead were laid on wooden biers or placed in wooden chest-shaped sarcophagi. Most of these coffins have disappeared without trace, but from the few that have been preserved we can gain a general idea of their shape, and even of their colour. The coffins from the Katsambas tombs were painted blue, a colour which seems to have had some special significance, since it is often found on the walls and roofs of sepulchral chambers and on ritual vessels and utensils, especially incense burners. Wooden coffins were later replaced by clay sarcophagi and a new type of tub-shaped clay coffin. The famous painted stone sarcophagus which was found in a Post-Palace tomb near Hagia Triada— although it had originally been used in an earlier period— showed scenes connected with the cult of dead kings. A cult of the dead was evidently part of the Minoan religion, for the actual burial service seems to have been only the first of a whole series of "memorial services", perhaps held at fixed intervals over a long period of time. Judging from the groups of clay figurines found in the outer chambers of the Kamelares tholos tomb, these ceremonies included funeral banquets, the offering of gifts to the dead, and ritual dances. Grave goods of all types were left by the side of the dead: food, clothes and toilet articles, braziers to heat

Left: the peasants march along in pairs holding farm implements; at their head is a long-haired chief with a long staff on his shoulder. Centre: a group of singers; the leader is playing the sistrum.

Right: another detail from the same vase: a drunken marcher stumbles and seems to collapse to the ground. (Herakleion Museum)

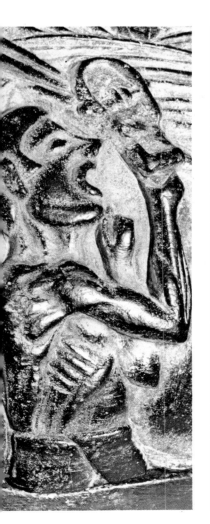 

the chambers, lamps to dissipate the darkness, and incense burners to spread perfumes and incense. The fact that these practices continued to be observed over a long period of time has helped us to form a clearer picture of life in the New-Palace Period.

The dead continued to be supplied with the various articles needed in everyday life until the bodies had completely decomposed, when the bones were removed to make room for new burials. It is evident that special care was taken over the removal of the main sections of the skeleton— the skull and the long bones of the arms and legs—for these were often placed in separate pits inside the tomb, while the smaller grave goods were piled into special pits. Extra space was made by cutting recesses or tributary passages into the sides of the tomb or by partially widening the main chamber.

After the doorway of the tomb had been blocked up, the entrance passage was filled with earth so that no one could enter the tomb to disturb the dead or to pillage the grave goods. Watchmen were appointed to look after the main cemetery areas, and a special guard was assigned to the royal tombs.

LIFE DURING THE NEW-PALACE PERIOD

The extensive remains unearthed at the New-Palace centres and the large numbers of grave goods found in tombs of this period have enabled us to reconstruct a much fuller picture of the life of this period than of either of the two preceding periods (the Pre-Palace and the Old-Palace ones). However, some aspects of New-Palace life, particularly those which concern the political and social organization, remain something of a mystery, and, in the absence of definite evidence, we can do no more than form plausible hypotheses on the basis of the material available.

The many cemeteries and tombs which have been investigated (either in the course of systematic excavations or as a result of chance discovery) have provided us with a wealth of anthropological material, much of which has not yet been studied as thoroughly as it deserves. It is clear, however, that the race which inhabited Crete in this period continued to belong chiefly to the dolichocephalic Mediterranean type; but there was also some admixture of other types, which eventually produced a mesocephalic type. Brachycephalic skulls are rare; perhaps the appearance of this type on the island may be explained by the penetration into Crete of northern peoples from the mainland during the Middle Helladic Period. With the expansion of the Minoan sea empire, it was natural that the original Mediterranean type would become crossed with others. This did not mean, however, that there was any substantial change in the racial composition of the population of Crete in the New-Palace Period.

Social Organization

The social organization seems to have undergone no radical change, though it had to be adapted to the new conditions of life both in the towns and in the country. Because of the rapid accummulation of wealth, the role of the old noble class, which had previously formed the aristocracy, now diminished in importance. This class was gradually replaced by the swiftly rising class of *nouveaux riches*, for whom privilege was based solely on wealth. The merchants and sailors built large and splendidly decorated mansions for themselves in the Cretan harbours and even on isolated islands like Pseira. The production of goods of all types, especially at the large palace centres, led to the creation of a middle class of artisans. After the institution of a feudal system on the island—our chief evidence for this is the appearance at this period of country villas or farmsteads, which were evidently dwellings of local chiefs—agriculture and irrigation were organized on a more systematic basis, and there was a consequent improvement in the standard of living of the peasant population. The new farming methods were apparently successful, for the farmhouses contained vast numbers of magazines full of pithoi and other special storage installations. Some of their contents have been identified from a study of the carbonized remains; they included cereals, pulse, fruits, olives, and grape seeds. In matters of agriculture, the Cretans were far more advanced than their neighbours in the Aegean islands or Helladic Greece, and it is not surprising that there are many legends that mention Crete as the source of improved methods of farming. Agricultural tools had been perfected, and many of them, like the pick and the mattock, bear an amazing resemblance to their modern counterparts; spades, like the plough, except for its point, were doubtless made of wood. In eastern Crete, several examples of a special type of dibble have been unearthed. Finally, sickles in combination with threshing-flails appear on the famous Harvester Vase from Hagia Triada, which is believed to represent peasants returning home from their fields.

The chief problem facing Cretan farmers was that of irrigation. In periods of drought, special ceremonies were held with the object of persuading the divinity to send rain; and these rituals are connected with small amulets which formed a special class of Minoan seal-stones. However, the farmers also took the precaution of building a special irrigation system with a network of water canals linked together in a systematic way. The irrigation system at Lasithi known by the name "linies", which has a multitude of ditches and canals linked together in a giant chess-board pattern, was undoubtedly first dug in Minoan times, as it is highly improbable that it is of Classical or Byzantine origin or that it belongs to the period of Venetian occupation. Only in recent years have the canals been cleared and the system put into operation again. Similar, though much more extensive, irrigation works were dug by the Minyans of Orchomenos in the Lake Kopais basin in Boiotia.

Crafts

Crete was an island of cottage industries; in their most organized form, these became palace industries, but there was never any attempt to establish independent workshops wholly given over to the production, and perhaps sale, of goods. Such a system was evidently unknown at that period. The products of various Minoan industries will be discussed in detail below in the section on Minoan art. For our knowledge of certain industries, however, such as weaving, embroidery, and knitting, the products of which have long since perished, we have to rely on painted or sculptural representations of clothes and knitted garments. Of the loom we know only that it was upright with loom weights of the double convex disk type rather than the oblong variety common in earlier times. The women did their weaving moving to and from the loom. Basket working was imitated in stone or clay utensils, which shows that some sort of container like the modern demijohn was evidently not unknown.

The aromatic and therapeutic herbs of Crete are in great demand today among manufacturers of perfumes and drugs. Some of these herbs still retain their prehistoric names: *minthe* (mint), *eleliphaskos* (sage), *diktamon* (Cretan origan), *apsinthos* (wormwood), *selinon* (celery), etc. It is not surprising, therefore, that, in Minoan times too, herbs formed the basis of a whole branch of industry. (The subsequent development of this industry in the Mycenaean region can be followed with the help of the Creto-Mycenaean tablets). Workshops unearthed at the palace of Zakros and elsewhere contained special utensils which were presumably connected with the preparation of aromatic substances for export. The resin from aromatic plants was used in the making of incense.

Another branch of industry was concerned with the production of colouring materials. Naturally, most of these were minerals, which were especially useful in fresco painting, but some animal and vegetable substances were also used. Huge numbers of murex shells have been found in all the settlements, especially the coastal ones. Purple was evidently exported too, for a vast mass of murex shells has been found at Kouphonesi, an island off the southeastern corner of Crete.

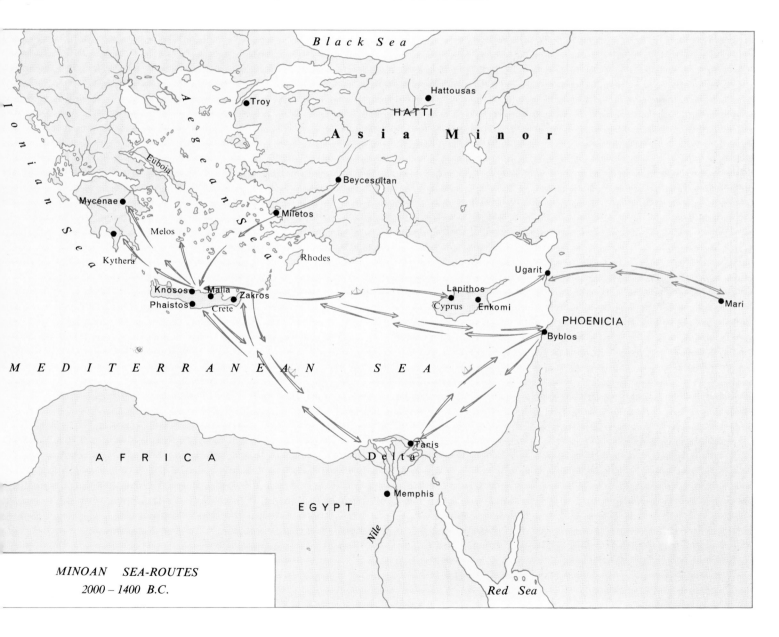

MINOAN SEA-ROUTES
2000 – 1400 B.C.

Minoan Crete was in direct sea communication with the whole of the Eastern Mediterranean and controlled all the sea routes. Minoan ships sailed to Egypt, the Syro-Palestinian coast, Asia Minor, the Aegean islands, and mainland Helladic Greece. They carried the products of Minoan workshops, which were in great demand, *to the Near East and returned carrying raw materials from these lands. The map shows the communication links of Minoan Crete, between 2000 and 1400 B.C., with the other large centres of that period in mainland Greece, the Aegean, Asia Minor, Cyprus, Egypt, and Phoenicia.*

Carved on the famous Prince's Cup of black steatite from Hagia Triada are two figures believed, respectively, to be a prince and an official. The prince (right) has an erect posture, long hair, wears jewellery, and holds a sceptre in his right hand. The other figure (left) holds a sword over his right shoulder and a sickle-shaped implement in his other hand; his appearance is generally simpler and he wears less jewellery. (Herakleion Museum)

Royal Commerce

A portion of Crete's agricultural produce and the greater part of her industrial production was destined for export. She traded mainly with the islands of the Aegean, mainland Greece, and the chief centres of Anatolia, the Near East, and Egypt. Stylianos Alexiou has put forward convincing arguments for the theory that Cretan trade in Minoan times was organized and substantially controlled by the palaces and that the merchants were in fact "employees" of the king. Even if this view is considered too extreme, there is no doubt that the palaces did play an important role in developing trade contacts, especially with the large foreign markets, since the chief products of both farmer and artisan were stored in the palace centres, and the palace itself was the chief producer of luxury goods which were in demand abroad. Choice wines and perfumed oil were transported in special vessels, the most popular being the false-necked stirrup jar.

Timber in abundance came from the cypress and cedar forests of Crete. Some was used at home in the massive timber ties in the walls of the palaces, but much was exported to countries like Egypt and Mesopotamia, where it was in short supply. Cretan ships also put in along the Phoenician coast to load timber from the cedar forests of Lebanon. Egyptian sources tell us that, during the reign of the Pharaoh of the 18th dynasty, the Kephtiu continued to trade with Egypt.

Egyptian sources often mention the Kephtiu, and tomb paintings of the 18th dynasty show them, among envoys of tributary nations, bringing gifts to the Pharaoh. The Kephtiu were evidently Minoan Cretans, for in the tomb paintings we can easily recognize their characteristic clothing and hairstyle, and most of the gifts they carry are undoubtedly Minoan products: rhyta, amphorae, prochoi, moulded vessels, skilfully fashioned kraters, cups of Vapheio type, etc. The most important paintings are those found in the tombs of Senmut, User-amon, Rekhmire, and Menkheperrasenb. The dress of the figures shown in the last two tombs betrays some Mycenaean influence. It seems probable that in some cases the Kephtiu-Cretan contingent included colonists from the Syro-Phoenician region.

From the Old-Palace Period onwards, Crete had maintained direct sea communication with the rest of the Eastern Mediterranean, and her ships were specially designed and fitted out for lengthy voyages. Her links with Egypt had now become much closer. The arms made for Queen Auhotep betray signs of Minoan workmanship.

The concensus of opinion among pottery experts is that Crete exported very little pottery to Egypt and the East in the second and third New-Palace phases, because all the pottery from this period found in these countries seems to have originated in Mycenaean centres. Although this theory ignores the fact that many vessels unearthed in Egypt are unmistakably Minoan in character and very often decorated in the marine style, (the most famous of these being the *nautilus oinochoe*, now in the Museum of Marseilles), it is quite probable that a certain proportion of Cretan products were channelled into foreign markets through trading stations established in Mycenaean centres.

The special honour accorded the Kephtiu and the envoys from the "islands of the Green Sea" in the Egyptian texts is an acknowledgement of the growing power of Minoan Crete and her rapid colonial expansion in the Aegean.

Some scholars (like P. Demargne) have failed to appreciate the close nature of the links between Crete and the East, especially the Syro-Phoenician region, and have on the contrary overestimated the extent of Mycenaean influence both in this region and the East generally. In their view, the spread of Mycenaean civilization alone is sufficient to account for the appearance of the hybrid Aegean-Eastern culture which developed in the Near East at this point. However, the civilization which evolved in Phoenicia (as the successor to Canaanite civilization) shows distinct signs of Minoan influence. C.F.A. Schaeffer, the excavator of Ugarit (modern Ras Shamra), rightly recognizes that there were Minoan settlements on the Phoenician coast and that many characteristic Minoan elements are present in both house and grave architecture in the region of Ugarit. In sacred texts, chiefly hymns, found in this important Phoenician city, there are clear signs of Cretan influence. Later, of course, Mycenaean influence became paramount, for eventually Crete itself was absorbed into the Mycenaean world.

Thalassocracy

Without naval supremacy (the Cretan thalassocracy, so often referred to in Greek legends), there could have been no Minoan expansion in the Aegean. Cretan naval supremacy was unchallenged in the first phase of the New-Palace Period. The Mycenaean centres had not yet been founded, and there was extensive Cretan colonization in the Aegean islands. In the two subsequent phases, up to the destruction of the Minoan centres c. 1450 B.C., there was a unified Creto-Mycenaean expansion with little sign of overt rivalry. It was only after the destruction of about 1450 B.C. that Mycenaean Greece displaced Crete as the leading power in the Aegean.

Crete could not have maintained her naval supremacy for so long without a systematically organized fleet capable of controlling sea routes, harbours, and naval bases. Such a fleet was also necessary to protect the island from surprise attack. The fact that peaceful and stable conditions prevailed on Crete and that the towns, even at the main palace centres, were unfortified shows that the navy maintained a constant vigilant watch over her coasts. There could have been no large-scale Minoan expansion if large numbers of ships had not been available. According to

legend, king Minos undertook many expeditions, both large and small, to various parts of the Mediterranean, and it seems probable that these were in fact colonizing expeditions. The ships depicted on New-Palace seal-stones and seal impressions appear better built and equipped than their predecessors of the Old-Palace Period. This may be accounted for to some extent by the fact that the engravings had become more naturalistic and more details could be shown; but, in general, it looks as if the ships themselves were now more complex; they are many-masted, equipped with rigging, rows of oars, rudders, rams, gunwales, and occasionally small deck cabins. A clay model of a ship from Hagia Triada, though somewhat crudely fashioned, clearly shows the rigging, the bridge, and the hold. With their high prows (which often terminated in a figurehead) and their heavy keels, Minoan ships were equipped to withstand even the roughest storms on the open seas. The building of harbours on the south and east shores of Crete, at Matala, Kommos, Hierapetra, Makrys Gialos, Zakros, and Palaikastro ensured swift and direct communications with the East and Egypt. For ships sailing round the island there were harbours east of Knosos at Malia, Mirabello, Pseira, Mochlos, and Seteia, and west of Knosos at Rhithymna (modern Rethymnon), Suda, and Balchania (modern Chania). There was evidently no special war fleet even in the culminating period of Minoan civilization. The merchant ships were sufficiently well equipped to defend themselves and, if necessary, to take the offensive. The naval base at Zakros was particularly well placed to exercise control over the eastern Aegean, to export, and to receive imports (tusks and bronze talents were found in the palace magazines there).

Political power in Minoan Crete rested on a theocratic base. Both private and public life were deeply influenced by religion, and religious rituals were an essential part of everyday life. Below: a 15th century steatite seal-stone from Knosos, perhaps showing a priest. (Herakleion Museum)

Despite the peaceful conditions of their life, the Minoans displayed considerable interest in armaments. They produced both defensive and offensive weapons of all kinds: among them, spears and javelins with extended and reinforced points; long hammered swords strengthened by a special midrib (the best examples have been found in sacred deposits in the cave at Arkalochori); strong daggers, often with gold nails in the handles; body-length, figure-of-eight shields, "pinched-in" at the waist to lessen the weight; and helmets with cheek guards and often with long curving crests. A second type of helmet built up of horizontal bands of split boars' tusks seems to have been more characteristic of Mycenaean Greece than Crete, but its technique is certainly Minoan, for there are several representations of it in early Minoan art.

Political Power

From the time of the founding of the old palaces, political power in Crete had been centred in the hands of the kings. This system rested firmly on a theocratic base, and as we can see from the arrangement of the sanctuary rooms in the palaces, the king also acted as the high priest. At the palace of Malia, various emblems of his power have been discovered. As well as his crown of lilies and long peacock feathers, the priest king also wore a necklace of lilies as a symbol of his religious authority; and he was represented accompanied by the sacred griffin. We do not know what meaning should be attached to the title "Minos", if indeed it is a title analogous to the Egyptian "Pharaoh", as many scholars believe. Other names attributed by legend to members of the royal family undoubtedly have a religious significance: Pasiphae (full moon), Ariadne (most pure), Europa (obscure new moon). Perhaps queens and princesses holding the highest religious offices took on such names, and their titles were later translated into these Greek forms during the period of Achaian rule at Knosos.

Nothing is known of the specific functions of the other dignitaries and officials of the Court, except that there was a hierarchy headed by the members of the royal family. There is nothing to suggest that the queen was more important than the king, or even equal to him, though she could probably succeed him in office if the next male heir was under age. She did have a particularly important religious function, however, as the main representative of the chief Minoan deity, the Mother Goddess. The palace bureaucracy was evidently extended, and archives were kept in a much more systematic way than in the previous period. Important officials lived either inside the palace itself or in houses adjoining, or just outside the palace walls. Some of these buildings were used for administrative purposes as well.

Minoan religion will be discussed in detail in another chapter, but we may remark here that, in Minoan Crete, life and religion were so closely bound up together that it is difficult to discuss them as separate subjects. Religious festivals and ceremonies were regarded as important social events, holidays for both Court and people. The offerings of first fruits which filled sanctuary magazines at the palaces and elsewhere were in fact an early form of tax, levied by the kings to enable them to carry out their extensive programme of public works.

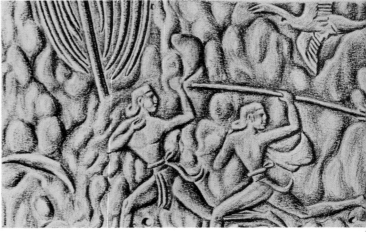

204

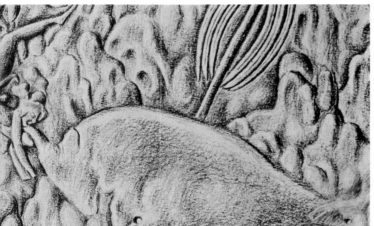

Private Life

Our knowledge of the private life of the Minoan Cretans is based on what we have been able to discover about the conditions of life at the large palace centres. Not only was the standard of living on Crete surprisingly high, but there was a certain delicacy and charm about Minoan life completely absent in the main centres of the contemporary civilizations of Egypt and the East. A characteristic feature of Minoan society was the freedom of women. Not only did they take part in all social activities, but they were allowed to develop and express their own personalities without hindrance. Their interests were by no means confined to the house and domestic duties. They even took part in dangerous athletic games, such as the ritual bullsports, and accompanied their menfolk on hunting expeditions. On such occasions, they had no hesitation in abandoning their elegant robes and donning the male "kilt", so that their movements would be unimpeded. They seem to have been regarded as the equals of men in such athletic activities, and in dancing displays they naturally took the chief role. The ladies of the Court evidently lavished great care and attention on their appearance, for their toilet rooms in the palaces were equipped with beauty aids of all kinds. They made skilful use of cosmetics to emphasize the red colour of their lips and the white of their cheeks. A dark tint was used to make the eyes seem larger, and the eyebrows were plucked with tweezers. The toilet rooms also contained shiny bronze mirrors with beautifully engraved wooden or ivory handles and small decorative toilet boxes. It was the workmen digging at Knosos who gave the name "Parisienne" to the elegantly dressed priestess on one of the frescoes. There was a great variety of fashion in the clothes worn by the women, and we must resort to modern *haute couture* terminology to give an accurate description of them. The most common garment was a "topless" dress with a tight fitting open bodice which left the breasts bare (or covered only by transparent tulle), beautifully made belts, and a skirt with tiers of flounces. There was a great variety of head coverings (berets with buckles, tiaras, hats) and an even greater variety of hair styles. Very often the hair was piled high on top of the head and skilfully arranged in complex styles sometimes with the aid of ribbons, diadems, hairnets, and concealed toupees. Especially popular were small ringlets framing the forehead and cheeks. By contrast, the clothes worn by Minoan men retained all their original simplicity. The usual garment was a kilt which hung loosely down from a belt (chiefly of metal) which was tightly drawn in at the

Moulded representations of religious and ceremonial subjects have provided a wealth of information about the private life of the Minoans. Top row: round dance on a sacred circular floor, from the tholos tomb at Kamelares (near Hagia Triada); the height of the figures is c. 14 cm. Right: clay figurine of a bare-breasted woman in the attitude of supplication; the clothing and hairstyle are characteristically Minoan. Bottom row, left; ivory pyxis with a masterly rendering of the capture of a bull by expert huntsmen. The dramatic event illustrated on the pyxis is shown in the middle row. Bottom row, right: gold-and-ivory bull jumper (taurokathaptes) making his daring leap; there is a wonderful sense of movement in this figure. Part of a moulded group showing bull sports, from the palace of Knosos. (Herakleion Museum)

waist. This both emphasized the lithe, slim-waisted body of the Minoan men and allowed great freedom of movement. A type of ceremonial kilt which reached down to the knees was introduced later, probably from the Mycenaean region.

The horse-drawn chariot seems to have appeared at the same date, c. 1600 B.C., in both Crete and mainland Greece. A seal from Knosos shows a horse bound with ropes near a ship, perhaps a symbolic representation of the introduction of this animal to the island. However, there is no evidence to suggest that horses were used for riding and racing either in Crete or in the Mycenaean region. Their sole function seems to have been to draw the light chariot, which was first used for hunting and, in later periods, to carry heavily armed warriors to battle. In Crete, there are many early representations of chariots on seals, seal impressions, and frescoes, and this suggests that the chariot may have been in use there even before the Mycenaean Age.

Athletic games and competitions, usually combined with religious ceremonies, were a regular feature of Cretan life. Frescoes, reliefs on stone vessels, seal-stones, and seal impressions give us some information about the chief contests— wrestling, boxing, jumping, and running. The agility and skill displayed by the competitors can have been achieved only through long years of training. The boxers wore special helmets, gloves, and leather leggings, while the wrestlers were elegantly attired and decorated with jewellery. The jumpers performed dangerous leaps through hoops or over upright swords.

The most dangerous contests, which were also those requiring the greatest boldness and skill, were the bullsports. We know all the details of this sport because it is portrayed in innumerable seal engravings and on frescoes. The athlete grasped the bull by its horns, flung himself into the air in a double somersault and, after passing over the bull's back, landed on the ground. Other people stood by to steady his landing, if necessary. Modern bullfighters claim that such a contest would prove fatal to the participants, even if the bulls used were relatively tame. The Minoans, however, seem to have been masters of the art of bull leaping, even if they did sometimes take a few precautionary measures, like sawing off the ends of the bulls' horns. It is probable that the Spanish bullfight, and consequently the Mexican rodeo, are descendants of the Minoan bullsports, for the intervening stages have been observed in some clay bull-fighting groups found in the Balearic Islands. Furthermore, we know that Crete was in contact with Tartesos, the Iberian peninsula of modern times.

The bullsports evidently developed out of the practice of

In Minoan Crete, athletic competitions were a popular feature of everyday life. The most spectacular event was the bull-jumping game, which was performed in combination with religious ceremonies. Above: a scene of bull jumping, from a fresco in the palace of Knosos. This was a dangerous contest: the athlete unflinchingly faced the charging bull and grasped it by the horns; as the bull tossed its head, the athlete flunked himself up, somersaulted over the horns and the bull's back, and landed on the ground behind it. The fresco shows the three stages of the jump. Below: four details of athletic games, from the conical rhyton from Hagia Triada: a bull-jumping scene, showing the athlete being tossed over the bull's head, and scenes of boxing, wrestling, and jumping contests. (Herakleion Museum)

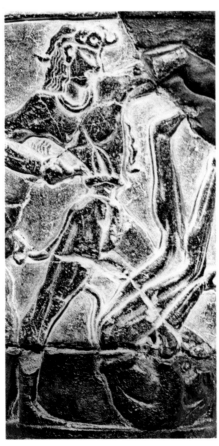

The interior walls of Minoan dwellings were decorated with frescoes on a great variety of subjects: spirals, rosettes, plants, flowers, rocks, animals, birds. Right: part of a frieze with partridges, from the 'Caravanserai' at Knosos (16th century B.C.) Facing page: bluebird from the House of the Frescoes at Knosos (c. 1500 B.C.). Perhaps the whole fresco showed the royal gardens with exotic birds. (Herakleion Museum)

hunting and trapping wild bulls. Various methods and devices were used, all relying chiefly on the specialized skills of the huntsmen. Bull hunting was a popular theme in Minoan art, and there are many interesting representations of it, often executed with great skill and verve. A typical example comes from an ivory pyxis found in a tomb at Katsambas. It shows bull-hunters with spears and lengths of material, which perhaps served the same function as the red cloak of the modern bullfighter. The bull had to be captured unharmed; hence, the use of rush nets, lassoes, and cleverly positioned traps.

The Minoans played various games involving the use of draughts, dice, and knuckle bones. Many remains of such games have been found, including a complete "draughtboard"—a fine piece of intarsia work using crystal, cyanos, faience, ivory, and gold and silver leaf. It dates from the New-Palace Period and may have been a gaming table used by the royal family.

NEW-PALACE ART

Architecture

A much fuller appreciation of Cretan palace architecture may be gained from the extensive remains of the new palaces than from the surviving scattered ruins of the early ones. The characteristic trend towards the picturesque, the varie-

gated, the charming is immediately evident. In the plan of the palaces, there is a sense of centrifugal movement away from the central court, and yet at the same time a feeling that this court is the gravitational centre of the palace, around which circle the corridors linking the various apartments. Light-wells, interior courts, and exterior porticoes create a chiaroscuro effect, and the deliberate avoidance of symmetry in the arrangement of the buildings and façades adds even greater variety to the overall composition. At many points, long corridors lead unexpectedly into spacious well-lit rooms with splendid fresco decoration. The picturesque effect is increased both by the liberal use of bright colours throughout the palace, especially on the timber sections and the downward-tapering columns, and by the striking interior decoration. Today we find it difficult to imagine the fairy-tale atmosphere of the interior of a Minoan palace. Even in its most monumental sections, like the large propylaia and the throne rooms, the building retains its manageable "human" proportions: it has no air of the indestructible and the eternal about it like the architectural monuments of Egypt, nothing to proclaim the grandeur of the kings, like the palaces of the East. In some sections, there are rows and rows of small rooms, which perhaps seem inappropriate to a large palace, but we should remember that the main residential quarters and ceremonial halls were situated on the upper floors and that the narrow rooms at ground level were mainly used as cult or service areas. It is scarcely surprising that, in later legends connected with Crete, the Palace of Minos was remembered as a labyrinth. Minoan architecture more than any other (except perhaps

Japanese, which sprang from a similar conception of the sacred quality of nature) preserved the closest possible links between man and the natural world, and there seems no reason to doubt that this unique style of palace architecture in fact originated in Crete. Some scholars have felt it necessary to search for prototypes in the East and Anatolia and have found similarities to Cretan palaces in palaces at Mari on the Euphrates, Alalakh in northern Syria, Ugarit in Phoenicia, and Beycesultan in Anatolia. However, in spite of some external similarities, the basic architectural principles on which these Eastern palaces are built differ completely from those of Minoan palace architecture. The only exception is the palace at Ugarit, but in it there are many elements attesting Minoan influence. In the palaces of the East, the basic principle is an analytic arrangement of buildings in an enclosed area, while in Minoan palaces the buildings spread out in a synthetic arrangement around a central open area. Minoan architecture was certainly influenced by the architectural styles which prevailed in other countries at that period; on the other hand, the architecture of the East and Egypt also betray considerable Minoan influence, especially in the field of interior decoration.

Murals

Fresco-painting, among other techniques of interior decoration, was one of the chief ways in which the Minoans gave expression to their delight in the natural world and to their feeling for grace and charm. Minoan frescoes always retained a purely decorative character even when they showed scenes of human figures or animals. Great care was taken that they should blend in well with the architecture; indeed they usually enhanced it. Most of the subjects of the paintings were purely decorative. Although we do not know all the details of the technique of fresco-painting, recent studies have shown that the main colours of the background were applied in layers to the wall plaster while it was still damp, thus forming a surface of stable colours on which details could be added and fixed with viscous substances when the wall was dry. The colours used in this fresco-painting were inorganic, mostly deriving from mineral substances. On frescoes stored for a long period during and after World War II in subterranean cellars of the Herakleion Museum, the colours of the restored parts have either disappeared or undergone a radical change, while the colours of the original work have been preserved intact.

Minoan decorative art in the culminating period was characterized by the use of bright saturated colours. This method of decoration was often used, though in a slightly different way, by other contemporary peoples and survived into Archaic and Classical times. But it was never used with such telling effect as in Minoan painting, where it created a sense of movement and *joie de vivre* entirely in keeping with the atmosphere of the surroundings. Avoiding grandiloquence, it gave rather a tender and innocently youthful expression to the Minoan sense of wonder at the mysterious world of nature. The paintings are imbued with a feeling of movement; there is nothing static about the figures or the arrangement of the decorative motifs. These motifs, arranged in friezes or spread over a whole surface, consist mainly of running spirals, rosettes, rings, and tresses, often with supplementary plant subjects twined between or inside them. Where the friezes or the roof decoration were worked in relief, the alternation of light and shadow on the surfaces created a picturesque effect.

Although it is difficult to reconstruct the scenes on Minoan frescoes, Evans attempted to restore some of the subjects with the assistance of the painters Gilliéron, father and son. We should be wary in our judgments of these restorations, since they detract from the original fragments. The museum at Herakleion has developed new systems which allow the original sections of the fresco to stand out clearly against the restored background and to be moved away for further study. Many scholars would prefer to dispense with restoration altogether, even if this made the subjects difficult to recognize.

The word "naturalistic" is often applied to Minoan fresco-painting, but, in fact, although the subjects are drawn from the natural world, the rendering of the figures and shapes is as a rule conventionally decorative. Contrary to what we would expect in naturalistic painting, green is scarcely ever used for vegetation and plants, and rocks, and animals are painted in a most improbable variety of colours which have no relation to their natural ones. Flowers too are shown in mixed, and often exotic, colours. It is often difficult to see what plant or animal is portrayed. Human figures are painted as freely moving coloured silhouettes. For crowd scenes, an impressionist technique is used: the heads and bodies are rendered by a single brush stroke, and the red colour of the male and the white of the

female skin are shown by large blobs of paint. The artists are fond of painting decorative details on clothes and birds' wings and of showing the veins of variously coloured rocks. Because of the curious "horseback perspective" which makes the shapes in the background frame the picture as if they were suspended from above, the natural landscapes seem crowded and enclosed. All these naturalistic scenes had the same basic purpose: to extol the sacred quality of nature.

There are some superb paintings of animals in their natural surroundings; the background is often simply a dense thicket. But the royal menagerie, which included blue apes and exotic birds, is shown inside the lavish gardens of the palace. Partridges fly by in pairs or hide in shadowy hollows close to running water. The marine world, too, is wonderfully portrayed. Fish, octopuses, sponges, and coral inhabit the soundless world of the sea-bed, while dolphins break the surface of the water, and flying fish or argonauts play in the foam of the waves. The reflection of the sunlight in the water produces the conventional scaly effect in the rendering of the sea.

It was not the habit of Minoan art (as it was of Eastern and Egyptian art) to immortalize the achievements of leaders or to portray historical events, even the most important ones, for the edification of future generations. Not a single inscription has been found on a Minoan fresco. The natural world and religious ritual were the two principal themes: but even so, fresco-paintings, often done in miniature, give us some insight into the elegant, busy life of the palace. Such are the scenes represented in the frescoes of the palace sanctuary and the sacred grove at Knosos. One scene, now unfortunately fragmentary, but which once included the elegant "Parisienne" priestess, shows the ceremony of holy communion at which priests dressed in women's clothing participate. Some scenes of everyday life evidently concealed a religious implication: one fresco of a girl kneeling to pick flowers in a flower-filled meadow perhaps shows the young goddess, as in the Persephone myth at the moment that she was abducted to the Underworld while gathering flowers.

The most exciting fresco scenes are those showing the bullsports and the capture of sacred bulls. Every phase of the action in these dangerous games is vividly portrayed, and we can almost feel the excitement in the air as the acrobat somersaults upwards over the horns of the charging bull. A relief from the northern entrance at Knosos portrays a captured bull snorting and panting after the long chase.

In the frescoes which date from the last phase of the palace at Knosos, procession scenes are common and the drawing becomes more pompous, formal, and symmetrical, though this does not appreciably detract from the liveliness of the composition. There is evidence of new influences, undoubtedly Mycenaean, since Crete was presumably ruled by an Achaian dynasty during that period. Among frescoes from this phase are those showing a long procession, the priest-king, griffins surrounding the sacred throne, and athletic games combined with griffins in relief.

Left: a masterpiece of Minoan art: a rhyton of rock crystal found in the repository of the sanctuary at the palace of Zakros along with other ritual vessels (1500-1450 B.C.). The turned ring at the neck is formed of crystal pieces with intermediate foils of gilded faience; the crystal beads of the handle are threaded onto a bronze wire. (Herakleion Museum)

Vase-painting

Fresco-painting directly influenced its sister art of vase-painting. The transition from the polychrome Kamares style to the naturalistic styles was a lengthy process, not a sudden change, as many scholars have thought. Marine and plant subjects were introduced gradually in polychrome ware and always retained a purely decorative function. As the shapes took on importance, polychromy gave way to a bicolour technique of decoration: white decoration on a background which was no longer black, but brown or violet. Towards the end of the first New-Palace phase, plant and marine subjects had begun to be rendered with greater naturalness, although they were still conventionally decorative. Famous examples of this style are the vases with white lilies from Knosos and the small jars with dolphins from Pachyammos. On another group of vases, there are expressive relief renderings of plant and marine subjects on a brown background.

The vase painters soon realized that a more striking effect could be achieved by rendering the naturalistic motifs in a dark colour on a light background; hence this technique was adopted in the two chief naturalistic styles which now emerged: the plant and the marine styles. Always mindful of the fact that vase-painting had a purely decorative purpose, the artists chose only subjects which were flexible enough to be easily adapted to the curving surface of the vases. They avoided scenes with human figures or quadrupeds, since these would have become distorted on round surfaces. Even birds were not introduced before the last phase of the New-Palace Period. A great variety of colour was still used on the vases, though it was now much less important than in the polychrome technique proper. Delicate flowers were shown in white, bands were painted in orange, and colouring effects were produced by the oxidizing action of the fire. Little attempt was made to divide up the surface of the vase into bands or frames, so that there was a free field for the motifs, which included marine creatures, vegetation, creeping plants, scattered flowers, plants with long slender stems, octopuses, argonauts, murex shells, star-fish, coral, and sponges. Sometimes, subjects were borrowed from fresco-painting: friezes or nets of spirals, rosettes, arc patterns, garlands, crowns of leaves, and necklaces. On ritual vessels, religious symbols are common. In the last New-Palace phase at Knosos, vase-painting, like fresco-painting, shows a tendency towards a more grandiose tectonic style with greater emphasis on harmony and symmetry. The same decorative subjects are used, but they are now more stylized and architecturally arranged. Evans called this the "Palace Style".

The shapes of vases became more slender and dynamic as the main weight was gradually transferred from the base to the shoulders, and eventually a round projecting base had to be added in order that the vase should balance properly. More and more new shapes were introduced as the uses of the vases became increasingly specialized. Particularly striking was the development of the large three-, four-, and nine-handled amphorae with their charming decoration and tectonic shape. There were large numbers of ritual vessels, chiefly spherical, conical, or ovoid rhyta, which were suitable for the offering of libations.

In the section dealing with private life in the New-Palace Period, we have already described the utensils that served various practical purposes. In Minoan Crete, such everyday utensils were carefully fashioned, and usually had considerable aesthetic as well as functional value.

Faience working made great progress in Minoan Crete and produced many decorative objects, which were inlaid on furniture, boxes, etc. Examples of this art are the two faience plaques shown above, which were found in the temple repositories at Knosos along with the figurines of the snake goddess. The first plaque *(left) shows a wild goat suckling her young, while the second (right) is a relief representation of a cow with her calf. These exquisite pieces of Minoan craftsmanship may be symbolic representations of the Mother Goddess, the goddess of fertility. (Herakleion Museum)*

Stone Carving

Great progress was made in stone carving in the New-Palace Period. The technique of cutting hard stones had been perfected, and the artists worked skilfully in basalt, porphyry, liparite, obsidian, rock crystal, and veined marble, producing a great variety of boldly shaped artistic types. Soft stones, like chlorite and steatite, were also used. Wherever vessels had specially complicated details in their shapes —turned necks, sometimes with a double lip, unusual stems, or bases—the component pieces were worked separately and then joined together with special metal dowels, or by special glues which sealed any cracks through which liquid might escape. Sometimes glue was used to join the main sections of the vase as, for example, in the famous rhyton known as the Harvester Vase, on which the glue line cuts through the middle of the relief decoration. Some of the finest examples of stone vessels have been found in the sanctuary treasuries, particularly at Knosos and Zakros: rows of superbly-worked rhyta in a variety of shapes, cups for holy communion, ceremonial jugs and amphorae, and skilfully carved ritual hammers. Some of the ritual vessels were carved into symbolic shapes or decorated with relief scenes showing religious ceremonies.

Among the most interesting vases from the point of view of both shape and material are: the ceremonial amphora with looped handles and double lip; the holy communion cups of obsidian and veined marble; the crystal rhyton with a turned ring at its neck and a handle of crystal beads threaded onto a metal wire (all from the palace sanctuary at Zakros); the bull-head and lion-head rhyta with additional inlaid material for the eyes and the tip of the muzzle (from Knosos and Zakros); and the sacred vessels decorated with superb relief representations of entire scenes (from Hagia Triada, Knosos, and Zakros). Of the last group, the most striking are: the Harvester Vase, a rhyton which shows a lively scene of a procession from some agricultural festival; a rhyton showing athletic contests and bullsports; a cup on which a young prince is portrayed receiving ritual offerings of animal skins (all three from the royal villa at Hagia Triada); and a rhyton showing a peak sanctuary and wild animals in opposing groups, or others running and climbing among the rocks (from the palace at Zakros). Relief vessels were often covered with gold leaf, so that they appeared to be made of solid gold, and the technique of the relief decoration obviously originated in the repoussé technique of decorating gold objects.

Stone lamps, chiefly of porphyry, were fashioned with great skill. Many of them were carved to represent papyrus or lotus stalks, flowerbuds, wreaths, etc. Some were provided with a base or stem (high or low), others (with two or more wicks) hung from hooks in a chandelier arrangement. Innumerable ritual objects were made of stone; we may note in particular the "tables of offering", which were produced in a great variety of shapes.

Miniature Sculpture

The materials used in miniature sculpture included various types of stone, more malleable materials like clay, faience, and ivory, and cast metals, both common and pre-

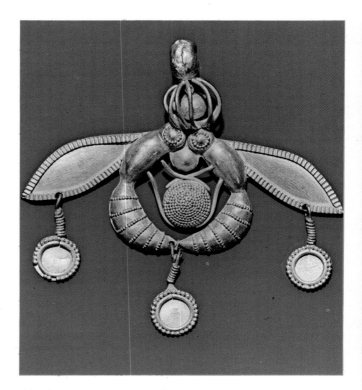

Stone carving and metal-work reached their culminating phase in the New-Palace Period. Jewellery and other objects were produced in original shapes with hammered, cast, granulated, or filigree decoration. Facing page: some examples of Minoan gold work and jewellery of the 16th century. Top: part of a gold pendant, a royal jewel with delicate filigree decoration, from Chrysolakkos at Malia: two wasps suck at a drop of honey; the small disc in the centre shows how expert the Minoans had become in the granulation technique. Middle: gold necklace bead in the shape of a small lion, from a grave enclosure in the Hagia Triada region. Bottom: gold necklace bead in the shape of a duck, with delicate granulation, from the palace at Knosos. This page: decorated gold double axes, Minoan religious symbols, dedicated at the sanctuary in the Arkalochori cave. These axes were completely buried under rocks which fell from the roof of the cave when it collapsed during the earthquake of c. 1600 B.C. (Herakleion Museum)

213

cious. Following an ancient tradition, the artists produced beautifully moulded figurines and votive figures of animals. Clay models of peak sanctuaries too continued to be produced in the first New-Palace phase and were now more carefully and pleasingly modelled than in the previous period. We have already spoken of the clay cult figurines from Piskokephalos with their varied attire and skilfully "piled up" hairstyles. This type of figurine is found in all the later periods in both palace and house shrines. The most valuable figurines were those made of faience or ivory, or a combination of gold and ivory. Working with these sensitive materials, the artists were better able to suggest the whiteness and warmth of the skin and the decorativeness of garments and hairstyles. The surface glaze of faience, particularly, helped to give a more natural look to the colours of garments. The best examples of faience figurines are the snake goddesses from Knosos, while from Palaikastro we have some superb ivory figures of children (perhaps deities). The clearly childlike features on the faces of these figures provide an excellent illustration of the delicacy of the ivory worker's art. A superb work both in its rendering of movement and in its sensitive imitation of living flesh is the gold and ivory bull-jumper from Knosos. Unfortunately, very little of the gold work of this figure has been preserved and the now corroded state of the ivory makes it difficult for us fully to appreciate this unique masterpiece. The sculptor succeeded in imparting a sense of the lightning speed with which the jumper performed this daring leap. The body of the figure stretches out like a piece of elastic and gives the impression that it is hurtling through the air. Unfortunately, the other figures in this group, including the bull itself, have been lost; but several important fragments from similar groups have been found at Knosos in recent years.

Faience and ivory working and the use of inlay techniques produced a host of imaginatively conceived and skilfully fashioned works of art, an example of which is the pyxis from the Katsambas tomb, which shows the capture of a wild bull. The strength and liveliness of the composition are remarkable. Mirror handles were engraved with great delicacy and skill, and the inlaid plaquettes in furniture were adorned with various scenes and varied decoration. Faience working produced many delicate objects moulded into a variety of shapes, such as the bull-head and lion-head rhyta, the small charming flower vases, and the skilfully made toilet articles. Inlay technique was used on boxes, furniture, and gaming boards (like the draught-board from Knosos). The technique of combining various materials to produce luxury objects was as highly developed in Crete as anywhere in the East or Egypt, and the delicacy and charm of the Cretan products was certainly unequelled anywhere. Pieces of inlay work are surely the faience plaquettes with naturalistic scenes of a cow suckling her calf and of a wild goat watching over her young.

Seal-stones, on which the Minoans engraved miniature figures and scenes in relief, are among the finest works of art produced in the New-Palace Period. Top: chalcedony seal-stone set in gold, showing a lion and tamers. Middle: gold ring decorated with a cult scene. Bottom: cyanos seal-stone set in gold, showing a god or hero with a lion. (Herakleion Museum)

Metal-work

The countless metal figurines which have been found represent either votaries, male and female, in the attitude of prayer, or small votive animals. One of the most charming examples of metal-work is the model of two wild goatlings reposing in carefree mood, from the sanctuary in the royal villa in Hagia Triada. The most numerous and interesting examples of figurines, however, come from the sacred caves, especially that at Psychro, which many scholars identify with the Diktaian cave. The most important cult figurines would undoubtedly have been fashioned from gold, but, unfortunately, not a single one of these has been preserved.

The wholesale pillage of most of the Cretan palaces and the two royal tombs has undoubtedly deprived us of some of the finest products of metal-work, which may have been equal, if not superior, to the finds in the royal tombs at Mycenae, although the fact that many of the Mycenaean finds are incontestably Cretan in character is some small compensation for the loss of their prototypes. From the finds in Crete we can also form some idea of the achievements of metallurgy in the culminating phase of its long development. Metallurgy was concerned chiefly with the production of utensils for ritual and everyday use, arms, gold objects, and jewellery, and its techniques had now been perfected. Metal objects, hammered or cast, were given engraved, embossed, inlaid, or granulated decoration. Most of the shapes were entirely original, and some remarkable works of art were produced. Bronze utensils had acquired a new firmness and trimness of shape and were decorated in a variety of ways. Particularly interesting are the amphorae, *hydriae* (water pitchers), jugs, basins, hand bowls, cauldrons (tripod or round-based types), cups, goblets, and lamps. The decoration is often repoussé or cast. Moulded on the lips of the hand bowls is marine, plant, or sacred-symbol decoration.

Many of the tools in everyday use—for wood and stone cutting, metal-work, and farming—were themselves works of art. The craftsmen evidently liked to use tools in which they could take both pride and pleasure. Toilet articles, particularly, were exquisitely made; some are so delicate that some scholars believe them to be surgical instruments. Cult objects, especially double axes, were carefully made and often splendidly decorated. One of the best examples, a bronze axe decorated with a dense pattern of lily stalks, was found in the sanctuary treasury at Zakros. In the cave at Arkalochori, many decorated and inscribed double axes of bronze, silver, and gold were found.

Weapons too were often works of art in themselves. The blades of the long fighting swords were hammered into elastic and functional shapes, well adapted to their purpose. Ceremonial swords, on the other hand, had decorated hilts and were obviously not intended for combat. The ivory or gold-plated hilts were embellished with a variety of subjects, both decorative and representational, and the rounded or mushroom-shaped pommels were often of agate or other precious stones. The technique of the gold-plated dagger with inlay decoration on the blade, of which many specimens have been found in the royal tombs at Mycenae and elsewhere, was evidently Cretan in origin, since similar daggers have come to light in Minoan settlements on the Aegean islands; and daggers with scenes incised on the blade have been found in Crete itself. On spears, the ring which fastened the point to the shaft often had miniature engraved decoration.

The subjects of seal engraving were drawn by the Minoans chiefly from the world of nature; scenes were rendered on stones of all kinds with great precision, sensitivity, charm, and imagination. Above: two large seal-stones from Knosos; the first —of sard—is decorated with a naturalistic representation of bulls; the second—of haematite—shows a lioness attacking a bull. Both seals are dated c. 1400 B.C. (Herakleion Museum)

Gold ornaments were undoubtedly the most striking products of metal-work. There had been a steady development of the goldsmith's art throughout the Pre-Palace and Old-Palace periods, and by New-Palace times all the techniques of working gold had been perfected, and an unprecedented variety of objects was produced. Necklaces were made from beads of all types, often moulded into the shapes of plants, flowers, fruits, small sea-creatures, insects, or quadrupeds. Sometimes, beads in the shape of small lions, bull-heads, feline creatures, deer, or wild goats were mixed with spherical, amygdaloid, or drop-shaped beads. Hairpins often open out into buds or flowers. Among the finest examples of gold work are the various pendentives with filigree or granulated decoration. The most famous are: the bee or wasp pendant from Malia; another ornament which shows the deity as the "Mistress of Wild Beasts" with birds and snakes, from the Aigina treasure, which presumably came originally from Crete; and the ornament in the shape of a young bull's head from the treasure of Zakros. A medallion in the centre of a diadem from this same Zakros treasure showed the goddess as the "Mistress of Wild Goats", framed by octopuses and spiral motifs. Some earrings in the shape of bull-heads, no doubt similar to those referred to by Homer as μορόεντα (berry-like), have very fine granulation. Gold rings were among the finest products of metallurgy: the bezel was often decorated with miniature scenes, usually religious in character.

Great progress was made in seal engraving in the New-Palace Period as the techniques of carving precious or semi-precious hard stone were improved. The prevailing seal shapes were the flattened cylinder, the lentoid, and the amygdaloid type, since these provided the best surfaces for the rendering of representational subjects. In no other branch of art, except perhaps fresco-painting, do the figures move so freely as in these miniature representations. The subjects are drawn both from nature and from religious ritual, and are copied to some extent from the fresco subjects. However, miniature engraving in its turn was to influence the technique of miniature fresco-painting.

Minoan taste always favoured the miniature, the charming, the delicate, and so it was natural for seal engraving to develop into a principal art form. The variety of the decorative and representational subjects portrayed is overwhelming. The vast numbers of clay seals and seal impressions which have been unearthed not only increase our knowledge of Minoan life, but are themselves masterpieces of the glyptic art. Some seals, engraved on special stones, like jasper, represented magical objects and were used as charms or amulets. Even today in Crete, such stones are thought to have magic properties, in particular the power to help mothers produce milk for their infants—hence their modern name: milkstones.

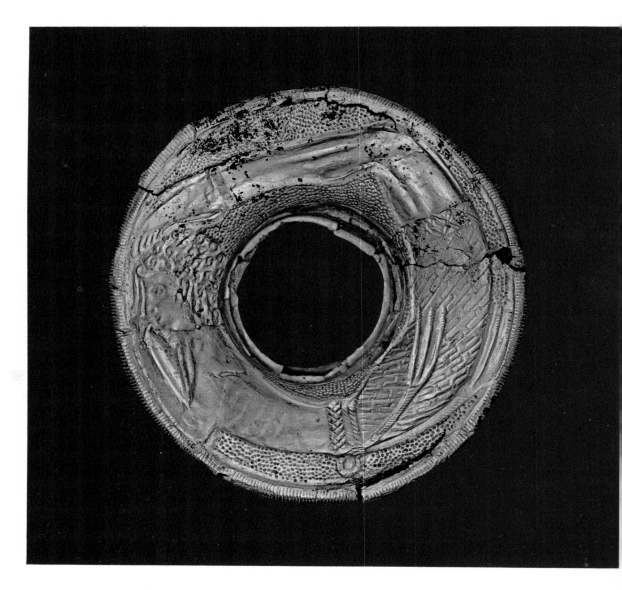

Gold covering of the hilt of a ceremonial sword, showing a sword-jumper, from the palace of Malia. It dates from the New-Palace Period (1700-1600 B.C.). The body of the acrobat is bent in a dangerous salto mortale *above the sword blade. (Herakleion Museum)*

MINOAN LINEAR SCRIPT

In a previous chapter we have explained the reasons for the continued use of the hieroglyphic script in the early part of the New-Palace Period even though a linear syllabic script, known in its early form as protolinear, had already been introduced alongside it at the close of the Old-Palace Period. The new script developed naturally as a stylized and simplified version of the old hieroglyphic characters, adapted to include abbreviations, combinations of syllabic signs, and more determinative elements. Ideographs were still used to render concrete meanings in pictorial terms, and these were of enormous help to the first students of the Minoan script in their efforts to guess the subjects of the texts. Some of the texts, like those incised on some of the frescoes at Knosos, on some jars, and on ritual stone utensils of the type found at Apodoulou in the district of Rethymnon are closer to protolinear, which means that Linear Script A must have developed directly out of the protolinear script. Unlike Linear Script B, which was used in Crete only at Knosos, Linear A was in use over a wide area, even throughout the islands and Helladic Greece, although examples of it outside Crete are comparatively rare. On Cyprus, the early Cypro-Minoan script seems to have developed out of Linear A, but then followed a completely independent course. Many local variations of Script A can be distinguished, but in general they all bear great resemblance to one another. Among the best-known are the "magic" texts, written spirally on the insides of two conical cups found in the house of the monolithic pillars near the palace at Knosos. These texts were written in cuttlefish ink, which shows that writing in ink on a suitable material was quite usual. There can be no doubt about the religious nature of the texts carved on the vessels used in sacred rituals, tables of offering, stone ladles, ritual cups, etc. The inscriptions on such objects present regular repetition of a group of four or five syllabic signs which, with the aid of the phonetic values of Linear B syllabic signs, have now been read: *Asasara* and *Asasarame*, names which are thought to be attributive epithets of the chief Minoan goddess. Brief inscriptions, of one or two signs each, in Linear A have been found on silver and gold axes in the cave at Arkalochori. Some of them have been read *Dâ Mâ: Mother Earth.*

Most of the palace texts in the New-Palace Period were incised on clay like the hieroglyphic archives at the palaces of Knosos, Phaistos, and Malia. The difference is that the tablets, which are now rectangular in shape, contain the main texts and no longer only the labels of the archives which were written on other material. So, for the first time we have real archives, and it is quite common to find texts written on both sides of the tablet in regular syllabic, somewhat careless, script with the usual complement of ideographs and numbers. They are obviously records of accounts; most of them contain lists and show amounts and sums. The arithmetical system is substantially the same as the one used in the hieroglyphic script; it is still decimal, using vertical lines for ones, dots or horizontal lines for tens, small circles for hundreds, and circles with four small lines radiating from the circumference for thousands. And it is interesting that there are special signs for various classes of fractions. Many of the syllabic signs used are also found in compound forms or in combination with small determinative signs. The basic

Linear Script A, a simplified and stylized version of the old hieroglyphic script, was perfected and came into general use in the New-Palace Period. Above: a Minoan cup, on the inside of which Linear Script A signs have been written in cuttlefish ink. (Herakleion Museum)

syllabic signs number approximately 85. The writing was from left to right and from the top of the tablet to the bottom, i.e.. as we write today. Only in rare cases was the tablet ruled before the text was written, and the text was often divided into sections with short introductory phrases. From these and various other indications, it is clear that the registers were often continued on a whole series of tablets which thus formed a complete unit.

Most of these archives have been found at the summer palace of Phaistos, at Hagia Triada, and at the palace at Zakros. At Hagia Triada, about 150 tablets were preserved, 90 in relatively good condition, the rest fragmentary; at Zakros, only 15 have been discovered. The small number of tablets found does not reflect the true extent of the original archives, since special conditions are necessary for their preservation, in particular, baking in a very hot fire. The conflagration which destroyed the palace helped towards the preservation of some tablets, but a great number dissolved into clay and disappeared. Only isolated tablets in this script have been preserved in the large palaces and other centres.

So far, the subject matter of these archives has been a matter of speculation, but, now that Linear B has been deciphered, efforts to decipher Linear A have been redoubled with revived hopes that the phonetic values of the signs would not have undergone a substantial change when the script was adapted to form the syllabary of Linear B. Texts which have been rendered with such hypothetical phonetic values

217

Texts in Linear Script A were incised on clay tablets, the majority of which have been found at Hagia Triada and Zakros. Above: two tablets from the Hagia Triada archives. (Herakleion Museum)

remain almost unintelligible. In an attempt to explain this, many scholars maintain that the language used, undoubtedly the Minoan language, was completely different from any other known ancient language. But a script with the difficult, imperfect, and free spelling system presented by Linear A is open to many complicated interpretations, so that it is not surprising that other scholars have managed to recognize in some of these mysterious texts elements of Semitic (H. Gordon), Luvian (L.R. Palmer and G. Huxley), and a proto-Indo-European tongue (V. Georgiev). Relying entirely on the general form of the tablets and on the ideographs, the early more systematic students characterized the texts as trade records and accounts (Arthur Evans, J.L. Myres) or as religious (J. Sundwall). In some cases, the second characterization seems far more probable; the Zakros archives, for example, are without doubt sanctuary archives. One of the tablets appears to be a list of double axes. It is also possible that many of the tablets from Hagia Triada were concerned with sacred matters, since they were discovered together with many sealings bearing religious representations, seal-ring impressions, and seal-stones of the members of the priestly hierarchy.

The main Linear A archives come from the last phase of the New-Palace Period and are therefore dated c. 1450 B.C. On the evidence of isolated inscribed monuments, it would seem that at that time the same script was in use at both Knosos and Malia.

MINOAN COLONIZATION

Greek legends often speak of Cretan settlements in the Aegean during the reign of Minos. Rhadamanthys and his followers had scattered throughout the Aegean islands —Rhadamanthys himself on Euboia, Staphylos on Peparethos

(modern Skopelos), Oinopion on Chios, Anios on Naxos, Euanthes on Thasos. With them they had brought the cultivation of cereals, the vine, and the olive. Oinopion and Staphylos, and Anios's daughters—Spermo, Oino, and Elais—had names characteristic of these cultivations. A sentimental tie between Minos and Dexithea led to the establishment of a colony at Koresos on Keos. Minos himself during his campaign in Attica, established a colony, Minoa in the Megarid, and many more Minoans settled in the Aegean, even in the Western Mediterranean. Other colonies like those of Membliaros on Thera and of Kadmos in Boiotia were thought to be of Phoenician origin, but they had more of a Cretan character, perhaps because there was Minoan colonization on a grand scale in Phoenicia. Membliaros was eventually named Anaphe. The Cretan Althaimenes had established himself on Rhodes. Trouble between Cretan dynasties led to the emigration of Sarpedon to Lykia. Miletos, setting out from the Cretan town of that name, settled in Karia and founded the town of Miletos there, which always acknowledged the Cretan town, Milatos, as its mother city. Milatos lay east of Malia. The Karians and the Lykians had always been considered of Cretan descent, and many place-names in southwest Asia Minor were related to Cretan ones. There was no definite tradition about Kythera, but the cult of the Kytherian Aphrodite, like that of the Paphian Aphrodite on Cyprus, was closely related to the cult of the Cretan goddess.

The legends said nothing definite about Cretan settlement in mainland Greece, although sacred myths referring to Crete were associated with the most important sanctuaries such as Delphi, Olympia, and Eleusis. But there were links with places such as Phoenicia and Lykia, where there were undoubtedly Cretan colonies. There was a widespread belief that the founders of the Mycenaean dynasties had come from distant lands—Egypt, Lykia, and Phoenicia. The Minyans who developed a great civilization of Creto-Mycenaean character and whose name was presumably related to the name Minos, settled at various favourable spots, like Iolkos in Thessaly, in Boiotian Orchomenos, and later in Pylos.

There is no doubt that the legend was based on the historical reality of a wide colonial expansion by the Minoans, especially in the New-Palace Period, and there is archaeological evidence for this at the places connected with the legend. Evans believed that the Mycenaean civilization had its origin in this colonial expansion. The whole problem will be considered in the relevant chapter. Here, we shall confine ourselves to summarizing what is known of the Minoan settlements in the Aegean.

It would appear that, at the beginning of the New-Palace Period, one of the most important colonies was founded on Melos, where a trading station, Phylakope, had already been established in the Old-Palace Period for dealing in obsidian.

Archaeologists have unearthed extensive remains of the second settlement, which presents features familiar from Minoan architecture. The stone-built, two-storey houses with their timber ties, stone and wooden staircases, typical rooms, interior fresco decoration with marine, plant, and representational motifs, the drainage system, the paved roads, all undoubtedly point to a Minoan settlement. Its most flourishing period seems to have coincided with the second phase of the New-Palace Period, which corresponds to Late Helladic I or Early Mycenaean. At the same time, on Keos, in the sheltered gulf of Koresos on the small peninsula of Hagia Eirene, a very similar settlement was passing through its most prosperous period. On the landward side, there was a wall with gates and towers, similar to the wall which existed a little later at the settlement at Phylakope. At the Keos settlement, all the features of Minoan town-planning and house architecture have been recognized. Particularly impressive are the paved roads with gutters, the stone staircases of the houses, the solid construction of the walls with ashlar masonry at vital points. Everywhere pottery and other objects of Cretan type were found. A special type of building, however, was the sanctuary, which was found close to the eastern gate; it comprised an ante-room, shrine, inner chamber (*adytum*), and priests' apartments.

Chance finds have confirmed that there were similar Cretan settlements in many other Cycladic islands. The settlement at Peparethos (Skopelos) can claim the most striking piece of evidence: a royal tomb, unearthed at Staphylos, which may well have belonged to the original founder of the colony from Knosos. It contained a sword larger than the swords in the royal tombs at Mycenae and covered with embossed gold plate, clay and bronze vessels of both Minoan and Mycenaean types, a bronze double axe, seal-stones, and other ornaments.

On Kythera, a flourishing New-Palace colony succeeded the Old-Palace settlements, which were no more than trading stations. A Minoan settlement has been discovered at Trianta, on Rhodes, which, it would seem, was destroyed at the same time as all the other Minoan centres, c. 1450 B.C. Judging by the grave goods in the rock-cut graves of the cemeteries, there must have been similar Minoan settlements on Kos and Karpathos. On Kythnos, a hoard of bronze implements of Cretan type was found. There are also many indications that the settlements of Lykia and Karia were closely connected with Crete, and this has been borne out by the excavations at Miletos and, more recently, at Iasos. In Phoenician territory, especially at Ugarit, the Cretan settlements had expanded beyond the level of trading stations and constituted proper colonies. A civilization developed there of mixed Asiatic and Mycenaean character.

Special mention should be made of Thera (Santorine), where recent excavations by Professor Marinatos have produced a wealth of evidence for the long flourishing and sudden destruction of this important centre. This destruction coincides, and is connected, with the destruction of all Minoan centres of civilization in Crete and the Aegean.

Linear Script A was in use at all Minoan centres during the first phase of the New-Palace Period. The writing was from left to right. Left: a summary chart of the 90 signs of Linear Script A. The arithmetical system, like that of the hieroglyphic script, was decimal: vertical lines for units, dots or horizontal lines for tens, circles for hundreds, and circles with rays projecting from the circumference for thousands, (below, left).

LATE MINOAN THERA

Historical Background

Thera was certainly not without a history before the recent discoveries of Professor Spyridon Marinatos. Its geology and volcanology had been studied in a series of papers and books, of which those by F. Fouqué and H. Reck were the most interesting. It was known that the island was inhabited before the great eruption. In Classical times, it was colonized by Minyans and Spartans, and the ruins of its capital were excavated and published by Baron Hiller von Gaertringen. The first prehistoric ruins had in fact been found earlier, but it is only now that we have a clear idea of the importance not only of Minoan Thera itself but also of Crete and of the historic effects of the huge eruption which occurred in the middle of the sixteenth century B.C. The consequences of that eruption at the very time when the Aegean Bronze Age was at its peak, and Crete was enjoying its golden age of art, prosperity, and peace, were tremendously important. They literally changed the course of history and civilization throughout the Aegean and, more generally, in the rest of Europe.

It was precisely in this period that Minoan Crete, prosperous and omnipotent, had extended its influence abroad, an influence based upon moral and artistic supremacy and technical superiority rather than upon military activity. We find traces of this influence, which in some instances may be characterized as colonization, from Thessaly to the Cyclades and from the coast of Asia Minor to the Aiolian Islands,

especially Lipari. This highly sophisticated civilization which was rather matriarchal in character, suddenly vanished from the Mediterranean; with practically no gap, it was succeeded by the Mycenaean civilization: venturesome, warlike, and clearly patriarchal in character. Fortunately, the bearers of this civilization did not come too late to drink from the springs of Minoan culture. Although that did not change the basic character of those professional warriors, it did give them the opportunity to join a real civilization many centuries before this happened for the other kindred members of the Indo-European family who happened to settle in more extended and fertile, but less civilized, lands.

Geological Backround

The changed character of Aegean civilization was the result of the great volcanic eruption which gave the island of Thera its present shape. This island was the result of thousands of years of volcanic activity. Originally, there were only two rocky islets of non-volcanic origin. The larger is Hagios Elias, which today is the highest peak on Thera (567 m.). Probably at the end of the Tertiary Geological Period, that is some two million years ago, the first volcanic craters began to be formed southwest of the Hagios Elias limestone rock

The volcano of Thera during its eruption in 1926; thick smoke rises from the crater of Nea Kamene. In the foreground, modern Thera. To the left, Akroteri, where a once flourishing settlement on prehistoric Thera has recently been unearthed. In this area thirty-five centuries ago, a disastrous volcanic eruption wiped out the brilliant Minoan civilization.

The present-day shape of Thera and the contour of the sur-rounding sea-bed are a result of a cosmogonic upheaval, c. 1500 B.C. After the gigantic eruption, a whole section of the island sank on to the sea-bed, and a submarine crater, a caldera, was formed with an area of 83 square kilometres—the largest in the world. The circumference of the caldera is outlined above sea level by the half-moon shape of Thera and by Therasia and Aspronesi. In the centre of the gulf, the small islands of Palaia and Nea Kamene have appeared. Above: the crater of a volcano on Nea Kamene.

There were three or perhaps four of them. With time they emerged above sea-level, they were then united and formed the modern Akroteri area, where the present excavations are taking place.

As time elapsed, more cones were formed to the north through volcanism. There may have been eight or more of them. After a long series of eruptions, the ejected lava and other volcanic materials turned these cones into a single island, in which Hagios Elias and the rest of the non-volcanic rocks were incorporated. Then all these volcanoes, the one after the other, became extinct. After thousands of years, this circular island (one of its names was Strongyle, which means the Round One) acquired humus, flora, and fauna, and almost certainly some of its craters were transformed into fresh-water lakes. The first human traces appear about 3,000 B.C. Since all volcanic islands are fertile, prosperous settlements were soon established on the island, though it is certain that earthquakes repeatedly destroyed the buildings on it. From the recent excavations we now know that the towns and buildings were immediately erected anew and more splendidly. The island prospered in the shadow of the great neighbouring island of Crete and its Minoan rulers.

The Minoan Eruption

About 1500 B.C., a rather severe earthquake not only destroyed Thera, but also inflicted damage to the buildings at Knosos. It is known that such quakes may serve as triggering for the awakening of a dormant volcano. Something of this sort happened at Thera. Soon after the earthquake, and while people were busy removing the debris and sheltering themselves provisionally among the half-fallen houses, the action of the volcano or volcanoes suddenly began and soon became terrific. Huge masses of pumice were ejected; they soon covered land and sea and were later transported everywhere by the waves. Then followed the ejection of volcanic powder, and for several days this powder covered the sky and darkened large areas around the volcano, apparently as far away as Egypt. The whole island was buried

A number of beautiful frescoes were discovered during the recent excavations at Akroteri, Thera. Above: the Springtime fresco from Room Δ2; volcanic rocks and their sides are covered with *red lilies, some about to open and some in full bloom; frolicsome swallows exchange pleasantries and kisses in the air. (National Archaeological Museum, Athens)*

under a thick layer of pumice and powder, fifty or more metres high. Then came the paroxysmal moments. The sides of the volcanic cone, hollowed internally by the terrible heat which transforms rocks into pumice and powder, became clefts and fissures, and the sea poured into the volcano's hollowed belly. A terrific explosion or, more exactly, a series of explosions followed. The central part of the island, which hitherto was a high volcano, exploded and sank into the abyss of the earth, together with two sections of the northern and western parts of the island's circumference. A great hollow space, called a caldera (from the Spanish word meaning cauldron), was created from this sinking. Originally, it was about 800m. deep, but because it was partly filled with the debris of the collapsed volcano, its present depth is 200 to 400 m. The sea entered this almost circular cavity, and thus the largest caldera in the world (together with the Crater Lake in Oregon) was formed. It is slightly elliptical in form, roughly 8 and 10 km. in diameter. One half of the island, about 83 sq. km., disappeared under the sea.

Historical Consequences

All Cretan palaces present clear signs of repeated destruction and rebuilding. These can be satisfactorily explained as the result of earthquakes. The last destruction or destructions, however, which occurred between 1500 and 1450 B.C., was a wholesale one. No palace survived, that at Knosos being the only exception. In general, scholars attributed this almost total destruction to an invasion or invasions from abroad. As a rule, it was the Achaians who were held responsible.

In 1932, Professor Marinatos, while trying to discover Amnisos, Minos's legendary arsenal, found pumice deep in the basement of a building near the shore. Since pumice is a purely volcanic material, pumice in Minoan layers was a most significant fact. Two years later, he expressed for the first time the opinion that Crete must have been destroyed not by man but by the huge eruption of Thera. His theory was published in detail in 1939.

Professor Marinatos had previously studied the eruptions

of similar volcanoes. There is a sister volcano of the Theran type, known as Krakatau or Krakatoa, in Sunda strait, between Java and Sumatra, on the small Rakata island. The eruption of this volcano on 26th-27th August 1883, is absolutely analogous to that of prehistoric Thera and gives us a clue to the violent character of such eruptions. Here are the main events: huge quantities of pumice covered the island and the surrounding sea, obstucting free navigation in neighbouring ports for several months; the volcanic ashes turned day into night within a radius of over 150 km.; the extra fine particles of this dust reached the stratosphere (about 30 km. high), floated in the atmosphere for months, and were transported thousands of kilometres away; the explosions were heard more than 2,000 km. away, and the sound waves circled around the Earth three times before calming down. Most catastrophic, however, was a series of tsunamis (tidal waves). They were about thirty metres high as they invaded the costal districts of Java and Sumatra with terrific speed. They carried away boulders, locomotives, rails, and whole ships. Several little towns and settlements were shaved off, and 36,000 people lost their lives.

The exploded area in Krakatoa was only 22.8 sq. km. as against 83 sq. km. in Thera. By analogy, on the basis of disappeared surface area, the explosive power in Thera must have been four times greater. Although there are different estimates, one thing is beyond any doubt: Crete, only sixty miles distant, must have suffered terrific losses. Tsunamis swept off everything along the coasts of the island. The fall of volcanic ash destroyed the crops, and fluorine poisoned living beings. A series of earthquakes, which are typical before or after every eruption of the Thera volcano, destroyed the palaces and inland settlements. The eastern part of Crete suffered more severely than the rest of the island. It is by no chance that in just this Eteo-Cretan part of the island the tradition about Crete remaining for some time without inhabitants was still alive in the days of Herodotos.

If the Minoan eruption on Thera had only the magnitude of the Krakatoa eruption, it is estimated that the noise would have been heard as far away as Gibraltar, Scandinavia, the Arabian Ocean, and Central Africa. The clouds of ash, gases, and vapour which were poured out of the volcano must have plunged the Southern Aegean and the Eastern Mediterranean into impenetrable darkness for many days. Given, then, that the caldera of Thera is much bigger than the subterranean crater created by the Krakatoa eruption, and that the depth of the sea between Thera and Crete is much greater than that near the volcano in the Indian Ocean, we may form some idea of the effects of the Theran eruption on Crete and the other shores which lay within reach of the volcano's fury. It is estimated that, within a period of 20 to 30 minutes from the final eruption of the volcano and the submersion of the final section of Thera, the tidal waves would have engulfed the northern shores of Crete and, in about three hours, the shores of southeastern Mediterranean from Tunisia to Syria. We can be positive in saying that the destruction of known and already excavated sites in Crete (Amnisos, Nirou, Malia, Gournia, Pseira, Mochlos) was due to the tsunamis. Recently, a new and interesting site was added, the palace of Zakros. The eruption of Thera had repercussions in Egypt too. The appearance of the Keftiu in paintings of Egyptian tombs about 1500 B.C. and during the following generation may be an indirect result of the partial abandonment of Crete.

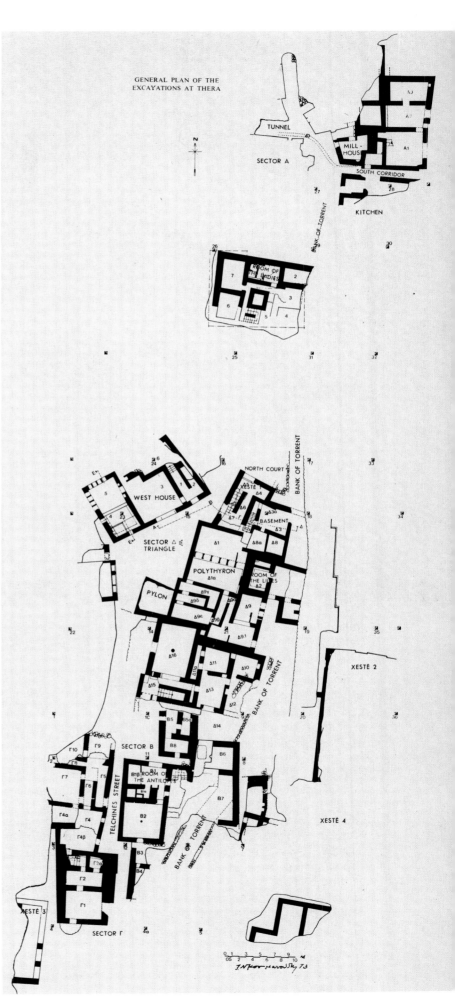

The Antelopes fresco from Room B1, facing Mill Square, Akroteri, Thera. There are six antelopes; two of them are represented *above in an amorous moment; the execution reveals discerning familiarity with animals. (National Archaeol. Museum, Athens)*

Excavations on Thera

Professor Marinatos's theory was published in the English periodical *Antiquity* for 1939. As was to be expected, scholars were sceptical and asked for more evidence based on excavations. Owing to World War II and the post-war difficulties in Greece, it was only in 1962 that local search in Thera began with a view to selecting the most suitable place for an excavation. It was known that the exploiting of the volcanic ashes of Thera for the construction of the Suez Canal in 1866 had revealed traces of habitations with abundant ceramic finds. The geological researches of Fouqué revealed similar traces in the district of Akroteri. At Fouqué's invitation, two young French archaeologists, Gorceix and Mamet, found and partly excavated ruins of destroyed houses to the north as well as to the south of the Akroteri village. Later, the Saliveros family found similar traces at Kamaras (Potamos) to the east of Akroteri. These were excavated by von Gaertringen's staff. Minor finds had also appeared in several parts of the island, so that no less than ten localities with hidden antiquities were listed by Mari-

natos. The question was in which one of these places the excavation should start. The classical method of investigating the depths of the earth by means of trenches was ruled out on account of the huge layers of pumice. After several years of study, it appeared to the excavator that geographical, climatological, and other reasons pointed to the Akroteri district as the most likely place for the capital of Thera. A field was chosen near the right bank of a torrent descending from Akroteri southwards to the sea. The rest was God's work, for the point chosen hides indeed the most residential quarter of the town, which seems to extend from the southern to the northern shore. Beyond this, the northernmost quarters of the town were swallowed by the abyss of the caldera.

In 1967, Professor Marinatos began excavating. The results have been very encouraging, although naturally it would be premature to construct from the finds a picture of the life of a Minoan settlement during its most flourishing years. However, it is clear that Akroteri was a busy centre before the volcanic destruction. The inhabitants were fishermen, traders and farmers; they cultivated corn and pulse.

The delightful fresco of the Boxing Children, discovered on the south wall of Room B1. This is the earliest representation of boxing-gloves. (National Archaeological Museum, Athens)

This fresco of the Fisherman holding two strings of mackerel was in an excellent state of preservation when found, together with the fresco of the second Fisherman, in the northeastern corner of Room 5 in the West House at Akroteri. This is the earliest specimen of complete nudity in Minoan-Mycenaean art. (National Archaeological Museum, Athens)

This historically significant frieze, painted in miniature style along the walls of Room 5 of the West House at Akroteri, represents an expedition. Above: Town 2 and warships, among them the flagship. Below: the rest of the fleet and Town 3. (National Archaeological Museum, Athens)

they ground the corn, extracted oil from olives, reared flocks of goats and sheep, and fished with nets.

Like any volcanic island, Thera was rich in alkalis and therefore very fertile. Results of the latest excavations show that there was also an exceptionally well-organized export trade, mainly in oil. The biggest, most beautiful, and earliest group of stirrup jars and ewers, peculiar vessels used for transporting oil, were unearthed on Thera, and several of them had inscriptions or signs in Linear A. They are the prototypes of similar jars made about 250 years later which bore inscriptions in Linear B. The stirrup jars from Thera had perfect 'bottling' systems and carried tags on which details of quality and origin were evidently noted. The commercial tradition of the island is clearly evident, and the richness of the houses testifies to a comfortable and sophisticated life comparable to the palace life on Crete.

During the excavations, vessels were found containing seeds of barley, lathyrus (fava), vetch pea and other types of pulse, sesame, and remains of sea creatures. The Therans practised metal-working and weaving, and they weighed their goods with lead and stone weights.

Like all Mediterranean peoples, the inhabitants of Thera were very fond of the so-called 'sea-fruits'. Traces and shells have been found of sea-urchins, limpets, sea and land snails. Some vessels contained flour, garlic and onions, oil, and perhaps other substances which have not yet been analysed. Recently, the shapes of various pieces of furniture have been reproduced by pouring fine gypsum into the hollows in the ash. A striking example is a whole bed with amazing detail, including the fine string which held the material or skin of the mattress.

The Therans lived in houses of two or three storeys, well-built and decorated with frescoes. In the construction of the houses, they used timber ties familiar from Minoan architecture, and the same type of doors and windows with stone jambs and lintels have been found. Even the doors of the upper storeys have been preserved. The floors of several upper rooms had a paving of regular slabs, and in the wall of one house a perpendicular drainpipe was discovered. The Akroteri settlement was divided into two by a paved road, which has been named "Telchines Street" ("Coppersmiths Road"). The stones are still shiny from once constant use.

One group of buildings presents some palace features, which means that there was some form of central authority on Thera; perhaps it was this palace centre which controlled the movement of merchandise between Crete, further lands and the Cyclades. The excavation of this section has only just begun, but all the indications are that it will bring to light monumental buildings constructed of ashlar masonry.

Art was highly developed in the Thera settlement. Considerable sections of frescoes have been found in some houses. One of these shows agile lifesize monkeys climbing about among the mountain rocks. Vegetation on the ground and swallows in the air above enliven the landscape, and there are also clumps of crocuses. There is a splendid painting of an 'African'. Other sections of the frescoes show spiral patterns in beautiful combinations.

Left: the Miniature frieze from the north wall of Room 5 of the West House at Akroteri: a sea-battle scene with landing troops and drowning soldiers. This page: a detail from the Blue Monkeys fresco. (National Archaeological Museum, Athens)

Excavation of a building with frescoes that have been preserved in position on the walls has recently been put in hand. One is a delightful scene portraying nature at the beginning of spring. Red lilies shoot up everywhere between the rocks. Swallows exchange pleasantries and kisses in the sky. It may be that the imposing rocks of the landscape will give us at least a general idea of the appearance of Thera before the volcanic eruption that hurled half the island into the sky and buried the other half under volcanic ash.

The painted decoration on clay pots shows artistic sensitivity and preserves the polychromy of earlier periods. There are two kinds of pottery: the mat-painted local and the imported, which is mostly Minoan but also Mycenaean. In both cases we have first-class products, and this is also true of the rest of the finds. Considering that the catastrophe occurred at the peak of the Mediterranean Bronze Age, it is no wonder that everything should be so exquisite. There are many stone vases, tools and implements, some metal vases, and only a few objects made of precious materials (gems, ivory, or silver) since the inhabitants took anything precious with them. Of imported objects, there are a few vases from the old excavations, two ostrich-egg rhyta, and a recently found canaanite jar. But the most precious products of Minoan art are the frescoes, and every excavation season seems to yield a new unexpected treasure.

The Most Recent Excavations

At every 25 to 30 yards, Telchinon Street, which runs from south to north, broadens into a little square, around which lie the most prominent houses (see General Plan). The room which yielded the Antelopes and the Boxing Children opens on to the first square, otherwise known as the Mill Square. Further north, the Triangle Square was discovered with the façade of the West House, already famous for its frescoes. Immediately to the north of it lies the semi-excavated House of the Ladies, in which a little room, bearing all the characteristics of a house-sanctuary, was decorated with a cult scene containing a group of noble-looking ladies.

These buildings were all ordinary houses made of rubble work; but to the east and to the south of them lies another series of four or five magnificent mansions made of squared tuff stones in ashlar masonry. From the ancient Greek technical expression for such a building system, these mansions have been called Xesté (that is, hewn stone) and numbered 1 to 4. Only one of them, Xesté 3, has been sufficiently excavated, and that only because it was the most severely damaged of all. It had two verandahs in the eastern façade. One of those characteristic religious recesses of the Minoan palaces known as lustral basins was found in this mansion. Among other precious items of pottery and stone implements found in it, the most precious were no less than about ninety square metres of frescoes.

The other mansions are in a better state of preservation up to the second, and one of them up to the third, storey. They have not been excavated yet, but one of them, Xesté 4, surely contains frescoes. Just as the 1973 season was about to close, a fifth ashlar-masonry building began to appear

The Young Priestess: this fresco, found in Room 4 of the West House at Akroteri, shows a priestess offering a cake in a bowl. (National Archaeological Museum, Athens)

close to, and to the south of, Xesté 4. It is obvious that these great buildings differ from the other houses of the town. It also appears that the quality of their frescoes is somewhat superior to that of the earlier ones. But it would be premature to go into greater detail about these prominent constructions. Only a brief description of the frescoes found during recent seasons is here possible.

Most famous is a little room (Δ2), beyond doubt a little house sanctuary, the frescoes of which have been entirely preserved on its walls (p. 222). It contains the Springtime fresco, whose purpose was to adorn the shrine of the Great Earth Mother. What is represented may be described as the festival of the meadows at springtime in the Mediterranean. A series of volcanic rocks, the clefts separating them, and the sides of the hillocks are all covered with lilies, some about to open and some in full bloom. Swallows flying singly or in pairs enliven the landscape and symbolize the tender moments of Nature being reborn. The design is clear and the colours luminous. Life and serenity characterize this work of the unknown landscapist.

At about the same time, the frescoes of the Antelopes and of the Boxing Children (p. 224 and i) were discovered in Room B1, facing the Mill Square. There are six antelopes, two of them represented in an amorous moment; the design is vivid, and the execution reveals discerning familiarity with animals. The fresco of the Boxing Children, apparently a brother and a sister, displays good rendering of the delicate anatomy of children's bodies, between six and seven; their mock-fighting is full of earnestness, and, incidentally, this is the first appearance of boxing-gloves.

Another room in the same quarter contained a fresco of a herd of Flying Monkeys, climbing upon the mountain rocks (p. 225). As in the case of the Springtime fresco, the design runs over the corners on all the walls of the room. This painting was badly damaged, but the main composition is quite clear, and the animals are rendered in a masterly manner. In connection with this, as well as with the Antelopes painting, the question arises as to where we may imagine these animals to be living. It is improbable that they lived on the island of Thera, since they belong to a typically African fauna. The recently found Miniature fresco, to be described below, may suggest a solution to this problem.

In the House of the Ladies there was a painting of a group of three women, one of whom may possibly be a seated goddess; a peplos and other offerings are being presented to her. A number of large sea-daffodils (*pancratium maritimum*) and a star motive (p. 227) form the background of this painting. The noble appearance and beauty of these women are suggestive of the period of European aristocracy of the late eighteenth century.

The West House too yielded a great art treasure. Already during the early part of its excavation, the Banners (now proven to be stern-cabins of warships) and the Young Priestess (p. 226) had been found. The latter is a *Krokopeplos* (clad in a saffron-coloured peplos) offering a cake in a gold-and-silver bowl. But that was only the beginning. The following year, as the excavation was about to be completed, two painted fishermen were found, one of whom, as by a miracle, was in an excellent state of preservation (p. iii). He stands over one metre high, holds two strings of mackerel

One of a group of women from the house shrine of the House of the Ladies. (National Archaeological Museum, Athens)

in his hands and has a shaven head with only a few locks; this is also the first specimen of complete nudity in Minoan-Mycenaean art.

But even more precious was a frieze, painted in miniature style, of which more than six metres in length have been preserved. The artistic value of this work is great, but even greater is its historical significance. It is an episode which, like a movies strip, narrates the events of an expedition. A fleet of seven warships and several smaller ships and boats, three towns, cattle, wild beasts, and no fewer than 80 persons participate in this adventure. The action takes place in a subtropical landscape, and it is hard to imagine any other land but Libya.

The preserved parts of the frieze are painted along the north, east, and south walls of Room 5 of the West House. At the beginning part of the frieze there stands a high and steep hillock right on the shore, on the top of which there is a gathering of several persons. Then follows the scene of a sea-battle, in which the silhouettes of drowning soldiers are little masterpieces (p. ii and iv). Warriors armed with body-shields, boar's tusk helmets, swords, and great naval spears, are landing. The first 'town' may be a mere hamlet with sheep-folds; there are herds and herdsmen there.

Along the east wall there is a subtropical landscape (p. 228), the basic element of which is a stream, surely not a great river such as the Nile. Palms make up the chief flora, and among the fauna we can discern ducks, flamingos (or ibises), panthers, and roe-deer. A griffin is flying over the hills. The landscape is a windy one.

The main subject is painted on the south wall. To the left is the second town. In the mountains above it, a lion pursues a herd of stags. Otherwise, the town presents a peaceful aspect. There are people gathered on the roofs or walking in the streets. There is also a scene of conversation by the brook between a man and a woman, both wearing fur mantles.

A kind of promontory appears to the right of the town, and the fleet is sailing past it. Seven ships in all, in two parallel columns are advancing towards the right. Only one, the "Peleia" ("Dore"), has sails. All the others are propelled by paddling in the shallow waters. Among them is the flagship in full colours.

The most advanced ships have already reached the third town, the boats of which hasten to welcome them. The ladies greet the arriving guests from the towers, and the children run to and fro in excitement.

It would be premature to try to tell of the true meaning of this whole action, so full of realism and apparently of historical significance. It appears to represent cordially friendly connections between the Aegean and a certain part of Libya, probably some part in the Great Syrtis. There must have been strongly Minoanized settlements there just as there must have been Libyan elements and inhabitants in the Aegean world. Tradition is our great help in such instances. Mycenaean myths like those about Aigyptos and Danaos or the Argonautic expedition are links between the Aegean and certain Libyan localities, such as Kinyps and Tritonis. Concerning Thera in particular there is the curious tradition that the island was born out of a lump of Libyan earth. Thus, the Theran colony of Kyrene would be like returning to lands where forefathers had once established connections.

THE FINAL CATASTROPHE
Widespread Destruction of Minoan Centres

Although the Minoan centres of Crete suffered extensive and repeated seismic destructions, life and civilization on the island went on without interruption, steadily developing and improving. One of these destructions at the beginning of the New-Palace Period was so complete that radical renovation of the buildings was required. However, the geological upheavals in the eastern Aegean were not over. The volcano on Thera showed obvious signs of renewed activity. It is not certain if the catastrophe of about 1600 B.C., at the period, that is, when the chief Mycenaean centres were being founded, was due to the initial eruption of the volcano. This was the view originally put forward by Marinatos, the excavator of Amnisos. The remains which had been discovered on Thera (long before Evans's excavations on Crete)

This subtropical landscape was painted along the East wall of *Room 5 of the West House at Akroteri. The main element is a*

beneath the thick layer of volcanic ash were assigned to this period. Later, it was shown beyond doubt that this volcanic eruption must have taken place c. 1500 B.C. (1520 B.C., according to Marinatos).

Professor Marinatos's view that there was widespread destruction of Minoan centres by the terrible eruption of the volcano is finally beginning to be accepted by scholars after coordinated research by geologists and archaeologists. There have been differences of opinion as to whether the destruction was the result of many successive eruptions or of a single catastrophic eruption. The evidence of archaeological research points to the first as the most likely; there were, that is, destructions in the Minoan centres caused by two successive eruptions, c. 1500 B.C. and 1450 B.C., of which the latter had annihilating consequences. The eruptions were accompanied by terrible earthquakes and volcanic waves that swept over the shores of Crete. Unfortunately, the excavators of the various Minoan centres did not, at the outset, envisage the possibility of such a calamity, and much evidence for it was passed over unnoticed. There had also been doubts about whether the destruction of the New-Palace centres was simultaneous, and only recent excavations, particularly at the palace of Zakros and at Knosos, have led towards a satisfactory solution of the problem of dating and of interpreting the evidence connected with the volcanic destruction.

Almost exactly the same phenomena have been observed in all the New-Palace centres that have been excavated. Obviously, the final calamity came almost as a complete surprise; it was total and accompanied by widespread fires that reduced most of the buildings to ashes. Fires of this sort, occurring simultaneously in almost all the settlements, would be difficult to attribute to enemy activity, especially since no traces have been found anywhere of intervention by foreign bands or of uprising by mutinous mobs. On the contrary, in many places we can observe the ruins of a wall, for instance, which was torn up from its base and flung down in one piece, or huge blocks which had been hurled a long distance—phenomena which can only be attributed to destruction by earthquakes. Catastrophes of this sort are almost always accompanied by great fires; this must have been especially true in areas where the lighting was by oil lamp and where the cooking fires would have spread easily. If the earthquakes began with small warning tremors, the inhabitants would have had time to get away, taking their valuable possessions with them. However, simple earthquakes could not have resulted in the total abandonment of sites that had been occupied for centuries. In great seismic catastrophes, panic often led to mass migration, but nearly always people returned before long to continue life in the same place. In this case, the explanation for the devastation that followed, especially in the coastal belt of Crete, has now been provided by a study of the phenomena that accompanied the huge eruption of the Theran volcano.

During the excavation of the Palace of Zakros, which began in 1962 and is still continuing, phenomena were studied which could only be interpreted as being the result of a volcanic eruption. Whole walls of hewn porous stone had fallen in one piece as a result of sudden enormous pressure. Similarly, other thick walls of very large bricks had collapsed with their bricks still in rows; the jars in the same underground storage rooms were heaped together against the west wall; ash which may have been of volcanic origin was found piled up to the level of the jar-lips. Quantities of pumice have been found in the banks of earth which covered the palace; sections of the palace had been hurled into the air and shattered as if they had been hit by bullets. Perhaps this also accounts for the widespread scattering of many utensils of the upper floors which have been found all over the palace area. Pieces of the famous relief rhyton of the peak sanctuary were scattered in four separate places. Some of these phenomena could have been caused by the same gigantic volcanic wave which swept over the northern shores and, to a lesser extent, the eastern shores of the island. It is not yet certain, but it may be regarded as highly probable, that numerous pieces of a spongy material containing sulphur and molten metal found in the palace area were hurled from the crater of the volcano of Thera, which was about 130 kilometres from Zakros.

stream of water bordered by palm trees, ducks, flamingos, pan-   thers, and a flying griffin. (National Arch. Museum, Athens)

A New Dynasty

However terrible the results of the volcanic eruption which sank two-thirds of Thera beneath the waves, thereby creating the largest caldera in the world, these alone could scarcely account for the abandoning of nearly all New-Palace centres, many of them lying in a radius which would have left them almost unaffected, did we not take into account the further consequences of this great catastrophe. The ash from the volcano would have covered the greater part of central and eastern Crete to a depth of certainly more than 40 centimetres, thus rendering most of the land barren or extremely difficult to cultivate. The water would have undergone many changes and most of it would have become unwholesome or poisonous. The ruling classes must have been persuaded that the deity wished to be rid of their presence. A flood of migrations was the natural consequence.

The once rich regions were abandoned, and the few inhabitants who remained had little inclination or energy to rebuild the ruins. Many years passed before the same places were inhabited again; some remained forever deserted. Only at Knosos do we see the palace founded again, almost in the same form, except for minor alterations. There, however, the archive tablets in Linear Script B, the predominance in the pottery of the palace style, which was based on new principles known in the Mycenaean region, the appearance in the architecture of new non-Minoan elements, all confirm that a new dynasty, Achaian-Mycenaean in character, had already established itself there. We may suppose that the new settlers were aided by the disturbances that followed the great destruction. Yet, the fact that Minoan life and civilization continued without any break leads us to accept the view that the first Achaian settlement was established with the support of the Minoan population, who thus found a way to regain part of their lost prosperity.

MINOAN RELIGION
The Vegetation Cycle and the Divinities

The succession of the seasons, vegetation, and the withering of plants and trees made a deep impression on primitive man. Every winter he wondered if the trees would ever bear fruit again, if the seed which was buried in the earth would shoot up in the spring. The longed-for return of spring filled him with joy. But again the reaping of the corn, the dog-days which dried up the grass, and the falling leaves in the autumn disturbed him deeply. The alternation of these feelings led to the personification of the basic elements in the eternal drama. In man's imagination, Nature took on the form of a Great Mother, while he saw vegetation as a Divine Infant, a Young God, who is born, dies, and is resurrected every year.

The relation between these two deities is not very clear. Sometimes, it appears to be the relation of lovers, a relation, however, which is not always brought to consummation, because the Young God dies sometimes a little before, sometimes a little after, his marriage to the Goddess. Elsewhere, she seems to be his mother, or his sister, or sometimes simply his companion. In these variations and under a variety of names, this divine couple also appears in the myths of the East, Egypt, Asia Minor, and Greece, and this helps us to form some idea of the apparently analogous religion of Minoan Crete, whose sacred texts have been lost for ever.

The Young God was not the only "mortal" figure in pre-Greek religion. It would appear that the Aegeans also believed in a young goddess who died and was born again. Ariadne, princess of Knosos and daughter of Minos, was both a moon and a tree goddess, and she died every year.

This religion did not disappear with the Minoan civilization; it continued to exist, altered and mixed with new elements in Archaic and Classical times, and so, thanks to Greek and Latin writers, some names of pre-Greek deities have come down to us. We know Diktynna and Britomartis. The first is undoubtedly the goddess who lived and was worshipped on the sacred mountain of Minoan Crete, Dikte, the great mountain with the cave where the Young God was born. The second name, it would seem, was the epithet of the Goddess Daughter and means "Sweet Virgin". These

then are the expressions in the Minoan religion of the two forms which Nature assumed: sometimes venerable, terrifying, and omnipotent; sometimes gentle, charming, and full of kindness. The Young God who died also had two natures: sometimes, he was the strong tamer of wild beasts, griffins, and winged game; at others, he was weak like a child or a flower—he was alternately called Belchanos and Hyakinthos.

The Minoan goddess appears in many different forms, and some students of religion believe that these represent separate deities. But it is probable that not even the devout votary of the Minoan Age could himself say with any certainty whether he believed in one goddess or many. In her various representations, the goddess appears: on the peak of a mountain; between lions; as the *Oreia Meter*—the Mother of the Mountain (we know this name from Asia Minor cults in Hellenistic and Roman times); as well as the Lady of Wild Beasts (*Potnia Thērōn*, as the Greeks were to call Artemis), because the presence of lions and panthers emphasized her power and majesty.

The goddess is represented sometimes seated below her spreading sacred tree, sometimes standing, holding snakes in her hands, or with one large snake coiled round the whole of her beautiful body. The snake is either the symbol of the infernal world, or the good "spirit" which protects the home, and at the same time perhaps the expression of the unpredictable, the abrupt and startling apparition of the supernatural in out-of-the-way country places.

Sometimes, doves (birds which make their nests in the big old temples of the East and in Cretan sanctuaries and were perhaps for that reason considered holy) flutter their wings on the shoulders and cheeks of the goddess or sit on her head. Sometimes, she holds in her hands, or has placed in her hair, the fertilized flower of the "sleep-bringing poppy", whose juice lulls her small creatures, the infants, or brings the votary to ecstasy and visions. Sometimes, she is the *Kourotrophos*, the maternal goddess who holds in her arms the Kouros, the young boy, the Divine Infant; elsewhere, she brandishes a sword like a warlike champion of

230

the Minoan kingdom; elsewhere, she sails away on her boat to far-off mythical islands.

Many of these symbols were inherited by the goddesses of historical times: Artemis, Aphrodite, Athena. But the Minoan goddess is more clearly linked with the powerful female divinities of Asia Minor: Kybele—Kybebe or the Great Mother of Phrygia; the Idaian Mother; Ma; the Ephesian Artemis. In cult scenes, there sometimes appear, as well as these deities, various fantastic daemons with human bodies and the heads of birds or animals. These strange daemons water the sacred tree, adore the goddess, accompany and protect the Young God. Perhaps these figures come from magic rituals in which priests wore animal masks; the disguise was intended to frighten and ward off evil spirits or to force the daemons to aid fertility.

Epiphany and Sacred Marriage

In the culminating years of the Minoan civilization, large cult statues were rare. In Crete, there were no large temples as in the East and Egypt, but only small palace, house, or country shrines. The images of the deity were adapted to the dimensions of the place of worship. It would seem, also, that a distinct, clearly Minoan conception of the deity led the votary to prefer small, more familiar representations of it. The large static stone figures which connect the divinity with a particular place of worship were foreign to him; he felt himself closer to the small fragile portable figurines which stood on a dais in a small room, as modern icons stand in a house iconostasis today.

The votary undoubtedly believed that even human beings could become incarnations of the deity for a short time or for ever. Members of the royal family, the king himself and the queen, the young princes and princesses, all play the part of deities in the rites and accept offerings from the worshippers. The queen, seated on her carved alabaster throne in the palace of Knosos, represents the goddess and takes part in the ritual, guarded to left and right by griffins painted on the wall. A crowd of votaries wait for her to appear before the sanctuary, and on feast days members of the priesthood carry her all round the township on a sedan chair.

There were, however, visionary epiphanies as well. Priests and priestesses, throwing themselves ecstatically into an orgiastic dance, see the goddess descending from heaven with windswept hair and sitting for a moment close to her small sanctuary or its altar.

The Minoan votary felt the deity as something mysterious, fleeting and intangible, which appeared only for a moment in human shape or in the shapes of various sacred animals —the bull, the bird, the snake, the wild goat, or a young cow suckling its calf with maternal tenderness. This explains certain myths of historical times which echo earlier beliefs as, for example, the legend of the marriage of the queen-goddess Pasiphae with the divine bull which leapt out of the sea, and the legend of the abduction of Europa by the Zeus-bull.

This vigorous, half-wild animal which originally had a practical function on Crete—the fertilization and propagation of the herd that gives milk, meat, and skins to the community—soon took on a deeper religious meaning, and his erotic union became an element in homeopathic magic that determined all natural fertility. As in the East, so in Crete,

Faience statuette of the 'snake goddess' from the treasury of the sanctuary at Knosos (New Palace Period). (Herakleion Museum)

the bull is identified with the heavens and the sun, which fertilizes the earth with rain and heat, while the female figure, the sacred cow, is associated with the moon, whose shape is reminiscent of horns. Thus, the marriage of the bull and the cow is at the same time the marriage of sun and moon.

Later, the roles of the participants in this sacred marriage are played by the king and queen of Knosos; the Greek name of the queen, Pasiphae, meaning "full of light" (and being the translation into Greek of some unknown Minoan name), shows exactly the connection of the queen-goddess with the moon. Her son, the Minotaur, a man with a bull's head, is also called Asteriōn, because he, like his father, is identified with the starry heavens.

We need not be surprised that the Minotaur dies, and that the sacred bull of Crete, (the pre-eminently sacrificial animal) is a "suffering god", for, in the East also, the "bull of heaven" and, in Egypt, Apis are eventually killed.

Another figure in Greek mythology, Amaltheia, who reared the "divine infant" that had been abandoned in the wilderness, was the wild goat of Minoan Crete, an animal full of vigour, sometimes shown with wings, who like a bull is linked with a natural fertility cult.

Sacred Caves and Peaks

The deity was also worshipped in caves. The striking stalactite formations in the caves of Dikte and Amnisos would have assumed a supernatural character in the reflections of torches and the meagre light of day. At Amnisos, in the Cave of Eileithyia, who was the goddess of love and reproduction, the central stalagmite and another smaller one by its side were regarded as "natural" images of the Goddess Mother and the Divine Infant. A low wall was built around them, and for centuries votaries left vessels there with milk and honey to secure the good-will of the goddess and her aid when a child was expected.

In the Diktaian Cave where, as the Greeks related later, another mother goddess, Rhea, hid her new-born son, Zeus, the votaries offered small bronze figurines which represented themselves in the attitude of worship. In this way they could remain ever close to the goddess. Small models of animals, mainly bulls, were substituted for the real slaughter of sacrifice. Bronze double axes and large swords in another

cult cave near Arkalochori show that there a warlike divinity was worshipped.

Worship was also offered on the high peaks of mountains and hills, for instance, at Asterousia, Juktas, Phileremos. The extensive view and the absolute stillness, broken only by the sudden leap of the wild goat or the flight of an eagle, made a great impression on the votary. He felt that these remote airy places were the most suitable ones for the presence of the supernatural and its worship. Sanctuaries were built on these peaks about 2000 B.C. and remained there to c. 1700 B.C. when, because of some unknown religious change or for some other reason perhaps connected with the destruction of the early palaces, most of these shrines ceased to be used.

On festival days a crowd of pilgrims set off from the villages of the plain, carrying vessels with offerings and votive gifts, and ascended slowly to the summit. There they gathered round the sanctuary and in the evening they lit a huge fire that could be seen from far off in all the villages of the plain, from where other worshippers watched the ceremony. Into the fire they threw clay images which represented the worshippers, their hands outstretched in supplication or salute, or clasped to the breast as if the votary was surrendering himself to the divinity. They also offered models of limbs of the body that were in pain or which had been healed with the help of the goddess, and models of birds, oxen, and other animals, and of a strange insect which was regarded as sacred, because it had a small horn. No doubt the fire, which was purposely built on a high place to be nearer to heaven, was intended to help the sun recover the strength it had lost during the winter. This fire, like the fires of St. John today, was probably lit at the summer solstice, when the days are at their longest. Throwing the images into the fire had an expiatory purpose and was equivalent to the votary himself leaping into the flames.

The Cave of Eileithyia near Amnisos (the port of Minoan Knosos), where the fertility goddess was worshipped. The votaries laid their offerings, usually milk and honey, around the stalagmites to ensure the blessing of the goddess.

Large New-Palace seal-stone made of sardonyx (Knosos). The goddess, standing between winged griffins who attend her, holds aloft an arc-shaped symbol from which a double axe rises. The face of the goddess shows the anti-naturalistic trend of the art of the Late New-Palace Period. (Herakleion Museum)

Shrines in Palaces and Houses

Many sections of the palaces and houses in Minoan Crete show religious features (horns of consecration, carvings of double axes and other symbols on the walls, etc.), but there are also special places of worship of a standard shape. The most typical are: the "triple shrines" which comprise three connected rooms with the central one on a higher level than the other two; the crypts with a central pillar; and the lustral basins.

Double axes, stars, and tridents were carved on the pillar in the crypt, and on the floor around it the votaries left small cups with offerings or poured various liquids into the basins and hollows in the paving as a libation to the daemonic being who inhabited the pillar. Similar examples of aniconic, and substantially fetishist, worship in later periods are the sacred stone of Kybele at Pessinous in Asia Minor and the *baityloi*, stones within which some supernatural power dwelt. Representations of pillars with birds seated on them or with sphinxes, griffins, or lions chained to them show that the pillar too had some cult significance and perhaps symbolized the sanctuary.

Lustral baths were rooms, access to which was down a small staircase. Libation vessels, rhyta, ceremonial utensils, and small clay cups which were found in such areas show that the worshippers carried out ritual acts there and made libations. The sanctified water which collected at the bottom of the basin was used for purifications and aspersions.

In late Minoan times, sanctuaries appeared which, it would seem, no longer belonged to the palace or to one house, but to the whole community, and this is important from the historical point of view. Such sanctuaries have been found at Knosos, Gournia, Karphi, Gazi, and elsewhere; these too are small rooms, usually with a dais built along the length of one wall, on which figurines were placed. Sometimes, there were also double axes and horns on the dais; in front of it, was a small altar where offerings were placed.

Idols of the Deity

As far back as the Neolithic Age, figurines of the Great Goddess appear in Crete which show her naked and plump, like the venerated mothers with many children in the then still matriarchal clans of Neolithic Crete. This type of figurine survived in certain small stone amulets which the men of later times still wore. The goddess also appears naked in the marble figurines of Cycladic type, which circulated in Crete in the Pre-Palace Period and which have been found in tholos tombs. Their similarity to the large cult statues of the Cyclades leads us to believe that these figures do not represent concubines or maidservants of the dead, but the goddess herself who accompanies and protects him as she did when he was alive.

On a vessel from Malia, the fertility goddess is again represented naked, boldly displaying the pubic triangle. Such representations were not indecent to the primitive mind, because human reproduction, like that of animals and plants, doubtlessly had a religious significance. However, representations of erotic scenes are entirely absent from Minoan art.

In later, more advanced, phases of the Minoan civilization, complete nudity disappears, and about 1600 B.C., in the famous Knosos statuettes with the snakes, the goddess appears dressed in the heavy robes of a court lady. Only the breasts protrude naked from the garment, which covers the rest of the body. Thus, there is still emphasis on the feminine and maternal character of the Great Goddess.

In the communal sanctuaries of Late Minoan times, the votaries worshipped large clay figurines having a variety of symbols on their heads (birds, horns, poppies, snakes) and both arms raised in a gesture suggestive of prayer. The attitude expresses a salute or benediction addressed to the votary. Perhaps its origin lies in the gestures of the priestess-dancers who represented the epiphany of the goddess or in the similar attitude of eastern deities entreating high gods on man's behalf.

Tree Worship

Great importance was attached in Minoan religion to sacred trees; and the pre-eminently sacred tree was the olive. The age-old olives of Crete, sprouting eternally from their ancient, almost dead, trunks, doubtlessly impressed Minoan man. The longevity of this tree and its importance to life explain why the olive was regarded as sacred at a period when man looked upon oil (like corn) as a basic necessity of life. Low enclosures crowned with horns were built round sacred trees; double axes and altars were placed outside them to receive offerings. Other sacred trees were the kind that shed their leaves in winter. In representations on gold royal rings, the votaries, men and women, stood by them sorrowfully mourning the falling of the leaves in autumn, or celebrating their reappearance in spring with an orgiastic dance.

Sacred Symbols

Minoan religion preferred a symbolic to a representational expression of the deity. One of the most sacred symbols is the pair of horns, often found together with a double axe or a branch from the sacred tree, and placed on a dais in the sanctuary or on an altar as the main cult object. Without doubt, the pair of horns is meant to be a concise representation of the bull's head (which was hung in the sanctuary or tomb after the sacrifice) and of the divine bull itself.

Even more important was the *labrys*, or double axe, which began simply as a tool in daily use and a weapon and developed into a symbol of supernatural power not only in Crete but also in Asia Minor and in many other places. Perhaps it was associated with lightning (which strikes and hurls down tall trees) or with the sacred bull which was sacrificed with this sort of weapon. The cult double axe was larger and finer than the one in everyday use; it had a semi-circular edge, incised, relief, or bored decoration, and was fixed on large wooden stands supported on stone bases. Sometimes, the double axe is shown on the head of the goddess as she stands upright between her sacred animals; sometimes, she holds it herself in both hands.

Another sacred symbol is the knot which often appears in conjunction with the double axe. The Minoans, like other peoples, attributed to the knot various magic, tutelary, and healing powers. Its tying ensured the possession of a loved one, and its loosening made birth easier. Chiefly, however, the knot binds and subdues daemons. A typical representation is of a goddess or priestess holding a griffin bound with the sacred knot.

Some defensive weapons, like the great figure-of-eight shield (made from bull-hide) and the helmet, took on by their very nature magic and tutelary powers. Perhaps these weapons were associated with the warlike nature of the goddess. Small amulets in the shape of a shield have also been found. The cross, the star, the curved cross, and the wheel are also sacred symbols, all connected with the stars or the sun.

Cult Utensils and the Priesthood

A typical Minoan ritual vessel is the *kernos* (cluster vase). The best known example is the stone kernos from Malia which has many rounded hollows in the circumference and a large bowl in the centre. This vessel must surely have been used for offerings of the "first fruit" of every type of agricultural produce. From a passage in Athenaios we learn that similar kernoi were used in historical times in the worship of Demeter and contained small quantities of cereals: wheat, barley, oats, various leguminous plants, oil, milk, wine, honey, sheep-wool, and even a string of dried figs or the sweetmeats of various fruits. And to this day in Crete, the priest blesses the "first fruits" of the earth each year in the church with the lovely prayer: "Lord, bless this bread, the wheat, the wine, the oil; and multiply them; and sanctify those who partake of them". The fruits that have been blessed are then shared among those present, the owner of the land, and the priest. The same sort of ceremony was probably carried out in Minoan times: a blessing and a prayer for plentiful crops, and at the same time a thanksgiving offering to the deity. The kernos is like a wreath of fruit, which symbolizes the circle of the year and secures fertility.

For liquid libations, the so-called *rhyton* was used. These rhyta had both a mouth through which they could be filled and a hole from which the water could be poured out. From the rhyton, which was held by the priest at the time of the libation, the water ran out into the lustral area or into a clay pipe and from there into the bosom of Mother Earth while a suitable prayer was slowly intoned, imploring nature to imitate the magic human ritual and send rain.

Some rhyta in the form of a bull, or a bull's head, were doubtless used to offer the blood of the sacrificed sacred animal. More rarely, they are in the shape of a lion's head, a sea triton, or a man. One rhyton in the form of a woman has the effluence holes in the breasts as if the goddess herself were offering a mother's milk to her creatures. Another rhyton from Gournia, certainly intended for the sacred fertility rites, shows a pregnant woman and has the effluence hole at the pudendum.

Worship took several forms. The votary presented himself at the sanctuary or to the invisible deity, not kneeling or bowed, but upright, his fist clenched and raised to his forehead. There followed the ritual act, usually the blood

Cult finds from the Minoan period. This page: model of a room of worship from the tholos tomb at Kamelares with four figures perhaps of the dead, seated on stools; two votaries stand to offer food on the small tables of offering in front of the dead.

less offering of fruit and wine. However, there were also blood sacrifices of bulls and other animals. Their blood was offered to the gods or to the underworld deities and the dead, while the seven-stringed lyre and the flute accompanied the ceremony.

The priests sometimes wore animal skins, taking the part of daemons, perhaps with the intention of gaining some magic power over the daemons they represented. Sometimes, they wore strange eastern tunics, with slanting bands, and on their shoulders they carried cult axes and stone hammers; they often dressed in women's garb, thus taking on the sex which dominated the Minoan pantheon and priesthood. Women's dress was also worn in Asia Minor at a later date by the eunuch priests of Kybele. The priests and priestesses concerned themselves with sacrifices and libations, the offering of prayers, the singing of hymns, even with exorcisms and magic. Cups with phrases written inside them whose meaning remains unknown were perhaps used to bind spirits or to give healing properties to the contents.

Dancing was extremely important in the cult. Women danced below the sacred olive trees or stretched out their arms in invocation of the goddess who came back in spring from the depths of heaven. On a Kamares ware fruit-stand from Phaistos, a goddess with flowers in her hands is shown standing between two priestesses who dance for her. The dancing women from Palaikastro who circle round the figure of the lyrist are also performing some act of worship.

Bullfights and Other Festivals

The most important festivals were the bullfights or, more precisely, bullsports—games and contests with bulls, which took place, it would appear, in spring, the season when men and nature are reborn. The contest was based on the sacred nature of the bull and its importance in the fertility cult. Similar contests took place in other fertile regions, such as the Indus Valley, Asia Minor, and Thessaly.

Perhaps the bullsports had their origin in contests between bulls, like those which were held in Egypt (in the sanctuary of the divine bull, Apis) and in China; quite soon, as was natural, men began to take part and to fight with the bulls. The development of the Cretan bullsports was en-

Left: model of a sanctuary with three pillars that support the beams of the roof on square capitals; above these sit three doves, symbols of the presence of the deity in the sanctuary. Right: clay cult figurine of the goddess from the sanctuary of Gortys *(Post-Palace Period); the goddess wears a rayed crown, above which protrude small snakes; more snakes coil through her hands which are raised in a gesture of benediction, and a dove perches on her neck. (Herakleion Museum)*

couraged by the frequent capture of wild bulls for the practical, magical, and sacrificial purposes already mentioned.

The bull was captured alive, and without being wounded, by means of a net-trap; or the practised hunter suddenly grasped him by the horns and held him motionless with his weight until he could be tied up. Later, this dramatic and dangerous scene was repeated in the theatral area of the city so that the whole population might enjoy the spectacle. The contest was made more exciting by the performing of daring acrobatic feats. Men and women grasped the bull's horns and leaped onto its back in various attitudes, then jumped down to the ground again.

The participation of women gave the Minoan bullfight overtones of an erotic game with this beautiful, virile animal. Fertility rites and the myth about the love of the queen-goddess Pasiphae and the bull have perhaps some connection with the Minoan bullsports. The bull was sacrificed later; it was never killed during the bullfight. The athletes were unarmed, they fought with their bodies only. Thus, the bull-fight remained a charming sport, in keeping with the character of the whole Minoan civilization.

However, there were other contests and games on festival days: boxing, and wrestling, and swinging on swings suspended from the sacred trees, and processions of priests and musicians. After the harvesting of the crops, the men who had reaped and winnowed the fruit formed a procession with the high priest at the head while a group of musicians accompanied by the *sistrum* sang the thanksgiving hymn to the deity.

In other processions, priests and worshippers proceeded in silence holding the libation vessels in outstretched hands. Elsewhere, the votaries walked along carrying valuable vessels with offerings which they were to lay devoutly before the queen-goddess or to empty out at the spot where the libations were made.

Worship of the Dead and the After-life

There is evidence for a belief in some sort of survival of the dead in Crete as early as Neolithic and Pre-Palace times. The dead were buried in hollowed out rocks and, later, in tholos tombs, and vessels containing food, meat, seafood, and even milk, honey, and wine were left beside them. The vessels were always uncovered, with the lids left by their side, so that the dead might eat and drink. These were left not only as provisions for the journey to the other world, but chiefly because it was thought that the dead man continued to exist inside the tomb and had the usual needs, at least until the body was completely decayed. For this reason, the living left by his side everything that he needed in his daily life: not only food, but also blades for shaving, bronze implements, weapons, jewellery, seals. After the decomposition of the body, the dead man would seem to have less importance. The remains were removed or heaped up and sometimes burned to purify the tomb, which then became the site for new burials.

But certain finds show that even in this early phase, as in all ages, there was more involved than the simple human affection and solicitude of the living for their lost ones; in man's imagination, the dead had become connected somehow with the world of the divine and the supernatural.

The presence in the tombs of kernoi for multiple offerings, of animal-shaped rhyta, and Cycladic-type figurines of the goddess show that during the burial acts of worship had been performed, directed either towards the dead themselves or more probably to the deities and the underworld powers, who were thus called to receive the dead and take them under their protection.

Clearer examples of worship of the dead, however, appear at the end of the Pre-Palace Period, when offerings unconnected with the burial were left in small rooms built specifically for this purpose outside the tholos tomb. Small cult vessels (made of stone so that they would last for ever and be distinguished from the common vessels in everyday use), pitchers with wine and other liquids, and clay cups (sometimes upturned to show that the offering was directed to the interior of the earth), all were heaped up in these rooms on the days of funeral ceremonies. It is evident that, as time went on, increasing importance was attached to dead members of the clan; the ancestors were by then closely associated with the chthonic deities who, if propitiated, could favourably influence natural production.

This attitude, however, did not last long. In Old-Palace, and even more so in New-Palace times, the development of powerful royal families reduced the importance of the clans. The basic social unit was no longer the clan but the family. The natural consequence was a gradual decrease in the worship paid to dead ancestors of the clan, with whom the family was no longer closely associated, since the family had its own distinct forefathers.

The graves were now family, or sometimes individual, tombs, and there were no longer any external cult rooms like those of the Early Minoan tholos tombs. However, some ritual objects (alabastra and libation vessels) which have been found inside the same tomb, particularly in Palace times, show that even then there were acts of worship during burial. There were even tables of offering, like those in the shrines, usually placed over the pit where the bones of earlier bodies had been piled in order to save space. Perhaps the aim was to propitiate the dead who had been put aside. Censers were used for ritual purposes and also to counteract the bad smell in the tomb when it was opened for a new burial.

The ritual acts which took place during the funeral were directed chiefly to the deity. But certain eminent dead— kings, queens, high priests, princes—still received worship.

Left hand page, top: stone libation vessel, from the New-Palace Period, in the shape of a bull's head, probably for the offering of blood from the sacrificed bull; the eye of the sacred animal is of rock crystal, and the white band on the muzzle is of shell; the horns were of wood covered with gold leaf (Herakleion Museum). Bottom: detail from a relief rhyton with carved representation in steatite; it shows the depositing of offerings at a peak sanctuary situated on a rocky summit of the mountain and flanked by four poles for flags; a young man bows low before the sanctuary to lay a basket of offerings. The rhyton is dated to the New-Palace Period, between 1500 and 1450 B.C. (Herakleion Museum). This page, left: bronze figurine of the New-Palace Period showing a young man in the usual attitude of worship: the body is arched and tense, the right hand is held to the forehead, and the left arm pressed straight by the side. This is probably the attitude of salute or supplication. The man wears the Minoan loin cloth, a necklace, and bracelets around the wrist and ankles. (Herakleion Museum)

On this polychrome stone sarcophagus, which was found in a tomb at Hagia Triada, there are representations of typical scenes of offerings, sacrifice, and other sepulchral ceremonies. This page, top: one of the long sides of the sarcophagus: a priestess pours out the blood from a sacrificed bull between two double axes, another brings more blood in buckets, and a musician plays a seven-stringed lyre; three men in animal skins offer two calves and the likeness of a ship to the dead man who stands on the right. Below: detail of the procession: the priestess with the buckets and the lyrist. Below, right: detail from the other long side of the sarcophagus: the table on which the bound bull is to be sacrificed; the blood is collected in a bucket while a man plays a double flute. The cult scene is continued on the short side of the sarcophagus (above, right), which shows two female deities arriving at the sanctuary in a chariot drawn by griffins. (Herakleion Museum)

This is shown by the clay representations of offerings, dances, and funeral meals from the tholos tomb of Kamelares, and particularly by the sacred crypts with a central pillar in the royal tomb of Knosos and in the tomb at Archanes, as well as by the bull sacrifice which evidently took place at Archanes.

On the coffin from Hagia Triada, there is a representation of the sacrifice of a bull and other animals, and also the offering of fruit and wine, in front of the sacred tree, and this perhaps shows some connection between the dead man and the vegetation god who dies and is born again. Two goddesses come to the sanctuary on a chariot drawn by two winged griffins, perhaps to protect the dead ruler, while the priests offer him a boat (as befits a sailor king) to travel to the Isles of the Blessed beyond the Ocean where, as Homer says,

> *Snowfall is never known there, neither long*
> *frost of winter, nor torrential rain,*
> *but only mild and lulling airs from Ocean*
> *bearing refreshment for the souls of men—*
> *the West Wind always blowing.*

> (*The Odyssey*, IV. 566)

Some connection with Egypt, either through direct influence or from some common origin and parallel development of ideas, is evident in these representations, particularly in the offering of the boat, in the animal skins worn by the dead man and the priests (showing some connection with zoomorphic daemons), and in the setting up of the dead man during the ceremony before the tomb and behind a sacred branch, which perhaps symbolizes rebirth. Perhaps Egyptian influence also accounts for the pair of scales which is sometimes found in tombs; they were to be used in the other world for weighing the soul to determine if it had been just.

It is very probable that when, in the course of time, their first simple ideas had matured, the Minoans began to believe in the survival of the soul beyond the grave and distinct from the body, and hence also in retribution. This is shown by the legends of Hades and the Elysian Fields, which were preserved in Homer and which were probably of Minoan origin. According to Evans, the use of blue colour on certain tombs of about 1400 B.C. symbolized the sky, whither the soul of the dead man would go after judgment. On the so-called ring of Nestor from the western Peloponnesos which, if it is genuine, must come from Crete, there are representations (again according to Evans) of scenes from the after-life. A dead couple are introduced into the mysteries of the other world, where the roots of the Tree of Life grow, and present themselves for judgment before the Great Goddess and a priest-griffin who sits on the throne.

Cult themes painted on Post-Palace clay coffins—double axes, horns, griffins, boats, divine or hieratic figures who pray or descend from heaven—show the connection which still existed in men's minds between the dead and the supernatural world.

At the end of the Post-Palace Period, cremation of the dead was introduced into Crete, perhaps from Central Europe or from Hittite Asia Minor. This new type of burial shows a new and simpler conception of death. Gradually, however, in this area too, there came about a mingling of new beliefs with the old religion of the Aegean.

THE MYCENAEA

The Age of Golden Mycenae

HISTORICAL BACKGROUND

The Helladic Bronze Age reached its culmination in its last period, called the Mycenaean Age or Late Helladic (c. 1600-1100 B.C.). For the first time, and more than three centuries later than Crete, southern mainland Greece achieved a high level of civilization with town and, later, palace organization, monumental art, and a system of writing. It is now considered certain that this civilization, which far surpassed every Helladic predecessor in achievement, was introduced by Greek tribes, since the area of its development coincides precisely with the region where the Greek nation, which had already reached an archaic form, was finally to settle.

Up to the last quarter of the 19th century, nothing was known about Mycenaean civilization. Epic and legend alike were thought best relegated to the world of myth. But in the summer of 1876, in the forgotten region of Mycenae, Heinrich Schliemann made some amazing discoveries which gave substance to the Mycenaean legend. Myth and epic now took the form of history.

Almost a century has passed since that beginning—the first landmark in Mycenaean and, more generally, Aegean archaeology—and the work still continues both at Mycenae and at other places that once knew the splendid civilization which has come to be known as Mycenaean after its first and chief centre. For the gleaming gold articles in the royal tombs at Mycenae, whose discovery unexpectedly vindicated Schliemann's faith in the veracity of the epic poems, were not sufficient to give a complete picture of a great civilization, much of which is still obscure. But from that moment their light illuminated the path for later systematic research, first by Chrestos Tsountas, the founder of the study of Greek prehistory, and later by Alan J.B. Wace, Carl W. Blegen, and their successors.

But for all that, for the Mycenaean civilization to be properly understood and placed in a more general historical context, one more archaeological miracle was necessary—the excavations and discoveries of Arthur Evans at Knosos. In time, the dazzle of the first splendid finds became diffused as research continued into the basic problems of Mycenaean civilization and its connections with the Minoan. In the end, it became clear that the consequences of Schliemann's discoveries were as important to Greek history as they were to archaeology.

The successful campaign of 1876 had been motivated exclusively by an "amateur's" profound faith in the truth of myth and legend. Despite reservations and hesitations on the part of sceptics, everyone was finally compelled to admit that legend had been proved true on all basic points. Schliemann was very much closer to the truth than the *ex cathedra* sages of his time. The recent chance discovery, in the autumn of 1951, of the second circle of shaft graves at Mycenae confirmed once again the truth of the legend. For all the extensive excavations on Greek soil, nowhere has such a hoard of gold objects been found to equal those heaped up at Mycenae—the city which legend called "rich in gold". The scholars who were most involved in the study of Mycenaean civilization had been convinced of its "Greekness" even before any definite proof came to light and long before its script was deciphered. So the Mycenaean Age must now take its proper place in Greek history; it is its immediate predecessor, the heroic age of ancient Greece, for which more and more evidence, both direct and indirect, is being collected through archaeological and historical research.

The half millennium or so which the Mycenaean Age covers corresponds to the Late Bronze Age in Greece or, more simply, the Late Helladic Period. The name *Mycenaean* however, by which it is usually known, is not an accidental choice; the role of Mycenae in the development of this civilization justifies its claim to be the "capital" city, and excavations continue to confirm its sovereign position—the position held by the seat of the Atreid kings in the epic poems. The term *Late Helladic* is also justified archaeologically, since research has shown that the Mycenaean Age constitutes the natural development and continuation of the Middle Helladic Period over almost the whole of mainland Greece. In other words, it is substantially the last division of the Helladic Bronze Age.

More important than the archaeological terminology is the determining of the correct place of the Mycenaean civilization in history—its position on the road to historical evolution. And it is clear now that the Mycenaean Age was the period in which the Greek nation began to take its final form. Research has shown that during the Mycenaean Period not only had the main groups of Greeks settled down in the country, but the great divisions of the Greek language into dialects had also been formed. So this period can no longer be regarded as pre-Greek, but emerges as the immediate past of historical Greece—the age to which the racial memory naturally turned and where its heroic tradition was rooted.

Today we have abundant archaeological evidence to prove the unbroken racial continuity of Hellenism from Mycenaean times down to the archaic and later periods, i.e. from pre-history to history. But the admiration by the ancient Greeks of the "bronze race", the reference of the idea of Panhellenism back to the Mycenaean Age (Thucydides), and the association of this age with the hero-ancestors of the whole nation were not inspired by "archaeolog-ical" evidence; they were clearly derived from the direct operation of an inherited tradition.

To deny today the "Greekness" of the Mycenaean world would not simply take away, as Tsountas writes "the wonderful backcloth of Greek history which throughout antiquity never ceased to inspire poets and craftsmen"; it would amputate the very roots of Greek civilization.

Chronology and Geography

The dates for the beginning and the end of the Mycenaean or Late Helladic Period have been fixed with a fair degree of certainty, after correlation with the chronology of Crete and by comparing the latter with the chronology of Egypt. For instance, the second New-Palace phase at Knosos coincides with Early Mycenaean (Late Helladic I) and the 16th century B.C. approximately; the beginning of Late Helladic is believed to coincide with the inauguration of the 18th Dynasty in Egypt (1580 B.C.), which is the beginning of the greatest period of Egyptian power.

There are three main subdivisions of the Late Helladic or Mycenaean Age: Early (Late Helladic I: 1600/1580-1500 B.C.); Middle (Late Helladic II: 1500-1425 B.C.); and Late (Late Helladic III: 1425-1100 B.C., if we are to include the final phase, the Sub-Mycenaean). The first two subdivisions make up the archaic period of the Mycenaean Age and were relatively brief. The third lasted much longer, almost three centuries; it is, therefore, divided into three main phases which correspond broadly to the 14th, 13th, and 12th centuries B.C.

These subdivisions, particularly the smaller ones, do not always correspond to historical phases; they refer mostly to changes in pottery. Even so, there is an obvious graduation in the development of the main successive phases (Early-Middle-Late). The Early Mycenaean, as the experimental or transitional phase, is quite different from the Late Mycenaean, the age of Achaian sovereignty, which includes the high point of Mycenaean power (c. 1350 B.C.).

The geographical boundaries of Mycenaean civilization have also been clearly determined. Almost all the Greek provinces enjoyed the benefits of this civilization, which saw the first flowering of the Greek spirit. Almost every important ancient city or great sanctuary had its Mycenaean precursor. The monumental remains, however, are more numerous from Thessaly southwards, on the eastern mainland and particularly in the Peloponnesos.

It is certainly no accident that the great Mycenaean centres where palace installations have been excavated or are known to have existed (Mycenae, Tiryns, Pylos, Athens, Thebes, Orchomenos, Iolkos) are all centres of important mythological cycles. The epic poems also reflect to some extent the conditions which existed in Mycenaean times, and it has become generally accepted that the famous Catalogue of Ships in the *Iliad* (II. 484 ff.) portrays the topography of the Late Mycenaean Period. Mycenae was the greatest centre from the very dawn of Mycenaean times to a short while before the final collapse of the Mycenaean world. Here better than anywhere else we can see evidence for the critical phase in the formation of the new civilization (the transition from Middle to Late Helladic and the first phase of the latter) in the two circles of shaft graves, i.e. circular walls enclosing deep grave pits in which eminent persons were buried. The first circle was excavated by Schliemann in 1876; the second by Papademetriou, Mylonas, and others (1951-54). Fortunately, both circles had escaped pillage and contained gold treasures and other grave goods. That unrivalled masterpiece of Mycenaean architecture, the tholos tomb commonly referred to as the "Treasury of Atreus"; the magnificent Lion Gate on the acropolis of Mycenae, where there are remains of the palace of the Atreids; and the comparatively well preserved palace and the amazing walls at Tiryns are among the most important and best known remains of Mycenaean civilization.

The second great centre was evidently Pylos, in fertile Messenia. Carefully excavated, it has given us treasures to rival those of the Argive centres. The Palace of Nestor on the hill of Eglianos, first noted by Constantine Kourouniotis, was eventually excavated a few years ago by Carl W. Blegen, along with a series of early tholos and chamber tombs excavated by Kourouniotis and Marinatos. Marinatos also excavated the early settlement at nearby Peristeria, in Kyparissia.

Lakonia has not yet been fully explored, nor has the Palace of Menelaos been discovered. Perhaps the discovery of the incomparable gold cups at Vapheio (Chrestos Tsountas) is sufficient, along with the evidence of other finds, to show that this area too was an important Mycenaean centre. In Attica, only a few fragments of a Mycenaean wall have been preserved on the acropolis of Athens (Spyridon Iakovides), while other remains have been discovered at Menidi and Spata, at Eleusis, Thorikos, and Marathon. In Boiotia, there have been finds, both in the past and recently, at the "Palace of Kadmos" and in Kadmeia, the acropolis of Thebes, (Antonios Keramopoullos), and these sites promise much for the future. The royal tholos tomb at Orchomenos known as the "Treasury of Minyas", (Schliemann) testifies to the importance of this site in Mycenaean times. Finally, in Thessaly, Iolkos, the point from which the Argonauts are said to have set sail, is perhaps the most northern of the Mycenaean palace centres (D.R.Theocharis). Recent excavations have also revealed important remains in Achaia, at

Aerial view of the acropolis of Mycenae, the city 'rich in gold', centre of the resplendent civilization known as Mycenaean. Mycenae was built on a naturally fortified hill overlooking the Argive plain, at the crossroads of communications in the Peloponnesos. The palace of the Achaian kings and the dwellings of the nobles were encircled by Cyclopean walls rising from the rocky fringe of the hill. This view shows the walls, traces of the palace on the summit, the Lion Gate, and the two grave circles where the treasures of the Mycenaean rulers were found. The acropolis of Mycenae covered an area of approximately seven acres.

Olympia, and in Triphylia where Dörpfeld excavated the tholos tombs of Kakovatos.

The architectural remains and the small finds which have come to light in the excavations are the chief source of our knowledge of Mycenaean civilization. From 1876 onwards, Greek and foreign scholars have worked together to compose a coberent picture of Mycenaean life and culture. Special tribute is due to the memory of those great men whose outstanding work has enriched our knowledge of this period: Heinrich Schliemann, Chrestos Tsountas, Alan J.B. Wace, Carl W. Blegen, Georg Karo, Arthur Evans, and Michael Ventris.

EARLY MYCENAEAN TIMES

Late Helladic I

The Early Mycenaean Period (c. 1600/1580 B.C.-1500 B.C.) is at the beginning an extension of the Middle Helladic Period. It is the transitional and experimental phase. Many traditional elements (e.g. Minyan pottery) survive and continue down to the end of the period and, in some places, even beyond it. It is a phase known to us almost entirely, or chiefly, from graves, so that it is impossible to reconstruct a proper picture of the civilization of this period.

As we have seen, at the end of the Middle Helladic Period, there is evidence of some change in the Helladic area at approximately the same time as the new palaces were being founded in Crete (c. 1700 B.C.). The once purely agricultural culture of mainland Greece had emerged from its isolation and, as if to make up for lost time, was making vigorous preparations for new developments. Typical Helladic products, such as the Minyan ware, were spread more widely over the country (Chalkidike, Aitolia, Northern Sporades, etc.), and choice products of the more advanced coastal centres were channelled into the interior.

Progressive trends in development must have been concentrated in the coastal centres and in some exceptionally favoured inland settlements, like Mycenae. We may suppose that flourishing coastal settlements such as Lerna, Aigina, Eleusis, Chalkis (Manika-Leukanti), Brauron, Iolkos, etc. had already developed some maritime activity, at least within the Aegean. Other changes in the size of graves and the number of burials (Eleusis), fortifications, which must have been the result of collective activity (Malthe, Aigina), and the manifest influence on pottery of Minoan and Cycladic styles may also be regarded as signs of some more general change. Obviously, the old narrow agricultural organization was a thing of the past. Other more profound changes can only be guessed at. For example, it must be supposed that the movement of Greek-speaking (Proto-Greek) tribes southwards had already been completed, that the filtering of the races eventually resulted in the absorption of the older "Aegean" Proto-Greek population, and that these changes intensified the receptivity of the Middle Helladic world for new developments. This world was now ready to put to good use the lessons it had learned from the neighbouring advanced civilization of Crete and the Cyclades. Consequently, both archaeologist and historian look in the final stages of Middle Helladic for indications of a change in the economy and of a more general preparation for a radical change in the culture. But the conditions which brought about this change, the origin of the amazing treasures in the shaft graves at Mycenae, and the role and influence of Minoan Crete are problems which are still being discussed.

Remains of skeletons show that the Mycenaeans of the period of the golden tombs were tall and warlike figures (the skeleton in grave V of Circle A was 1.82 m. in height, i.e. gigantic for that period). So, we may connect the shaft graves with the Achaians who, in the Middle Helladic Period, moved from Thessalian Achaia towards the south.

It has been proved that Mycenae was a highly flourishing Mycenaean centre. One factor which contributed to this was its favourable position on a naturally fortified hill overlooking the Argive Plain and at the junction of the most important roads of the Peloponnesos. This explains the wealth in the hands of its powerful and ambitious rulers, but the rich and exquisitely worked grave goods of the royal tombs tell us nothing about the general cultural level either in the region of Mycenae or, more generally, in the Greek world. The archaeological evidence on the summits of Mycenaean acropolises is certainly very meagre, especially at Mycenae itself, though some palace sites with thick banks (Thebes, Iolkos) have not yet been properly excavated. We can form some idea of the life at Mycenae at the end of the Middle Helladic Period and at the beginning of Mycenaean times from the remains of the smaller but important settlement at Peristeria. The dwelling of the ruler on the naturally fortified acropolis was a large simple house with stone-built foundations and floors of beaten clay, following in its construction a Middle Helladic pattern. There is nothing that can be compared, even remotely, with the settlements of the second New-Palace phase in Crete or Thera. So there is a manifest difference between the cultural level and that implied by the richness and art of the grave goods.

But if we turn to the problem of the origin of the treasures in the shaft graves, there is no doubt that the objects found there have an overall Minoan and Cycladic look about them. No observation of details can alter this impression or lessen the strength of Minoan influence. Without the previous existence of the splendid civilization of Minoan Crete and of the Cyclades, it would have been impossible for the treasures of the shaft graves or for Mycenaean civilization itself to exist.

Regular communication and exchange of goods brought more general influences from Minoan and Cycladic Greece, though not a complete transplantation of civilization. It was the native cultural elements of mainland Greece which formed the body of the Early Mycenaean civilization that received the imported overseas elements.

Relative newcomers on the threshold of such a highly advanced civilization as that of Minoan Crete, the Middle Helladic people seem to have been dazzled by the external

The impressive relief of the Lion Gate, symbol of the strength of the mighty kings of Mycenae. Two standing lions, three metres high, face each other over the massive lintel, adding to the grandeur of the entrance to the acropolis, which is fortified with Cyclopean ramparts. This is the most ancient Greek monumental relief sculpture. Beyond the Lion Gate is Circle A of royal tombs.

HEINRICH SCHLIEMANN (1822-1890), the great pioneering German excavator of Troy and Mycenae. From childhood, he had dreamed of bringing Homer to life again by discovering the world of the Iliad *hidden beneath the soil of centuries. A tireless traveller and an erudite scholar, he learned both ancient and modern Greek and, late in life, took up the study of archaeology. After his excavations had brought to light the 'treasures of Priam' on the hill of Hissarlik, he came to Mycenae in 1876 and, guided by the legend which had been handed down by Pausanias, he proceeded to unearth the circle of shaft graves behind the Lion Gate and their unrivalled treasuries of grave goods. In spite of all the criticism which has been made of his methods of excavation and his 'mania for treasures', the fact remains that Schliemann opened up a whole world for archaeology by revealing to the dazzled eyes of the world the civilization known as Mycenaean. The dreams of a man of vision had been given substance and his faith in Homer justified beyond expectations.*

CHRESTOS TSOUNTAS (1857-1934), the greatest figure in the heroic age of Greek archaeology. After taking over the excavations at Mycenae from Schliemann in 1886, he devoted himself methodically and quietly to the excavation of the vast cemetery, the tholos tombs, the acropolis, the remains of the palace and dwellings, the road, and the aqueducts. In his first great publication, Mycenae and the Mycenaean Civilization *(1893), remarkable for both its style and content, he gave, for the first time, a general picture of this civilization in a systematic account of everything that Schliemann had discovered and of everything that subsequent excavations had brought to light. Later, by his excavations in the Cyclades and his exemplary accounts of them, he laid the foundations for the study of the previously unknown Cycladic civilization. In the early years of this century, he turned his attention to Thessaly. His excavations at Sesklo and Dimeni were the great turning points in his work and opened up new horizons in the study of Greek prehistory.*

grandeur of the first such civilization with which they came into close contact. The first phase of their acquaintanceship was necessarily imitative, and this is clearly the explanation of the treasures in the shaft graves. The Mycenaean rulers retained the austere tastes of their ancestors and lived in the same simple surroundings, as befits a military people. On the other hand, they were attached to the goods they had acquired through toil and sacrifice in their turbulent lives and took care that their belongings were deposited with them in their graves. They were, after all, their personal acquisitions. The living had acquired, should have acquired, or could still acquire their own.

Directly or indirectly, Minoan influence proved beneficial. Cretan sea power controlled organized trade in the Aegean, creating at the same time the conditions necessary for economic cooperation and fruitful exchange. Within the framework of an advanced civilization there is room for parallel peaceful activity. We cannot know exactly how much the Mycenaeans learnt from the Minoans, but it is certain that towards the end of the Early Mycenaean Period, c. 1500 B.C., they had developed considerable naval skill and commercial independence, since we find them established at Miletos.

The transformation of Middle Helladic into Mycenaean was complete, and this evolution was to have important consequences for the future of civilization in the Aegean.

ARTHUR JOHN EVANS (1851-1943), the British archaeologist who rediscovered the lost civilization of Crete, the brilliant civilization to which he gave the name Minoan. *He began his excavations at Knosos in 1900 and continued them till 1935, when he left Crete at the age of 84. Never before had one man done such huge archaeological and interpretative work in such a confined area. It was with Evans that archaeology in the Aegean began to be pursued seriously, systematically, and on a large scale. Our knowledge of the Minoan civilization was increased by the amazing monuments he unearthed, and the historical interpretation of it was aided by his monumental publications, especially his classic works,* Scripta Minoa *and* The Palace of Minos at Knossos, *in which his amazing erudition and interpretative power reveal the measure of his genius. It was natural that such a stupendous work would be the target of criticism. Many extreme theories put forward by Evans have now been disproved or abandoned. But the continuing criticism shows how much his work remains alive.*

ALAN J.B. WACE (1879-1957), the distinguished British archaeologist who devoted his life to the excavation of Mycenae. He had been brought up on humanist studies and was a tireless researcher and a versatile scholar, equally at home discussing popular art, classical philology, or the interpretation of prehistory. He and Carl W. Blegen, the American archaeologist, drew up a timetable of evolution in prehistoric Helladic Greece, continuing and completing the foundation work of Tsountas. For Wace, Mycenae was not a heap of dead ruins, but a living place with its origins in legend and epic and a history which continued right up to the present day. Moderate in his judgments, but positive in his opinions, Wace was soon convinced of the 'Greekness' of the Mycenaeans and their language, and he lived to see his views confirmed. He did much excavation work, but at the same time found time to teach and to publish his findings and conclusions in a most exemplary manner. The value of his work, whether it deals with prehistoric Thessaly or with Mycenae, will never be diminished.

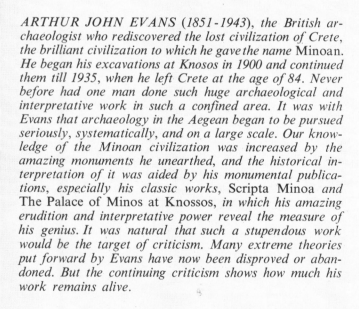

The Helladic Mycenaeans were ready to expand throughout the whole of the Aegean the moment that the Minoan retreat began (after 1500 B.C.) and naturally they began to take the initiative more and more from the declining Minoan world, whose cultural advances they continued in both the Aegean and the Eastern Mediterranean.

Late Helladic II: A Creto-Mycenaean Blend

The second Mycenaean period (1500 B.C.-1425 B.C.) is the period when the power of Mycenae was firmly established. The blending of various influences gave this phase a distinct "Creto-Mycenaean" character, but there are no indications of any clear break with the previous period. Perhaps it was only the consequences of the eruption of the volcano on Thera (end of 16th century B.C.) that brought about the change, at least indirectly, through the destruction of many Cretan centres. The rulers of Knosos still controlled the Aegean up to the middle of the 15th century B.C., but in many places, e.g. at Miletos, Mycenaean influence increased at the expense of Minoan. Helladic trading activity became widespread, and Helladic products began to reach distant shores, even as far away as southern Italy. On Rhodes, a proper Mycenaean station was founded—a step towards expansion to the East.

THE ORIGIN OF MYCENAEAN POWER

The Problem

The luxurious quality and fine artistry of the finds that came to light during Schliemann's excavations of the royal tombs of Mycenae made it immediately obvious that a highly advanced civilization had been discovered. Archaeologists and historians at once began to argue about its origins. Schliemann maintained that it was the very civilization which was described in the Homeric poems and that, without a doubt, the royal dead belonged to the dynasty of the Atreids. Indeed, in the dead man with the grandiose gold mask he recognised Agamemnon himself, the leader of the Achaians in their expedition to Troy. Some other scholars believed that the origin of the newly discovered civilization was Phoenician.

Sporadic excavation work which followed showed that the Mycenaean civilization was widespread, not only in southern mainland Greece, but all over the Aegean. Some scholars, pointing out the similarity of Cycladic and Cretan finds to the objects and buildings unearthed at Mycenae, claimed that Crete was not unrelated to the origin of Mycenaean civilization.

When, after the proclamation of its autonomy in 1898, large-scale excavations began in Crete, the problem seemed to be solved. It was proved that the Minoan civilization had a very long evolution in Crete, whence it had spread to the islands of the Aegean. In its last phase, the Late Minoan, it was similar in many aspects of its life and culture to that of Mycenaean Greece. Further, legend spoke clearly of a Cretan thalassocracy and extensive colonization in the Aegean. On the basis of these facts, Arthur Evans had no hesitation in stating that the origin of Mycenaean civilization lay in Minoan colonization. "Pan-Minoanism" suddenly became fashionable, and most scholars were convinced that the Minoan civilization had been transplanted in an identical form to the Aegean Islands and mainland Greece.

In the meantime, excavation work went forward at the most important Mycenaean centres. Soon enough material was available to study the evolution of Mycenaean civilization from its beginning to its end, to determine its position in the more general framework of the development of Helladic civilization and its connection with the Cycladic and Minoan civilizations. It was now certain that the Mycenaean civilization in mainland Greece had been created in a purely Middle Helladic framework and that apart from the transplantation of numerous Minoan and, to a lesser extent, Cycladic elements, there had been no change brought about by any other foreign influences from the North or the East.

Now scholars were noticing more and more the differences rather than the similarities between Mycenaean and Minoan civilization—differences in way of life, customs, habits, dress, religion, and in the general direction and basic characteristics of their art. The arguments among scholars, particularly between Evans, the chief exponent of the colonization theory, and Wace, who supported the theory of a local evolution under Minoan influence, developed into a real polemic. Evans set forth his arguments in his great work on Knosos and in special books and studies. Wace showed great moderation and confined himself to a summary of the conclusions drawn from his excavations at Mycenae. Scholars were divided, though most leaned towards Evans's view.

In 1939, a large part of the archives of the palace at Pylos was unearthed by Kourouniotis and Blegen. These archives were immediately seen to bear an amazing similarity to the archives in Linear Script B found at Knosos. Evans was triumphant: both the language and the writing at Mycenaean Pylos were obviously Minoan. Finally, however, the views of Wace's supporters prevailed. When the Creto-Mycenaean texts of Linear Script B were deciphered in 1952, it was proved almost conclusively that not only were the archives of the Mycenaean centres written in an archaic Greek language, but so were the archives of Knosos which belonged to its final phase, approximately from 1450 to 1380 B.C. Some scholars now began to talk of the establishment of an Achaian dynasty at Knosos and the introduction into Crete of genuinely Mycenaean elements of a Greek character. Others went even further: perhaps the whole last Minoan period, Evans's Late Minoan, had a Mycenaean character which might have been interpreted as an early settlement of Achaians in Crete. Naturally, more moderate opinions were also expressed which recognized a pre-eminently Minoan influence in the creation of Mycenaean civilization.

These differences of opinion show that the problem has not yet found a final solution. To form a clearer picture, we must make a sober study of the arguments put forward by the two chief factions and place them in a wider historical context so that each should acquire its true demonstrative strength.

Evans's Theory

Evans's theory may be summarized as follows: The Mycenaean civilization made its appearance suddenly, and in Minoan dress. Life changed abruptly, and the cultural level reached the level we have recognized at Knosos around 1600 B.C., at the end of the first New-Palace Period. From being farmers and stockbreeders the inhabitants suddenly became, in the chief centres at least, townsmen, artisans, merchants, and sailors. They enjoyed the same comforts as those which had been developed on Crete: both men and women wore Minoan clothes, their jewellery followed Minoan fashions; and, in general, they adopted the habits of life which had been known in Crete for centuries. Their religion, according to this theory, took on a Minoan character and used similar symbols and vessels. Tools and weapons and the products of artists and artisans became almost like their Cretan equivalents. Even the burial customs changed

The treasures of the shaft graves of Mycenae, which were unearthed during Schliemann's excavations in 1876, revealed the existence of a once splendid civilization, and their great quantity and exquisite art dazzled the world. Above, right: diadem from Circle A (16th century B.C.), a composition in gold plate, which perhaps decorated a royal sarcophagus. Below, left: decoration on the sides of a hexagonal casket from Circle A (c. 1500 B.C.); on the relief gold plate which covers it, there are lively representations of lions who tear antelopes to pieces or pursue deer. Below right: gold rhyton in the shape of a lion's head, 16th century B.C., from a royal tomb of Circle A at Mycenae. (National Archaeological Museum, Athens)

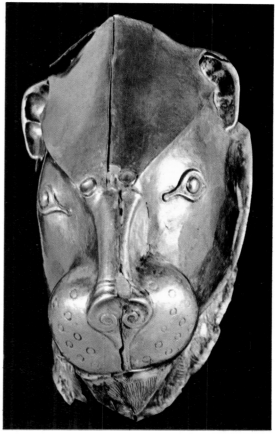

and now reflected Cretan beliefs in after-life. The provision of rich grave goods for the dead was sanctioned and became general. All this striking "Minoanizing" appeared suddenly, precisely at a period when the new palaces and settlements of Crete were suffering widespread destruction, at about the same time as Minoan settlements on the Aegean Islands were resuscitated, and when new ones, in the form of colonies, were being founded. So, according to Evans, this sudden "Minoanizing" could only be explained by the theory of a colonizing settlement of Minoans at favourable or controlling sites in the Helladic region.

Evans compared this colonial thrust of the Minoans with the expansion of Greek civilization and the creation of colonies in wide zones of Asia Minor and on the shores of Macedonia, Thrace, the Black Sea, Sicily, and southern Italy. He accepted, however, that the indigenous Helladic population—substantially Greek—continued to live, self-sufficient, by the side of the Minoan colonists, even welcoming the Minoans at first and offering no resistance, since they were reaping the fruits of a civilization more advanced than their own; and only in a later phase, when the natives had assimilated the helpful lessons of Minoan civilization, did they rise and resist. It was thus that the Minoan dynasties were overthrown, and indigenous Achaian dynasties established. Evans insisted that the history of this development could be traced in legend and in the Homeric poems. In his opinion, the early appearance in Mycenaean Greece of a warlike spirit and an interest in armaments and fortifications was the outcome of the Minoan rulers' awareness of their vulnerable position among a foreign subject population. Evans found it easy to reconcile with his view the influences which the Helladic world had exerted, during the Mycenaean Age and even earlier, on Minoan civilization. Indeed, he attributed to such influences the origin of the tectonic "palace style" during the last phase of the palace of Knosos.

Wace's Theory

Wace conceded that the Middle Helladic world had been "Minoanized" to a large degree. But he stressed that, despite all the Minoan influence, the basic character of the civilization on the mainland, underneath its foreign dress, remained Helladic and the transmitters of it continued to be the same elements who had evolved the Middle Helladic civilization. Many peoples, he pointed out, embraced the main elements of a higher civilization without losing their own identity but by impressing the seal of their own culture on whatever they adopted. The people who evolved the Mycenaean civilization had basically a very different character from the Minoans; they were chiefly distinguished by the organizing spirit of men who had become conscious of the value of the human factor; their thought had advanced to the abstract level of a higher logic which strove to impose on all creation its own laws of inner truth, those laws precisely which would later be applied by the Greeks on a much

Grave goods from royal tombs of early Mycenaean times. Above, left: gold ring from Circle A at Mycenae with a hunting scene engraved on the bezel. Below: gold seal-stone in the shape of a flattened cylinder with a representation of a hero struggling with a lion. (National Archaeological Museum, Athens)

broader scale during the Geometric, Archaic, and Classical periods. They took foreign elements to themselves in order to assimilate them and make them their own just as later, during the orientalizing period, they assimilated elements they had taken from the East in order to progress more swiftly, after a stage of vigorous maturing, to the creation of higher art forms which we know as Archaic. The character of the Helladic Greeks was essentially aggressive and warlike, and this produced the epic heroic spirit which is expressed in the Homeric poems. In art, they imitated the Minoans as faithfully as they could, although in other fields they kept their preference for abstraction and tectonic organization. The laws of harmony and symmetry were more highly valued than naturalism. Symmetry and the warlike spirit were evident in all their creations, even in the products of the Minoan craftsmen whom they employed. They loved weapons and took great delight in the exercise of them. The horse and the introduction of the light chariot gave a particular tone to their contests, and we see this reflected in the epic poems.

Thus, although many aspects of Minoan life and culture were inherited, the application of the laws of inner truth resulted in new forms of expression in every branch of art from vase-painting to the engraving of seal-stones. Much was assimilated from the sophisticated character of Minoan life, but basically the Mycenaeans retained a liking for plainness of quite another order in which the masculine and aggressive spirit was more prominent in their culture. A preference for monumental sculpture is also clearly evident. According to Wace, there was an early trend towards mass production in art and standardization of products, which were thus more easily circulated in markets abroad.

Religion too, despite its externally Minoan character, showed an obvious trend towards an anthropomorphic multi-figure pantheon, the one which was to appear later in the epic cycle. Its early appearance is proved by the references to the gods on the Linear B tablets from the archives of the Achaian dynasty at Knosos. The tablets reveal a new political, social, and economic organization which was begun in early Mycenaean times and which was certainly not early Cretan.

These and many other similar arguments of Wace and his supporters were persistently challenged by the handful of Evans's supporters who still remained. Evans himself was no longer alive to face the new arguments based on the decipherment of the Linear B tablets, which, it appeared, proved that the language of the people who transmitted the Mycenaean civilization was without any doubt Greek.

If, however, it is accepted that it was the Achaian Greeks who developed the Mycenaean civilization, and Cretan colonization is ruled out, some logical explanation is still required for the abrupt change and sudden "Minoanizing" in art. Wace originally explained this sudden change by postulating a surprise pirate operation carried out by the Middle Helladic people against the rich centres of Crete around 1600 B.C. According to this theory, their operation was successful in spite of the vigilance of the Minoan fleet. The palace of Knosos was set on fire, and a great wealth of spoils, a host of Knosian prisoners, among them experienced artists and craftsmen, were carried off in the ships of the Middle Helladic invaders back to their lands.

However, it has been proved that the catastrophe of 1600 B.C. on Crete was due to earthquake and not to hostile invasion. While the seismic destruction would admittedly have provided the most opportune conditions for a pirate raid, such a large-scale operation would have had to be planned long before the earthquake, of which naturally there could have been no warning. The power of Crete was not based on a land organization but on its fleet, so a surprise attack could hardly have been feasible. And, again, if we suppose that a surprise attack was successful at one centre, there were so many other powerful centres to repulse the invaders. The theory of the sea-might of Crete being routed by Middle Helladic raiders seems improbable. Even if this were accepted as a possibility, we must still ask why the all-conquering invaders abandoned the rich island without reaping greater profit of it. Instead, we find the palaces being rebuilt on a grandiose scale and the Minoan kingdoms being reorganized. There is also the question of why the Minoans did not attempt a counter-invasion, particularly at a period when the Middle Helladic centres had not been organized and fortified. In any event, a large-scale invasion would certainly have required some coalition of forces, but no sign of any such preparations has been found. Further, the treasures which are adduced as Cretan spoils do not date only from the years around 1600 B.C., but come from a much broader period from 1600 B.C. to 1450 B.C.; and they could hardly be the spoils from continuous pirate operations. If even a few of the graves of circle B at Mycenae are of an earlier date, the invasions must have begun in the 17th century, which would imply many successive conquests and devastations at Knosos. If most of the objects had been fashioned by Minoan craftsmen who had been carried off in a raid, the argument about spoils loses all point. The treasuries of Vapheio, Midea, Myrsinochori, Pylos, and

Peristeria belong to the years after 1600 B.C. and, consequently, could not have formed part of the spoils of a pirate invasion around that date. The dispersion of abducted Minoan craftsmen over the whole extent of the Mycenaean world also seems improbable. And it would certainly be impossible to explain how a pirate operation could have resulted in a wholesale change in the life, religion, art, and way of thinking and feeling of a population which had remained for centuries at an almost unchanged level of agrarian culture.

Finally, the theory has been put forward that the Egyptians took on a large number of armed mercenaries from the Middle Helladic region to drive the Hyksos out of the Nile valley, that the reward in gold—of which there was plenty in Egypt—paid to the expeditionary force accounted for the sudden wealth of the Mycenaean centres, and that the fighters who returned from Egypt brought with them the custom of burying the dead with valuable ornaments. This is the theory proposed by Marinatos, and it has now been adopted by many archaeologists and historians. The main evidence adduced by the adherents of this theory are the gold masks of the Mycenaean tombs, the embalmed remains in the fifth tomb, and the great quantity of gold found at Mycenae.

ARCHITECTURE
Domestic Architecture

There are very few remains of Mycenaean settlements from the early period; and those that have been preserved

This page: Circle A of shaft graves, which lies inside the walls, behind the Lion Gate; nineteen bodies, including those of two infants, had been buried in this circle—perhaps kings and members of the royal family.
Right: tholos tomb of the 15th century B.C. near the palace of Nestor at Pylos; the vault of the tomb has been restored.

are in bad condition. Certain scholars have, therefore, concluded that the original houses, even the palaces, were exceptionally simple in design and constructed of poor materials. But this view cannot be reconciled with the otherwise advanced level of Mycenaean life, the highly organized social, political, economic, religious, and private life attested to by the rich finds in the royal tombs and the extensive cemeteries. Nor is it in keeping with the monumental form of grave architecture which, it has been proved, made its appearance at a very early date. The disappearance of the older buildings on the Mycenaean acropolises is quite natural since extensive levelling, propping, and artificial terracing were carried out before the new palaces were built. In Crete too, similar works resulted in the disappearance of large sections of the early palaces, but there the great extent of the palace area and the building of the palaces on separate levels of the hillside helped to preserve a fair number of early sections from which we can form some idea of the early buildings. A few features of the original architecture have been preserved at Mycenae and Tiryns, such as large foundations, bases of large columns, support walls, etc. Remains of simple buildings were also found at Ephyra, Prosymna, Asine, Midea, and Eutresis, though we can learn little from them. The best evidence comes from the extensive building group at Peristeria in Triphylia, one of the most ancient Mycenaean palace complexes. In the same region, there are some of the earliest tholos tombs and remains of a grave circle with grave finds similar to those in the royal tombs at Mycenae.

Excavations at Mycenae have shown that the original acropolis was very small, that it was not surrounded by walls but by a simple enclosure, and that the main approach

A shaft grave from Circle B at Mycenae (outside the walls) with skeletons of three men and a woman. The dead body on the left had been buried in a supine position with the legs open and a sword at its side. Rich grave goods accompanied the dead: masks of a gold-silver alloy, swords with handles of precious metal, decorated vessels, a gold cup, and other objects.

was direct from the road which climbed the southwest side of the hill, ending at a ramp which sloped in exactly the opposite direction from the one taken by the later ramp up the hill, i.e. it climbed from south to north.

Tomb Architecture and Funerary Customs

The amazing wealth of the grave goods in the royal shaft graves on the acropolis of Mycenae was in striking contrast to the simplicity of the actual construction of the graves themselves. All six in the first circle were spacious but simple pit shafts with a lining of stone; the ledge formed by the investment walls was used as a support for beams, on top of which slabs were laid to cover the shafts and prevent water from seeping in. In one of the graves, the ends of the beams were encased in bronze to prevent rot.

The royal tombs were found in two circles, originally outside the main acropolis, on the slope which held the Middle Helladic cemetery and perhaps part of the dwelling area. In the Late Mycenaean Period, the first circle was enclosed within the wall, no doubt to protect the graves from possible pillage and to turn the royal cemetery into a cult area.

The graves of the second circle differed both in construction and in the richness of the grave goods. There were also many more bodies than graves. Although some of the graves in the second circle had been disturbed or destroyed, the number of Mycenaean graves was not less than 14 and the dead numbered more than 24, compared with 19 (including two infants) in the first circle. The great number of graves and burials in the second circle makes it impossible that they were all of kings, queens, and heirs apparent; the number of royal persons would have been disproportionately large for the short period of 100 to 150

years. It has been suggested that the lower circle was used for princes and other persons related to the reigning dynasty, but this view assumes that the two circles were contemporary, and this is not certain. The burials in the second circle are held to have begun considerably earlier, in the last phase of the Middle Helladic Period, a little after 1650 B.C.

One of the problems which has particularly occupied researchers and students of Mycenaean civilization is the precise dating of the tholos tombs. Most of them had been completely looted, and the few objects which remained were scattered about. It would appear that the looting took place in ancient times because two of these grave monuments, one at Mycenae and the other at Orchomenos, had been characterized as the θησαυροί, the treasuries, of Atreus and

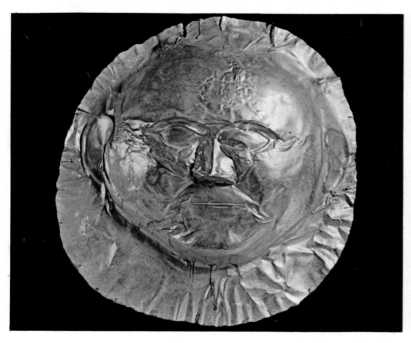

Minyas. When Pausanias visited Mycenae, the inhabitants proudly showed him the first, and told him about the site of the burial of Agamemnon and his retinue on the acropolis and of the graves of the outcasts—the murderous couple, Aigisthos and Klytaimnestra. It was this information that Schliemann relied on when he explored the acropolis for the graves of the royal dead. It is clear that historical memory had retained some vague recollection of the burials in the two royal circles, although history had turned into legend, and there was some confusion between different periods.

Evans considered it completely out of the question that the royal dead could have been buried in such slapdash constructions as the graves of the upper circle, especially since the monumental tholoi had been constructed in the same or a slightly earlier period. He had no doubt that the latter were to be dated in the Early Mycenaean Period. He was certain too that the most important monumental tholoi, like the treasury of Atreus and the tholos tomb of Klytaimnestra, as their sculptured decoration which was saved from destruction and the few grave goods which had escaped the attention of the pillagers testified, belonged to this period. He, therefore, maintained that the Mycenaeans had placed the royal dead in the monumental tholos tombs and that in the Late Mycenaean Period the dead were hastily moved when some danger of pillage suddenly appeared. Their removal was facilitated by the fact that the dead were enclosed in wooden, probably anthropomorphic, sarcophagi, on which the gold decoration of bands, diadems, rosettes, etc. and

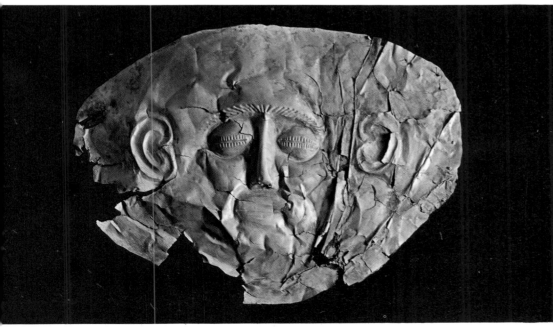

The curiously-shaped gold masks which were found in the royal grave circles at Mycenae (16th century B.C.). Top row, from the left: gold mask from Circle A; the impressive face of a bearded man with Greek features; Schliemann thought this mask belonged to Agamemnon. The next two are also royal masks from Circle A.
Bottom row, left: royal mask from Circle A.
Centre: electron mask of a member of the royal family from a grave of Circle B.
Right: royal mask from Circle A; in spite of the stylization, individual features have been rendered which differ from those on the other masks.
(National Archaeological Museum, Athens)

257

the gold masks were fitted. Following Schliemann, Evans pointed to the imperfect embalming of some of the dead in support of the view that the burial customs betrayed undoubted Egyptian influence. This theory of Evans about the removal of the dead, although apparently logical, was proved wrong after the discovery and careful investigation of the second royal circle. Removal of the dead was then shown to be quite out of the question. In the meantime, Wace was trying to determine the chronological sequence of the nine tholos tombs. Using various criteria, clearly typological, he divided them into three groups, taking the most primitive as the earliest and the more skilfully constructed and monumental as the latest. Finally, he dated these tholos tombs in the Middle Mycenaean Period and the first phase of the Late Mycenaean. Other scholars, such as Mylonas, date all of them in the last Mycenaean period, up to the middle of the 13th century B.C.

Three tholos tombs, at Midea in the Argolid, Vapheio in Lakonia, and Myrsinochori near Pylos, contained grave pits in which royal dead had been buried. They had escaped pillage, and their rich treasuries could be dated with certainty in the Middle Mycenaean Period. The tombs could not have been built later than 1500 B.C. Other tombs have now been discovered of this and even earlier periods. Of particular interest are two tholos tombs in the region of the Palace of Pylos, three tholos tombs at Peristeria in Triphylia, of which the smallest contained some grave goods similar to those of the Mycenae shaft graves, the tholos tombs at Kakovatos, and the one at Vourvoura in Kynouria. Even earlier is the tholos tomb at Osman Aga in the Pylos region.

It may, therefore, be considered certain that the tholos tombs were a sudden development in grave architecture contemporary with the appearance of the new Minoan elements in the Mycenaean world (c. 1600 B.C.). The view that the tholos came from Crete, though fully justified by the results of recent investigations on that island, which have confirmed that this type had a continuous development there from the Pre-Palace Period, is not accepted by all scholars.

Since the rich provision of grave goods for the dead was a custom almost certainly foreign to the Middle Helladic world, while in Crete it had an earlier history, it would seem that this custom was introduced into the Mycenaean region from Crete. The immediate impression created by the funeral ornaments is that of a display of barbaric luxury, but such an impression does not in fact correspond to reality. According to one view, numerous gold ornaments adorned the wooden sarcophagi and the funeral shrouds that were wound round the dead. This was the function too of the innumerable pieces of gold plate or foil cut into various decorative and representational shapes with perhaps some symbolic religious significance. The funeral masks, which are comparatively clumsy objects (as they were made in a hurry), and rather conventional, did not lie directly over the faces of the dead, nor did the wide and weighty diadems rest directly on their heads. The way in which the leaves and flower buds are crushed is reminiscent of modern funeral wreaths when their flowers have wilted. Most of these golden ornaments were specially made for use in funerals. Everything contained in these tombs emphasized the care taken to provide symbolically all the basic necessities of life: food and drink, clothing and ornament, even entertainment. Some

objects were intended to dispel the darkness of the chamber and to lead the dead man along the path to the underworld. Religious symbols and representations secured him the protection of the divine powers. The presence of these powers was shown in rare cases by small figurines which were found close to the dead. It was natural that "the glorious deeds of men" which were so important in their life should be represented in miniature sculpture and narrated on funeral steles. The great variety of decorated arms is witness to the Mycenaean spirit of domination. While it is difficult to reach definite conclusions about Mycenaean beliefs concerning the after-life, we are quite justified in supposing that the needs of the dead man had to be satisfied until his body had decayed.

There is no evidence that members of the royal retinue followed their masters to the grave, or that there were ever systematic human sacrifices. The slaughter of prisoners during the burial of heroes who had fallen in battle, of which we read in the epic poems (burial of Patroklos), does not mean that it was the established custom to offer human sacrifices. The prisoners were responsible for the death of the hero and, besides, they were regarded as simple possessions.

In some tombs, there were traces of the wheel tracks of the funeral chariot which took the dead down into the tomb. In one of the tholos tombs at Tragana, these tracks were continued artificially even beyond the entrance threshold. The dead were usually interred in a supine position, very rarely with contracted legs. In three of the tombs of the second circle at Mycenae, skeletons of two men and a small girl were found with their legs half-open. Except for the jewellery and the direct attachments to the dead, the grave goods were usually placed along the two short sides of the grave. Gold cups were often placed in the hands of eminent persons, and this was how the cups in the royal tombs at Vapheio and Midea were found. The provision of grave goods in the rectangular and tholos tombs was much the same, although our information about the latter is limited since very few of them have escaped pillage. The gold masks were found only on the royal dead. Only one mask, of a gold-silver alloy, was found in the graves of the second circle.

In the tholos and rock-cut tombs, the entrance was usually walled up with a stone barrier after the dead had been laid inside the tomb, but it is not certain whether or not the *dromos* was filled in too, at least in the case of the tombs with a monumental façade. Perhaps the façade had already been built while the persons for whom the tomb was intended were still alive. There are many indications that graves were covered with *tumuli*, mounds of earth enclosed by a low wall, from one side of which the way (*dromos*) to the inside began.

According to one theory, the chamber tombs also originated in Crete, where the small burial caves had been formed

Left page, above: gold brooch (16th century B.C.). Below: representation of two figures on a gold ring; according to Evans, the subject is the 'sacra conversazione' of the great goddess and the young god; others believe that it represents a scene from daily life. This page: bronze figurine of a young man of Minoan appearance and dress but of Helladic character; the position of the arms is unusual, and it has been suggested that he holds a butterfly or grasshopper between the palms of his hands. (National Archaeological Museum, Athens)

in many instances by additional cutting into the rock in order to widen the chamber or to form recesses and a regular approach. These burial caves developed naturally into burial chambers hewn in soft rock. In the Early and Middle Mycenaean Periods, their development is analogous to that in Crete. Later, the rock-cut tombs of Crete show strong Mycenaean influence.

The chamber tombs which form extensive cemeteries in all Mycenaean centres were more likely to escape pillage than the big tholos tombs whose positions were well known. According to legend, the chamber tomb of Hyrieus in Aulis which had been built by Trophonios and Agamedes was pillaged through the removal of a single stone without the seals of the door being broken. It would appear that the oracle of Trophonios at Levadeia was also a tholos tomb. Glaukos, son of Minos, was laid in a similar subterranean construction. Tholos tombs, however, were not always built underground. The Vapheio tomb protruded at the level of the peak of a hill, and a whole series of tholoi in Aitolia-Akarnania and a tomb at Iolkos (the Kapaklı tomb) all lay on a level stretch of land, not hidden in a hillside.

Naturally, the size, shape, and decoration of a tomb were in accordance with the social position of the family or clan to whom it belonged. Many members of the same family or of the same clan would be buried in one tomb. Generally, the rich tombs were numerous in the Early and Middle Mycenaean Periods. In the bigger ones, the dimensions of the chambers were 5.50 x 6.50 metres and the height up to 7 metres. The roof was rarely level, but it usually formed a gently curving vault. Steps, recesses, and passages connecting with side chambers were common.

It is difficult for us to reach any definite conclusions about the beliefs of the Mycenaeans of the 16th and 15th centuries. Perhaps some sort of belief in a judgment in after-life or an imitation of an old Minoan custom is shown by the gold scales, with butterflies on the balances, intended for the weighing of the soul, which were found in the royal tombs of the first circle at Mycenae, and by the many other bronze scales which accompanied the dead in the chamber tombs. The belief in a judgment in after-life by Minos, Rhadamanthys, and Aiakos, the first two Minoan and the third Mycenaean, survived even in historical times.

The traces of fires in the burial chambers may perhaps be explained by the need for purification of the dead and the cleansing of the area of any infection.

PUBLIC AND PRIVATE LIFE, 16TH AND 15TH CENTURIES B.C.

It is difficult to form a complete picture of the life of the Early Mycenaean Period since the palaces and chief

Early Mycenaean life is illustrated on seal-stones, which are often masterpieces of miniature art. Numerous seal-stones have been found in graves at Mycenae, Tiryns, Midea, Vapheio,

Pylos, and Thebes. Left: representation on a sardonyx seal-stone of a lion attacking a bull (15th century B.C.). Middle: a bearded head, perhaps of a king, in amethyst (16th century

centres of habitation are unknown. The rich grave goods, especially those which have been found in the royal tombs, give us some knowledge of the cultural level, but there are no archives or tablets like those of the Late Mycenaean Period to help us formulate more concrete conclusions even of a hypothetical character.

It seems certain that, in the larger Mycenaean centres at least, royal dynasties were established which exercised more or less absolute control over a comparatively extensive region. Naturally, many of these dynasties would be related to one another, as they are in legend. The power of the kingdom of Mycenae is evident from its great wealth and the monumental architecture of its royal tombs. The palace at Mycenae must have been equally superior. It would appear that, like Knosos in Crete, Mycenae kept a distance between herself and the other centres. But it is difficult to be sure if the king of Mycenae was *primus inter pares*, as was the ruler of Knosos.

The organization of the Mycenaean settlements must have been based on military supremacy rather than on any theocratic concept. If the earliest dynasties were indigenous, the political organization must have been based on old native customs, perhaps of a fairly democratic character, since in Middle Helladic settlements there is no evidence at all of any centralized authority. The king may have surrounded himself with experienced counsellors from the

B.C.). Right: chariot with two horses, charioteer, and warrior on a sardonyx seal-stone (15th century B.C.), from the tholos tomb at Vapheio. (National Archaeological Museum, Athens)

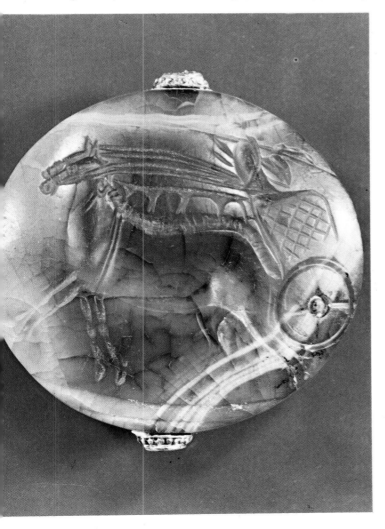

class of nobles, and we may even assume a sort of hierarchy headed by the king, as in Crete, but here the theocratic base must have been considerably weaker.

The other members of the royal family must also have been regarded as distinguished personages, for they received special funeral honours. The tombs of the queens and princesses often contained exquisite small swords, showing that women took part in the activities of the court. In hunting scenes depicted on gold rings and seal-stones, women of noble class appear along with the men. Later, they were shown on frescoes taking part in hunts and bullfights, as in Crete, perhaps indicating that on mainland Greece women had similar freedoms.

Mycenaean commerce must have been controlled by the king, as in Crete. The Mycenaeans gradually displaced the Minoans in foreign markets. How may this change be explained? We talk of a Minoan thalassocracy, but we should remember that it was substantially Creto-Mycenaean before becoming wholly Mycenaean. Is it then possible to distinguish Mycenaean from Minoan ships? In the representations, chiefly on seal rings, seal-stones, or seal impressions from the Early and Middle Mycenaean Periods, the ships are in no way different from Minoan ones. And it is certain that the latter continued to carry out their double mission, commercial and military, of keeping the sea routes under their control. The Minoan trading stations, particularly in the Syro-Phoenician region, could now multiply their commercial links with the Mycenaean centres. The Mycenaean ships would have had mixed crews of both natives and Minoans. The Mycenaeans soon picked up the naval art, and from land-lubbers were transformed into seamen.

The classes of craftsmen were as varied as those in Crete, perhaps more so, since production had to be adapted to the requirements of local consumption. Native craftsmanship could no longer compete with Minoan; it had to change and, in changing, it took refuge in imitations, which were not always successful or effective. So, the way lay open for wholesale adaption to Minoan fashions, which led to the swift disappearance of native production. As a result, Early Mycenaean art took on a pronounced Cretan character.

Some scholars have maintained that the miniature representations on seals imitated Minoan originals in dress, weapons, jewellery, etc., while Mycenaean life itself was in fact different from the Minoan. But from the evidence of the tombs, at least the royal ones, it appears that the men wore the Cretan kilt and the women dresses of Cretan fashion. Changes in dress came at a later date, when a type of breeches replaced the men's kilt with its cod-piece.

In their daily life, the Mycenaeans enjoyed all the comforts which the Minoans had known for centuries: recreational games, athletic sports, dancing displays, baths, etc. The boudoirs were as well equipped as those of the Minoans, and the men took considerable trouble with their appearance and adorned themselves with various pieces of jewellery, as had been the custom in Crete. The gradual development of the warlike spirit, however, went hand in hand with the cultivation of a more masculine appearance. The men now wore beards and moustaches, but clipped their hair so that it would not impede movement in combat.

There has been considerable argument about bull-fighting in Mycenaean times. Had bullfights become established in mainland Greece as they were in Crete, or were the Mycenaean representations of them simply imitations? The depiction of the capture of a bull in rush nets is so common that it seems probable that bull-fighting was an established practice. If the bull was captured unhurt, he may have been used in bullfights.

ART, 16TH AND 15TH CENTURIES

The art of the Mycenaean world from its early to its culminating period may be divided into three phases. In the first, production is of three kinds: native of a Middle Helladic character, Minoan, and imitation Minoan. In the second phase, an assimilative one, art takes on a Creto-Mycenaean character with Minoan shapes prevailing. In the last phase, production is chiefly of native inspiration.

In the Early Mycenaean Period (1600 B.C.-1500 B.C. approximately), the rich grave furnishings and tomb architecture help us form a satisfactory picture of the development of art.

Pottery

Pottery production may be divided into the three categories mentioned above: native, Minoan imitation, and Minoan production. Objects of Minoan production either came directly from Crete or were made by Minoan craftsmen established in the Mycenaean region. The imitations were generally imperfect, though sometimes faithful and artistic. Pottery of mixed Helladic and Minoan character also appears along with the imitative, but not at the beginning of the period. However, genuine Minoan vessels are very rare in Greece. From the vessels in grave circle A at Mycenae, for example, only one is considered to be genuinely Minoan. Native production is confined to two characteristic categories: the Minyan and the matt-painted ware. Minoan influence is obvious in both. A usual technique was that of the yellow Minyan ware decorated with small motifs in one or two colours. On the matt-painted ware, the technique remains the same, but the decorative motifs show the influence of the Minoan curvilinear subjects and of the plant style. In this category there are also some vessels betraying Cycladic influence, especially jugs with necks twisted backwards and mastoid protuberances, as well as amphorae with depictions of birds and strange daemons. The few specimens of pottery from Crete are easily distinguished by the technique, the shapes of the pots, and the decoration. Most of these vessels belong to the second Palace Period (16th century B.C.). The vessels are mainly in the plant style or decorated with running spirals and other typical motifs of that period. In the Middle Mycenaean Period, the marine style also appeared with its characteristic subjects. The local "Minoanizing" production developed a few special features which, to some extent, show independent developments in the

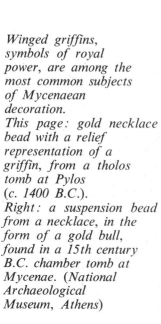

Winged griffins, symbols of royal power, are among the most common subjects of Mycenaean decoration.
This page: gold necklace bead with a relief representation of a griffin, from a tholos tomb at Pylos (c. 1400 B.C.).
Right: a suspension bead from a necklace, in the form of a gold bull, found in a 15th century B.C. chamber tomb at Mycenae. (National Archaeological Museum, Athens)

Mycenaean region. Favourite shapes are the loaf-shaped alabastra and the Ephyraean goblets (*kylikes*). The latter take their name from ancient Ephyra in Korinthia, where the first specimens were found. Isolated plant and marine subjects decorate the cheeks of these beautiful vessels.

In the last phase of the Middle Mycenaean Period, the so-called palace style evolved, and we can follow its parallel development at Knosos throughout the period of the Achaian dynasty. The tectonic and conventional decoration in this style betrays the new spirit, undoubtedly local Helladic, inherited from the Middle Helladic Period. The most interesting examples were found in tholos and chamber tombs at Mycenae, Prosymna, Vapheio, the Pylos region, the Triphylia region of Messenia, and at Athens and Thebes. This Mycenaean pottery can easily be distinguished from other native production by the local varieties of the clay, the way in which the vessel was baked, the exceptionally gleaming varnish, and the removable decoration. The peculiarities in the shape and decoration of the vessels help us to determine more precisely the centre of production. Wherever imitation Minoan or Creto-Mycenaean pottery is found, the hesitant or inexperienced hand of the decorator may be recognized by the absence of a vigorous line, and in many cases it is the flabbiness of the shapes of the vessels that betrays the local potters. These special characteristics make Mycenaean pottery easily distinguishable even when it is discovered in countries distant from Greece. Pottery found in the settlement on the Lipari Islands near Sicily

Above: scene of fighters engaged in single combat, engraved on a gold seal-bead, from a royal tomb of Circle A at Mycenae (16th century B.C.). (National Archaeological Museum, Athens)

and in Egyptian tombs of the 18th dynasty was immediately recognized as Mycenaean.

We know little about the progress made in the plastic arts, because few houses or shrines have been discovered and because it was not customary to place figurines in graves with the dead, as it was in the Cyclades and indeed in this same Mycenaean region at a later date. The group of large clay figures of characteristic Minoan types from the temple on Keos does not seem to be early Mycenaean, since the settlement is regarded as a Minoan colony.

Stone Carving

In stone carving, there are many representative examples to prove that the craftsmen faithfully followed the Minoan tradition, and in fact, in certain cases, it is very difficult to distinguish native work from Cretan imports. Wonderful stone vessels have been found in both the first and second grave circles at Mycenae. From the second circle comes a charming vessel of rock crystal with a handle worked in the shape of a duck's head and neck; from the first circle, a vessel of bold design with three large looped handles and an undulating lip. Also found here were the communion cups with their conical bodies on tall turned stems, conical and egg-shaped libation rhyta of semi-precious stone (particularly porphyry, Spartan basalt, alabaster, veined and speckled marble), lamps shaped as flowers or buds. Tables of offering, low or raised on a tall foot, were common too. Relatively small stone jars were decorated with medallions

and bands imitating ropes (tholos tomb of Klytaimnestra). Even vessels of steatite with a variety of scenes rendered in relief were not unknown at this time in the Mycenaean region. A typical example is a vessel from Mycenae with a relief representation of an octopus, very similar (though more stylized) to the one which decorates a fragmentary rhyton from Knosos. A fragment from Epidauros was decorated with a whole scene of men on a beach; in the sea is a dolphin and perhaps a ship.

The Mycenaean decorative style is more characteristically expressed in architectural sculpture: continuous series or nets of spirals, rosettes and half-rosettes surrounding both sides of a perpendicular central band, zig-zag bands, etc. As in Crete, half-columns flank the entrances to monumental tombs. There has been considerable argument about the funerary steles which were erected over the tombs of dead officials. Now it has been shown that the early ones were decorated with various subjects, mainly scenes of contest either in the chase or in war, rendered in a style rather more Minoan than conventionally Mycenaean.

Minoan influence is more obvious in the miniature engravings of the seal-stones and the miniature metal work of the seal-rings. The seal-stones could easily travel from place to place and pass down from generation to generation. Great numbers of them came from Crete and the Minoan colonies or were handed down as ancestral heirlooms. This makes it difficult to distinguish the genuinely Mycenaean variety. As in Crete, the main shapes are lentoid, amygdaloid, and the flattened cylinder that gives a rectangular sealing surface. The majority of the representations on seal-stones are indeed masterpieces of miniature art. Scenes of battle and the chase are depicted in a lively manner and with feel-

ing for the drama of the moment, though in a somewhat decorative style. Beautiful gold rings were found at Mycenae, Tiryns, Midea, Vapheio, Pylos, and Thebes. A majestic winged griffin appears on a flattened cylinder seal from a tholos tomb at Pylos. A considerable number of the seal-stones are set in gold. Two wonderful amygdaloid seal-stones from the tholos tomb at Myrsinochori have representations of the dramatic capture of a bull in a net and of another wounded bull; the back is decorated with a cross-hatch pattern with added inlay. The richness of this type of jewellery is in striking contrast to Middle Helladic simplicity. Proper use of the veining was made according to the Minoan technique. The seal was really a jewel and was worn along with other stones in necklaces and bracelets, or in rings, and this explains why beautiful stones were used. One of the best seal-stones was found in the accumulation from an old excavation: the goddess, her arms raised, sits side-saddle on a strange animal and crosses, or almost flies over, a rocky landscape. The tholos tombs of Dendra, Vapheio, and Myrsinochori have given us a large number of fine seal-stones with interesting subjects; apart from the numerous religious representations, there are representations of scenes from private life, and of the fauna of the land, sea, and air: hunters pursue bulls, figures drive along in a smart chariot, men tame lions, waterfowl fly about, dolphins leap up, quadrupeds suckle their young.

Metal-work

The best known branch of art in the Early Mycenaean Period is that of metal-work. The royal tombs were lavishly

quipped with metal utensils, arms, implements, and jewellery. By contrast, there are few remains of miniature metal-work igurines.

Mycenaean bronze vessels are almost facsimiles of the Minoan, with the same technique in the flattening of the plate, the cutting, the pinning, and the soldering. So it is difficult to speak of purely Mycenaean metal-work bronze vessels before the middle or even the last part of the Middle Mycenaean Period. At that time, bronze household utensils appear that must have been the pride of their owners. As in later times, it was essential for every good household to possess a large quantity of utensils of this sort, which were handed down from generation to generation as dowries or heirlooms: amphorae, jugs, pitchers, basins, bowls, round-bottomed or tripodal cooking-pots, cups, goblets, and lamps. Hoards of such bronze utensils have been found in the Mycenaean region, concealed below house floors or in hiding-places, where they were evidently placed for safety.

Utensils of precious metal (gold, silver, gold-silver alloy) and gold jewellery were so numerous in the royal tombs of Mycenae that the city's reputation of being "rich in gold" seems entirely justified. The technique used in the fashioning of gold objects appears to have been Minoan, although in Crete itself very few utensils of precious metal have been found. Some scholars believe the explanation is that Crete was poor in gold, and so the Minoan craftsmen had to resort to gilding stone and clay utensils.

The wealth of these precious utensils gives us some idea of the grandeur of the royal banquets and of the high standard of living, at least at the court. The working of the gold, the hammering, soldering, welding and lining, the strengthening of certain sections, the engraving, and the methods of decoration (both inlay and repoussé) were all techniques which had been known in Crete for centuries. Particularly fine are the chalices, goblets, many types of cups, and the various jars from the boudoir. On silver vessels, gold lips and other gold inlays were common. The inlay technique made it possible for scenes or decorative motifs to be shown, as on the silver-gold cup with the altar of vegetation from a royal tomb at Mycenae. However, the main decoration was done in repoussé. Spirals, rosettes, branches, arcades, furrows were all thus rendered in relief. The world of the sea-bed is depicted with even greater charm on metal than on clay utensils, and dolphins are shown making graceful leaps. Subject-rendering has passed the narrow limits of decorative pottery: animals are depicted in relief moving with amazing agility, often in the "flying gallop"; there are lions, cat-like creatures, deer, bulls, or supernatural beings like griffins. These subjects were the stock-in-trade of Minoan artists too, but Mycenaean work, especially in the latter part of the Middle Period, displays a feeling for harmony and tectonic approach which clearly distinguishes it as native Helladic.

The most outstanding of the utensils made of precious metal are those decorated with "contest" motifs, such as the capture of wild beasts, the hunting of dangerous or particularly nimble game, as well as battles and sieges. The most famous are certainly the two gold cups from the tholos tomb of Vapheio. Identical in shape and technique, they differ in their decoration. Each shows the capture of wild bulls by a different method. In one, the hunted bull falls into rush nets hung between trees just as he is springing to attack the hunters. The second shows a more idyllic scene: the capture is effected by using a female animal as decoy; while the bull is busy flirting, oblivious to danger, the expert hunters lasso his foot in a noose. Evans believed that the artist was inspired by the relief frescoes on the north-gate "bastion" of the palace of Knosos. A stemmed silver cup from the royal tholos tomb of Midea shows the dramatic scene of the hunting of a boar with the help of trained hunting dogs. Two silver utensils with powerful and skilfully composed representations were found in the royal tombs of the first circle at Mycenae. The first is a large krater with a scene of epic combat between two groups of armed warriors. The liveliness of the movements, the dramatic feeling in the composition, the multiplicity of forms, and the picturesque effect of the whole are all typically Minoan, while the balance in the movements and in the positions of the warriors reveals a predominant characteristic of Mycenaean conception. There is another masterly rendering, on a conical silver rhyton, of a whole scene outside a besieged city. It shows a landing operation with all the vigour of epic narration: boats approach the beach (one rower can be discerned), and men swim to the shore. The waves are rendered by scaly cross-hatching. The town is defended by heavily-armed soldiers with the aid of archers and slingers; on the walls, the unarmed population is depicted watching the battle with much gesticulation.

More silver utensils would certainly have been preserved if the metal were not so easily destroyed by oxidization. Some have a very neat shape, e.g. a group of goblets (kylikes) from a rock-cut grave at Mycenae. A silver jug from the royal tombs of the acropolis is decorated with running spirals on arc patterns. The craftsmen often added moulded ornament to the lips of gold and silver vessels or to the handles. On the gold goblet known as the "Cup of Nestor", two small birds, perhaps wild doves, perch on the lips as if to drink the contents. Sometimes, utensils made of precious metals, particularly rhyta, were moulded into various plastic shapes. The best examples come from the royal tombs of Mycenae: a gold rhyton in the shape of a lion's head, on which the features of the animal have been rendered with great vigour and liveliness, though in a somewhat conventional manner; another, of silver, in the shape of a bull's head with gilded horns and eyes inlaid with gold and silver and a large gold rosette on the forehead; a third moulded into the shape of a deer with branching antlers. A characteristic example of Mycenaean work is a hexagonal wooden gold-plated pyxis with dense relief decoration resembling wood carving; between nets of spirals, lions tear antelopes to pieces or chase deer.

Many other objects used as funerary ornaments for the king and other nobles were also worked in metal. Gold masks, which were evidently used in the Early Mycenaean Period, cannot be regarded as very important works of art, except perhaps the mask which, Schliemann thought, belonged to Agamemnon himself. Here the features are impressive, and the face is rather of the regular bearded Greek type. The other masks present rather strange faces —fleshy with staring eyes and bald craniums. The gold breastplate of one of the royal dead was decorated with a dense spiral pattern. The breasts were indicated by small circles, each with a dot at the centre. One infant was completely covered in gold plate without decoration.

The funerary ornamentation was completed by the addition of diadems or half-diadems with rosettes and flower-buds. According to one theory, some adorned the sarcophagi, being placed like rays starting from ellipsoidal bands. There has been some argument about the numerous plates cut into various shapes which decorated the wooden covers of the sarcophagi. These were presumably nailed to the wood or sewn into the shrouds in which the royal dead were wrapped. The shapes include rosettes, crosses, stars, and small discs with various motifs. Other plates were cut to represent figures: oysters, tritons, octopuses, butterflies, supernatural beings, or small figures of divinities, such as naked goddesses with doves; or sometimes they were cut in the shape of a sanctuary with its three-columned wings. There were also butterflies adorning the balances of the scales which weighed the soul to determine its value.

Apart from the funerary ornament in the tombs, there was also a wealth of jewellery which had been worn by the members of the royal family and the nobles while they were still alive. This was much more solidly constructed in a variety of materials besides gold. Gold plate and leaf cover bone, ivory, wood, and sometimes leather. Buttons, accessories, and small tabs with a central notch come from leather belts and straps of swords and daggers, serving as ornaments or as fasteners. Small four-spoked wheels were similarly used as decoration on leather goods. There were open-work lunate earrings; fastening rings for the hair; heavy and light bracelets (one with a multi-leaved rosette of various metal plates depicting a flower); breast-chains worn by dignitaries (one with a row of two-headed eagles); necklaces with many kinds of beads decorated with plant, marine, and animal subjects; breast pins; and large attachments with religious or decorative subjects, most of them of symbolic significance. There are some rare examples of solid gold ornaments, among them a beautiful pin in open-work gold plate which represented the vegetation goddess holding necklaces in her hands. In the necklaces as well as gold beads, there were precious or semi-precious stones—amethyst, rock crystal, various agates, jasper, and cyanos. The beads were spherical, amygdaloid, spindle shaped, flattened cylinders, drop-shaped, and so on.

Weapon-making

The fashioning and decorating of metal weapons made outstanding progress, as was natural in a region where the warlike spirit manifested itself so early. The famous swords in the royal tombs of Mycenae have mostly decorated handles covered with gold plate. Usually the top of the handle is in the shape of an apple or a mushroom, and the heel of the blade has a rounded end; later, however, the tip becomes square or ends in a cross- or horn-shape. Perhaps these very long swords were intended more for a display of grandeur than for use in war, although their blades were quite sharp enough to despatch an adversary. They are usually more than a metre in length. Often the gold plate and the ivory have beautiful representational decorations. On the pommel of one sword, the bodies of four lions curve in torsion, bringing their heads together. A little later, the hilt is strengthened by an extension along the length of the stem and by the addition of a row of nails, and the blade is broadened so that it may be used like a sabre. The median rib, which at first was simply a reinforcement, is now decorated with a series of representations of animals—horses, deer, or griffins in "flying gallop"—or with decorative motifs like small shields or spirals. Along with these splendid weapons, there were other shorter ones, such as smaller side swords or simple daggers. These were used in hand-to-hand fighting to wound the adversary on the neck above his covering shield, in the way shown on miniature representations. The daggers, being royal weapons, were the finest of all, and were used even by queens and princesses. The striking metal-work technique on some of the daggers might almost be called "metal-painting". Using niello, i.e. an alloy of lead, silver, borax, and sulphur, the craftsmen worked whole scenes on the broad spine of the dagger in different shades of coloured metal. Scenes of contest, which are common, are rendered with great vigour and charm. The best of these daggers come from the royal tombs at Mycenae, but isolated specimens have also been found at Prosymna, Vapheio, Myrsinochori, Aigion, and Thera.

Among Mycenaean offensive weapons, Cretan-type spears, darts, and *sagynai* (type of hunting javelin), often decorated with small engraved representations, can be recognized. The arrow-heads of bronze, though often of obsidian or silex, resemble swallow-tails or a wedge with a stem. As in Crete, few Mycenaean defensive weapons have been preserved, for most were made of perishable material. In representations, however, and in miniature depictions, there are both the figure-of-eight shield and the semi-cylindrical; the latter, "tower-like", as the epic poems say, covered the whole body of the warrior, thus rendering the breast-plate, the mitre for the abdomen, and the greave superfluous. A semi-circular projection on the top of the shield served to protect the head when the shield was raised slightly. Since the warriors were hampered in their movements by these heavy weapons, they needed the aid of light-armed troops, the archers and the slingers, as we see on the siege rhyton. The effectiveness of offensive weapons meant that defensive weapons had to be similarly efficacious. Suits of armour at the end of Middle Mycenaean times were of bronze and very heavy. The bronze armour from the Dendra tomb, for instance, consists of a series of bronze belts jointed together with the breastplates and shoulder-coverings. Layers of skins were no longer sufficient protection. Rows of pieces of boar-tusk, fixed between the bands, reinforced the leather cover of the helmet, which eventually became no more than the lining. Crests, often long and curving, decorated the tops of helmets. Leg protection was by means of leather straps, like modern gaiters. These were later replaced by one-piece bronze greaves.

The combatants were transported to the field of battle with the help of light chariots drawn by one or two horses. These were used both in battle and in the chase. Our knowledge of the Mycenaean chariot comes solely from representations of it; we see its wicker body side-pieces and rails, the joint between axle and pole, and the harness with yoke, bridle, and reins. The only fragments which have been

preserved are of bridles which were of bronze; these have been found in the tomb of Klytaimnestra and in the annex of Kadmeion, which is perhaps of a later date.

Bronze implements of the Early Mycenaean Period are similar to those of Crete; later on, differences gradually begin to appear. The main categories were the stone-cutting and wood-cutting implements as well as some that were intended for the cutting and working of leather. The bronze instruments used in the boudoir were as varied as those of Crete: mirrors, razors, tweezers, and caskets for jewellery or make-up.

When working with delicate materials, such as ivory, wood, faience, or glass, the Mycenaean craftsmen copied Minoan originals. Ivory dogs had been added on to a wooden casket from the royal tombs at Mycenae. On another pyxis from Myrsinochori, the decoration was neat spirals and coils. A plaquette from Mycenae shows a goddess sitting on rocks. Ivory combs are decorated with similar charm. On a comb from Myrsinochori, for example, wild cats are depicted chasing waterfowl. Luxury bronze mirrors found in tholos and chamber tombs had carved handles; on two specimens, young girls are shown sitting opposite each other holding mirrors or birds.

Vessel of rock crystal, found in a prince's grave of Circle B at Mycenae (16th century B.C.) and regarded as a masterpiece of Mycenaean stone carving. The plasticity of the duck's head *and the liveliness of its eye, the movement and grace of the com-position, reveal artistic sensitivity as well as technical proficiency. (National Archaeological Museum, Athens)*

The Centuries of Achaian Sovereignty

EXPANSION

The fire which broke out in the palace of Knosos "one spring morning with a strong south wind" a little after 1400 B.C. did more than reduce the huge and complex palace building to ashes; it paralyzed the administrative and economic centre of the island, thus concluding a gradual but steady process which resulted in the removal of the seat of power from island Crete to mainland Greece. This process had begun much earlier, and all the efforts of the Achaian overlords of Knosos to check it had failed. Already, before the end of the 15th century B.C., Mycenaean trading stations had appeared on the doorstep of the chief Minoan ones on Melos, Rhodes, and Kythera, which they were obviously set to replace. Mycenaean products had begun to reach the markets of the East and to become ever more widespread at the expense of Cretan exports. And if the letter of the Hittite King to his rebellious and usurping subject Madduwattas is in fact to be dated in the period 1400-1395 B.C., as has recently been proposed (and not c. 1200 B.C., as was generally accepted before), then the Achaians, or at least some Achaians, must have already raided the shores of Asia Minor, a region which had never ceased to attract them. The finds from excavations and, to a certain extent, the substratum of memory which is reflected in myth and legend, help us to form a picture of a new, vigorous, and rapidly advancing civilization which, having assimilated such elements of Minoan civilization as were useful to it, particularly the organization of the central authority and trade on the pattern of the cities of the East, was now ready to displace and replace its teachers. The destruction of the palace at Knosos relegated Crete to a secondary position, from now on always following in the wake of the Mycenaeans, adapting itself to the new order of things, but no longer making history itself. The way was now open for Mycenaean trade to expand, free from organized competition.

Greece and the Eastern Mediterranean at the Beginning of the 14th Century B.C.

During this period, the population of Greece lived in villages and small townships of which about 130 are known to us today. These settlements, scattered from Tempe to Tainaron, are numerous in Attica and Boiotia, more scattered in Thessaly and the Peloponnesos, and completely absent in Epeiros, Aitolia and Akarnania, the Ionian Islands and, with the exception of one or two mountain villages, Achaia. Already one of the basic characteristics of Hellenism had emerged: its orientation towards the Aegean. Most of the settlements were concentrated in certain regions and around some larger centres, one in Thessaly (Iolkos), two or three in Boiotia and Euboia (Orchomenos, Thebes, Chalkis), four in the eastern Peloponnesos (Corinth, Mycenae, Tiryns, Menelaïon, and the Gulf of Gytheion), and two in the southwest Peloponnesos (Pylos, Kyparissia). Overseas expansion had already begun, as shown by the settlements at Naxos, Delos, Kythnos, Seriphos, and Melos, i.e. the Cyclades and the islands nearest to mainland Greece. Mycenaean products had spread as far as the Lipari Islands of Sicily; they were particularly popular at Troy, on the Syrian coast (Alalakh, Ugarit, Tel Sukas, Akkar, Byblos), in Palestine (Hazor, Gezer, Lachish), in Jordan (Amman), and in Egypt—that is, wherever the Cretan merchants had already prepared the way. Immediately after the decline of Crete, the Mycenaeans hastened to establish trading stations at Taras and Ugarit and two colonies, one at Miletos, which was built on the burnt-out ruins of the earlier Minoan city, and the other at Ialysos on Rhodes, which absorbed the neighbouring Cretan settlement. Moreover, they began to colonize Cyprus, where the first groups of Arkadians arrived from Triphylia and Pisatis. These newcomers, who settled at Maroni and Enkomi among the indigenous population, brought the place-name *Alasia* from their native land, and this eventually came to denote the whole island. The increasing similarity of the products of Mycenaean craftsmanship, especially pottery, and the gradual effacing of local differences show that the contact between these centres, especially within Greece, was close, continuous, and unhindered. This is confirmed too by the swiftness with which all artistic and technical innovations became general regardless of their place of origin.

Achaian activity in the surrounding world met with conditions which were favourable or which at least did not impede peaceful development. Egypt under Amenhotep III (1405-1367 B.C.) was passing through a period of great wealth and power. To the north, in the region of the Upper Euphrates, the very powerful state of the Mitanni was on friendly terms with Egypt, especially since the daughter of the king of Mitanni had married the Pharaoh. Between these two great states lay the cities of Canaan (i.e. Syria and Palestine), which enjoyed a status of semi-independence under the slack and continually alternating suzerainty of the two big powers. In the prevailing conditions of peace and tranquillity, these cities were able to progress and prosper and had developed into civil entities with flourishing craft industries and commercial organizations. Further north, in the depths of Asia Minor, the Hittite state was facing constant upheavals, disorders, and raids from neighbouring peoples which prevented its expansion to the south and west,

to the shores of Cilicia, where the independent state of Arzawa lay. The ascension of Shuppiluliumash I to the Hittite throne (1375 B.C.) and the death of Amenhotep III (1367 B.C.) brought about a radical change in the factors which were preserving the status quo in the Near East as well as a change in the relations of the various states. Shuppiluliumash, one of the most powerful figures in ancient history, managed within a few years to pacify his state, to occupy Northern Syria (1370 B.C.), and to overthrow the Mitanni kingdom (1340 B.C.), which was also invaded by the Assyrians. Further, the death of Amenhotep brought the heretical dreamer Akhenaton (1367-1350 B.C.) to the Egyptian throne. Akhenaton spent his life trying to impose on Egypt a religious reform of his own inspiration, with the result that the actual administration of his kingdom was sorely neglected. His immediate successors were incapable of restoring the kingdom to its former strength and so, from the middle of the century, after intrigues, rebellions, border changes, and local clashes, the centre of power moved northwards, and the cities of Canaan came more under the influence of the Hittites than of Egypt, though without major wars or destruction, especially in the coastal belt. Thus the life of this region, which was the commercial crossroads of the then known world, changed very little, even though the balance of power had been overthrown at Egypt's expense.

In the Western Mediterranean, i.e. in Italy and Sicily, and in the North, in the Balkan peninsula, the situation was completely different. These countries were in a semi-savage state of primitive agricultural culture without cities or any organized authority. Apart from raw materials (liparite) and some products from the far North (amber from the Baltic) which they brought down the rivers of Europe, these peoples had little to offer. The exchanges, usually for weapons and jewels, were effected through trading stations which the Achaians themselves had set up (e.g. at Taras and at Ischia). These exchanges were very limited and not vital to the Mycenaean economy.

Initial Development

The expansionist tendency of the Achaians outside Greece, and especially towards the rich and advanced countries of the Near East, though still somewhat hesitant and always following in the familiar footsteps of the Cretans, kept pace with a much more vigorous expansion into the interior of Greece itself, especially into the more fertile areas, and also along the main routes of communication. In the first half of the 14th century B.C., the settlements almost doubled in number. They extended northwards to the Axios Valley, west to Akarnania and the coast of Epeiros (Parga); they multiplied in Lokris, Phthiotis, and particularly in the valley of the Alpheios, on the road, that is, by which the mountain people of Arkadia went to Elis, Triphylia, and the sea. Sporadic settlements began to appear in Ithaca and Zakynthos. There were new ones too in the Aegean (on Skyros, Skopelos, Kimolos, and Paros); and, on Rhodes, they now occupied the whole northern section of the island. They were particularly dense, however, in Boiotia, Attica, Korinthia, and the Argolid, and even more so, proportionately, in the Thessalian plain. So mainland Greece presented a noticeable increase in its population, which came about in an entirely normal and peaceful way without any addition or invasion of new elements. On the contrary, a wave of emigration had begun of the indigenous population who began to travel to ever more distant places, and this continued and gathered momentum during the next two to three hundred years. There is no doubt that the country made great progress, and there must have been a corresponding rise in the standard of living based on improved methods of agriculture and the better exploitation of productive regions—the very regions where the greatest concentration of settlements is observed. But a general improvement in living conditions is not possible without systematic measures being taken on an extensive scale and over a wide area by a strong political and economic power capable of controlling whole regions, of programming works, and of implementing its plans.

The second half of the 14th century is the period of the strengthening of the central authority in mainland Greece, of economic organization, and of the first communal enterprises. Shortly after 1350 B.C., an intricate system of dykes, ditches, and tunnels was constructed to drain the Kopais swamp and to give the farmers of the Orchomenos region one of the most fertile pieces of land in the whole of Greece. At the same time, the first Cyclopean walls at Tiryns were built and, later, the walls at Mycenae, probably inspired by Hittite prototypes; extensive palaces were built on these two acropolises, and also at Pylos and Thebes. These palaces never formed part, even as self-sufficient and independent units, of a populous fortified city with a more or less extensive dominion, as was the case in Cyprus and the East, nor were they purely and simply the dwellings of the ruler and his retinue. From the first they imitated their Cretan prototypes, and their character never altered; each one of them was at the same time the seat of the ruler, the administrative centre of a basically agricultural region, and the co-ordinator of its economic activity. The imposing construction of the palaces and the kind of authority they represented show clearly that their power was as beneficent as it was great, and the sites of the settlements which were under the control of the palaces leave no doubt that peace and prosperity prevailed.

So, the 14th century is the age in which Mycenaean Greece, freed from the competition and, to a certain extent, the opposition of Crete, availed herself of the chance to organize her kingdoms in accordance with the precepts she had learned from her former rival, to enter into direct and regular contact with the surrounding world, and to develop the system which was to provide a framework for her great period of prosperity. The warlike groups of farmers and stockbreeders developed into a compact population of cultivators and craftsmen, the tribe chieftains into rulers,

and the buccaneers and pirates into colonists and merchants. The change which had begun to manifest itself in the period of the shaft graves had been finally completed.

The Hegemony

After the first hesitant steps of 1400 B.C. and the exploratory expansion of 1350 B.C., there followed the most glorious period of Mycenaean civilization, the period which saw the explosive expansion of the Achaians and the establishment of their sovereignty in the Eastern Mediterranean, which they were to retain until the last decades of the 13th century.

The culmination of this vigorous period occurred in the first half of the century, and there is striking evidence for it in the developments within Greece itself during those years. The settlements in mainland Greece and the Ionian Islands increased by 112; and to these were added another one in Chalkidike, four on Kos, eight on Rhodes, four on Kalymnos, Karpathos, and Leipso, six on Lesbos, Psara, and Samos, and five in the Cyclades. Thus the total of known sites rose to 413. Greek settlements were not to reach this number again until the 5th and 4th centuries B.C. Most of them were established among already existing settlements, which clearly shows the great increase in population in one or two generations. The most noticeable increase in density is observed in Messenia, which had the greatest concentration of population, then Lokris, Euboia, the highlands of Achaia, and Lakonia around Sparta. New centres appeared at Libatho on Kephallenia, and on Zakynthos; in other words, there was a great increase in settlements in the Alpheios Valley, Messenia, and Euboia, even greater in the Dodecanese (Kos, Rhodes), a clear expansion to Lokris, the Ionian Islands, and Achaia, and a limited but indubitable expansion to Epeiros. By now the whole of Greece, apart from Epeiros and the mountains of the Peloponnesos, was densely inhabited, and the population lived in both old and new settlements concentrated for the most part either in certain areas (Argolid, Achaia, Gulf of Gytheion, and the Plain of Libatho) or round some large centres such as Larisa, Iolkos, Orchomenos, Thebes, Chalkis, Athens, Corinth, Olympia, Kyparissia, Pylos, Messene, and Menelaïon. We do not always know the actual centre of each group of settlements, and their distribution does not always coincide with that of historical times, but their arrangement into clearly discernible groups shows that, apart from the large palaces and their immediate dominions, there were many other smaller groups of towns and settlements dependent on, or at least under the control of, the richest and strongest town in their region.

This geographical and administrative division into many small hegemonies is confirmed by the information that has come down to us in the epic poems. At the end of the second book of the *Iliad*, there is a list of the Achaians who fought at Troy with mention of the cities or regions they came from, the names of their leaders, and the number of ships provided by each expeditionary force. This "Catalogue of Ships", as it is called, is one of the early sections of the epic, and the verse must have been originally composed in Mycenaean times. Philological analysis shows that the Catalogue as a whole makes up a small independent epic with its own introduction and invocation to the Muses; it describes the

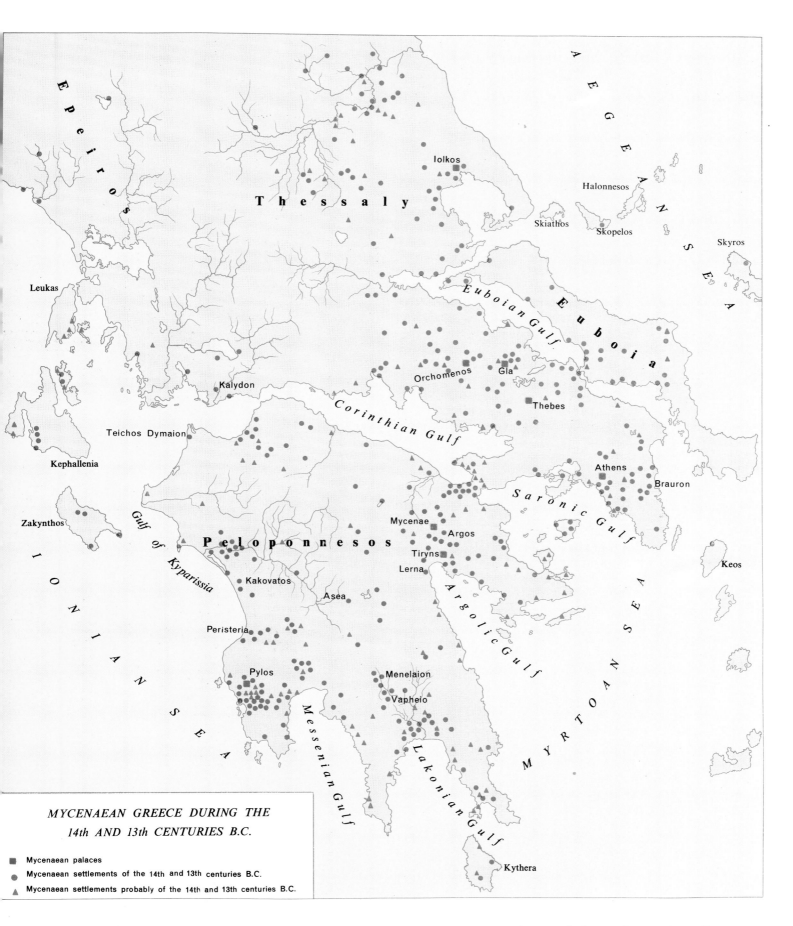

**MYCENAEAN GREECE DURING THE
14th AND 13th CENTURIES B.C.**

■ Mycenaean palaces

● Mycenaean settlements of the 14th and 13th centuries B.C.

▲ Mycenaean settlements probably of the 14th and 13th centuries B.C.

Mycenaean civilization reached its peak in the 14th and 13th centuries B.C. As appears from the map, the central Helladic area, from the Northern Sporades to the Ionian Islands and from Northern Thessaly to Kythera, was densely populated. The Mycenaean palaces of Messenia, the Argolid, Attica, Boiotia, and Iolkos were centres of particularly populous regions. Concentrations of population are also observed in Lokris, Euboia, the mountainous areas of Achaia, and Lakonia. At this period, political and economic life was at its most flourishing within Greece, and the Mycenaeans also expanded their interests overseas.

271

battle order of the Greeks as it must have been when they set off for Troy and not during the tenth year of the war, when the narration of the *Iliad* begins. A comparison of the Catalogue with the rest of the epic shows that there are differences between the two texts on important questions: for example, on the position and importance given to the Boiotians (prominent in the Catalogue, slight in the *Iliad*); on the extent and importance of the kingdom of Agamemnon (he is referred to in the *Iliad* as ruler of the Argolid and many islands, while the Catalogue assigns these to Diomedes, leaving Agamemnon with only Mycenae and the north shore of the Peloponnesos); on the kingdom of Achilles (according to the Catalogue, he rules over a small region at the mouth of the Spercheios, in the *Iliad* over an extensive region which stretches to Iolkos and Pelion); and on the kingdom of Odysseus (he appears in the Catalogue with his dominion cut in two by the much more powerful state of Meges, which the *Iliad* has removed to the country of the Epeians). This basic evidence and a host of other indications show that the Catalogue and the *Iliad* were written separately; they were combined at a much later date without any serious attempt to make even the most important pieces of information consistent.

Historical and archaeological research too has shown that the Greece of the Catalogue was very different from the Greece of the 9th and the 8th centuries B.C., the period, that is, when the *Iliad* was composed. It describes a political division very different from the one that was created after the invasion of the Thessalians and the descent of the Dorians, whom indeed it completely ignores. Of the 164 places it mentions, 60 or more have been shown to be Mycenaean on the evidence of excavations or through their connection with old myths and legends. The rest could very well be Mycenaean but in any case not a single Dorian site is mentioned. The chief proof, however, is that about one-quarter of the total number of sites mentioned (e.g. Nisa, Kalliaros, Bessa, Augeiai, Mideia, Arne, Eiones, Rhipe, Stratie, Enispe, Parassie, Elone) were not known to the Greeks of historical times nor to the Ionian bards who composed the *Iliad*. Indeed about 40 of the sites are mentioned only in the Catalogue. Their names and particularly the characteristic epithets which accompany them (rich in grapes, windswept, white) could not possibly have been preserved unless we accept that the Catalogue was compiled at a period when these place-names were known and in use and that, when later they changed along with the more general geographical and political situation in Greece, the memory of them survived through their preservation in the oral epic tradition. In other words, the Catalogue, despite various additions and changes made to it from time to time, is basically a work of the Mycenaean Period and echoes the conditions which existed then. Each group of the Achaian forces was associated usually with one leader but with several towns or regions. The Catalogue is thus a further proof that Mycenaean Greece was organized not into isolated and self-governing cities but into small states covering a wider area, corresponding, more or less, to natural geographical regions, each governed in most cases by one ruler. This agrees with the archaeological evidence. It may be noted too that all the kingdoms of the Catalogue that have been identified (since they contain cities or regions known to us today) appear to fit very well with the groups of settlements which have been excavated in modern times.

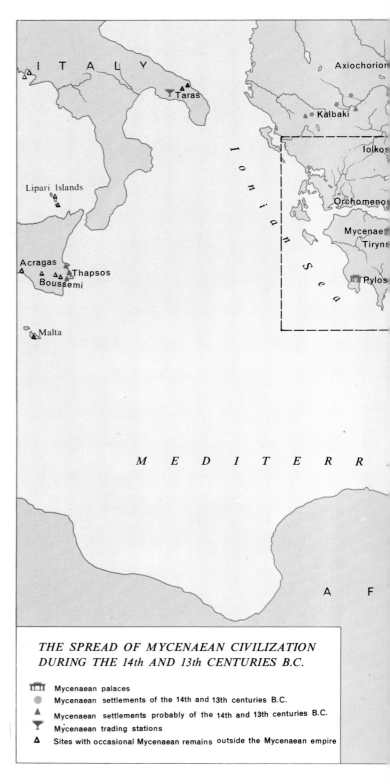

THE SPREAD OF MYCENAEAN CIVILIZATION DURING THE 14th AND 13th CENTURIES B.C.

▥ Mycenaean palaces

● Mycenaean settlements of the 14th and 13th centuries B.C.

▲ Mycenaean settlements probably of the 14th and 13th centuries B.C.

⊤ Mycenaean trading stations

△ Sites with occasional Mycenaean remains outside the Mycenaean empire

The centres of these kingdoms communicated with each other and with the rest of their own region by means of well-constructed carriage roads; these had small guardposts at intervals to keep track on traffic and protect the road, if necessary. They formed an organized road network, remains of which have been found in Crete as well as in mainland Greece. From Mycenae they led off to different points in the Argolid, the Corinthian Gulf, and to Epidauros. In Boiotia, they provided a link via Leuktra between the coast of the Corinthian Gulf (Libadostra) and the Thebes-Orchomenos region and the acropolis of Gla; in Messenia, they started from Pylos and ended in the region of Kalamata. This network, of which new sections are

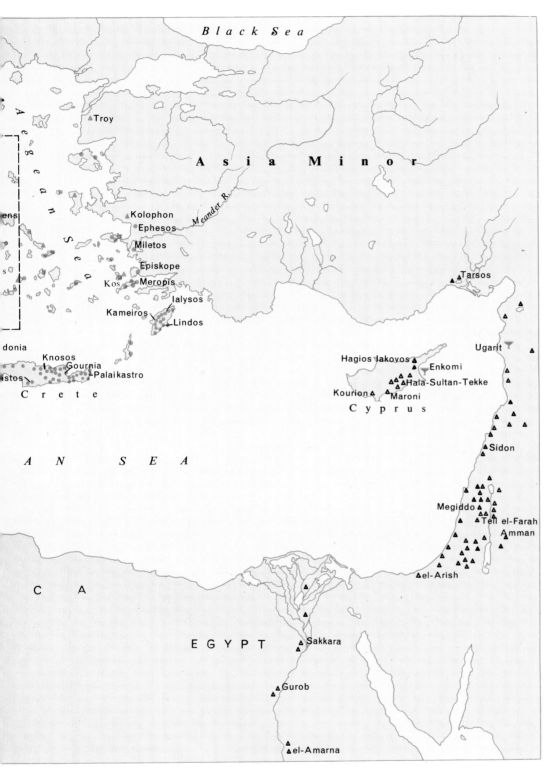

Map labels:

Black Sea

Asia Minor

Troy

Kolophon
Ephesos
Miletos
Episkope
Kos — Meropis
Ialysos
Kameiros — Lindos

A e g e a n   S e a

ens
s

donia
Knosos — Gournia
istos — Palaikastro
C r e t e

Tarsos

Ugarit
Hagios Iakovos — Enkomi
Hala-Sultan-Tekke
Kourion — Maroni
C y p r u s

A N   S E A

Sidon

Megiddo
Tell el-Farah
Amman

el-Arish

C   A

EGYPT — Sakkara

Gurob

el-Amarna

In the 14th century B.C., the Mycenaeans began their explosive expansion beyond the confines of the Achaian hegemony in mainland Greece (enclosed in broken line on map). Achaian settlements became denser in the Dodecanese and Crete, flourishing colonies were founded in Asia Minor, and trading posts organized on Cyprus. Mycenaean influence and trade contacts spread as far as Southern Italy, the Syro-Palestinian coast, and Egypt.

continually being uncovered, secured better and easier communications than the haphazard road system of Classical times. Close and regular contact between the various large regions was thus assured, and this made for cultural unity and a constant interplay of influences. Roads and other large public works, like the drainage installations at the Kopais Lake and, a little later, the fortifications on the acropolis at Gla, show that there must have been some political bond between the various rulers which secured their mutual cooperation for large-scale projects. The evidence from both archaeology and legend confirms the apparent supremacy of certain palaces (Mycenae, Tiryns, Pylos, Thebes, also Athens, Iolkos, and, earlier, Knosos).

This would have been possible only if their administrative influence extended over an area much wider than their immediate region. It has sometimes been suggested that the whole Mycenaean world was gathered into a single kingdom, that the smaller regions belonged in some way to the king of Mycenae, and that the whole formed an "empire"—to use the word by which it has become customary to call the great states of that period, particularly those that had possessions outside their ethnic boundaries. But this does not seem to have been the case. Certainly, the purely archaeological evidence shows that Mycenae and the Argolid were pioneers in the shaping and developing of certain fashions and trends in the life and culture of the time, but there is no

273

evidence, even indirect, on the Pylos tablets to indicate any kind of subordinate role. Further, legend and epic have retained the memory of clashes, even wars, between Mycenaean states. The generalship of Agamemnon in the Trojan expedition was simply the result of an agreement among all parties that he should command the expeditionary force in the theatre of operations; and, in fact, Achilles had no hesitation about challenging and actually violating that agreement.

It is, therefore, highly probable that the political arrangement of Greece in the 13th century B.C. corresponded to the picture presented by the excavations: the country was divided into four or five large, and about as many smaller, "federal" states, corresponding to the large palaces. The palace was both the dwelling place of the monarch and the administrative and economic centre of his dominion. The palaces were large building complexes of several storeys, with extensions and annexes for the family apartments, storerooms, workshops, archives, and various other uses, and probably with the houses of the palace staff, of whom there was a great number with varied and specific functions. For instance, apart from the general servants, there were women whose sole duty was the preparation and supervision of baths (λεωτροχόωοι). The overlord, like his equivalent in Crete and the cities of the East, gathered the contributions of his subjects into the palace buildings, where he also stored and maintained all battle equipment (chariots, suits of armour, weapons); from the palace, he directed farming and animal rearing, made raw materials (such as copper) available to the craftsmen and artisans, and controlled all these activities with the help of a group of scribe-accountants.

At the summit of the social pyramid was the monarch, the *Wanax* as the tablets call him, leader of the armed forces, highest judicial authority, and controller of production and commerce. However, he was not identified with the chief priest, or regarded as in any way divine, like the kings of eastern countries. Immediately after the monarch came the almost equally important office of the *Lawagetas*, the polemarch or army chief. Both owned areas of land for their own exclusive use and had at their disposal a personal retinue of palace guards, heralds, and servants.

The gods and their sanctuaries were also assigned property, both land and movable goods, which was looked after by priests of various ranks. From the tablets it emerges that there was also a body of high-ranking officials, though their role is not very clear, who seem to have formed an executive class. In the smaller centres, which were dependent on a central authority, there were councils of notables (senators) and local leaders of secondary importance, like the *Korete* and the *Porokorete*, among whom are mentioned kings (*Basileu*), who must have been some sort of community leaders.

There was some kind of standing army stationed at various points in the kingdom. In the Pylos kingdom, ten such stations are mentioned, none of which have yet been identified. The soldiers seem to have been divided into decarchies; their numbers, which evidently varied according to circumstances but never exceeded one to two hundred, are always given in multiples of ten. The ordinary hoplites were foot soldiers. They wore helmets with a covering of boar tusks, short corselets, and leggings; they carried a small circular or semi-circular shield and fought with bows,

A chief characteristic of the life of the Achaians, even from early Mycenaean times, is their warlike spirit. The blades of the famous swords from Mycenaean tombs were decorated with scenes of war, single combat, and hunting. On this fine bronze blade of *a dagger from Circle A at Mycenae (16th century B.C.), there is a representation of a lion hunt; the hunters are dressed in waist clouts and armed with shields, bows, and javelins. (National Archaeological Museum, Athens)*

Details from the everyday life of the Mycenaeans are shown in scenes imaginatively rendered on the gold cups found in a tomb at Vapheio in Lakonia (16th century B.C.). Above: detail of a scene of idyllic charm, showing the capture of wild bulls: the huntsman has resorted to trapping the bull by using a female animal as decoy; while the bull flirts, oblivious to danger, the huntsman passes a rope noose over his hind foot. (National Archaeological Museum, Athens)

spears, and swords.

The officers of this army came from the class of the *Moropa* (moiroppas = the possessor of a moira, i.e. a lot?), landowners, and local officials who were also the commanding officers of the regional units. Alongside these were the *Eqeta* (followers), directly dependent on the sovereign, who secured their services by granting them the necessary property requirements, some form of dress or uniform, and the greatest part of their military equipment.

The storerooms of the palaces contained all types of arms: heavy bronze suits of armour (like the one found at Dendra), which protected the whole body of the warrior, and war chariots (a weapon borrowed from the East), used in formation fighting as the chief striking force of that period. These chariots and their attachments were issued to the *Eqeta*, who apparently formed a select body of heavily armoured chariot fighters serving close to the ruler. On some tablets, however, the *Eqeta* are assigned to various local units under the command of a *Moropa*, perhaps to secure (as John Chadwick supposes) direct communication with the palace by means of their swift chariots. Some such mission, evidently peaceful, since the warriors are lightly armed with only helmet and spear, is depicted on a fresco from the

palace of Pylos. There was a plentiful supply of ships, o which the ruler had several in use for missions of a defensiv nature, manned by oarsmen of whom he kept a register i his archives.

Below this class of administrative officials and arm officers, came the main body of the population—farmers stockbreeders, and artisans. On the last rung of the socia scale was the large slave population, mainly foreign prisoner of war, who made up the necessary labour force and carrie out work of all kinds.

Ownership of land was fixed by a system of which th details are not yet clear. There were first the "precincts" o the ruler and the *Lawagetas*: these were the legal property o whoever occupied these offices. Then, there were the *kama* which apparently the palace granted to certain persons in re turn for services or in exchange for goods. The *ktoinai* (estates were divided into two basic categories: the *kekemena* o the tablets (*kekeimena*?), which were the collective property of the community, and the *ktimena*, which belonged to in dividuals or to the sanctuaries of the gods. The owners eithe cultivated the estate themselves or rented it to tenants. Th tenant then paid the owner in kind in proportion to th area of the land and the quantity of seed he needed for sow

The small and manoeuvrable chariot with one or two horses was widely used for a variety of purposes in public and private life. In battle, it transported the warriors to the point of assembly; in times of peace, it was used for long journeys and hunting expeditions. Below: two Mycenaean warriors with a chariot on a

fresco from the palace of Pylos; they wear short tunics and hel mets with a covering of boars' tusks. The chariot is the ligh diphros. We can see the round rail, the warrior-charioteer hold ing the bridle, the axle, wheels, and pole of the chariot. (Fresc completed by Piet de Jong).

ng. Similar systems were in force elsewhere, as, for example, n Mesopotamia.

Animal rearing was organized on a similar basis. Its most important products were wool (for clothing) and hides. Various pasture animals (sheep, goats, pigs) and pack animals (oxen, horses, asses) were reared. A number of shepherds harged with the care of herds belonging to the palace or to private citizens grazed them in the open or in special enclosed reas, and, every so often, specially appointed supervisors eceived the agreed quantity of animals for slaughter, as vell as cheese, wool, and hides. Other farmers were in charge of pigsties, where they kept and fattened specially chosen nimals; others looked after pack animals (oxen) and horses sed for drawing chariots and for riding.

Parallel with farming and animal rearing, the development of arts and crafts and the expansion of trade created a second broad field of economic activity, and the rulers vere not slow to recognize its importance. The palace archives show that the kings employed a large number and a great variety of artisans and craftsmen, who were often oused in the palace area. The artisans obtained the materials of their trade from the palace storerooms; on returning the inished products of their art, they were remunerated for

Scene from private life from a fresco in the palace of Pylos: Mycenaeans with short tunics out hunting, marching in formation; some are armed with spears, one leads a hound. Hunting was a popular form of exercise for the Mycenaeans. (Fresco completed by Piet de Jong).

A warlike people, the Mycenaeans were skilled in the use of defensive and offensive weapons. Above: ivory head of a warrior: he wears a helmet with a covering of boars' tusks and sidepieces; the knob at the top served perhaps to hold the crest. (National Archaeological Museum, Athens)

their work with food or land for cultivation. The ruler also employed a large number of administrative employees, court functionaries, and professional men appointed to carry out precisely specialized duties. For instance, the tablets refer to the similar but clearly distinct occupations of woodcutter, carpenter, ship-builder, and furniture-maker.

The making of materials and garments was in the main the concern of the women; there were the *pektriai*, who carded the wool, the *elakatiai*, who spun it, the *histeiai*, who wove it, and the *lineiai*, who made linen fabrics. Their work was then handed on to the tailors or seamstresses, who sewed the clothes, and to the fullers who washed and whitened them. The preparation of bread also involved several categories of people: the *sitochooi* shared out the grain to the *meletriai*, who ground it and handed the flour over to the *artopoqo* (baker), who kneaded and baked the bread. There is mention, too, of doctors, perfumers, goldsmiths, bronzesmiths, potters, bowmakers, and builders. The transportation and export of goods, which had been produced under the supervision of the ruler, was undertaken by the energetic and venturesome class of sailors and merchants.

Export and general communication with foreign countries was chiefly by sea. There were sailing vessels with one mast and oars, sometimes with figure-heads on the prow representing birds, animals, or fish. At a period when the distinction between commerce and piracy was not always clear, most ships were used indiscriminately for peaceful or hostile missions. There seems to have been one type of ship, however, which was used exclusively for fighting purposes; it was long and narrow in shape, and, therefore faster and more manoeuvrable, and equipped with a long ram. There is no doubt that Mycenaean ships controlled the sea routes of the whole of the then known Mediterranean, and their crews were ready to sail in voyages of exploration to the most distant places. The memory of these adventures has been preserved in the legend of the Expedition of the Argonauts. Colonies were founded (Miletos, Ephesos, Episkope, Halikarnassos, and perhaps Kolophon) and trading stations organized (Ugarit, Enkomi, Kition). Without doubt, some merchant families settled among the natives at Taras and in Cyprus (Arpera, Aradippou). The links with southern Italy and Sicily were closer than in earlier times, as is shown by the remains which have been found at Ischia, Vivara,

Brindisi, San Cosimo, Bari, and Malta as well as at Thapsos and at another five or six settlements in Sicily. Troy VI was destroyed in 1275 B.C. by a terrible earthquake, but Troy VIIa, which was built on its ruins, continued to exchange goods with Greece. However, the most striking penetration of the Achaians was in the southeast Mediterranean where their products literally flooded the coast and part of the hinterland. Excavations have brought to light considerable Mycenaean finds in fifty or more sites on the coast of Canaan along the Orontes and the Jordan Rivers, in the interior of Palestine, and in Jordan. In Egypt, there have been Mycenaean finds at about nine sites from Aswan in the south to el Arish in the Sinai Peninsula in the east, i.e. on the ancient road to Palestine. This shows that communication between the Achaians and the Egyptians was both by sea and overland.

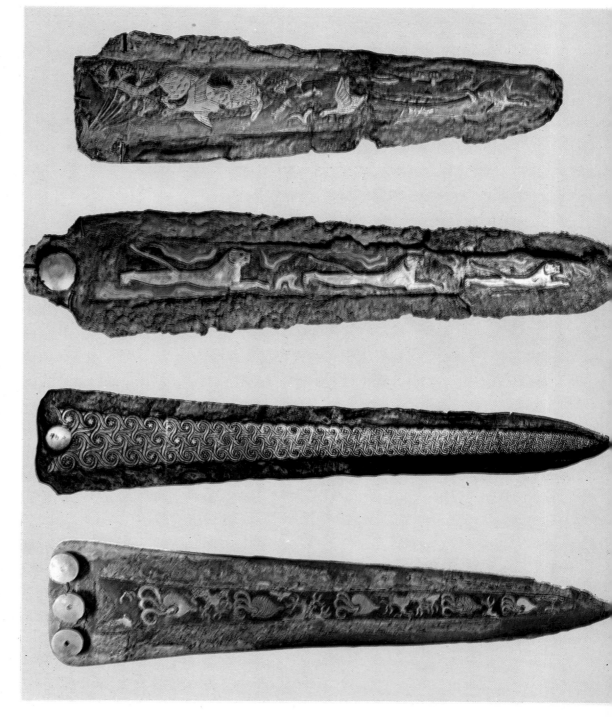

The richness, size, and variety of the weapons found in the royal tombs bear witness to the vigorous fighting tradition of the Mycenaean world. This page: four daggers with inlay decoration: the first shows papyri, birds, a river, fish, and a feline creature attacking; the second, lions in the 'flying gallop'; the third, spirals and rosettes; and the fourth, coral and nautiluses (16th century B.C.). Right: two massive royal swords with handles set in gold, from the 16th and 15th centuries B.C. (National Archaeological Museum, Athens)

The Eastern Mediterranean up to the End of the 13th Century B.C.

The activities of the Achaians in the Eastern Mediterranean were carried out against the background of a world which had been pacified and reorganized after forty years of vicissitudes and upheavals.

The breaking up of the Mitanni kingdom on the Upper Euphrates by the invasions of the Hittites and the Assyrians in c. 1340 B.C. brought the two great powers of the age, the Hittites and the Egyptians, into direct conflict and led to a period of continuous friction between them. There were successive political intrigues, and the semi-independent cities and states of Syria and Palestine were constantly changing allegiance; in the main they drew away from Egyptian influence and either joined the Hittites or formed independent federations. The Hittites, under Shuppiluliumash and his son Arnuwandas III (1335-1334 B.C.), exploited the weakness of the successors of Akhenaton, the last Pharaohs of the 18th dynasty, and in the disturbances and upheavals which they themselves had deliberately provoked, managed to extend their borders and influence southwards. Moreover, the brother and successor of Arnuwandas, Murshîlish II, managed to subjugate the kingdom of Arzawa (1330 B.C.), and thus Hittite power now stretched over almost the whole of Asia Minor and North Syria, while their invasion of Palestine created serious problems for Pharaoh Horemheb. This tough soldier, who ascended the Egyptian throne in 1335 B.C., organized the state and the army and managed to stabilize to some extent the borders with Palestine. In 1325 B.C., he even tried to extend them by provoking a rising against Murshîlish in Syria, with its centre

Two of the dead in the 5th royal tomb at Mycenae wore pectorals. One, known as the 'Breastplate of Agamemnon', was gold and decorated with spirals. (National Archaeological Museum, Athens)

at Carchemish, but Murshîlish had no difficulty in suppressing it. The successors of Horemheb, the Pharaohs of the 19th dynasty, benefited from his reorganization work and continued his policy of re-establishing Egyptian power in Syria. When Seti I ascended the throne, he lost no time in organizing an expedition to the north (1308 B.C.) against the various towns and tribes that had defected to the Hittites. He reached Kadesh on the Orontes, but his efforts had no lasting results, and the Hittites were not long in recovering Kadesh and the surrounding region. In the twenty years that followed, local intrigues and minor disturbances continued, and the new Hittite king, Muwattalish (1306-1282 B.C.), began to gather his army and his allies in preparation for the inevitable clash.

In 1285 B.C., Rameses II set off at the head of a large army with the object of making war on the Hittites and re-establishing Egyptian power in Asia Minor. The reckoning with Muwattalish took place at the battle of Kadesh, which ended with the complete rout of Rameses and the final abandoning of Egyptian projects for expansion northwards. Neither, however, were the Hittites to attempt expeditions to the south. Muwattalish concluded a treaty which fixed the borders of the two states at Beirut. Rameses always respected the treaty and never violated the frontier. Later, in 1269 B.C., the brother and successor of Muwattalish, Hattushilish III, signed a peace and non-aggression treaty with Rameses, making the existing state of affairs official. Thus, the outcome of the battle of Kadesh was a lengthy period of peace and tranquillity based on the balance of power between the Hittite and Egyptian kingdoms. This peace lasted approximately to the end of the century and secured for the whole of the Near East safe movement of men and merchandise and unhindered communication among administrative centres. There was even an "official" and permanent postal service between Egypt and Asia Minor.

The Mycenaean *Koine*

The 13th century B.C. saw the zenith of Mycenaean civilization. Founded on the successful adaptation of Cretan prototypes, internal organization, and orientation towards the sea, it owed its prosperity to its widespread and regular contacts with the surrounding world. In the interior of the country, the great palaces created and maintained conditions necessary for regular and profitable exchange of goods and for the export, mainly from the Argolid, of various cultural fashions of both native and foreign inspiration. This systematic and continuous interplay of influence led to the creation of a civilization which found identical expression in mainland Greece, the Aegean, and the Eastern Mediterranean. The art, architecture, weapons, dress, jewellery, cult utensils, and burial customs were everywhere the same; the products of craftsmen, not simply uniform but quite clearly standardized. Brisk and unceasing trade carried Mycenaean goods across the sea to flood Egypt, Canaan, and the coasts of Asia Minor with vessels of various shapes and sizes. Most of them contained perfumed oil, an essential protection for the skin in hot climates. These were luxury vessels, usually of clay, sometimes faience. The presence of the Achaians is indicated chiefly by pottery, though arms were also exported, mainly of the luxury type (parade swords and daggers), as well as jewellery and various utensils and trinkets made of good quality wood and ivory. Wine was probably exported too; and perhaps fabrics, as suggested by the decorative motifs on objects of eastern provenance. All these were exchanged for tin from Asia Minor and the Caucasus; wine, ivory, spices, perfume, and purple cloth from Canaan; bronze from Canaan and, particularly, Cyprus; silver, materials (or yarn), and perhaps horses from the Troad; gold, faience objects, alabaster, semi-precious stones, ostrich eggs, and generally luxury goods from Egypt; and liparite from southern Italy.

These are the products of which we can still find traces today; there may have been others. But on the evidence we have, it seems that there was some imbalance between the many and varied imports and the relatively few exports. There was evidently import of raw materials and export of finished products, mainly pottery.

The Achaians often followed in the wake of their products; they travelled in search of work, and finally settled in places where they met favourable conditions. In Cyprus, there was already a large community of Achaians who managed to keep in touch with developments in mainland Greece and yet give their products a clearly local character. At Ashdod, and in other parts of Palestine, vessels have been found which were made from local clay and materials, but which were otherwise Mycenaean in every way. From the wreck of a Phoenician boat found off the Halikarnassos peninsula, we learn that a usual method of trade at that period was for the craftsmen to travel by ship, making their wares either during the voyage or at the various ports of call. Some tried their luck as mercenaries in the service of the Egyptians or the Hittites, but only as individuals or in small groups, because they do not seem to be included in the lists of tribes mentioned in the relevant sources, nor can they be distinguished from their appearance or arms in any representations. Most of the Achaians who left Greece established themselves as colonists or merchants in the islands and at various points along the shores of the Eastern Mediterranean. The striking increase in the number of settlements on such places as Rhodes, Kos, and Cyprus does not admit of any other explanation. This continuous influx of men, techniques, and products had a profound effect on the civilization of the Eastern Mediterranean, though today only scant material evidence for this is visible: in an Egypt preoccupied with the introduction and, later, the rejection of Akhenaton's religious and artistic reforms, Mycenaean influence had little effect, but on the shores of Canaan and in Cyprus there was large-scale imitation and adoption of Mycenaean miniature-art motifs, such as the various ways of depicting animals (particularly in motion), trees, and olive branches, as well as elaborate and detailed decorative motifs (overlapping scales, web of tri-curved arches, curvilinear meanders), which appear mainly on ivory reliefs and seal-stones. The influence and spread of Mycenaean art resulted first in the creation of new fashions in art and, then, in the transplanting of more basic and complex elements of life and culture in the whole of the Eastern Mediterranean. There they left their clear mark and eventually led to the formation of a common civilization with its spiritual centre in mainland Greece. Though basically Aegean in character, this civilization had assimilated various Cretan and eastern influences; and in spite of its mainland origin, it was entirely dependent on the sea for expansion and enrichment. It covered, apart from mainland Greece, most of the Aegean Islands, the Dodecanese, Cyprus, and various points on the opposite coast. This homogeneous civilization, made up of so many scattered communities of men from the same nation speaking the same language, has, with some exaggeration, been compared to the similar phenomenon in the Hellenistic Age and called the *Mycenaean Koine*.

As has already been noted, this koine was surrounded in mainland Greece by less advanced populations, among whom its influence penetrated only gradually. It had various centres, of which the most important was in the Argolid, though there were many other Mycenaean communities gathered round the large palaces and kingdoms in the northeast and southwest Peloponnesos, Boiotia, and Thessaly, i.e. the largest and most productive regions of the country. Among these, there were other smaller regions, like the area around Athens, Eleusis and the Thriasian Plain, and the Tetrapolis at Marathon. Legend has retained the memory of disputes and clashes between the different tribes (the Pylians and Arkadians v. the Epeians, for example) or small wars between isolated cities and states (Thebes v. Orchomenos or Athens v. Eleusis), but generally relations between them were peaceful and often friendly.

The 13th century was the period of the greatest progress

Shields, either in the shape of a figure-of-eight or semi-cylindrical and tower-like, were the chief defensive weapons of the Mycenaean warriors. This page: fresco with a representation of a figure-of-eight shield hanging on a wall; it was found in 1970 at Mycenae in a room built next to the wall; behind, on the wall, is a band decorated with a spiral pattern.

281

and prosperity at Mycenae. In the middle of the century, the acropolis area was doubled when the west wall was built. The acropolis enclosed one of the two old royal grave circles (called Circle A) and was further reinforced by the construction of two imposing fortified entrances, the Lion Gate and the North Gate. Similar constructions, technically perfect, grandiose, and imposing, were the late tholos tombs, the so-called tombs of Atreus, Klytaimnestra , and the Lions. Outside the acropolis, the Mycenaean ruler had a series of workshops and commercial installations, and when, in 1240 B.C., the palace was damaged by extensive fire, he rebuilt it, bigger and grander than ever, adding a whole wing on the eastern side.

It is not clear if this activity should be connected with a change of dynasty (according to legend, after an oracle, Atreus, son of Pelops, succeeded the fourth scion of Perseus and a kinsman of his, Eurystheus), but if this was the case, the change must have taken place smoothly without hostilities or upheavals, since the new rulers treated the graves of the old kings with great care and reverence and continued the same work and way of life without interruption. A similar development can be seen at Tiryns, where the fortifications of the acropolis were extended and a new palace built, and also at Pylos, where the great palace complex was constructed. In Boiotia, on a rocky rise in the Kopais Lake, the vast acropolis of Gla with its double palace was built, which does not seem to have been inhabited systematically or for any length of time; it was apparently a communal defensive enterprise undertaken by the towns of the region. The acropolis of Athens was also enclosed by walls in imitation of the fortifications in the Argolid, and at Gla. This shows that Athens was the chief city of Attica, where the numerous settlements were then enjoying a period of peace, progress, and prosperity.

The most important event in this period was the complete destruction of the palace of Thebes. By virtue of its wealth and strength, its wide and multifarious contacts, Thebes occupied the same position in Boiotia and the Greek mainland as that held by Mycenae in the Peloponnesos. Thus, from the moment that either of these cities aspired to dominate Mycenaean Greece, the reckoning between them was inevitable. Excavations have confirmed that the destruction of Thebes came suddenly and during a period of prosperity and intensive commercial activity: there were inscribed vessels from eastern Crete and the Peloponnesos in the storage rooms, agate jewellery was abandoned half-finished in the workshops of the stone-cutters, and there was a collection of lapis lazuli objects (mainly cylinder seals) from various periods and of mainly Asiatic origin. The palace was never repaired or rebuilt, though life continued in the city. It is significant that the Catalogue of Ships, which lists most of the Boiotian cities, does not even mention Thebes or its king. Ancient tradition recorded two successive expeditions of the Peloponnesians (curiously without the participation of Mycenae) which ended with the capture of Thebes, the extermination of the family of the Labdakids, and the destruction of the city, which was aban-

Opposite page: the famous suit of armour from the Dendra grave: it consists of a series of bronze bands attached to the breastplate, the collar, and the epaulets (Nauplion Museum). This page: two Mycenaean helmets. Above: a bronze helmet from Knosos from the period of the Achaian dynasty (Herakleion Museum) Below: a boar-tusk helmet in three bands.(Herakleion Museum).

282

doned by all surving inhabitants on the advice of Teiresias. There is no doubt that the fire and the destruction of the palace were due to an internal war, a confrontation between the two large neighbouring, and eventually rival, federations—the Peloponnesian with its centre in the Argolid, and the Boiotian under the leadership of Thebes—and that the result was a complete victory for the Argives.

Legend, as it has come down to us in the Theban epic, and as Aischylos presents it in the *Seven against Thebes*, tells us that there were two successful expeditions against Thebes. In the first, Polyneikes was accompanied by the Argives Adrastos, Amphiaraos, Kapaneus, Parthenopaios, and Hippomedon, and the Aitolian Tydeus; the second, which ended in the capture of Thebes ten years later, was undertaken by the *Epigonoi* (descendents), i.e. Alkmaion and Amphilochos, the sons of Amphiaraos, Aigialeus son of Adrastos, Sthenelos son of Kapaneus, Promachos son of Parthenopaios, Euryalos son of Mekisteus, Thersandros son of Polyneikes, and Diomedes son of Tydeus. Pausanias (IX.9) mentions that both sides had allies and mercenaries, the Argives from Messenia and Arkadia, the Thebans from Boiotia and Phokis. "This war between Argos and Thebes was, in my opinion, the most memorable of all those waged by Greeks against Greeks in what is called the heroic age... the Argive army marched from the middle of the Peloponnesos to the middle of Boiotia, while Adrastos collected his allied forces from Arkadia and the Messenians; and likewise mercenaries came to the help of the Thebans from Phokis and the Phlegyans from the Minyan country..."

The Achaians and the Eastern Mediterranean

Before losing his palace, and probably his life, the king of Thebes evidently traded with Crete and collected valuable objects from Asia Minor, Mesopotamia, and the Near East. Luxury goods similar to these (faience objects, iron jewellery, and ostrich eggs) have also been found at Mycenae and at various other points in mainland Greece. In the middle of the 13th century B.C., the links with the Western Mediterranean were broken. Various tribes had moved south from Italy and established themselves in the Lipari Islands, at Thapsos, and in other parts of Sicily, with the result that trade was disrupted, and further attempts at colonization, always feeble in the West, were discouraged. In the East, however, there was still regular and vigorous trading through posts like Ugarit, through the advanced settlements of the Dodecanese and Cyprus (to which the flow of colonists continued), and through colonies like Miletos. This last city, Mycenaean from the beginning of the 14th century B.C., was destroyed a little after 1300 B.C., but immediately rebuilt and fortified by a strong wall reinforced with ramparts. After 1250 B.C., it came under Hittite influence for a short time (referred to as Millawanda on Hittite tablets), but preserved its Mycenaean character. The only permanent Achaian settlements in Asia Minor were at Miletos, Iasos, Episkope, and in the Halikarnassian peninsula; and it is indicative that these were concentrated in the same region, opposite Rhodes, Kos, the Cyclades, and the Peloponnesos. This region belonged to Arzawa, a federation of cities and districts corresponding to Lykia and Pisidia, and its history is typical of that of the

The Achaians maintained regular trade exchanges and cultural links with the whole of the Eastern Mediterranean in the 14th and 13th centuries B.C. As appears from the map, the Mycenaean centres were in touch with the Asia Minor coast from Troy to Halikarnassos, with the Syro-Palestinian coasts, and with Egypt. Links with the Western Mediterranean were broken in the middle of the 13th century B.C. after the descent of northern tribes from Italy into Sicily.

COMMUNICATIONS AND TRADE-ROUTES DURING THE MYCENAEAN PERIOD
(14th and 13th centuries B.C.)

— — — — — By sea
·················· On land

whole of the western part of Asia Minor, i.e. the coastal belt and its hinterland. It lay on the periphery and under the control of the Hittite Empire, against which it took every opportunity to rebel. Independent up to the beginning of the 14th century B.C., it was conquered by Shuppiluliumash in 1370 B.C., rebelled against Murshîlish II in 1334, was subdued in 1331, and took part in the battle of Kadesh as an ally of Muwattalish in 1285 B.C. A few years later, in the reign of Hattushilish III (1275-1250 B.C.), it made a vain attempt to defect, and a second uprising against his successor, Tudkhalijash IV (1250-1220 B.C.) was equally unsuccessful.

Another very powerful federation of twenty-two cities and districts lay in the part of the Asia Minor peninsula which stretches from Sardis to Troy, watered by the Kaÿstros, the Hermos, and the Kaïkos and corresponding to the later

Lydia and Mysia. The Hittites called it *Assuwa*, a name connected with Homer's *Asios* meadow (the Kaystros valley) and the place-name *Asia*, which eventually came to denote the whole continent. In its most flourishing period, before Tudkhalijash subdued it in two successive expeditions c. 1230 B.C., its dominion stretched from Karia to the Hellespont. The last two cities in the catalogue of Tudkhalijash, which begins from Lukka (Lykia) and proceeds, it seems, from south to north, are Wilusa and Truisa. Some have tried to identify these with Ilion (Wilios) and Troy; though linguistically possible, this is anything but certain, especially in the case of Wilusa. There were no Mycenaean settlements in this area, except perhaps at Kolophon, where a tholos tomb has been found. Traces of trade exchanges or other cultural influences are extremely scant. The exception, of course, is Troy, the only city which maintained close and regu-

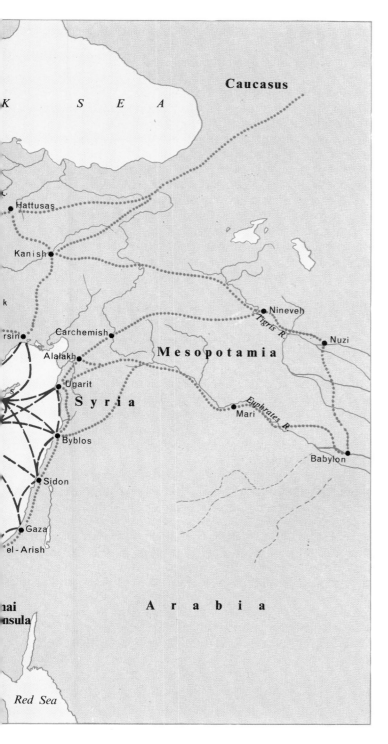

Millawanda in 1300 B.C. and administered it through a local ruler. Its gods (along with those of Lazpash, i.e. Lesbos) were called upon to heal the sick Murshîlish; the king of Ahhijawa sent gifts to the Hittite court; his brother was a guest there for some time; and when Shuppiluliumash wanted to be rid of his queen, he exiled her to Ahhijawa. So, the relations between Ahhijawa and the Hittite Empire were generally friendly, though the two states were not equal in power, at least in the eyes of the Hittites. In an extract from a treaty between Tudkhalijash IV and the king of Ammuru, the original text reads: "the king of Egypt, the king of Babylon, the king of Assyria, and the king of Ahhijawa", but the last phrase was later erased.

However, there was a certain amount of friction. During a period of hostilities, Ahhijawa supplied, or tried to supply, the enemies of the Hittites, the Assyrians, through the harbours of Syria. Also, when Tudkhalijash was fighting in the region of the River Seha (Meander), the king of Ahhijawa appeared in person in Asia Minor under conditions which are by no means clear.

The best, and most readable, source, and the one which typifies the relations between the two countries, is a prolix epistle from the king of the Hittites to his "brother", the king of Ahhijawa, written either by Murshîlish II or by Muwattalish, the victor of Kadesh, at the period when Hittite power was at its zenith. Both the content and tone of the letter show that the writer was obliged to endure the sort of behaviour at the hands of the recipient and his people which he was not accustomed to forgive in others. "I am", he writes, "in the country of Lukka. As soon as I arrived at the town of Salappa, Tavagalavas asked me to accept him as my subject. So I sent a high official to escort him to me, but he insulted him publicly and declined to come, asking me to make him a tributary king without his even appearing before me. Then, although I had warned him to withdraw his men from the region of Iyaalanda, he formed an alliance with my enemies and made war on me, forcing me to devastate the region and to send away the inhabitants. However, I did not touch the town of Atriyia, respecting its treaty with Millawanda. I did not bother about

Scene of parting and embarkation on a Mycenaean ship, perhaps inspired from a scene in an epic narrative and rendered on a gold ring from the Treasure of Tiryns. (National Archaeological Museum, Athens)

lar contact with the Mycenaean. There is no doubt that the rest of the Assuwa coastline was kept closed to the Achaians.

There are no Achaian sources to tell us anything of the links between the Mycenaean world and western Asia Minor, and archaeology can do little more than confirm the existence of such links, suggest their nature, and estimate their importance, thereby giving a representational picture of the situation in the eastern Aegean in the 13th century B.C. There were, however, written sources in the Boğazköy archives which give us some important information and a number of historical details.

From these sources (of the 14th and 13th centuries B.C.), it emerges that on occasion a certain role was played in the affairs of Assuwa by the state, the king, and various other persons from a country called *Ahhijawa*. Ahhijawa, which was never conquered by the Hittites, captured the city of

my prisoners-of-war, because we had no water and I hadn't enough men. So Pijamaradu comes along and takes my prisoners and takes refuge in Millawanda. I told him to come back and wrote to you to complain... But when my brother's emissary came, he brought me neither greetings nor gifts, but said to me: 'He has written to Atpas: send Pijamaradu to the Hittite king'. So I went to Millawanda. I went there because I was thinking: 'The words I have to say to Pijamaradu must be heard by my brother's subjects'. But Pijamaradu had escaped by ship. My accusations were heard by Atpas and Avajjiana. Why do they continue to hush them up? Because he is a relative of theirs? Finally, I made them swear an oath, and they will report the matter to you faithfully. I sent for Tavagalavas, but he had left saying he feared for his life, although I had given him a guarantee through my emissary. You sent me word to receive him but not to take him with me. So that you won't think I don't pay attention and attach importance to what you say, I went there myself and told Atpas to fetch him to me in accordance with your instructions. And if he is still afraid, I am ready to leave a hostage from among my own kinsmen in his place. But he continues to insist that he is afraid. In the meantime, Atpas asked for my protection and support, and I agreed, since he is your man, provided you were first asked and raised no objection; but this he refused! I also gave a guarantee to Pijamaradu that if he appears before me, he won't be hurt in any way, and that I will pledge him my support in the way I will explain to you. If he is happy with that, all right. If not, then I shall send him back to you, and in the meantime a courtier and relative of my queen shall remain in his place. Assure him too that if he obeys me, he will get his country back. As for the 7,000 prisoners of mine whom he brought to your country, I shall send one of my men for them; you interrogate them, keep whoever wishes to stay, and send me back whoever wishes to return. I hear that Pijamaradu is boasting that he is preparing to attack me, using your country as a refuge and base of operations. Do you condone that? If not, send him to me here, or establish him in whatever part of your kingdom you wish, but prevent him from making war on me so long as he is with you, since we are friends. I have sent my army to Millawanda on a friendly mission,

purely and simply to stop his followers going after him. Please write and tell me what you have done about it all... So now we have been reconciled after that incident over the city of Wilusa over which we went to war. What else is needed? When someone admits to another that he is to blame, then that other should not repulse the one who admitted he was wrong. My own guilt which I admitted to my brother, he forgave me and I shan't act again against my brother. Such a thing would not be right... But my brother wrote to me: 'You called me a coward and you act offensively toward me'. You see, my brother, I was young then; if I ever wrote you anything offensive, I did it without thinking. If you are going to hold that against me, you know very well how such words easily escape the lips of a military commander who may sometimes curse his men if someone in the battle seems slow or cowardly. Insults come out easily then. Why should I say that to you with illwill? Let those words be judged by the celestial sun-god, to see if I am guilty of illwill, if I acted insultingly towards you. But now, an insulting word has escaped the lips of my brother too and has reached the Great King, the King of the Hatti. Let us, therefore, investigate the matter. Send me, brother, one of your subjects. And I will condemn the one who brought you these words, the words which must be wiped out and forgotten. He will be beheaded. But if it is your man who distorted your words, then he too must be beheaded... Thus the responsibility for these words will be borne by those who carried them, and the words will be judged by the celestial sun-god."

The all-powerful king of the Hittites could hardly be more conciliatory. Although his troops had taken Millawanda without resistance, it is clear that without the goodwill of his "brother", he cannot capture the two rebels who have insulted him, snatched a considerable part of the spoils of war, and who now, having escaped across the sea, were preparing to invade his empire. Obviously well aware of the weakness of his position, he swallows every insult, gives all possible guarantees, accepts the guilt for what has happened in the past, and asks no more than to secure his seaboard, with every possible sacrifice on his part. This attitude is only understandable if we suppose that Ahhijawa, unlike Millawanda, lay in a position where it could not be

Remains of the acropolis of Troy with a view over the Scamander valley and of the Hellespont in the background.

The expedition of the Achaians against Troy was undoubtedly a historical event. The capture of Troy, which became the theme of a great epic cycle four centuries later, testifies to the strength and vigour of the Mycenaean state during the last decades of the 13th century B.C. Left: a dramatic scene from a similar siege is depicted on the famous rhyton from the acropolis at Mycenae: Achaian warriors attempt a landing before the walls; some swim to the shore, others climb the walls, while, from the ramparts, the besieged defend the city with bows and slings. (National Archaeological Museum, Athens)

attacked by the Hittite army—that is to say, across the sea (where Pijamaradu also fled)—and that it possessed a large enough fleet to constitute a real threat.

The kingdom of Ahhijawa, then, was not as great or as strong as the Hittite Empire, Egypt, Babylonia, or Assyria, but it was independent and maintained generally friendly relations with the Hittites, from whom it was separated by the sea. The two states had a common frontier at Miletos, which belonged to the king of Ahhijawa. In whole, and in part, the kingdom of Ahhijawa was suitable as a base of operations for expeditions to Asia Minor whose coasts, however, lay a long way from the capital of Ahhijawa and the seat of its king and received visits from him only on rare occasions and in exceptional circumstances, so that he could have only indirect knowledge of what was happening there. Finally, Ahhijawa was a sea power to be reckoned with, and its ships traded at the harbours of Syria. The whole of this description (especially the mention of the suzerainty over Miletos, which was exclusively Mycenaean

all through this period) fits Greece perfectly, or rather it would fit one of the Greek kingdoms that was powerful in the Aegean and in regular contact with the East.

The identification of the Hittite name *Ahhijawa* with the Mycenaean *Achaia* presents linguistic difficulties because of the inexplicable rendering of the central syllable *ai* in the form *ija*. This continues to perplex philologists; and it is a serious discrepancy which cannot be overlooked. However, the rest of the evidence seems overwhelming, and we may safely conclude that, even without the evidence of an equivalent name, Ahhijawa may be identified with the land of the Achaians—either the whole or a very large part of it. D.L. Page has recently put forward serious arguments in support of an identification with Rhodes, but in fact Rhodes was not only comparatively small in area, but it had not even been fully colonized by the Achaians in the time of Tavagalavas. So, the country of Ahhijawa must be sought among the states of mainland Greece, probably of the Peloponnesos.

....
I will tell the lords of the ships, and the ships numbers.
  Leïtos and Peneleos were leaders of the Boiotians,
with Arkesilaos and Prothoenor and Klonios;
they who lived in Hyria and in rocky Aulis,
in the hill-bends of Eteonos, and Schoinos, and Skolos,
Thespeia and Graia, and in spacious Mykalessos;
they who dwelt about Harma and Eilesion and Erythrai,
they who held Eleon and Hyle and Peteon,
with Okalea and Medeon, the strong-founded citadel,

Kopai, and Eutresis, and Thisbe of the dove-cotes;
they who held Koroneia, and the meadows of Haliartors,
they who held Plataia, and they who dwelt about Glisa,
they who held the lower Thebes, the strong-founded citadel,
and Onchestos the sacred, the shining grove of Poseidon;
they who held Arne of the great vineyards, and Mideia,
with Nisa the sacrosanct and uttermost Anthedon.
Of these there were fifty ships in all, and on board
each of these a hundred and twenty sons of the Boiotians.
  But they who lived in Aspledon and Orchomenos of the Mi

CITIES AND PLACES	LEADERS	SHIPS
BOIOTIANS		
Hyria, Aulis, Schoinos, Skolos, Eteonos, Thespeia, Graia, Mykalessos, Harma, Eilesion, Erythrai, Eleon, Hyle, Peteon, Okalea, Medeon, Kopai, Eutresis, Thisbe, Koroneia, Haliartos, Plataia, Glisas, Lower Thebes, Onchestos, Arne, Mideia, Nisa, Anthedon	Peneleos, Leïtos, Arkesilaos, Prothoenor, Klonios	50
Minyan Orchomenos, Aspledon	Askalaphos, Ialmenos	30
PHOKIANS		
Kyparissos, Pytho, Krisa, Daulis, Panopeus, Anemoreia, Hyampolis, Lilaia	Schedios, Epistrophos	40
LOKRIANS		
Kynos, Opoeis, Kalliaros, Bessa, Skarphe, Augeiai, Tarphe, Thronion	Aias (son of Oïleus)	40
ABANTES (Euboia)		
Chalkis, Eiretria, Histiaia, Kerinthos, Dion, Karystos, Styra	Elephenor	40
ATHENIANS		
Athens	Menestheus	50
SALAMINIANS		
Salamis	Aias (son of Telamon)	12
ARGIVES		
Argos, Tiryns, Hermione, Asine, Troizen, Eiones, Epidauros, Aigina, Mases	Diomedes, Sthenelos, Euryalos	80
MYCENAEANS		
Mycenae, Corinth, Kleonai, Orneiai, Araithyrea, Sikyon, Hyperesia, Gonoessa, Pellene, Aigion, Aigialos, Helike	Agamemnon	100
LAKEDAIMONIANS		
Pharis, Sparta, Messe, Bryseiai, Augeiai, Amyklai, Helos, Laas, Oitylos	Menelaos	60
PYLIANS		
Pylos, Arene, Thryon, Aipy, Kyparisseeis, Amphigeneia, Pteleos, Helos, Dorion	Nestor	90
ARKADIANS		
Pheneos, Orchomenos, Rhipe, Stratia, Enispe, Tegea, Mantineia, Stymphelos, Parrhasia	Agapenor	60

REEKS IN THE TROJAN WAR

Askalaphos led these, and Ialmenos, children of Ares,
whom Astyoche bore to him in the house of Aktor
Azeus' son, a modest maiden; she went into the chamber
with strong Ares, who was laid in bed with her secretly.
With these two there were marshalled thirty hollow vessels.

Schedios and Epistrophos led the men of Phokis,
children of Iphitos, who was son of great-hearted Naubolos.
These held Kyparissos, and rocky Pytho, and Krisa
the sacrosanct together with Daulis and Panopeus;
they who lived about Hyampolis and Anamoreia,

they who dwelt about Kephisos, the river immortal,
they who held Lilaia beside the well springs of Kephisos.
Following along with these were forty black ships,
and the leaders marshalling the ranks of the Phokians set them
in arms on the left wing of the host beside the Boiotians.

Swift Aias son of Oïleus led the men of Lokris,
the lesser Aias, not great in size like the son of Telamon,
but far slighter. He was a small man armoured in linen,
yet with the throwing spear surpassed all Achaians and Hellenes.
....
Iliad, II. 493-530, trs. Richmond Lattimore

CITIES AND PLACES	LEADERS	SHIPS
EPEIANS (Elis)		
Bouprasion, Elis, Hyrmine, Myrsinos, Olenian Rock, Alesion	Amphimachos, Thalpios, Diores, Polyxeinos	40
DOULICHIONS (?)		
Doulichion, Echinai	Meges	40
KEPHALLENIANS		
Ithaca, Neritos, Krokyleia, Aigilips, Zakynthos, Samos	Odysseus	12
AITOLIANS		
Pleuron, Olenos, Pylene, Chalkis, Kalydon	Thoas	40
CRETANS		
Knosos, Gortys, Lyktos, Miletos, Lykastos, Phaistos, Rhytion	Idomeneus, Meriones	80
RHODIANS		
Rhodes, Lindos, Ialysos, Kameiros	Tlepolemos	9
SYMAIANS	Nireus	3
Syme		
DODEKANESIANS		
Nisyros, Krapathos, Kasos, Kos, Kalydnai islands	Pheidippos, Antiphos	30
MYRMIDONS		
Pelasgian Argos, Alos, Alope, Trechis	Achilles	50
Phylake, Pyrasos, Iton, Antron, Pteleos	Protesilaos	40
Pherai, Boibe, Glaphyrai, Iolkos	Eumelos	11
Methone, Thaumakia, Meliboia, Olizon	Philoktetes (Medon)	7
Trikke, Ithome, Oichalia	Machaon, Podaleirios	30
Ormenion, Hypereian spring, Asterion, Titanos	Eurypylos	40
Argissa, Gyrtone, Orthe, Elone, Oloosson	Polypoites, Leonteus	40
ENIANES - PER(R)HAIBIANS		
Kyphos, Dodona, region of the Titaresios	Gouneus	22
MAGNESIANS		
Pelion, region of the Peneios	Prothoös	40

The Trojan War

A little before the end of the 13th century B.C., the kingdom of Mycenae had reached the peak of its power and activity. The acropolises were enlarged, the fortifications strengthened, and water supplies secured within the walls. At Mycenae, where the annexes of the palace and some houses to the west of the acropolis were destroyed by fire, probably after an earthquake, a northeast extension to the enceinte with various buildings and a subterranean spring were constructed.

At Tiryns, after one or perhaps two fires and alterations to the palace, the lower acropolis was built, almost doubling the fortified area, as well as various buildings and tunnels below the wall. At the same time, the fortification at Athens was completed, and an underground spring was constructed inside the walls. The palace complex and the acropolis at Gla were burned and abandoned perhaps because, after the destruction of Thebes, the victorious Argives were not disposed to leave such an important fortification close to Orchomenos and the neighbouring cities. The section of the Cyclopean wall which has been found in the eastern part of the Isthmus seems to belong to this period too. Perhaps it was left half-finished because it was considered superfluous after the destruction of Thebes.

According to epic tradition, it was the powerful, vigorous, and ambitious generation of these years which undertook the expedition against Troy. The legend which has come down to us, chiefly through the *Iliad* but also in other smaller and often fragmentary sources, tells the following story about the cause of the war: Aphrodite had promised Paris, son of Priam, king of Troy, the most beautiful woman in the world, and he was encouraged to abduct the lovely Helen, wife of Menelaos, king of Sparta. Menelaos at once called upon Helen's former suitors to come to his aid, invoking the oath they had sworn to her father, Tyndareus, to join in alliance with Helen's husband against anyone who should try to take her from him. Under the command of Menelaos's brother, Agamemnon, king of Mycenae, a host of local rulers and former suitors of Helen gathered with their warriors from all over Greece (from Thessaly to Crete and from the Ionian Islands to Rhodes) and set out on the great expedition against Troy with 1186 ships and thousands of men. But Priam too had many strong allies who are listed, like the Achaians, in the second book of the *Iliad* (II. 816-877). First, after the Trojans, come the inhabitants of the Troad and the whole Hellespont region under Aineias, Pandaros, Adrestos, Amphios, Asios, Hippothoos, and Pylaios. Then follow the peoples of the northern shores of the Aegean (Thracians under Akamas and Peiroos, the Kikones under Euphemos, and the Paiones from the Axios Valley under Pyraichmes); of the coasts of the Propontis and the Euxine (the Phrygians under Phorkys and Askanios, the distant Paphlagonians under Pylaimenes, and the Halizones of Alybe under Odios and Epistrophos); and of western Asia Minor, whence came the Mysians under Chromis and Ennomos, the Maionians from the region of Tmolos under Mesthles and Antiphos, the Karians under Amphimachos and Nastes, and the Lykians under Sarpedon and Glaukos.

In a variation of the myth, which is not mentioned in the *Iliad*, the Achaians, sailing for Troy, disembarked by mistake on the coast of Mysia, where the ruler, Telephos, son of Herakles, tried to repulse them and was wounded by Achilles. The next morning, the Achaians discovered their mistake and realized that Telephos was not only their compatriot, but also a relative of the Heraklid rulers of the Dodecanese, Tlepolemos, Pheidippos, and Antiphos. So they hastened to be reconciled with him and to tend his wound. He gave them fresh provisions and showed them the route to Troy, though he himself remained neutral in their quarrel with Priam. The siege of Troy which followed lasted ten continuous years. A permanent Achaian camp was established on the shore, and there were frequent fights on the plain in front of the city, with the Trojans sallying forth unhindered to do battle. Throughout the entire expedition, the Achaians were supplied by sea, having captured the islands of Lesbos and Tenedos. Their leaders attempted personal expeditions in different directions, capturing and plundering other, smaller, cities like Killa and Kolonai. Aias crossed into the Thracian peninsula where he forced the king, Polymnestor, to abandon his alliance with Priam; later, he turned his attention to Phrygia, where he destroyed the kigdom of Teleutas and abducted his daughter Tekmessa. Achilles made off with Aineias's herds from Ida and destroyed twelve coastal towns with his fleet and another eleven in the hinterland (among them Thebe and Lyrnessos). Finally, in the tenth year, Troy was taken through the strategem of the Wooden Horse, and the Achaians set off on their journey homewards.

For the Greeks of historical times, the Trojan expedition was an accepted fact, an event of great national importance, of which they felt justly proud; and the heroes who had taken part in the war were regarded as real people. "There appears to have been no common action in Hellas before the Trojan War", writes Thucydides, (I. 3) "...for these separate Hellenes,...owing to their weakness and isolation, were never united in any great enterprise before the Trojan War. And they made the expedition against Troy only after they had gained considerable experience of the sea."

Heinrich Schliemann shared the faith of the ancients in Homer. This led him, in 1870, to search for ancient Troy on the hill of Hissarlik (= little fort), and he excavated the greater part of the site with the help of W. Dörpfeld. Excavations were resumed in 1932-38 by a team from the University of Cincinnati under Carl W. Blegen. The excavations brought to light a large and very ancient city that had been continuously inhabited from 3000 B.C. to the beginning of historical times. At every period of its history, the city was more closely linked with the coast than with the Asia Minor hinterland. It passed through seven main successive prehistoric phases, one built on top of the other, and these are numbered Troy I-VII. The city was inhabited again during the Geometric Period (Troy VIII) and the Hellenistic Period (Troy IX). The successive cities were from the beginning fortified by strong and well-constructed ashlar walls. The biggest, most splendid, and longest-lived of all the cities was Troy VI, which was built c. 1800 B.C. Its civilization, completely different from that of the previous stratum, had much in common, particularly in pottery, with the contemporary civilization of mainland Greece, and it is thought that its founders were a branch of the Greek-speaking tribes who established themselves in Greece during that period and who reached the Troad during

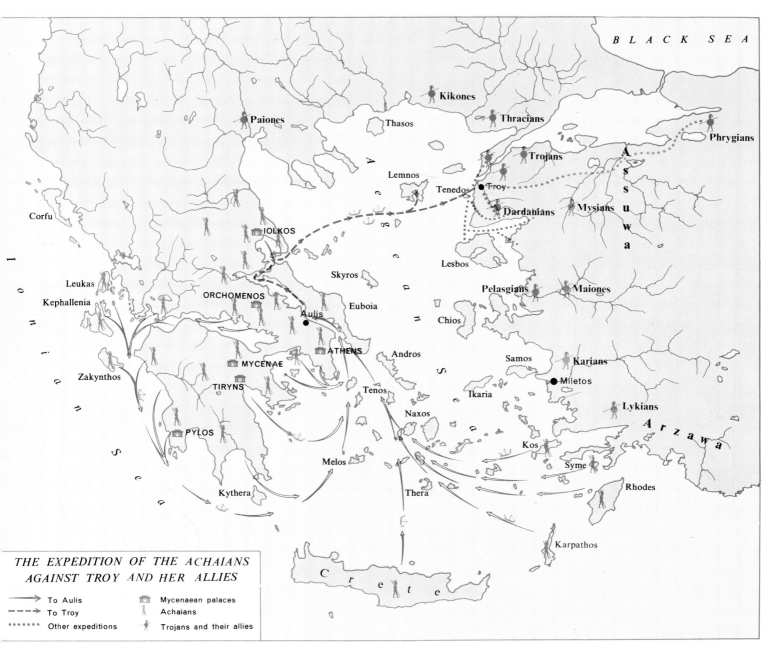

THE EXPEDITION OF THE ACHAIANS
AGAINST TROY AND HER ALLIES

→ To Aulis   🏛 Mycenaean palaces
--→ To Troy   🧍 Achaians
····· Other expeditions   🏹 Trojans and their allies

Expeditionary forces from all over Mycenaean Greece took part in the siege of Troy. According to legend, the local rulers of Thessaly, the Sterea, the Ionian Islands, the Peloponnesos, Crete, and Rhodes hurried to join the expedition, providing a total of 1186 ships and many thousands of men. They gathered, *as is shown on the map, in the Euboian Gulf, and from Aulis the fleet sailed for Troy. Their adversaries too had formed a strong confederation, which, according to Homer, included the inhabitants of the Hellespont and the shores of the Euxine, and those of Thrace and Macedonia.*

the course of the same general movement southwards.

From animal bones found at Troy, it appears that these people introduced the horse into this region. Later levels contained much Mycenaean pottery, which suggests that they were in regular contact with Greece. A great quantity of clay loom weights found in the houses of the town show that the inhabitants practised weaving, particularly of woollen fabrics, judging by the large number of bones of sheep and goats that have been found. This rich and prosperous city was destroyed a little after 1300 B.C. by earthquake and fire. The surviving inhabitants immediately repaired the walls and founded the next city, Troy VIIa, on the ruins of the old. The new city had smaller houses, hastily-built with badly matched materials, often with party walls (the earlier ones had been detached) and crowded in dense rows even along the length of the inside of the wall, where there

had previously been a road. In almost all the houses, many large jars were found buried up to their lips in the floor. This had enabled the inhabitants to store large quantities of food and water without using up living space.

It appears that this city had to house many more inhabitants than before. Its end came suddenly, during the last period of the Mycenaean koine, when it was destroyed by fire. Human skeletons have been found among the ruins. Archaeological evidence shows that a large number of people took refuge in Troy VIIa, and that the town was beseiged for a long period. Finally, around 1200 B.C., the enemy managed to capture the fortress and destroyed it thoroughly and mercilessly.

The historical sources for the period, though scanty, complete the picture. The Achaians, as emerges from the Tavagalavas letter, had direct contact with the Hittite Empire

291

during its most flourishing period and traded with it through Rhodes and Miletos. Peace prevailed in this region since the Hittites ruled Arzawa and had Assuwa under their control.

However, towards the end of the 13th century B.C., the Hittite Empire, harassed by internal agitations and threatened on its eastern borders by the Assyrians, began to weaken. The first signs of trouble had already appeared in the reign of Tudkhalijash IV (1250-1220 B.C.). He had been obliged to suppress two successive insurrections by the Assuwa confederacy and to occupy Miletos for a space of time, though with great difficulty (he was obliged to address a series of written circulars to his subjects, complaining about the state of morale and discipline in the army and the corruption of local administrators, and to adjure his officials to respect and apply his instructions faithfully). During the reign of his successor, Arnuwandas IV (1229-1190 B.C.), matters became even worse, unrest was general, and the Hittite forces, perhaps under pressure from the Assyrians, were forced to withdraw from the coast, abandoning Assuwa, which they had subdued at such great cost, and leaving a political vacuum behind them. It was natural that the Achaians would attempt to exploit the situation

in order to push their settlements farther afield to points to which they had been unable to penetrate up to that time, while the cities and peoples of Assuwa would hasten to re-form and strengthen their confederacy.

The catalogue of Priam's allies contains certain references which make it clear that it had been composed at about the period when these events took place. There are certain discrepancies between the catalogue and the rest of the epic which show that the former had been composed separately and inserted into the main body of the *Iliad* at a later date. For example, while according to the catalogue (2.858) the Mysians live in Asia Minor, according to the *Iliad* (13.5) they live in Thrace. The leader of the Kikones in the catalogue (2.846) is Euphemos, but elsewhere in the *Iliad* (17.73), Mentes. The bow of Pandaros is a gift from Apollo in the catalogue (2.827), but the *Iliad* (4.105-111) attributes its manufacture to a "horn-cutter", who made it from the horns of a wild goat that Pandaros himself had killed. Further, the catalogue betrays such a limited and imperfect knowledge of the topography of western Asia Minor that it could not be the work of the Ionian bards of the 9th and 8th centuries B.C. who composed the main body of the epic, for they lived in Asia Minor and had travelled all

Dramatically realistic battle scenes from Mycenaean times have been preserved on the frescoes in the Palace of Pylos. Left: warriors with helmets, leggings, and kilts, armed with daggers or spears, are carrying out the mass execution of men dressed only in animal skins (13th century B.C.). Right: on the upper band of the fresco, two men fight in single combat; a third is running away; on the lower band, two men on the ground are evidently hors de combat. The Mycenaean warriors on the fresco are uniformly dressed, except for two who wear helmets with a long straight nose-piece. (13th c. B.C.). (Restored by Piet de Jong)

292

A krater from the acropolis of Mycenae shows six warriors marching along, armed with helmets, shields, and spears. The representation comes from the last Mycenaean period after 1200 B.C. (National Archaeological Museum, Athens)

over it. It ignores, for example, cities and places well-known in that period, such as Smyrna, or it mentions places and epithets that the Ionians had in the meantime forgotten and were no longer able to identify—places such as Alybe, or the "dense-leaved" mountain of Phthires outside Miletos.

So the catalogue of the allies of Priam is earlier than the main body of the *Iliad*. Just as the Catalogue of Ships reflects the political organization of Greece late in the 13th century B.C., so the catalogue of Priam's allies gives a rough and incomplete, yet generally faithful, picture of the situation in Asia Minor at the same period. It must be, at least in part, the remnant of some Mycenaean epic which among other things listed the cities and regions of western Asia Minor that allied with Troy against the Achaians during the invasion of their country.

Thus the memories retained in epic and legend, the evidence of the excavations, and the historical sources for the period all show that around 1200 B.C. the Achaians, taking advantage of the weakness of the Hittites, attempted a large-scale and lengthy expedition to Asia Minor with the object of establishing themselves firmly on that part of the coast which they had been unable to penetrate up to that time, i.e. the region of Assuwa. The expedition ended in the capture and pillage of some towns, but not in the establishment of the Achaians in the region. This is shown by the findings of the excavations and by the legends that describe the return journeys; the Achaians returned home probably because they were unable to subdue the whole federation. One of the incidents of the expedition, perhaps the most important, was the siege and capture of Troy; this became the subject of a great epic cycle composed four centuries later in Ionia with the *Iliad* as the chief section. The cycle eventually came to include references to the period earlier than the Trojan War, such as various smaller epics

(e.g. one describing the single combat of Tlepolemos and Sarpedon) or persons (e.g. Aias the Telamonian), and at the same time it preserved the memory of many genuinely Mycenaean elements (e.g. the helmets with the boars' tusks or the shape of Aias's shield) as well as many names of people and places which had in the meantime been forgotten.

DECLINE

At the period of the Trojan expedition and during the first years of the 12th century B.C. that followed, various centres, both large and small, in mainland Greece—acropolises, palaces, and settlements—were destroyed, chiefly by extensive fires. Scholars have sometimes tried to prove that these destructions were due to some single common cause of great historical significance, perhaps an invasion by foreign or neighbouring peoples (Dorians, Illyrians, or other unidentified tribes, generally of northern origin). If this is the case, it is strange that they left no trace of their passing, apart from a series of burnt-out buildings, and no trace whatsoever of their settling—no new or special techniques, forms, or any cultural evidence. This led V.R. Desborough, the latest and most systematic supporter of the invasion theory, to suppose that the invaders, after destroying everything they had found in their path and forcing a large number of inhabitants to take refuge in Cyprus and Achaia, abandoned the country in their turn, proceeding in some unknown direction. Other scholars attribute the fires to internal clashes and disorders which became general when the central authority was weakened as a result of the long absence of the leaders from their country and the failure of the Trojan expedition. While the possibility of some such disturbances of a local and restricted nature is

293

not entirely ruled out, there is still no real evidence for it, and it should be pointed out that the cases of destruction from fire definitely confirmed in the whole of Mycenaean Greece number only eight in all, and these are well scattered: Krisa in Phokis, Gla in Boiotia, a part of the settlement of Zygouries in Korinthia, sections of the acropolises of Mycenae and Tiryns in the Argolid, the palace of Englianos and the settlements at Nichoria in Messenia, and Menelaïon in Lakonia. The destruction of Gla, which in any case was never permanently inhabited, is dated to the previous period and seems indeed to have been premeditated. Of the other seven sites, Mycenae, Tiryns, and Nichoria continued to be inhabited without any interruption (at Mycenae in fact a new row of storerooms was built on the inside of the north wall). This leaves only four sites that were permanently abandoned. For a country as densely populated as mainland Greece in the 13th century B.C., the number of destructions is very small, and they are widely scattered among other centres that remained unaffected. This makes it unlikely that there could have been any hostile invasion on a large or small scale. Pylos, the last stronghold on the road of any south-bound invaders from the north who would have already crossed Phokis, the Isthmus, and the Argolid, could certainly not have been caught unawares by such an invasion. And yet the tablets from Englianos, which are contemporary with the burning of the palace, talk of every sort of everyday administrative matter, but nowhere mention any increase in military preparations or special security measures in the region. The only remotely relevant text mentions the despatch of 30 rowers to a place called Pleuron and lists another 400 or so rowers, present and absent. But these naval preparations, even if they were for war, could scarcely have been intended to deter a horde of invaders who were crossing the Peloponnesos on land, burning acropolises and devastating the country.

There is no doubt that the destructions did take place; but they would not be rare occurrences in settlements built with a great deal of exposed timber, where there were open fires and no efficient means of extinguishing them. Some destructions may have been due to hostilities, though only on a local and restricted scale, since there is no sign of any interruption in the life on any of the major acropolises or in wider areas. More important from the historical point of view is the progressive abandoning of certain centres in mainland Greece (Eutresis, for example), in the rich and prosperous Argolid (Berbati, Prosymna), and in Lakonia and Messenia, without any destruction through any external cause. R. Carpenter recently proposed that this should be attributed to a radical change in the climatic conditions which then prevailed in the Eastern Mediterranean. Even the slightest rise in temperature of the earth's atmosphere lessens the extent of the cold polar zone and causes a corresponding shift of the air currents (the Etesian winds, *meltemi*) from the temperate zone towards the poles—and in the present case, towards the north. Wherever these winds blow they ensure a certain percentage of humidity; when they move from a zone (in this case, the Aegean and surrounding area), the level of humidity there falls, and this causes lengthy periods of drought and consequent widespread famine. Similar disasters, often very tragic, but always of purely local extent and importance, were not unknown in that period, and written sources (Egyptian, Hittite, and Syrian) occasionally mention them. Such a prolonged and radical climatic change as that postulated by Carpenter, however, is not mentioned in any of these sources, nor would it now be possible to prove that it ever did occur, unless it could be shown that the abandonment of settlements in Greece eventually resulted in certain zones or at least in an extensive region being completely deserted because it had become barren. But since no section of the country was completely deserted, the reason for the abandonment of these centres must be sought elsewhere.

The "Peoples of the Sea"

The period of peace and tranquillity which followed the Hittite-Egyptian treaty after the battle of Kadesh lasted

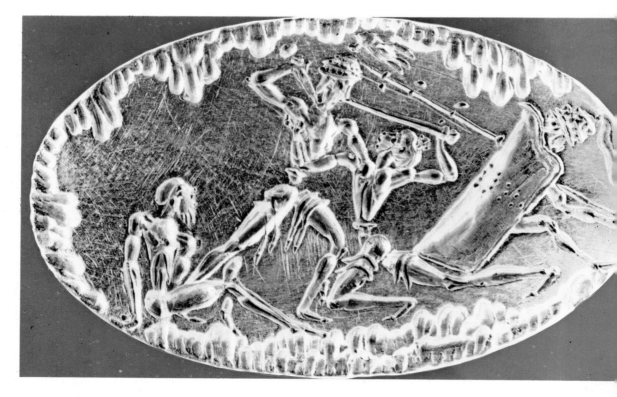

A wonderfully dramatic representation of a battle on a gold ring from Mycenae. The men fight hand to hand in mortal combat. A wounded man drags himself along the ground, while another warrior, armed with a spear, tries to help his companion. The ring was found in Grave Circle A at Mycenae. (National Archaeological Museum, Athens)

Mycenaean influence is manifest all along the Syro-Palestinian coast. The chief features of Aegean art can be recognized in this ivory relief found at Ugarit. It depicts a bare-breasted goddess sitting in front of a rock, flanked by two goats rampant; in her hands she holds stalks of grass. (Musée du Louvre, Paris).

as long as the two powers maintained their strength and influence. Towards the end of the century, however, Egypt faced a series of invasions in the Nile Delta by the Libyans and the Meshwesh, with the later help of various groups of raiders who were named on Egyptian inscriptions *Trsh* (Tursha or Teresh = Tyrsenians or Tyrrhenians?), *Lk* (Lukka= Lykians), *Shkrsh* (Shekelesh or Shakalsha = Sicilians?), *Shrdn* (Sherden or Shardana = Sardinians?) and *Ikwsh* (Ekwesh, Akawasha, or Akaiwasha). Most of these peoples were from Asia Minor, evidently from the coast, and have been identified with peoples who, it is believed, emigrated a little later to various points in the Western Mediterranean, giving their names to the places where they settled (Tyrrhenia, Sicily, Sardinia). The Lukka (or Luqqa) are surely the Lykians; they had fought at Kadesh as allies of the Hittites. The Akaiwasha have been identified by many with the Achaians and the Ahhijawa, but this is not possible, since the Egyptian sources explicitly state that the Akaiwasha practised circumcision, an Egyptian and Semitic custom entirely foreign to the Greeks.

The attack of the "Peoples of the Sea", as the Egyptians called this small expeditionary force, which was accompanied by the women and children of the Libyans and all their possessions, was repulsed by Merneptah in 1219 B.C. and dispersed before the raiders could establish themselves on Egyptian soil.

Meanwhile, the situation in the Hittite Empire had deteriorated considerably. Arnuwandas IV died childless in 1190 B.C., and this was the cause of a series of disturbances and palace intrigues. Matters were not improved when his brother, Shuppiluliumash II, ascended the throne. Within the country, ambitious nobles and army officers were constantly plotting and organizing uprisings and defections from the central authority. The Assyrians made continuous raids on the once all-powerful Empire and occupied much Hittite territory in the region of the Upper Euphrates. Every new indication of weakness led to the defection of various tributary rulers and allies. The last glimpse of glory of the Hittite Empire seems to have been the naval victory over the fleet of Alasia (Cyprus) in 1185 B.C. and the imposition of a gold and copper tax on this island. But even this was a short-lived triumph. Within a few years, dissolution and ruin set in through a series of events that upset the political balance of power—always precarious—in the Near East and brought on the scene, or permitted the appearance of, new powerful forces, such as the Phrygians and the Assyrians. It is not known whether this stormy interlude had its beginnings in flight from famine, uprising against the Hittites, or pressure by other invaders (the Phrygians?). We cannot tell how or where the trouble started. All we can be sure of is that at this period western Asia Minor was passing through a period of great instability and confusion. Although the expedition of the Achaians against Assuwa (which had scarcely recovered from the Hittite offensive) did not bring about its capture, the whole federation must have been considerably shaken by this event and by the destruction of five or six, and possibly more, of its cities. At the same time, it would appear that there was serious famine in some parts of the hinterland; Egyptian and Syrian sources mention the despatch of at least two large consignments of grain: the first in 1222 B.C. from Merneptah to Pitassa (the region of the Salt Lake Desert); the second, of about 450 tons, forty years later, from the king of Ugarit to Ura in western Cilicia. It was in this disturbed situation, c. 1178 B.C., that a number of tribes began to move from various points in Asia Minor in the direction of the coast and thence southwards. Known today by the names given to them by the Egyptians, they are, again, the Shekelesh, and with them the Peleset (Philistines), the Denyen (a people of eastern Cilicia), and the unidentified Djekker and Weshesh. But now it was no longer a question of an invasion by warriors but, at the beginning at least, of a largely unorganized movement of populations—men, women, children, and all their possessions—which swept down the coast on land and sea devastating the country. This motley horde attracted in its passing various groups of adventurers who wanted to profit from the general pillage, deserters from the Hittite forces and their allies, and uprooted inhabitants of the region who had to choose between starving in their ruined homeland and joining the descending swarm of invaders. By the time these hordes reached Lykia, the threat had become greater than anything the Hittite Empire could deal with on its own. The Great King hastened to request help from every quarter, even from those of his vassals (the ruler of Ugarit, for example) who were under no obligation to give him military aid. "The enemy is advancing against us," he writes to king Ammurapi of Ugarit, "and there is no number... our number is... whatever is available look

for it and send it to me." The danger was so grave and so obvious that everyone hastened to his aid with all their forces, none sooner than Ugarit, aware that its own time was approaching. The tablets from its last days give a very vivid picture of events in 1176 B.C. and 1175 B.C., when even Egypt had begun to feel alarmed. Ammurapi tried to organize the defence, hastily concluding treaties with his neighbours (probably the king of Amuru). At the same time, he despatched his army and fleet to Lykia to help the Hittites, even though that left his kingdom exposed to raids from small hostile fleets that took the opportunity to devastate his country. Some of his ships stopped at Cyprus, and the king there, who had been asked to keep an eye on naval activity, was in time to warn him that the enemy fleet had appeared and to advise him to take precautionary measures. But the king of Cyprus was soon in trouble himself, because part of the fleet from Ugarit defected to the enemy who then proceeded to disembark on Cyprus, plunder the coast, and pillage Enkomi, Kition, and several other towns in the interior. In the meantime, the invaders on the mainland who had already burnt Khattushash (Boğasköy), captured and destroyed Mersina (Mersin) and Tarsos (Tarsus), and defeated the troops of the Hittites and of Ugarit in the region of Mt. Amanus. They now poured down onto the Syrian plain and reached Mukish, immediately north of Ugarit. Ammurapi himself now hastened there to take his place at the head of his army, leaving his mother in charge of affairs at home. One of the last texts from the city is a brief and dramatic report from a district governor to the ruler Žrdn, who had evidently requested information: "To Žrdn, my lord, say: thy messenger has arrived... our food in the threshing floors is sacked and also the vineyards are destroyed. Our city is destroyed, and mayst thou know it!" Immediately afterwards came the turn of Ugarit itself; it was destroyed so thoroughly that it was never resettled, and even its site was forgotten. The same fate was shared by Alalakh, Hamath, Carchemish, and Tell Abu Hawwam; Tell Sukas and Sidon were rebuilt. The horde of invaders

The discovery of objects of eastern origin in mainland Greece makes it clear that there were close commercial and cultural links between the Mycenaean world and the countries of the Near East and Egypt. Above, left: Egyptian cartouche with hieroglyphic inscription. Right: two cylinder seals, the first Egyptian, the second, Syro-Hittite. All were found at Perate in Attica. The first seal depicts an anthropomorphic winged demon in an ankle-length robe with lozenge decoration. The second shows a winged demon holding an antelope upside-down. (National Archaeological Museum, Athens)

crossed Canaan unchecked and were brought up only at the borders of Egypt, where Rameses III routed them on land and sea. But he did not succeed in driving them off altogether, because the Philistines at least managed to establish themselves permanently in Palestine.

The Repercussions

This disaster, that resulted in the break-up of the Hittite Empire, the destruction of so many cities, and a change in the composition of the population of Asia Minor and Palestine, did not affect Greece or the Aegean Islands. But its consequences for the Mycenaean world were almost equally ruinous. Canaan, because of its geographical position and easily negotiable terrain, was the crossroads—and so, also the main theatre of war—of the Eastern Mediterranean, the terminating point of both the caravan routes from the interior and the shipping routes from the sea. With the passing of the centuries, its cities had developed a well-organized but precarious system for regulating contact and exchange of goods between the cities of the Aegean, Asia Minor, Mesopotamia, and Egypt. Its main ports, such as Ugarit, had whole districts given over to the establishments of merchants who received cargoes and sent them on to their own countries or channelled them, along with locally made products, to more distant markets. Thus Canaan became the nerve centre of an intricate network of commercial links, aiding, controlling, and maintaining a balance in the economic activity of the surrounding countries. The countries that lay on the periphery of this network were dependent on it in varying degrees according to the variety and sufficiency of their own products and their own capacity to maintain direct trade contacts with foreign markets. Mycenaean Greece, which lay on the periphery of this zone of exchange, did not produce enough for her own needs, nor was she able to keep in direct contact with the countries of the East, except by sea. Her participation in the economic life of the then civilized world was not possible without

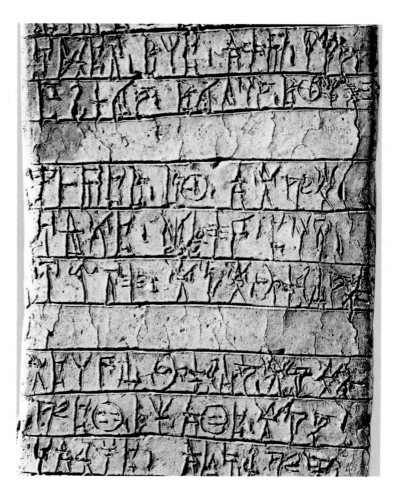

The destructions which occurred at the beginning of the 12th century B.C. in acropolises, palaces, and settlements of mainland Greece could not have been due to enemy invasion. From a deciphered tablet from Pylos (list of coastguards and officials, above) we learn that there was a permanent garrison stationed in ten departments of the state. A hostile surprise attack is out of the question at Pylos, the most southerly Mycenaean centre of the Peloponnesos. (National Archaeological Museum, Athens)

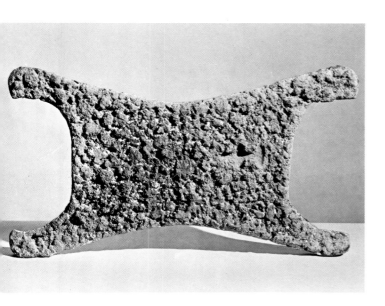

The open sea roads allowed the safe transport of merchandise and raw materials between the Aegean and the Near East. The valuable bronze used in the workshops of the Achaian kings came mainly from Cyprus. Above: a bronze talent from Mycenae (Numismatic Collection, National Archaeological Museum, Athens)

the aid of intermediaries, i.e. the ports of Syria and Palestine, since the other regions of the Mycenaean koine (the Dodecanese, Cyprus, and the southwest shores of Asia Minor) had only indirect and limited contact with the East. So the destruction of the cities of Canaan had a profound effect. The "Peoples of the Sea" did not, at the beginning at least, replace those they had destroyed, but left only ruins and ashes behind them. Thus, the threads of contact between the Aegean and the East were broken, and the movement of products and men between them was disrupted.

The chief consequence was the loss of the capacity for coordinated commercial and economic planning on a large scale and under a unified control, such as had been organized on the Mycenaean side by the palaces for almost two centuries. Their wealth and power had been based not so much on the productive capacity of their separate regions as on their fruitful overseas contacts. Now, although the rulers were still in a position to gather up the products of their own country and make them available for export, they could no longer channel them into foreign markets with the same ease. Even more serious was the fact that the products which the rulers imported had ceased to be readily available in large quantities. Wholesale supply and distribution were no longer

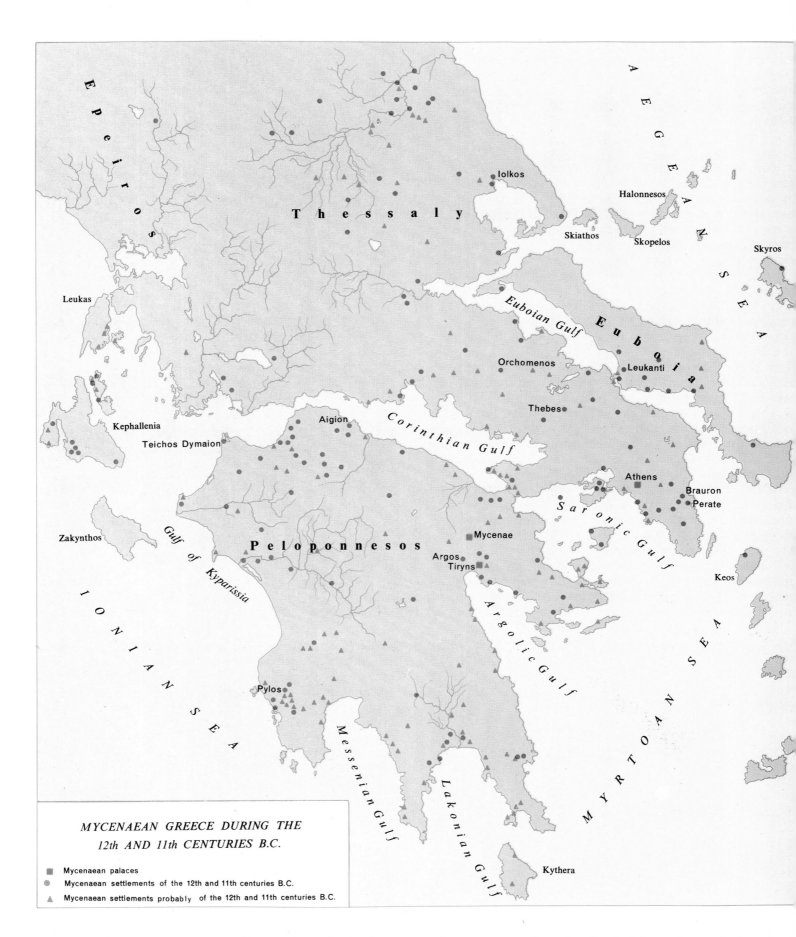

MYCENAEAN GREECE DURING THE
12th AND 11th CENTURIES B.C.

■ Mycenaean palaces

● Mycenaean settlements of the 12th and 11th centuries B.C.

▲ Mycenaean settlements probably of the 12th and 11th centuries B.C.

The decline of the Mycenaean world coincides with the descent of the 'Peoples of the Sea', who swept through the lands of the Near East. The commercial centres were destroyed, and there were grave repercussions in Mycenaean Greece. The communication route between the Aegean and the East had ceased to exist.

The movement of merchandise had been disrupted, the palace were no longer in a position to co-ordinate production and distribution. As appears from the map, the population in mainland Greece thinned out as more and more Achaians abandoned their country. The period of dispersion had begun.

feasible, and it became increasingly difficult for the rulers to coordinate and control the commercial life of the country. The overseas sector of the centralized palace economy found itself suddenly in a vacuum, paralyzed, and forced to fall back on domestic production. The weakening of a system that had always strengthened central authority resulted in the diminishing of the power of the palaces and the splitting-up and decentralization of the various regions of the Mycenaean state. In other words, the destruction of the commercial centres of Canaan brought about the decline of the palaces in Greece and the break-up of the Mycenaean koine, the essential element of which had been centralization and coordination of economic and cultural activity. This development is well illustrated in the pottery of the period, which now no longer shows general standardization, but develops different features in different places—with marked local traits in Crete. Great variations in the standard of living from place to place are also evident.

The Dispersion

The Achaians naturally lost no time in trying to restore the previous order of things. Their preoccupation with overseas markets and the inability of mainland Greece to return to the old standard of living resulted in a great wave of emigration to the known and familiar regions of the Near East. In the period of ten to fifteen years following the descent of the "Peoples of the Sea", Mycenaean settlements on Rhodes increased from 21 to 36 and now covered the whole island, while on Cyprus newly-arrived Achaian colonists rebuilt Kition and Enkomi, colonized Sinda, Kourion, and Palaipaphos and founded a new settlement at Palaikastro-Maa. Another group established themselves at Tarsos (Tarsus), which had been abandoned by the Hittites after its destruction. The colonies at Miletos, Ephesos, and in the Halikarnassos region continued to be inhabited and indeed were probably strengthened.

This emigration had repercussions in mainland Greece. The country suddenly became very sparsely populated. Of the 328 known settlements, only 137 continued to be inhabited. The greatest gaps appeared in Messenia, Triphylia, and Pisatis (from where Cyprus was probably colonized), then in Lakonia, the Argolid and, to the north, Boiotia, Phthiotis, and Lokris. It must be strongly emphasized, however, that although the population thinned out, no region was completely abandoned. Of the 45 or so sites in Messenia and Triphylia, six continued to be inhabited and as many again of the 11 or 12 along the stream of the Alpheios; in Lakonia there were still Amyklaion and five or six of the 15 or so towns of the Gytheion Gulf. On the acropolis at Mycenae, the storerooms of the north wall continued to be used; the northeast wall was repaired as well as the east wing of the palace, although on a smaller scale; some rooms were built in the interior of the northeast extension and in the west section close to the royal grave circle; and the building by the Lion Gate called the Granary was enlarged. Maintenance and supplementary work rather than any new building was carried out at Tiryns, where the palace had been rebuilt after the fire at the end of the 13th century B.C.; the tunnels of the lower acropolis continued to be maintained and used. The acropolis at Athens and the palace at Iolkos continued to be inhabited without interruption. At the same time, some new centres were established in Ithaca and Kephallenia,

and especially in Achaia and Elis, now more densely inhabited than before. Settlements also appeared in Attica (Keratea, Perate), Aigina, Euboia (Leukanti), Chios (Emporió) and Naxos.

By about 1150 B.C. the picture was complete. The settlements, though fewer and more scattered, were still found in all the areas where there had been settlements before; they were actually denser now in the region of Larisa and the (Thessalian) Peneios; in Attica, particularly the Mesogeia plain and the east coast; around Corinth; in the Argolid and Pylia and the gulf of Gytheion; along the Alpheios River; in the region of Aigion and Patras; in the mountainous region of Achaia; Kephallenia and Ithaca It is significant that most of the abandoned settlements lay in the hinterland, while the ones that survived and the ones that were newly founded were, almost all, on the coasts and islands. In other words, while the hinterland suffered steady decline and depopulation, there was clearly a movement of the remaining population towards the coasts—westwards to Achaia, Elis and the Ionian Sea, eastwards to Attica, the Lakonian Gulf, and the Cyclades, and overseas to the Dodecanese and Asia Minor. The Aegean was still a secure area, and the Achaians continued to be closely linked with the sea which, as the experience of two centuries had taught them, was both a means of communication and a source of wealth.

So, the internal structure of the Mycenaean world changed radically within the space of twenty-five years. The palaces, whose power had been based on the systematic cultivation of large agricultural areas and the coordination of imports and exports, were now replaced by many smaller — one might almost say civic—centres, each with a much smaller region under its control, little political strength, and limited capacity for production and trade. The attempts by these cities to re-establish their links with the surrounding world and to restore the old system of commercial exchange in the now disturbed Eastern Mediterranean resulted in the establishment of a second, smaller and short-lived, koine which included: the coastal centres of Attica and the eastern Peloponnesos (Perate, Asine, Monemvasia); Naxos, Melos, and probably other Cycladic islands too; Crete, where new settlements were founded at Phaistos and Gortys; the Dodecanese (Rhodes, Kos); and Cyprus, which received a second great wave of immigrants c. 1150 B.C. and became now completely Achaianized. It was through Cyprus that the other centres of the Mycenaean koine maintained their indirect contact with the East. With Egypt, there were more direct links. Archaeological finds show evidence of the importation of jewellery and luxury goods, and there were doubtless other products of which no traces remain today. These goods were exchanged mainly for pottery, particularly vessels filled with perfumed oil. These were decorated in the typical manner of the time, the so-called close style (which had originated in the Argolid), and with spectacular island motifs borrowed chiefly from Crete and the Cyclades. This type of pottery has been found not only in Mycenaean settlements in Asia Minor (Miletos, Iasos, Episkope), but also at other places on this coast (Troy VIIb, Pitane); it even reached southern Italy in small quantities. In Canaan, it has been found only in Tell Sukas and Beishan. The distribution and influence of Mycenaean pottery is interesting from the historical point of view. In Palestine, for example, the Philistines (the only part of the invading horde which settled permanently on the land it had occupied) developed a brand of pottery with a distinct local character but with manifest borrowing of Mycenaean elements. This shows that Mycenaean civilization, the only one, apart from the Egyptian, that survived the upheavals in the Aegean and the Eastern Mediterranean, was still sufficiently widespread and brilliant to impress newcomers. The Philistines, whether they had been familiar with Mycenaean culture before, or whether they met it now for the first time, evidently admired it enough to want to imitate it, and came into contact with it often enough to have the chance to do so. In general, however, the various centres of the small koine now maintained trade links more with Cyprus and the Aegean than with the foreign countries that supplied luxury goods. Thus, valuable materials, like gold, ivory, and semi-precious stones, previously available in large quantities to challenge the skills of a host of specialized craftsmen, now became rare, and there were obvious attempts at economy in using them. There are indications that, as time went by, the Achaians were obliged to renounce the luxuries of life and to restrict themselves to the essentials of everyday living. At the same time, because of the break-up of the Hittite Empire, which had jealously guarded the monopoly on the production and working of iron, this metal began to circulate more widely in Greece. It had previously been used only for jewellery, but now it began to be used for weapons and tools as well.

Disintegration of the Mycenaean World

The decrease in the population and the general drift towards the coasts and the sea resulted in the neglect, even the complete abandoning, of extensive areas of farmland in the interior. It was natural that these regions should attract some of the mountain tribes who lived on the periphery of the Mycenaean world. Though Mycenaeanized to some extent, they still retained a strong local character, and were much in contact with, and influenced by, their northern neighbours. About the middle of the 12th century B.C., they began to descend to the plains and to penetrate the empty areas of abandoned farmland. This descent, recently confirmed by archaeological finds, was known to the ancients through the legend according to which, sixty years after the Trojan War, the Thessalians from Thesprotia invaded Aiolis, displacing the Boiotians to Kadmeia, which, as we know from the Catalogue of Ships, they had already settled in part and called Boiotia. Herodotos writes (VII. 176): "The wall (of Thermopylae) had been built by the Phokians for fear of the Thessalians when these came from Thesprotia to dwell in the Aiolian land which they now possess." And Thucydides (I. 12): "The present Boiotians were driven from Arne by the Thessalians in the sixtieth year after the capture of Ilion, and settled in the district now called Boiotia, but formerly Kadmeia; (only a portion of these had been in that land before, and it was some of these who took part in the expedition against Ilion)."

This movement of neighbouring and less advanced peoples into the empty regions (which was to happen again and again in Greece's history) was the forerunner and perhaps the cause of more serious population movements. These never had the character of an organized expedition or took

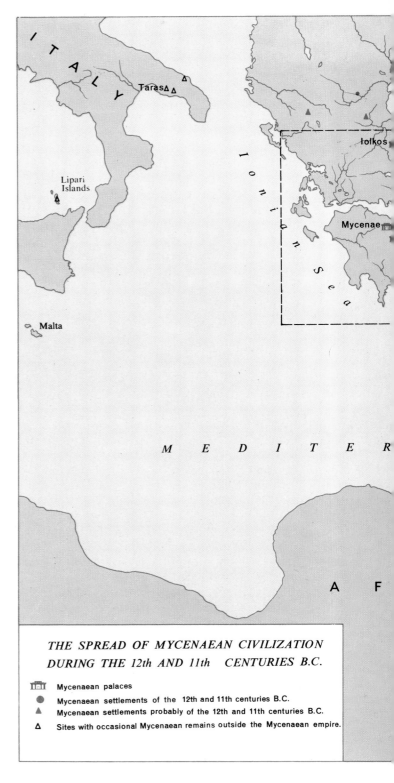

THE SPREAD OF MYCENAEAN CIVILIZATION DURING THE 12th AND 11th CENTURIES B.C.

- 🏛 Mycenaean palaces
- ● Mycenaean settlements of the 12th and 11th centuries B.C.
- ▲ Mycenaean settlements probably of the 12th and 11th centuries B.C.
- △ Sites with occasional Mycenaean remains outside the Mycenaean empire.

on any systematic form, but they proceeded at a slow, almost hesitant pace. Yet, eventually, they brought about a change in the composition of the northern population of the country and led to a series of disorders (among which perhaps should be included the destruction of Iolkos shortly after 1150 B.C.). Through these newcomers Greece was now directly linked with Illyria, the Balkans, and the countries of Central Europe—with civilizations producing artifacts which, still well scattered and separated from their lands of origin, reached Attica and the Argolid at the end of the century. There, as in the rest of the Peloponnesos, life continued without any sign of hostile activity. At Mycenae, the fire in the granary and the neighbouring houses seems to have been

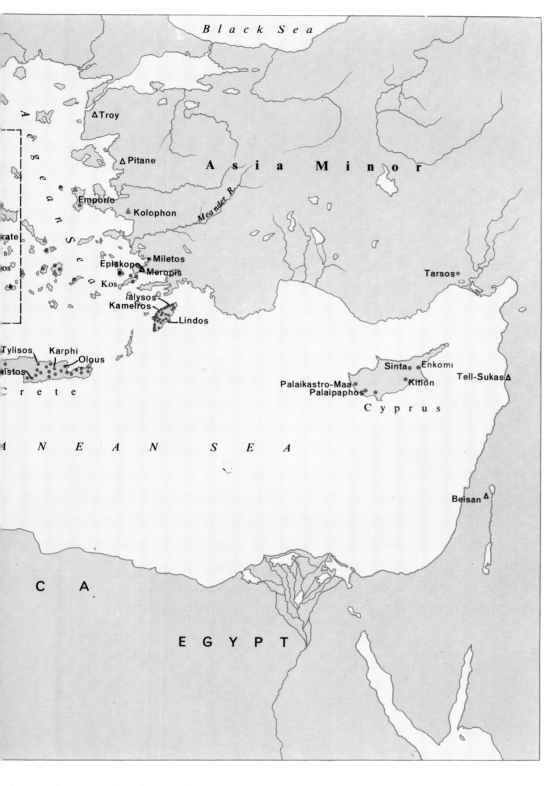

The upheavals which took place in the Eastern Mediterranean led eventually to the break-up of the Mycenaean political and economic organization. Mainland Greece passed into a period of decline, and the country became depopulated as a wave of emigration to the East began. Neighbouring peoples started to move southwards into the abandoned regions. The expatriate Achaians founded new settlements in Crete, Rhodes, southwest Asia Minor, Cyprus. By the middle of the 11th century B.C., Mycenaean civilization was at an end.

due to chance rather than to the capture and plunder of the acropolis. Thus, as time passed, more and more of the country was occupied by these bands of newcomers, though generally without destruction or devastation.

In the 12th century B.C., particularly after the middle of the century, a great wave of emigration began as men abandoned their motherland to seek their fortunes elsewhere. Many Achaians, perhaps the most vigorous and active among them, left Greece to settle in the East, close to the sources of wealth and plenty, unwittingly creating the conditions which were to favour future Greek colonization of the Mediterranean. In Greece, they were replaced by rough backward populations, for whom life in mainland

Greece among the ruins of Mycenaean prosperity represented an improvement in living conditions far greater than that the Achaians sought when they emigrated to the East.

This process was still in its beginning and was to take a long time to reach completion. However, it had already brought about a general lowering of resistance and vitality in mainland Greece. The gradual decline of the hinterland began to affect the coast and the islands, and there seemed no possibility of reversing the trend. A little after 1100 B.C. and in the first quarter of the 11th century B.C., the last attempts to revive the overseas economy foundered. The last acropolises were abandoned as well as some settlements which had lived off the overseas economy, such as

Leukanti, Perate, and Phylakope. This development must have been generally peaceful without hostilities or violence. This is evident from the settlements on Naxos and Kos, and the peaceful penetration and perhaps settlement of the Achaians as far away as Stratonikeia in Asia Minor.

At the same time, however, there were some sporadic destructions on the shores of the Eastern Aegean (Emporió, Miletos), perhaps to be connected with events also taking place in Crete at that time: the destruction and abandoning of coastal settlements (Malia) and the founding of settlements of refugees, or fugitives from the coast, in the mountain regions distant from the sea (Karphi). There is no doubt that the break-up of the small koine may have turned many sailors and islanders to piracy and adventuring. The Aegean at the beginning and, particularly, the middle of the 11th century B.C. must have been in a state of turmoil. There was no longer any power capable of keeping the seas safe for navigation. After the efforts of almost a century, the Mycenaean world had exhausted its creative energy and passed into a period of decline and struggle for survival. At the same time, a fundamental readjustment had begun which would in time create new trends and lead this world to new destinies.

WRITING DURING THE LATE MYCENAEAN PERIOD
Linear B

In previous chapters we have followed the development of prehistoric script in the Aegean area from the Early Bronze Age to the first phase of the Late Bronze Age. Evans's conviction that a prehistoric script existed in the Aegean had been proved correct, but Evans did not at first realize the extent of the problems connected with its discovery. As more and more material came to light, and the number of tablets in Linear Script B (as he called it to distinguish it from the preceding hieroglyphic script and Linear A) reached 3000-4000, he realized how important its decipherment was from the historical point of view. Evans had well-founded hopes that decipherment was feasible, for despite the fact that no bilingual text had been discovered, there were many clues in the script itself: the inclusion of many ideograms (i.e. signs that depict the objects they denote); the fact that the archives were clearly a system of accounts; and the strong likelihood that the syllabic signs had phonetic values similar to those of the Cypriot syllabic signs, which had been known for a long time. He jealously guarded the rights of the decipherment of the Knosian texts for himself for nearly all his life, avoiding publication of the material, with the sole exception of the hieroglyphic and some of the Linear A texts; these were published in 1909. Only in 1935 did he decide to publish about 120 texts after J. Sundwall had published another 38. This delay in publication hindered attempts to decipher the script.

Evans, however, often spoke at length about the character of the Knosian archives, basing his assumptions mainly on the analysis of the ideograms; and he succeeded in classifying the tablets into categories. The preservation of the tablets was clearly due to chance; they had been baked hard in the fire that had reduced the palace to ashes. Usually the scribes simply dried the tablets in the sun before storing them, classified, in small chests and baskets. Those that had not been baked by the fire crumbled to pieces. It is certain that only a small part of the archives has been preserved, perhaps no more than a tenth of the whole. Given that these tablets represented the inventories of one, or at the most, two years, one can form some idea of the original extent of the Knosian archives.

Up to 1939 no archive of tablets had been found in the large Mycenaean centres. So, it was taken for granted that the script was a monopoly of the Cretan scribes and that systematic archives were not kept in Mycenaean palaces. True, some inscribed vessels, particularly false-necked stirrup jars, had been discovered in most of the Mycenaean centres (as many as 30 at Thebes), but these were vessels which could easily have been transported with their contents and which could probably have come from Crete. But in 1939 the palace of Pylos was discovered, and with almost the first blows of the pickaxe hundreds of tablets were revealed. They finally numbered 1250 pieces. In the meantime, other tablets were found at Mycenae, most of them in the palace annexes outside the acropolis, and recently some dozens of tablets have been found at Thebes. Consequently, there can now be no doubt that the Mycenaean centres inherited from Crete the custom of keeping systematic archives in a manner so similar to the Minoan that at first almost everyone was convinced that Cretan scribes, employed on the mainland, were responsible for them. Indeed, many believed that the language too was Minoan, since it contained the same groups of syllabic signs and exactly the same ideograms. The new discoveries simply increased the complexity of the historical problems connected with the Creto-Mycenaean archives.

In ancient times, chance discoveries had confirmed the existence on Greek soil of very ancient texts written in unknown prehistoric scripts, not unconnected with Egyptian and Eastern scripts. Evans mentions two characteristic instances. When Agesilaos and his army were in Boiotia, a strange tomb was discovered by chance at Haliartos, and everyone believed that it was the tomb of Alkmene, the mother of Herakles. Most intriguing was a bronze tablet found there with what seemed to be very ancient writing on it. Because the letters resembled Egyptian hieroglyphics, the tablet was sent to the king of Egypt for decipherment. The king entrusted the interpretation of it to his priest Honuphis who, after lengthy study and much poring over ancient books—he had to produce some satisfactory answer—concluded that the tablet dated from the time of Proteus and that it contained a general exhortation to the Greeks to stop their dissensions, to apply themselves to letters and philosophy, and to institute a contest in honour of the Muses. This anecdote is related by Plutarch in his life of Agesilaos.

The second case relates to a chronicle translated from a Greek original of the 4th century A.D. by a certain Lucius Septimius. This was a chronicle of the Trojan War attributed to Diktys, a companion of Idomeneus, and consequently an eye-witness of that historical event. In the prologue, there was mention of the circumstances of the discovery of the chronicle. In the year A.D. 66, during Nero's phrenetic tour of Greece, a grave was laid open at Knosos after a terrible earthquake. It was found to be the grave of the renowned Diktys. Passing shepherds saw a tin chest in the yawning chasm and opened it expecting to find treasure, but instead they discovered clay tablets with incomprehensible signs of writing on them. These were presented as a gift to Nero who, supposing the script to be Phoenician, entrusted the decipherment of the tablets to Phoenician experts. They declared the tablets to contain a chronicle of the Trojan War written by the Cretan Diktys. Many considered this chronicle a literary fake contrived by Septimius, but a fragment of a papyrus of the 3rd century A.D. proved that there really was a Greek original, known, it seems, to the Byzantine chroniclers Malalas and Kedrenos. It seems that, when the cunning Phoenicians realized that they had to give the Emperor some plausible explanation, they invented the story of the chronicle of Diktys, which was later elaborated even further until it became pseudo-historical.

The tablets in Linear B differ in many respects from those in Linear A. The tablet itself is now hardly ever rectangular; the prevailing shape is that of a long, narrow leaf, showing obvious influence from palm leaves on which texts were written principally in cuttlefish ink. Most of the texts were written along the broader width and read from left to right like our modern European script; here and there they were continued on the back of the tablet. The scribes often used different groups of signs in varying sizes for headings, sub-titles, and inscriptions designating the contents. No doubt there were certain strict rules laid down by palace bureaucratic procedure. The ruling and regular dividing up of the contents of the tablets was a common practice. In comparison with the somewhat untidy looking tablets in Linear Script A, the later ones are quite well arranged and often calligraphically written. We can see the scribes' corrections and the spots where parts of the text have been re-written after the original writing had been erased. When the tablets were no longer required,

they were reduced to mud, which was used for making new tablets. Study of the various signs showed that they were about 90 syllabic signs and many more ideograms. Some syllabic signs similar to ideograms were recognized as syllabic from their position in the text.

The arithmetical system differs very little from that of Script A; the tens are again represented by horizontal lines, and the units by vertical. There are many addition and subtraction sums, and Evans distinguished a series of percentage tablets, on each of which the amounts added up to 100. There are no fractions like those in Script A, but there are different categories of compound numbers which are used as measures of length, weight, and capacity. Evans saw clearly that the texts were lists, tables, and records that made up a system of accounts and that they dealt with palace personnel (men, women, and children were distinguished by special ideograms), domestic animals and herds, and a variety of different goods: manufactured utensils, kinds of clothing, weapons, etc.

It was obvious that Script B had been formed by adapting the syllabic signs of Script A in various ways. Some new signs had been added; old ones had been altered; and some signs had been retained from the older scripts, the pictorial and linear hieroglyphic or the proto-linear.

The Decipherment

The texts were still awaiting decipherment. Some scholars made repeated attempts to interpret the script, while others confined themselves to statistical studies of the signs in the inscriptions and their various combinations. Working from similarities with the Cypriot syllabic script, A. Persson read

The third phase of the development of the Aegean script, Linear B, is an adaptation of the syllabic signs of Linear A. Decipherment by Michael Ventris showed that the language of the new script was archaic Greek. Left: a clay tablet with signs in Linear B from the Palace of Knosos, dated c. 1380 B.C. (Herakleion Museum)

on the lip of a jar the word Ποσειδάϝονος. V. Georgiev read texts which he considered to be in a Proto-Indo-European language, related to Hittite but which included many pre-Greek elements. E. Sittig, basing his work on a statistical study of correspondences with the Cypriot syllabary, produced some quite unacceptable readings. Even more fantastic was the interpretation of the Czech B. Hrozný, who took the phonetic values of similar signs from many different scripts. Evans, on the other hand, was more prudent and confined himself to conclusions based on a study of the ideograms. The Finn J. Sundwall proceeded with similar caution. Important help came from A. Cowley, who managed to read on the tablets the words which characterized men, women, and children, and from Alice Kober, who was the first to recognize declension changes in the words and gender endings.

The decipherment was finally achieved in 1952 by an amateur, the young architect Michael Ventris, helped in the linguistic field by John Chadwick from the University of Cambridge. For a time Ventris, using army methods of code-breaking, worked systematically on the assumption that the language of the tablets was related to Etruscan. He made his conclusions known only to a small group of specialists, and in his 20th work-note (1951) he posed the question: "Might the language of these texts be Greek?". A year later, he published, with Chadwick, his famous paper *Evidence for Greek Dialect in the Mycenaean Archives*, in which he declared the most probable hypothesis to be that the Creto-Mycenaean texts were written in a very archaic Greek dialect and in which he gave the first results of their decipherment. A few years later, in 1956, after his sudden death, came the publication of *Documents in Mycenaean Greek*, which contained 300 texts. There, it was revealed how the decipherment had been achieved.

Ventris began his work by drawing up a sort of grid. Syllabic signs representing syllables of a single vowel or of a consonant and a vowel were separated out, and those of them that had the same vowel were placed in vertical columns while those that had the same consonant but a different vowel were placed in horizontal columns. On the assumption that the language was Greek, he made some observations about the probable declension changes of case and gender. In determining the values of the syllables, he was helped by certain hypothetical readings of words which had been recognized with the help of ideograms or through their special use in the texts, e.g. as collective nouns. He thus obtained phonetic values for some syllables and, when these were replaced in the text, they set off a kind of chain reaction among the other syllables. When placed back in position on the grid, they automatically indicated the value of many other syllables, hypothetically at first, but later with a greater degree of certainty. It was noted then that for these phonetic values to be valid for a general decipherment, certain spelling rules must have been observed; such rules, the postulation of which at first glance seemed very bold, were in fact only natural in an old script that had had to be adapted to a new language, the Achaian-Mycenaean in this case. On the basis of these rules, however, short words could be read in as many as twenty or more ways. The correct rendering of longer words too became problematical. For example, there was no distinction between long and short; the *i* of dipthongs was not indicated except as an exception; the final or initial *s* before a consonant was not written; liquids and nasals were omitted before consonantal syllables; the *l* and *r* followed by a vowel were indicated by the same sign; there was no distinction between syllables with a smooth, medium, or rough consonant of the same category; in syllables with a double consonant or with two consonants, there was analysis into two syllables with a repetition of the vowel, and so on. Texts rendered with this spelling system were very difficult to transcribe and even more difficult to interpret correctly; but the two scholars thought this very natural in such an early script. With some effort, passages were read that seemed logical enough and fitted to the character of the tablets and, in most cases, to the ideograms they contained. What seemed strange was the repetitive rendering of the same word both by an ideogram, and in syllabic script. Some suspected that such correspondences had been used from the beginning in determining the phonetic values of syllables and that, consequently, the correspondences of words and ideograms did not confirm a correct decipherment. However, some tablets with exact correspondences between syllabic script and ideograms were not yet known when Ventris and Chadwick were working on the script. These tablets have confirmed the correctness of the decipherment. The most im-

Clay tablets with Linear Script B signs were found in all Mycenaean centres. They were preserved for about 33 centuries only because they were baked hard in the fires which re- *duced the palaces to ashes. Above: clay tablet from the palace of Knosos with signs in Linear B. (Herakleion Museum)*

HIERO GLYPHICS	LINEAR A	LINEAR B	HIERO GLYPHICS	LINEAR A	LINEAR B

Tablets with inscribed texts in the prehistoric script of the Aegean were first discovered by Evans during the excavations at Knosos. Evans classified the material and drew up tablets which showed the development of the script from the hieroglyphic stage to Linear B. Left, above: comparative table with the successive phases of simplification; in the first column, the hieroglyphics; in the second, the Linear A signs; and in the third, the corresponding signs of Linear B. Below: the arithmetical system of Linear B: the units are vertical lines; the tens, horizontal; the hundreds, circles; the thousands, circles with four rays; the tens of thousands, circles with rays projecting from the circumference and a horizontal line in the centre; there are no fractions in the Linear B system.

UNITS		⎮⎮⎮ ⎮⎮	=	5
TENS	—	≡ =	=	50
HUNDREDS	○	○○ ○○	=	400
THOUSANDS	⊕	⊕⊕ ⊕○	=	4000
TENS OF THOUSANDS	⊖	⊖⊖ ⊖⊖	=	40000
EXAMPLE	⊕	⊕⊕ ⊕⊕ ○ ○ = = ⎮⎮⎮ ⎮⎮	=	14268

portant of these are the tablet with the tripods and the tablet with types of equines. The first presents an amazing correspondence of the words "tripod, tripods, depas, four-eared, three-eared, without ears", with accompanying pictorial ideograms, and the second a correspondence of ideograms depicting three different types of equines with the words "horse, colt, ass". It would be difficult to attribute such correspondence to mere coincidence. Thus, even scholars who had at first been reluctant to accept that decipherment had been achieved, finally came to accept Ventris's conclusions. There are still some scholars who remain sceptical and express serious reservations. The decipherment, they maintain, is still hypothetical, and the texts that have been read must not be used as historical documents. In their opinion, confirmation should be awaited from future discoveries of new archives. Other scholars remain completely unconvinced and point out, in special studies and publications, the weaknesses of Ventris's method. They have experimented with artificial texts, using similar methods of transcription and interpretation, and have produced results apparently no less logical. The objections are certainly serious, but Ventris's supporters have succeeded in refuting most of the opponents' arguments. We may conclude by saying that the whole problem of the decipherment is still being examined by scholars, and final judgment is suspended until more evidence is brought to light by future research.

MYCENAEAN RELIGION

Our knowledge of the religion of the inhabitants of mainland Greece during the Mycenaean Period is very limited. It is based mainly on representations of presumed religious subjects engraved on trinkets, rings, seal-stones, and small stones. These representations make up, one might say, the illustrations of a book for which the text has to be written. Because these pictures are open to so many different interpretations, theories about Mycenaean religion have often been based on shaky foundations. An example was Evans's theory, once universally accepted, that the Minoan and the Mycenaean religions were one and the same, or rather that the Minoan religion had been adopted and copied by the inhabitants of mainland Greece. This theory had the support of even that eminent student of ancient Greek religion, M.P. Nilsson.

The decipherment of Linear B sowed the first seeds of doubt about the soundness of this theory. The names of the gods worshipped during late Mycenaean times and the offerings made by the Mycenaeans to them are recorded on some of the tablets from Pylos and Knosos. On a tablet from Pylos we read:

For Poseidon	1 gold cup, 2 women
For Zeus	1 gold cup, 1 man
For Hera	1 gold cup, 1 woman
For Hermes	1 gold cup, 1 man

This means that the most important gods of the Olympian pantheon—Zeus, Hera, Potnia Athena, Poseidon, Hermes, and others—were worshipped in mainland Greece in the 14th and 13th centuries B.C. These gods were completely different from the Great Goddess or the goddesses of Minoan Crete, who were worshipped exclusively before 1450 B.C., i.e. before the establishment of an Achaian dynasty at Knosos.

Excavations in this century, on the other hand, have shown that the inhabitants of Mycenaean Greece were descendents of the first Greek-speaking tribes who established themselves in this region as early as 1900 B.C. From then until the end of the Mycenaean Age, there are no indications of any invasion in this region by foreign peoples to whom might be attributed the introduction of the cult of the gods mentioned in the tablets. It is evident that the cult of the Olympian gods came to Greece with the first Greek-speaking tribes at the beginning of the Middle Helladic Period, and that these continued to be the great gods worshipped by the inhabitants.

The religion which these first Greek-speaking tribes brought with them must have been aniconic, for we have no representations of the gods they worshipped. It would appear also that their cult rites were celebrated in open spaces or in sacred groves, since excavations have failed to unearth any temples or sacred buildings. When the Greek-speaking tribes were firmly established on Greek soil, they came at first into contact and, later, into regular communication with the inhabitants of Minoan Crete, who had an advanced religion with rich ceremonial. From it they adopted such elements as did not conflict with their own beliefs. These new elements were blended with their traditional cult to form a Mycenaean religion basically different from the Minoan.

Gods and Goddesses

It would seem that at an early stage the Mycenaeans adopted the Minoan goddess of vegetation, fertility, and trees. As farmers, they saw in this goddess the personification of their beliefs and yearnings. The imposing figure of the Minoan goddess, with her prominent bare breasts, aptly symbolized the re-awakening of nature. In imitation of Minoan originals, the handmaids of the goddess are also depicted with ample bosoms. It was thus believed that the fertility of the goddess and her handmaids would be transferred to the cultivated earth and would increase its productivity. We find an early representation of this goddess of vegetation and trees on the engraved bezel of a gold ring from Mycenae, which dates from the beginning of the 15th century B.C.

On seal-stones we see the picture of yet another goddess who holds in either hand an animal, wild or tame, or sometimes a bird. She is the Potnia Therōn, the "Lady of Wild Things"—the goddess of untamed nature who protects animals and grants them fertility but who can also annihilate them. As stockbreeders, the Mycenaeans needed the help of such a goddess and in Minoan archetypes found the expression of their beliefs and yearnings for divine protection for their herds.

A goddess is clearly represented in some clay female figurines, typical finds from the last period of the Mycenaean Age. The lower part of the body is usually cylindrical in shape, while the broad upper part is given a wing-shaped appearance by the stylized raised arms. These figurines have their origin in the Minoan goddess of benediction.

Our knowledge about the religious beliefs of the Mycenaeans comes mostly from engraved representations on jewellery and seal-stones. Above: religious scene on a gold ring from Tiryns: the goddess sits on a folding chair, her foot resting on a stool; behind her is a bird; four daemons approach holding pitchers, perhaps containing the 'first fruits'. (National Archaeological Museum, Athens)

On a beautiful seal-stone from Mycenae, the goddess is represented with raised arms flying in the air as she rides on her mythical animal. Other female figures with elliptical torsos probably represent handmaids of the goddess or divine nurses. Some identify the goddess of untamed nature with Artemis, and the goddess of vegetation and trees with Demeter, although the name of the latter is not mentioned on any of the tablets found so far. An ivory group of two women and a child was found at Mycenae and identified by Wace with Demeter, Persephone, and Iakchos, but there is no indication that this group represents divinities or has any religious character; it is more likely that it shows simply nurses with a child.

The Mycenaean pantheon included a war goddess—a warlike people could scarcely be without one—though her depiction was not anthropomorphic. It would appear that the Mycenaeans could find no archetype for her in Minoan art and were obliged to create one for themselves. She is represented by a *palladion* (an anthropomorphic protective standard), a figure-of-eight or bicircular shield fixed on a mast. A head projects from the top of the shield, and a spear protrudes at the side. There is an early representation of this palladion on a gold ring from the acropolis of Mycenae, and a later one on a plaster tablet, again from Mycenae, this time from the so-called "House of Tsountas". On this tablet, two women with covered breasts adore the palladion, which

is placed between them. At the side is an altar with concave sides. The picture has not been preserved in good condition, and there are doubts about the head, hands, and feet of the palladion. On fragments of frescoes found at Mycenae in 1970 there is a representation of a figure-of-eight shield crowned by what seems to be a head with a helmet. It would appear that now the standard form of the palladion becomes clear. The head is painted white, which indicates that the deity is a goddess. This symbolic representation is in the aniconic tradition of Mycenaean religious art and perhaps originated in an arms cult, a common phenomenon among primitive warlike tribes. The chief symbol of the cult was the figure-of-eight shield, evidently still in use during the 15th century B.C. Apparently, this shield retained its religious significance even after another type of shield had replaced it in the Mycenaean armoury. We find frescoes with figure-of-eight shields at Knosos, Tiryns, Thebes, and in a building of perhaps sacred character at Mycenae. It is curious that the Mycenaeans imagined their war divinity as a goddess and not as a god. We may perhaps identify her with the Potnia Athena mentioned on the tablets.

No representations have been found of the gods, such as Poseidon or Zeus. This is perhaps because the Mycenaeans did not find in the Minoan pantheon an archetype worthy of the divine power and importance of their own gods. In later Minoan art, the Great Goddess is often accompanied by a god who is her consort, son, or companion. This god holds only a subordinate place in the Minoan pantheon, and was perhaps even a latecomer to it. Even his figure is smaller than that of the goddess. It was impossible for the Mycenaeans to identify their great gods with such a minor deity. Therefore, in depicting their gods, they remained faithful to the aniconic tradition. We have some evidence for the actual cult of the gods from the tablets found at Pylos and Knosos. Finally, it must be mentioned that the Mycenaeans did not adopt the snake goddess of the Minoan religion. She seems to have been alien, even perhaps opposed, to their beliefs.

Shrines and Sacred Places

Our knowledge of Mycenaean places of worship comes from two pieces of gold plate with embossed representations found in grave Circle A at Mycenae, from various gold rings with decorated bezels, and from seal-stones. These show that the Mycenaeans built small cult buildings on the tops of mountains or hills. The sanctity of these buildings is indicated by the horns of consecration which decorate the façade. Some have three rooms like the Cretan sanctuaries. Apart from these small shrines, there were also outdoor *temene* surrounded by a low wall which enclosed one or more trees of a sacred grove. *Baityloi* (sacred stones), sacred columns, piles of stones or earth (altars?), tables of offering, and other sacred objects were placed in the temene. Perhaps these sacred areas continued the tradition of the open-air cult areas which, it would appear, were used by the first Greek-speaking inhabitants of mainland Greece.

Excavations so far have not revealed sacred precincts or special temples. In the Mycenaean Age, there were evidently no temple buildings like those of historical times. Only at Keos (settlement at Hagia Eirene — John Caskey) has a building been found whose contents (clay figures of women) show clearly that it was a temple. But even this has more of a Minoan than a Mycenaean character. At Eleusis (Constantine Kourouniotis), the oldest building below the megaron-shaped Telesteria of historical times seems to have been the first temple of Demeter in Greece, built in the middle of the 15th century B.C. However, its original contents have not been preserved to give us definite

information about its purpose. During the last phase of the Mycenaean Age, a room in the dwelling of the ruler was used as a shrine for family worship. There is an example in the Late Mycenaean dwelling at Asine (A. Persson): clay figurines of the goddess of benediction were found on a raised bench in one room. And in the palace of Pylos (Carl Blegen), there is one room, separated from the rest, which seems to have been a shrine. In the curious group of buildings unearthed at Mycenae in 1968 (William Taylour), one room was evidently a cult area. In its gallery, there was a storeroom or repository, which contained many clay statuettes of a unique and almost barbaric type. Finally, a fresco discovered in 1970 (George Mylonas) in a room of a similar building complex shows the war deity, the palladion, surrounded by figure-of-eight shields. In another part of the fresco, a goddess could be clearly distinguished. It is important to note that no statues of gods, as we know them from historical times, have either been found or seen depicted in cult representations. Evidently, the Mycenaeans, like the Minoans, did not make large statues of their gods.

The Cult

The cult of the gods was extremely simple. The usual method of worship was to say prayers in an attitude of reverence, with one hand raised and the other clasped to the chest, and to offer gifts. On seal-stones, we see votaries approaching the shrines with priestly step and devout solemnity, carrying small offerings and cult utensils. In the cult of the goddess of fertility and untamed nature and during prayers at the sacred precincts, an important role was played by orgiastic dances of men and women. By means of these dances, the worshippers thanked the goddess and called on her to hear their prayers and grant fertility to the earth and the herds. They deposited flowers and fruits for the vegetation goddess on the tables of offering and altars in the sacred precincts and shrines. To the great gods, Poseidon, Zeus, etc., they may have sacrificed animals. An agate seal-stone found at Mycenae shows a boar on a sacrificial table. The priest, dressed in a heavy robe, prepares to cut out the entrails of the animal. Other animals sacrificed to the gods were: bulls, cows, wild goats, even deer. The sacrifices

Two religious representations on Mycenaean jewellery, the one on the left on a gold ring, that on the right on a jasper ring, both from Mycenae. Left: the goddess of vegetation, seated, receives offerings of sacred lilies from two women and a girl; in the background is the double axe, the Minoan cult symbol. Right: a bearded man holds a lion in either hand. (National Archaeological Museum, Athens)

This superb ivory group was found at Mycenae in 1939: two women, similarly attired, watch over a child. This triad, depicted elsewhere also, may be connected with the legend of the orphan infant who is saved and brought up by two or more divine nurses. (National Archaeological Museum, Athens)

were accompanied by the pouring of various libations from sacred utensils, the rhyta. Sometimes, the rhyta were in the shape of a bull's head (there is also a gold rhyton in the shape of a lion's head), but in most cases they were funnel-shaped clay vessels with a hole in the bottom.

Libations were also poured from ceremonial jugs, similar to those used by the Minoans. On small glass tablets, which have been found chiefly at Mycenae, we find representations of Minoan daemons with lion trunks and strange leather mantles standing on their hind legs and pouring libations on altars, sacred branches, and sacred columns. These daemons, "forerunners", according to Tsountas, "of satyrs and the mythical creatures of the forests" of historical times, are thought to represent the followers of the goddess of vegetation and nature.

The tablets indicate that the libations were of oil, honey, wine, and water. Sometimes, the offerings to the gods included valuable vessels, often of gold or silver, and even slave men and women who served in the sanctuaries. Shrines and altars were decorated with branches from sacred trees and bathed in perfumed oil.

The conception of many, if not of all, cult objects (horns of consecration, rhyta, concave-ended altars) was imported from Crete. Only one symbol was not adopted by the Mycenaeans: the double axe. For the Minoans, the double axe had the same symbolic significance as the Cross has for the Christians. But for the Mycenaeans it was only a tool for the killing of sacrificial animals. At the beginning of the Mycenaean Period, we do find representations of double axes that were perhaps part of the cult, but after the middle of the 15th century B.C., the double axe lost its religious and symbolic importance in Mycenaean religion. Sacrifices and sanctuaries were supervised by priests and priestesses, who also administered sacred property. It appears that, during sacred rites, the priests wore rich heavy robes that covered their whole bodies. About the priestesses, we have little information, but it would appear that for the cult of the goddess of fertility and nature they wore the Minoan dress that left the breasts bare. It is believed that in Crete the king was also the high priest, but, in Mycenaean Greece he evidently left all sacred duties and offices to the priests and priestesses.

There is no evidence to support the theory that there was a cult of the dead during the Mycenaean Age. All we know is that the dead were buried with great reverence and care, perhaps in accordance with a rich burial ritual.

Ceremonies

The pictorial representations of religious ceremonies show only individual worship. There are no representations of communal worship, nor scenes of religious ceremonies with the participation of a large crowd. From the evidence of the tablets at Pylos, it has recently been suggested that religious ceremonies with popular participation took place every month, but there is no real confirmation of this theory. Some representations from the palaces of Tiryns and Thebes of the last phase of the Mycenaean Age have come to light which show a procession of women holding various objects in their hands. The procession suggests a popular festival, but there is no other information about it.

The few representations of contests with bulls and the famous gold cups from Vapheio that show the trapping of wild bulls are not enough to prove that bullsports had a religious character in the Mycenaean world. Dancing, particularly the orgiastic dance, was a basic element in the cult of the vegetation and nature goddess. But dancing of spectators in public religious festivals does not seem to have been usual, as it was in Crete.

We may conclude that the religion of the Mycenaeans was to a large degree aniconic, and altogether much simpler than that of the Minoans, although it had borrowed many elements from Crete. At heart, however, it preserved its own character. All the elements that formed the basis of Greek religion in historical times were inherent in the religion of the Mycenaeans.

BUILDING AND ARCHITECTURE, 14TH TO 11TH CENTURY B.C.

Dwellings

The Mycenaeans lived in settlements which consisted of separate groups of usually independent houses, without party walls. Most of the settlements were agricultural, consisting of small, one-storey buildings with one or two rooms. In the bigger centres, and particularly around the palaces, the houses were more crowded together, bigger and more complex, often with basement, ground floor, upper storey, and various auxiliary rooms and spaces, i.e. kitchens, storerooms, stables, sometimes workshops. Usually the dwellings were separated by narrow irregular passages, here and there formed into wider and somewhat straighter roads, but generally there was no overall plan or arrangement.

The basic building unit was the megaron. This comprised a square room with a built open hearth and a vestibule, the *aithousa*; often, between the vestibule and the main room (the *domos*), there was another ante-room, called the *prodomos*, which separated the domos still further from the open air and protected it from the weather. In some houses, and particularly in the smaller ones which had no extra rooms, there was a small *opisthodomos*, a "back room". The dimensions of the megaron determined the number of interior supports to the roof. One or two columns stood in the façade between the jambs of the aithousa, and two or four in the interior of the domos, arranged symmetrically around the hearth. The megaron usually opened on to a court around which auxiliary rooms were built. The basement was used mainly as storage space, and the upper floor, if any, as the family apartments.

There is no certain evidence about the structure of the roofs of Mycenaean houses; there are no traces of tiles or covering slabs. However, the proportions of most of the rooms, the distribution of the interior supports, and various constructional details suggest that, while the smaller and more temporary buildings may have had sloping or arched roofs made of brushwood, grass, or other similar materials, the larger buildings must have been covered by constructed flat roofs, similar in construction to those of modern Greek island houses. The roofs were supported on the inside by columns similar to the Cretan ones—wooden, apparently in one piece with low capitals, and tapering towards the bottom. They often had flutings, either close, narrow and vertical (there were 64 flutings on the columns of the *propylon* at Pylos) or diagonal and spiralling, decorated with various designs.

The same basic features are found in the construction of the palaces, though these were built on a much grander scale, over a more extensive area, and constructed of much more durable and luxurious materials. The main palace complex was enclosed on all sides by auxiliary rooms and apartments situated on its perimeter and forming a continuous enclosure with their exterior walls. There were various small auxiliary doors and one main entrance, the propylon, which led into a large court, either through an outer court as at Tiryns, or through a series of smaller areas, as at Mycenae and Pylos. The court was surrounded by porticoes, one of which acted also as the vestibule of the three-part megaron.

The domos measured 12.90×11.50 m. at Mycenae, 12.90×11.00 at Pylos, and 11.80×9.70 at Tiryns. It was the largest and most magnificent room in the palace, and was also the throne room. The throne was placed on a low dais in the middle of the right-hand wall in front of the large circular low hearth built exactly in the centre of the room between the four symmetrical columns which supported the roof. The domos of the palace of Pylos also had an interior gallery, which evidently communicated with the apartments of the upper floor.

The megaron and court were surrounded by a large number of small and large rooms linked by corridors, smaller courts, auxiliary entrances, and staircases leading to the upper storeys. The doorways (which did not always have closing doors) and windows let in sufficient daylight to illuminate the inner rooms.

At Pylos and Tiryns (perhaps also at Mycenae, but here a large part of the palace has been lost without trace), there was a second, smaller megaron, while at Tiryns there was even

In the palaces of the Mycenaean kings, the biggest and most imposing area was the throne room. Above, right: reconstruction of the richly decorated throne room in the Palace of Pylos; in the centre, a large circular hearth built between four columns in the middle of the right-hand side of the room stood a throne set on a low dais; various frescoes adorned the walls, while the ceiling and floor were also richly decorated (Reconstruction by Piet de Jong). Below: the hearth in the big throne room as it was found during excavations at the Palace of Pylos; the border of the hearth is decorated with a flame pattern.

In the Palace of Pylos there were bathrooms and a complete drainage system. Right: bathtub as it was found in a room of the palace.

a third one, smaller still, which opened on to the same inner court. There were also bathrooms, guest rooms, and the living apartments of the king and his family, which seem to have been situated on the upper floors. The remaining rooms were mainly workshops and storerooms, full of shelves and containing the various products made by the palace craftsmen. There were also rows of large jars holding the produce of the surrounding region. Some of the rooms were intended to house the administrative employees of the palace and the archives. At Pylos, the latter were found immediately after the main entrance before the court of the megaron. In their entirety and not taking into account the various possible annexes and extensions beyond the main building complex, the palace installations, including the living spaces and working areas of the king and his large staff, covered a densely occupied area of about 1 or 2 acres. All the buildings, and the well-planned drainage system which served them, were built to last. Even today we can see traces of careful and systematic maintenance and renovation.

Citadels

The most characteristic and certainly the most striking example of Mycenaean architecture is the *acropolis*—the citadel, fortified by strong Cyclopean walls, where the king's palace and the dwellings of the nobility were situated. In time of danger, the king's subjects all took refuge inside the walls of the acropolis. It should be noted that not all the large palaces were fortified (Pylos, for example, had no walls), nor did those that were fortified always belong to the greatest and most powerful kings. There are large citadels not only at Mycenae, Tiryns, Gla, Athens, and Mouriatada, but also at Eutresis, Midea, Dorion, Keos, and Thorikos. The walls, imposing and massive, were of a thickness which varies from 17 m. (eastern and southern section at Tiryns)

to 3.60 m. (eastern corner at Athens). The average was 7.50 at Tiryns, 5.50 at Gla, and 5 at Mycenae. Their height is over 8 m. at Mycenae and 7 m. at Tiryns. The walls were generally built on the tops of rocks and on heights which were naturally fortified but also suitable for habitation. The enceinte followed the irregular curve of the brow of the hill. Only at Gla and at some points at Tiryns was an attempt made to give the curve of the walls a more regular form by breaking it up into a series of small straight sections with shallow setbacks at the points of contact. Thus, the whole took on a more systematic and planned appearance.

The building of the acropolis, therefore, was simply the fortifying of the area formed by the crest of the hill. The acropolis at Tiryns had a surface area of about 5 acres, at Athens about 6 acres, and at Mycenae about 7 to 8 acres, while at Gla the acropolis, built through the communal efforts of many local cities, occupied a whole island in the middle of Lake Kopais of over 50 acres in area.

The walls of the citadels were broken by openings at well-spaced intervals. These were formed into gates of varying dimensions and importance. Gla had four entrances, while at Mycenae, Tiryns, and Athens there were only two, a large and an auxiliary one, set a good distance apart and at points which corresponded to the main natural accesses to the citadels. The gates were more regular in construction than the rest of the walls, and one at least, the Lion Gate at Mycenae, was decorated with a relief built into the wall above the lintel. In their construction, the greatest possible care was taken to ensure that they were not only impressive but also particularly strongly fortified. For this purpose, the outer area of the gates, which always took the form of a ramp (natural at Mycenae, Athens, and Gla, artificial at Tiryns), or a staircase (as in the secondary entrance at Athens and Tiryns), was shaped into a narrow court or path between two arms of the wall (Tiryns), or between the wall and a specially built tower (Mycenae, Athens), or between two tower-like ramparts (Gla). Thus, charges against the gates were broken by the upward slope, and the attackers reached them in small numbers, crowded together in the confined narrow area before the gate, gaining no protection from their shields against the rain of missiles which the defenders would hurl down from the walls above. These defensive tactics necessitated the gathering and easy movement of a large number of defenders on the walls, and this explains why the walls were thicker near the gates and at easily assailable points in the fortifications, and also why the thickness of the walls was more than 1.50-2.00 m.—more, that is, than would be required by purely technical considerations in the case of walls of the height and construction of the Cyclopean ones. In the walls of Tiryns and Mycenae, there were also small vaulted openings, which facilitated communications in time of peace and could be easily blocked in the event of a siege. These openings were found in relatively late sections of the fortifications, perhaps because the idea of their construction came only after many years of building experience.

The citadels of Mycenae, Tiryns, and Athens had other installations too: sloping tunnels which led from inside the walls to underground springs or water veins, thus securing a water supply to the fort in the event of siege.

Other Cyclopean constructions comparable to the walls are the viaducts which were built at various points in the Mycenaean road network. They consisted of two corbelled walls, facing each other and meeting at the top at an acute angle, thus forming a narrow, and therefore strong, arch over which the road ran. Arches constructed in this manner—with an acute-angled corbel-vault—could not span wide spaces, and their use was therefore confined to the bridging of uneven patches of ground, mainly ravines and torrent beds.

TOMBS

Mycenaean tombs were of three types: shaft graves, chamber tombs, and tholos tombs. The first, and simplest, consisted of a long narrow perpendicular shaft, covered after the burial with rough stone slabs which sometimes rested on a narrow ledge cut out of the inner wall of the shaft at a height of about one metre from the bottom. The rest of the shaft was then filled in with earth.

The chamber tombs were small underground rooms, dug deep into a hillside wherever feasible. A narrow open trench,

Below: reconstruction of the inner court of the Palace at Pylos. The open court was overlooked by imposing and richly decorated *façades with pillared porticoes and balconies; through the door on the left was the throne room. (Reconstruction by Piet de Jong)*

The monumental tholos tombs were built during the last period of Mycenaean power. Top, right: the remains of the tomb at Orchomenos, which is called the Treasury of Minyas, 'richest among men'. In Pausanias's day, it was still intact; the object of general admiration, it was considered equal to the Treasury of Atreus at Mycenae. The entrance was 5.60 m. high and 2.76 m. wide. To the left is a door leading to a side chamber, which was specially built, not cut into the rock like the one in the Treasury of Atreus. Middle: the famous tholos tomb at Mycenae, known as the Treasury of Atreus; at the end of the dromos is the monumental façade with the door, a huge inner lintel (weighing 120 tons), and the relieving triangle which transfers the load from the lintel to the jambs. Bottom: the remains of the tholos tomb at Koryphasion (Pylos); according to legend, it is the tomb of Thrasymedes, son of Nestor. Right, the Ionian Sea and, left, the Gulf of Pylos.

the *dromos*, led down to the door of the tomb, which was usually cut into the middle of one of the sides, in most cases on the axis of the length of the chamber, but sometimes at an angle to it. The narrow jambs which flanked the door did not stand vertically, but sloped slightly inwards so that the top of the opening was narrower than the bottom. The slope of the dromos walls corresponded to that of the door jambs. Practically vertical in the early tombs, they became progressively more inclined in later ones, until, by the end of the 13th and particularly the 12th century B.C., the dromos had taken on the shape of an upturned wedge. The lintel was usually flat, though in a few cases it was given a gentle curve.

The door led into a relatively shallow passage — the *stomion*—cut into the rock. At some points it had the same width as the entrance, in others it became narrower or wider as it led into the chamber. After the burial, the door and the outer part of the stomion were blocked up with a dry-stone wall, and the dromos was filled in. The chamber itself was left free of earth.

The chambers were square, ellipsoidal, or horseshoe-shaped. They had a flat floor and vertical walls. The roof was usually flat, but sometimes hipped or sloping down towards the back or towards the entrance. Some of the tombs had a low ledge along the length of one of the walls to hold the grave goods. Many tombs had small low niches cut into their walls, and sometimes into the walls of the dromos. Even more common were pits dug in the floor of the tomb, either large ones covered with slabs in which the dead were laid, or smaller ones in a variety of shapes in which bones and grave goods from earlier burials were deposited when the tomb became full up. A few tombs were extended by means of small side-chambers hewn out of one of the sides.

The chamber tombs, being dug into the earth, were naturally undecorated. In very rare cases (e.g. a few tombs in the Argolid, at Thebes, and Halikarnassos), there was sculptured decoration on the façades, or a coat of stucco, plain or coloured, on the door frame, the sides of the dromos, or the walls of the chamber.

While the shaft graves and chamber tombs can be termed works of architecture only in the sense that they are spaces which have been given a definite shape, the tholos tombs are proper buildings which incorporate fundamental constructional elements. They were the tombs of kings, rulers, and noblemen and are, therefore, fewer in number than the shaft graves and chamber tombs contemporary with them.

The tholos tombs are, in fact, a more splendid and luxurious version of the chamber tombs. They have the same design: a dromos leads to a chamber entered through a door and a stomion. Here, however, the dromos is level or on an imperceptible incline, its walls are vertical, and the door and the chamber are built with huge stone blocks. The tomb is sometimes built at ground level (in which case it is covered over by an artificial mound) and sometimes cut deep into the side of a hill. The building is on the corbel system; the tombs are beehive-shaped with a circular floor. The diameter varies from 3.50 to 4.00 m. in the small Messenian tombs to 14.50 m. in the Treasury of Atreus at Mycenae. In earlier tombs, the height is less than the diameter (except in a few "pointed-top" tombs at Menidi, Marathon, and Korone), and, in later tombs, the height and diameter are approximately the same. The doorway is flanked by jambs built on a stone threshold and supporting massive flat lintels (usually two or three together), which cover the whole of the passage-way and support the section of the tholos above them.

The most splendid examples of tholos tombs come from the last period of Mycenaean power, during the 13th century B.C., when building techniques were well advanced, and much experience had been gained in the use of materials. The dromoi, façades, and chambers are built of four-sided stone blocks laid in horizontal, almost isodomic, courses. There are relieving triangles in every case, the doorway is closed by regular doors, while the façade and the walls of the chamber are splendidly decorated. Two of the largest tholoi, the so-called tomb of Atreus at Mycenae and that of Minyas at Orchomenos, have a small square side chamber, and all the tombs have one or more pits in the floor which were used as repositories for bones and grave goods.

The Treasury of Atreus

The most magnificent and the best preserved Mycenaean tholos tomb is the Treasury of Atreus. Built about 1250 B.C., it is indeed a royal building of imposing dimensions, perfect in construction, and richly decorated. It was built about 400 m. southwest of the acropolis in the side of a low hill which was at that time inhabited. The dromos, with vertical and parallel side walls, was 36 m. long and 6 m. wide. The floor of the dromos was plastered with white clay, the walls covered with regular pseudo-isodomic layers of squared conglomerate blocks, and the beginning of it was blocked by a low cross wall of similar construction. The monumental façade of the tomb, 10.50 m. high, had a door in the centre, 2.70 m. wide at the bottom, 2.40 m. at the top, and 5.40 m. high. The door was framed by sculptured *fasciae* and flanked on either side by a half-column of greenish marble. These half-columns rested on low square bases and were decorated with sculptured chevrons. Above the door and the lintel was the relieving triangle, concealed behind a slab of coloured marble (only a few pieces survive, but enough to show that it was carved with horizontal spirals and half-rosettes) and flanked by two half-columns, smaller and more slender than the lower ones, and decorated with carved winding spirals instead of chevrons. Inside the passage-way (5.20 m. long) was the threshold, covered with wood or bronze, and the huge double doors. The inner part of the stomion (about 3/4 of the whole) is covered by an enormous monolithic lintel weighing 120 tons. Its interior face was carved to follow the curve of the vault, which rises up in 33 regular ashlar courses of massive stones to a height of 13.20 m. The floor of the tomb, like that of the dromos, was plastered with white clay. Traces of bronze nails at various points in the side walls show that some additional decoration, perhaps bronze rosettes, had been nailed to the walls.

On the north side of the chamber, a second, smaller, door leads into a square side chamber, 6 × 6 × 6 metres. Today we can see only the bare irregular walls, as they were originally hewn out of the rock; but originally, they were covered by thin stone slabs with sculptured decoration like the walls of the similar side-chamber in the Treasury of Minyas at Orchomenos. Probably there was a pillar or column in the middle to support the roof covering. After it had been built, the huge tholos was covered by a mound of earth which protected the vault from damp and other damage and kept the stone courses in their proper position.

Building Methods

There are two main types of Mycenaean building, distinguished both by the manner and the materials of their construction; first, ordinary structures, like houses and palaces; second, Cyclopean structures (i.e. built of massive boulders), such as fortifications, bridges, and tholos tombs.

Mycenaean houses rested on strong foundations of undressed stones, held together by nothing more than some insulating white clay spread in the bed of the foundations and between the joints of the stones. These foundations were continued up to a considerable height in underground rooms in the form of strong stone walls which acted as supports for the upper storeys. The ground floor areas too had a thick well-built stone base which supported a light upper structure of crude bricks held together by a network of solid timber ties. The surfaces of the walls were protected by an insulating layer, usually of clay reinforced with chaff, and the biggest and most luxurious houses had frescoes painted on a coat of stucco. This method of construction was proof against earthquakes but not against damp or fire. This explains why Mycenaean buildings were in such constant need of repair and were so frequently destroyed.

The palaces were more carefully built and maintained than ordinary houses, though the technique of their construction was basically the same. They were also more systematically planned and built with more varied and valuable materials. They were influenced by Cretan prototypes and closely resembled one another in design and construction, with perhaps a few local variations due to the availability of different building materials. The floors were all plastered. In some parts of the megaron at Mycenae, gypsum slabs were laid over the floor, while at Tiryns the floor of the bathroom next to the large megaron consisted of a single huge slab of hard limestone, measuring $3.00 \times 4.00 \times .70$ m. and weighing 20 tons. Most of them, however, were covered with stucco, painted over in places with various decorative patterns. The thresholds were sometimes of wood, but usually consisted of large slabs of limestone or conglomerate, smoothed and worked on the visible raised part of their surface, but left rough and irregular on the lower sections which were hidden by the floor plaster of the areas connected by the doors. The sides of the threshold supported the massive lintels, and in the corners shallow round cavities were carved out to take the bronze-cased rods which protruded from the bottom part of the wooden doors, and on which the doors turned. The outer doors were evidently completely faced with bronze and decorated with bronze ornaments. Windows must have been similarly constructed. It is certain that they had wooden frames and probably also wooden shutters.

The columns in the rooms and outdoor areas were made from tree-trunks and rested on stone bases, which, like the thresholds, had their foundations either in the natural rock or in a suitable substructure of small stones. The circular upper surface of the column base was smoothed, while the

Sixteen kms. from Mycenae, on a small rise in the Argive Plain, the citadel of Tiryns was built with a Cyclopean enceinte. The walls, which have a perimeter of 700 m., enclose an area of 20,000 square metres. The main gate is on the eastern side. Historians are puzzled by the existence of two strong citadels within such a short distance of each other.

316

rest, which was hidden beneath the floor covering, was left rough-hewn. The walls, .50 to 1.00 m. thick, were constructed of undressed stones (large ones for the façades, smaller ones for the filling) up to a height of about one metre. Above that they were continued with crude bricks and a timber framework. In the court of the megaron at Mycenae and in the palace of Pylos, the façade was built of quadrilateral blocks of stone placed in regular ashlar layers. The blocks were not parallel-sided but cut so that they tapered towards the back, giving their upper and lower surfaces a trapezoid shape. This ensured full contact at the vertical joints on the outer surface, while inside a small triangular space was left between each two blocks. This was filled with clay and small stones, so that the blocks were firmly joined to the fill of the wall behind them. In general, the walls in the palaces were given a more systematic facing than those of ordinary houses, and better materials were used. On the inside walls there was stucco painted with frescoes, and on the outside walls an insulating layer of mud, reinforced with small pebbles or straw and most probably whitewashed. Some rooms, such as the bathroom at Tiryns or the vestibule and anteroom of the megaron at Pylos, had wooden panelling, and the walls of the storerooms and other auxiliary rooms were covered with clay.

The fortification walls and the tholos tombs were built entirely of large stones, usually huge boulders. More precious and finer materials (bronze, wood, marble) were added rarely, and then only in small quantities for decorative purposes. This decoration, however, pales into insignificance beside the massive and imposing construction of the walls themselves. Their great weight and mass make them seem like a natural extension of the hill on which they are built.

The foundations of the walls always consisted of the natural rock itself. The surface was prepared either by the rough levelling of irregular ground or by the filling in of cavities with small stones, held firmly together by yellow clay, which made the bed of the foundations level. The first massive stone layers supported the rest of the wall, which was built, in the same way in each case, of large irregular limestone boulders (dragged into position up an artificial ramp with the aid of rollers and crowbars), roughly hewn and fitted together without any joining material. These boulders presented a unified and vertical surface. In the region of the gates at Mycenae, the façade was built from a type of conglomerate found close to the acropolis. This type of stone divides naturally into horizontal layers, which can easily be cut into rectangular pieces and used in ashlar building.

The two faces of the wall were built of these huge boulders, 1.00×3.25 m. in length, some placed as headers, and some as stretchers. Wherever it was necessary to give more support to adjacent or upper blocks, small stones were wedged between them, while the core of the wall between the two faces was loosely filled with field stones, sometimes held together by a little clay. This construction was solid and resistant, provided the width of the wall did not exceed a reasonable limit. Wherever the construction was particularly massive, there was a danger that the weight of the filling material, as it gradually settled in the course of time, would exert too much pressure on the faces and eventually split them apart. In the tower at the entrance to the Acropolis of Athens, this eventuality had been guarded against by the construction of an interior cross-wall which linked the two sides together and supported a part of the fill, thus considerably lightening

One of the galleries in the Cyclopean walls of Tiryns. These passages had a width of 1.65 m. and a vertical wall height of 1.75 m. The upper sections of the walls (built on the corbel system) converge to form a pointed arch. The tunnels led to the storerooms of the citadel.

317

the load on the façade.

There were small variations in the construction of the walls from place to place and from one building phase to another, but the general picture is always the same. In and around the gates, more or less uniform blocks of stone were generally used. At Tiryns the rest of the walls were constructed, in the early years, of small and naturally symmetrical blocks, and in later years of large irregular blocks, while at Mycenae the stones used in the last building phase are small and with more, or more obvious, traces of hammer dressing than the earlier ones.

In Cyclopean constructions, as in all other types, the most sensitive and vulnerable point is the gateway, because here the upper layers (a weight of hundreds of tons) are not founded on the rock, but are suspended over an empty space, supported only by the lintel, itself the weakest part of the door-frame. The jambs, which rest directly on the ground or on the threshold, are in much less danger, and therefore, in some cases, especially in the tholos tombs, they were constructed of successive layers of smaller blocks, like the wall. The thresholds could be built in one of two ways, depending on the amount of wear and tear they were expected to withstand. In the tholos tombs, which were entered only on rare occasions, the thresholds were constructed of slabs so delicate that they could not even support

the weight of the jambs. Particularly good examples are the treasuries of Atreus, Klytaimnestra, the Genii, and Minyas. There, the thresholds were laid in position after the building of the door and the surrounding section of the tholos and simply spanned the space between the jambs. In the Treasury of Atreus, the threshold consisted of three pieces cut slantwise in the middle so that a triangular space was left between them. A wedge-shaped piece was fitted into this space. Its dimensions were precisely calculated so that, when it was placed in position, the outer pieces were pushed out towards the sides and wedged firmly between the two jambs. Then the threshold was completely covered with wood or bronze so that the joints and ill-fitting shapes of the pieces were hidden from view. By contrast, the thresholds in the gates of the citadels were crossed many hundreds of times a day by men and animals, and had to be of an appropriate thickness and weight. They were constructed of monolithic stone slabs, much more massive than was required by functional considerations, and were reinforced in the centre.

The lintels too consisted of massive monolithic slabs, but even so they were unable to support the load above them. A way had to be found of lightening or transferring the weight. The first method (used in some of the earlier tholos tombs—Menidi, Mouriatada) was to leave a series of gaps in the upper stone courses; but this was only partly effective

and in any case feasible only when the doorways were narrow. The second and only really effective method was the construction of an arch above the lintel which transferred the load to the jambs.

The Mycenaean arch was not a true arc (that would have required finer building materials and a more precise calculation of shapes and dimensions), but was built in the much simpler corbel manner. On the two sides of the opening, each layer of stones protrudes out a little more than the last, so that the greater part of the weight is borne by the layers below, and only a small section hangs in space. Thus, two symmetrical slanting walls are formed, which meet to form between them a triangular space, known as the relieving triangle, which considerably lightens the load on the lintel. This space was usually closed (for reasons of safety as well as aesthetics) with relatively light slabs of stone, sometimes decorated with reliefs, as is the case in the Lion Gate at Mycenae. The same system was used to lighten the load in openings on the inside of Cyclopean structures like galleries, or passages leading down to underground springs or bridges. By far the most effective use of this corbel technique is in the tholos structures, where each ring of stones protruded a little more than the last towards the centre so that the diameter was gradually reduced, and a vault was constructed which could span a very large space, always provided that the height

of the vault was approximately equal to the diameter of its floor. The perfect state of preservation of the Treasury of Atreus, which has suffered no damage except at the hands of pillagers, shows how safe and durable such a method of construction is when employed with proper care.

Roads

The Mycenaeans also built an extensive road network, sections of which can still be seen today. Their roads were 3.50 to 4.50 m. wide and carefully planned to avoid sharp inclines. In mountainous country, they were sometimes cut into hillsides and supported by specially built Cyclopean embankment walls up to 4 m. high, and sometimes running over massive viaducts. Their foundations were of stones and earth covered with rubble to a thickness of about 25 cm., while the surface (which is preserved today at only a few points) was of trodden earth, clay, and pebbles.

The Drainage Works of Lake Kopais

The greatest technical achievement of the age was undoubtedly the draining of Lake Kopais. This was undertaken, according to ancient sources, by the Minyans of Or-

The Mycenaean walls are of solid and lasting construction. They are built of irregular blocks, 1.00 to 3.25 m. long. Close to the gates, however, a special effort was made, particularly at Mycenae, to use uniform material for the façades of the wall—rectangular pieces of conglomerate, built in almost isodomic layers. Left: part of the fortified area at Mycenae. Right: entrance to the Mycenaean citadel and the Lion Gate; above the massive lintel is the relieving triangle, which brings the weight to bear on the two jambs.

chomenos, who thereby secured for themselves a large and very fertile area of farmland. Later, the Thebans—led, according to legend, by Herakles—occupied the area, destroyed the works, and allowed it to revert once more into marshland. From the traces of the works which remain today, we cannot tell exactly when the installations ceased to function or how they were destroyed, but they indicate that when they were in use they were both brilliantly conceived and amazingly effective. Lake Kopais was not successfully drained again until 1889, thirty-two centuries after the Minyans achieved it. Lake Kopais lies in a flat sunken stretch of land of about 200 square kilometers surrounded (except to the southwest) by mountains and rocky hills with high and steep slopes. Two rivers, the Melas and the Boiotian Kephisos, as well as several small streams, ran down into the Kopais basin. Every winter they flooded their banks and turned the whole area into a large shallow lake. The water began to rise in November, and by March was 3 to 5 m. deep. The level dropped between April and October, when the lake turned into a swamp. This was because, in the summer, when there was a smaller volume of water in the rivers, the natural swallets (katabothrai), which ran out of the lake at various points in the bank, were able to draw off the reduced volume of water and carry it away eastwards to Skorponeri, Larymna, and Hylike. These swallets, which were distributed in five groups along the north and east shores (Mavromati, Moulki, Vrystika) and particularly at the northeast tip of the lake (Paliomylos, Spitia, Binia, Megale Katabothra, Kasnesi), formed the basis of the Minyan drainage network.

The basic idea was simple and bold: the water from the rivers, instead of being allowed to flood the plain, needed to be collected and channelled into the swallets, after these had been suitably widened and strengthened. So, a system of dykes and enbankments was built , some of the swallets were widened and deepened (at Kasnesi, for example) and a large underground drainage tunnel was cut into the hillside.

The dykes had a width of 40 to 50 m. and whatever height was necessary (today they are preserved only up to 1.50 m.), and their sides were protected by massive stonework. They were built on the inside of the lake basin along the banks so that an irregular channel with an average width of 40 to 60 m. was formed between the dykes and the lake bank. At points where the bank was low or insecure, a second dyke was constructed along it, opposite the first, with its lake side reinforced with stones. Only very scanty remains of these dykes are preserved today on the eastern side, but in the Mycenaean period they formed a complete peripheral moat which collected the water and led it into the swallets. On the northern side, too, where the two main rivers, the Kephisos and the Melas, run into the lake, the dyke was made especially strong (today we can still see remains with a breadth of more than 66 m.) with two Cyclopean walls built on its inside as a backbone, each 2 m. thick, and 27 m. apart.

Thus, the bulk of the water was channelled to the northeast corner of the lake close to the acropolis of Gla and the part of the shore where most of the swallets began. To ensure a regular outflow, an emissary canal approximately 9 kms. long and 60 to 80 m. wide was dug between two banks 40 m. and 50 m. wide respectively. Their inner slopes were reinforced with Cyclopean walls 3 m. thick. This canal, which drew off the water from the rivers at a point close to the modern village of Topolia, followed first a curving, then a straight course, collected on its way some of the water from the

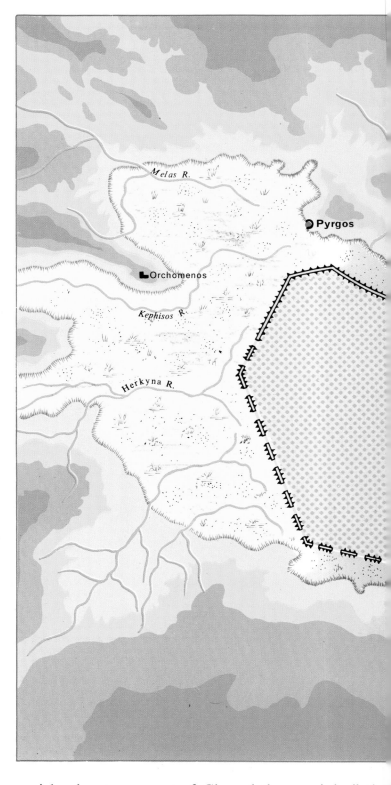

peripheral waterway east of Gla and then carried all the water into the swallet at Binia. None of the swallets was capable of taking such a tremendous volume of water, and so it was necessary to supplement them with an artificial emissary tunnel carved into the rock. This began at Kephalari and followed a curving course in a northeasterly direction beneath the neck of land which was crossed by the ancient road to Larymna. This tunnel, which has not yet been completely explored, is a technical achievement of no mean quality. Over a total distance of 2,230 m., the Mycenaeans dug 16 vertical square shafts at intervals of 100 to 200 m. and 18 to 63 m. in depth, according to the contours of the ground. When they reached the desired depth, they began

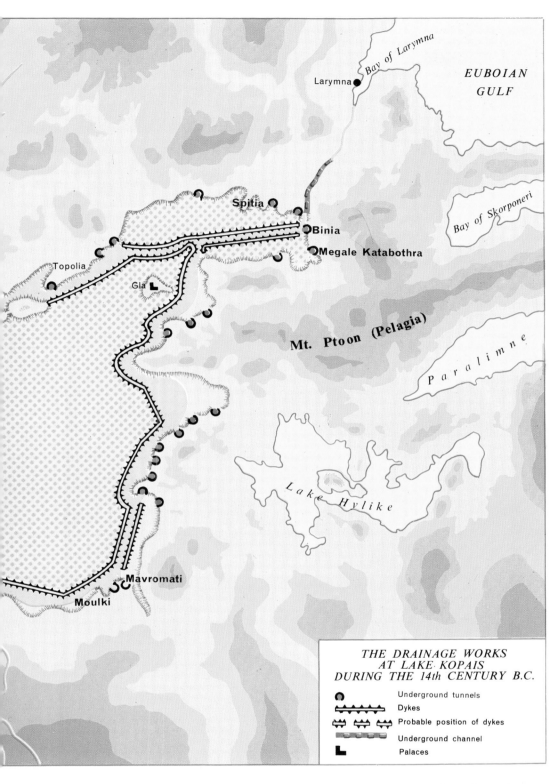

THE DRAINAGE WORKS
AT LAKE KOPAIS
DURING THE 14th CENTURY B.C.

○ Underground tunnels
Dykes
Probable position of dykes
Underground channel
L Palaces

During the zenith of the Mycenaean period (14th century B.C.), the vast drainage works at Lake Kopais were carried out, daring in conception and admirable in execution. The waters of the rivers and torrents which flooded the plain were channelled into canals 40 m. to 50 m. wide and brought towards the east end of the lake, where an emissary canal led them into the swallets (katabothrai). Because the swallets were incapable of carrying away such a huge volume of water, the Minyans of Orchomenos constructed an artificial underground tunnel 2,230 m. long. Left: map of the district with a plan of the Mycenaean installations showing the dykes, the peripheral canals, and the underground tunnel.

to tunnel sideways to link the shafts together. The tunnel started from a mouth in the lake shore 2.50 m. below the average level of the lake bed and followed a steady 11% gradient. There are indications, particularly in the last two shafts to the north, that the digging of the tunnel was done in both directions simultaneously and that the gradient was originally intended to be more gradual than it finally became. At the points which have been explored, the tunnel walls are vertical up to a height of 1.43 m. and then slant inwards up to 1.75 m., where they meet the horizontal roof, 1.45 m. wide. In other words, a conduit was formed capable of draining large quantities of water and with the additional advantage that it was more easily accessible for repair or

inspection than the natural swallets.

The gigantic drainage works of Lake Kopais were regularly inspected and systematically maintained. At the most vital point, the area near Topolia where the catchment area of the two rivers, the emissary canal, and the channel of the east side all met, an acropolis was built on the islet of Gla, and there were other smaller fortifications and lookout points along the bank and on the hillsides overlooking the lake.

At the end of the Mycenaean period, this whole complex was abandoned. From the traces which remain we cannot tell whether there was a violent destruction or whether the works were simply neglected and gradually ceased to function after the disappearance of the central authority (probably the confederation headed by Orchomenos) which had built and maintained them. In historical times, the various installations had fallen into disuse for the most part, and various attempts made from time to time to build new drain-age works or (as we learn from an inscription from Roman times) to repair and maintain a part of the old network were only partially successful and did not prevent the waters from regularly inundating the plain.

MYCENAEAN ART, 14TH TO 11TH CENTURY B.C.

Art had reached full maturity in Greece at the beginning of the 14th century B.C. Cretan prototypes had been assimilated and adapted, the secrets of technique had long been mastered by Mycenaean artists, and their work had acquired its own characteristic appearance, distinguished chiefly by the tectonic arrangement of shapes and the comparative simplicity of the decoration.

The political power of the Mycenaean world, its division into small states which were in regular communication with one another, and its strong links with the rest of the Eastern Mediterranean created a framework in which art could develop and, at the same time, determined what influences would affect it and what general direction it would take. The Mycenaean artists had no difficulty in obtaining materials, and worked in secure conditions under the protection and on behalf of local rulers. Their products could be swiftly and safely transported and, thanks to the flourishing economy, were in great demand not only in Greece itself but all over the Eastern Mediterranean. The import of various eastern products meant that there was a continuous and fruitful interchange of ideas and borrowing of techniques. The great demand for Greek products naturally resulted in increased production and standardization; palace models were copied on a wide scale to meet the demands of foreign customers. Shapes became simplified and stylized: great numbers of craftsmen had to be recruited to cope with the ever-increasing demand, and this led to a lowering in the quality of products and a mechanical repetition of fashionable subjects. This is particularly evident in vase-painting, the most popular form of handicraft: the subjects which made more demands on the individual talent of the artist (scenes from nature, for example) were either avoided altogether or rendered in a stylized fashion of facile combinations of simple geometric shapes. Ivory-working and seal-engraving suffered the same fate in that the sculptural rendering of figures was abandoned and replaced by simple engraving of the outlines and conventional decoration with no modelling of the planes. The progressive trend towards simplification and increased production is even more obvious in the work of the goldsmith and the jewellery-maker.

The political changes in the 12th century B.C. resulted in the closing of the large palace workshops. A host of small local workshops, each with its own style and techniques, swiftly replaced them, though no individual artistic traits emerged as a result of this decentralization. The general decline in the standard of living and the shortage of good quality materials led to the abandoning of the more aristocratic art forms, such as gold and ivory working and seal engraving. Vase-painting became increasingly stylized to the point of abstraction and sought variety not in the creation of new subjects but in the endless combination of old ones. In its last phase (a time of fatigue and decadence), Mycenaean art abandoned most of its usual forms of expression and natural models and confined itself to the me-chanical repetition of carelessly rendered abstract and lifeless motifs.

Painting

Examples of Mycenaean painting have been preserved only on frescoes and on vases. Frescoes, painted on plaster, decorated the palaces and the houses of the wealthy. Vase-painting consisted of monochrome linear representations of figures and scenes drawn on vessels of certain shapes.

Of all the arts which the Mycenaeans learnt from the Cretans, fresco-painting was the one they copied most faithfully. Apart from extending the repertoire of subjects to include some motifs of their own warlike inspiration, Mycenaean artists altered nothing either in technique or in the manner of rendering the figures. This faithful imitation gave Mycenaean fresco-painting the static and inflexible quality which usually characterizes traditional art and checked its development. There is no observable difference between the fresco technique of the last palace at Knosos and that of the mainland centres in the latter part of the 13th century B.C. for all the two hundred or more years which separate them, and it is consequently impossible to use stylistic criteria to date them.

With only a few exceptions (a small votive tablet, an early funerary stele, originally carved, later stuccoed over and painted, and a painted full-relief woman's head from Mycenae), all examples of painting on plaster come from the interior decoration of the palaces and buildings of various Mycenaean centres, particularly Thebes, Mycenae, Tiryns, Pylos, and Orchomenos. Very few paintings were found in their original position, i.e. on the wall surface. Most had come unstuck and fallen among the ruins of the houses. Others, which in some cases had been destroyed by fire, had been discarded even during Mycenaean times and replaced by new frescoes which were often copies of the old ones. Many of the frescoes found in the palace of Pylos and most of those from Tiryns come into this category. In most cases, however, we can make a fairly accurate guess about which part of the building the frescoes originally came from. A dado, sometimes monochrome, sometimes with decorative patterns or coloured veins in imitation of marble, ran along the bottom of the wall, and the main pictures were painted above this. At some points in the buildings, in corridors for example, or close to auxiliary passages, the walls were painted to look like cloth, i.e. curtains or tapestry.

For all their variety of subject, the compositions fall into two basic and easily distinguishable groups. The first, which is repeated in almost identical form in the palaces of Thebes, Pylos, Mycenae, and Tiryns, consists of rows of women, painted almost life-size, walking in procession, holding various objects (pyxides, flowers, vessels) as offerings to some deity. The second group comprises various representations inspired by the daily life and occupations of the Mycenaeans and includes a host of subjects in a limited number of combinations. There are plants (flowers, olive branches, trees), sea-creatures (dolphins, octopuses, argonauts), birds and animals (bulls, dogs, horses, deer, boars) and imaginary creatures (griffins, sphinxes), men, chariots, and pieces of architecture (e.g., façades of houses), as well as a variety of abstract decorative designs. All these, usually painted on a small scale, are combined in scenes of war (Mycenae, Pylos), hunting (as in the scene of the boar hunt from Tiryns), religious ceremonies (sacrifice scene from Pylos), as well as other genre scenes (such as the two charioteers from Pylos). Finally, in some cases, the two groups are present together without any obvious link between them, as in the

scene of the lyre-player between griffins in the throne room at Pylos.

The design is always two-dimensional, without depth or perspective. The figures are simply flat shapes, usually drawn in sharp black outline and painted in bold colours against a monochrome background. Figures are shown in profile, though with eyes drawn frontally. The skins of animals and the plumage of birds are often rendered with crosses, rosettes, wavy lines, and other supplementary ornament which has no relation to reality. In human bodies the flesh of women is always left white, while that of men is painted brown. The colours are always and everywhere the same, without gradations and without any correspond-

Mycenaean fresco-painting imitates the Minoan both in technique and the rendering of figures. However, a fresco-painting found at Mycenae in 1970 surpasses its Cretan models in the natural-ness of the rendering and the excellence of the design. The Mycenaean woman wears a necklace and bracelets. The black mass of hair is broken up with lighter bands.

323

ence to reality, particularly in the case of animals and plants, which are often painted red or blue. In addition to the white of the whitewashed surface of the wall, the colours used are: red (light and dark), brown, yellow ochre, blue, black, and (rarely) green. The figures in the composition are often arranged in horizontal rows, one on top of the other, sometimes separated by lines which are supposed to represent the ground, though often these lines are left out, and the levels of the figures merge into one another (as in the bull hunt from Tiryns), creating a kind of perspective effect which enlivens the composition. In other words, the Mycenaean painters—like all their contemporaries—were completely ignorant of perspective and shading, and used colours in a conventional way, indifferent in most cases to the verisimilitude of the result. Their designs, however, were fairly naturalistic. The artists had a talent for suggesting movement, and the overall impression given by their pictures (which was more important to them than the realistic rendering of detail) was pleasing and convincing. They managed to give life to the most stylized and rigid shapes.

When a room was to be decorated with frescoes, the walls were first covered with a layer of clay, usually of a yellowish colour, reinforced with chaff. Then the rough surface of this undercoat was given two or three thin and uniform coats of stucco. The top coat was carefully smoothed over. On top of this, the frescoes were painted in the technique we now call *alfresco secco*, i.e., not on the still damp newly-whitewashed wall, but on the dry plaster, which was dampened in sections and covered with paint dissolved in a thin lime solution. Analysis has shown that the Mycenaean painters used mineral colours almost as they found them or with very little mixing. The white was, of course, the white of the stucco itself, the black came from charcoal produced by the combustion of organic substances, probably bones, the yellow was simple ochre, and the light red, burnt ochre. The powder of some iron oxide, usually haematite, made the dark red, the blue was pounded or melted glass, the green the powder of a copper oxide (malachite, for example), and the brown was earth rich in manganese.

Before applying the colours, the artist incised some guide lines on the wall surface, using a taut thread and a sharp tool for straight lines, and compasses for circles. He next made the preliminary sketch, i.e., a basic sketch of the shapes of the composition, in a light reddish or yellowish colour. Then he coloured in the background and painted first the general outline, then the details, and finally the surfaces of the figures. He usually painted the background before the figures so that these were left white, and sometimes the painter decided to leave them without colour altogether. Where the background was light in colour, it was painted over the whole surface of the wall except for the parts which had to be left white, and the figures were later painted on top of it. Where the background was dark, it stopped at the outlines of the preliminary sketch of the figures.

The *alfresco secco* technique gave the painter more time to work comfortably than the true fresco technique, but obliged him to paint the wall in separate relatively small sections. This is why he often divided the background into broad wavy or straight vertical strips painted in different colours or in different shades of the same colour, with the paint applied in coats of varying thickness. The artist

Sections of frescoes from Mycenae, Pylos, and Tiryns of evident Minoan influence. Left: a female figure wearing a head-dress

with a crest, the type usually worn by princesses; from Mycenae, 13th century B.C. (Nauplion Museum). Middle: fragment from

generally imitated standard models and soon acquired a familiarity with his subjects and a proficiency in technique which enabled him to work with the swiftness required by his material. However, the speed with which he painted and the resultant shackling of his creative imagination led to hurried and often careless renderings of subjects with bold but unsteady outlines, confused borders between various colours, and affected, if not positively unnatural, proportions in the figures. The same criticism may be made of all Mycenaean painting, with only one exception: the picture of a female figure (perhaps a goddess) from the late 13th century B.C., which was discovered in 1970 in a room of a house built on the inside of the west wall of the acropolis of Mycenae. The liveliness and grace of the design, the unforced naturalness of the movement, the trueness of the features and proportions, and the fine workmanship in the rendering of details, all make this fresco a masterpiece of Mycenaean painting and of ancient Greek painting generally, placing its unknown creator among the great artists of all times.

Vase-painting

The second category of Mycenaean painting, vase decoration, was more elementary in conception and execution and also more standardized than fresco-painting. The first examples appear in the 14th century B.C., and production continued well into the 12th century B.C. Most of the finds, however, come from the middle period, the 13th century. Two types of vase—kraters and stirrup jars—were more richly decorated than the others. There is also a group of painted clay *larnakes* (sarcophagi) from a later period, found in the cemetery of Tanagra. The majority—and certainly the best—of the decorated vessels have been found outside the Greek mainland, in Cyprus, where there were local factories, and at various points on the Syrian and Palestinian coast. They were evidently a luxury product, in great demand both in Greece and abroad. Their place of origin seems to have been the Argolid, since many were found at Corinth, Mycenae, Tiryns, Argos, and Berbati. In the 12th century B.C. they also began to be produced in Attica and on Naxos.

The subjects of the vase-paintings included human figures (men and women), animals, birds, fish, marine and plant life, and a variety of objects connected with man and his activities. The compositions were more or less standardized. One of the main groups, often painted on kraters, included chariots, drawn by one or more horses with a driver, carrying often a passenger and one or two escorts. The decoration was supplemented by a variety of unconnected motifs (fishes, flowers, vases, rosettes, geometric patterns). Vessels decorated with scenes of chariot racing have been found in great quantities in all the countries into which Mycenaean civilization penetrated. It is evident from their wide diffusion that they had some special use and significance in funeral ceremonies.

The larnakes from Tanagra served a similar function. The work of two or three contemporary craftsmen, they were decorated with rows of women singing dirges, or simply with women's profiles, and, in one instance only, with a chariot race and a bullfight. Other compositional groups appear only sporadically or even singly in the finds made

 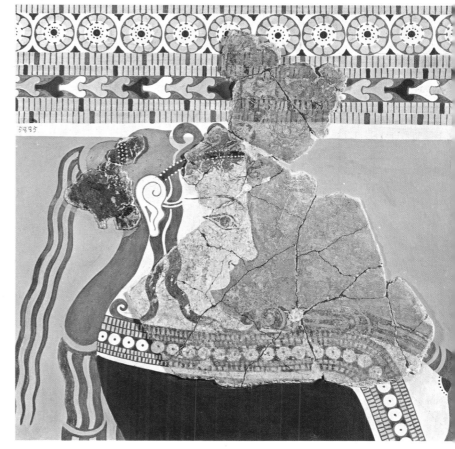

... fresco from the palace of Pylos: two men dressed in animal skins; 13th century B.C. (Chora Triphylias Museum). Right: frag-ment from a fresco showing a procession of women; from the palace at Tiryns. (National Archaeological Museum, Athens)

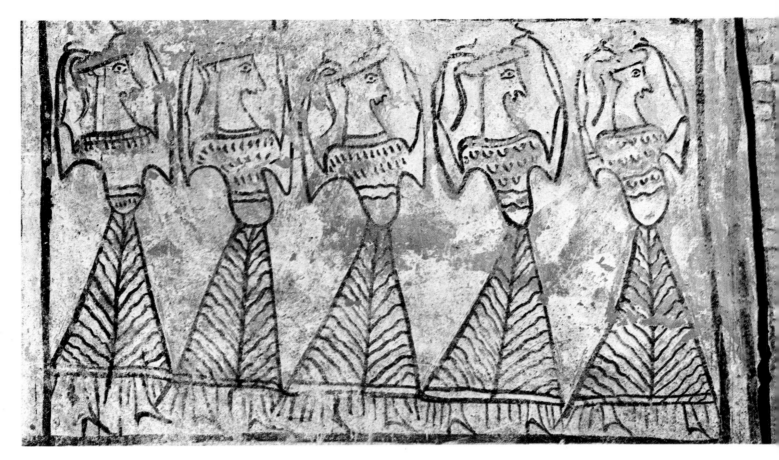

so far: animals in a line or facing each other; a ship with armed officials on the deck and members of the crew (painted smaller) in the hold; a goddess on a three-legged throne welcoming a procession of armed worshippers. Later works from the 12th century B.C. show a landscape with birds and a wild goat between clumps of bushes and a date palm; a lamenting woman bidding good-bye to a row of Mycenaean warriors depicted as marching to battle with upraised spears. These compositions are certainly influenced by fresco-painting; the last indeed is practically a duplicate of a representation of warriors painted on stucco on a funerary stele from Mycenae, and the border, painted with figures of deer which surround it is identical to the one on a fresco from Tiryns. After 1200 B.C., a revival of the 16th century Minoan marine style produced a group of vessels, nearly all stirrup jars, decorated with octopuses whose tentacles enclose fish, birds, and a variety of unconnected supplementary decoration. The octopuses are stylized, almost abstract, with symmetrically drawn tentacles, yet very decorative.

In general, vase-painting produced sketches rather than pictures. The figures, like the rest of the decoration on the vases, are monochrome, painted in the usual reddish or brown colour, sometimes broken up by small white dots or lines; they are compact silhouettes or, more rarely, outlines with the basic details sketched inside them or given in white paint on a dark background. As always happens with children's drawings and immature painting, the proportions of the figures are unnatural and affected, the design abstract without any plasticity, the basic features emphasized in an almost symbolic fashion. The trend towards stylization became more marked as time went by. The figures in the composition are generally placed side by side, and the meaning of the picture is suggested by the movement and stance of the figures, not by their expression or

their respective positions. Human figures are depicted only on later vases, and are of two distinct types: the Minoan, with a fine sharp profile, oval or round eye, and an ear which is not actually drawn but left as a gap between the hair; and the Helladic type, which we know from the funeral masks at Mycenae and the silver vessels with inlay decoration from Mycenae and Pylos. This second male type is usually dressed, often armed, and has a large nose, a beard or a weak jaw, and asymmetrical circular ears. The animals, birds, and fishes are well drawn in outline, but their details are rendered by conventional and often purely decorative patterns (crosses, spots, wavy lines), while the flowers and plants are abstract geometrical patterns which bear no relation to their real shapes.

Mycenaean vase-painting, then, is the work not of artists but of craftsmen who had neither the means nor the imagination to produce original works of art. The limitations of their technique and their inability to develop their craft beyond the established prototypes and to create new forms of expression are more evident here than in the work of the fresco-painters.

Pottery

The Mycenaeans used an enormous number and variety of vessels (about 80 known types) with more or less standard shapes and only very minor variations, such as in the number of handles, the shape of the lip and the base, and so on. They can be classified according to their uses into perfume-holders (these are the most luxurious vessels), containers for solids, containers for liquids, various types of drinking vessels, and ritual utensils (kernoi, rhyta, etc.). The ritual utensils have a greater variety of shape and individual detail

Figures were painted on the clay larnakes *(coffins) found in the cemetery of Tanagra. The painting of coffins was a Minoan custom which appears in some Helladic regions after the 13th century B.C. Left: the two long sides of the* larnax *from the cemetery at Tanagra, showing a procession of lamenting women with their hands raised to their heads; they are dressed in the Minoan fashion. (Thebes Museum)*

The most common vessel is the stirrup jar, which was intended to contain perfumed oil. This curious vessel, with its round body, low base, long narrow neck, and upright handle supported on a vertical stem with a discoid top, was invented in Crete but immediately adopted by the potters of mainland Greece, who continued to produce it all through the Mycenaean period. More than any other kind of vase, the stirrup jar illustrates the duration and diffusion of Mycenaean civilization.

Other common shapes are the *kylix* with a high stem and circular base, the jug, the *alabastron*, and, towards the end of the period, the *skyphos* and the *stamniskos*. All these vessels, the work of professional craftsmen, were moulded on the wheel from pure clay, and their surface was usually coated with a slip, i.e. a fine covering of thin clay, sometimes the same as the clay used in making the vase, but usually lighter in colour. Over the slip, the decoration was painted in black, red, or brown with a thin brush. The shades of the colours could be varied by using different thicknesses of paint or different methods of firing the pot.

Many vessels, particularly those in household use, were unpainted, while others, chiefly imitations of metal prototypes, were painted all over. Many of the most common vases were decorated in a sparse and simple fashion with bands which emphasized the various parts of the vessel—the mouth, the meeting of neck and shoulder, the largest diameter, the handles, and the base. In other vessels, particularly the stirrup jars, alabastra, kraters, and "luxury" vessels generally, the decoration consisted of combinations of various simple and more complex motifs, some inspired by the natural surroundings, others geometric. They were placed in horizontal bands, or covered the main surfaces as their chief feature of decoration. After 1400 B.C., the

decorative motifs no longer sprawled freely over the surface of the vessel, nor did they have the individual character which was the chief mark of the palace style of the 15th century B.C. They were given standard shapes and arranged in neat bands or placed inside borders. This trend became increasingly evident during the 14th century B.C. The prevailing shapes were the stirrup jar, the kylix, the jug with regular or cut-away neck, and the low round alabastron which, however, began to disappear towards the end of the century and was replaced by a type of small alabastroid vessel with a narrow cylindrical or slightly conical body. The decorative motifs included many marine and plant subjects (murexes, octopuses, argonauts, papyri, or lilies), with stylized but not rigid shapes, and with enough variety in the manner of their execution for their prototypes to be still easily recognizable.

In the 13th century B.C., the great demand for Mycenaean pottery, both within Greece and abroad, resulted in the mass production of vessels with standardized shapes and decoration. A few local fashions persisted in the peripheral workshops of Rhodes, Cyprus, and, to a lesser extent, Crete, but otherwise uniformity was total. To the previous shapes, there were now added the skyphos, the krater, and the three-handled jar typical of Rhodian pottery. In the decoration, marine subjects became rarer, and plants, particularly flowers, more common. All the decoration, however, had now become stylized beyond all recognition. The motifs became purely conventional patterns dictated by the shape of the area to be decorated.

The break-up of the Mycenaean *koine* at the beginning of the 12th century B.C. brought this period of standardized production to an end. The general trend continued to be the same everywhere. The shapes became more upright and angular, oval or conical, with an increasing preference for conical bases. Stylization of decorative motifs was carried to extremes. Kylikes and kraters were no longer produced, but stamniskoi, small lekythoi and *oinochoai* (trefoil-mouthed jugs) became popular. There were two main decorative styles which developed parallel to each other. One has been called the Granary Style, after the building in the acropolis at Mycenae where examples of it were first found in large quantities. It was used chiefly on simpler vessels. A large part of the surface of the vessel was painted, and very simple decorative motifs added (often wavy or zig-zag lines in the reserved unpainted zones). The second style is called the Close Style and was used for the decoration of "luxury" vessels, particularly stirrup jars, pyxides, and ring-shaped vessels, as well as skyphoi, oinochoai, hydriai, and small lekythoi. Many kinds of stylized motifs were painted in dense patterns all over the vase. Whatever motifs did not lend themselves to stylization (chiefly marine and some plant motifs) were abandoned. The shapes were almost all geometrically arranged in simple or complex patterns (zig-zags, wavy lines, angles, triangles, spirals, concentric arcs) and were often sketched rather than drawn. Some flowers had become so abstract and stylized that it would be impossible to identify them if the previous semi-abstract stage of their rendering had not been known to us. All these patterns were drawn in an increasingly complex way and in arbitrary combinations (flowers juxtaposed with angles, triangles with semi-circles); they were no longer placed side by side but combined to form balanced and in most cases symmetrical compositions with the motifs facing each other or in a series of broad bands which took up a large part of the surface of the vessel. Later, the subjects became even more complex and carelessly drawn. They were combined in even denser patterns, and the greater part of the vase surface was covered with decoration.

There was still some pictorial decoration in this period, but it was confined mainly to stirrup jars and had a very restricted repertoire of subjects. Chariots became rare and finally disappeared altogether, while the human form and some animals were still drawn, as for example on some stirrup jars from Perate and on the Warrior Vase from Mycenae. One group of vases was decorated with octopuses (Naxos, Dodecanese, Attica).

The chief characteristic of 12th century B.C. pottery is its great variety. No two vessels are exactly alike. There is a clear effort on the part of the vase-painters to avoid repetition. This tendency, along with the general decline of Mycenaean civilization and the severing of its links with the East from where it had drawn much inspiration, swiftly exhausted the imagination of both potter and vase-painter and led to the abandoning of the more demanding Close Style and the general adoption of the simpler Granary Style, the forerunner, in its last phase, of the Sub-Mycenaean and Geometric Styles.

Sculpture

The Mycenaean sculptors, like their Cretan teachers, worked in stone, clay, plaster, ivory, and semi-precious stones. They produced sculpture in the round and relief work, as well as seal-stones with engravings which would come out as embossed decoration on the seal impression. Ivories and seals have survived in great numbers and great variety, but little remains of works in stone, plaster, or clay, and so our knowledge of Mycenaean sculpture is incomplete.

The following sculptures in the round have been found: the plaster head of a woman or sphinx and some large clay statuettes of men, women, and coiled snakes from Mycenae; a man's head, also of clay, from Asine; another fragment of a head from the Acropolis at Athens; and hundreds of small stylized terracotta figurines of women, animals, and birds which have been found at most Mycenaean centres.

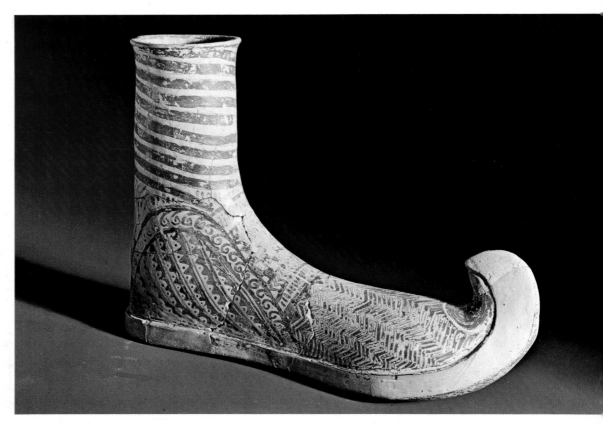

Mycenaean pottery includes vessels of a religious or ritual character. Right: libation vessel in the shape of a winged shoe, perhaps of local type, from Voula, Attica. It seems that Apollodoros's myth about the winged sandals stolen from the nymphs by Perseus was of Mycenaean origin. (National Archaeological Museum, Athens)

Two examples of stylized Mycenaean pottery. Left: ritual vessel with three feet and three animal heads (two of deer and one of a bull), from a tomb at Volimidia. (Chora Triphylias Museum)

Right: stylized terracotta figurine of a woman from Mycenae with a tubular body and stunted arms; necklaces and bracelets are painted at the neck and on the arms. (Nauplion Museum)

There are also some vessels moulded in the shapes of animals and various other objects, most probably imitations of more valuable metal or stone originals. With a few exceptions, unremarkable because of their stylization and uniformity, all these works belong to the latter part of the 13th century B.C. and to the 12th century B.C. Consequently, they must represent the last phase in the relatively unchanged tradition of Mycenaean sculpture. This is shown by their similarity to the earlier Minoan terracotta statues found on Keos.

The head from Mycenae is made of white plaster with the details (hair, eyes, mouth, ears, and two dotted circles on the cheeks) painted on in the fresco technique. The head has been fashioned with greater care and skill than the clay heads from Athens or Asine, also painted white and given added colour. The features of the Athenian and Mycenaean heads are fairly regular, with more or less correct proportions and no sharp contrasts. The Asine head has round protruding eyes, a large pointed nose, a pointed chin (perhaps a beard), and discoid ears. The hair is gathered into pigtails which look as if they had been stuck on as an afterthought—it is altogether more roughly modelled and carelessly executed than the other two heads. All three,

however, have one basic characteristic in common: although they are free-standing sculptures, they have none of the roundness and the gradual modelling of the features achieved in more highly developed sculpture, but are worked in four separate planes (face, back of head and two profiles) which meet rather than merge together.

The figurines are even more rudimentary and conventional. The large ones have cylindrical tube-like bodies, spherical heads with long, pointed noses, and incised mouths. The eyes and hair are sometimes moulded, sometimes painted. Short, stunted arms are raised on either side of the body or crossed over the chest. In the small figurines, which are completely stylized imitations of the large ones, cylindrical from the waist down with plank-like torsos and flat, wing-shaped arms, abstraction has reached such a point that the general shape of the human body is barely recognizable, and there are no moulded details except for a slight protuberance for the nose, two small discs at the breasts, and sometimes a pigtail down the back. The remaining features (eyes, clothes, jewellery) are sketched on the clay wherever the figurines are not painted all over. Most are the usual mass-produced types of women's figures with upraised or crossed

329

arms. There are some others, basically similar in shape, which show a woman holding a child in her arms or on her shoulders, or seated on a throne or on the saddle of a pack animal, or kneading dough; and also a rudimentary group of chariot and charioteer. Equally rudimentary are the figures of animals (usually bulls or oxen). Where there is no particularly obvious feature, like horns or a mane, it is often impossible to say with any certainty what animal is represented. The moulded vessels made for religious or ritual use are also given functionally stylized shapes. The features are rendered roughly and clumsily, the details no longer moulded but painted on in a conventional manner. Some vessels represent birds; there is also a pack animal loaded with wine-skins, a rhyton in the shape of an ox-head from Karpathos, a fish-shaped rhyton from Tiryns, and two high boots with upturned points.

The only examples of Mycenaean relief sculpture, carved on stone, which have been preserved are the Lion Gate relief in the acropolis at Mycenae and a few fragments from the decoration of the side chamber of the Treasury of Atreus. There are also some architectural features with sculptured motifs (spirals, rosettes, stylized flowers, etc.), such as the half-columns and the façade of the Treasury of Atreus and the roof of the side chamber of the Treasury of Minyas at Orchomenos.

The most important of these is the large and imposing Lion Gate relief, the only known example of Mycenaean monumental sculpture. It was discovered intact and in its original position. The rest of the reliefs were found in scattered fragments, often so few and so small that it is impossible to reconstruct the design of the whole.

The Lion Gate relief is carved on a slab fitted into the space of the relieving triangle over the lintel. It shows two symmetrical lions standing on their hind legs facing each other and resting their front paws on a small concave-sided altar which stands between them. On top of the altar is a column crowned by a capital which supports part of an entablature. The heads of the lions, which were carved separately, are now missing. They were probably worked in a softer, more malleable type of stone, though, judging by the size of the dowel holes in the slab, it must have been heavy and fairly massive (perhaps steatite). The bodies of the two animals and the column between them are carved in relatively low relief with the muscles and the various planes of the body shown roughly but boldly. The proportions are rather conventional, and there is little detail; but the sculpture as a whole gives an impression of naturalness and creates an effect of impressive vigour and imposing strength. The same characteristics are seen in the fragments from the Treasury of Atreus. These show a small-scale relief of the head and neck of a bull in front of the leafy branches of a tree.

The carving of these reliefs in an age when tools were of stone and bronze was a long and laborious process. The technique had come from Crete and, chiefly, from the Cyclades. The basic tools were the emery chisel and the bronze drill and saw, which cut into the hard stone by grinding it with sand or emery powder. The saw was a simple straight or sickle-shaped blade without teeth, or sometimes simply a piece of wire, while the drill was a bronze tube, like the modern carpenter's auger, 1.6 cm. in diameter. It was turned by the regressive pulling of a rope or bow, and it left a thin straight cylinder of stone in the centre of the drilled hole which could later be broken off easily. Relief sculpture was done in the following way: first, the sculptor drilled a serried

Clay chariot with two horses (perhaps a children's toy) found in a chamber tomb at Megalo Monasteri in Thessaly, 13th century B.C. (Volos Museum)

330

row of holes along the outlines of the shapes of the composition, and then converted these into a continuous irregular channel by cutting out the cylindrical centres of the holes and the thin walls between them; he used stone hammers or emery cutting tools to take off the part of the surface which was to form the background and the saw to cut narrow channels wherever the curve of the relief permitted; finally, he smoothed out the rough parts of the background and the figures and effaced the traces of tool marks by rubbing them with sand or emery powder. Sometimes, (as in the reliefs from the Treasury of Minyas) he used compasses, instead of the tubular drill, for the circles, and this resulted in less regular shapes. On small surfaces and for delicate work as, for example, in the carving of close patterns of decorative motifs, he used small stone or bronze chisels. The carving of reliefs with such rudimentary tools and techniques must have required a tremendous amount of work and inexhaustible patience, which makes the achievements of the Mycenaean sculptors all the more noteworthy.

Ivory-carving

Ivory-carving and pottery making were the only two branches of Mycenaean art which succeeded in graduating from Minoan imitation to the production of entirely original works of high quality, which in their turn influenced the artists of Crete and the East. A large number of excellent ivory sculptures from Syria and Palestine are imitations of Mycenaean originals (e.g. the Vegetation Goddess on the cover of a pyxis from Minet-el-Beida). Others betray so many diverse influences that it is difficult to determine

Two of the most important works of Mycenaean sculpture. Left: part of a clay figurine of a woman, painted with brown-black varnish; the hair has been shaped into two spirals on the forehead and falls in waves to the shoulders (Nauplion Museum). Above: a woman's head in plaster from Mycenae; it is completely covered with white paint, with details in red and black. (National Archaeological Museum, Athens)

their origin, particularly when we remember that many of them were the work of itinerant craftsmen who absorbed influences from all over the Eastern Mediterranean and who produced work in whatever style and technique seemed to appeal to the local market.

Ivory from Syria and Egypt was used in the carving of small free-standing figures. Examples are a group of two women and a child, a small head and a lion from Mycenae, and a small statue of a woman from Prosymna. There is also an enormous number of embossed reliefs, sometimes carved on plaques, pyxides (usually the cylindrical variety), combs, mirror handles, sword hilts, tool handles, and inlays on chariots, furniture, and various utensils like those mentioned in the Pylos tablets. Ivory objects of Mycenaean make have been found in various parts of Greece and the Near East, but the main groups come from Mycenae (the most important centre of ivory-carving), from Delos, and from Megiddo in Syria and, to a lesser extent, from Argos, Athens, Menidi, Spata, Enkomi, and Ugarit. Inlays had the shape of sea-shells, spiral bands, figure-of-eight shields, lilies, ivy leaves, rosettes, and columns and other pieces of architecture. The pyxides are carved with various decorative motifs: simple spirals, leaf spirals, astragals (as on the cylindrical pyxis from Routsi in Arkadia), or more

Reliefs are extremely important in the sculptural decoration of Mycenaean monuments. Above: relief decoration on the roof of the side-chamber of the Treasury of Minyas at Orchomenos, with spirals, flowers, and rosettes in harmonious combinations. Below: relief decoration on a funeral stele of porous stone, from Grave Circle A at Mycenae; on the upper part, a row of continuous spirals; on the bottom part, a hunting scene or, according to another interpretation, a chariot race. (National Archaeological Museum, Athens)

intricate designs. The plaques usually show the figures of men and animals, real or imaginary. One group of plaques of mixed Mycenaean and Eastern character from Syria and Palestine were decorated with trees or olive branches.

The animals appear alone or in groups and occasionally with human figures. One of the most beautiful examples is the plaque from Megiddo which shows a seated griffin with its head erect and its symmetrical wings spread out to the left and right, like the facing sphinxes from Mycenae. This small sculpture is skilfully carved, with great attention to detail and a variety of planes. In spite of its small dimensions, it has a monumental character and is reminiscent in its general features of the Lion Gate relief. The other compositions usually show animals fighting: lions attacking griffins, or bulls, or a man. But there are also more idyllic scenes: bulls among trees, lions against a background of foliage, and animals grazing or resting.

The most important portrayal of human figures is the free-standing group from Mycenae (as skilfully executed as its minutely carved Cretan prototypes), which shows two seated women whose shoulders are covered by the same *peplos* (shawl) and a small child standing between their knees. The group stood on a base, probably of wood. It presents a great contrast to the large plaster and clay sculptures of the period, for here there is a sense of natural movement, the details and proportions of the human figure are faithfully rendered, and there is an unforced gradation of planes.

There are many fine examples of figure reliefs in ivory: a seated goddess from Mycenae; warrior heads from Mycenae, Spata, and Cyprus; two women facing each other on mirror handles from Mycenae; and the warrior on the Delos plaque, who is shown standing in front of a large figure-of-eight shield with a helmet on his head and a spear in his hand. The contrast between the slim waist and the rippling muscles of a robust body is a naturalistic detail which shows how much progress the Mycenaean craftsmen had made, without, however, forgetting the prototypes of their Cretan teachers.

These works are typical of the 14th century. In the 13th century, the reliefs were rudimentarily modelled and became low and flat, so much so that some of them are incised rather than sculptured. This group includes a small head sculptured in the round from the acropolis of Mycenae. The width of the face is out of all proportion to the height, the chin is weak, and the top of the head is almost flat. The eyes are rendered in a conventional manner with a low outline and flat pupils, and the hair by dense rows of fine incised lines.

After 1200, when the material became scarce, decoration became limited to motifs and lines merely traced on the ivory. Thus, when the Mycenaean *koine* first took shape, more and better ivory was imported: ivory work became extremely popular, and there was a widespread demand for small artifacts (though increased production led to deterioration of quality). Finally, with the decline of Mycenaean economic and commercial life, the art of ivory-carving was almost completely abandoned.

Ivory, a soft and delicate material, was easily cut with a saw. The engraving was done with a bronze knife or with a hard stone blade and the surface was smoothed over with sand or some similar type of crystalline powder. If a piece of ivory was too small for the craftsman's purposes, he engraved additional pieces and fitted them all together with dowels (small projections on one piece that fitted into corresponding holes in the other). Sometimes, especially in combs, the pieces were fitted together with narrow projecting strips inserted into corresponding slits.

Seal-engraving

By 1400 B.C., Mycenaean seal-engraving had passed into a period of decline. The best examples of this art had been produced earlier, in the 16th and 15th centuries B.C., when Minoan influence was still direct and strong. There was an evident, if brief, revival in the 13th century B.C.; the seals from this period are of good workmanship and decorated with a great variety of subjects, but they still cannot be compared to the masterpieces of the earlier centuries.

A few seal-stones from this last period have been found in the royal tomb at Dendra, the tholos tomb at Menidi, the cemetery at Perate, and on the acropolises of Mycenae and Athens. They are worked chiefly in agate, sard cornelian, steatite and, in a few cases, onyx, chalcedony, amethyst, and jasper.

There was great variety in the decorative motifs: animals, imaginary creatures, men, plants, pieces of architecture. Often a carnivore, usually a lion, is shown hunting and overcoming his victim, generally a deer, a cow, or an ox. There are also animals flanking pillars (as on the Lion Gate) and, more rarely, cult scenes or a struggle between a man and a lion. There is only one scene from marine life—an octopus among dolphins on a clay seal from the Palace of Pylos. The chief characteristic of Late Mycenaean seals is the breaking up of the shapes of the composition. The designs are simplified, parts of the body are rendered by mere lines or broader surfaces with few gradations, carved separately and then linked together with knobs at the joints, i.e., the join is now optical, not organic, as in earlier seals. We are left with only hollow silhouettes without properly plastic forms, and it is often difficult to recognize the subject of the composition.

Metal-work

Metal-work, practised in Greece from the Early Bronze Age, made great progress during the Mycenaean period. The commonest metal in use was bronze, but gold and silver were also used. The products of Mycenaean craftsmanship, known to us chiefly from the grave goods in the royal grave circles at Mycenae, were in great demand in the Eastern Mediterranean, where they were often presented as valuable gifts to kings and rulers. The metal-working tradition persisted to the end of the Mycenaean Age. The Pylos tablets refer to ritual vessels, rhyta in the shape of an ox-head with golden horns, silver and gold cups, and jugs decorated with sea-shell and spiral motifs. However, the later works lack the brilliance of those of the earlier period. The niello technique was gradually abandoned, and the last examples of this once widespread and popular method of metal-working are two silver vessels with inlaid rows of male heads from Mycenae and Pylos and a dagger from the grave

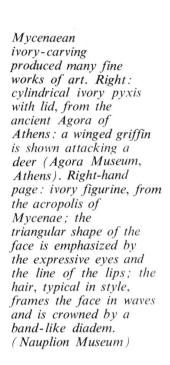

Mycenaean ivory-carving produced many fine works of art. Right: cylindrical ivory pyxis with lid, from the ancient Agora of Athens: a winged griffin is shown attacking a deer (Agora Museum, Athens). Right-hand page: ivory figurine, from the acropolis of Mycenae; the triangular shape of the face is emphasized by the expressive eyes and the line of the lips; the hair, typical in style, frames the face in waves and is crowned by a band-like diadem. (Nauplion Museum)

at Pharai in Achaia.

Very few vessels (of either the luxury or everyday variety) survive from the period after 1400 B.C., and some of these, particularly the later ones, are clumsily made. The shapes, however, had not changed, and the vessels seem to have been in widespread use, since many clay vessels imitate metal prototypes, and some kylikes covered with tin leaf are imitations of rarer and more valuable silver vessels.

More numerous, and more interesting, are examples of metal tools (razors, knives, tweezers, chisels, awls, axes) and weapons (swords, daggers, spears, arrow-heads, helmets, and the suit of armour from Dendra). All are made of bronze and worked in a simpler manner than in earlier years. They were cast or hammered into the desired shape and usually left undecorated. Only the swords and a few of the daggers had a little decoration on their hilts: engraved ivory plaques, gold or gilt double-headed studs and, more rarely, fine gold sheet which encircled and held the covering of the handle. On the blades, inlay decoration had been replaced by simple carvings along the length of the medial rib which was now lower and slightly curved. The long and finely-worked parade swords, produced by only two or three large workshops, stopped being produced after 1400 B.C. and were replaced in the 13th century by a new type of sword of eastern origin, shorter and with an almost flat blade and a T-shaped handle. The old gold or ivory pommel at the end of the handle had been replaced by a flat transversal crescent, while the bottom of the handle was now equipped with a quillon, i.e. a guard in the form of two projections which protected the swordman's hand. These swords, simpler and more practical than the earlier ones, were made in all Mycenaean centres in large quantities. There were many small variations, but in general this shape of sword remained unchanged to the end of the Mycenaean period.

Jewellery

The finest work on precious metals and semi-precious stones was done in the 16th and 15th centuries B.C., when the best jewellery was produced. After 1400 B.C. there were no further innovations in the techniques of jewellery-making. As time went on, precious metals and semi-precious stones became increasingly rare and, after 1200 B.C., they were almost completely replaced by glass and other artificial materials.

The most common piece of jewellery was the finger-ring. Sometimes it was a plain circular band, sometimes it had an ellipsoidal and slightly conical bezel, usually undecorated. In a few cases, the bezel was engraved with scenes similar to those on seal-stones, more rarely there was an inlay of some other material, e.g. amber or enamel. Earrings were less common and came almost exclusively from Cyprus, where they were produced and used in all the main settlements. The shapes (ox-heads, crescents, rings) were more or less standardized. There were hair fasteners, with two or three coils to hold plaits, and also bracelets, either simple closed circles or (from the 12th century B.C.) open circles

with tapering ends, wound round one another so that the diameter of the bracelet could be adjusted.

The most common pieces of jewellery were the small beads used in necklaces, bracelets, and diadems. An enormous variety of these has been found, some in simple geometric shapes, chiefly spherical or round and flat, but also barrel-shaped, looped, ellipsoidal, cylindrical, quadrilateral, and lozenge-shaped. Others are stylized imitations of the seeds and pips of various fruits (corn, pumpkins, acorns), or the outer husk of picris and poppy; others of leaves and flowers (papyrus, lily, ivy), or animals (ox-heads, sea-shells, argonauts). Yet others are cut into the shape of various decorative motifs (rosettes, figure-of-eight shields, pendent spirals, etc.). There is also a very typical variety of cylindrical gold beads decorated with serried rows of minute granules. The jewellery was made of various metals: gold, silver, lead, and, more rarely, iron (then the most precious metal, difficult to come by, because it was produced only in small quantities by the Hittites and very sparingly exported), or of various alloys of metals (gold and silver or gold and bronze). Most were plain, either cast or hammered, but some were decorated with filigree, granulation, or plain inlaid enamel. Some beads were made of wood or clay coated with fine gold leaf. During the 13th century B.C., Mycenaean craftsmen began to use chiefly artificial materials (glass, melted glass, faience) as cheap imitations of semi-precious stones and precious metals. With these materials they made luxury type polychrome vases, various inlays and decorative objects (rosettes, plaques with embossed patterns), amulets, handles of various objects, bezels of rings and beads, all of which were exported to countries as far away as England and Hungary.

Music

The little knowledge we have of Mycenaean music has been gleaned indirectly from a study of fresco-paintings showing musical scenes and from an examination of the few fragments of instruments that have been found; and our interpretation of the evidence is assisted by a comparison with what we know of Cretan and Cycladic music. Our chief evidence comes from actual pieces of two ivory lyres from Menidi, a small bronze votive lyre from Amyklaion, the picture of another in the hands of a lyre-player on a fresco in the throne room at Pylos, and some small fragments from Mycenae which are probably part of a lyre or flute. There is no evidence for the existence of the sistrum or cymbals, which were known in Crete, or of the trumpets, drums, and castanets, which were played in Egypt and the countries of the East. Mycenaean music, so far as we can judge, was usually played by only one musician, not by groups of players with a variety of instruments, as was the custom elsewhere. Although we have no definite proof that the flute was played, we do know that this instrument existed both in the Cyclades and Crete in the form of a double flute, which perhaps suggests that a rudimentary form of two-voice polyphony was known and practised.

The lyres, like the Minoan ones, were generally in the shape of an inverted horseshoe, closed at the top by a straight horizontal yoke and fitted at the bottom with an additional cross joint (the *chordotonon* of Classical times), which was usually curved. Strings of equal length were stretched between these two bars, the gaps between them narrowing towards the bottom. Each string played only one note. The lower curved section of the horseshoe was of equal thickness or slightly thicker than the two arms, which means that the sound-box of the instrument was rudimentary, or even non-existent, as in the phorminx in later times. The lyres from Menidi and Amyklaion, like the Minoan ones, had eight strings, that from Pylos only five. The latter was therefore limited to a five-note scale and suitable only for accompaniments. All the evidence suggests that the usual, if not the only, form of musical entertainment in Mycenaean times was singing or melodic recital to a simple accompaniment of one or two instruments.

Literature

The centuries of the rise, flourishing, and decline of Mycenaean civilization saw also the birth and shaping of almost all the myths and legends which were to supply the material for epic poetry, tragedy, and the other genres of later Greek literature. Yet the Mycenaean Period itself has left us no texts to compare with those of later periods, no single fragment of literature, at least in its original form. The palace tablets, written in a script which cannot reproduce the true phonetic values or the delicate shades of meaning (much less the prosody) of the spoken language, are simply brief and often abbreviated records of accounts with no pretensions to elegant expression. They are important in that they prove that the Achaians spoke a type of Greek which was very close to the artificial archaizing idiom used by later poets, particularly those who composed the epic poetry which has been preserved to this day. There is no doubt that these poets took their themes and material from earlier works handed down by oral tradition. We must now ask: how early were these works? What was their original form? Can they be regarded as true works of literature?

Philologists have shown that the epic poems of the 9th and 8th centuries B.C. were the final written versions of a cycle of poems which had been handed down through many centuries of oral tradition. They were the end products of a process common to all oral poetic cycles: the handing down from one generation of bards to another not only of legends and themes, or even whole epic compositions, but especially of a large number of formulas, i.e. standard phrases in the appropriate metre which constituted whole lines (As soon as early rose-fingered Dawn appeared), or

half-lines (much-enduring godlike Odysseus), or just stereotyped combinations of two words, usually of noun and epithet, (glancing-helmed Hector, long-shafted spear). These formulas made up the bulk of the material of the poems. The bards knew them all off by heart and used them according to the requirements of sense and metre in every new narrative poem they composed, indifferent to the fact that many of these expressions had become obsolete or that their precise meaning was no longer appropriate. It has been calculated that about one-fifth of the Homeric poems is made up of formulaic lines and that, in the 28,000 lines of the *Iliad* and the *Odyssey*, there are about 25,000 recurrent shorter formulas. The great number and variety and the immutability of these phrases enabled the bards to compose verses swiftly and easily, since they relied on memory as well as inspiration. It shows too that these expressions had emerged as a perfected instrument after a long process of assembling and polishing. It proves, in other words, that the epics had a life of centuries, not only as myths and historical traditions, but also as poetic composi-

In Mycenaean metal-working, separate figures or shapes made of metal leaf were glued on to a vessel or a sword blade on a background consisting of an alloy of silver, bronze, lead, and sulphur. Below: silver cup from a tomb at Mycenae decorated with a row of inlaid male heads. In the upper row, bearded heads of gold and black niello. (National Archaeological Museum, Athens)

tions. This is true not only of the Homeric poems, i.e., the Trojan cycle which was composed in Ionia after the 8th century B.C., but also of a host of other epic sagas (the Theban cycle, for example, or other smaller fyttes which sang the deeds of local heroes, like Minyas, Theseus, or Herakles). These sagas are mentioned in ancient sources, but only a few fragments of them survive. These poems, composed in Boiotia and other parts of mainland Greece, and a few other minor ones, such as the 8th century B.C. dedication on the "cup of Nestor" found at Ischia, were in the same poetic idiom and metre as the Ionian epics and included some of the same formulas. Yet they were composed at a time when the Ionian poems had not acquired the form in which they were later to be known in Greece. So there are two parallel and independent branches of the oral poetic tradition, similar enough to suggest that they have a common original which was composed before the dawn of the Geometric Period and the colonization of Ionia. We can determine the date of the original from the factual and linguistic evidence in the epic poems themselves. First, they mention

and often give detailed descriptions of objects completely unknown after the end of the Mycenaean Period, e.g. Meriones's helmet and Aias's shield. Second, they present a picture of Greece quite different from that of historical times; for example, they completely ignore the existence of the Dorians in Greece, and the Catalogue of Ships reflects a geographical and political division of Greece which ceased to exist after the 10th century B.C. Third, the poems include words which are found on the Knosos and Pylos tablets as terms in everyday use but which later disappeared from everyday speech; for instance, the word *amphiphoreus*, which was later replaced by the simpler form *amphoreus* (amphora), was retained in the poems only because of metrical considerations.

The roots of the epic cycles must, therefore, be sought in the Mycenaean Period. There is no doubt that the nuclei of the poems had been composed in the same dactylic hexameter verse that was used in later historical times and that the poems were sung by Achaian minstrels at a time when the heroes of the poems were still alive.

Some evidence of Mycenaean music comes from the frescoes. The lyre was already in use in early Mycenaean times. Below: musician with five-stringed lyre and bird; the lyre, which is

similar to the Minoan type, is shaped like a horseshoe; it normally had eight strings. Fresco from the throne room at the palace of Pylos. (Reconstruction by Piet de Jong)

A MYCENAEAN DYNASTY AT KNOSOS (1450-1400 B.C.)

Shortly after 1450 B.C., an Achaian dynasty was established at Knosos. The existence of Mycenaeans in Crete was definitely confirmed when the Linear B tablets were deciphered in 1952. The quarrels between the 'Pan-Minoan' and the 'Helladic' factions were at an end, but there still remained the question of how the Achaians came to gain a foothold in Crete.

In the second half of the 15th century B.C., an eruption of the volcano on Thera had catastrophic results in Crete and over much of the Aegean. Tidal waves, earthquakes before and after the eruption, and a rain of ash from the volcano turned Crete into a disaster area and dealt the flourishing Minoan civilization a shattering blow, from which it never recovered. The palaces collapsed in a heap of ruins, and all central authority was paralyzed. It would seem that the Mycenaeans took this opportunity to establish themselves at Knosos, but we cannot know if their appearance there was the result of occupation, a dynastic marriage, or a *coup d'état* by some Mycenaean general in the Minoan fleet.

The sources for our knowledge of this period (Late Minoan II) had always been archaeological, and our conclusions had been based mainly on the correlation and analysis of pottery styles and architectural innovations. It was, therefore, an event of tremendous importance when, for the first time in our study of prehistoric Crete, completely new evidence came to light. The decipherment of the Linear B tablets found at Knosos and dated precisely to this period provided us with a wealth of helpful information.

Perhaps for the first time there was now an obvious concentration of power at Knosos. This palace was the only one to be rebuilt after the volcanic disaster. The palace archives and the remains which have been excavated (the throne room at Knosos, the frescoes, the so-called palace style pottery, the large amphorae, and the Ephyraean goblets) all testify to the establishment of Mycenaeans in Crete.

Mycenaean influence is most evident in the throne room and the other architectural finds from this period which have been unearthed at Knosos. This building group, dated to the last constructional phase of the palace, is incorporated in the old ground plan. The aim of its construction is clear: to give the palace an official throne room corresponding to those which we know in the palaces of Mycenaean Greece (Mycenae, Tiryns, Pylos). The griffins which guard the throne are similar to those on frescoes at Pylos. Even the *alabastra* found in the throne room at Knosos are of a type which prevailed in the Helladic region. Some scholars see additional evidence of Mycenaean influence at Knosos in the stone friezes with relief decoration of triglyphs and half-rosettes and in the fluted columns.

There is clear Mycenaean influence too in both the shapes and decoration of the pottery of the period, which is in the so-called palace style. This type of pottery is found only at, and in the vicinity of, Knosos, in the palace and the surrounding buildings, in the warrior tombs, and in the graves at Katsambas, the port of Knosos. There are three characteristic shapes: the big three-handled amphorae, the squat alabastra, and the so-called Ephyraean goblets. The decoration consists of simplified versions of earlier Minoan subjects and old naturalistic motifs, eventually stylized into lifeless and abstract designs. In general, a new tectonic decorative trend is observed in the design.

These features were not adopted elsewhere in Crete, though a few sporadic examples found in other regions are doubtlessly not accidental. They were genuinely Mycenaean features, foreign to Minoan tastes. The Minoan population gradually recovered from the disastrous effects of the eruption and continued living all over Crete, although now under the lax suzerainty of the newcomers at Knosos. There is no archaeological evidence to suggest any clash between

Mycenaeans and Minoans. Even at Knosos, various buildings erected round the palace at this period have no special Mycenaean features. In many parts of Crete there was frenzied building activity at this time, and it seems that there was a return to prosperity on the island.

At Knosos in the 15th century, a new martial spirit prevailed. Even Evans noticed that the once peaceful character of Minoan life had taken a markedly warlike turn during the last palace period. For the first time in the region round Knosos warrior tombs were built, and the dead were buried with all their bronze equipment: helmets, swords, daggers, and spears. Frescoes at Knosos show young, armed, white-skinned soldiers leading black mercenaries from Nubia. On another fresco from Knosos there are representations of shields hanging on the wall. Helmets with their covering of boars' tusks became a decorative motif in pottery. The palace archives provide a wealth of information about the number and condition of the chariots and their equipment,

about the horses which drew them, and about the battle gear of the leading class. It has been suggested that, since there are no large plains in Crete, the chariot never played an important military role, but was used mostly for religious processions. The same cannot be said, however, about the defensive and offensive weapons, ideograms of which appear on the Knosos tablets. The breastplates and helmets, the swords and spears are clear evidence of the militarism which prevailed.

From the Linear B tablets from Knosos we learn something of the political organization during the period of the Achaian dynasty on Crete. It is almost the same picture as that presented later by Mycenaean Pylos. The ruler of Knosos, we read on the tablets, was the *Wanax*. He controlled the military, political, commercial, and perhaps even the religious life of the region. There is no doubt that this title was assumed by the Achaian prince who occupied Knosos, and that it was inherited by his descendants. The political

The throne room at Achaian Knosos (1400 B.C.). On this alabaster throne standing in its original place, sat the last ruler of Knosos. On the wall are griffins among plants on a red background. The bottom zone of the wall is painted to look like marble. (Restoration of wall decoration)

339

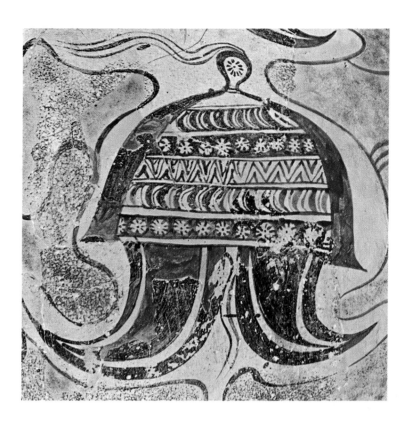

Representation of a Mycenaean helmet on a palace amphora from a tomb at Katsambas, the port area of Knosos. The helmet has a covering of boar's tusks and hair from a horsetail. It comes from the period between 1450 and 1400 B.C. (Herakleion Museum)

We may assume that wool was the chief source of Crete's wealth. The export of materials to Egypt, perhaps even to Mycenaean Greece, is confirmed by other sources, e.g. pictures of Cretans offering Minoan materials to the Pharaohs, and by the widespread use in Egypt of Cretan decorative motifs, evidently copies from imported Minoan cloths.

This information concerns only one branch of the commercial activity of the Cretans. But we can extend our speculations to other fields as well. The palace owned not only flocks of sheep, but also goats, pigs, various pack animals, and agricultural produce. Exports probably included saffron, oil, and timber. The existence of a palace economy is also proved by the discovery of pottery in the palace style of the Achaian period and of a stone cutter's workshop in the palace of Knosos. The Mycenaean dynasty continued the old Minoan commercial policy and perhaps taught it to the Achaians of mainland Greece as well. The palace gathered in the contributions of its subjects, stored them or made them available to craftsmen, and later supervised their export and exchange for other products.

Among the various stone vessels which came to Crete from Egypt at this period was a vessel of great historical significance: an alabaster amphora filled with perfume. It came from the royal Egyptian workshop and bore the mark of the great Pharaoh of the 18th dynasty, Tuthmosis III. Other evidence that contact was maintained between Crete and Egypt during the period of Achaian rule at Knosos is supplied by the fresco paintings of black-skinned Nubians. It would appear that Crete retained her naval strength even after the volcanic disaster, and it is reasonable to suppose

system seems to have been feudal, as it was at Pylos, but perhaps with a stronger theocratic element inherited from the earlier Minoan tradition. The tablets also confirm the theory that there was a central authority at Knosos since the palace controlled neighbouring Amnisos and Tylisos, Phaistos and Inatos in southern Crete, Lyktos in central Crete, Lato and perhaps Seteia and Itanos in the east, and Sybrita, Kydonia, and Aptera in the distant west.

Most of these places are mentioned on a large collection of tablets from Knosos (more than 800 texts in all) which refer to flocks of sheep and to wool. These tablets were in a good state of preservation and could be systematically studied. They gave us some exceptionally valuable and often detailed information about stockbreeding, trade, and economic activity at Knosos and confirmed the pre-eminent role of the palace and its bureaucracy.

The palace had a large number of herds, mainly of rams, which were entrusted to the care of shepherds scattered all over Crete. In the archives, the scribes record the name of the shepherd and the location of his pastures with a detailed list of male and female animals and a list of missing animals. The number of animals in a flock varies between 30 and 400, but in most cases it is fixed at exactly one hundred. Other tablets are records of the wool obtained from the animals and the amount to be taken by the palace on the basis of a calculation of the wool obtained from each animal. The controlling hand of the palace is evident everywhere. The number of animals listed on the tablets is about 80,000— a huge number for Crete at that period. We must conclude that they were reared not for meat, but for wool; and wool was obtained in greater quantity from rams.

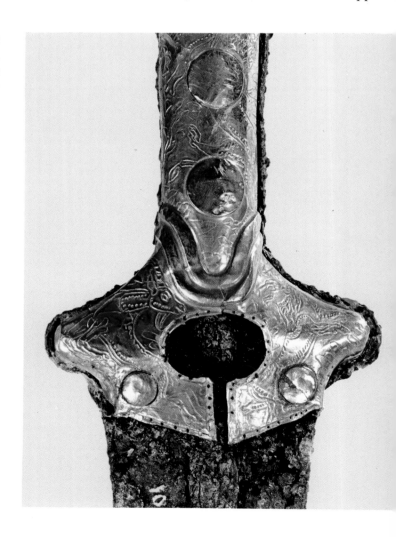

that the Mycenaeans were astute enough to realize the importance of maintaining the Cretan harbours and expanding their own maritime activities.

Minoan supremacy and commercial strength were both now fast declining in the Aegean. The old trading stations at Phylakope on Melos, Ialysos on Rhodes, and Kythera gradually gave ground before the rival Mycenaean stations which had been established on the islands earlier. Mycenaean pottery was in demand all over the Eastern Mediterranean. The Achaian rulers of Crete obviously made no attempt to help check the decline of Minoan merchants, who had always been their most dangerous rivals in the markets of the Aegean, the East, and Egypt. On Crete itself, however, the rulers at Knosos were kindly disposed towards the Minoan population since they relied on their support and good-will.

The period of Achaian supremacy at Knosos was the last great period of Minoan art. Mention has already been made of architecture and pottery. Fresco painting, gold and metal working (especially the fashioning of bronze vessels and arms), ivory work, and seal engraving were all still practised. In the latter, strong Mycenaean influence is again evident: there is general stylization of old motifs, tectonic arrangement of shapes, and a new preference for heraldic compositions which usually show early Minoan cult scenes.

Religion was now a blend of old Minoan and new Achaian elements. The cult of the great goddess in peak sanctuaries, sacred caves, and house sanctuaries continued. In the palace tablets, new Achaian deities are mentioned for the first time: Zeus, Potnia Athena, perhaps Poseidon. The Knosos tablets mention the offerings that were made to these deities: oil, barley, figs, wine, honey. However, we must rule out the co-existence of two separate cults, one Mycenaean connected with the palace, the other Minoan persisting in the rural areas. Since there are no traces of clashes between the two sections of the population, Achaian and Minoan, in 15th century Crete, it is hardly likely that there could have been controversy over such a sensitive matter as religion. So, it must be supposed that the Achaian ruler of Knosos and the members of his family must have successfully fulfilled the function of the last Minoan priest-king who, in the eyes of his subjects, assumed a divine role during religious ceremonies.

Evidently, Minoan burial customs too were adopted by the Mycenaean rulers of Knosos. The old Minoan royal tomb at Isopata was used again in this period for the burial of a member of the Achaian court. The frescoes on the sarcophagus from Hagia Triada show that the burial for which it was used was carried out in accordance with the old Minoan ritual of royal burials.

A little after 1400 B.C., a second disaster occurred. The palace of Knosos was destroyed by fire, the cause of which is uncertain. Some scholars attribute the fire to chance, others to natural causes, yet others to an uprising by the subject Minoans. The last Cretan palace, after long centuries of history, ceased to exist, and with it the Minoan civilization itself was extinguished. Perhaps the Achaian rulers sought to establish a new seat of power at Knosos or in the surrounding region, but they could do nothing to check the decline. Mycenaean Greece was now without a rival.

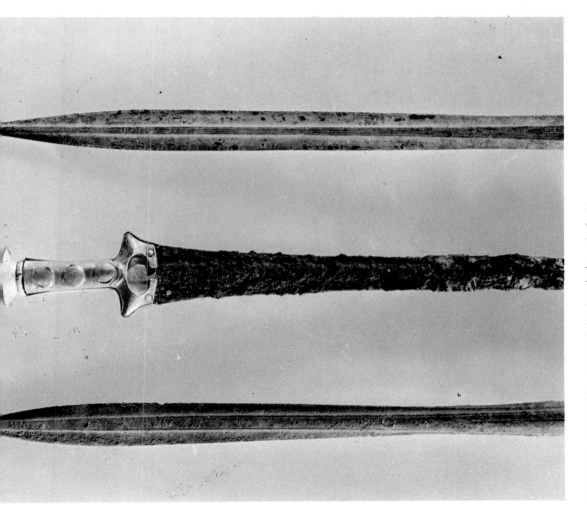

The Mycenaean art of weapon-making and decoration was transplanted to Crete after the establishment of the Achaian dynasty at Knosos. Left: bronze sword (in the middle) with gold-encased handle and bronze spear-points from the tombs at Knosos, where the dead of the Achaian military aristocracy were interred. Left page: part of the gold-encased handle of a sword with a representation of lions chasing wild goats. From Zafer Papoura, cemetery of Knosos, second half of the 15th century B.C. (Herakleion Museum)

POST-PALACE CRETE

The final destruction of the palace of Knosos shortly after 1400 B.C. was a fateful landmark in the history of Minoan Crete. The long tacit rivalry between Minoans and Mycenaeans was finally brought to an end. The Mycenaeans reigned supreme in the Aegean and in the markets of the Eastern Mediterranean. Crete was no longer a leading power.

The decline, however, came in gradual stages. For a long time there were still strong links with the glorious past. At the beginning of this period particularly, there is abundant evidence of prosperity all over the island. But politically Crete was now but a province, no longer capable of providing any competition to Achaian Greece.

There are literary as well as archaeological sources for this period: various myths which probably contain some historical truth have come down to us. The most important information is the one mentioned by Homer:

> One of the great islands of the world
> in midsea, in the winedark sea, is Krete:
> spacious and rich and populous, with ninety
> cities and a mingling of tongues.
> Akhaians there are found, along with Kretan
> hillmen of the old stock, and Kydonians,
> Dorians in three blood-lines, Pelasgians—
> and one among their ninety towns is Knossos.
> Here lived King Minos whom great Zeus received
> every ninth year in private council...
>
> *The Odyssey, XIX. 172-179*

Homer gives a faithful picture of Post-Palace Crete. It is one of the great islands of the world. It is densely populated. A conventional number of cities is given: 90 (100 in the *Iliad*). Only a few of these were known to Homer, mainly those mentioned in the Catalogue of Ships (Knosos, Gortys, Lyktos, Miletos, Lykastos, Phaistos, Rhytion), and some others which happened to be mentioned incidentally in the poem, like Amnisos. There are remains of buildings from this period in Crete, but they have not been properly excavated. The best known are at Chondros Viannou, Gournia, Archanes, Chania, Palaikastro, Zakros, and Hagia Triada. The tremendous number of cemeteries which have been found proves once more the accuracy of Homer's descriptions.

The population of Crete is made up of native Minoans, Achaians, and Kydonians. The Achaians established themselves there, as we have seen, after 1450 B.C.; hence the myth which speaks of the founding of some cities by Agamemnon in western Crete (Pergamos, Lappa, Tegea) and the existence of place-names like Gortys, Arkadia, Pharai, and Phalanna. The Achaians participated in the founding of Polyrrhenia. According to legend, the Spartan herald of Agamemnon, Talthybios, led Achaian colonists from Mycenae to Crete. The origin of the Kydonian tribe is problematical, but they are thought to have occupied western Crete since scholars agree that Kydonia was located there.

Among the inhabitants of Crete, Homer mentions not only Achaians and Kydonians, but also Eteo-Cretans (the "Kretan hillmen of the old stock"), Dorians, and Pelasgians. Eteo-Cretans were the original Cretan population who had become mixed with the Achaians and who abandoned central Crete after the Dorian invasion. According to Strabo, they lived in southern Crete, and their existence is also

established in eastern Crete in later years. At the beginning, they probably also remained in other parts of the island, but they seem to have become absorbed by Greek tribes at an early date. The Dorians came at a later date, and Homer's reference to them is an anachronism. Finally, the Pelasgians remain a complete mystery. No wonder that the language of the Cretans was "a mingling of tongues" (*memigmene*).

Memories of Minoan Crete were still clear. Homer remembers Knosos and Minos. Elsewhere, he mentions Rhadamanthys and Deukalion, Daidalos and Ariadne. But the Cretan hero in the *Iliad* is the son of Minos, Achaian Idomeneus, who, with his friend and relative Meriones, son of Molos, has a prominent place in the poem on account of his valour and prestige. Idomeneus is a powerful king and participates in the Trojan War, with 80 ships, which places him third in naval strength after Agamemnon and Nestor. Evidently, he is the personification of the might of Post-Palace Crete.

The extent of Idomeneus's power in Crete is not clear. From the *Iliad* it would appear that power in Post-Palace Crete was concentrated in the hands of one ruler. This is not confirmed by excavations, since no palace from this period has so far been found. The megara at Hagia Triada and Tylisos were perhaps the seats of strong local chiefs, but not of kings. In spite of the spread of settlements and cemeteries of this period all over Crete, particularly in the West, it appears that the region round Knosos was the real centre of the island. The cemeteries round Knosos, at Katsambas, for example, are among the richest in Crete. Archanes, where an unpillaged royal tholos tomb from this period was found, is also close to Knosos.

The picture of Post-Palace Crete is further enriched by archaeological evidence. Despite the destruction of the last palace, life continued without any clear break. Post-Palace Crete had not been absorbed into the Mycenaean world. The differences between Crete and Achaian Greece are greater than the similarities. Crete kept her own customs and civilization. She may have recognized the sovereignty of the ruler of Mycenae. Yet, the cultural and religious differences between the two regions show that the suzerainty of Mycenae was not oppressive; nor were old Minoan memories effaced so as to render Crete particularly receptive to Mycenaean influences.

After the final destruction of the palace of Knosos, some sites, like Pseira, Nirou Hani, and Mochlos were abandoned. Humbler buildings were founded on the imposing ruins at other sites. Some regions were now inhabited for the first time. Certainly the most characteristic example of "re-occupation", as Evans called it, was at Knosos. The palace area was inhabited again, this time by ordinary people who cleared the ruins and made makeshift repairs to some sections. The entrance of the north propyla underwent some modification. The southern propyla became storerooms for *pithoi* (large storage jars). A pottery kiln was installed close to the light-well in the queen's megaron. Particularly interesting was the spread of settlements in western Crete. Perhaps conditions were more favourable in this part of the island, because it communicated more easily with the Peloponnesos, or perhaps the Cretans were now obliged to develop their own natural resources, since they no longer controlled

During the period of the decline of Minoan art, sculpture produced only works of a religious character. The Minoan goddess was still worshipped in small sanctuaries, and figurines usually show her with raised arms and dressed in a cylindrical garment. Above, left: clay figurine of the goddess from the sanctuary at Gazi, near Herakleion; on top of the wreath on her hair are doves and the symbol of the horns of consecration. Right: clay figurine of the Minoan poppy goddess from the same sanctuary; three poppy calyces rise from the wreath on her head. (Herakleion Museum)

trade in the Aegean; and Egypt, the old source of wealth, was inaccessible to them. Very few Egyptian objects from this period have been found on Crete, and no Cretan objects at all have yet been found in Egypt. There is no doubt that official trade between the two countries had ceased. Crete still had some indirect influence abroad, however; it is conjectured that Cretan craftsmen who could not find work in their own country offered their services to the court of Amenhotep III and Akhenaton and to the palaces of Mycenaean Greece.

Many of the new settlements in western Crete were founded at convenient points, while in the rest of the island low knolls were preferred. Evidently, there was no fear of foreign invasion, and life continued peacefully. The port of Knosos continued to be inhabited, and there is evidence of links with Cyprus. A typical example of a settlement is at Chondros Viannou, a small farming community, where there were many houses with interior courts and hearths. Isolated houses found in other regions (Palaikastro, Zakros, Gournia) are of excellent construction with spacious arrangement of rooms, reminiscent of the contemporary houses in Tel-el-Amarna. They present an unexpected picture of prosperity. At Hagia Triada, a whole "agora" was found: eight rectangular storerooms containing many pithoi and a common vestibule in front, supported by alternating columns and pillars. The study of architecture alone shows that civilization in Crete continued without a break. Mycenaean type megara such as those at Tylisos and Hagia Triada were not found in any other regions.

Evidence from other arts points to the same conclusions. The royal workshops were no longer functioning, but Cretan craftsmen had lost none of their skill, and the old Minoan repertoire of motifs was inexhaustible. The working of stone vessels was not common, and few new shapes were invented, but the old ones were still regularly produced, and some heirlooms of earlier periods continued to be used. Metalworking was more popular. Bronze was used for making weapons rather than vessels. Earlier types of swords, spears, and various sorts of razors continued to be used, particularly at the beginning of the period. At the same time, new types of knives and swords appear. Bronze mirrors are common. The bronze vessels preserved in a tomb at Knosos and in another at Archanes are particularly interesting for the variety of their shapes and decoration.

Ivory and gold work was much practised. Ivory was used for the handles of bronze mirrors, combs, and inlay work. Older Minoan subjects, like the cow suckling her calf, appeared again for the first time in ivory work of this period. Particularly interesting is the ivory inlay on the front side of a footstool from Archanes: large and small figure-of-eight shields alternate with column-shaped plaques, and its two handles are decorated with ivory plaques showing warrior heads wearing helmets with a covering of boars' tusks. As in other branches of art, the Minoan tradition continued unbroken despite Mycenaean influences. In gold working and miniature work, however, it is more difficult to distin-

In the 13th century B.C., decline is evident in all branches of art in Achaian Crete. Frescoes have almost vanished. Only the surfaces of sarcophagi are painted over with various decorative subjects. Below: sarcophagus from Episkope of Hierapetra with representations of wild goats, bulls, and dogs as well as human figures in chariot racing scenes. (Hierapetra Collection)

344

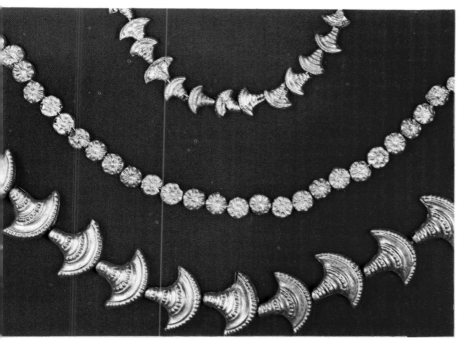

In most branches of art, the Minoan tradition continued unbroken on Crete during the first half of the 14th century B.C. Only in gold and miniature work is it difficult to distinguish Mycenaean from Minoan products. For example, the gold beads in the shape of rosettes and papyri (above, left) and the necklace of sard and gold (right), all found in an unpillaged royal tomb at Archanes. The rosettes and small papyri evidently decorated the fringe of the dress of a princess-priestess. (Herakleion Museum)

guish Mycenaean from Cretan products. Gilt bronze seal rings, gold beads in the shape of rosettes, argonauts, and papyri, as well as beads of various shapes in faience, sard, rock crystal, and ivory are found as much in Crete as in the rest of Greece during this period. Exceptionally fine examples of gold jewellery are the granulated earrings in the schematic shape of bulls' heads, doubtless the work of Cretan goldsmiths. Also of interest are some gold rings from Archanes and a gold primitive mask from Mouliana.

The general decline in Minoan art is particularly well illustrated in seal-engraving. At the beginning of this period, Cretan craftsmen still used semi-precious stones and produced both lentoid and amygdaloid seals and cylinder-seals engraved with interesting subjects: lions tearing bulls to pieces, waterfowl, chariots, cult scenes. But before long, soft steatite stone had become the most commonly used material, the seals were all made in the simple lentoid shape, and the repertoire of subjects was restricted to animal scenes.

In pottery, where there was a clear continuation of the trends of the previous period, the same tendency towards simplification is observed. The Mycenaean-inspired repertoire of shapes and decorative motifs becomes restricted. The distinguishing features of this pottery are a greater proportion of painted vases and a fondness for animal and plant subjects. The decorative motifs, however, became increasingly stylized and eventually turned into completely lifeless forms. The pottery followed the general trends of the period: the so-called Mycenaean *koine*, the later granary fashions, and the close style. The last examples of frescoes are on the painted floor of the Mycenaean shrine at Hagia Triada (dolphins and polypods) and on a sarcophagus from the same site dated to the beginning of this period. Only rectangular and bath-shaped coffins have surfaces large enough to take paintings. Some of the sarcophagi are covered with simple decorative or animal motifs, others with double axes, horns of consecration, griffins, and chariot

races. The sarcophagi from Episkope (Hierapetra) are covered with motifs associated with the worship of the dead.

At the beginning of the Post-Palace Period, the dead were still interred in shaft graves; there were also burials in pithoi and in sarcophagi inside rock-cut chamber tombs similar to those of Mycenaean Greece. In fact, with a few differences, burial customs in Crete were similar to those on the Greek mainland. In both regions, there was the custom of building cenotaphs; stone built tombs with a *dromos* (a runway to a tholos or chamber tomb) and a burial chamber (square or circular) with a vaulted roof were used for the burial of high-ranking persons. The side chamber of a tholos tomb at Archanes, which had escaped pillage, contained the remains of a woman, probably a princess, and a dazzling collection of grave goods: various objects made of gold, semi-precious stones, bronze, glass paste, ivory, clay, and two beads of iron, then a rare and precious metal. A horse had been sacrificed in the dead woman's honour. The skull of a sacrificed bull was found among the material blocking the door, showing that the dead woman received the divine honours traditionally accorded by the Minoans to their royal dead. More evidence for this comes from the representations on the sarcophagus from Hagia Triada.

The Minoan goddess continued to be worshipped in small house shrines during the Post-Palace Period. In the so-called Shrine of the Double Axes at Knosos, the floor was strewn with pebbles; placed on a bench at the back of the room were horns of consecration, figurines of worshippers and, in the centre, a small figurine of the goddess with arms upraised. Sculpture in this period was concerned almost exclusively with cult subjects. The cylindrical shape given to the clothes of the cult statues from the shrines at Gournia, Gazi, Gortys, Pangalochori, Sachtouria, and Myrsine is in line with the general trend towards simplification and stylization of shapes evident in every field, especially vase painting, in this final phase of Minoan art, now in its decline.

CYPRIOT CIVILIZATION IN THE MYCENAEAN PERIOD

Geographical Position and Cultural Development

Although Cyprus is only the third largest island of the Mediterranean (after Sicily and Sardinia), its role in history has always been of great importance. Its civilization may not have been as dazzling as that of Crete, but it has an equally long history. For thousands of years, two great civilizations, one of Aegean and one of Eastern origin, existed side by side and in close contact on this island, which covers an area of only 9,251 square kilometres.

Although the sea formed the natural defences of the island and secured her independence, Cyprus could not avoid being within view of her neighbours: her northern shores are a mere 68 kilometres distant from the mountains on the opposite coast, while the promontory of Hagios Andreas, the most easterly point of the island, is only 121 kilometres from Syria. On the other hand, the southern shores of the island are 422 kilometres distant from Egypt and 400 kilometres from Rhodes, while Athens is 800 kilometres away. So, geographically, Cyprus belongs to the farthest end of the Eastern Mediterranean basin, and it is not surprising that over a period of several millennia she developed close commercial links with her neighbours and received their cultural influences.

What is surprising is that, after assimilating these influences, Cyprus managed to defy the laws of geography, to find her way to the West by forging indissoluble links with the Hellenic world, and to become culturally a part of it from the Late Bronze Age to this day. Steadfastly attached to the Greek world, while at the same time always open to Eastern influences, Cyprus developed a peculiarly distinct civilization, a blend of Hellenic and Eastern cultures, in which elements from both were assimilated and combined with boldness and imagination to give Cyprus her special character in the history of the Eastern Mediterranean.

Our picture of Cypriot civilization in the Prehistoric Period is at present incomplete because, despite intensive archaeological activity during the last forty years, the excavations have not yet covered settlements from every period of the island's history. In the main, only cemeteries have been studied. Moreover, the so-called Cypro-Minoan script, potentially an important source for our knowledge of the period, has not yet been deciphered. The only literary sources we have are indirect and often not fully understood references to Cyprus on a few Eastern texts dated between the 18th and 11th centuries B.C.

We can, however, form a general idea of the life on prehistoric Cyprus. The fertile central plain of Mesaoria, between the mountain ranges of Troodos (1,953 m.) and Pentadaktylos (1,019 m.), has been the centre of the agricultural life of the island from times immemorial. It had the same fertile soil and enjoyed the same favourable climate as the plain of Phaistos in Crete. Cereals as well as a great variety of vegetables and fruits were grown in abundance. The mountain sides were covered with trees: chiefly pine, cedar, cypresses, all of which provided good timber for ship-building. Strabo tells us that in his time her forests were impenetrable and stretched down to the edges of the plains.

There are small fertile valleys surrounded by low tree-clad hills. It was on these hills, close to springs, that large neolithic settlements were founded in the 6th millennium B.C. In the last phase of the Neolithic Period, contact was made for the first time with the peoples on the shores of the mainland opposite. Blades made of obsidian—a stone not found in Cyprus—have been found among the remains of the Neolithic settlements.

The Appearance of Bronze

Around 3000 B.C. the neolithic sites were abandoned, perhaps as a result of some natural disaster. The appearance and increasing use of bronze on the island during the subsequent period of about five centuries was the signal for new and rapid development. This was the so-called Chalcolithic Period, a transitional period between the Neolithic and the Early Bronze Age. Numerous settlements were founded on the island. There was a new pottery style, the "red-on-white" pottery, abstract geometric motifs, and statuettes of clay or steatite, most of them showing the mother goddess. The Chalcolithic Period ended c. 2500 B.C. Two centuries later, c. 2300 B.C., the Early Bronze Age began.

The existence of copper on Cypriot soil ensured the swift development of a flourishing economy, but also caused the great powers of the times to turn covetous eyes upon the island. Syrian and Egyptian records mention taxes (mainly in copper) paid by the Cypriots to the Egyptian Pharaoh or the rulers of Syria, but it is not yet known when these taxes were introduced or what events led up to their imposition.

The appearance of new settlements during the Early Bronze Age shows that there was an increase in the population. Since only cemeteries have been excavated so far, we know very little about the architecture of the period. Our knowledge comes from a single dwelling excavated at Alambra and a few scattered ruins at Ampelikou. These buildings had rectangular rooms with stone foundations and an upper structure of bricks. The roofs must have been flat.

Excavations of various cemeteries have brought to light a variety of finds, on which events of daily life and religious scenes are depicted. The cemeteries are outside the settlements, on the hillsides. The graves are either rock-cut chamber tombs (Hagia Paraskeve Vounous) or natural caves on the edges of plains.

In pottery, the traditional Cypriot shapes faced competition for a short time from a new type of vessel, which appears to have come from southeast Asia Minor. The Cypriot tradition prevailed, however, and by the end of the Bronze Age Cypriot potters were producing an extraordinary

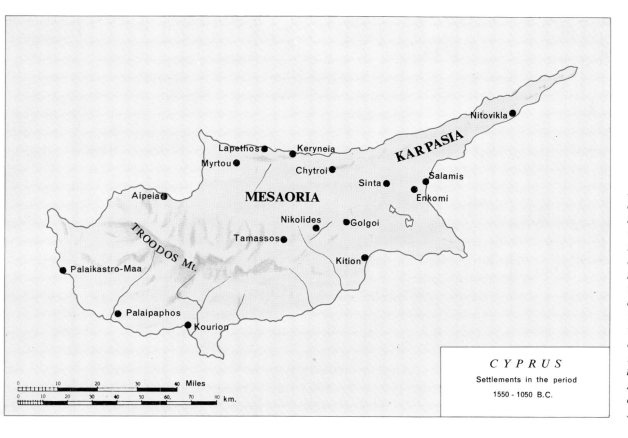

variety of vessels: large complex vessels with rich incised decoration, cups with spouts decorated with moulded birds, ox-heads, and human and animal forms in scenes from daily life.

The tombs of this period contained gold and silver ornaments, necklaces, flat clay figurines with incised decoration and zoomorphic vases, all of which testify to the skill and to the sense of humour of the Cypriot artists. Bronze weapons and tools have also been unearthed, and there are some interesting compositions in clay, such as a representation of a ceremony inside a sanctuary and one showing oxen pulling a plough. The steady evolution of religious beliefs is shown by the clay group from Vounous and the groups from Kotsiates. Among the most recent finds in the necropolis of Kotsiates, a village near Idalion, are two clay models of sanctuaries depicting three *xoana* with ox-heads, fixed to the wall; on the ground is the figure of a woman in front of a large amphora, evidently pouring a libation. The three statues are reminiscent of the three relief figures in the sanctuary at Vounous. A similar model of a sanctuary from the Middle Bronze Age comes from Kalopsida. Apparently, bull worship was practised all over Cyprus, and the sacred symbol of the cult was the triad of figures found in various groups from Vounous, Kotsiates and Kalopsida. These sanctuaries are rather like the sanctuaries of Çatal Hüyük in Asia Minor in spite of the time difference. The Cypriot of the Bronze Age contemplated the cycle of life and death with awe, and on this he based his religious beliefs. Like the later Greeks, he associated life and death with two symbols: the bull and the snake.

The civilization of the Early Bronze Age was more complex than that of the Stone Age. There was a better organized society, and the mining of copper had opened up new cultural and economic horizons. The export of copper to neighbouring countries brought Cyprus into contact with the great peoples of Asia Minor, Syria, and Palestine. The island amassed great wealth and also absorbed many influences from the East. There was now regular trading with all the countries of the Near East and, on a restricted scale, even with Crete. The resulting prosperity aided the development of a sophisticated culture on the island, and this was maintained all through the Bronze Age. The Cypriots welcomed foreign influences, but always succeeded in assimilating them and in preserving the distinctly Cypriot character of their culture.

The Middle Bronze Age

The Middle Bronze Age (2100-1600 B.C.) is not marked by any particular cultural innovations. It is really just the transitional phase between the Early and the Late Bronze Age. The island retained its important position in the Near East, and there are a few hints of the changes which were to come about in the next period.

Various objects of Cretan origin appear during this period. We know that the Cretans of the Middle Bronze Age engaged in trade with Syria, and it is not unlikely that their ships sometimes anchored in the small bays of the north coast of Cyprus.

There are remains of Cypriot architecture of the Middle Bronze Age at Kalopsida, in the eastern part of the island, where a house has been unearthed. It has eleven rectangular rooms arranged along the three sides of a central court. There are more numerous remains of military architecture from the last part of this period. The uneasy atmosphere which prevailed in the Eastern Mediterranean prompted the inhabitants of the island to construct fortifications along

A hunting scene engraved on the long side of an ivory pyxis from Enkomi: panic-stricken animals gallop along wildly; hunters, some on foot, some riding in a chariot, pursue the animals, shooting arrows after them; a large bird flies above the richly adorned horses

the northern shores. The most important is the fortification wall at Kreni, near Keryneia, which was stoutly built with large stones and reinforced with towers. Today it is preserved up to a height of 2 m. More fortifications have been unearthed at Nikoledes, in the middle of the island, and at Nitovikla. The latter shows some eastern influence and is similar to the Boğazköy fortifications.

Grave architecture had by now become more compact; many burial chambers (e.g. at Lapethos, and Karmi) are arranged around a common corridor. The earliest known grave *stele* from Cyprus comes from this period: a somewhat clumsily rendered human form cut into the wall of the *dromos* of a tomb (possibly influenced by Egyptian prototypes). Other types of tomb unearthed at Palaioskoutella near Nitovikla are similar to tombs found in Syria and Palestine, and this perhaps suggests that the Hyksos settled in the eastern part of Cyprus after the 17th century B.C.

While the towns on the northern coast of the island suffered a steady decline, the towns in the south and east, which traded with Syria and Palestine, became increasingly prosperous. Large settlements here developed into proper towns with harbours and important outlying districts. Kition and Enkomi, for example, which were only small agricultural settlements in the Early Bronze Age, developed swiftly after the 17th century B.C.

Although there was some contact with Minoan Crete at the beginning of the Middle Bronze Age, there are no traces of Cretan influence on Cypriot art. Very few fragments of Cypriot vessels have been found on Crete, or Minoan ones on Cyprus, which makes it unlikely that there was close contact between the two islands. By contrast, a great number of Cypriot vessels have been unearthed in Syria, Palestine, and Cilicia; there was evidently regular contact with these countries; products from Syria and Palestine came to Cyprus in great abundance towards the end of the period.

Art continued to find bold and imaginative expression. Pottery styles became more ambitious, linear motifs were painted on a white background, and care was taken to improve both the quality and the decoration of the vessels. Moulded human or animal forms or those of fantastic creatures were often added to the vessels.

However, Cypriot civilization was not yet autonomous. This was a period of change and development that prepared the way for the great civilization of the Late Bronze Age which was to follow.

Late Bronze Age: The Culminating Period

The brightest and most creative period of prehistoric Cyprus was the Late Bronze Age, 1550-1050 B.C. In these five centuries, Cyprus became a most important political and cultural centre in the Eastern Mediterranean. But the main event in this period, the one which has determined the subsequent history of the island to this day, was her attachment to the Mycenaean way of life. From then on, she became a most vigorous outpost of Hellenism in the Eastern Mediterranean.

The terrible eruption of the volcano on Thera, which resulted in the destruction of Minoan civilization on Crete, took place some time at the beginning of this period. At the first International Conference on the "Volcano of Thera" in 1969, it was claimed that the tidal wave which swept away the coastal cities of Crete reached the Nile Delta and the Syro-Palestinian shores and must also have affected Cyprus. According to one theory, the group burials on the northern

and a hound runs by the side of the chariot; a wounded bull turns to face his horns towards the pursuers. Hunting scenes, like all scenes of combat, were favourite subjects in Mycenaean art. (British Museum, London)

shores of the island, the steady decline of the towns in that region, and the founding of towns in the south and east coasts after 1500 B.C. are all a consequence of that same volcanic eruption which caused devastating destruction on Crete and Thera.

The destruction of the important Minoan centres around 1500 B.C. was an important landmark in the history of Cyprus during the Late Bronze Age. The Mycenaeans, who had now developed their own flourishing civilization, began to displace the Minoans and to rob them of their commercial supremacy in the Eastern Mediterranean. Cyprus was ideally situated as their advanced base in the East. Mycenaean merchants established themselves in the large centres on the south and east coasts and began to trade with the Syro-Palestinian coast and with Egypt. The existence of copper on the island must have been an added attraction, and Cyprus soon became the main centre of Mycenaean culture and commerce in the Near East.

The relations between the island and the Mycenaeans in the 14th and 13th centuries B.C. are something of a mystery. Did Mycenaeans establish colonies on Cyprus from 1400 B.C. onwards, or did they simply trade with the island? Were the Mycenaean products, particularly the great number of vases which have been found in Cyprus, imported from Greece? The most recent excavations at Enkomi and elsewhere have failed to produce evidence of Mycenaean colonization between the 14th and 13th centuries B.C. The civilization retained its distinctly Cypriot character until the end of the 13th century B.C., when certain important changes definitely indicate that Mycenaean colonists settled on Cyprus around 1230 B.C. Although there is no direct evidence anywhere of violent destruction, there are signs that some Cypriot towns were abandoned as a result of some natural disaster, perhaps the terrible droughts that afflicted many countries in the Eastern Mediterranean. A layer of

clay covers the abandoned dwelling area at Kition. Both Kition and Enkomi were rebuilt on a new plan and in a different architectural style. Cyclopean walls with ramparts and huge gateways were also constructed at this period.

Finds of Mycenaean vessels in the style which was popular in the Argolid about the end of the 13th century B.C. suggest Achaian establishment on the island. It was precisely at this period that the large centres in the Peloponnesos, like Mycenae and Pylos, were suffering steady decline, and the Achaians, seeking new places to settle, began to emigrate to the islands of the Aegean and to Cyprus (Enkomi, Kition, Palaikastro-Maa, Sinda, Palaipaphos). Certain religious customs of this period also testify to the arrival of Achaian colonists on the island.

After 1230 B.C., Cyprus made rapid progress in every sphere in spite of a short period of disturbance and upheaval, during which many centres were destroyed in raids by the "Peoples of the Sea", as the invaders were called in Egyptian texts. Enkomi, Kition, and other cities in the centre of the island were destroyed, as was Ugarit on the Syrian coast opposite. The kings of Ugarit and Alasia (the name by which Cyprus is referred to in the Eastern texts) were fully aware of the menace presented by the "Peoples of the Sea". In their correspondence, engraved on clay tablets which have been found at Ugarit, the king of Cyprus warns his ally, evidently a king on the Syrian coast opposite, that the enemy fleet has made its appearance. He then inquires about the position of his ally's army and armaments, and advises him to fortify his cities, collect his army and weapons together, and prepare to meet the enemy. The king of Ugarit replies: "Father, the enemy fleets have arrived and burnt our cities. Our country has been destroyed by the seven ships of the enemy." This correspondence shows that there was an alliance between Cyprus and Syria and gives a first-hand account of the dramatic upheavals in the Eastern

Mediterranean caused by the raids of the "Peoples of the Sea". They were eventually defeated by Pharaoh Rameses III in 1191 B.C. on the borders of Phoenicia.

It was in this turbulent period, about the end of the 13th century B.C., that the first recorded naval battle in history took place; it was between the Hittites and the Cypriots. The tablet which refers to the battle was found at Boğazköy in 1963; it is a very important historical document. The Hittite king, Shuppiluliumash II, writes: "...and the ships of Alasia (Cyprus) stopped before the foreign ships three times in the middle of the sea. And I completely wiped them out ... I captured all the ships, and, in the middle of the sea, I set fire to them. A great enemy force from the country Alasia came against me, and I completely vanquished them. And I ordered Alasia to pay me tribute..." This tribute took the form of gold and copper. The Hittite text is our only source of information about this event, about which at any rate there has been no confirmation so far from any other source.

After the destruction of Ugarit during the 12th century B.C., refugees from the Syro-Palestinian coast began to arrive in Cyprus and to settle there, and at the same time more Achaian colonists arrived from Greece. Life revived in the Cypriot towns. Commerce flourished, though still not to the same degree as before, and wealth accumulated on the island. In 1075 B.C., however, there was another great disaster; the archaeological evidence suggests that this time it was an earthquake. The inhabitants of Enkomi gradually began to abandon their city and to settle in the coastal town of Salamis, which was to play an important role in historical times. By 1050 B.C., Enkomi was completely deserted. At Kition, the dwellings were repaired, and life continued as before. But in 1000 B.C., this city was abandoned too, and its port disappeared, perhaps silting up.

The Late Bronze Age ended c. 1050 B.C. In spite of the various upheavals and disasters during that period, Cyprus made great progress in every sphere of activity. The soil was fertile, and the land was endowed with important natural resources. The blend of Eastern and Aegean cultures on the island produced a peculiarly multiform and complex civilization whose vigour was evident in every branch of art.

There are large gaps in our knowledge of the cultural history of the island, because the only Late Bronze Age centre which has so far been properly excavated is Enkomi. Our information about public and private life, therefore, is based mainly on the remains which have been unearthed at this site and on sporadic finds from other towns.

Architecture

Very few buildings from the period before the Achaian settlement have been discovered. The remains excavated at Enkomi (rebuilt by the Achaians after 1230 B.C.) were built over the ruins of older dwellings. This city—like Kition, Sinda, Kourion, and Palaikastro—was fortified with a Cyclopean wall, ramparts, and strong gates. At Kition and Enkomi, the base of the walls consisted of layers of bricks on a strong base formed by two courses of large monolithic stones. The ramparts were rectangular and built of ashlar stones. The width of one of the ramparts at Kition is 18 m. It is preserved today up to a considerable height.

Architecture and town-planning at Enkomi made great progress during the last phase of the Late Bronze Age. The area of the town has been precisely determined; it stretches 400 m. from north to south, 350 m. from east to west. Intersecting roads, 3 m. wide, connect the sectors of the city with each other and lead to the gates in the walls. The city was built on an amazingly regular plan. The houses, like those at Kition, have the shape of a Π and a small courtyard in front. In the northern part of the city, the houses were built in proper "blocks". The seven roads which separate them are 3 m. wide and 32 m. apart. They all meet a bigger road which runs from south to north and ends at the gate in the north wall. At the crossroads of the two main roads in the centre of the city, there is a paved square surrounded by public buildings. One of these buildings is built with ashlar blocks, reminiscent of classical Greek architecture. The largest house, perhaps the palace, has a wide and imposing façade with an entrance and wide windows, and is built of large ashlar stones. Although its basic shape is that of the Eastern tripartite house, it presents some of the features of a Mycenaean megaron. There are indications that the houses had an upper storey.

Two sanctuaries have also been unearthed at Enkomi. One is an imitation of a Greak sanctuary. It has the anteroom in the main part of the sanctuary and a large porous stone pillar in the middle to support the roof. Close to the base of the pillar is a well. The other is a large sanctuary found at Kition during recent excavations. The outer wall is built of large ashlar blocks, and the building is on the same plan as the sanctuary of the horned god at Enkomi. In the shrine there was a rectangular altar and, by its side, the horns of consecration, the symbol of Aegean religion. This altar is dated to about 1200 B.C., i.e. after the Achaians had settled in the city. A large amount of copper slag was found at Enkomi and Kition, and copper workshops were unearthed in the northern sections of these two towns built close to the wall so that the eastern and southern winds would disperse the dangerous fumes.

Towards the end of the Bronze Age, the burial customs on the island showed marked Mycenaean influence. In the cemeteries at Kourion (Kalorizike), Lapethos, and Salamis, tombs with long straight *dromoi* were found cut into the soft rock. An 11th century tomb at Kalorizike contained the head of a gold sceptre and the incinerated remains of a woman placed inside an amphora. The custom of cremation, previously unknown in Cyprus, had evidently been introduced by the Achaian colonists.

Pottery

The Cypriot potters of the Late Bronze Age must have been very imaginative, for they produced an enormous number and variety of vessels. The numerous pottery finds on the island have enabled scholars to determine cultural influences and the countries which were in contact with Cyprus during this period.

The export of copper to the countries of the Near East

led to the establishment of close commercial and cultural links between Cyprus and her neighbours. The import of foreign works of art had an effect on native production. Artists, inspired by foreign types of vessels, produced new vessels of their own, decorated with an eye for detail and lively imagination. *Oinochoai* (vessels for dipping wine from the krater and pouring it into the drinking-cups) with a metallic appearance, cups with a white surface and painted designs, relief decoration, are all reminiscent of the skilfully wrought jewellery of the East and are excellent examples of Cypriot work in the middle of the 16th century B.C.

Cyprus had particularly close trade links with Egypt. Cypriot vessels containing opium dissolved in honey were exported in great quantities to the Nile region, and Egyptian exports to Cyprus included gold, alabaster, glass, and various faience objects. From Palestine there came vessels with bichrome decoration depicting birds and fishes.

The two centuries of Mycenaean presence were a period of great economic and cultural development. Thousands of Mycenaean vessels dated to the period between 1400 B.C. and 1230 B.C. have appeared and keep appearing both on Cyprus and on the Syro-Palestinian coast. It is difficult to

Cypriot craftsmen produced a special type of ivory work, a blend of Aegean and Eastern styles. Below: two sides of a mirror

handle from Enkomi. Left: a warrior fights with a winged griffin. Right: a lion attacks a bull. (British Museum, London)

judge whether these were imported from Greece or produced on the island. The problem, in other words, is to determine whether the Mycenaeans originally came to Cyprus as merchants to set up trade contacts or whether they arrived with the intention of establishing colonies.

On the basis of the archaeological evidence, two theories have been put forward. According to one, the Mycenaean merchants who established themselves in cities on the south and east coasts were accompanied by craftsmen from Greece who found employment in the local workshops and produced various art objects, chiefly pottery. They used Mycenaean techniques although they were influenced to some degree by Eastern products. So, a new mixed style of pottery was created, the so-called Cypro-Mycenaean style.

According to the second theory, all the Mycenaean vases were imported from Greece. Their similarity to Cypriot and Eastern vessels is accounted for by the fact that the potters and vase-painters of the Peloponnesos adapted their work to suit the demands of the Cypriot market. This theory is at present being tested with the help of chemical analysis.

For the time being, however, our knowledge must be confined to conclusions based on archaeological evidence. Most of the Mycenaean vessels found on Cyprus seem to have been produced on the spot by Mycenaean craftsmen who imitated the style and technique of Helladic vessels. Influence from native production and some deference to Eastern tastes affected the development of the art of the emigré Mycenaean craftsmen. Much the same thing seems to have happened on Rhodes in the 8th and 7th centuries, when Phoenician craftsmen there produced perfume-holders of faience which were used by Phoenician merchants for carrying perfume from the East.

The earliest example of a Cypro-Mycenaean vase is the wide-mouthed *krater* (mixing-bowl), which rarely appears in Greece after 1400 B.C. Its appearance coincides with that of the first specimens of the pictorial style created, according to some scholars, by the first Mycenaean craftsmen who settled in Cyprus. The whole surface of the vessel is divided into vertical bands symmetrically decorated with geometric patterns and painted representations. The subjects in the early period are birds, fish, octopuses, bulls, chariots, as well as human figures who appear along with the animals and chariots. On a krater from Kourion there is a representation of women watching a chariot race. There are also some mythological subjects; on a krater from Enkomi the artist has tried to depict a Homeric scene: Zeus holding the scales of Destiny in front of the warriors who are setting out to battle.

Bulls are a favourite subject in Cypro-Mycenaean art. The picture of bulls on a krater from Enkomi is reminiscent of Aegean representations of this subject. On one side, the bulls are galloping along; on the other side, they stand quietly allowing the herdsmen to stroke them (cf. the gold cups from Vapheio in the Peloponnesos).

General view of prehistoric Enkomi in eastern Cyprus. This site was unearthed only in the last few years. The town was well-planned—note the network of intersecting roads. Copper work-shops were found here, where once copper ore from Mt. Troodos was converted into copper ingots to be loaded on to ships for export.

At the beginning of the 14th century, the pictorial subjects become purely decorative, and various filling ornaments are used to cover almost the whole surface of the vase. This is known as the Tel-el-Amarna style after the Egyptian city of that name (destroyed in 1375 B.C.), where many painted vessels were found.

From the middle to the end of the 14th century B.C., the decorative element prevails in vase-painting. Compound groups with chariots give way to simpler scenes. The bodies of bulls, birds, and other animals are filled with small lines or dots, so that the picture has the effect of weaving or embroidery. This style continued for a whole century to 1230 B.C. Some fine vessels in this technique found in Cyprus and in the town of Ugarit are thought to be the work of a single artist, the so-called "Bull protome painter".

The prevailing style in the middle of the 13th century is typified in the work of the "swallow painter". Although the subjects have become simplified, the painter manages to endow his work with verve and a sense of movement and to decorate the surface of the vase with great charm.

The Cypro-Mycenaean style of pottery, which had survived for two centuries, now passed into a period of decline. In its last phase, it imitated the engraved patterns on ivory objects. There are a few fine examples of this work in which the rendering of the details of the shapes is successfully achieved by the alternating of fine and thick lines. The bodies of the bulls, including leg muscles and other details, are

Clay model of a sanctuary found in 1970 in the village of Kotsiates. It shows three forms with ox heads and a female figure standing before a large amphora. (Cyprus Museum, Nicosia)

The Achaians brought their Creto-Mycenaean religion with them to Cyprus. Above: a country shrine at Myrtou contained this monumental altar, built of hewn stones and crowned by the Aegean religious symbol of horns of consecration.

rendered in a very skilfully realistic manner. In general, however, Cypro-Mycenaean pottery steadily degenerated and finally disappeared altogether around the end of the 13th century B.C.

In the 12th century B.C., a second wave of Achaian colonists arrived in Cyprus and introduced a new pottery style, the granary style, in which the decoration consisted of horizontal wavy lines. Links between Cyprus and Crete also became closer during the last years of the Late Bronze Age, and the shapes of Cypriot vessels were influenced by both Late Minoan and Eastern pottery.

Pottery was not the only product of Cypro-Mycenaean art in the 14th and 13th centuries B.C. At Enkomi and Kition, specimens have been found of metal objects with inlay decoration, enamelwork, goldwork, and seal engraving. One of the finest metal vessels is a silver cup with inlaid gold and niello decoration found in a 14th century B.C. grave at Enkomi. It is similar to the famous cup from Dendra in the Peloponnesos.

A unique vessel found at Kition is a faience *rhyton*, (vase in the shape of a funnel or cone) with its surface covered by a thick layer of blue enamel. The decoration is divided into three zones: the first contains two galloping bulls and a goat; the second, scenes of the hunting of wild bulls; and the third, running spirals. The bodies of the animals are either painted yellow or shown by inlaid red enamel. This vessel, dated to the 13th century B.C., is a good illustration of the different influences which affected Cypriot work. The shape is clearly Aegean, but the representations are both Aegean and Eastern in character, while the composite enamel technique is probably of Egyptian origin.

Gold working too produced some fine examples of mixed Aegean and Eastern work. Many gold diadems with embossed decoration found in graves have both Eastern and Aegean decorative subjects: sphinxes, lions, goats, human heads, figure-of-eight shields, etc. Necklaces too have been found with beads in the shape of figure-of-eight shields, and also pendants in the shape of pomegranates with granulated decoration and rings.

Seal-engraving also shows both Aegean and Eastern influence, proving that Aegean art did not become familiar to the Cypriots only through the import of products, but had deeper roots on the island. The representations of Mycenaean youths and other Aegean subjects on cylinder seals (like the one from Enkomi) were the work of Mycenaean artists established on Cyprus. Other representations show Eastern influence or are a mixture of the two styles.

Ivory carving was another art practised by Cypriot artists in the last phase of the Late Bronze Age. The great number and individuality of the ivory products shows that they were made in native workshops. The blending of Eastern and Aegean influences is particularly evident here. (A school of ivory carving had been operating in northern Syria from the 15th century B.C.). Examples of Cypriot work are a mirror handle and a *pyxis* (jewellery box) from Enkomi and a mirror handle from Palaipaphos.

Two bronze statuettes found at Enkomi are important both as works of art and as evidence for the import of Mycenaean religious beliefs and customs. One of the statues, found in the town sanctuary, shows a horned god, standing upright, wearing a kilt and a sheepskin conical helmet with large horns. He is the Arkadian "Horned Apollo" (*Apollon Keraiates*). This solid bronze statuette, 0.55 m. high, is the largest found from this period. The beautiful features and smile of the god are to some extent the forerunners of Archaic Greek sculpture. In a second and later sanctuary at Enkomi, there was another bronze statue of a horned and bearded god. He holds a spear in his right hand and a shield in his left. He stands on a base which has the shape of a copper ingot, and he is therefore thought to be the protector of this metal on Cyprus.

Copper

The copper mines were the chief source of wealth on Cyprus and ensured the swift political and cultural development of the island. After the Hyksos had been driven out of Egypt, a new period of peace began in the Eastern Mediterranean—the *Pax Aegyptiaca*—and, on Cyprus, conditions became favourable for progress in both public and private life. Up to that time, settlements had been built on the northern shores, where they were protected by the natural barrier of the mountain ranges. However, now that peace reigned, the settlements in the north gradually declined in importance. From the end of the Middle Bronze Age, new centres began to develop on the south and east coasts, and it was from here that the export of copper, the chief commercial activity of the island, was organized. The change in the position of the settlements was to have a great effect on the evolution of social institutions. The commercial centres with natural harbours developed into large towns: Enkomi, Kition, Palaipaphos. In the centre of the island, industrial areas grew up where copper ore was mined.

The chief sources of copper lay in the foothills of the Troodos range of mountains. A Hittite tablet refers to copper in the "Takata" mountain, and this has been identified with Mt. Troodos. On tablets from Egypt and Ugarit, on the other hand, Cyprus is called the "copper country". It appears

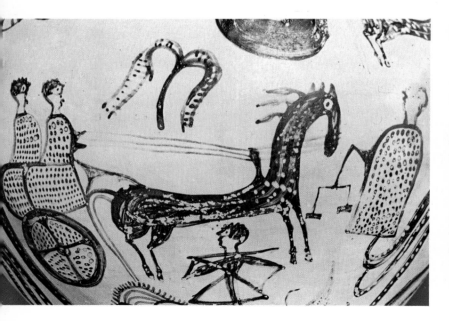

Mycenaean painted pottery styles were imported into Cyprus in the middle of the fourteenth century B.C. by craftsmen who settled in the island along with Mycenaean merchants. Above, left: detail from painting on a Cypro-Mycenaean amphoroid krater *that was found in a tomb at Enkomi: a chariot with two charioteers and a figure holding scales. Right: a bull and a goat painted on a* krater *from Enkomi. (Cyprus Museum, Nicosia)*

from the archaeological evidence that the ore was not worked on the spot, but sent by pack animal to the large centres on the east and south coasts. This is proved by the existence of special workshops in the northern sector of Enkomi and the copper slag found at Kition. In smelting the ore, the craftsmen gave the copper the shape of ingots, and it was in this form that it was loaded onto ships for export. The ingots found at Enkomi are dated to the 12th century B.C. A shipwreck recently found on the seabed off the southern shores of Asia Minor was carrying Cypriot copper ingots. Such ingots must also have been exported in preceding centuries, since they are mentioned in the correspondence between Pharaoh Akhenaton and the king of Alasia on Tel-el-Amarna tablets (14th century B.C.). Perhaps the ingots found in the palace of Zakros on Crete came from Cyprus too.

Economic Life

The mining and export of copper was not the only aspect of economic activity on Cyprus. Farming too played an important part in the economic life of the island and was a stable source of wealth. Archaeological evidence shows that the Late Bronze Age was a most flourishing and prosperous period. The island had become an international commercial centre. Ships from all over the Mediterranean visited her harbours to pick up cargoes of copper and, since the economy was based on exchange of goods, the Cypriot market was flooded with many valuable products: gold, precious stones, ivory, alabaster, glass, and faience objects.

There was regular contact with the Syro-Palestinian coast throughout the Late Bronze Age. It is not certain whether there were trade links with Cilicia, but many scholars believe that Cyprus traded with Egypt through Ugarit.

There was a great increase in trade with the Aegean after 1400 B.C. The Hellenization of the island by the Mycenaeans took place in a peaceful manner. The island became a hive of activity: there were prosperous cities, busy harbours, and a multitude of workshops. There were highly specialized craftsmen: potters, goldsmiths, silversmiths, enamel-workers, coppersmiths, and seal engravers. However many craftsmen may have come from Greece or the East, the large scale production of works of art on the island shows that the Cypriots themselves were skilled and specialized craftsmen, while the ruins of Enkomi suggest that they were also able builders and town-planners.

Religion

In the Chalcolithic Age, the Cypriots worshipped a female deity. Statuettes from this period, found at Erimi, show her as the Mother Goddess, the goddess of fertility. The idea of fertility is also personified in zoomorphic representations of the deity: the snake, which represents its chthonic nature, and the bull, which symbolizes fertilization. Later, there are manifest influences from Creto-Mycenaean religion, testifying to the colonization of the island by

Scenes from daily life are shown on this famous rhyton *from Kition. There are three zones of decoration on the enamelled surface: the first shows galloping bulls and a goat; the second, a hunting scene; and the third, spirals. (Cyprus Museum, Nicosia)*

Two Cypriot cult statues. Left: a clay figurine from Enkomi representing the goddess of fertility. Right: solid bronze statue of the horned god, Apollon Keraiates of Arkadia, wearing a *belt round his waist and a conical cap on his head; this is the largest specimen (55 cm.) of metal-work from the Mycenaean period in Cyprus. (Cyprus Museum, Nicosia)*

Achaians from the Peloponnesos. An inscription from Pyla near Larnax shows that the worship of the Arkadian "Horned Apollo" continued on the island until the 4th century B.C. Ox-heads, used as masks during the sacred ritual, were found around the statue of the god. The multitude of cups found in the same sanctuary must also have been used during ceremonies there. The stone column which supported the roof in one of the sanctuaries at Enkomi was perhaps connected with the Creto-Mycenaean cult of the "sacred pillar". A 4th century B.C. inscription from Tamassos refers to the cult of Apollo Alasiotas, perhaps a later form of the god of Alasia (Cyprus) in the Late Bronze Age.

There is more evidence of Creto-Mycenaean cults in other parts of the island. A country shrine near Myrtou contained a monumental altar of ashlar stones crowned by horns of consecration. A similar religious symbol has recently been found close to the built altar in the sacred precinct at Kition. The second bronze statue of the god which was found at Enkomi stood on a base in the shape of a copper ingot. This god has, therefore, been called the divine protector of this metal on Cyprus; he must have been the chief symbol of the Cypriot religion, since the production of copper was the source of the island's prosperity.

Administrative System

Since we cannot read the Cypriot texts, we have no information about the administration of Cypriot cities. We know that Late Bronze Age Cyprus was ruled by kings, since foreign monarchs often addressed themselves to the rulers of Cypriot towns, calling them sometimes "father", sometimes "brother". The uniformity of level in the material civilization of the Cypriot cities shows that these kings were on friendly terms with one another. Besides, this was essential to the successful and profitable mining and export of copper.

A mid-11th century B.C. grave at Kourion contained the head of a golden sceptre, which terminated in a ball with two eagles and had inlay enamel decoration. This must surely have belonged to the "sceptre-bearing" king of Kourion.

According to an Egyptian text, there was a queen called Hativa on Cyprus in 1085 B.C. A certain Ben Amon, says the text, travelled to Byblos to arrange the sale of timber. After many adventures, he came to the country of Alasia and, when pursued by a hostile mob of natives, took refuge with Queen Hativa. He communicated with her through an interpreter, for the queen did not know Egyptian.

The Cypriot Script

About 1500 B.C., a system of writing, different from that of the Minoans, appeared in Cyprus. It is called the Cypriot syllabic script, and all attempts to decipher it have so far failed, for there are no bilingual texts to help.

The signs in this script are linear (i.e. combinations of straight and curved lines), and they are found incised on clay tablets, and either incised or painted on vessels. Towards the end of the 2nd millennium, the signs were also engraved on bronze surfaces.

The Cypriot tablets were fired in the usual way and not dried in the sun like the Creto-Mycenaean ones. The engraving seems to have been done with bone tools, many of which have been unearthed during excavations (Enkomi, Kition, Palaipaphos). So far, seventy-six signs and five numerals have been recognized.

The first definite example of Cypriot writing is on part of a rectangular clay tablet of about 1500 B.C. found at Enkomi in 1955. The writing is incised on one face of the tablet in three rows separated by lines. The signs are fairly large and complex and in many respects similar to the signs of Cretan Linear A. There are examples of writing from the period between 1400-1150 B.C. on both vessels and tablets. The famous clay cylinder from Enkomi (13th or 12th century B.C.) has its whole surface covered by writing in 27 rows with divisions between the words.

An interesting example of an Aegean script of Cypro-Minoan character has been found at Ugarit. The signs are similar to the ones on the Enkomi tablets. The discovery of Cypro-Minoan writing on the Syrian coast need cause no surprise. Ugarit was an important commercial centre, and a community of Cypriot merchants was established there.

From the last phase of the Late Bronze Age (1150-1050 B.C.) there is a great variety of objects with writing inscribed on them: bronze bowls, tools, farm equipment, votive rods, Eastern-type cylinder seals, loom weights, and inscribed tablets from Enkomi. In addition, there are the inscriptions on clay vessels. Our knowledge of the script of this period is sketchy, but the great number and variety of inscribed objects and the spread of the script to many parts of the island show that it was in general use towards the end of the Bronze Age.

There have been many attempts to trace the origin of the Cypriot script of the Bronze Age and to decipher it. The successful decipherment of the Cypriot syllabic alphabet of the Classical period during the latter half of the 19th century encouraged philologists to formulate certain theories about the earlier script. The Cypriot syllabic script which appeared on the island around the end of the 8th century B.C., to be replaced in part by the Greek alphabet in the 4th century B.C., was the last form of the Minoan linear system of writing. In 1905, A. Sayce showed that there was a second script on Cyprus similar to the classical one but earlier, and it was this second script which was evidently in use during the Bronze Age.

Two theories have been put forward about the origin and evolution of this script. According to the first, it was the Minoan Linear A script that was the forerunner of the Cypriot Bronze Age script. The Cypro-Minoan, or Cypro-Mycenaean script as Evans called it, was then succeeded by the Cypriot syllabic script of the Classical period. The second theory states that the script was imported into Cyprus from mainland Greece during the period of Achaian colonization c. 1230 B.C. However, the archaeological evidence (e.g. the 16th century tablet from Enkomi with writing similar to Linear A) proves that the Cypriot script must be earlier than the Mycenaean colonization.

It has been suggested recently that since there is no archaeological evidence for direct links between Cyprus and Crete, the Cypriots must have learnt the script from Minoan merchants who had settled in the commercial centres on the Syro-Palestinian coast.

The Name "Alasia"

After 1700 B.C. Cyprus was known in the East as the country of copper. It is called *Alasia* on Hittite tablets, in the archives of Mari and Alalakh, in the correspondence with the Pharaoh Akhenaton, on the texts from Ugarit, and perhaps in the Old Testament (if Elisia is in fact to be identified with Alasia). It is doubtful whether the name came from *Alaseïon* in the Peloponnesos, since the Mycenaeans came to Cyprus in the 14th century B.C. Besides, the name *Cyprus* was known to the Achaians, because Linear B tablets mention *Cypriots*. The eastern texts in which the Cypriot king is addressed as "brother" or "father" deal with historical events confirmed by archaeological evidence, such as the invasion by the "Peoples of the Sea" and the devastation of the country.

Because Alasia was known abroad as a place from which copper was exported, Alasia was at first identified with Enkomi, the first large Mycenaean town to be excavated on Cyprus. Copper workshops abounded there, and apparently Enkomi controlled the smelting and export of the metal. Later, however, it was discovered that two other coastal cities, Kition and the city close to the Salt Lake near Larnax, both had extensive copper workshops, so that it is now considered more appropriate to attribute the name Alasia not to a single town but to the whole island.

The Greeks in Cyprus

There were three successive phases of Greek settlement in Cyprus: (1) in the 14th and 13th centuries B.C., when merchants and craftsmen arrived in the coastal cities, (2) at the end of the 13th century B.C., when Greeks colonized the island, and (3) in the middle of the 12th century B.C.

The influence of the newcomers from Greece was always strong and made itself felt in every aspect of life, so that Cyprus not only became completely Hellenized but preserved the Mycenaean tradition throughout her later history. Even when Greece was passing through a period of upheaval during the so-called Dorian invasion, the Mycenaean way of life continued uninterrupted in Cyprus, and the institution of the monarchy was preserved in Cypriot towns until the 4th century B.C.

Mycenaean penetration of the island was entirely peaceful; the Greeks came as colonists, not as invaders. Cypriot religion adopted many elements from Creto-Mycenaean cults. The Cypriot dialect, as it has developed through the centuries, is in many respects similar to the dialect of Arkadia, the region from which the Achaian colonists had come. Cyprus has become a sort of repository of Greek traditions.

In spite of its remote position in the Eastern Mediterranean, far distant from Metropolitan Greece, surrounded by foreign peoples, and close to the powerful civilizations of the East, Cyprus has remained a Greek island. Successive invasions throughout her history have not been able to destroy her deeply rooted Greek character, which has persisted on Cyprus from the 14th century B.C. to the present day.

Greek legends have retained the memory of the coloni-

zation of Cyprus by the Achaians after the Trojan War. Myths are not always reliable. Sometimes they contain a kernel of historical truth, sometimes they are no more than stories made up after the event to serve some political purpose. Some of the legends concerning the colonization of Cyprus by the Achaians, however, have recently received striking confirmation, e.g. the legend according to which Salamis on the eastern coast of Cyprus was founded by Teukros, son of Telamon, king of the island of Salamis. Isokrates says that "Teukros arrived on Cyprus, colonized Salamis, naming it after his native island, and begat the line of kings who rule Cyprus now." Aischylos in the *Persai* refers to the island of Salamis in the Saronic gulf as the "mother-island" of Salamis,

Cypro-Mycenaean metal-working (gold-working, inlay decoration on various metallic objects, seal engraving) made great progress during the 14th and 13th centuries B.C. Below, this page head of a gold sceptre from Kourion; the top of the sphere ter-

the town on Cyprus. Pindar, referring to Cyprus, says, "And Teukros, son of Telamon, lives there." The scholiast of Pindar adds, "Teukros came to Salamis after the sack of Troy, and having been suspected by Telamon of being responsible for the death of Aias, he fled to Cyprus, which he colonized and ruled." When, thirty years ago, the Mycenaean city of Enkomi, two kilometres southwest of Salamis, was unearthed, it was generally believed that the legend referred to the colonization of Enkomi by Teukros and the Achaians at the end of the 13th century B.C. Recent excavations at Salamis, however, have shown that Salamis was founded at the beginning of the 11th century B.C., when Enkomi was beginning to decline. The pottery of this period shows

Eastern influence, and this tallies with a legend mentioned by Virgil, that Teukros, before settling at Salamis, went to Sidon and requested the aid of King Belos: "and I well remember Teukros who came to Sidon when he was exiled from his country and sought a new kingdom with the aid of Belos, who at that time held rich Cyprus under his glorious sovereignty" (*Aeneid*).

At Kourion where, according to Herodotos, there was a colony of Argives, excavations have shown that Achaian colonists settled there and introduced pottery styles and burial customs from Mycenaean Greece. Particularly interesting is the legend quoted by Pausanias which attributes the founding of Paphos to Arkadian settlers: "Agapenor com-

minates in two eagles whose bodies have scaly decoration in the cloisonné technique. This page, top row: silver cup from Enkomi with semi-globular body and wish-bone handle, decorated with ox-heads, lotus flowers, and rosettes in gold and niello.

Right: square four-legged bronze support decorated with bulls in relief. Below: gold diadem from Enkomi, made of an oblong sheet of gold decorated with two rows of winged sphinxes in repoussé. (Cyprus Museum, Nicosia)

manded the Arkadians at Troy. After the fall of Troy, the storm that broke on the Greeks as they sailed for home carried Agapenor and his Arkadian fleet to Cyprus, where Agapenor founded Paphos and built the sanctuary of Aphrodite at Palaipaphos." The legend confirms what is known of Kinyras, king of Paphos and priest of the temple of Aphrodite, who lived at the time of the Trojan War. According to tradition, Agapenor succeeded in expelling Kinyras and in becoming ruler of Palaipaphos. Excavations there have unearthed many finds from the 12th century B.C.

The links between Cyprus and Arkadia are proved by the similarity of the Arkadian and the ancient Cypriot dialects. Recent excavations on the coast at Paphos, at a site called Palaikastro-Maa, have revealed a small town founded by Achaian colonists at the end of the 13th century B.C. This seems to have been the first settlement of the Achaians before they spread to the rest of the island. Like Enkomi and Kition, the town is fortified by Cyclopean walls. A great deal of pottery of Mycenaean style has been found there.

Some legends attribute the founding of Cypriot cities to other heroes of the Trojan War: Keryneia was founded by Kepheas, Golgoi by the Sikyonian Golgos, Lapethos by the Lakonian Praxandros, and Aipeia by Demophon. In some cases, archaeological finds have not confirmed the veracity of these legends, but more recent findings tend to indicate

that there is some historical truth behind some of these myths. The Achaians perhaps did not found new cities, but preferred to settle in the old ones, which they gradually Hellenized. In any case, the colonization of Cyprus by the Achaians after the Trojan War, which is mentioned in many legends handed down through the Classical Period, was an historical event for which there is now ample archaeological evidence.

The Mycenaean colonization and Hellenization of the island had a profound effect on the life of the Cypriots during historical times. Not only has Cyprus retained her Greek character from the Late Bronze Age to the present day, but she also preserved many elements of Mycenaean civilization long after such elements had disappeared from the rest of the Hellenic world. As late as the 5th century B.C., the king who lived in the palace at Vouni asserted his opposition to the Persian dynast by converting the central part of the palace into a Mycenaean megaron. In the 2nd century A.D., an eminent citizen of Salamis, who was the Gymnasiarch of the city, proudly bore the name Diagoras, son of Teukros. There are many Homeric elements in the modern Cypriot dialect, both in its vocabulary and syntax. The conclusion is that, over a period of more than three millennia, Cyprus managed to retain her Greek character intact—an achievement which cannot be matched by any other area beyond the Aegean.

HIEROGLYPHIC									
LINEAR A									
LINEAR B									
CYPRO-MINOAN									
CLASSICAL CYPRIOTE									

The prehistoric Cypriot script has not yet been deciphered. It is syllabic, but different from the Minoan linear script. Some scholars believe that it developed out of the Minoan, others that it was imported from mainland Greece. Above: table showing the evolution of the signs of the Cypriot script from the hieroglyphic to the syllabic alphabet of the Classical Period.
Below: two tablets from Enkomi inscribed with texts in the Cypriot script; the first is from the 16th century B.C., the second, from the period between 1400 and 1230 B.C. (Cyprus Museum, Nicosia)

THE SUB-MINOAN AND SUB-MYCENAEAN PHASE

The one and one-half centuries (1150-1000 B.C.) between the final years of the Creto-Mycenaean Period and the beginning of the Protogeometric Period are known as the Sub-Mycenaean phase on mainland Greece and as the Sub-Minoan phase on Crete. It is the borderline phase between prehistoric and early historical times.

MAINLAND GREECE

In the Mycenaean world, in spite of the breaking up of the palace kingdoms c. 1130 B.C., the Late Bronze Age culture continued for another century, though there was an evident decline in prosperity and vigour and a need to adapt to changing conditions. With the disappearance of the old social organization and the palace bureaucracies, the scribes who had compiled records of the tribute due to the kings now found themselves unemployed, and their script (Linear B) fell into disuse. There were no more orders for valuable vessels or ornaments made of gold, ivory, and precious stones, and the goldsmiths and engravers could no longer pursue their craft. Decline was inevitable. Architecture suffered too: no more large buildings were constructed, and it was no longer considered necessary to lavish money on monumental fresco decoration.

No doubt the general decline in art, rather than any lack of religious fervour, accounts for the small number of cult figurines of the Mother Goddess found from this period. All the religious representations now had a somewhat flaccid appearance, which was only natural after the disappearance of the monarchy and the public sanctuaries at the palaces.

Burial customs, however, remained basically the same; only where it was absolutely necessary were any changes made. In the more secure districts (Attica, Achaia, Kephalenia, etc.) where, after a period of upheavals, destructions, and migrations, the population now concentrated, extensive cemeteries were built (Kerameikos, Salamis) with cist or simple earth-cut tombs instead of the old costly tholos or chamber tombs used for family burials. This simple type of grave, known in mainland Greece since the Early Bronze Age, led to individual, rather than multiple, burial, though it was also adopted in order to save space at a period when the increase in population was creating problems. Inhumation was by far the most common way of disposing of the dead, but cremation was also practised.

The increasing number of elements of eastern and northern origin which appeared at this period does not necessarily reflect any change in the racial composition of the population, but rather illustrates the readiness of the people to adopt anything which could be put to practical use in their changing way of life. For example, from the time that the pleated chiton became fashionable, bronze and iron fibulae and pins became popular everywhere and began to be regarded as essential accessories. During the same period, iron came into general use. Iron has rightly been called a "democratic metal", for it is a cheap and easily worked material. Most metal products, especially weapons (swords, daggers, spear heads) were still made of bronze, and those that were made of iron were imitations in the new material of earlier Mycenaean types.

Objects made of metal and other precious materials last for generations, and then they decay and disappear. They, therefore, provide little evidence to help construct a picture of cultural evolution. Pottery, on the other hand, which is in everyday use and considered too cheap to be worth collecting, is often preserved intact so that changes in pottery styles provide the best available evidence for the study of cultural changes.

Sub-Mycenaean pottery follows the trends which appeared in the last Mycenaean phase. There is a liking for simplicity and a return to abstract geometric subjects, which had been traditional in Helladic Greece before there was any influence from Minoan naturalism. Motifs from the complex close style also survive, but these have now sadly degenerated and are so carelessly executed that it is often difficult to recognize what they depict. Of the Mycenaean shapes, the stirrup jar, the skyphos, the small amphora, and cups are still produced. Later, lekythoi, jugs, trefoil-lipped oinochoai, and amphorae become more popular. The shapes undergo a gradual transformation. The spherical vessels become slenderer, ellipsoidal, or bi-conical, while gradually the bases become conical.

The decoration of the pottery at the end of the 12th century B.C. (especially of that of the granary style) mainly consists of simple subjects, wavy lines, zig-zags, bands, various linear compositions, hatched triangles, and semicircles, all arranged in patterns which emphasize the shape of the vessel and draw attention to its main parts. The pottery style of the Sub-Mycenaean phase continues without a break until it eventually reaches maturity and perfection in the subsequent Protogeometric Period, when complete harmony of shape and decoration is achieved.

CRETE

In about 1200 B.C., at the time when most of the Mycenaean centres disappeared, disturbances in mainland Greece had their repercussions in distant Crete, changing the distribution of the population and of the settlements. Settlements on the south coast were gradually abandoned, though not necessarily as a result of destruction, while other settlements which had been abandoned earlier after long centuries of flourishing life during Minoan times were now reinhabited.

Minoan civilization preserved its own character intact until about 1130 B.C., when some changes came about that were evidently connected with the destruction of Mycenae on the mainland and the general break-up of the Mycenaean world. A general upheaval caused by the arrival of newcomers on the island (probably only in central Crete) forced the inhabitants, or the newcomers, to flee to new remote settlements, which they founded for greater safety in mountainous regions, e.g. Karphi in the eastern part of central Crete, Kavousi more to the east, and the acropolis of Gortys in the southern part of central Crete.

In this transitional period (from 1150-1000 B.C.), known as the Sub-Minoan phase, non-Cretan elements appear in architecture, pottery, and miniature work. Late Mycenaean pottery styles from the mainland and the Aegean (the Dodecanese and Cyprus) influence or displace native

Minoan styles. There is more substantial evidence for Crete's links with Cyprus in the iron ore and iron weapons which were imported from Cyprus at this period. Imports from the Balkan peninsula and the Adriatic via Greece and the Aegean were pins and fibulae and a type of finger-ring or earring with spiral terminals—a popular type of jewel in Greece and Central Europe.

In spite of all the various foreign influences, the Minoan tradition survived, especially in the sphere of religion. Cult areas, religious symbols, and burial customs all kept their Minoan character. It was a long time before the customs introduced by groups of newcomers or invaders had any real effect on the traditional Minoan way of life. In the end, however, Minoan culture was forced to capitulate, and Crete was absorbed into the wider world of Helladic Greece.

Pottery

The transition from the Late Minoan to the Protogeometric Period is clearly shown in the pottery of the intervening Sub-Minoan phase. At first, there is a determined effort to retain the old Minoan repertoire of shapes and decoration, i.e. the traditional rich style which demands considerable skill on the part of the artist; but this style is now mixed with some elements from the Argive close style. Stirrup jars, pyxides, cups with pouring spouts, flasks, all the old Minoan shapes are decorated with bold designs in this style: rows of triangles and arcs, simple or fringed lines, abaci, and a variety of plant and marine subjects,

all completely stylized and bearing little resemblance to the original forms.

Part of the evidence for the changes which came about in Crete just after the beginning of the final phase of the Minoan Period is the appearance of a non-Minoan pottery style, different both in the shapes used and in their decoration. Many examples of this pottery have been found at Knosos, Karphi, two new sites on the Mesara plain, Phaistos and Gortys, as well as in graves at Phaistos. The style evidently became more and more widespread in central and eastern Crete, influenced the existing Minoan style, and in the end transformed it into Sub-Minoan. Of the new shapes, the krater was of Cypriot origin, while the cup, the skyphos, the kalathos, the belly-handled amphora, the trefoil-lipped oinochoe, and the bird vases were probably Helladic. Decoration was restricted to simple linear designs, particularly wavy lines and triangles, especially on stirrup jars. Often part of the vessel, usually the bottom part, was left unpainted. This, too, was a common feature of Helladic pottery.

In the arrangement of various decorative subjects, the Mycenaean panneled manner may be observed. This continued to be used in the subsequent Protogeometric style and became a distinguishing feature of Cretan Protogeometric pottery.

Pithoi and larnakes (sarcophagi in which the dead were buried) were given painted decoration in the restricted style of the vases. There are many examples of such painted sarcophagi from the Sub-Minoan phase. One of the chamber tombs at Gypsades (Knosos) contained a larnax with wavy

In Crete, the so-called Sub-Minoan phase (1150-1000 B.C.) was a period of decline, and only in religion was Minoan tradition still alive. Above, left: clay model of a sanctuary from Archanes, showing the goddess through the open door. Right: figurine of the Minoan goddess; her bell-shaped dress opens at the front to show her feet, and her hands are raised in the attitude of prayer. The figurine of the goddess was found at Karphi, Lasithi. (Herakleion Museum)

decoration on the body and lid; while burial in an individual larnax was an old Minoan practice, the simple decoration is in the prevailing style of the Sub-Minoan phase. In earlier times, religious subjects and scenes of funerary worship were often painted on the sarcophagi.

Cult Statuettes and Miniature Work

The figure of the benevolent Minoan goddess, with her arms upraised in the traditional attitude of prayer, is the most common statuette found in the sanctuaries of the Sub-Minoan phase. The general decline in art is well illustrated in the gradual degeneration of these figurines, once the finest products of Minoan sculpture, into lifeless objects, which by the end of the Sub-Minoan phase were mass-produced on the potter's wheel.

Large clay statuettes of the Minoan goddess (up to 63-67 cm. high) have been found on the altar of a communal shrine at Karphi on Mt. Dikte. Typologically, they resemble the earlier statuettes from the sanctuary at Gazi (the dove and poppy goddesses). But the latter have symmetrical shapes, greater plasticity in the face, and a more lively expression. The goddesses from Karphi have the same bell-shaped dress, sometimes open at the front to show the feet, which were made separately from the rest of the body. The huge ill-proportioned arms are raised in an attitude of prayer, either vertical or inclining slightly forwards. The face is cold and expressionless. On the head of the goddess is a diadem with her official symbols: birds or a pair of horns.

The Dorians had already arrived in Crete when a minute clay shrine (now in the Herakleion Museum) was made at Archanes. The door is open to reveal the Minoan goddess, her arms raised in prayer, sitting in her circular shrine.

Miniature work in the Sub-Minoan phase was mainly affected by the increasing use of iron, rather than bronze, especially in weapon making, and the import of foreign products. The most common weapon was the single-blade iron knife with bronze nails in the handle, which was introduced from the Eastern Mediterranean, probably via Cyprus. But the earlier types of Cretan weapons continued to be made, though now in the new material. Iron objects, however, are not numerous, and they are usually found, perhaps by coincidence, in areas where cremation was practised. (This custom first appeared in eastern Crete).

For the first time a new article of personal adornment appears: the fibula. There are two types, made of bronze or iron: the violin-shaped and the arched fibula. The arched fibula, which developed directly out of the Central European violin-shaped fibula, was popular in northern Greece and was probably introduced by the newcomers or invaders on the mainland and in the islands. Another new accessory introduced at this period was the pin used to keep the new fashionable chiton round the shoulders.

Very little jewellery was worn at this period. The once dazzling variety of jewels made of gold, semi-precious stones, and glass paste was replaced by cheap clay or steatite jewellery. Even seal-stones, once produced in such abundance on Crete, were now rare, and the few that have been found were evidently used as loom weights. Bronze rings of the old simple type were still made in large quantities; and the newcomers brought with them a new kind of finger-ring or earring which terminated in spirals.

One of the last interesting examples of clay-modelling from the Sub-Minoan phase on Crete is this ceremonial vessel from Karphi, Lasithi, dated in the 11th century B.C. It shows a three-wheeled cart pulled by three bulls. (Herakleion Museum)

363

Linguistic and Ethnic Groups in Prehistoric Greece

FIELDS AND METHODS OF RESEARCH

Ancient Greek, Latin, and Byzantine texts provide much information about what the Greeks from Homer's time onwards knew, or thought they knew, about the Greek tribes of the period before the first millennium B.C. and the other peoples who had settled in Greece and the Aegean before the arrival of the Greeks. There are three schools of thought about this literary evidence: two directly conflicting, and one halfway between them. One school is disposed to accept the information supplied in ancient texts on the grounds that it must echo real legends and memories of the past, so that it gives ready credence to every scrap of information without questioning whether it is genuine or not. The opposing school dismisses it all as the fabrication of later poets, genealogists, and local scholars, so that it refuses to accept even the most weighty testimonies. Only scholars who take the trouble to test the evidence in the various ways that it is customary to check written historical sources succeed in clearing the cluttered ground and in opening up a real channel of communication between ourselves and the witnesses of the past. The information which has come down to us is, alas, extremely scant. Sometimes we know nothing more than that a certain group existed. In other cases, we are told when and where it lived. More detailed information—about its religion, internal organization, or migrations—is rarely forthcoming. Fortunately, the literary evidence is supplemented by the findings of the philologist, the archaeologist, and the student of myth and religion.

Since it was discovered that Greek and many other languages had a common origin, philologists have made great progress in piecing together the grammar and vocabulary of this "mother language" (usually called Indo-European) and in establishing the form which the Greek language must have taken before it began to break up into various dialects. Another broad and important field of research is the study of Greek dialects with the purpose of discovering their origin and determining their mutual relation and the movements of the groups who spoke them. Many theories have been put forward, all conflicting on important points, because there is no basic agreement about the selection, dating, and interpretation of the dialect phenomena. A third field of philological research opened up when it was realized that many Greek words, including names of Greek gods and heroes and place-names in the Greek lands, were remnants of languages which had been spoken before the immigration of the first Greek-speaking tribes. The search gradually widened until all the countries of the Mediterranean, Central Europe, and the East had been ransacked for traces of the linguistic and ethnic groups who lived there before the first historical languages were spoken. In addition, it was realized that the etymologies of the names of certain ethnic groups, gods, and mythical heroes might lead to some conclusions about the origin of, and the affinities between, the groups which used those names.

Archaeological finds have given us a wealth of evidence about civilizations on Greek soil in the Stone and Bronze Ages. Neither these civilizations nor the wide breaks which separate them (indicated by widespread destructions of settlements, retrograde steps in techniques or in life in general, introduction of important innovations) can be automatically linked with any special ethnic group, as is usually the case with languages and dialects. Such a connection is not entirely ruled out, however, and there have been several attempts to establish it by indirect means. Archaeological finds assist in the study of the ethnic and linguistic groups in prehistoric Greece chiefly by throwing light on areas which are not covered by legend or philological research, and by providing a definite chronological framework within which events may be given their proper place and sequence.

The study of myth and religion cannot offer much help where the Stone and Bronze Ages are concerned; only in rare cases is there direct testimony or indirect evidence that a particular myth or cult was associated exclusively with one people or tribe.

THE MEDITERRANEAN SUBSTRATUM

In the ancient Greek legends, the most frequently mentioned pre-Greek peoples are the Pelasgians and the Leleges; less often do we hear of the Karians, the Tyrrhenians, and the Phoenicians; and only very occasionally of the Aones, the Ektenes, the Haimones, the Hyantes, the Kaukones, the Kylikranes, the Temmikes, and others. Philological research has shown that these peoples belonged to at least two linguistic groups, and the etymology of the race-names and of the names of gods and heroes which can be attributed to these peoples enables us to assign them to one group or the other.

During the period from the late 19th century to the years between the two world wars, it was generally believed that all the words of the Greek language, all the names of the gods and heroes worshipped by the Greeks, and all the place-names in Greece and the Aegean which did not have a Greek structure and etymology were the remnants of a linguistic substratum which has been called by turn "Aegean", "Anatolian", and finally "Mediterranean", because traces of it were found first around the Aegean, then in Asia Minor, and finally in the Balkans, the two other peninsulas of southern Europe, and even in southern France and North Africa. From the inter-war period onwards, more and more convincing evidence has come to light of another substratum that was in fact Indo-European. This will be discussed at length below. It is sufficient to say here that some of the philologists responsible for the discovery of this linguistic substratum deny the existence of a purely Mediterranean substratum, while others deny the existence of an Indo-European substratum and maintain that only Mediterranean languages were spoken in Greece before the arrival of the Greeks.

Both views are extreme. It can no longer be denied that the Greek language has preserved words and names which come from other Indo-European languages. But it is certain too that some words and names have remained which cannot be recognized as Indo-European, but present characteristics known to belong to other linguistic families.

The ethnic name *Leleges* (*Λέλεγες*) has *Lex* in the singular, without the initial *le-*. The *le-* which appears in the plural is no more than the prefix which differentiates plural from singular in the language of the Hatti, a people who lived in Asia Minor before the Indo-Europeans. So, the Leleges must have spoken the same language as the Hatti.

The names of the *Tyrrhenians, Ektenes,* and *Kylikranes* can be assigned to the Mediterranean substratum, because they cannot be given an Indo-European etymology and because the suffix -*ān*- which they contain is not Indo-European, but Mediterranean, though this did not prevent it from being used later in the formation of the names of Indo-European races, including Greek ones.

According to the ancients, Kadmos, the founder of Kadmeia and of a dynasty in the Boiotian town of Thebes, had come originally from Phoenicia (in Greek, *Phoinike*). On the basis of this information, some modern historians have supposed that this city and other regions where there were legends about Kadmos were in fact once inhabited by Phoenicians and other Semitic peoples during the Bronze Age. Students of the Semitic languages derive the name *Kadmos* from the root **kadm-* which means "forward", "before", "east". The majority of scholars are unconvinced by this theory, but still cannot agree on the origin of Kadmos and his Phoinikes. They have identified them variously with Greeks, Mediterraneans, Minoans, and Illyrians. The name of Kadmos was given: to a mountain and a river in Karia, near its borders with Lydia and Phrygia, where Phoenicians never immigrated; to a rock on the coast of southern Illyria; and to a tributary of the Thyamis (Kalamas) in Epeiros. A sacred pole planted in the ground and provided with a human head was called by the Thebans *Dionysos Kadmos* or *Dionysos Orthos* (erect, upright). Kadmilos, a divine figure in the mysteries of Samothrace, was identified as the ithyphallic Hermes. The Cretans of historical times used the word *kadmos* with the meanings of δόρυ (spear), λόφος (hill, crest), ἀσπίς (shield). The idea common to these meanings is height. This explains why the name *Kadmos* was given to mountains and rocks, to a sacred pole, and to an ithyphallic god. But why was the same name given to rivers? We can find the answer in the Greek verb κέκαδμαι, κέκασμαι (I am prominent, I excel, I shine). The meaning of being prominent is suitable for hills and eminences, and the idea of shining is suitable for rivers, since their waters reflect light. This etymology of *Kadmos* is a second argument against the hypothesis of Semitic origin. Some scholars have correlated the root of the name *Kadmos*, the Cretan *kadmos*, and the Greek κέκαδμαι, κέκασμαι with Sanskrit *çaçaduh, çaçadunah-* (to excel, to be strong), Gaulish *cadr* (valiant, strong), and Latin *Camenae* (goddesses of springs). For a long time, the present author espoused this opinion; he now considers it unlikely in view of the fact that the mysteries of Samothrace belonged to the Tyrrhenians, who were one of the peoples of the Mediterranean substratum. As concerns the ethnic name *Phoinikes*, there are two different opinions: according to the one, it is derived from the Indo-European *gʷhon-os* (blood, murder), whence Greek φόνος (murder), φοινός (red); according to the other, it goes back to a Semitic race-name *Puni*, whence the Latin *Puni* (Phoenicians, Carthaginians). The former etymology has lost its probability since the reading of Mycenaean texts gave the words *ponike, ponikija*, which obviously stand for *phoinike, phoinikija*, for, if *phoin-* had been derived from gʷhon-os, it should have appeared in these texts as *qonike, qonikija* (since in Mycenaean the original Indo-European *gʷ* is not changed into *p*). The latter opinion too is improbable, because (a) as regards the name *Puni*, it should have taken in Greek the form Πύνοι, which is not the case, and (b) as regards the name *Phoinikes*, it is known that the names *Phoinix* and *Phoinike* have a distribution which is incompatible with that of the Semitic Phoenicians: Phoinix was the name of a mountain and a stronghold in Karia and of a river in Lykia, both being regions into which the Phoenicians never penetrated, while Phoinike in Epeiros was likewise beyond the limits of their expansion. At any rate, the ethnic name *Phoinikes*

was not born on the coast of Lebanon but in Epeiros. It was given by the Greeks to the people who lived on the Lebanese coast because the latter used to dye material in φοινόν, a deep red colour, and because there was a tribe called *Puni*, whose name sounded to the Greeks as the equivalent of *Phoinikes*. After excluding both the Indo-European and the Semitic origins of the names *Phoinike, Phoinikes*, there remains no alternative but to assign them to the Mediterranean substratum.

Place-names which are widespread in the Iberian peninsula, southern France, Italy, the Balkans, Greece, Asia Minor, and the Caucasus have been preserved from the same substratum. All have monosyllabic roots with a vowel which is sometimes given as *a*, sometimes as *e*: e.g. *Kar-/Ker-, Kal-/Kel-, Gar-/Ger-, Sal-/Sel-, Tab-/Teb-*. It would appear that the Indo-Europeans who preserved these place-names had some difficulty in pronouncing a vowel which had a phonetic value somewhere between *a* and *e*. As a rule, each of these roots is included in place-names which have some common feature, so we may conclude that each root stood for the name of that feature in the ancient language. For a long time, it was generally thought that the same linguistic stratum had given us place-names and words ending in *-s(s)a, -s(s)os, -ttos, -nda, -ndos, -nthos*, and *-ymna*. Recently, however, some scholars have attributed them to the Indo-Europeans who preceded the Greeks. The question is very difficult and still open.

The preservation of these linguistic elements makes it clear that the language from which they are derived was in use in Greece and the other Mediterranean countries when the first Indo-Europeans arrived. The arrival of the first Indo-Europeans in Greece is dated at the beginning of the Bronze Age. So, the people who spoke this language must have been predominant in Greece even earlier, in the period up to the end of the Neolithic Age, and in some parts up to the beginning of the Bronze Age. When did they come to Greece? At present, no answer can be given to this question.

The Leleges settled in many regions of Greece, particularly Thessaly, Euboia, Lokris, Boiotia, the Megarid, Aitolia, Akarnania, Leukas, Elis, Lakonia, the Cyclades, and parts of western Asia Minor. In Greece, they disappeared quite early under the pressure of successive waves of Indo-Europeans. In Asia Minor, they survived longer. The *Iliad*, which gives us a picture of the political and ethnic situation at the end of the Mycenaean Age, mentions the Leleges as allies of the Trojans and locates them close to Troy. Other communities of Leleges submitted to the Greeks in Ionia. In Karia, the Leleges were conquered by the Karians and lived for several centuries as a subject race until they were finally absorbed into the Karian population. It was because of this gradual mingling of the Leleges with the Karians that the Greeks in classical and later times regarded them as the same race.

The Tyrrhenians are usually mentioned as inhabitants of the islands of the northern Aegean and of the shores of northwest Asia Minor. A few remnants of this race survived up to the first centuries of the first millennium B.C. The Ektenes are said to have lived in Boiotia. The Kylikranes are mentioned as enemies of Herakles somewhere in central Greece, which means that they still survived in Mycenaean times.

The people who first bore the ethnic name *Phoinikes*

and worshipped *Kadmos* came to Boiotia from Epeiros, where both names are met: town *Phoinike*, river *Kadmos*, rock *Kadmos*, country *Kammania* (which may have originated from *Kadmania*); in Epeiros we also meet the ethnic name *Phoinatoi*, which is closely related to the name *Phoinikes*. In fact, the only difference between the two ethnics lies in their suffixes: *Phoin-ik-s*, *Phoina-to-s* (same formations: *Boio-to-s*, *Thespro-to-s*, *Apodo-to-s*, etc.). The Phoinatoi (an ethnic name postulating a place-name *Phoina*) may then have been a branch of the Phoinikes who remained in Epeiros until historical times. According to Greek legends, Kadmos displaced the Temmikes and the Aones from Boiotia. A comparison with other Greek legends shows that it is very rare for events which took place earlier than the beginning of the Late Bronze Age to be remembered. We may, therefore, suppose that the movement of Kadmos's people from Epeiros to Boiotia occurred at the earliest in the transition from Middle to Late Helladic times.

THE INDO-EUROPEANS

Many languages, both ancient and modern, of Europe, the Middle East, India, and central Asia (some of which have been transplanted to America, Africa, Australia, and the Oceanic islands in recent times) are related in varying degrees. Of the ancient languages in this group, only those in which we have texts are of interest to us: chiefly Greek and Latin; but also Sanskrit and Avestan (languages of the ancient Indians and Iranians); Hittite cuneiform, Hittite hieroglyphic, Luvian, and Palaian (languages of the peoples of Asia Minor in the Bronze Age and, sporadically, during the first centuries of the 1st millennium B.C.); and Tocharian (spoken in central Asia). Other ancient languages in this group are known hardly at all. The comparative study of Gothic and of modern Celtic, Germanic, Baltic, and Slavic languages helps us to form a partial picture of the main features of their forerunners. As for ancient languages which ceased to exist without leaving extensive texts or any successors (Osco-Umbrian, Messapic, etc. in Italy; Dako-Mysian, Thracian, and Illyrian in the Balkans; Lydian, Karian, Lykian, Phrygian, etc. in Asia Minor), our knowledge is limited to a few words and names found on short grave inscriptions or mentioned by Greek and Latin writers.

The relation between these languages is evident to some degree from the striking similarities between them, e.g. Greek and Latin have the same words for *I* (ἐγώ, *ego*), *father* (πατήρ, *pater*), *I bring* (φέρω, *fero*). More often though we have no more than eloquent correspondences, as between: the Greek πέντε, the Latin *quinque*, and the English *five*; the Greek ἵππος the Gaulish *epo-*, the Latin *equus*, the Sanskrit *aśvas*, the Old English *eoh*, the Old Irish *ech*; Greek εἰμί, Avestan *ehmi*, Lithuanian *esmi*, Old Slavonic *jesmi*, Sanskrit *asmi*. But in most cases, the relation between words is not immediately obvious at all and can be traced, often with considerable difficulty, only by expert philologists using appropriate methods.

The links, evident or not, between these languages concern a small part of their vocabulary and a large part of their grammar. Their common vocabulary includes mainly the numerals, the personal and some other pronouns, words which express degrees of kinship, names of animals and plants, and a few of the most common verbs. The grammatical relation between the languages emerges from both phonetics and inflexion, i.e. the manner of declining nouns, adjectives, and pronouns and conjugating verbs, the comparison of adjectives, derivations, etc., as well as from their syntax.

On the basis of these facts, philologists have concluded that the ancient languages mentioned above are all derived from one earlier language, which they call Indo-Germanic or Indo-European (since its successors spread from India to Europe). This language must have split up into dialects before the peoples who spoke it began to migrate in various directions. Eventually, the original language ceased to exist altogether. The external cause of its disappearance was the splitting up of the peoples who spoke it into groups who moved away from their original homeland and ceased to be in contact with one another. The internal cause was the gradual development of new idiomatic expressions in the language spoken by each separate group. Each group enriched its original vocabulary with words borrowed from other languages or words which it made up itself, and at the same time some of the words inherited from the original language were forgotten. There were alterations in the phonological system: some old sounds vanished, others came to be pronounced differently, and some new sounds were created. Finally, similar changes came about in the declension of nouns and pronouns and the conjugation of verbs.

After the existence of an Indo-European language had been established and some of its features determined, the question arose: did this linguistic entity correspond to an ethnic one? Some scholars believe that it did, and have even gone on to claim that the original Indo-Europeans were not just a people but a particular race, the so-called "northern race", with distinct physical and biological traits and with their own mental, moral, and spiritual qualities. However, repeated measurements of skeletons from graves contemporary with the arrival of the Indo-European groups in various countries show that relatively few of the bodies were of the "northern" type. The majority presents features of other European or Near East types, or a mixture of these. It seems probable, therefore, that the people who spoke the ancient Indo-European language did not belong to a distinct human race, or at least they had ceased to belong to one long before they began to break away into smaller groups. However, during the period in which the original Indo-European language was used (even after some internal differences in dialect had emerged), those who spoke it can probably be regarded as having belonged to a group of tribes, some of which may have been of a common origin. This group must have split up into smaller ones, each with its own leaders, land, life, and migratory movement. As these smaller groups gradually moved further away from each other, they came to form new and separate peoples.

It is difficult to determine the original homeland of the Indo-European language and people. In tackling this problem, we notice that the Indo-European languages have some names of animals and plants from the temperate zones in common, but no common names for animals and plants from the arctic or tropical zones. Some scholars look for the Indo-European homeland in central Europe or further east, since some of these languages have a common word for the beech tree, others a common word for salmon.

Archaeologists have tackled the problem indirectly. They have associated certain types of vases, weapons, dwellings, and graves with the Indo-European tribes and suggested certain regions where they may have settled, all between central Europe and the Urals-Baikal line.

In the period between the two world wars a vigorous debate began between the supporters and the opponents of the theory that many Greek words and many names of gods, heroes, men, and places in Greece were the remnants of one or more Indo-European languages distinct from Greek. The fact is that both sides have shown exaggeration in stating their positions. If we take all the hundreds of words and names which have at one time or another been proposed as remnants of the pre-Greek Indo-European linguistic substratum, and if we discount all those which do not satisfy the rules of etymology, we are still left with ample evidence to support the theory that Indo-Europeans appeared in Greece before the arrival of the first Greek-speaking tribes, and enough information to help us determine some of the features which characterized the language or languages which they spoke. These are mainly phonetic. Recently assigned to this substratum are also the suffixes: -*s(s)*- (e.g. Kaukasa, Marpessa, Amphissa, Antissa, Argissa, Larisa, Halikarnassos, Parnassos, Amnisos, Ilisos, Kephisos, Lykabettos, Hymettos, kyparissos, narkisos); -*anth*- and -*inth*- (e.g. Erymanthos, akanthos, Korinthos, terevinthos, hyakinthos, minthe); -*ymn*- and -*ynn*- (e.g. Kalymna, Larymna, Diktynna).

The philologists who specialize in tracing non-Greek elements of Indo-European origin in the Greek language do not agree about the number of original languages which must be postulated. According to the pioneers of this type of research, all non-Greek words are derived from a single language, conventionally referred to by them as "Pelasgic", which may have had two dialects. A more recent theory proposes that there were originally three main languages. The whole question remains open.

We have already noted that of the various peoples whom the Greeks regarded as their predecessors, the Ektenes, Kadmeians-Phoinikes, Kylikranes, Leleges and Tyrrhenians, belonged to the Mediterranean substratum. We shall now see that the rest, the Aones, Dryopians, Haimones, Hyantes, Kaukones, and Pelasgians, all had Indo-European names, and that some of them can be connected with civilizations of the Early and Middle Bronze Age.

HAIMONES

The ethnic name *Haimones* (Αἴμονες) may be given several plausible derivations: from the Greek adjective αἴμων,

which means "bloody" or "sanguine", or from an identically-sounding Greek word which means "zealous" or "clever", or from the noun αἶμος, which means "bush" or "area covered with bushes" and which is also the name of *Mt. Haimos*.

From ancient records memories have been retained to the present day which place the Haimones in Thessaly, more particularly in the Dorian plain in the regions of Larisa and Iolkos. Furthermore, these people may be responsible for some place-names (*Haimon, Haimonia, Haimoniai*) and some names of heroes (*Haimon, Haimonios*), all of which are located in Boiotia, Aitolia, and southern Arkadia.

Most of the regions mentioned above have yielded specimens of chalcolithic "crusted ware". There are close parallels of this in the late Neolithic phases in the cultures of Gumelnica (Western Bulgaria), Vinča (Serbia), Lengyel (Hungary). So, it is reasonable to suppose that the Haimones came to Thessaly from one of these regions (near Mt. Haimos?), where they developed the "crusted ware" style c. 3000 B.C. and subsequently colonized some sites in Boiotia, Aitolia-Akarnania, and Arkadia.

PELASGIANS

No less than seventeen theories have been put forward about the identity of the Pelasgians and their relation to other peoples. Some scholars refuse to believe that the Pelasgians ever existed at all as a distinct people. Others admit that the name *Pelasgoi* once belonged to a definite people, but maintain that in the ancient texts which survive the word *Pelasgoi* has taken on a general meaning and been used indiscriminately to describe various pre-Greek tribes. Indeed, both theories express the perplexity that one feels when first faced with the vague and often contradictory statements made by ancient writers about the Pelasgians. Recently, attempts have been made to assign some definite character to the Pelasgians by supplementing the testimonies of the ancients by the findings of philologists, archaeologists, and students of religion. This has produced a great variety of often unexpected results. Some of the theories put forward are entirely fanciful or based on an arbitrary selection of often flimsy evidence; some which were once considered plausible have since been disproved. We shall mention only two recent theories.

According to the first, the Pelasgians were an Indo-European people. This theory was first put forward in the years between the two wars, when there was still no certain evidence to support it. The students of non-Greek Indo-European elements in the Greek language had settled on "Pelasgic" simply as a convenient name for the language

The map shows the distribution of Indo-European tribes in Greece in the Early Bronze Age. There are indications that the following tribes lived in Greece before 2000 B.C.: the Haimones in regions of Thessaly, Aitolia, Boiotia, southern Arkadia; the Dryopians in the Spercheios Valley; the Proto-Achaians in Achaian Phthiotis, Athamania, and Aitolia; the Kaukones in northern Elis, Triphylia, and Messenia; the Pelasgians in central Epeiros, Krestonia, Achaian Phthiotis, Phokis, Attica, Euboia, and the Peloponnesos; and the Hyantes in Boiotia, Phokis, Western Lokris, and Aitolia.

THERMAIC GULF

A E G E A N   S E A

I O N I A N   S E A

Phoinike ●

Kadmos R.

Thyamis R.

● Dodona

Inachos R.

Achelaos R.

● Larisa

Spercheios R.

Euboian Gulf

Corinthian Gulf

Athens ●

Saronic Gulf

Gulf of Kyparissia

Lerna ●

Argolic Gulf

M Y R T O A N   S E A

Messenian Gulf

Lakonian Gulf

INDO-EUROPEAN PEOPLES
IN GREECE DURING THE EARLY
BRONZE AGE

	Haimones		Pelasgians
	Dryopians		Kaukones
	(Proto)-Achaians		Hyantes

from which these elements were derived, and it was not until 1958 that the name of the Pelasgians was assigned an etymology which actually connected it with the "Pelasgic" language. In other words, it was suggested that the rules of phonetics which had been established for the Pelasgic language made it perfectly possible that the name *Pelasgos* was derived from the Indo-European roots: *bhel- (to flower, to flourish) and *osgho (branch). A compound word *bhel-osgho-s, which would then mean "flowering branch", through a series of mutations, became *Pelasgos*: first, the rough *h* in *b^h* dropped, because it was followed by the similarly rough *h* in *gh*; the *b* which remained became *p*; the *g^h* became *g*; and the *o* turned into *a*. This etymology is perfectly sound from the phonetic point of view. All the changes which take place conform to rules which were not drawn up intentionally to explain them (which, unfortunately, is often the case) but which had already been seen to apply to other remnants of the pre-Greek Indo-European substratum. But the derivation of the ethnic *Pelasgos* from *Bhelosghos* was not supported semantically by the actual sense of the word; there was at that point nothing to show that *Pelasgos* meant "flowering branch".

The second of the two recent theories is a most enterprising but unconvincing attempt to identify the Pelasgians with the Illyrians.

Some light may be thrown on the origin and relations of the Pelasgians by the legends connected with the hero Pelasgos. According to myths told in Arkadia, Argos, and Thessaly—all three being separate regions in which the Pelasgians had settled—the hero Pelasgos was associated with better methods of providing food for mankind: at Argos and in Thessaly, he was associated with the cultivation of cereals and the preparation of bread; in Arkadia, with the discovery of the nutritive potential of the acorn. We may note here that the ancient Greek word for *oak* (δρῦς) is derived from an Indo-European root which means "tree" generically. We may therefore suppose that Pelasgos, before he became a hero, was the personification of a vegetative spirit which made trees bear fruit and corn ripen. In even earlier times, this spirit must have been identified with every tree and plant. The ancient poet Asios tells us that "the earth gave up" (ἀνέδωκε) Pelasgos on the wooded mountains. The phrase "earth gave up" makes us think immediately of a plant shooting up out of the ground, and the use of the plural "mountains" suggests that the birth of Pelasgos did not occur only once, in one place, and at a certain time, but that it symbolized the birth of every tree. There is also indirect evidence for the link between Pelasgos and vegetation: according to one legend, probably Thessalian in origin, Pelasgos had a son called *Chloros* (green): finally, Pliny provides some helpful evidence by mentioning that a certain type of laurel was called *pelasgum*. This material, then, has given us some information about the religion of the Pelasgians and has also enabled us to connect the Pelasgians with the pre-Greek Indo-European substratum, since the original identity of Pelasgos as the personification of growth and fruit-bearing fits well with the meanings suggested by the derivation of the name *Pelasgos* from *bhel-osgho-*. The root *bhel-* means not only "to flower", but also "to sprout", "to swell", "to become green". *Pelasgos* must originally have meant the branch at leaf-bearing or blossom time and later the spirit which made the branch bear leaves and flowers. The Pelasgians were the people who worshipped

this spirit and believed that they owed their existence to it.

The direct and indirect information we have about the Pelasgians and about toponyms connected with their name make it possible to associate them with certain definite regions: the Thracian shores of the Black Sea, the Propontis, Krestonia (north of Chalkidike and west of the Strymon), central Epeiros, Pelasgiotis, Achaian Phthiotis, Phokis, Euboia, Attica, Argeia, Sikyonia, Achaia, Arkadia, Crete, some islands of the Aegean, South Aiolis, and Ionia.

Various Greek legends mention the Pelasgians as the immediate forerunners of the Arkadians in Arkadia, the Danaans in Argos, the Ionians in the southern Peloponnesos and Attica, and of various Greek tribes in Thessaly. Since the Danaans arrived at the end of the second phase of the Early Helladic Period, and the other Greek-speaking tribes at the end of the third phase, and since there was a unified civilization in Greece throughout the first two phases of the Early Helladic Period, it seems reasonable to suppose that the Pelasgians settled in Greece from the beginning of this period.

The Pelasgians in mainland Greece had been absorbed by the Greek population before the end of the Mycenaean Age. The Pelasgian tribes who by that time were on the move in Boiotia and Attica were invaders from Thrace. Perhaps the same was true of the Pelasgians who are mentioned in the *Odyssey* as inhabitants of Crete along with the Eteo-Cretans, Kydonians, Achaians, and Dorians. There were Pelasgians on the Ionian coast when the Greeks migrated there. The *Iliad* gives some information about the country of the Pelasgians who sent military aid to the Trojans. Several places have been suggested as their homeland, but the only one that fits Homer's description is the Thracian shore of the Black Sea.

Pelasgian communities survived in Krestonia and the Propontis down to the 5th century B.C. Greeks who came across them noted that these two groups spoke the same language in spite of the distance which separated them and that their language differed from that of neighbouring peoples, i.e. the Tyrrhenians, Thracians, and Phrygians.

PROTO-ACHAIANS

Although the Achaians of the Mycenaean Age were undoubtedly a Greek people, their name does not appear to be Greek. We call the first people who bore this name Proto-Achaians to distinguish them from the Greek-speaking Achaians of the Mycenaean Age.

Ten etymologies have been suggested for the name *Akhaios*, but only one seems to make sense. This derives the word from the Indo-European root *ak^w- (water), which is semantically plausible, because a spring in Messenia was called Achaia, and a river which flowed into the eastern Black Sea was called Achaious. Furthermore, the phonetic combination *ach* is found in many names of rivers: Acheloos, Inachos, Achamas, Achates, Acheles, Achardeos. Perhaps Achilles was an ancient water god. Leaving aside other evidence for this (and the references to the worship of Achilles as a god in various parts of Greece), we will mention only that some Greek colonies on the Black Sea worshipped *Achilleus Pontarches* (Lord of the Sea) as a god. The root

* ak^w- in Greek would have given ap- or at-, depending on the vowels which followed and the dialect. On the other hand, it must be borne in mind that the pre-Greek Indo-European substratum changed * k^w to k and that at least one language or dialect of this substratum changed the k to kh. This then must have been the language which gave the Greeks the names: Achaians, Achilles, Acheloos, Achamas, Achates, Acheles, Inachos.

As we shall see below, the Greek Achaians spread into various Greek lands from Achaian Phthiotis, so they must have settled in this region after the Proto-Achaian population, from whom they took their name and certain cults. Other Proto-Achaians were perhaps settled in Athamania and Aitolia, regions where there are rivers called Inachos and Acheloos. There are many names of rivers and places, and of gods, with the root ach- in central and eastern Greece, the Peloponnesos, the Aegean islands, and the coast of western Asia Minor, but it is difficult to say which of these are Proto-Achaian and which are Greek Achaian.

Outside Greece, we find a people called Achaians on the eastern shores of the Black Sea. In the same region, there are rivers called Achaious and Achardeos and a settlement called Achaia. Some post-classical writers claim that these Achaians were Greek colonists, but there is no agreement about their place of origin or about the circumstances of the colonization. The texts in question are not very reliable, so altogether this claim would seem to be no more than a speculation on the part of Greek scholars in the Alexandrian Age. This people might have been a branch of the Proto-Achaians, in which case the names mentioned above would correspond to their settlements.

DRYOPIANS

Strabo says the Dryopians were not Greeks. We have no reason to doubt this assertion, because groups of Dryopians survived in Greece up to Classical times, and the Greeks had plenty of opportunity to acquire first-hand knowledge of them. In the Mycenaean Age, the Dryopians lived in the Spercheios Valley. According to one legend, they were driven out of there by Herakles.

The name Dryopes (Δρύοπες) is Indo-European; it breaks down into the root *dru- (tree, oak) and the suffix -op-, known in many race and place-names in the Greek mainland, Illyria, and Thrace and in other Greek words which denote various kinds of birds and insects. The name of the Deuriopes or Douriopes (Δευρίοπες, Δουρίοπες) in Illyria is derived from the same root: dru-, deur-, and dour- are all related to the same Indo-European stem.

OTHER PRE-GREEK INDO-EUROPEAN PEOPLES

We have very little information about the Aones, the Hyantes, or the Kaukones. The first two are mentioned as the very ancient inhabitants of the region around Thebes, even earlier than Kadmos's Phoinikes. The Hyantes too settled in Boiotia, but also in Phokis, Western Lokris, and Aitolia. The Kaukones controlled northern Elis and parts of Triphylia and of Messenia. Other Kaukones lived in Paphlagonia. Indo-European etymologies have been proposed for all these names, but there is no means of checking them. All of them, however, look like Indo-European formations.

References to Karians as early inhabitants of mainland and island Greece in various Greek texts have no historical basis. The names of places and gods which are usually mentioned as Karian residues there bear no relation to the name of the Karians; the *kar- root which they contain is a stem of the Mediterranean substratum to be found everywhere from Spain to the East. The ancients were misled by these names (the name of the Karians is not derived from *kar- but from *kawer-), and also by the mistake of confusing Leleges and Karians.

In recent years, it has been suggested that the Greek lands were inhabited by Luvians who came from Asia Minor to mainland Greece c. 1900 B.C. and to Crete two centuries later. But the linguistic evidence rests on a narrow base and is not sufficient to convince us that the phenomena which are attributed to the Luvians are exclusively Luvian and not common to other peoples too. All attempts to prove this theory on the basis of archaeological evidence have failed.

THE PROTO-GREEKS

Danaans

In the Homeric poems, the names Danaoi (Δαναοί), Achaioi (Ἀχαιοί), and Argeioi (Ἀργεῖοι) are used to denote the Greeks of the Mycenaean Age. Classical writers often use these names in the same sense, but some refer to the founder of the Danaan race as a foreigner, an Oriental who came to Greece from Egypt with his fifty daughters. Some modern historians have thought that these texts echo stories about the Danaans coming originally from a country of the Near East and have tried to find evidence in support of such a theory. None of their ingenious arguments, however, can be regarded as convincing.

It has also been proposed that the name of the Danaans contains an Indo-European root * danu- (dampness, cool, drop, water, river), and that the Danaans emigrated to Greece from the borders of the Eurasian steppes. The chief arguments may be summarized as follows: the root * danu- has been preserved in the ancient Indo-Iranian languages and in many river names: Tanais (Don), Danastris (Dnjestr), Danapris (Dnjepr), Danuvius, Danubius, Δάνουβις (Danube), all north of the Black Sea; Tanew in modern Poland; Eridanos (Eder?); Rhodanos (Rhône) in western Europe; Apidanos, Apidon, Eridanos, Iardanos, Tanaos in Greece. Indian mythology gives the name Danu to a goddess, the mother of the dragon Urtra, and also to a group of daimons who are associated with springs. In the Avesta, an Iranian national epic, a hostile people is called Danawo-, and this corresponds letter for letter with the earlier form of the name of the Danaans: Danawoi (Δαναϝοί).

The derivation of the name Danaos (Δαναός), Danaides (Δαναΐδες), Danae (Δανάη), and Danaoi (Δαναοί) from the root danu is confirmed by the fact that the legendary figures who bore these names all had connections with water. Greek myths credit Danaos and his daughters with the discovery of springs and the construction of wells, and say that Danaos made Argos εὔυδρον (well-watered) when previously it had been ἄνυδρον (waterless). Further, it has been observed that the names of some of the Danaids (the daughters of Danaos) are those of springs. These facts can be supplemented with various other pieces of information. The legend according to which the Danaids beheaded the sons of Aigyptos and buried their heads under the waters of Lerna may be based on a memory of human sacrifices on the shores of the lake and of the burial of heads on the lake bed in order to increase the volume of the water; similar or equivalent magic rituals are known from folklore studies. Perhaps the same ideas were behind the myth according to which Danae had been fertilized by golden rain. Primitive communities attribute to rain the power to make women fertile, and for that reason on certain days of the year women shower themselves with artificial rain, believing that in this way they will secure their own fertility and also the fertility of domestic animals, fields, and trees.

Close to Lake Lerna, with which the Danaids were associated, in a region which is rich in myths about the Danaids and Danae and in legends connected with the Danaans, and not far distant from the Tanaos River, lies a carefully excavated settlement. After a destruction dated c. 2100 B.C., this settlement was reinhabited by a new people. Among the pottery finds from the period of reoccupation there were some fragments of vessels with decoration in the style associated with the third phase of the Kurgan culture, i.e. the phase (from 2300 B.C. onwards) during which there was an explosive expansion of this culture from the modern Ukraine to the Caucasus, Asia Minor, the Balkans, and central and northern Europe.

It seems probable, therefore, that it was a band of Danaans who destroyed Lerna c. 2100 B.C.; that they founded the new settlement there and lived alongside the older inhabitants of the region. Myths and names connected with the Danaans are found in Attica, Boiotia, Phokis, the Spercheios Valley, Achaian Phthiotis, Larisa, and Crete. Kurgan pottery of the fourth phase is said to have been found at Eutresis in Boiotia and at Hagia Marina in Phokis, i.e. in two of the regions mentioned above. However, if, as the experts maintain, the Kurgan pottery of the fourth phase is the sort known as "Schnurkeramik" or "coarded ware", then we must add the regions where this latter type of pottery has been found. The Kurgan culture is characterized chiefly by pit graves built up on the inside and covered by a tumulus. In a recent study, all the tumuli of the Early, Middle, and Late Bronze Age in Greece and Albania were attributed to the peoples of the Kurgan culture. But the list should be restricted only to tumuli over tombs (for it includes among others the mound at Lerna, which is not a tomb tumulus), and then only to those which, like the graves they cover, present all the distinctive features of Kurgan graves. Only when a proper list has been drawn up of all the sites where coarded ware has been found and all the sites where Kurgan tumuli exist, shall we be able to make a definite comparison of their distribution with the distribution of traces associated with names and myths of the Danaans.

What of the *Danuna* of Cilicia? According to the Phoenician text of the bilingual late 8th century B.C. inscription of Karatepe, the rulers of the Danuna traced their origin to a certain *Mps*. This has been identified with *Mopsos* (*Μόψος*), who is mentioned in several Greek texts as the leader of colonists in Cilicia and the founder of various cities in that country. In the Hittite text of the same Karatepe inscription, the name of the ancestor is given as *Mu-ka-sa-sa*, i.e. *Muksas*. The fact that *ps* and *x* or *ks* were evidently interchangeable (as illustrated too in the name of a figure in Lydian mythology who is alternately mentioned as *Mopsos* and *Moxos*) has led philologists to recognize two different attempts to render an old Indo-European sound k^w followed by *s*. So, the rulers of the Danuna were Indo-Europeans. Further, the mention of Mopsos or Moxos as the founder of the ruling dynasty of the Danuna affords a better indication for a link between them and the Danaans than the mere similarity of their names, Danuna-Danaans, which could have been coincidental. Various heroes called Mopsos or Moxos and related place-names are known in regions where there are traces of Danaans not only in Cilicia but also in Syria and Palestine (hero *Mopsos*; the city name *Dana*; the river name *Jordan*, which is not Semitic, but closer in sound and meaning to *Iardanos*, which is the name of rivers in mainland Greece and Crete); in Pontos (the city names *Moxoupolis*, *Danae*, *Danati*); and in Greece. In Greece especially, the facts in question lie within very small areas: in Attica (*Eridanos*, *Mopsopia*), in Boiotia (*Danaos*, *Proitos*, *Mopsos*), in the Larisa region (*Danae*, *Akrisios*, *Mopsos*, *Mopsion*). The fact that traces of the Danaans outside Greece are found not only in Cilicia but also in Pontos, Syria, and Palestine, makes it unlikely that the Danuna of Cilicia were Danaan colonists from Greece. It is more probable that the Dorians, the Danuna, and the other peoples who bore this name and who were associated with the Danaans and Mopsos in Pontos and in Syria-Palestine were all branches of the people who are called by the name *Danawo* in the *Avesta*.

Which way did the Danaans come into Greece? The character of several finds at the Lerna layer which was reoccupied after the destruction of c. 2100 has led archaeologists to believe that the newcomers had spent some time in the Aegean area. Other indications of the same layer point to some link with Troy in particular. And the very fact that the Danaans settled exclusively in the eastern part of Thessaly and of southern Greece suggests that they came over the Aegean. Furthermore, the chronological difference between the third phase Kurgan pottery at Lerna and the fourth phase Kurgan pottery at Eutresis and Hagia Marina suggests that probably a first wave of this culture landed in the Argolid, while a second went further north to Boiotia and Phokis.

Independent research has established that around 2300 B.C. northwest Asia Minor was conquered by invaders from Thrace who had originally come from the Ukrainian steppes. Their Thracian homeland is the area of the "mound culture of Bulgaria", a term which denotes the same culture as that now referred to as Kurgan. The general picture of the line of advance of the people of this culture shows them as having come from the Ukraine to Greece, via Thrace and the Troad, where they acquired the Trojan and Aegean features evident in the finds at Lerna.

It should be noted that the destruction which took place at Lerna around 2100 B.C. was not an isolated event. At the same period, there were destructions and changes at other sites in the Argolid, Korinthia, Attica, and the Cyclades.

ABANTES

The Abantes, according to the *Iliad*, were a Greek race who had settled in Euboia. Aristotle and Arrian, however, consider them to be Thracians, who had originally inhabited a city in Phokis called Aba or Abai. Modern scholars are equally unable to agree about the origin of the Abantes. Some believe Homer, others Aristotle, others go their own way and associate the Abantes with the Illyrians, or the Leleges, or the Karians.

The name *Abantes* is Indo-European both in form (with a *-nt*-suffix) and in its root. There are two rivers called *Abas*, one south of the Caucasus, the other in Italy. So, this name includes the Indo-European stem *ab-* which means "water", "river". The place-names *Arethousa* and *Kanathos* in Euboia and other parts of Greece where the Abantes settled have a *th* in place of the Indo-European *dh* as required by Greek phonetic rules, while Thracian and other Indo-European languages have a *d*. So, the *Iliad* gives the correct information about the homeland of the Abantes, and Aristotle must have been mistaken in thinking that they were Thracians. Probably he was misled by the fact that the city Aba, like other sites in Phokis, was in fact inhabited by Thracians who invaded Greece at the end of the Mycenaean Age. The Abantes settled in many regions of mainland Greece as well as in Euboia: Argos, Sikyon, Phokis, Epeiros. Abantes and Amantes are mentioned in southwest Illyria too (the interchanging of *m* and *b* is a common phenomenon both in Greek and in other languages). It seems probable then that the Abantes appeared at Argos and Phokis at the same time as the Danaans and elements of the Kurgan culture. This and the fact that the name *Abas* is found in the Caucasus as a water name make it probable that the Abantes came to Greece in the same wave of migration which brought the Danaans. The group of Abantes in southwest Illyria and Epeiros followed a different route along with the main body of Greeks.

THE MAIN BODY OF PROTO-GREEKS

The scant traces of the Kurgan culture in Greece have been unearthed only at a few sites, always in layers which correspond to Early Helladic III (c. 2100-1900 B.C.) and usually along with indications of the presence of Danaans and Abantes. It would then appear that during that period these were the only two Greek tribes to have arrived in Greece. On the other hand, the important and widespread cultural changes which took place between the end of the Early Helladic and the beginning of the Middle Helladic (c. 1900 B.C.) seem to indicate that it was only during this period that large masses of Greeks arrived. Before that, they had settled in southwest Illyria, Epeiros, western Macedonia, and northwestern Thessaly. For this, there is historical, archaeological, and linguistic evidence:

1. It has already been noted that one group of Abantes settled in southwest Illyria and another group in Epeiros. We shall see below that the most northerly traces of the Ionians are found south of the Khasia mountains, and of the Boiotians in the northern part of the Pindos Range. The Greek tribes who flooded into Greece at the end of the Mycenaean Age came from Pindos and Epeiros. But even after these emigrations, there were still Greeks living north of Khasia and Kambounia and west of Pindos.

2. In Thessalian Argissa, the Early Bronze Age ended with a violent upheaval, and there are indications that a new people settled there in the Middle Bronze Age. The pottery of this period is similar to that found in western Macedonia at the end of the Early Bronze Age. The fact that several early Bronze Age settlements in Macedonia did not survive into the Middle Bronze Age also shows that some groups moved from southwest Macedonia to Thessaly around 2000-1900 B.C. Since there appears to have been no change in the population of Thessaly from that date to the Mycenaean Age, when Thessaly was definitely inhabited by Greeks, these groups must have been Greek.

3. As we shall see below, the earliest dialect differences which emerged in the Greek language are an indication of the distribution of the Greek tribes throughout the country: Ionians south of Khasia, Arkadians north of Khasia, Aiolians northeast of the Arkadians, and other Greek tribes west of north Pindos (Tymphe, Smolikas, Grammos).

When did the Greek tribes with which we are concerned arrive in southwest Illyria, west Macedonia, Epeiros, and northwest Thessaly? Certainly after the beginning of the penetration of the Kurgan people into the Balkan peninsula, which is dated to about 2300 B.C., but not later than 2100 B.C., because the splitting up of the Greek language into the different dialects which had appeared in these regions by 1900 B.C. was a process which could not have been completed in less than two centuries.

Today we know the names of thirty-two ancient Greek tribes of the Mycenaean Age, but we can find traces of only six of these before 1900 B.C.: the Abantes and Danaans, who arrived in Greece with those names c. 2100 B.C.; the Ionians and Boiotians, whose names can be traced back to the area of expansion of the main body of Greeks before 1900 B.C.; and of the Arkadians and Phlegyans, who bore totemic, and therefore very ancient, names.

On the contrary, evidence for the dialect differences in the Greek language before 1900 B.C., though incomplete, still covers the whole range of the language spoken by the tribes who lived in northwest Thessaly, western Macedonia, and southwest Illyria up to this date.

The history of the Greek language and its dialects in the centuries before there were any written records has to be traced retrospectively. Some light is thrown on the phase which interests us here by certain links which have been observed among the basic Greek dialects: Ionic-Attic; Arkado-Cypriot; Aiolic; West Greek and the Mycenaean or Achaian dialect, which became known when the Linear B tablets were deciphered.

1. Arkado-Cypriot and Aiolic are more closely related to each other than either is related to any other Greek dialect. This has led many eminent philologists to conclude that Arkado-Cypriot and Aiolic were the descendants of an earlier Greek dialect, which they called Central Greek. Recent attempts to show that Arkado-Cypriot and Aiolic are not closely related have not been successful. Since there was no geographical proximity after 1900 B.C. between the speakers of the Aiolic dialect, who

were in Thessaly and some parts of central Greece, and the speakers of Arkado-Cypriot, who were in the Peloponnesos, we are bound to suppose that the link between these two dialects goes back to the period before 1900 B.C.

2. The existence of features common to Ionic-Attic and Arkado-Cypriot admits of a satisfactory interpretation only if it is assumed that they originated in the period when the Ionians and Arkadians had a common border in northern Greece. The contact between them must have been prior to 1900 B.C., since after this date the Ionians and Arkadians spread into the areas we have mentioned above.

3. The few features shared by Arkado-Cypriot and West Greek are usually attributed to the influence on Arkadian of Western dialects in the Peloponnesos. But how did this influence reach as far as Cyprus since the period of her colonization by Arkadian-speakers ended just when the Western tribes were settling in the Peloponnesos? These links too must then go back to a period when the Arkadians were in contact with the Western tribes within a relatively small area, so that dialectal phenomena could have been transmitted from one group to the other. This period must have been earlier than 1900 B.C., since after that date the Arkadians were in the Peloponnesos and the Western tribes in Epeiros, western Macedonia, and southwest Illyria.

4. Still fewer are the very features common to Aiolic and to West Greek; so, they may have evolved independently. Even if they are due to the geographical propinquity of the speakers of these dialects, they need not necessarily be dated before 1900 B.C., because the two groups had common borders even after this date, and because Aeolic-speaking tribes moved down into the plains of Thessaly from eastern Pindos, where there were influences from the Western dialect.

We can see, then, that the dialect differences indicate two main lines of development: one represents the preliminary stage of the dialects which were spoken in historical times; in it we can recognize the early characteristics of the Ionic and Western dialects and the characteristics of Central Greek, from which Aiolic and Arkado-Cypriot were to emerge. The second line of development crosses the first, because it links one section of Central Greek, i.e. the one which was to be transplanted to the Peloponnesos and to develop into Arkado-Cypriot, with both Ionic and West Greek. Thus, Central Greek was split up into two sectors, one of which had some features in common with the Ionic and some with the Western dialect, while the other sector had neither. The links can be illustrated by a diagram:

	NE sector of Central Greek (later Aiolic)
Early stage of West Greek	SW sector of Central Greek (later Arkado-Cypriot)
	Early stage of Ionic

Ionic and West Greek were spoken in the regions which have already been mentioned as the homes of the Ionians and the Western tribes: northwest Thessaly and Epeiros, respectively. We now see that the Central dialect should be located in western Macedonia.

The Ionic and Central dialects were separated by the mountains of Khasia and Kambounia; the Central and West Greek by the mountains of north Pindos (Tymphe, Smolikas, Boion, Grammos) and Vernon. These mountains determined the spread of the dialect phenomena which came to characterise the Ionic, Central, and Western dialects. They were not, however, impassable barriers: northwest Thessaly is in contact with western Macedonia, and western Macedonia with Epeiros. This brought about the spread of dialect phenomena which linked Ionic with Arkado-Cypriot, and Arkado-Cypriot with West Greek. Accordingly, the branch of the Central dialect from which Arkado-Cypriot emerged must have been spoken before 1900 B.C. in the basin of the upper Haliakmon. This means that the branch of the Central dialect from which Aiolic evolved must have been located further east, and this explains the absence of common features in Ionic and Aiolic and definitely shows that the few features which are common to Aiolic and West Greek are not due to contact between these two sectors earlier than 1900 B.C.

THE GREEK GROUPS 1900-1150 B.C.

The sharp break in culture which marks the transition from the Early to the Middle Bronze Age in Thessaly and southern mainland Greece around 1900 B.C. was the result of the expansion of one section of the main body of Proto-Greeks into these lands from the regions where they had previously settled. Another group moved down along the length of the Pindos Range and the axis of Epeiros-Aitolia. A third group were content to occupy the lands abandoned by the emigrants. There were no more migrations of Greeks on such a large scale and of such historical importance until the end of the Mycenaean Age, c. 1150 B.C. Small sporadic movements of various groups in the intervening period had no important results. So, from 1900 to 1150 B.C., the history of the formation of the Greek people followed an unbroken course.

The direct and indirect consequences of the large-scale migrations of about 1900 B.C. and of the smaller sporadic movements which followed are threefold:

(a) The earlier inhabitants were subdued, driven away, wiped out, or absorbed. Nevertheless, the Danaans in the Argolid and the Leleges in Eastern Lokris retained their independence up to the beginning of the Late Bronze Age; the Dryopians in the Spercheios Valley and the Kadmeians in Boiotia held on until the 13th century B.C.; the Abantes of Euboia remained autonomous until the end of the Bronze Age.

(b) The Proto-Greeks split up into groups; the individual characteristics of the original dialects multiplied, widening

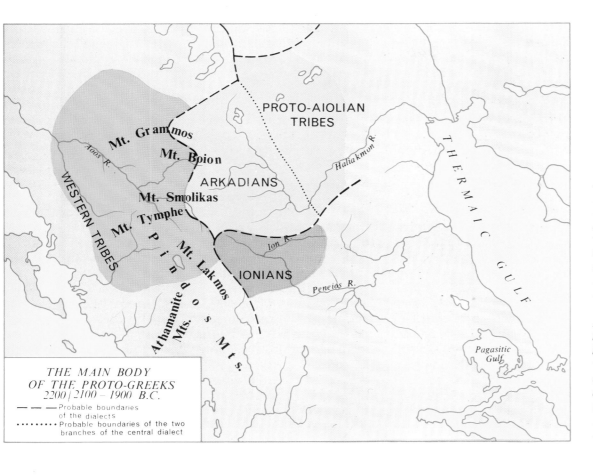

Between 2200/2100 and 1900 B.C., the main body of Proto-Greeks had settled in Epeiros, western Macedonia, and northwest Thessaly. The original language of the Proto-Greeks split up into three branches: the Western, Central, and Ionic. On the map, these branches are separated by a broken line, while the two variants of the Central dialect (Arkado-Cypriot and Aiolic), in the area inhabited by Arkadians and Proto-Aiolian tribes, are separated by a dotted line.

the distance between them so that new dialect branches were formed; many of the original tribes broke up, because they had become separated into smaller groups during the migrations or for other reasons.

(c) The interchange of influences between the Proto-Greeks and the earlier population led to cultural proximity; in some cases, the Proto-Greeks completely absorbed the earlier inhabitants; in other cases, new combinations were formed out of the mingling of exclusively Proto-Greek elements.

The first two developments resulted eventually in the transformation of the Proto-Greek tribes into the Greek tribes of the Mycenaean Age. In alphabetical order, these were: the Abantes, Achaians, Ainianes, Aiolians, Aithikes, Aitolians, Arkadians, Arktanes, Athamanians, Boiotians, Dolopes, Dorians, Epeians, Graioi, Hellenes, Ionians, Kephallenians, Kouretes, Lapiths, Lokrians, Macedonians, Magnetes, Minyans, Molossians, Myrmidons, Per(rh)aibians, Phlegyans, Phokians, Phthians, Pierians, Thesprotians, and Thessalians.

Ionians

The Ionians bore this ethnic name at least as early as the period when they inhabited northwest Thessaly, for a river there is called *Ion*. Etymologies of the name of the Ionians (᾿ΙάϜονες, ῎Ιωνες, ῎Ιανες) from ἰέναι, ἰᾶσθαι, ἰός, etc. are all unacceptable, chiefly because they fail to show that the name had a corresponding sense. Similarly unsuc-

cessful are the attempts to show that the word was borrowed by the Ionians from a people who lived in Asia Minor.

The name *Ion* was given not only to the river in northwest Thessaly mentioned above, but also to the Alpheios River. Furthermore, there is a legend concerning the *Ionides*, the nymphs of a spring of Kytheros, which is a tributary of the Alpheios in the Olympia region; there is also mention of the *Ionaion* grove, which was close to the Alpheios. A hero, Ion, who is mentioned somewhere near Olympia, was the companion of the *Ionides* and bathed in the Alpheios; he must have been the personification of the river Ion-Alpheios, to whom the *Ionaion* grove was dedicated. But the son of Xouthos, Ion, who was the recognized ancestor of the Ionian race, had also been a river god; in Attica, it was believed that he was buried in the deme which was called *Potamos* (river), and he received sacrifices customarily offered in river worship rituals. The name *Ianiskos*, a healing god in Attica and Sikyon, is a diminutive of *Ian*, a variant of *Ion*. Further, this function connects him with the *Ionides* of Olympia, since these nymphs were believed to have healing powers and were worshipped under the name *Iatroi* (healers). One of them was called *Iasis* (cure). The words ἴασις, ἰατρός, ἰᾶσθαι all come from the Indo-European root *is- (to give warmth, to give life, to heal, but also: vehemence, force, violence). The latter meanings are appropriate to the nature of violent rushing streams, such as the Ion in northwest Thessaly and the Alpheios.

The Ionians, therefore, worshipped rivers, which they named *isawones, iaones, iones*, and personified them in a god whom they called *Isawon, Iaon, Ion*. Their ethnic name shows that they identified themselves with the element they worshipped, a usual phenomenon in ancient religions.

The dialect spoken by the Ionians when they left northwest Thessaly must have been closer to the common Greek language than to the familiar Ionic-Attic dialect.

It is quite probable that already at this time the Ionians celebrated the festival of Apatouria, since this festival was common to all Ionian communities and is of a very ancient character. The appellation Apatouria, which Athena had in Troizen, was a name left by the Ionians who lived there in prehistoric times.

The ancients believed that the Ionian tribes—the Aigikoreis, Argadeis, Geleontes, and Hopletes—originated in various social classes or castes. Some modern scholars have accepted this view as well as the ancients' interpretation of these names; others believe that they correspond to religious groups or to administrative divisions in Attica. But none of these theories can be regarded as correct. These names can be interpreted only as corresponding to actual early divisions of the Ionian tribe. The name *Hopletes* (Ὅπλη-τες) has been linked with the words *hoploteros, hoplotatos* (ὁπλότερος, ὁπλότατος = more recent, most recent), and this seems appropriate, since all the official lists of tribes have the Hopletes in the last place. Evidently, the Hopletes were members of a tribe which, at a later date, was added to the list containing the first three tribes. The addition was made by the Ionians of Attica, since the Hopletes are only mentioned at all in Attica, at Miletos, where there were

Athenian colonists, and at Kyzikos, a colony of Miletos. The other three tribes which are found in most Ionian cities must have existed before the period of migrations during which the Ionians scattered over the area to be described below.

In historical times, there were Ionians in only one area of the Greek mainland: Attica. The rest inhabited Euboia, the Cyclades, Ionia, and other distant colonies. Some trustworthy legends, however, mentioned the Ionians as having lived in earlier times in the Megarid, Korinthia, Epidauros, Kynouria, and Achaia. On the other hand, Homer's word that Euboia was occupied by the Abantes at the end of the Mycenaean Age shows that Euboia must have become Ionian at a later date.

Taking into account all the information we can glean from legends and all the traces of the Ionians (names, dialectal features, cults, etc.), which we find in various areas, we can draw the following conclusions: after leaving northwest Thessaly, the Proto-Ionians procceeded southwards; one group remained in southwest Thessaly, others pushed further on to western Lokris, the eastern mainland, the Argolid, Korinthia, Kynouria, Achaia, Pisatis, and northern Triphylia.

One part of the original Ionian settlements later submitted to other Greeks. Achaians, Minyans, Phlegyans,

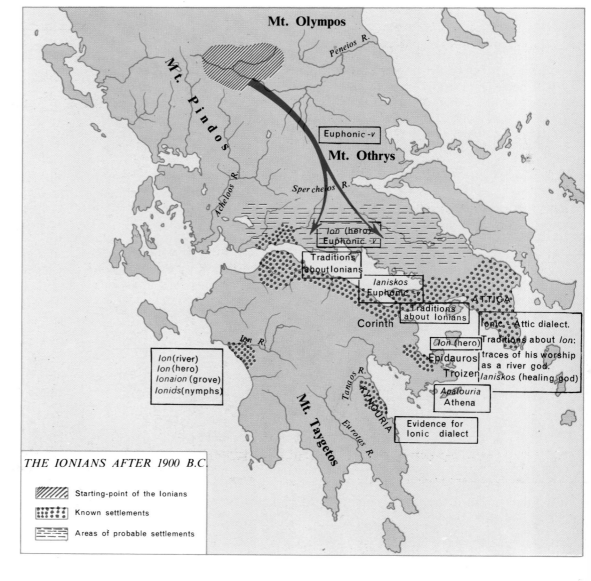

About 1900 B.C., a section of the Proto-Greeks moved away from their original homeland and spread throughout the Greek mainland. Other smaller and sporadic movements took place in the centuries which followed. Eventually, these Proto-Greeks were formed into the familiar Greek tribes of the Mycenaean Age. Of these, the Ionians who inhabited northwest Thessaly moved southwards. One small group stayed in southwest Thessaly, others moved further south and settled, as shown on the map, in Western Lokris, Attica, Megarid, Korinthia, Achaia, Pisatis and northern Triphylia, Kynouria, and western Argolid.

THE IONIANS AFTER 1900 B.C.

Starting-point of the Ionians

Known settlements

Areas of probable settlements

Lapiths, and others subdued or broke up the Ionian settlements in the eastern mainland as far as the borders of Attica and the Megarid and the northeast Peloponnesos. Other Achaians conquered northern Triphylia and Pisatis. At the end of the Mycenaean Age, Ionians still held Attica, the Megarid, Epidauros, Troizen, Kynouria, and Achaia. But Ionian populations continued to live as a subject race in the areas mentioned above.

In the meantime, the Ionians themselves had assimilated other racial elements. Some ancient texts express the opinion that the Ionians were Hellenized Pelasgians. This idea has no basis in fact, except to the extent of being an extrapolation of traditions connected with certain Ionian groups of historical times in whom the memory of Pelasgian ancestors was preserved. We shall see below that Lapiths and Molossians settled in Attica during the Mycenaean Age and were assimilated into the Ionian population so rapidly and to such a degree that their heroes came to be recognized as national heroes of the Athenians, and their clans became accepted into the circles of Athenian aristocracy. The creation of the Hoplete tribe mentioned above had the sole purpose of providing the cadre for the grouping together of people of non-Ionian origin who at some later point were recognized as members of the Ionian community which ruled Attica.

Arkadians and Arktanes

According to our hypothesis, the Arkadians settled in western Macedonia before 1900 B.C. The etymology of their name from *ark(t)os* (bear) suggests that they practised totem bear worship. There is more evidence for this in the Arkadian myth which presents the mother of Arkas as a bear or as a nymph transformed into a bear. So, on the basis of this and of their religion we may conclude that their name was extremely ancient.

This name makes its appearance in the actual Sterea Hellas and Athamania. Some myths mention Arkadians as allies of Herakles in wars against peoples of Thessaly and of regions situated in central Sterea Hellas, and one legend gives this name to the inhabitants of Opous on the shores of the Maliac Gulf. Themisto, who is mentioned in various myths as the mother of Arkas, is associated not with Arkalia, but with Athamania (she is said to be the wife of Athamas and the daughter either of Inachos, the river which flows through this country, or of Hypseus, the king of the Lapiths of Pindos); so there were myths about Arkas in his country too. Close neighbours of the Athamanians were the Arktanes (᾽Αρκτᾶνες), whose name is almost identical with that of the Arkadians (᾽Αρκάδες). The Arktanes who handed down the myths about Arkas in Athamania and the Arkadians of present-day Sterea Hellas were sections of the tribe which did not reach the Peloponnesos.

In 1900 B.C. the Arkadians spoke one of the two variants of Central Greek, the one which had features not only of Central Greek (and perhaps already some of the later Arkado-Cypriot dialect), but also some in common with Ionic and some with the Western dialect. After the Arkadians had settled in the Peloponnesos, some innovations were introduced, exclusive to Arkadian. The area in which the new dialect was spoken extended beyond the borders of the region called Arkadia in historical times towards the Argolid, Lakonia, Messenia, and Triphylia, all regions which were later occupied by the Achaians.

While the Arkadians of Sterea Hellas and the regions of the Peloponnesos, excepting Arkadia and a part of Triphylia, were absorbed by newcomers, fellow Arkadians in central Peloponnesos who survived to historical times themselves absorbed their predecessors, the majority of whom were Pelasgians. It was thus that Pelasgian legends about Pelasgos came to be regarded as Arkadian myths, and it was believed that the Arkadians were Hellenized Pelasgians.

THE PROTO-AIOLIANS

The Aiolic, which evolved from the northeast variant of the earlier Central Greek, was spoken on the islands of Lesbos and Tenedos, and on the adjacent coast of Asia Minor. But Lesbos was colonied by Greeks after the end of the Mycenaean Age, and the Asia Minor coast even later. So where were the Aiolic-speaking people before the end of the Mycenaean Age and earlier?

The traditions about Aiolian colonization in Asia Minor mention as the mother countries various regions in Thessaly, present-day Sterea Hellas, the Peloponnesos, and some islands of the Aegean. Furthermore, dialectal phenomena suggesting an Aiolic substratum are observed in these and some other regions. The Aiolic dialect, however, could not have evolved uniformly from one end to the other of such an extensive and broken-up area. Its original birthplace must have been a much more compact and isolated region. Thessaly answers to this description; and there is other evidence in its favour: (1) In historical times, the inhabitants of Pelasgiotis (in eastern Thessaly) spoke a variant of Thessalian which was intermediate between Aiolic and the variant of Thessalian spoken in Thessaliotis (in southwestern Thessaly) which is considered closer to the language brought by the Thessalians when they occupied this country after the end of the Mycenaean Age. (2) The Mycenaean dialect has several features in common with the Aiolic. This is easily explained by the fact that the Achaians, who spoke Mycenaean Greek in the Peloponnesos and in Crete, had emigrated from southern Thessaly. Their dialect was already formed to a large extent at the beginning of the Late Bronze Age (c. 1600 B.C.), when one section of the Achaians of Thessaly migrated to northeast Peloponnesos. Since a dialect can only take shape if the people who evolve it live for a considerable length of time in the area where the dialect is being formed, it is reasonable to suppose that the Greek elements who called themselves Achaians entered Thessaly around 1900 B.C. By that date, all the speakers of the northeast variant of Central Greek must have arrived.

To these distant ancestors of the historical Aiolians we can attribute neither a race-name nor any other distinguishing characteristic. We do not even know if they were one tribe or many. At any rate, by the end of the Mycenaean Age, they were split up into several tribes. But there is no trace of the name of any one of them north of Thessaly.

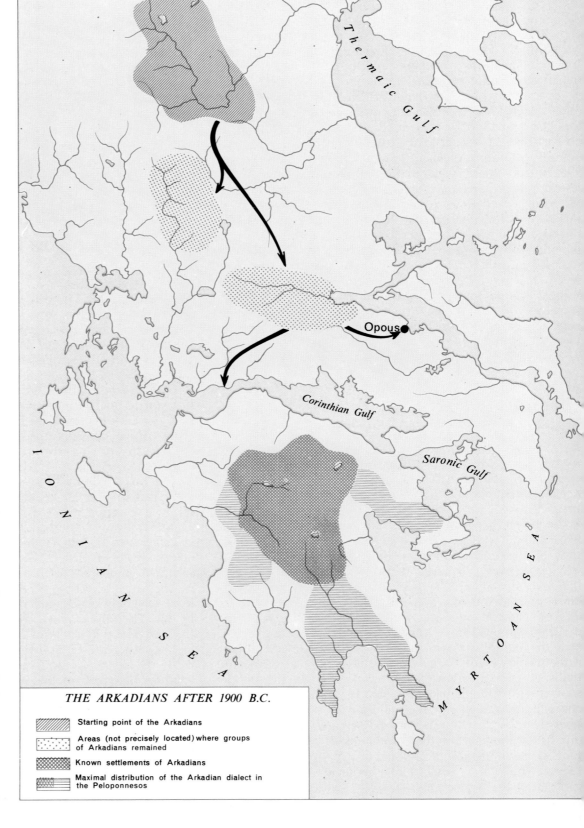

The Arkadians, who presumably inhabited western Macedonia before 1900 B.C., moved southwards during the great migratory movement of the Proto-Greeks and settled in central and northern Peloponnesos. The Arkadian dialect was formed during the last phase of this movement and spread throughout almost the whole of the Peloponnesos. By historical times, however, only the Arkadians in central Peloponnesos had survived by absorbing their predecessors in that region. The rest of the Arkadians, in the neighbouring regions and in the mainland, were absorbed by the tribes who settled later in those regions.

THE ARKADIANS AFTER 1900 B.C.

Starting point of the Arkadians

Areas (not precisely located) where groups of Arkadians remained

Known settlements of Arkadians

Maximal distribution of the Arkadian dialect in the Peloponnesos

Achaians

The most important of the tribes of this group is that which later came to be known by the name *Achaioi* (Ἀχαιοί). In the Homeric poems, this name is used hundreds of times to denote the Greeks as a whole in the period during which the events described in the epics took place. However, in three passages in the *Iliad*, the same name is attributed to a particular Greek tribe which lived in the region that came to be called Achaian Phthiotis, in the Argolid, and in Messenia. Legends mention migrations of groups of Achaians from Achaian Phthiotis to the Argolid, Lakonia, and Messenia, as well as other movements of Achaians from the Argolid to the other two regions of the Peloponnesos. They also refer to the occupation of Olympia by Achaians before the descent of the Aitolians to Elis. According to other legends, the Achaians of the Argolid, Lakonia, Messenia, and the Olympia region were annihilated, displaced, or reduced to subjection by the Dorians and the Eleans; some, however, fled to the north coast of the Peloponnesos, which has since been known as Achaia. The Achaian Phthiotians of historical times were also believed to have descended from the early Achaians.

In historical times, both the Achaians of Phthiotis and the Achaians on the north coast of the Peloponnesos spoke sub-dialects of West Greek. For that reason, some scholars have concluded that the Bronze Age Achaians should also be assigned to the same linguistic group; others have identified the Achaians with the western tribes as a whole, Dorians included, and have cast doubt on the validity of the ancient legends which explicitly distinguish Achaians from Dorians and which say that the latter migrated to the Peloponnesos after the end of the Mycenaean Age and occupied lands which belonged to the Achaians. A third theory, based on the "Aiolisms" in the language of the Homeric poems, states that the Achaians spoke Aiolic. Yet a fourth modern opinion, following Homer, considers the Achaians to be all the Greeks south of Macedonia in the Mycenaean Age. All these theories, and many others less widely accepted, which are omitted here, have now been superceded by the view that the Achaians of the Mycenaean Age were the ancestors of the Arkadians and the Cypriots of historical times. Before the decipherment of the Mycenaean Linear B tablets, the arguments in support of this theory were that there were remnants of the Arkadian dialect in the Argolid, Lakonia, and Messenia, all three being regions which were once inhabited by Achaians, and also that there were traces of the presence of Achaians in Cyprus, where the Arkadian dialect had been transplanted. Now that the Mycenaean script has been deciphered, many scholars believe that this theory has been confirmed by the new evidence.

We shall confine ourselves here to a discussion of this last theory, the one which has had the support of the majority of scholars ever since it was first formulated in 1886. All the main and subsidiary arguments put forward in support of this theory before the decipherment of Linear B aimed at showing that during the Mycenaean Age Arkado-Cypriot was spoken wherever there were Achaians, and, conversely, that there were Achaians wherever Arkado-Cypriot was spoken. There is other evidence, however, from which it emerges that (1) the distribution of the Achaians covers only one part of the area where Arkado-Cypriot was spoken: (2) the Achaians did not speak Arkado-Cypriot. We draw the first conclusion from the following observations: (a) Unlike the Argolid, Lakonia, Messenia, the Olympia region, Crete, and the Dodecanese, Arkadia has no legends about Achaians. This is particularly significant, because the Arkadians of historical times, with unimportant exceptions, were the descendants of the ethnic groups who inhabited the country before the end of the Mycenaean Age, while in the Argolid, Lakonia, Messenia, the Olympia region, Crete, and the Dodecanese, the Achaians had been subdued by the Dorians; (b) A passage in Herodotos (IX. 26) tells us that the inhabitants of Tegea in Arkadia differentiated themselves from the Achaians; (c) The ethnic *Achaios* which

is given on an inscription to a Cypriot does not apply, as is often thought, to the Cypriots as a whole. On the same inscription, another Cypriot is called *Salaminios*, from the name of the Cypriot town of which he was a citizen. So, the name *Achaios* here applies only to a citizen of a Cypriot town called * *Achaia*. This place-name, the similarly Cypriot place-name *Achaiōn Akte*, and the name *Achaiomanteis*, which was given to the priests of some unknown Cypriot cult, do not indicate that all the Cypriots were Achaians, but make it more likely that these names originated among a small group of Cypriots. If this was the only evidence we had, we might have been able to concede that, while all the people who spoke the Arkadian dialect in the Bronze Age were not Achaians, the latter did form one group of Arkadian-speakers chiefly in the Argolid, Lakonia, and Messenia, where there are indisputable traces of the Arkado-Cypriot dialect and evidence of the presence of Achaians. But this concession is impossible even on the strength of the evidence which existed before the decipherment of the Mycenaean Linear B tablets. For, both the ancient legends and the cults of the Achaians point to Thessaly, where not the Arkadian but the Aiolic dialect took shape. The decipherment of the tablets, as we shall see below, upsets rather than confirms the theory that the Achaians are to be identified with the Arkado-Cypriots. From these texts it emerges that Mycenaean evolved from Aiolic, as it is suggested by the legends and cults that the Achaians of the Greek South came from Achaian Phthiotis.

The decipherment of the Linear B tablets by Michael Ventris and John Chadwick gave us a wealth of evidence about the Achaians; it is in fact not only new, but also the first direct and, therefore, the most reliable evidence available. So it was realized that the answer to the old question, "Who were the Achaians?" depended on the answer given to the newly-formulated question, "What is the relation between the Achaian (or Mycenaean) dialect and the known Greek dialects of historical times?". As it is, many of the suggested answers to this second question, especially those which have been widely accepted, are influenced either by answers which had already been given to the first question or by opinions about the origin of the Greek dialects which had been formulated before the decipherment of Linear B.

When Ventris and Chadwick published the results of the decipherment, they first expressed the opinion that the dialect of the Mycenaean tablets was an archaic form of "Achaian", that is, of Arkado-Cypriot, since they did not question the then generally held opinion that Arkado-Cypriot was the dialect spoken by the Achaians. But most of the characteristics of the dialect of the tablets, which they thought identified it as Arkado-Cypriot, were in fact simply archaisms, that is to say, features which were once common to the whole of the Greek language but which later disappeared from all Greek dialects except the dialect of the Mycenaean tablets and Arkado-Cypriot.

It was not long before Chadwick and, soon after him, Ventris abandoned their first theory and declared that the dialect of the tablets was the common ancestor of Aiolic and Arkado-Cypriot. On the basis of the phenomena they had observed and the interpretation they had placed on it, they should have identified Mycenaean with Aiolic. They justified their hesitation in drawing this conclusion by invoking "historical reasons", which is another way of saying that they were still under the influence of preconceived ideas.

Another scholar, E. Risch, identified the dialect of the Mycenaean tablets with the "Southern" dialect, which he himself had suggested earlier as the common ancestor of Arkado-Cypriot and Ionic-Attic and which he had dated to the Mycenaean Age. This theory overlooks phenomena which establish a close link between Arkado-Cypriot and Aiolic and many other phenomena which dissociate Arkado-Cypriot from Ionic-Attic, and dates the birth of these two dialects to a period after the Mycenaean Age on the basis of no reliable arguments. When all the dialectal evidence is considered together, Ionic-Attic and Arkado-Cypriot emerge as strongly differentiated dialects in the Mycenaean Age, while the "Southern" dialect disappears altogether. Besides, the identification of Mycenaean with the "Southern" dialect rested on partial selection and interpretation of evidence. In fact, Risch noted the relation of Mycenaean to both Ionic-Attic and Arkado-Cypriot, but failed to note its relation to Aiolic; and although he observed that Mycenaean had some innovations exclusive to itself, he failed to realize that this fact argued against his own theory that Mycenaean was the mother language of Ionic-Attic and Arkado-Cypriot. For, in such a case, these dialects would have inherited the innovations of Mycenaean. The only possible conclusion is that Mycenaean had evolved as a separate dialect.

The relation, overlooked by the majority of Mycenaean scholars, between Mycenaean and Aiolic has been put forward by a few specialists, perhaps not always on the basis of conclusive arguments, but without negating links with other dialects, particularly Arkadian.

It is only recently that some attention has been paid to the innovations which belong exclusively to the Mycenaean dialect. Many scholars have noted these Mycenaean peculiarities, but have hesitated to draw the obvious, indeed the only possible, conclusion.

We shall not attempt to review all the theories which have been put forward about the identity of the dialect on the Mycenaean tablets. We have discussed only those theories which have been widely accepted.

There are many sides to the problem of the Mycenaean dialect, and each must be carefully studied if we wish to piece together a comprehensive solution. The dialectal phenomena in the Mycenaean texts (excluding phenomena once common to the whole Greek language which have survived in the Mycenaean dialect and are therefore misleading) can be divided into the following groups:

(1) *Exclusively Mycenaean*: (a) sporadic loss of the digamma, still conserved in the other Greek dialects; (b) palatalization of *k* and *g* before *ẏ*; (c) plural instrumental -*os;* (d) suffix -*wont-* in place of -*went-* in the formation of place-names; (e) dual nominative-accusative of *a*- stem feminines in -*o;* (f) dual nominative-accusative of *a*- stem masculines in -*ae;* (g) singular dative -*ei* in place of the locative; (h) extension of dual oblique cases -*oi* -*oiin* of the first and second declensions to the third declension; (i) extension of the use of derivatives in -*eus;* (j) extension of the use of derivatives in -*ta;*

(2) *Mycenaean and Aiolic*: (a) tendency to eliminate *e* and *i* between consonant and vowel; (b) *o* in place of *a* in *enewo, enotos* (for *enea, enatos*); (c) extension of the use of adjectives of material in -*ios* instead of a genitive; (d) patronymics in -*eios;*

(3) *Mycenaean and Arkado-Cypriot*: (a) dual oblique cases of the thematic flexion in -*oiyn;* (b) plural dative of the third person of the personal pronoun *spheis;* (c) possibly, adverbial suffix -*da;*

(4) *Mycenaean, Aiolic, and Arkado-Cypriot*: (a) *a⟩o* before or after a nasal or a liquid; (b) *o⟩(o)u;* (c) preposition *peda;* (d) extension of the *o* vocalism of Indo-European nasal or liquid sonants; (e) tendency to replace athematic infinitives -*nai* by thematic -*(e)n;* (f) construction of some prepositions with the dative-locative instead of the genitive-ablative; (g) preference for the form *apu* of the preposition *apo;*

(5) *Mycenaean, Aiolic, Arkado-Cypriot, and Ionic-Attic*: (a) assibilation of *ti, te, tu;* (b) preference for the *e* vocalism in *hieros.*

The Mycenaean dialect, therefore, does not correspond to any of the Greek dialects known before the decipherment of the Mycenaean tablets; not only does it have some completely individual features, but the phenomena observed both in it and in other dialects make up a unique whole in Greek. Combinations of the latter phenomena reveal the links between Mycenaean and other Greek dialects whose date, location, and character can be determined. Links between Mycenaean and Arkado-Cypriot should be located in the Peloponnesos and be later than those between Mycenaean and Aiolic, which must be placed in Thessaly, since it is known from other evidence that the Achaians, to whom the Mycenaean dialect is attributed, came down to the Peloponnesos from Thessaly. Since the first evidence for links between Mycenaean and Arkado-Cypriot is on tablets dated from 1400 B.C. onwards, the links must have been established at an earlier period. On the other hand, the phenomena which connect Mycenaean with Aiolic are to be dated between the beginning of the formation of the Aiolic dialect and the departure from Thessaly of the group of Achaians who came down to the Peloponnesos and Crete. Even if Aiolic had begun to be formed before the descent of the Proto-Aiolic-speaking groups into Thessaly c. 1900 B.C., very few of its characteristics would be earlier than that date, because the process of the formation of the dialect speeded up from the moment that the Proto-Aiolic speakers ceased to be in contact with the Proto-Arkadian speakers. The breaking off of contact between the Mycenaean and the Aiolic dialects and the establishment of connections between Mycenaean and Arkado-Cypriot occurred some time between 1900 B.C. and 1400 B.C. Since the phenomena which connect Mycenaean and Aiolic are far more numerous than those which connect Mycenaean and Arkado-Cypriot, it seems likely that the migrations of the creators and speakers of the Mycenaean dialect took place closer to 1400 B.C. than to 1900 B.C., perhaps about 1600 B.C. The fact that we find both Aiolic and Arkado-Cypriot in groups 4 and 5 above shows that the phenomena observed in these groups are derived from Central Greek. But how did phenomena from Central Greek appear in Mycenaean? They are too numerous to have all been taken by the Achaians from the Arkadians between 1600 B.C. and 1400 B.C. Some, if not all, must have come then from Aiolic. And if these are added to the phenomena of group 2, which are common to Mycenaean and Aiolic, it becomes obvious that the two dialects are not simply old neighbours, but in fact close relatives. The connections between Central Greek and Aiolic, Aiolic and Mycenaean, Mycenaean and Central Greek suggest that Mycenaean did not evolve directly out of the Central Greek dialect, but was an offshoot of Aiolic, through which it inherited the characteristics of Central Greek.

We also know something of the cults of the Achaians. They inherited two of their cults, together with their race-name, from the Proto-Achaians: the cult of Achilles, the water god, and of Achaia, goddess of earth, who was identified with Demeter. The other gods attributed to the Achaians (because they are found in most of the regions where groups of Achaians settled) had Greek names: Neleus, Pelops or Pelias, Agamemnon, Bias, Melampous. The first of these has been recognized by historians of ancient religion and by other scholars as an ancient god of Hades, and his name has been convincingly derived from νη-ἔλεος (pitiless, without mercy). Myths and cults connected with Neleus are found in Thessaly, western Boiotia, Attica,

Korinthia, Messenia, and Triphylia. Pelops is found in the Argolid, Eastern Lokris, Achaia, Pisatis, and Lakonia, but has his roots in Achaian Phthiotis, where the name *Pelopeia*, a derivative of *Pelops*, was given to a daughter of *Pelias*, a name which is itself a variant of *Pelops*. Both names are derived from πελιός (pale). The mother of Pelops, Kalyke, also belongs to Thessalian mythology. The ancient myths which present Pelops as coming to the Peloponnesos from Asia Minor are of posterior derivation. Agamemnon is associated with wells, healing springs, and sacred plane trees at Delphi, in Boiotia, at Kaphyai in Arkadia, in other regions of Greece (our sources do not specify which), and in Ionia. Apart from this evidence that Agamemnon was an ancient god of water and vegetation, there is the testimony of the ancients and archaeological evidence that Agamemnon was worshipped at Amyklai in Lakonia under the name

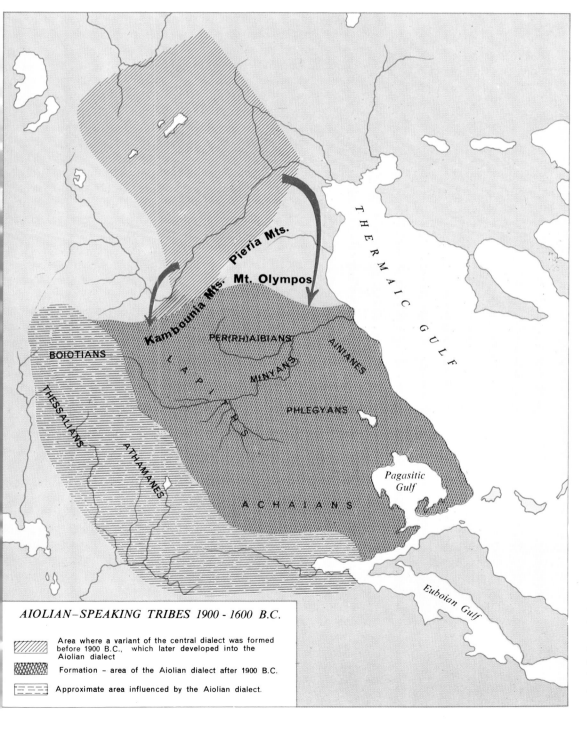

AIOLIAN–SPEAKING TRIBES 1900 - 1600 B.C.

Area where a variant of the central dialect was formed before 1900 B.C., which later developed into the Aiolian dialect

Formation - area of the Aiolian dialect after 1900 B.C.

Approximate area influenced by the Aiolian dialect.

The Central dialect of Proto-Greek was evolved in Macedonia and northern Thessaly before 1900 B.C. A variant of this dialect developed into the Aiolic, which came to be spoken in the whole of Thessaly. It was spoken by the Achaians, Lapiths, Per(rh)aibians, Minyans, Ainianes, and Phlegyans. This dialect also influenced the neighbouring western and southern regions, which were inhabited by Athamanians, Boiotians, and Thessalians.

Zeus Agamemnon along with his associate, goddess Alexandra. So, the cult of Agamemnon at a shrine near Mycenae was not directed to a heroified mortal, as has been suggested, but to the ancient god of the Achaians. Melampous, who was worshipped in historical times at Aigosthena in the Megarid and at Melampodeion in Arkadia, and Bias, a river god (there is mention of a river of this name in Messenia, and the name has an etymology from the word βία meaning "violence", "force"), appear as founders of Achaian dynasties and heroes of myths in southern Thessaly, the Argolid, and Messenia.

These, then, were the regions in which the Achaian cults known to us were located. By taking these findings, together with the conclusions which have emerged from the analysis of the dialect on the Mycenaean tablets, and comparing them with the information contained in the historical nuclei of the legends concerning Achaian migrations, it is possible to reconstruct a general picture of the formation and expansion of this tribe.

One or more tribes of Proto-Greeks who spoke a Pre-Aiolic variant of Central Greek arrived in southern Thessaly c. 1900 B.C. and subdued the resident population of Pre-Greek Proto-Achaians. After a long period of co-existence, the newcomers absorbed the Pre-Greek Proto-Achaians, but took over their name and at least two of their cults. They also embraced a section of the Greek tribe of the Athamanians who had also penetrated into southern Thessaly.

Around 1600 B.C., groups from this tribe, formed by the mixing of the ethnic groups mentioned above, moved southwards as far as northwest Peloponnesos. Perhaps this movement should be associated with the establishment of Achaians (indicated by the existence of traces of Achaian cults and myths) in Eastern Lokris, Phokis, Boiotia, and the Megarid. Legends have preserved the memory of clashes between the Achaians who settled in the region of Mt. Kyllene and the inhabitants of Phliasia and Stymphalia, while in the Argolic plain, they connect Achaian expansion with the marriages of Achaian leaders to the daughters of Danaos, which perhaps reflects the peaceful occupation of the land of the Danaans by Achaian people. This is supported by archaeological evidence, for there are no signs of any violent clashes in the Argolid during the Mycenaean Age. The dialect of the Achaians of northeast Peloponnesos, cut off from the Aiolic-speaking area, began to acquire its own characteristic features while, at the same time, its contact with the Arkadian-speaking sector resulted in its absorbing new influences.

According to legend, Lakonia was occupied by Achaians who came from Thessaly, Boiotia, and the Argolid. The cult of Hera Argeia confirms the Argolid as one of their places of origin, while the cult of Ino could have been introduced either directly from Thessaly or from one of the intervening stopping places of the Achaians where this cult was known. The legends which connect the Achaians of Messenia directly with Thessaly are confirmed by the fact that Neleus, Bias, Thetis, and the Nereids were known in Messenia, for all these had been brought by the Achaians when they moved from Thessaly to what today is Sterea Hellas and to the Peloponnesos. However, the dialect on the tablets found in the palace at Pylos, being the same as that on the tablets found at Mycenae and Knosos, indicates that the people who spoke this dialect at Pylos came not from Thessaly directly but from the Argolid, and that their migration must have taken

place after 1400 B.C. Whether these were the first Achaians who settled in Messenia, or whether they were preceded by others who came from Thessaly or elsewhere, the Achaian population settled among the earlier population of the Kaukones. From Messenia, the Achaians spread to the north, occupying Triphylia and Pisatis.

The form of the language on the Knosos tablets tells us that the Achaians who captured Minos's capital came from the Argolid and that they migrated to Crete sometime before the first decades of the 14th century B.C., at about the time that the first Achaian settlements appeared on Rhodes and at Miletos.

Lapiths

The Lapiths settled originally in the extreme west of Thessaly and Mt. Pindos, and from there they were in touch with Epeiros. Some memories of this period were preserved in the later myths of this tribe. The many-branched genealogical tree of Lapith heroes who appear, in the Late Mycenaean Age, to be active in eastern Thessaly and Greek regions further south begins with Hypseus, who is said either to have lived in the mountains of Pindos near the springs of the Peneios or to be the father of Themisto, who appears in Athamanian myths. One of the Lapith heroes, Polypoites, has the same name as one of the sons of Odysseus and Kallidike, queen of the Thesprotians. In a myth to be considered below, two Lapith heroes, Peirithous, father of Polypoites, and Theseus have an adventure somewhere in Thesprotia. Finally, the appearance of Lapiths and Molossians together in settlements in southern Greece suggests that these two tribes migrated there together from Pindos.

According to Homer, towards the end of the Mycenaean Age the Lapiths held the cities Argissa, Gyrton, Orthe, Elone, and Oloosson (which were in north Pelasgiotis and south Per(rh)aibia) as well as the cities Larisa and Mopsion and the mountains Ossa and Homalion, which are attributed to them by later writers. Post-Homeric writers tell us that the Lapiths had displaced the Ainianes and subdued one section of the Per(rh)aibians. The ethnic name *Ainianes* is derived from the name of a city which lay within the boundaries of the Lapith state in the period described by Homer. Lands of the same state belonged earlier to Phlegyans and Minyans. It emerges from these facts that the Lapiths spread out towards Histiaiotis and Per(rh)aibia perhaps after the middle of the Mycenaean Age.

Our sources mention a great number of Lapith heroes, many more than heroes of any other Greek tribe. Even if the list is confined to the earlier texts, which offer guarantees of authenticity, we can still find over twenty names.

Of these heroes, Aigeus and Theseus are associated with Thessaly, the latter more particularly with Magnesia and the city of Pherai. Also in Thessaly, as well as in the Spercheios Valley, are Ampykos, Polypoites, and Phalaros. Other evidence for the existence of Lapiths in the Spercheios Valley is the ethnic name *Lapitheios*, which is derived from the name of a town, *Lapithe*. In Phokis, we have the town Theseia and other traces of Lapiths; in Boiotia, Phalaros, Koronos, and other Lapith heroes.

The greatest concentration of Lapith legends and names south of Thessaly is in Attica. The clan of the Perithoïdai

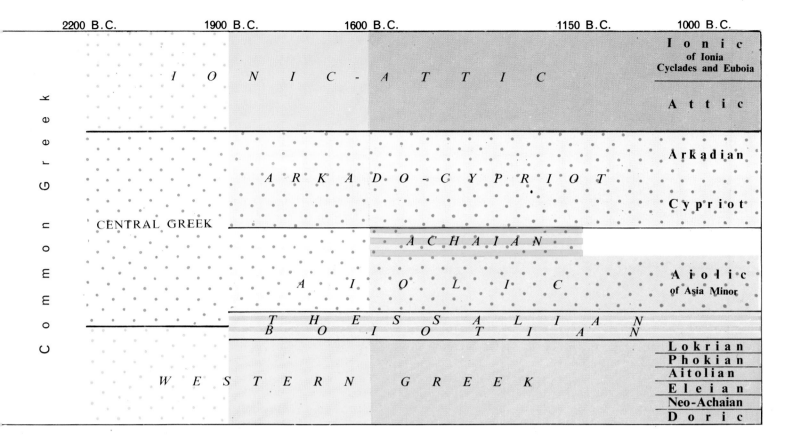

Diagram showing the splitting up of the Greek language into dialects, their mutual relation and their evolution. The Greek language split up into three dialects between 2200/2100 and 1900 B.C., during the period, that is, when the main body of Greek-speaking Indo-Europeans concentrated in a rather small area, which included Epeiros and a part of southwest Illyria, western Macedonia, and northwest Thessaly. Two of these dialects were very ancient forms of the Ionic-Attic and of the Western dialects of later times. The third, the Central, broke up later into Aiolic and Arkado-Cypriot. The splitting-up of this dialect must have begun after 1900 B.C., since one group of tribes who spoke the Central dialect migrated to the Peloponnesos and another to Thessaly, with the result that the original dialect underwent changes. Both the Aiolic, which evolved in Thessaly, and the Arkado-Cypriot dialect, which evolved in the Peloponnesos, kept many of the characteristics of the mother dialect. About 1600 B.C., one section of the Aiolic-speaking Achaians migrated to northwest Peloponnesos, where they began to add some innovations to the original Aiolic, and to be influenced by Arkado-Cypriot. The result was the Achaian dialect, which has become known to us as the language of the inscribed tablets from the Mycenaean palaces. In the meantime, in the regions where Aiolic and Western Greek influences crossed each other's path, the Thessalian and Boiotian dialects were formed. At about the same time, Ionic-Attic and the Western dialect reached their final form. After the end of the Mycenaean Age, the Achaian dialect disappeared. The great migrations of the Greek tribes during the second millennium B.C. resulted in the development of sub-dialects within each dialect. In the diagram, each dialect is shown by a different colour. Central, Arkado-Cypriot, Achaian, and Aiolic are shown in shades of red to indicate their close relation. Red dots on the bands of the filial dialects of the Central and on that of the Mycenaean indicate survival of Central characteristics in the dialects which grew out of it. Thessalian and Boiotian are not given any special colour, but are shown by alternating bands of the red and green colours of Aiolic and Western, respectively. In the course of time, each dialect took on more and more its own individual features. This development is shown by dots in the appropriate colour in the column for the period 2200-1900 B.C., by a light-shaded background of the same colour in the column for 1900-1600 B.C., and by a deeper-shaded background for the columns 1600 B.C. onwards.

who lived in the deme of the same name, close to Marathon, believed that they had descended originally from the Lapith hero Peirithous. Their name alone is eloquent enough testimony. Boutes, the ancestor of the Attic clan of the Boutadai, bore the same name as the father of Hippodameia, wife of Peirithous and mother of Polypoites. A third Attic clan, the Koronidai, and the village Koroneia had the same name as the Lapith hero Koronos. Koroneia was close to Brauron, in the deme of Philaïdai, which was inhabited by the Philaïdai, a clan of Molossian descent. Koronos was also said to be the father of Lysidike, mother of Philaios, i.e. of the ancestor of the Philaïdai. Another interesting point about the relations between the Lapiths and the Molossians,

and particularly the Philaïdai, is that the very rare name Kypselos is found among the Philaïdai of Attica and also in a Lapith clan who lived in northeast Peloponnesos. The Athenians linked Peirithous with Theseus, and this tallies with the mention of the latter in Hesiod as a Lapith hero. Hesiod could not have access to Attic sources, nor could the Athenians have been influenced by Hesiod in linking the two heroes, because Hesiod does not mention Peirithous. An Attic myth related that Peirithous and Theseus tried to carry away Persephone, wife of Aïdoneus, or Hades, the king of Thesprotia, to a region of Epeiros (we know exactly which region since the rivers Kokytos and Acheron and Lake Acherousia are specifically mentioned), but they fell into the hands of the king and were imprisoned in Hades. This myth could not have been made up in Attica; if it had been, it could not have been earlier than the 5th century B.C., since before that date the Athenians had no contact with Epeiros. But the 5th century B.C. is a very late date for the creation of such a myth. Firstly, the myth itself has a very ancient character; it is set in the kingdom of the dead, which is thought to lie in some region of Epeiros, and it is one of many stories in which the god or ruler of the Underworld subdues those who try to abduct his wife or one of the dead. Secondly, up to the 5th century B.C., Athenian legends about Theseus had crystallized around such matters as could have no connection with any adventure of this hero in Hades. It is more probable, therefore, that this myth came to Attica with the Lapiths, particularly the Perithoïdai, who came directly from Pindos, where they must have been in contact with Epeiros and the Thesprotians. Other Lapith heroes in Attica are Phalaros, Periphas, and Phorbas.

The Kypselidai in Corinth believed that they were descendants of the Lapith hero Kaineus and remembered that their ancestors had lived at Gonoussa, near Sikyon, until the arrival of the Dorians. Other traces of Lapiths in the same region are myths about Koronos, who is mentioned as the king of Sikyon, and about Elatos and Peirithous, who are associated with Mt. Kyllene. Since Sikyon and Gonoussa and other cities in the same region clearly show close links with Pelasgiotis and since there was a settlement of Per(rh)aibians at Pheneos, which borders on Mt. Kyllene, we may assume that the Lapiths of northeast Peloponnesos came from northern Thessaly and that they migrated from there along with other peoples of the same origin.

Groups of Lapiths came down as far as Lakonia. A ridge of Taygetos which pushes out into the Eurotas plain is called Lapithaios, and there are legends in this region about the heroes Lapithes, Ampykos, and Elatos and a myth which locates the Centaurs at Malea, whereas Homer mentions Mt. Pelion as the home of these monster enemies of the Lapiths.

The Centaurs are also said to have lived at Pholoe. This is because the myth moved with the Lapiths when they migrated from Thessaly to Elis. Here the legend states explicitly that Phorbas, son of Lapithes, left Thessaly and settled at Olonos, which is another name for Mt. Erymanthos. The same hero is said to have helped Epeios against Pelops. This myth is evidently an echo of the wars waged by Lapiths and Epeians against the Achaians of Olympia and Pisa, who are represented here by Pelops. Aigeus and Koronos too appear again in Elis. In the *Iliad*, the inhabitants of Elis are Epeians. But three out of their four leaders belong to Lapith dynasties, and the fourth is a descendant of a certain Pythios, who had come from Thessaly and could also, therefore, have been a Lapith. South of Elis, in Triphylia, a mountain was called Lapithos.

Phlegyans

The ethnic *Phlegyas* is a word which means a kind of eagle of dark red colour; it has the same root as the verb *phlegō* with the very characteristic Greek *ph* in place of an Indo-European *bh*. So the Phlegyans were a Greek tribe in spite of the fact that in the *Iliad*, although their existence was known, they are not mentioned among the Greeks who fought at Troy.

Phlegyas, the hero of the tribe, is closely connected with mythical figures in the Dotian plain and in the region of Lake Boibe, in the middle of eastern Thessaly. Since the *Iliad* attributes this country to the Lapiths, it follows that the Phlegyans had occupied it at an earlier period.

From the "Homeric" *Hymn to Apollo* and other ancient texts we learn that, in very early years, sections of this tribe had settled in Daulis and close to the Kopais Lake. They are remembered in myths chiefly for their aggressiveness and ferocity, qualities to which their neighbours could testify. The information about dates which can be gleaned from various sources suggests that the wars in which these people were involved took place before the end of the Late Bronze Age. The fact that they are not mentioned in the *Iliad* among the peoples living in Phokis and Boiotia shows that they did not survive there until the end of the Mycenaean Age.

The Phlegyans were one of the earliest peoples to worship Asklepios, a god whose roots were in Thessaly. At Titane in Sikyonia, whose name is connected with that of the mountain Titanos, situated on the borders of Pelasgiotis and Histiaiotis, Asklepios was worshipped under the appellation *Gortynios*. This appellation is related to a place-name having the form *Gyrton(e)* on the Dotian plain, which was the Thessalian homeland of the Phlegyans, and the form *Kyrtone* in the region of their settlements in Boiotia. The Phlegyans of present-day Sterea Hellas and Sikyonia, therefore, had migrated from Thessaly.

Minyans

Although ancient sources refer to the Minyans as a very ancient Greek tribe, some scholars have claimed that the Minyans were not Greek, others that they never existed at all. We shall not refute the arguments of the latter group here, but simply point out that the memories which were preserved about the Minyans in various parts of Greece were too vivid and too concrete to relate to an imaginary people.

Of the theories which claim that the Minyans were not Greek, we shall mention only the one which has had a large following ever since it was first formulated 150 years ago. According to this theory, the Minyans were related to the inhabitants of Minoan Crete. The evidence adduced is that the names *Minyas* and *Minos* have the same root. But the *i* in the second is long, while the *i* in the first is short. This makes it difficult to prove that the two names are related, whereas it suggests that the name Minyas is connected with the Indo-European * *minu-* (with a short *i*), which means "small" and which has survived in other Indo-European languages as well as in Greek.

In the *Iliad*, the Minyans appear as rulers of a part of western Boiotia, including the cities Orchomenos and Aspledon; there is no mention of them in Thessaly, where other ancient sources and documentary evidence place them.

West of Tempe and close to the borders of Thessaly and Macedonia, we find three characteristic names: *Minya*, the name of a city and a mountain directly connected with the name of the tribe; *Orchomenos*, name of a city and a mountain, which in Boiotia is that of the seat of the Minyans there; *Almon* or *Almonia*, the name of a city (in our sources it is identified with *Minya*), whose ethnic *Almones* appears in Boiotia again as the name of a village near Orchomenos. The occurrence of these three names together both in a small region of northeast Thessaly and in a similarly small region of western Boiotia suggests that Minyans migrated from the one region to the other. The memory of this migration was preserved in legends in Boiotian Orchomenos, according to which the founder and first king of the city was a son of Peneios, a river in Thessaly which ran through the region where the towns Minya, Almon, and Orchomenos were situated. The Minyans, of course, had arrived in Boiotia before the end of the Mycenaean Age, when the events described in the *Iliad* occurred. On the other hand, the earlier the migration, the more difficult it would have been for the legends to retain the memory of colonists coming from a region of Thessaly close to the Peneios. In the *Iliad*, the Thessalian homeland of the Minyans belongs to the Lapiths. So, it is probable that migrations of the Minyans from Thessaly to Boiotia can be linked with the spread of the Lapiths from western to eastern Thessaly.

Many trustworthy sources place the Minyans in another region of Thessaly, at Iolkos, and connect them particularly with the Argonaut expedition. Further, in neighbouring Achaian Phthiotis, we find another city called Orchomenos. The *Iliad*, however, says nothing of Minyans at Iolkos, but mentions other peoples as the inhabitants of this region.

The name *Minyeios* which appears in the *Iliad* as a river in northern Triphylia suggests that Minyans may also have settled in this region before the end of the Mycenaean Age. Herodotos mentions Minyan migrations to this area from Lakonia after the descent of the Dorians.

Per(rh)aibians and Ainianes

In the Homeric catalogue of Greeks who took part in the Trojan expedition, the Per(rh)aibians and Ainianes have a common leader and live in a region whose capital is the town of Kyphos; in the same region there is a place called Dodone and a river called Titaresios, a tributary of the Peneios. The ancient scholiasts of Homer thought that the region he was referring to was the northern part of historical Per(rh)aibia, because they knew of settlements there with the names Kyphos and Dodone or Bodone; they could identify the Titaresios with a tributary of the Peneios which had its source in the mountain called Titarion; and, finally, because they knew from various legends that in the period earlier than the one with which Homer was concerned, Per(rh)aibians and Ainianes held the country which the *Iliad* assigned to the Lapiths. Some modern scholars have endorsed the opinion of the ancient scholiasts and have recognized some of the geophysical features mentioned by Homer in the region in question. Others have doubted the validity of the evidence upon which the ancients relied and suggest that the country of the Per(rh)aibians and Ainianes was in Pindos and in the part of Epeiros around Dodona, where they too have found geographical features which correspond to Homer's description. On balance, however, the evidence favours the opinion of the ancients and

the scholars who follow them. Further, it is clear that the name of the Ainianes began as a race-name of the inhabitants of a town close to Tempe called *Ainia*. This tallies with the ancient legend according to which the Per(rh)aibians and the Ainianes from the plains of northeast Thessaly and lower Per(rh)aibia retreated into the more confined mountainous interior before the Lapith advance.

Other Aiolians(?)

Other tribes mentioned as settlers in Thessaly before the invasion of the Thessalians and the Magnetes are called Hellenes, Myrmidons, Phthians, and Dolopians. The last are known to us in the historical period. Of the first three we know nothing except that they are mentioned in the *Iliad* as subjects of Peleus. The centre of Peleus's kingdom was Achaian Phthiotis, but its boundaries extended beyond this region towards the eastern side of the Thessalian plain and towards the Spercheios Valley; Dolopia, north of Tymphrestos, also came under its suzerainty. Since we cannot tell when these tribes first came to Thessaly, we have no means of knowing whether or not they were Aiolic-speaking peoples. There is a further difficulty concerning the racial element present in the name of the *Hellenes* (Ἕλληνες). Since this name came to denote all the Greek-speaking tribes after the southward advance of the western group, it may originally have denoted the whole, or only a part, of this group.

One of the Greek tribes of prehistoric Thessaly who spoke the Aiolic dialect already bore the name *Aioleis* (Αἰολεῖς). Some remnants of this tribe are found later in Thessalian Magnesia and in the region of Pleuron and Kalydon in Aitolia. It seems that the sections of this tribe who moved across to the Island of Lesbos and the Asia Minor coast opposite gave their name to all the peoples who spoke Aiolic.

TRIBES BETWEEN THE AIOLIANS AND THE WESTERN GREEKS

From 1900 B.C. onwards, three Greek tribes, the Athamanians, the Boiotians, and the Thessalians, occupied a geographical and dialectal position which was intermediate between the Aiolian tribes of Thessaly and the Western Greek tribes of Epeiros.

Athamanians

Hekataios and Strabo both maintain that the Athamanians were a "barbarian" (i.e. non-Greek) race, but there is no doubt that the Athamanians believed themselves to be Greek. This emerges from the following excerpt from a letter sent between 205 and 201 B.C. from the Athamanian kings Theodoros and Amynandros to the inhabitants of Teos: "...and we do this, because we happen to be familiar with all the Hellenes, since we are related to the leader himself of those who bear the common appellation of Hellenes...". There is also objective evidence that the Athamanians were

Greek: the place-names in Athamania are without exception Greek, and seven out of the eight other Athamanian personal names known to us are Greek too. The majority of scholars, both in the past and today, have considered the Athamanians to be a Greek race.

As we saw above, the name of the river Inachos which runs through Athamania shows that the Athamanians settled there on top of a Proto-Achaian stratum. From this, they took the cult of Inacho, the daughter of Inachos, whom they married to their god who bore their own name, Athamas. Inacho˙ has become known by her abbreviated name, Ino. The existence of myths about Athamas and Ino in Achaian Phthiotis suggests that the Athamanians were settled there before 1600 B.C., because the distribution of myths about Ino in more southerly Greek regions matches the distribution of Achaians there. Ino and Athamas appear together again only in western Boiotia and, significantly, in the whole of the mythical cycle about them. So they were brought there not by the Achaians, but by the Athamanians. Furthermore, there is philological evidence that there was an Athamanian settlement in the Spercheios Valley.

Boiotians

The ethnic *Boiotoi* (*Βοιωτοὶ*) with its suffix -*to*-, which is characteristic of many race names concentrated in Epeiros, suggests a derivation from *Boion* (*Βόϊον*), a mountain mass of the northern part of the Pindos Range. This region must have been abandoned by the early bearers of this name at about the same time as the Proto-Aiolian tribes moved down from Macedonia to Thessaly and settled further south in central Pindos, where they remained for many centuries, almost to the end of the Mycenaean Age, when we find them once more on the move. That the Boiotians lived for a long time in central Pindos is suggested by the form of their dialect: half its characteristics are Aiolic, half Western. This was once thought to be the result of superimposing a dialect of the Western type, regarded as the original Boiotian dialect, on a dialect of the Aiolic type assumed to have been spoken by the Greek population of Boiotia in the Mycenaean Age. Later, however, it was observed that the dialect substrata in Greece had very little influence on the top strata and that, generally speaking, dialects which presented much the same features as the Boiotian were formed in areas where innovations from external centres of dissemination had crossed each other's path. It was, therefore, proposed that the Boiotian dialect had been formed in an area which lay between the Western and the Aiolic sectors.

Thessalians

The dialect which was spoken in Thessaliotis in historical times greatly resembles the Boiotian; it has the same mixture of Aiolic and Western dialect characteristics, though the latter are slightly less numerous. This dialect too was once thought to be the product of the mixing of a Western dialect, brought no doubt by the Thessalians, with Aiolic spoken by the early inhabitants of Thessaly. Later, it came to be regarded as the transition between Aiolic and West Greek. Adopting the latter interpretation, we conclude that from

1900 B.C. onwards the Thessalians lived somewhere between Thessaly and Epeiros and certainly close to the Boiotians. This conclusion is in accordance with the legend which mentions the *Thessalians* as having been neighbours of the Thesprotians at an earlier date.

THE WESTERN GREEKS

It has become generally accepted that the tribes of the Western dialect group who are found settled in southern Greece at the end of the second millennium B.C. and later migrated there from more northerly sites which they had occupied in Epeiros and perhaps in Illyria up to the end of the Late Bronze Age. Yet this theory takes account of only part of the evidence available.

Lokrians, Phokians, Aitolians, and Kephallenians

Of the peoples in present-day Sterea Hellas who spoke a variant of West Greek in the historical period, three are mentioned in Homer as living before and during the Trojan War in the same regions which they also held later: the Aitolians, the Phokians, and the Eastern Lokrians. This is confirmed by other evidence about the Aitolians and the Lokrians, and is not disproved by what is known of the Phokians.

Like the Athenians and the Arkadians, but unlike the immigrants of the 12th and 11th centuries (Dorians, Eleans, Boiotians, Thessalians, Ainianes of the Spercheios Valley), the Lokrians had no recollection of being newcomers. Their arrival in Sterea Hellas must have been much earlier than the end of the Mycenaean Age. Furthermore, the aristocratic clans of the Lokrians traced their descent from heroes of the Mycenaean Age, while the kings and noble families of the Dorians, Eleans, Boiotians, and Thessalians claimed ancestors among the leaders of the invasions and the later phases of occupation. Lokrian nobles bore the name *Aianteioi* (*Αἰάντειοι*) and were recognized as descendants of Aias and Oileus, familiar heroes of the epic cycle. Aias had his origin in an old daimon, who was the personification of the river Aias or Aoos, which has its source on Mt. Lakmos in the Pindos Range, whence it flows down into the Adriatic. Oileus too seems to have been of northern origin.

The presence of Aitolians on the northern shore of the Gulf of Patras before the end of the Mycenaean Age is confirmed by the legends of the Eleans, descendants of a group of Aitolians who immigrated to the Peloponnesos along with the Dorians. According to these legends, at the time when the Dorian invasion became imminent, not only were the Aitolians in Aitolia, but they had knowledge of the interior of the Peloponnesos as far as Elis. No less significant is the fact that the historical memories of the Eleans themselves did not extend beyond Aitolia.

According to Homer, at the end of the Mycenaean Age, the Kephallenians held Zakynthos, Kephallenia, Ithaca, Leukas, and Akarnania; and they maintained friendly relations with the Thesprotians who held the shores of Epeiros. As we shall see below, Odysseus, the hero of the Kephallenian tribe in the Homeric poems, also has a place in Thesprotian myths in Pindos and on the borders of Epeiros and Macedonia. We can scarcely suppose that the myths about Odysseus could have penetrated so deeply into Epeiros through the migration there of Kephallenians from Akarnania or the islands. The general direction of Greek migrations was from north to south, and this makes it more likely that the Kephallenians originally came from Epeiros. It follows that they too should be regarded as one of the tribes of the Western dialect group who migrated to the south before the end of the Mycenaean Age.

How long before the end of the Mycenaean Age did the Lokrians, Phokians, Aitolians, and Kephallenians settle in the regions where Homer places them? As we have seen, the Lokrians, Phokians, and Aitolians spoke variants of West Greek from which, with the addition of a very few innovations, the Doric of historical times emerged. This dialect presented great uniformity on the eve of the population movements which separated the Lokrians, Phokians, and Aitolians from the Dorians, Eleans, and the people who settled in Achaia. This uniformity implies that these tribes lived close together for a long period of time before

the population movements began. If the Western dialect reached the final stage of its evolution in Epeiros, the Lokrians, Phokians, and Aitolians must have settled in present-day Sterea Hellas a little before the end of the Mycenaean Age. But such a late date presents difficulties. We have seen that the Lokrian legends imply that this tribe reached Eastern Lokris well before the end of the Mycenaean Age. Since, on the basis of dialectal evidence, the movements of this tribe are connected with the movements of the Phokians and the Aitolians, about whom we have no corresponding legends, these tribes also must have arrived in Sterea Hellas at or about the same time as the Lokrians. As there is no archaeological evidence for mass movements between the beginning of the Middle Bronze Age and the end of the Late Bronze Age, it would appear that the movements of the tribes with which we are concerned here took place at the earlier date. As was pointed out elsewhere, however, the culture and dwelling conditions in the Middle Bronze Age were such that excavations of the corresponding strata do not enable us to recognize population changes with any certainty unless they were accompanied by widespread destruction. It seems, then, that the Western dialect reached its final form

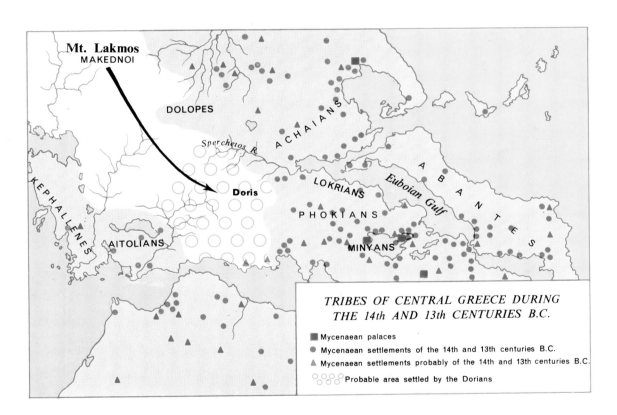

TRIBES OF CENTRAL GREECE DURING THE 14th AND 13th CENTURIES B.C.

■ Mycenaean palaces
● Mycenaean settlements of the 14th and 13th centuries B.C.
▲ Mycenaean settlements probably of the 14th and 13th centuries B.C.
○ Probable area settled by the Dorians

Before the end of the Mycenaean Age, Makednians (Macedonians), who had migrated from Mt. Lakmos in Central Greece, and tribes who inhabited the same region earlier united to form a new tribe, the Dorians. This name originally meant 'inhabitants of Doris'. Homer does not mention the Dorians, not because they did not live in Doris, but because this region formed part of a wider area which lay beyond Homer's visual field. On the map, the region which is thought to have been the homeland of the Dorians is indicated by yellow circles on a lighter background. The archaeological sites in what today is Sterea Hellas and in

part of Thessaly which are dated to the 14th and 13th centuries B.C. are also marked. It is to be noted that in the white zone, where the Dorians settled, there are only two sites, and these are on the shores of the Corinthian Gulf. The dearth of sites in this region is due not only to the fact that there have been fewer excavations in central Sterea Hellas than in the surrounding regions, but probably also to the mountainous character of the land itself, which must have obstructed the expansion of Mycenaean civilization. Homer ignores this whole region, probably because it remained beyond the scope of Mycenaean civilization.

in the area known today as Sterea Hellas after a long period, which must have begun at the beginning of the Mycenaean Age and during which the Lokrians, Phokians, Aitolians, and other tribes unknown to us lived in close contact with one another. Some of these took on the name of the Achaians after they moved to northern Peloponnesos; others became component parts of the Dorian tribe formed in central Sterea Hellas in the last third of the Mycenaean Age.

Dorians

The Dorians do not appear in the *Iliad*. In the *Odyssey* they are mentioned as one of the tribes in Crete. But there is both direct evidence and indications in legends that there were Dorians in Sterea Hellas, particularly in Doris, before the end of the Mycenaean Age. The fact that the *Iliad* is silent about them does not constitute evidence to the contrary, since the same poem omits any mention of a large area of Sterea Hellas, from Eastern Lokris and Phokis to Antirrhion, Lake Trichonis, and Akarnania.

The name *Dorieis* (*Δωριεῖς*) is obviously a typical ethnic in *-eus* derived from a place-name *Dori-* (*Δωρι-*). It, therefore, denotes the inhabitants of Doris. This ethnic then was created in Doris, and the sources which refer by this name to the ancestors of the Dorians before they settled in this region are guilty of anachronism.

The Dorians of the historical period were divided into three tribes: *Hylleis* (*Ὑλλεῖς*), *Dymanes* (*Δυμᾶνες*), and *Pamphyloi* (*Πάμφυλοι*). The eponymous heroes of the Dymanes and the Pamphyloi were believed to be sons of Aigimios who had led the "Dorians" to Doris. The eponymous hero of the Hylleis was said to be the son of Herakles who had acquired one third of Aigimios's kingdom for helping him against the Lapiths. Behind this myth is the recollection that there were two main component parts of the Dorian tribe, one which came to Sterea Hellas from some other region and one that was already settled there at an earlier date. The name of the *Pamphyloi* (*Παν-φυλοι*= all tribes) tells us that the tribe which bore this name had been formed by the union of many ethnic groups. Some modern scholars have suggested that the name of the Hylleis was Illyrian and, consequently, that the Hylleis were Illyrians. But their arguments are unfounded. Since it is known that the island of Korkyra was colonized by Corinthians, who were Dorians, the Hyl(l)aikos or Hylikos harbour there must owe its name to the Dorian tribe of the Hylleis and not to an Illyrian race. The mention of *Hylleis* or *Hylloi* (*Ὑλλεῖς, Ὑλλοι*) in Illyria must be given a different interpretation. The ancient writers who mention them not only fail to agree about which region they inhabited (somewhere in Dalmatia or Istria) but also, when they do offer some geographical information, they reveal their total ignorance of these regions. It seems then that these Hylleis or Hylloi were not actually seen by any ancient observer. Further, since they are referred to in our sources as descendants of Hyllos and Melite, a heroine in Korkyrian myths and eponymous of one of the Dalmatian islands colonized by the Korkyraians, it is reasonable to suppose that the stories about them were invented in Melite and in neighbouring Korkyra Melaina because some Illyrian race-name resembled the name of the Hylleis. Whatever this name was, the people who bore it had nothing to do with

the Dorian Hylleis. Another argument states that certain words used by the Dorians and the Eleans can be recognized as Illyrian. But even if we were to admit that these words were Illyrian—itself a doubtful assumption since they do not appear in any Illyrian text—they are still too few in number to prove that there was any significant percentage of Illyrians among the Dorian population.

Legends which survived among the Dorians and which have come down to us through Pindar, Herodotos, and other ancient writers, say that the earliest ancestors of the Dorians were *Makednoi* (that is, Macedonians), who migrated to Doris from Pindos, more precisely from the Lakmos region. Since it has already been seen that the Dorians took their name from Doris, where they formed themselves into one ethnic group by the union of the local inhabitants and the newcomers, it can readily be inferred that the name *Makednoi* and the mention of Pindos as their original homeland do not refer to the whole of the Dorian tribe but just to one of its component groups—not the Hylleis, however, because these had settled in present-day Sterea Hellas earlier. Ancient texts containing echoes of fragments of a very old lost epic about Aigimios say that the Dorians stood in danger of attack by the Lapiths, that the king of the Dorians, Aigimios, sought the help of Herakles in return for the reward mentioned above, and that Herakles repulsed the Lapiths and established the Dorians in a region from which he had driven out the Dryopians. It follows that the race which was led by Aigimios and helped by Herakles was not yet the Dorians but the Macednians. Herakles here is no more than the representative of a people in central Sterea Hellas. One of the texts mentioned above says that Aigimios's people at the time of the Lapith attacks were in Histiaiotis; others imply that they had already reached the northern part of present-day Sterea Hellas. The second version must be the earlier one, because it tallies with the mention of the alliance of the people who are represented by Herakles. The mention of the Lapiths as enemies of the "Dorians", i.e. the Macednians, does not conflict with this version since, as we have seen, there are traces of Lapith settlements in the Spercheios Valley.

From another group of texts, which echo neither the Aigimios epic nor Dorian legends, but an epic narration concerning the sack of Thebes by the Epigonoi, it emerges that at that period (the middle of the 13th century B.C.) one section of the Dorians was settled in Boiotia, more particularly in the region of Homole. The use of the Dorian race-name, which in this case is not an abuse of the term, shows that the fusion of the Macednians, the Hylleis, and other peoples into the new nation of the Dorians had already taken place.

Molossians, Thesprotians, and Macedonians

Whereas one section of Macednians penetrated into the present-day Sterea Hellas, groups of Molossians advanced towards Attica, Sikyonia, and Arkadia. The hero Apheidas, who appears as a descendant of Theseus, and the Attic clan of the Apheidantidai are connected with the Apheidantes, a subdivision of the Molossians. Mounichos, king of the Molossians in an unspecified country, has the same name as the

Thracian Sea

AEGEAN SEA

Cretan Sea

ACHAIANS

IONIAN SEA

Myrtoan Sea

Aoos or Aias R.
ABANTES
MOLOSSIANS
THESPROTIANS
MACEDONIANS
PER(RH)AIBIANS
TAINIANES
Titaresios R.
Peneios R.
LAPITHS
ATHAMANES
THESSALIANS(?)
BOIOTIANS(?)
DOLOPES
ACHAIANS
KEPHALLENES
DORIANS
LOKRIANS
PHOKIANS
AITOLIANS LOKRIANS(?)
ABANTES
MINYANS
ACHAIANS
IONIANS
EPEIANS
LAPITHS
Asopos R.
Inachos R.
ACHAIANS
ALPHEIOS R.
ARKADIANS
MINYANS
ACHAIANS
Eurotas R.
Pamisos R.
IONIANS
ACHAIANS
KEPHALLENES
ACHAIANS

THE GREEK TRIBES
END OF 13th CENTURY B.C.

The distribution of the Greek tribes just before the end of the Mycenaean Age: in Epeiros, western Macedonia, Thessaly, and there lived: the actual Sterea Hellas Abantes, Molossians, Thesprotians, Macedonia, Per(rh)aibians, Ainianes, Lapiths, Thessalians, Boiotians, Kephallenians, Aitolians, Lokrians, Achaians, Dolopians, Dorians, Phokians, and Ionians; in Euboia: Abantes; in the Peloponnesos: Achaians, Arkadians, Epeians, Minyans, Ionians; in Crete and Rhodes: Achaians. The smaller settlements of Lapiths, Molossians, and Athamanians are not marked. The names of the groups who lived in Thessalian Magnesia, the west of the Thessalian plain, central and eastern Boiotia, and the Isthmus region are not known. In southern Thessaly, along with the Achaians, there were tribes called Hellenes, Phthians, Myrmidons, and Aiolians, but their particular localities cannot be precisely established.

eponymous hero of Mounichia, as a companion of Theseus, and also as a grandson of Theseus. The first Mounichos is said to be the father of a certain Philaios, a namesake of the hero of Attica who gave his name to the Philaïdai clan. The latter Philaios appeared as the son or grandson of Aias (with whom he is connected etymologically also: *phil-* + *Aias*). As has been stated earlier, the name Aias was given to a river known as the Aoos, by which the Molossians dwelt before they spread into central Epeiros. Alkon, a hero of Phaleron, which is close to Mounichia, has the same name as a Molossian noble. Finally, the cults of Artemis in Mounichia and at Brauron, close to the deme of Philaïdai, have in common a ceremony, the *arkteia*, in which girls dressed up as bears.

We find the cult of Artemis Mounichia at Sikyon too. Since the cult statue was a wooden xoanon of the 6th century B.C. and since it is quite unlikely that the Sikyonians could have borrowed at such an early date an Athenian cult which was unknown outside Attica, this is very probably an indication that there was an early settlement of Molossians at Sikyonia.

The name *Apheidantes*, by which one of the demes of Tegea was called, and the name of Apheidas, a hero who was worshipped in that city, show that there was a colony of Apheidantes (a section of the Molossian tribe) in the

interior of Arkadia. Since this region was unaffected by the great migratory movements of the Western tribes, which took place after the Mycenaean Age, the penetration of the Apheidantes must be dated earlier than these migrations.

The main body of Macedonians and Molossians and other Greek tribes who remained north and northwest of Thessaly were to emerge on the historical scene only after the end of the Bronze Age.

Of the Greek tribes of Epeiros, we can at this point discern only the Thesprotians. According to the *Odyssey*, they held the Epeirot coast, maintained friendly relations with the Greeks of the Ionian Islands with whom they allied against the Taphian pirates, and permitted pilgrims *en route* for Dodona to pass through their country. From other sources we learn that they spread as far as western Macedonia and had a common frontier with the Bryges who lived in that region. Further, the legend of the Thessalians according to which the latter came originally from the country of the Thesprotians implies that the Thesprotians had spread as far as central Pindos, where the Thessalians should be placed before their expansion. The myths which have Odysseus settling at Trampya (close to modern Metsovo) and leading the Thesprotians to war against the Bryges are not a product of poetic fancy, as some believe, but are based on Thesprotian legends.

389

CRETO - MYCENAEAN HERITAGE

There were two "Golden Ages" in Bronze Age Greece: the New-Palace Period on Minoan Crete and the culminating phase of the Mycenaean period on the mainland. The Minoan civilization, eastern in character though not in spirit, was not only the finest achievement of the Aegean Bronze Age, but also the first advanced civilization to flourish on European soil. From its remote position in the extreme south-west corner of the continent, the Minoan civilization shone out brilliantly over both the Aegean and the mainland. Before its own light dimmed, it succeeded in illuminating the path ahead which the more primitive peoples of Helladic Greece could follow, and in providing, through its own achievements, the spark of inspiration they needed to create their own new civilization, the Mycenaean.

The Mycenaean civilization did in fact continue along the path paved by its predecessor up to the end of the Bronze Age, but it had a vigour and spirit of its own and a more decisive influence on later Greek history, since its own character determined to a large extent the character of Greek civilization in the subsequent Archaic period.

We have seen that the disintegration of the Mycenaean state did not bring about the end of the Mycenaean civilization. Nor did the eventual destruction of this civilization wipe out all its achievements. To some degree at least, the Creto-Mycenaean heritage survived and was handed down through subsequent generations. This happened at a critical turning-point in history: the transition between the Bronze Age and the Early Iron Age. The change in culture took place at approximately the same period throughout the whole of the Eastern Mediterranean.

The changes which came about during this period in the whole of the surrounding area had important results in Greece, now emerging from the obscure period called the Greek "Middle Ages". The term is misleading, but it does reflect our present ignorance of this new critical phase— only a temporary ignorance, however, for future research will no doubt throw light even on this dark period. In the circumstances, however, it is difficult to trace the path of the Creto-Mycenaean heritage. It is obscured in the general haze which surrounds both the superficial and profound changes which took place in this period and we can do little more than speculate about its character. Moreover, little help is provided by the pedant who seeks to match the information given in the epic poems with the archaeological evidence, ignoring the fact that the epics were not historical documents and that the rudimentary restoration of the past achieved by archaeology cannot be termed history.

There is no doubt, however, that a Creto-Mycenaean heritage existed. It has long been established by researchers that in spite of all the upheavals of the "Dark Ages", there was no break between the Mycenaean and post-Mycenaean world.

What exactly was this heritage and how was it handed down? How extensive was it and how significant from a historical point of view? To a great degree, these questions have already been answered in this volume in the chapters on the Mycenaean civilization and on ethnic and linguistic groups in prehistoric Greece. These answers will be supplemented by others in the second volume of this History dealing with post-Mycenaean and Archaic Greece. But before we leave the civilizations of Minoan and Mycenaean Greece, we naturally wish to consider for a moment how extensive and important their influence was on the evolution of Greece in the historical period.

There is plenty of evidence, gathered both recently and in the past, to show that elements of the Mycenaean civilization either survived into or reappeared in historical times: the idea of the city-state, the megaron-shaped plan of the Greek temple, the nuclei of the epics, the language of the Greeks. For all the excellent work being done in this broad field of research, the subject has not by any means been exhausted. Indeed, new fields of study have opened up especially after the decipherment of the Mycenaean script. Leaving on one side all other manifestations of culture, we may observe that the ethical values of the Mycenaeans alone played a decisive role in shaping the culture of historical Greece.

The heritage from the heroic age influenced not only the cults and myths but also the entire spiritual life and education of the Greeks in historical times. The idea of national unity had its roots in the heroic age, and again it was to this period that the Greeks turned whenever a treaty or alliance needed to be justified historically. It was the common tradition more than a common language or country which united the Greek race. The survival and transmitting of this tradition would naturally have been impossible had there been no racial continuity in Greece. The Mycenaeans at the end of the Mycenaean period—the people who handed down this tradition—were basically an Indo-European people. But they were also Greek. It was precisely this mixing of tribes and cultures which had produced the Mycenaean "miracle". Also, there is no doubt that some fairly substantial remnants of the Mycenaean population remained. They were subdued or transferred to areas where they could do no harm. Some were sent to distant coasts or islands, such as Cyprus, where there is no doubt that they had an influence on later developments. This is shown by the fact that the greatest cultural progress in historical times was achieved in Attica—a region not settled by the newly-arrived Greeks.

These Greek tribes from the north who were destined to complete the end of the Mycenaean civilization, whose collapse from internal causes was inevitable, were not capable of creating the new civilization by themselves. Their important function was to overthrow a world whose collapse was already inevitable. This is why the first centuries following their arrival, the "Dark Ages", are reminiscent of the similar period, c. 1900 B.C., when the arrival of the main body of Proto-Greeks resulted in a break in culture and a halt to progress.

These primitive peoples owed their cultural development, indeed their introduction to civilization, to the beneficial influence exerted on them by the neighbouring Minoan civilization. We have already seen how the fruitful creative spirit of Crete inspired the Helladic world. And we can appreciate how much the poorer the Mycenaean civilization would have been without the influence of the Minoan by noting the much lower level of civilization achieved by other European countries in the Bronze Age.

However, in spite of the apparent parallels between these two transitional periods—Minoan-Mycenaean and Mycenaean-post-Mycenaean—there was in fact a great difference between them: when the Middle Helladic world emerged as a distinct culture in the 17th century B.C., the neighbouring Minoan civilization was still flourishing. But when the north-western Greek tribes moved southwards the Mycenaean world was on the point of collapse. It was natural, therefore, that the latter migrations of the Greeks should result in abrupt changes. These were once interpreted as a consequence of some alteration in the racial composition of Greece, some break in the previous culture. The old belief that there was a great gulf between prehistoric and historical times was supported by the theory that the "northern" tribe descended into Greece c. 1100 B.C. bringing the Olympian gods and the Greek spirit to the "pre-Hellenic" world. But these theories have now been abandoned, for Greek history no longer begins with the coming of the Dorians.

The new age, which begins at the dawn of historical times, appears to be entirely different from the preceding one and, as we have seen above, there are historical reasons for this. The new age, however, is not completely cut off from the past. More and more evidence of Mycenaean influence is coming to light all the time. And it is certain that the racial continuity of the Greeks from the beginning of the second millennium will be established, whether or not the present interpretations of the Mycenaean texts continue to be accepted.

We now know that the Mycenaeans are part of the Hellenic World and tradition. Consequently, the heritage they bequeathed to later generations must have played an important role in forming the civilizations of both Archaic and Classical Greece.

BIBLIOGRAPHY

THE NATURAL SETTING

Abel, Othenio, *Lebensbilder aus der Tierwelt der Vorzeit*. Jena, 1922.
Andree, Julius, Neue Cavicornier aus dem Pliocän von Samos. *Palaeontographica* 67 (1926), pp. 135-175.
Aubouin, Jean, Contribution à l'étude géologique de la Grèce septentrionale : Les confins de l'Epire et de la Thessalie. *Annales Géologiques des Pays Helléniques* 10 (1959), pp. 1-525.
Beloch, Karl, Julius, *Griechische Geschichte*. 8 vols. Strassburg, 1912-1927.
Bequignon, Yves, *La vallée du Spercheios des origines au IV siècle*. Paris, 1937.
Brunn, J. H., Contribution à l'étude géologique du Pinde septentrional et d'une partie de la Macédoine occidentale. *Annales Géologiques des Pays Helléniques* 7 (1956), pp. 1-358.
Bursian, Conrad, *Geographie von Griechenland*. 2 vols. Leipzig, 1862-1868.
Casson, Stanley, *Macedonia, Thrace and Illyria*. Oxford, 1926.
Celet, Paul, Contribution à l'étude géologique du Parnasse-Kiona et d'une partie des régions méridionales de la Grèce continentale. *Annales Géologiques des Pays Helléniques* 13 (1962), pp. 1-446.
Dercourt, Jean, Contribution à l'étude géologique d'un secteur du Péloponnèse septentrional. *Annales Géologiques des Pays Helléniques* 15 (1964), pp. 1-418.
Gaudry, Albert, *Animaux fossiles et géologie de l'Attique*. 2 vols. Paris, 1862-1867.
Glotz, Gustave, *Histoire grecque*. Vols. I-II. Paris, 1925-1931.
Heldreich, Th., *La faune de la Grèce*. Athens, 1878.
Heuzey, L., *Le mont Olympe et l'Acarnanie*. Paris, 1860.
Kirsten, E., & Kraiker, W., *Griechenlandkunde*. Heidelberg, 1957.
Leake, William Martin, *Travels in Northern Greece*. 4 vols. London, 1835.
Lehmann, H., *Argolis I: Landeskunde der Ebene von Argos und ihrer Randgebiet*. Athens, 1937.
Maull, Otto, *Griechisches Mittelmeergebiet*. Breslau, 1922.
Melentis, Johann, K., Studien über fossile Vertebraten Griechenlands. *Annales Géologiques des Pays Helléniques* 11 (1960); 12 (1961); 14 (1963); 16 (1965); 17 (1966); 18 (1967); 19 (A) (1968); 21 (B) (1969).
Myres, John L., *Geographical History in Greek Lands*. Oxford, 1953.
Neumann, C., & Partsch, J., *Physikalische Geographie von Griechenland*. Breslau, 1885.
Philippson, Alfred, *Beiträge zur Kenntnis der griechischen Inselwelt*. (Petermanns Geographischen Mitteilungen, Ergänzungsheft 134). Gotha, 1901.
— *Beiträge zur Morphologie Griechenlands*. Stuttgart, 1930.
— *Die griechischen Landschaften*. Vos. I-II. Frankfurt, 1950/1951-1956/1958.
— *Das Klima Griechenlands*. Bonn, 1948.
— *Land und See der Griechen*. Bonn, 1948.
Roth, Johannes, & Wagner, Andreas, *Die fossilen Knochenüberreste von Pikermi in Griechenland*. Munich, 1854.
Schlosser, Max, Die fossilen Cavicornia von Samos. *Beiträge zur Paläontologie und Geologie Österreich-Ungarns und des Orients* 17 (1905), pp. 21-118.
Schneider, H.E., *Zur Quartärgeologischen Entwicklungsgeschichte Thessaliens* (Griechenland). Bonn, 1968.
Schoo, J., Vulkanische und seismische Aktivität des ägäischen Meeresbeckens im Spiegel der griechischen Mythologie. *Mnemosyne* 4 (1937), pp. 237 ff.
Schultze, J., *Neu-Griechenland: Länderkunde Ostmakedoniens und Westthrakiens*. (Petermanns Geographischen Mitteilungen, Ergänzungsheft 233). Gotha, 1937.
Stählin, F., *Das Hellenische Thessalien*. Stuttgart, 1924.
Thenius, E., Gab es im Wiener Becken eine Pikermifauna? *Anzeiger der Österreichischen Akademie der Wissenschaften* 8 (1949), pp. 185-192.

PALAEOLITHIC AND MESOLITHIC PERIODS

Chavaillon, N. & J., & Hours, F., Une industrie paléolithique du Péloponnèse : Le Moustérien de Vasilaki. *Bulletin de Correspondance Hellénique* 88 (1964), pp. 616-622.
Dakaris, S.I., Higgs, E.S., Hey, R.W., The Climate, Environment and Industries of Stone Age Greece : *Part I. Proceedings of the Prehistoric Society*, Cambridge, 30 (1964), pp. 199-244.
Higgs, E.S., Vita-Finzi, C. The Climate, Environment and Industries of Stone Age Greece : *Part II. Proceedings of the Prehistoric Society*, Cambridge, 32 (1966), pp. 1-29.
Higgs, E.S., Vita-Finzi, C., Harris, D.R., Fagg, A.F., The Climate, Environment and Industries of Stone Age Greece : *Part III. Proceedings of the Prehistoric Society*, Cambridge, 33 (1967), pp. 1-29.
Jacobsen, Thomas W., Excavations at Porto Cheli and Vicinity; Preliminary Report II : The Franchthi Cave, 1967-1968. *Hesperia* 38 (1969), pp. 343-381.
Kokkoros, P., & Kanellis, A., Découverte d'un crâne d'homme paléolithique dans la péninsule chalcidique. *L'Anthropologie* 64 (1961), pp. 438-446.
Leroi-Gourhan, A., & Chavaillon, J. & N., Paléolithique du Péloponnèse. *Bulletin de la Société Préhistorique Française* 60 (1963), pp. 249-265.

Markovits, A., Περὶ τῶν μέχρι σήμερον ἐρευνῶν ἐπὶ τῆς λιθικῆς περιόδου τῆς Ἑλλάδος. *Πρακτικὰ Ἑλληνικῆς Ἀνθρωπολογικῆς Ἑταιρείας* 1928, pp. 114-134.
Milojčić, V., Boessneck, J., Jung, D., Schneider, H., *Paläolithikum um Larissa in Thessalien*. (Beiträge zur Ur- und Frühgeschichtlichen Archäologie des Mittelmeer-Kulturraumes, vol. I). Bonn, 1965.
Müller-Karpe, H., *Handbuch der Vorgeschichte I (Altsteinzeit)*. Munich, 1966.
Sauter, Marc R., *Préhistoire de la Méditerranée: Paléolithique-Mésolithique*. Paris, 1948.
Schmid, E., *Die Seidi-Höhle: Eine jungpaläolithische Station in Griechenland*. (Colloque International de Spéléologie. Athens, 1963, pp. 163-174.
Sordinas, Augustus, Investigations of the Prehistory of Corfu during 1964-1966. *Balkan Studies* 10 (1969), pp. 393-424.
— Προϊστορικὴ ἔρευνα στὴν Κέρκυρα κατὰ τὸ 1965. *Κερκυραϊκὰ Χρονικὰ* 11 (1965), pp. 141-148.
— Προϊστορικὴ ἔρευνα στὴν Κέρκυρα κατὰ τὸ 1966. *Κερκυραϊκὰ Χρονικὰ* 14 (1968), pp. 77-83.
Stampfuss, R., Die ersten altsteinzeitlichen Höhlenfunde in Griechenland. *Mannus* 34 (1952), pp. 132-147.
Theocharis, Dimitrios R., *Ἡ αὐγὴ τῆς Θεσσαλικῆς προϊστορίας*. Volos, 1967.
Weinberg, Saul S., *The Stone Age in the Aegean*. Cambridge Ancient History. Vol. I, part 1. 3rd ed., 1970, ch. X.

NEOLITHIC PERIOD

Angel, J. Lawrence, Neolithic Ancestors of the Greeks. *American Journal of Archaeology* 49 (1945), pp. 252-260.
Benton, S., Hagios Nikolaos near Astakos in Akarnania. *Annual of the British School at Athens* 42 (1947), pp. 156-183.
Blegen, Carl W., *Prosymna: The Helladic Settlement Preceding the Argive Heraeum*. 2 vols. Cambridge, Mass., 1937.
— Excavations at Nemea 1926. *American Journal of Archaeology* 31 (1927), pp. 421-440.
Caskey, John L., Excavations at Lerna (Preliminary Reports). *Hesperia* 26 (1957), pp. 142-162; 27 (1958), pp. 125-144; 28 (1959), pp. 202-207.
Caskey, John L. & Elizabeth G., The Earliest Settlements at Eutresis: *Supplementary Excavations, 1958. Hesperia* 29 (1960), pp. 126-167.
Charles, R.P., Sur le Néolithique égéen et ses origines. *Κρητικὰ Χρονικὰ* 18 (1964), pp. 245-268.
Childe, V. Gordon, *The Dawn of European Civilization*. 2nd ed., London, 1927.
Delvoye, Ch., *Que pouvons-nous entrevoir de la vie économique de la péninsule grecque à l'époque néolithique*. Mélanges Georges Smets. Brussels, 1952, pp. 189-206.
— Remarques sur la seconde civilisation néolithique du continent grec et des îles avoisinantes. *Bulletin de Correspondance Hellénique* 73 (1949), pp. 29-124.
Evans, J.D., & Renfrew, C., *Excavations at Saliagos near Antiparos*. London, 1968.
Frankfort, Henri, *Studies in Early Pottery of the Near East*. Vol. II. London, 1927.
French, D.H., Late Chalcolithic Pottery in North-West Turkey and the Aegean. *Anatolian Studies* 11 (1961), pp. 99-141.
— Prehistoric Pottery from Macedonia and Thrace. *Praehistorische Zeitschrift* 42 (1964), pp. 30-48.
Fürst, C., *Über einen neolithischen Schädel aus Arkadien*. Lund, 1932.
Garašanin, Milutin V., *Zur Problem der Dimini-Wanderung*. Athenische Mitteilungen 69-70 (1954-1955), pp. 1-11.
Grundmann, Kimon, Magula Hadzimissiotiki: Eine steinzeitliche Siedlung im Karla-See. *Athenische Mitteilungen* 62 (1937), pp. 56-69.
Hansen, Hazel D., *Early Civilization in Thessaly*. Baltimore, 1933.
Hauptmann, H., & Milojčić, Vladimir, *Die Funde der frühen Dimini Zeit aus der Arapi-Magula, Thessalien*. Bonn, 1969.
Heurtley, W.A., *Prehistoric Macedonia*. Cambridge, 1939.
Holmberg, Erik J., The Neolithic Pottery of Mainland Greece. *Göteborgs Kungl. Vetenskapshoch Vitterhets-Samhälles Handlingar* 7 (1964), pp. 3-39.
— *The Swedish Excavations at Asea in Arcadia*. Lund-Leipzig, 1944.
Kosmopoulos, Walker Leslie, *The Prehistoric Inhabitations of Corinth*. Munich, 1948.
Kunze, Emil, *Orchomenos II: Die neolithische Keramik*. Munich, 1931.
Mellaart, James, *Earliest Civilizations of the Near East*. London, 1965.
Milojčić, Vladimir, Zur Chronologie der jüngeren Steinzeit Griechenlands. *Jahrbuch des Deutschen Archäologischen Instituts* 65/66 (1950/1951), pp. 1-90.
— Ergebnisse der deutschen Ausgrabungen in Thessalien, 1953-1958. *Jahrbuch des Römisch-Germanischen Zentralmuseums Mainz* 6 (1959), pp. 1-56.
Milojčić, V., Boessneck, J., Hopf, M., *Das präkeramische Neolithikum sowie die Tier- und Pflanzenreste*. (Die deutschen Ausgrabungen auf der Argissa-Magula in Thessalien I). Bonn, 1962.

Mylonas, George E., *Excavations at Olynthos I: The Neolithic Settlement.* Baltimore, 1929.
— Ἡ Νεολιθικὴ ἐποχὴ ἐν Ἑλλάδι. Athens, 1928.
— The Site of Akropotamos and the Neolithic Period of Macedonia. *American Journal of Archaeology* 45 (1941), pp. 557-576.

Rodden, Robert J., Excavations at the Early Neolithic Site at Nea Nikomedeia, Greek Macedonia (1961 Season). *Proceedings of the Prehistoric Society*, Cambridge, 28 (1962), pp. 267-288.

Schachermeyr, Fritz, *Das ägäische Neolithikum.* (Studies in Mediterranean Archaeology 6). Lund, 1964.
— *Die ältesten Kulturen Griechenlands.* Stuttgart, 1955.
— Dimini und die Bandkeramik. *Prähistorische Forschungen* (Anthropologische Gesellschaft Wien) 4 (1954), pp. 1 ff.
— *Prähistorische Kulturen Griechenlands.* Paulys Real-Encyclopädie der Classischen Altertumswissenschaft. Vol. XXII₂, cols. 1350-1548.

Sordinas, Augustus, Investigations of the Prehistory of Corfu during 1964-1966. *Balkan Studies* 10 (1969), pp. 393-424.

Sotiriadis, Georges, Προϊστορικὰ ἀγγεῖα Χαιρωνείας καὶ Ἐλατείας. Ἀρχαιολογικὴ Ἐφημερίς 1908, pp. 63-96.

Theocharis, Dimitrios R., Ἀνασκαφαὶ ἐν Σέσκλῳ. Πρακτικὰ τῆς ἐν Ἀθήναις Ἀρχαιολογικῆς Ἐταιρείας. 1962, pp. 24-35; 1963, pp. 40-44; 1965, pp. 5-9; 1966, pp. 5-7; 1968, pp. 24-30.
— Ἡ Αὐγὴ τῆς Θεσσαλικῆς Προϊστορίας. Volos, 1967.
— Ἐκ τῆς Προϊστορίας τῆς Εὐβοίας καὶ τῆς Σκύρου. Ἀρχεῖον Εὐβοϊκῶν Μελετῶν 6 (1959), pp. 279-328.
— Nea Makri: Eine grosse neolithische Siedlung in der Nähe von Marathon. *Athenische Mitteilungen* 71 (1956), pp. 1-29.

Theocharis, Dimitrios, R., Romiopoulou, Aikaterine, Deshayes, Jean, Ἀνασκαφαὶ Ντικλὶ Τάς. Πρακτικὰ τῆς ἐν Ἀθήναις Ἀρχαιολογικῆς Ἐταιρείας 1961, pp. 81-89.

Titov, V., *Neolit Grecij.* Moscow, 1969.

Tsountas, Christos, Αἱ προϊστορικαὶ ἀκροπόλεις Διμηνίου καὶ Σέσκλου. Athens, 1908.

Valmin, Natan, *The Swedish Messenia Expedition.* Lund, 1938.

Wace, A.J.B., Thessaly and Tripolje. *Eurasia Septentrionalis Antiqua* 9 (1934). pp. 123-134.

Wace, A.J.B. & Thomson, M.S., *Prehistoric Thessaly*, Cambridge, 1912.

Weinberg, Saul S., Excavations at Prehistoric Elateia, 1959. *Hesperia* 31 (1962), pp. 158-209.
— *The Relative Chronology of the Aegean in the Neolithic Period and Early Bronze Age.* Ehrich, Robert W., Chronologies in Old World Archaeology. Chicago-London, 1965, pp. 285-320.
— Remains from Prehistoric Corinth. *Hesperia* 6 (1937), pp. 487-524.
— *The Stone Age in the Aegean.* Cambridge Ancient History. Vol. I, part 1. 3rd ed., 1970, ch. X.

Zervos, Christian, *Naissance de la civilisation en Grèce.* 2 vols. Paris, 1962-1963.

NEOLITHIC CRETE

Alexiou, Stylianos, Ἀνασκαφαὶ ἐν Κατσαμπᾶ. Πρακτικὰ Ἀρχαιολογικῆς Ἐταιρείας 1954, pp. 369-376.

Dawkins, R. M., Excavations at Palaikastro, IV. *Annual of the British School at Athens* 11 (1904-1905), pp. 258-292.

Evans, Arthur, *The Palace of Minos.* Vols. I-II. London, 1921-1928.

Evans, J. D., Excavations in the Neolithic Settlement of Knossos, 1957-1960, Part I. *Annual of the British School at Athens* 59 (1964), pp. 132-240.
— Excavations in the Neolithic Mound of Knossos, 1958-1960. *Bulletin of the Institute of Archaeology*, London, 4 (1964), pp. 34-60.

Furness, A., The Neolithic Pottery of Knossos, *Annual of the British School at Athens* 48 (1953), pp. 94-134.

Hutchinson, R.W., Cretan Neolithic Figurines, *IPEK* 12 (1938), pp. 50-57.
— *Prehistoric Crete.* 3rd ed., Harmondsworth, 1965.

Levi, Doro, Gli scavi a Festòs. *Annuario della Scuola Archeologica di Atene* 19/20 (1957/1958), pp. 193-361; 23/24 (1961/1962), pp. 377-504.

Pendlebury, J. D. S., *The Archaeology of Crete.* London, 1939.

Platon, Nicolas, *Crète.* (Archaeologia Mundi) Geneva-Paris-Munich, 1966.

Zervos, Christian, *L'Art de la Crète néolithique et minoenne.* Paris, 1956.

NEOLITHIC CYPRUS

Catling, H.W., *Cyprus in the Neolithic and Chalcolithic Periods.* Cambridge Ancient History. Vol. I, part 1. 3rd ed., 1970, ch. IX(c).

Charles, R.P., *Le peuplement de Chypre dans l'antiquité: Étude anthropologique.* (Études Chypriotes II). Paris 1962.

Dikaios, P., *The Excavations at Erimi, 1933-1935.* Reports of the Department of Antiquities, 1936, I. Nicosia, 1938, pp. 1-81.
— *Khirokitia.* Oxford, 1953.
— *Sotira.* Philadelphia, 1961.
— *The Stone Age and the Early Bronze Age in Cyprus.* The Swedish Cyprus Expedition 4, Part Ia. Lund, 1962, pp. 1-204.

NEOLITHIC RELIGION

Clark, Grahame, *Archaeology and Society.* London, 1960.

Franz, L., Mittelgriechische Steinzeitidole. *IPEK* 8 (1932/1933), pp. 39-49.

James, E.O., *Comparative religion: An Introduction and Historical Study.* 3rd ed., London, 1969.
— *La religion préhistorique.* Paris, 1959.
— *La culte de la déesse-mère dans l'histoire des religions.* Paris, 1960.

Müller, Valentin, *Frühe Plastik in Griechenland und Vorderasien.* Augsburg, 1929.

Renfrew, Colin, The Development and Chronology of the Early Cycladic Figurines. *American Journal of Archaeology* 73 (1969), pp. 1-32.

Ucko, Peter J., *Anthropomorphic Figurines of Predynastic Egypt and Neolithic Crete with Comparative Material from the Prehistoric Near East and Mainland Greece.* London, 1968.

Weinberg, Saul S., *Ceramics and the Supernatural: Cult and Burial Evidence in the Aegean World* Matson, F., Ceramics and Man. Chicago, 1965. Neolithic Figurines and Aegean Interrelations. *American Journal of Archaeology* 55 (1951), pp. 121-133.

THE BRONZE AGE

Bernabò-Brea, L., *Poliochni: Città preistorica nell'isola di Lemnos.* Vol. I. Rome, 1964.

Blegen, Carl W., *Korakou: A Prehistoric Settlement near Corinth.* Boston-New York, 1921.
— *Zygouries: A Prehistoric Settlement in the Valley of Cleonae.* Cambridge, Mass., 1928.

Caskey, John L., Excavations at Lerna (Preliminary reports). *Hesperia* 23 (1954), pp. 3-30; 24 (1955), pp. 25-49; 25 (1956), pp. 147-173; 26 (1957), pp. 142-162; 27 (1958), pp. 125-144; 28 (1959), pp. 202-207.
— The Early Helladic Period in the Argolid. *Hesperia* 29 (1960), pp. 285-303.
— The Earliest Settlements at Eutresis: Supplementary Excavations, 1958, *Hesperia* 29 (1960), pp. 126-167.
— *Greece, Crete, and the Aegean Islands in the Early Bronze Age.* Cambridge Ancient History. Vol. I, part 2. 3rd ed., 1971, ch. XXVI(a).
— *Houses of the Fourth Settlement at Lerna.* Χαριστήριον εἰς Ἀναστάσιον Κ. Ὀρλάνδον. Vol. III. Athens, 1966, pp. 144-152.

Childe, V. Gordon, A Gold Vase of Early Helladic Type. *Journal of Hellenic Studies* 44 (1924), pp. 163-165.

Dor, L., Jannoray, J., van Effenterre, H. & M., *Kirrha: Étude de préhistoire phocidienne.* Paris, 1960.

Dörpfeld, W., *Alt-Ithaka.* Munich, 1927.

Frankfort, Henri, *Studies in Early Pottery of the Near East.* Vol. II. London, 1927.

French, D.H., *Anatolia and the Aegean in the Third Millennium B.C.* Cambridge-Athens, 1968.

Frödin, Otto, & Persson, Axel W., *Asine: The Results of the Swedish Excavations, 1922-1930.* Stockholm, 1938.

Fuchs, Siegfried, *Die griechischen Fundgruppen der frühen Bronzezeit und ihre auswärtigen Beziehungen.* Berlin, 1937.

Goldman, Hetty, *Excavations at Eutresis in Boeotia.* Cambridge, Mass., 1931.

Heath, Martha C., Early Helladic Clay Sealings from the House of the Tiles at Lerna. *Hesperia* 27 (1958), pp. 81-121.

Heurtley, W.A., Excavations in Ithaca, II: The Early Helladic Settlement at Pelikáta. *Annual of the British School at Athens* 35 (1934/1935), pp. 1-44.
— *Prehistoric Macedonia.* Cambridge, 1939.

Kunze, Emil, *Orchomenos III: Die Keramik der frühen Bronzezeit.* Munich, 1934.

Lamb, Winifred, *Excavations at Thermi in Lesbos.* Cambridge, 1936.

Matz, Friedrich, *Die Ägäis.* Handbuch der Archäologie, II. Munich, 1950, pp. 179-308.
— Zur ägäischen Chronologie der frühen Bronzezeit. *Historia* 1 (1950), pp. 173-194.

Mellaart, James, The End of the Early Bronze Age in Anatolia and the Aegean. *American Journal of Archaeology* 62 (1958), pp. 9-33.

Milojčić, Vladimir, Ergebnisse der deutschen Ausgrabungen in Thessalien, 1953-1958. *Jahrbuch des Römisch-Germanischen Zentralmuseums Mainz* 6 (1959), pp. 1-56.
— *Samos I: Die prähistorische Siedlung unter dem Heraion. Grabung 1953 und 1955.* Bonn, 1961.

Müller, K., *Tiryns IV: Die Urfirniskeramik.* Augsburg, 1938.

Mylonas, George E., *Aghios Kosmas: An Early Bronze Age Settlement and Cemetery in Attica.* Princeton, 1959.
— Ἡ Πρωτοελλαδικὴ καὶ ἡ Μεσοελλαδικὴ Ἐποχή. Ἀρχαιολογικὴ Ἐφημερίς 1937, pp. 40-47.

Papavasiliou, George, Περὶ τῶν ἐν Εὐβοίᾳ ἀρχαίων τάφων. Athens, 1910.

Renfrew, Colin, Cycladic Metallurgy and the Aegean Early Bronze Age. *American Journal of Archaeology* 71 (1967), pp. 1-20.

Theocharis, Dimitrios R., Ἀνασκαφαὶ ἐν Ἀραφῆνι. Πρακτικὰ τῆς ἐν Ἀθήναις Ἀρχαιολογικῆς Ἐταιρείας 1951, pp. 77-92; 1952, pp. 129-151; 1953, pp. 105-118; 1954, pp. 104-122; 1955, pp. 109-117.
— Ἀνασκαφὴ ἐν Παλαιᾷ Κοκκινιᾷ Πειραιῶς. Πρακτικὰ τῆς ἐν Ἀθήναις Ἀρχαιολογικῆς Ἐταιρείας 1951, pp. 93-127.

— Ἀσκηταριό: Προϊστορικὴ Ἀκρόπολις παρὰ τὴν Ραφίναν. *Ἀρχαιολογικὴ Ἐφημερὶς* 1953/1954, Vol. III, pp. 59-76.
— Ἐκ τῆς προϊστορίας τῆς Εὐβοίας καὶ τῆς Σκύρου. *Ἀρχεῖον Εὐβοϊκῶν Μελετῶν* 6 (1959), pp. 279-328.
Theocharis, Dimitrios R., Romiopoulou, Aikaterine, Deshayes, Jean, Ἀνασκαφαὶ Ντικλὶ Τάς. *Πρακτικὰ τῆς ἐν Ἀθήναις Ἀρχαιολογικῆς Ἑταιρείας* 1961, pp. 81-89.
Vermeule, Emily, *Greece in the Bronze Age.* Chicago-London, 1964.
Wace, A.J.B., The History of Greece in the Third and Second Millenniums B.C. *Historia* 2 (1953/1954), pp. 74-94.
Wace, A.J.B., & Blegen, Carl W., The Pre-Mycenaean Pottery of the Mainland. *Annual of the British School at Athens* 22 (1916/1918), pp. 175-189.
Weinberg, Saul S., A Gold Sauceboat in the Israel Museum. *Antike Kunst* 12 (1969), pp. 3-8.
— *The Relative Chronology of the Aegean in the Neolithic Period and Early Bronze Age.* Ehrich, Robert W., Chronologies in Old World Archaeology. Chicago-London, 1965, pp. 285-320.
Welter, Gabriel, *Aigina.* Berlin, 1938.
Zafiropoulos, Jean, *Histoire de la Grèce à l'âge du bronze.* Paris, 1964.

EARLY CYCLADIC CIVILIZATION

Caskey, John L., *Greece, Crete, and the Aegean Islands in the Early Bronze Age.* Cambridge Ancient History. Vol. I, part 2. 3rd ed., 1971, ch. XXVI(a).
Doumas, Christos, Κορφῆ τ' Ἀρωνιοῦ. *Ἀρχαιολογικὸν Δελτίον* 20a (1965), pp. 41-64.
— *The N.P. Goulandris Collection of Early Cycladic Art.* Athens, 1968.
Renfrew, Colin, *Cycladic Mettallurgy and the Aegean Early Bronze Age. American Journal of Archaeology* 71 (1967), pp. 1-20.
— The Development and Chronology of the Early Cycladic Figurines. *American Journal of Archaeology* 73 (1969), pp. 1-32.
Stephanos, Klon, Ἀνασκαφαὶ Νάξου. *Πρακτικὰ τῆς ἐν Ἀθήναις Ἀρχαιολογικῆς Ἑταιρείας* 1908-1911.
Tsountas, Christos, Κυκλαδικά. *Ἀρχαιολογικὴ Ἐφημερὶς* 1898, cols. 137-212; 1899, cols. 73-134.
Zervos, Christian, *L'art des Cyclades.* Paris, 1957.

PRE-PALACE PERIOD (see general bibliography on Minoan Civilization)

MIDDLE HELLADIC CIVILIZATION

Blegen, Carl W., *Korakou: A Prehistoric Settlement near Corinth.* Boston-New York, 1921.
— *Prosymna: The Helladic Settlement Preceding the Argive Heraeum.* 2 vols. Cambridge, Mass., 1937.
— *Zygouries: A Prehistoric Settlement in the Valley of Cleonae.* Cambridge, Mass., 1928.
Blegen, Carl W. & Wace, A.J.B., Middle Helladic Tombs. *Symbolae Osloenses* 9 (1930), pp. 28-37.
Buck, Robert J., Middle Helladic Mattpainted Pottery. *Hesperia* 33 (1964), pp. 231-313.
Bulle, Heinrich, *Orchomenos I: Die älteren Ansiedlungsschichten.* Munich, 1907.
Caskey, John L., Excavations at Lerna (Preliminary Reports). *Hesperia* 23 (1954), pp. 3-30; 27 (1958), pp. 125-144.
Dörpfeld, W., *Alt-Ithaka.* Munich, 1927.
Fimmen, Diedrich, *Die kretisch-mykenische Kultur.* 2nd ed., Leipzig-Berlin, 1921.
Forsdyke, E.J., The Pottery Called Minyan Ware. *Journal of Hellenic Studies* 34 (1914), pp. 126-156.
Frödin, Otto & Persson, Axel W., *Asine: The Results of the Swedish Excavations, 1922-1930.* Stockholm, 1938.
Furumark, Arne, *The Mycenaean Pottery: Analysis and Classification.* Stockholm, 1941.
Goldman, Hetty, *Excavations at Eutresis in Boeotia.* Cambridge, Mass., 1931.
Haley, J.B. & Blegen, Carl W., The Coming of the Greeks. *American Journal of Archaeology* 32 (1928), pp. 141-154.
Harland, James Penrose, The Peloponnesos in the Bronze Age. *Harvard Studies in Classical Philology* 34 (1923), pp. 1-62.
— *Prehistoric Aigina: A History of the Island in the Bronze Age.* Paris, 1925.
Holmberg, Erik J., *The Swedish Excavations at Asea in Arcadia.* Lund-Leipzig, 1944.
Hopkins, C., The Early History of Greece: The Origin of the Middle Helladic Culture. *Yale Classical Studies* 2 (1931), pp. 117-136.
Jannoray, J. & van Effenterre, H., Fouilles de Krisa (Phocide). *Bulletin de Correspondance Hellénique* 61 (1937), pp. 299-326; 62 (1938), pp. 110-148.
Keramopoullos, Antonios D., Θηβαϊκά, 1917. *Ἀρχαιολογικὸν Δελτίον* 3 (1917).
Mylonas, George E., *The Cult of the Dead in Helladic Times.* Studies Presented to David Moore Robinson. Vol. I. Saint Louis, Missouri, 1951, pp. 64-105.
— *Grave Circle B of Mycenae.* Lund, 1964.

— The Luvian Invasions of Greece. *Hesperia* 31 (1962), pp. 284-309.
— Οἱ Προϊστορικοὶ κάτοικοι τῆς Ἑλλάδος καὶ τὰ ἱστορικὰ Ἑλληνικὰ φῦλα. *Ἀρχαιολογικὴ ἐφημερὶς* 1930, pp. 1-29.
— Προϊστορικὴ Ἐλευσίς. Athens, 1932.
Myres, J.L., *Who were the Greeks?* Berkeley, 1930.
Romaios, K.A., Ἐκ τοῦ Προϊστορικοῦ Θέρμου. *Ἀρχαιολογικὸν Δελτίον* (1915), pp. 225-279.
Sotiriadis, Georges, Fouilles préhistoriques en Phochide. *Revue des Études Grecques* 25 (1912), pp. 253-299.
Schachermeyr, Fritz, *Die ältesten Kulturen Griechenlands.* Stuttgart, 1955.
— Luwier auf Kreta? *Kadmos* 1 (1962), pp. 27-39.
Vermeule, Emily, *Greece in the Bronze Age.* Chicago-London, 1964.
Wace, A.J.B., The History of Greece in the Third and Second Millenniums B.C. *Historia* 2 (1953/1954), pp. 74-94.
— *Mycenae.* Princeton, 1949.
Wace, A.J.B. & Blegen, Carl W., The Pre-Mycenaean Pottery of the Mainland. *Annual of the British School at Athens* 22 (1916-1918), pp. 175-189.

MIDDLE CYCLADIC CIVILIZATION

Atkinson, T.D. et al., Excavations at Phylakopi in Melos. *Journal of Hellenic Studies, Supplementary Paper No. 4.* London, 1904.
Buck, Robert J., Middle Helladic Mattpainted Pottery. *Hesperia* 33 (1964), pp. 231-314.
Caskey, John L., *Greece and the Aegean Islands in the Middle Bronze Age.* Cambridge Ancient History, revised ed. of Vols. I & II, fasc. 45, 1966.
Coleman, John E., Middle Bronze Age Burials in Ceos. *American Journal of Archaeology* 69 (1965), p. 167.
Scholes, K., The Cyclades in the Later Bronze Age: A Synopsis. *Annual of the British School at Athens* 51 (1956), pp. 9-40.

OLD-PALACE PERIOD (see general bibliography under Minoan Civilization)

THE DEVELOPMENT OF MINOAN SCRIPT (see general bibliography under Minoan Civilization)

MINOAN CIVILIZATION

Banti, L., Pugliese Carratelli, G., Levi, D., *Arte minoico-micenea.* Enciclopedia dell'Arte Antica Classica e Orientale. Vol. V, pp. 42-110.
Biesantz, H., *Die kretisch-mykenische Kunst.* Illustrierte Weltkunstgeschichte 1959.
Charbonneaux, Jean, *L'art égéen.* Paris-Brussels, 1929.
Demargne, Pierre, *Naissance de l'art grec.* Paris, 1964.
Evans, Arthur J., *The Palace of Minos.* 4 vols. and Index. London, 1921-1936.
Fimmen, Dietrich, *Die kretisch-mykenische Kultur.* 2nd ed., Leipzig-Berlin, 1924.
Fouqué, F., *Santorin et ses éruptions.* Paris, 1879.
Glotz, Gustave, *La civilization égéenne.* Paris, 1953.
Graham, James Walter, *The Palaces of Crete.* Princeton, 1962.
Hawkes, Jacquetta, *The Dawn of the Gods.* London, 1968.
Higgins, Reynold, *Minoan and Mycenaean Art.* London, 1967.
Hood, Sinclair, *The Home of the Heroes: The Aegean before the Greeks.* London, 1967.
Hutchinson, R.W., *Prehistoric Crete.* 3rd. ed., Harmondsworth, 1965.
Kantor, Helen J., *The Aegean and the Orient in the Second Millennium B.C.* Bloomington, Indiana, 1947.
Karo, G., *Kreta.* Paulys Real-Encyclopädie der Classischen Altertumswissenschaft. Vol. XI.
Marinatos, Spyridon, Amnisos, die Hafenstadt des Minos. *Forschungen und Fortschritte* 10 (1934), pp. 341-343.
— Ἀνασκαφαὶ Θήρας. *Πρακτικὰ τῆς ἐν Ἀθήναις Ἀρχαιολογικῆς Ἑταιρείας* 1967, pp. 124-150.
— Αἱ Ἀνασκαφαὶ τῆς Θήρας. *Ἀρχαιολογικὰ Ἀνάλεκτα ἐξ Ἀθηνῶν* 1 (1968), p. 213-220.
— *Excavations at Thera.* 5 vols. Athens, 1968-1972.
— Τὸ ἡφαίστειον τῆς Θήρας καὶ οἱ πολιτισμοὶ τοῦ Αἰγαίου. Πεπραγμένα τοῦ Β' Διεθνοῦς Κρητολογικοῦ Συνεδρίου. Vol. I. Athens, 1968, pp. 198-216.
— Περὶ τὸν θρῦλον τῆς Ἀτλαντίδος. *Κρητικὰ Χρονικά* 4 (1950), pp. 195-213.
— Thera. *Ἀρχαιολογικὰ ἀνάλεκτα ἐξ Ἀθηνῶν* 3 (1970), pp. 1-5.
— The Volcanic Destruction of Minoan Crete. *Antiquity* 13 (1939), pp. 425-439.
Marinatos, S., Hirmer, M., *Kreta und das mykenische Hellas.* Munich, 1959.
Matt, L., von; Alexiou, St., Platon, N., Guanella, H., *Das antike Kreta.* Zürich 1967.
Matz, Friedrich, *Kreta, Mykene, Troja.* Stuttgart, 1956.
— *Kreta und frühes Griechenland.* Baden-Baden, 1962.
— *Minoan Civilization: Maturity and Zenith.* Cambridge Ancient History, revised ed. of Vols. I & II, fasc. 12, 1962.
Ninkovich, D., & Heesen, B., *Santorin Tephra.* Colston Papers, Vol. XVII.

1965, pp. 413 ff., including a full bibliography of geological and vulcano-
logical subjects.
Palmer, Leonard R., *Mycenaeans and Minoans: Aegean Prehistory in the Light
of the Linear B Tablets*. 2nd ed., London, 1965.
Pendlebury, J.D.S., *The Archaeology of Crete*. London, 1939.
— *A Handbook to the Palace of Minos at Knossos*. 2nd ed., London, 1954.
Pernier, L., & Banti, L., *Il palazzo minoico di Festòs*. 2 vols. Rome, 1935-1951.
Platon, Nicolas, *Crète*. (Archaeologia Mundi) Geneva-Paris-Munich, 1966.
— *Cretese-miceneo*. Enciclopedia Universale dell'Arte. Vol. IV, p. 70.
Schachermeyr, Fritz, *Ägäis und Orient*. Vienna, 1967.
— *Die minoische Kultur des alten Kreta*. Stuttgart, 1964.
— *Die Prähistorischen Kulturen Griechenlands*. Paulys Real-Encyclopädie der
Classischen Altertumswissenschaft. Vol. XXII₂. Stuttgart, 1954, cols.
1350-1548.
Snijder, G.A.S., *Kretische Kunst*. Berlin, 1936.
Vercoutter, Jean, *Essai sur les relations entre Egyptiens et Préhellènes*. Paris,
1954.
Wace, A.J.B., *Crete and Mycenae*. Cambridge Ancient History, Vol. II. 1926,
ch. XVI.
Willetts, Ronald F., *Everyday Life in Ancient Crete*. London, 1969.
Xanthoudides, Stephanos, *The Vaulted Tombs of Mesara*. London, 1924.
Zervos, Christian, *L'art de la Grèce néolithique et minoenne*. Paris, 1956.

SEALS

Corpus der kretisch-mykenischen Siegel:
    I. Sakellariou, Agnes, *Die minoischen und mykenischen Siegel des National-
museums in Athen*. Berlin, 1964.
    II. Platon, Nicolas, *Iraklion: Archäologisches Museum*. Part 1. Berlin,
1969.
    IV. Sakellarakis, J.G., *Iraklion: Sammlung Metaxas*. Berlin, 1969.
    VII. Kenna, V.E.G., *Die englischen Museen*. Part 2. Berlin, 1967.
    VIII.   *Die englischen Privatsammlungen*. Berlin, 1966.
    XII.   *Nordamerika*. Part 1. Berlin, 1972.
Kenna, V.E.G., *Cretan Seals*. Oxford, 1960.
Matz, Friedrich, *Die frühkretischen Siegel*. Berlin-Leipzig, 1928.
Sakellariou, Agnes, *Die mykenische Siegelglyptik*. (Studies in Mediterranean
Archaeology, 9) Lund, 1964.

GUIDES

Alexiou, Stylianos, *Guide to the Archaeological Museum of Herakleion*. Athens,
1968.
— *Μινωϊκὸς πολιτισμὸς μὲ Ὁδηγὸν τῶν ἀνακτόρων Κνωσοῦ, Φαιστοῦ καὶ Μαλίων.*
Herakleion, 1964.
Blegen, Carl W., & Rawson, Marion, *A Guide to the Palace of Nestor*. Cincinnati,
1962.
École Française d'Athènes, *Guide des fouilles francaises en Crète*. Paris, 1966.
Palmer, Leonard R., *A New Guide to the Palace of Knossos*. London, 1969.
Pendlebury, J.D.S., *A Handbook to the Palace of Minos at Knossos*. 2nd ed.,
London, 1954.
Pernier, L., & Banti, L., *Guida degli scavi italiani in Creta*. Roma, 1947.
Wace, A.J.B., *Mycenae: An Archaeological History and Guide*. Princeton, 1949.

MINOAN RELIGION

Alexiou, Stylianos, *Ἡ μινωϊκὴ θεὰ μεθ' ὑψωμένων χειρῶν*. Herakleion, 1958.
Frazer, J.G., *The Golden Bough: A Study in Magic and Religion*. Abridged ed.,
London, 1968.
Hutchinson, R.W., *Prehistoric Crete*. 3rd ed., London, 1965. ('Minoan Reli-
gion', pp. 199 ff.).
Kerényi, Carl, *The Gods of the Greeks*. 2nd ed., London, 1961.
Marinatos, Spyridon, & Hirmer, Max, *Kreta und Mykenische Hellas*. Munich,
1959.
Matz, Friedrich, *Götterscheinung und Kultbild in minoischen Kreta*. Wiesbaden,
1958.
Nilsson, Martin P., *Geschichte der griechischen Religion*. Handbuch der Alter-
tumswissenschaft, Section 5, Part 2, Vol. I. Munich, 1967.
— *The Minoan-Mycenaean Religion and its Survival in Greek Religion*. 2nd
ed., Lund, 1950.
Pendlebury, J.D.S., *The Archaeology of Crete*. London, 1939. (Minoan Re-
ligion', pp. 272 ff.).
Persson, Axel W., *The Religion of Greece in Prehistoric Times*. Berkeley-Los
Angeles, 1942.
Picard, Charles, *Les religions préhelléniques (Crète et Mycènes)*. Paris, 1948.
Platon, Nicolas, *Crète*. (Archaeologia Mundi) Geneva-Paris-Munich, 1966.
('La religion', pp. 189 ff.).
Schachermeyr, Fritz, *Die minoische Kultur des alten Kreta*. Stuttgart, 1964.
('Götterglaube und Frömmigkeit', pp. 140 ff.).

MYCENAEAN CIVILIZATION

Aign, Bernhard, *Die Geschischte der Musikinstrumente des Ägäischen Raumes
bis zum 700 vor Christus*. Frankfurt, 1963.
Åkestrom, Åke, Some Pictorial Vase Representations from the Mainland in
Late Helladic Times. *Opuscula Atheniensia* 1 (1953), pp. 9-28.
Alin, P., *Das Ende der mykenischen Fundstätten auf dem griechischen Festland*.
(Studies in Mediterranean Archaeology, 1) Lund, 1962.
Andronikos, Manolis, *Totenkult*. Archaeologia Homerica, Vol. III. Ch. W.
Göttingen, 1968.
Barnett, R.D., *The Sea Peoples*. Cambridge Ancient History, revised ed. of
Vols. I & II, Vol. II, ch. XXVIII.
Biancofiore, F., *La civiltà micenea nell'Italia meridionale*. 2nd ed., Rome, 1967.
Biesantz, Hagen, *Kretisch-mykenische Siegelbilder*. Marburg, 1954.
Blegen, Carl W., *The Mycenaean Age*. Cincinnati, 1962.
Blegen, Carl W., & Rawson, Marion, *The Palace of Nestor at Pylos in Western
Messenia*. Vol. I: *The Buildings and their Contents*. Princeton, 1966.
Bulle, Heinrich, *Orchomenos I: Die älteren Anseidlungschichten*. Munich, 1907.
Carpenter, Rhys, *Discontinuity in Greek Civilization*. Cambridge, 1966.
Caskey, John L., *Greece and the Aegean Islands in the Middle Bronze Age*. Cam-
bridge Ancient History, revised ed. of Vols. I & II, fasc. 45, 1966.
Casson, Stanley, *The Technique of Early Greek Sculpture*. Oxford, 1933.
Chadwick, John, *Aegean History, 1500 - 1200 B.C.* Studii Classice, Vol. XI.
Bucharest, 1969, pp. 7-18.
Charitonidis, Seraphim I., Μυκηναῖος ἀγγειογράφος. Ἀρχαιολογικὴ ἐφημερὶς
1953-1954, Vol. II, pp. 101-106.
— Μυκηναῖος ἀγγειογράφος τῶν Παπύρων. Ἀρχαιολογικὸν Δελτίον 16 (1960),
pp. 84-90.
Daniel, Glyn, & Evans, J.D., *The Western Mediterranean*. Cambridge Ancient
History, revised ed. of Vols. I & II, fasc. 57, 1967.
Desborough, V.R.d'A., & Hammond, N.G.L., *The End of Mycenaean Civili-
zation and the Dark Age*. Cambridge Ancient History, revised ed. of Vols.
I & II, fasc. 13, 1962.
Desborough, V.R.d'A., The Greek Mainland, c. 1150-c. 1000 B.C. *Proceedings
of the Prehistoric Society*. Cambridge, 31 (1965), pp. 213-228.
— *The Last Mycenaeans and their Successors: An Archaeological Survey,
c. 1200-c. 1000 B.C.* Oxford, 1964.
Deshayes, Jean, *Les outils de bronze de l'Indus au Danube (IVe au IIe millénaire)*.
2 vols. Paris, 1960.
Drower, M., *Ugarit*. Cambridge Ancient History, revised ed. of Vols. I & II,
Vol. II. ch. XXI(b).
Furumark, Arne, *The Chronology of Mycenaean Pottery*. Stockholm, 1941.
— *The Mycenaean Pottery: Analysis and Classification*. Stockholm, 1941.
— The Mycenaean IIIC Pottery and its Relation to Cypriote Fabrics. *Opuscula
Archaeologica* 3 (1944), pp. 194-265.
Graham, J. Walter, Mycenaean Architecture. *Archaeology* 13 (1960), pp. 46-54.
Higgins, R.A., *Greek and Roman Jewellery*. London, 1961.
Hope Simpson, R., *A Gazetteer and Atlas of Mycenaean Sites*. London, 1965.
Huxley, G.L., *Achaeans and Hittites*. Oxford, 1960.
Iakovidis, Spyridon E., Τὰ Κυκλώπεια Τείχη. Ἀρχαιολογικὰ Ἀνάλεκτα ἐξ Ἀθη-
νῶν 2 (1969), pp. 463-472.
— Ἡ μυκηναϊκὴ ἀκρόπολις τῶν Ἀθηνῶν. Athens, 1962.
Kambanis, Michel L., Le dessèchement du lac Copais par les anciens. *Bulletin
de Correspondance Hellénique.* 16 (1892), pp. 121-137; 17 (1893), pp. 322-
342.
Kantor, Helene J., Ivory Carving in the Mycenaean Period. *Archaeology* 13
(1960), pp. 14-23.
Karo, Georg, *Führer durch Tiryns*. Athens, 1934.
— *Mykenische Kultur*. Paulys Real-Encyclopädie der Classischen Altertums-
wissenschaft. Suppl. VI. Stuttgart, 1935, cols. 584-615.
— *Die Schachtgräber von Mykenai*. 2 vols. Munich, 1930-1933.
Kenny, A., The Ancient Drainage of the Copais. *Annual of Archaeology and
Anthropology, University of Liverpool*, 1935.
Keramopoullos, Antonios, D., Θηβαϊκά, 1917. Ἀρχαιολογικὸν Δελτίον 3 (1917).
Kirk, A.G.S., *The Homeric Poems as History*. Cambridge Ancient History, re-
vised ed. of Vols. I & II, fasc. 22, 1964.
Lacy, A.D., *Greek Pottery in the Bronze Age*. London, 1967.
Lang, Mabel, *The Palace of Nestor at Pylos in Western Messenia*. Vol. II: *The
Frescoes*. Princeton, 1969.
Lencman, J.A., *Die Sklaverei im mykenischen und homerischen Griechenland*.
Wiesbaden, 1966.
Loud, G., *The Megiddo Ivories*. Chicago, 1939.
Macheprang, Mogens B., Late Mycenaean Vases. *American Journal of Ar-
chaeology* 42 (1938), pp. 537-559.
Marinatos, Spyridon & Hirmer, Max, *Kreta und das mykenische Hellas*, Munich,
1959.
Moon, Brenda E., *Mycenaean Civilization*. 2 vols. London, 1957-1961.
Mylonas, George E., *Ancient Mycenae: The Capital City of Agamemnon*. Prince-
ton, 1957.
— *Grave Circle B of Mycenae*. (Studies in Mediterranean Archaeology, 7)
Lund, 1964.
— *Mycenae: A Guide to its Ruins and its History*. Athens, 1967.
— *Mycenae and the Mycenaean Age*. Princeton, 1966.
Notopoulos, James A., Homer, Hesiod and the Achaean Heritage of Oral
Poetry. *Hesperia* 29 (1960), pp. 177-197.
Nylander, Carl, Troja-Philister-Achämeniden. *Berliner Jahrbuch für Vor- und*

Frühgeschichte 6 (1966), pp. 203-217.

Page, Denys L., *History and the Homeric Iliad*. Berkeley-Los Angeles, 1959.

Parry, Milman, see his bibliography in Lord, Albert B., Parry and Huso. *American Journal of Archaeology* 52 (1948), pp. 43-44.

Platon, Nicolas, Μινωϊκὴ λύρα. Χαριστήριον εἰς ᾽Αναστάσιον Κ. ᾽Ορλάνδον. Vol. III. Athens, 1966, pp. 208-232.

Reusch, H., *Die zeichnerische Rekonstruktion des Frauenfrieses im Böotische Theben*. (Abhandlungen der Deutschen Akademie der Wissenschaft, 29) Berlin, 1965.

Ridder, A. de, Fouilles de Gha. *Bulletin de Correspondance Hellénique* 18 (1894), pp. 271-310.

Rodenwaldt, Gerhart, *Der Fries des Megarons von Mykenai*. Halle, 1921.

Sakellariou, Agnes, Μυκηναϊκὴ σφραγιδογλυφία. Athens, 1966.

Sandars, N. K., Later Aegean Bronze Swords. *American Journal of Archaeology* 67 (1963), pp. 117-153.

Schachermeyr, Fritz, *Ursprung und Hintergrund der griechischen Geschichte*. Propyläen Weltgeschichte, Vol. III. Berlin-Frankfurt, 1962.

Schliemann, Heinrich, *Mycenae*. Leipzig, 1878.
— *Mycenae und Tiryns*. Leipzig, 1880.
— *The Prehistoric Palace of the Kings of Tiryns*. London, 1886.

Schuchhardt, Carl, *Schliemanns Ausgrabungen in Troja, Tiryns, Mykenä, Orchomenos und Ithaka im Licht der heutigen Wissenschaft*. Leipzig, 1890.

Stella, L. A., *La civiltà micenea nei documenti contemporanei*. (Incunabula Graeca, 6) Rome, 1956.

Stubbings, Frank H., *The Expansion of Mycenaean Civilization*. Cambridge Ancient History, revised ed. of Vols. I & II, fasc. 26, 1964.
Mycenaean Pottery from the Levant. Cambridge, 1951.
The Recession of Mycenaean Civilization. Cambridge Ancient History, revised ed. of Vols. I & II, fasc. 39, 1965.

Taylour, William, *Mycenaean Pottery in Italy and Adjacent Areas*. Cambridge, 1958.
— *The Mycenaeans*. London, 1964.
— *Tiryns: Die Ergebnisse des Ausgrabungen des Instituts*. 6 vols. 1912-1971.

Tsountas, Christos, Μυκῆναι καὶ μυκηναῖος πολιτισμός. Athens, 1893.

Tsountas, Christos, & Mannatt, J. Irving, *The Mycenaean Age*. Boston-New York, 1897.

Vermeule, Emily, *Greece in the Bronze Age*. Chicago-London, 1964.

Wace, A. J. B., Excavations at Mycenae. *Annual of the British School at Athens* 24 (1919-1920), pp. 185-209; 25 (1921-1923), pp. 1-434.
— *Mycenae: An Archaeological History and Guide*. Princeton, 1949.

Zevros, Christian, *L'art des Cyclades*. Paris, 1957.

MYCENAEAN RELIGION

Evans, Arthur J., Mycenaean Tree and Pillar Cult and its Mediterranean Relations. *Journal of Hellenic Studies* 21 (1901), pp. 99-204.

Mylonas, George E., *Mycenae and the Mycenaean Age*. Princeton, 1966.

Nilsson, Martin P., *The Minoan-Mycenaean Religion and its Survival in Greek Religion*. 2nd ed., Lund, 1950.

Palmer, Leonard R., *Mycenaeans and Minoans: Aegean History in the Light of the Linear B Tablets*. 2nd ed., London, 1965.

Persson, Axel W., *The Religion of Greece in Prehistoric Times*. Berkeley-Los Angeles, 1942.

Picard, Charles, *Les religions préhélléniques (Crète et Mycènes)*. Paris 1948.

Wace, A. J. B., & Stubbings, Frank H., *A Companion to Homer*, London, 1962.

MYCENAEAN SCRIPT

Bennett, Emmett L., *The Olive Oil Tablets of Pylos: Texts of Inscriptions Found 1958*. (Minos, Suppl. 2) Salamanca, 1958.
— *The Pylos Tablets: Texts of the Inscriptions Found 1939 - 1954*. Princeton, 1955.

Bennett, E. L., Chadwick, J., Ventris, M., *The Knossos Tablets: A Revised Transliteration*. 2nd ed., London, 1959.

Brice, W. C., *Inscriptions in the Minoan Linear Script of Class A*. Oxford, 1961.

Carratelli, G. Pugliese, *Le epigrafi di Haghia Triada in Lineare A*. (Minos, Suppl. 3) Salamanca, 1963.
— *Le iscrizioni preeleniche di Haghia Triada in Creta e della Grecia peninsulare*. Rome, 1945.

Chadwick, John, *The Decipherment of Linear B*. 2nd ed., Cambridge, 1967.

Chapouthier, Fernand, *Les écritures minoennes au palais de Mallia*. Paris, 1930.

Doria, Mario, *Avviamento allo studio del miceneo*. Rome, 1965.

Evans, Arthur J., *Cretan Pictographs and a Prae-Phoenician Script...* London, 1895.
Scripta Minoa. 2 vols. Oxford, 1909-1952.

Grumach, Ernst, *Bibliographie der kretisch-mykenischen Epigraphik*. Munich-Berlin, 1963. Supplement I (1962-1963). Munich, 1967.

Ktistopoulos, K. D., Πρῶται παρατηρήσεις ἐπὶ τῶν ἐπιγραφῶν τῆς Πύλου. Athens, 1951.

Palmer, Leonard R., & Boardman, John, *On the Knossos Tablets*. Oxford, 1963.

Ventris, Michael, & Chadwick, John, *Documents in Mycenaean Greek*. Cambridge, 1956.

THE MYCENAEAN DYNASTY AT KNOSOS

Alexiou, Stylianos, ᾽Υστερομινωϊκοὶ τάφοι λιμένος Κνωσοῦ (Κατσαμπᾶ). Athens, 1967.

Evans, Arthur J., *The Palace of Minos at Knossos*. 4 vols and Index. London, 1921-1936.

Furumark, Arne, The Settlement at Ialysos and Aegean History 1550-1440 B.C. *Opuscula Archaeologica* 6 (1950), pp. 150-271.

Hood, Sinclair, & De Jong, Piet, Late Minoan Warrior Graves from Ayios Ioannis and the New Hospital Site at Knossos. *Annual of the British School at Athens* 47 (1952), pp. 243-277.

Killen, J. T., The Wool Industry of Crete in the Late Bronze Age. *Annual of the British School at Athens* 59 (1964), pp. 1-15.

Marinatos, Spyridon, *The 'Volcanic' Origin of Linear B*. Europa: Festschrift für Ernst Grumach. Berlin, 1967, pp. 204-210.

Nilsson, Martin P., Ἡ μετανάστευσις τῶν Ἑλλήνων εἰς τὴν Κρήτην. Κρητικὰ Χρονικὰ 3 (1949), pp. 7-15.

Palmer, Leonard R., *The Interpretation of Mycenaean Greek Texts*. Oxford, 1963.

Pendlebury, J. D. S., Egypt and the Aegean in the Late Bronze Age. *Journal of Egyptian Archaeology* 16 (1930), pp. 75-92.

Popham, Mervyn R., The Destruction of the Palace of Knossos and its Pottery. *Antiquity* 40 (1966), pp. 24-28.
— *The Destruction of the Palace of Knossos: Pottery of the Late Minoan IIIA Period*. (Studies in Mediterranean Archaeology, 12) Göteborg, 1970.

Sakellarakis, John A., ᾽Ελεφαντοστᾶ ἐκ τῶν ᾽Αρχανῶν. Atti del 1o Congresso Internazionale di Micenologia. Rome, 1968, pp. 245-261.
— Παρατηρήσεις ἐπὶ τῆς σημειωθείσης εἰς ᾽Αρχάνας ΥΜ ΙΙΙ θυσίας ταύρου. Πεπραγμένα τοῦ Β´ Διεθνοῦς Κρητολογικοῦ Συνεδρίου, Vol. I. Athens, 1968, pp. 238-246.

Schachermeyr, Fritz, Das Keftiu Problem. *Jahreshefte des Österreichischen Archäologischen Institutes in Wien* 45 (1960), pp. 44-68.

Vermeule, Emily, *The Decline and End of Minoan and Mycenaean Culture. A Land Called Crete: A Symposium in Memory of Harriet Boyd Hawes*. Northampton, Mass., 1967, pp. 81-98.

MINOAN POST-PALACE PERIOD

Aposkitou, Martha, Κρήτη καὶ ῞Ομηρος. Κρητικὰ Χρονικὰ 14 (1960), pp. 147-172.

Desborough, V. R. d'A., *The Last Mycenaeans and their Successors: An Archaeological Survey, c. 1200-c. 1000 B.C.* Oxford, 1964.

Hood, Sinclair, Date of the 'Reoccupation' Pottery from the Palace of Minos at Knossos. *Kadmos* 5 (1966), pp. 121-141.
— 'Last Palace' and 'Reoccupation' at Knossos. *Kadmos* 4 (1965), pp. 16-44.
— *'Last Palace' and 'Reoccupation' at Knossos*. Πεπραγμένα τοῦ Β´ Διεθνοῦς Κρητολογικοῦ Συνεδρίου, Vol. I. Athens, 1968, pp. 173-179.
— The Last Palace at Knossos and the Date of its Destruction. *Studi Micenei* ed Egeo-Anatolici, fasc. 2. Rome, 1967, pp. 63-70.

Mylonas, George E., Athens and Minoan Crete. *Harvard Studies in Classical Philology*. Suppl. 1, 1940, pp. 11-36.

Palmer, Leonard R., & Boardman, John, *On the Knossos Tablets*. Oxford, 1963.

Platon, Nicolas, ᾽Ανασκαφὴ Χόνδρου - Βιάννου. Πρακτικὰ τῆς ἐν ᾽Αθήναις ᾽Αρχαιολογικῆς ῾Εταιρείας 1957, pp. 136-147.

Popham, Mervyn R., *The Last Days of the Palace at Knossos: Complete Vases of the Late Minoan IIIB Period*. (Studies in Mediterranean Archaeology, 5) Lund, 1964.
— Some Late Minoan III Pottery from Crete. *Annual of the British School at Athens* 60 (1965), pp. 316-342.

BRONZE-AGE CYPRUS

Åstrom, Lena, *Studies on the Arts and Crafts of the Late Cypriote Bronze Age*. Lund, 1967.

Catling, H. W., *Cypriot Bronzework in the Mycenaean World*. Oxford, 1964.
— *Cyprus in the Neolithic and Chalcolithic Periods*. Cambridge Ancient History, Vol. 1, part 1. 3rd ed., 1970, ch. IX(c).

Desborough, V. R. d'A., *The Last Mycenaeans and their Successors: An Archaeological Survey, c. 1200 - c. 1000 B.C.* Oxford, 1964.

Dikaios, Porphyrios, A Conspectus of Architecture in Ancient Cyprus. Κυπριακαὶ Σπουδαὶ 24 (1960), pp. 1-30.
— *Enkomi*. 3 vols. Mainz, 1969-1971.
— *A Guide to the Cyprus Museum*. 3rd. ed., Nicosia, 1961.

Furumark, Arne, The Excavations at Sinda. *Opuscula Atheniensia* 6 (1965). pp. 99-116.

Gjerstadt, Einar, The Colonization of Cyprus in Greek Legend. *Opuscula Archaeologica* 3 (1944), pp. 107-123.
— *Studies on Prehistoric Cyprus*. Stockholm, 1926.

Hill, George, F., *A History of Cyprus*. Vol. I. Cambridge, 1940.

Karageorghis, Vassos, *Corpus Vasorum Antiquorum: Cyprus*. 2 vols. Nicosia, 1963-1965.

— *Chypre.* (Archaeologia Mundi) Geneva-Paris-Munich, 1968.
— *Mycenaean Art from Cyprus.* Nicosia, 1968.
— *Nouveaux documents pour l'étude du bronze récent à Chypre.* (Études Chypriotes, 3) Paris, 1965.
Masson, Olivier, *Inscriptions chypriotes syllabiques: Recueil critique et commenté.* (Études Chypriotes, 1) Paris, 1961.
Merrilees, R. S., *The Cypriote Bronze Age Pottery Found in Egypt.* Lund, 1968.
Pouilloux, Jean, *Salamine de Chypre: Le site et ses problèmes.* Comptes Rendus de l'Académie des Inscriptions et Belles-Lettres 1966, pp. 232-256.
Schaeffer, Claude F.-A., *Enkomi-Alasia.* Paris, 1952.
— *Missions en Chypre, 1932-1935.* Paris, 1936.
— *Ugaritica V.* Paris, 1968, pp. 607 ff.
Sjoeqvist, Erik, *Problems of the Late Cypriot Bronze Age.* Stockholm, 1940.
Stubbings, Frank H., *Mycenaean Pottery from the Levant.* Cambridge, 1951.
Taylor, J. du Plat, et al., *Myrtou-Pighades: A Late Bronze Age Sanctuary in Cyprus.* Oxford, 1957.

SUB-MINOAN AND SUB-MYCENAEAN PERIODS

Desborough, V.R.d'A., The Greek Mainland, c. 1150-c. 1000 B.C. *Proceedings of the Prehistoric Society*, Cambridge, 31 (1965), pp. 213-228.
— *The Last Mycenaeans and their Successors: An Archaeological Survey, c. 1200-c. 1000 B.C.* Oxford, 1964.
Desborough, V.R.d'A., & Hammond, N.G.L., *The End of Mycenaean Civilization and the Dark Age.* Cambridge Ancient History, revised ed. of Vols. I & II, fasc. 13, 1962.
Furumark, Arne, *The Chronology of Mycenaean Pottery.* Stockholm, 1941.
— *The Mycenaean Pottery: Analysis and Classification.* Stockholm, 1941.
Hawkes, Jacquetta, *The Dawn of the Gods.* London, 1968.
Hutchinson, R.W., *Prehistoric Crete.* 3rd ed., Harmondsworth, 1968.
Marinatos, Spyridon, & Hirmer, Max, *Kreta und das mykenische Hellas.* Munich, 1959.
Mylonas, George E., *Mycenae and the Mycenaean Age.* Princeton, 1966.
Pendlebury, J.D.S., *The Archaeology of Crete.* London, 1939.
Styrenius, Carl-Gustaf, *Submycenaean Studies.* Lund, 1967.
Vermeule, Emily, *Greece in the Bronze Age.* Chicago-London, 1964.

LINGUISTIC AND ETHNIC GROUPS IN PREHISTORIC GREECE

Adrados, F.R., *La dialectologia griega come fuente para el estudio de las migraciones indoeuropeas en Grecia.* Salamanca, 1952.
Bosch-Gimpera, Pedro, *Les Indo-européens: Problèmes archéologiques.* Paris, 1961.
Brandenstein, W., Die Erforschung der Ortsnamen in Altkleinasien. *Zeitschrift für Ortsnamenforschung* 11 (1935), pp. 61-78.
— *Kleinasiatische Ursprachen.* Paulys Real-Encyclopädie der Classischen Altertumswissenschaft, Suppl. VI, Stuttgart, 1935, cols. 165-181.
— Festschrift Hirt, Vol. II, 1936, pp. 29 ff.
— *Zeitschrift der Deutschen Morgenländischen Gesellschaft* 42 (1938), pp. 303 ff.

Buck, Carl D., *The Greek Dialects.* Chicago, 1955.
Buti, G.G., *La casa degli Indoeuropei.* 1962.
Cardona, G. (ed.), *Indo-European and Indo-Europeans.* 1968.
Chadwick, John, Ἡ γένγησις τῆς ἑλληνικῆς γλώσσης. Ἐπιστημονικὴ Ἐπετηρὶς τῆς Φιλοσοφικῆς Σχολῆς τοῦ Πανεπιστημίου Ἀθηνῶν 12 (1961-1962), pp. 531-544.
— The Greek Dialects and Greek Prehistory. Greece and Rome 3 (1956), pp. 38-50.
— *The Prehistory of the Greek Language.* Cambridge Ancient History, revised ed. of Vols. I & II, fasc. 15, 1963.
Childe, V. Gordon, *The Aryans: A Study of Indo-European Origins.* London, 1926.
Crossland, R.A., *Immigrants from the North.* Cambridge Ancient History, revised ed. of Vols. I & II, fasc. 60, 1967.
— *The Indoeuropeans.* 1970.
— Past and Present 12 (1957), pp. 16 ff.; 13 (1958), pp. 88 ff.
Devoto, Giacomo, *Le origini indoeuropee.* Florence, 1962.
Georgiev, Vladimir, J., *Introduzione alla storia delle lingue indoeuropee.* Rome, 1966.
— *Die Träger der kretisch-mykenischen Kultur, ihre Herkunft und ihre Sprache.* 1937/1938.
— *Vorgriechische Sprachwissenschaft.* 2 vols. 1941-1945.
Gimbutas, M., *Bronze Age Cultures in Central and Eastern Europe.* 1965.
— The Indoeuropeans: Archaeological Problems. *American Anthropologist* 65 (1963), pp. 815 ff.
Hoffmann, Otto, *Geschichte der griechischen Sprache.* Leipzig, 1911.
Krahe, H., *Sprache und Vorzeit.* Heidelberg, 1954.
Kretschmer, Paul, Zur ältesten Sprachgeschichte Kleinasiens. *Glotta* 21 (1933), pp. 76-100.
— Die ältesten Sprachgeschichten auf Kreta. *Glotta* 31 (1944-1951), pp. 1-20.
— Die Leleger und die ostmediterrane Urbevölkerung. *Glotha* 32 (1952-1953). pp. 161-204.
— Die vorgriechischen Sprach- und Volksschichten. *Glotta* 28 (1940), pp. 231-278; 30 (1943), pp. 84-218.
Lochner-Hüttenbach, Fritz, *Die Pelasger.* Vienna, 1960.
Meillet, A., *Aperçu d'une histoire de la langue grecque.* 7th. ed., Paris, 1965.
Merlingen, Weriand, *Eine ältere Lehnwörterschicht im griechischen.* 2 vols. Vienna, 1963-1967.
— Das 'Vorgriechische' und die sprachwissenschaftlichvorhistorischen Grundlagen. Vienna, 1955.
Pisani, Vittore, *Le lingue indoeuropee.* 2nd ed., 1964.
Porzig, Walter, Sprachgeographische Untersuchungen zu den altgriechischen Dialekten. *Indogermanische Forschungen* 21 (1954), pp. 147-169.
Risch, Ernst, Die Gliederung der griechischen Dialekte in neuer Sicht. *Museum Helveticum* 12 (1955), pp. 61-76.
Sakellariou, Michel, *Dialectes et ethnè grecs à l'âge du Bronze.* 3 vols. in process of publication.
Schachermeyr, Fritz, *Ägäis und Orient.* Vienna, 1967.
Die ältesten Kulturen Griechenlands. Stuttgart, 1955.
Die minoische Kultur des alten Kreta. Stuttgart, 1964.
Prähistorische Kulturen Griechenlands. Paulys Real-Encyclopädie der Classischen Altertumswissenschaft. Vol. XXII$_2$. Stuttgart, 1954, cols. 1494-1548.
Windekens, A.J. van, *Le pélasgique.* 1952.

INDEX

Rakhmani, 76, 77, 82, Saliagos, 76, 77, Sesklo, 68, 73, 74, 75, 77, 81, Sotera (Cyprus), 86. See also civilizations
Cyclades, 18, 20, 29, 76, 81, 82, 97, 98, 99, 102, 105, 106, 107, 108, 109, 110, 111, 113, 119, 129, 131, 132, 133, 139, 140, 141, 169, 170, 219, 220, 224, 233, 246, 263, 270, 283, 299, 335, 336, 372, 376
Cyclopean walls, 312, 313, 316, Cypriot—,350
cylinder, clay, from Enkomi, 357
cylinder-seals, 345
cymbals, 335
Cypriot dialect, 358, 360
Cypriots, 358, 379
Cyprus, 27, 29, 82, 85, 86, 88, 121, 129, 130, 132, 150, 190, 217, 218, 269, 270, 278, 281, 283, 293, 295, 296, 297, 299, 300, 325, 327, 333, 334, 344, 346, 347, 348, 349, 350, 351, 352, 353, 354, 355, 357, 358, 359, 360, 361, 363, 374, 379

Daemons in Minoan religion, 229
daggers, 110, 119, 123, 127, 132, 150, 157, 167, 204, 215, 266, 334, 339, 361
Daidalos, 180, 187, 342
Dako-Mysian language, 367
Dalmatia, 388
Dana (Palestine), 372
Danaans, 370, 371, 372, 373, 374, 382
Danae (daughter of Akrisios), 371, 372
Danae (near Larisa), 372
Danae (Pontos), 372
Danaids, 372
Danaos (Boiotia) 371, 372
Danaos (son of Belos, founder of Argos), 371, 372, 382
Danapris [Dnjepr], 371
Danastris [Dnjestr], 371
Danati (Pontos), 372
Danu (Indian goddess), 371
Danube, River, 29, 371
Danubian region, 79
Danuna (Cilician tribe), 372
darts, 266
Daulis, 384
Dawkins, R.M., 116
decipherment of Creto-Mycenaean script, 243, 250, 302, 303, 304, 306, 338, 374, 379, 380, — of Cypriot alphabet of Classical period, 357
decoration : on royal daggers (Mycenae), 266, on diadems (Cyprus), 354, inlaid decoration on larnakes, 325, 326, on metal vessels, 353, on precious utensils, 265, on royal swords (Mycenae), 266, on vases, see vase-painting and pottery
decoration, interior, of palaces : Knosos, 183, 184, Mycenae, 322, 323, Orchomenos, 322, Pylos, 322, 323, Thebes, 322, Tiryns, 322, 323, 324
decoration, sculptured, at Treasuries of Atreus and Minyas, 330
deer, 46, 47, 54, fallow —, 25. See also cervus elaphus; reindeer
Delos, 140, 269, 333
Delphi, 381
Demargne, P., 203
Demeter, 234, 307, 381, temple of — at Eleusis, 308
demijohn, 201
Demophon (founder of Aipeia), 360
Dendra, 264, 334
Denyen (people of Cilicia), 296
deposit, hieroglyphic, 159
Desborough, V.R., 293
Deukalion (son of Prometheus), 342
Deuriopes [Douriopes], (Illyrian people), 371
Dexithea, 218
diadems, 123, 257, 335, 363
diadems, funerary, 266, 354
Diagoras son of Teukros, 360
Didymoteichon, 27
Dikaios, Porphyrios, 85, 86
Dikilim Tash, 100
Diktaian cave, 231, 232
Diktaian sanctuary, 197
Dikte, Mount, 229
Diktynna (pre-Greek deity), 230, 268
Diktys, 302, 303
Dimeni, 64, 72, 75, 77, 79, 80, 81, 100, 105
dinotheres, 22
Diomedes, 272, 283
Dionysos Kadmos or Orthios, 366

Disk of Phaistos, 155, 157, 160, 162, 187
Djekker (tribe), 296
Dodecanese, 19, 20, 270, 283, 297, 299, 361, 379
Dodona [Dodone, Bodone], 134, 386
Dolopes [Dolopians], 375, 386
Dolopia (north of Tymphrestos), 386
Domokos, 64
domos, 80, 310
Don, River, 50, 371
Dorians, 97, 293, 342, 363, 370, 375, 379, 384, 385, 386, 387, 388, 389
Descent of —, 272, 358, 386, 388
Doric dialect, 388
Doris, 388
Dorion (Peloponnesos), 136
Dörpfeld, W., 246, 290
Dotian plain, 368, 384
drainage systems in Cretan palaces, 146
Drama (place), 25
draught-board from Knosos, 186, 208, 214
dromos, 315, 345, 350
drums (musical instrumets), 335
Dryopians (Indo-European tribe), 368, 371, 374, 388
Dymanes (Doric tribe), 388

"Earplugs", 61
earrings, 345, 362, 363
East, the, 27, 29, 54, 56, 57, 58, 59, 61, 62, 63, 67, 72, 96, 97, 99, 100, 150, 152, 169, 170, 171, 175, 176, 190, 202, 203, 205, 209, 230, 231, 249, 268, 270, 274, 283, 287, 297, 299, 301, 331, 335, 341, 347, 349, 351, 355, 358, 365, Middle —, 26, 34, 56, 57, 59, 62, 63, 367, Near —, 26, 37, 40 49, 52, 55, 58, 59, 60, 202, 203, 269, 280, 283, 295, 299, 331, 347, 349, 350, 367, 371
economy : agricultural, 96, 102, 168, 246, agricultural and stockbreeding, 53, 57, 105, food-gathering, 53, 57, 59, food-producing, 57, 59, hunting, 57, maritime barter, 102, mixed, 58, 109, 110
Effenterre, H. van, 153
Eglianos [Englianos], 244, 294
Egnatia, Via, 29
Egypt, 37, 97, 107, 117, 120, 130, 131, 139, 150, 152, 162, 167, 175, 176, 185, 190, 202, 203, 204, 205, 209, 210, 218, 223, 226, 230, 235, 239, 243, 254, 269, 278, 279, 280, 281, 287, 294, 295, 296, 297, 299, 302, 331, 335, 340, 341, 344, 346, 349, 351, 354, 355, 371
Eiones (Argolis), 272
Ektenes (pre-Greek tribe), 365, 366, 368
Elais (daughter of Anios), 218
El Arish, 279
Elateia (Phokis), 68, 74, 81
Elatos (Lapith hero), 384
Eleans, 379, 386, 387, 388, 389
elephant, 25, 47 —, ancient (Palaeoloxodon antiquus), 25 —, southern (Archidiscodon meridionalis), 25
Eleusis, 135, 244, 246, 281, 308
Elis, 19, 47, 270, 299, 366, 379, 384, 388
Elone (Thessalian Phthiotis), 272, 382
embalming, 258
Emporio (Chios), 76, 299, 302
enamelwork, 353
England, 23, 335
Enkomi, 269, 278, 296, 299, 331, 349, 350, 352, 353, 354, 355, 357, 359
Enispe (Arkadia), 272
Ennomos (Mysian leader), 290
Epanome (on Thermaic Gulf), 100
Epeians, 272, 375, 384
Epeios (hero), 384
Epeiros, 19, 20, 25, 29, 45, 46, 47, 49, 51, 66, 75, 99, 134, 268, 269, 270, 366, 367, 370, 373, 374, 375, 382, 383, 384, 386, 387, 388, 389
Ephesos, 278, 299
Ephyra (modern Korakou), 255, 263. See also Korakou
epics, Homeric, 36, 250, 253, 259, 270, 272, 292, 293, 336, 337, 342, 379, Theban epic, 283, 337, Ionian epics, 337
Epidauros, 264, 272, 376, 377
Epigonoi, 283, 388
epiphany of Minoan goddess, 230, 231, 233
Episkope (Cyprus), 86, 278, 283, 299
Epistrophos (leader of Halizones), 290
eqeta (followers), 276
equus caballus, 25

Eretria, 72
Eridanos, River, 371, 372
Erimi (Cyprus), 88, 355
eruption of Thera volcano, 220, 221, 222, 225, 226, 249, 338, 348, 349
Erymanthos, 47, 368, —Mt., 384, — valley, 47
Eteo-Cretans, 342, 370
Etesian winds (meltemia), 33, 294
Etruscans, 127
Euanthes (founder of Thasos), 218
Euboia, 18, 19, 20, 22, 23, 29, 100, 101, 110, 135, 218, 269, 270, 299, 366, 370, 373, 375, 376
Euboian Channel, 20
Euboian Gulf, 22
Euphemos (leader of Kikones), 290, 292
Euphrates, 58, Upper —, 269, 295
Europa, 204, 231
Europe, 26, 29, 32, 34, 40, 48, 49, 51, 52, 54, 59, 60, 61, 77, 97, 106, 113, 117, 171, 239, 300, 362, 365, 367, 368, 372
Eurotas, River, 29, — plain, 384, — valley, 19
Euryalos (son of Mekisteus), 283
Eurystheus, 282
Eutresis (Boiotia), 101, 170, 255, 294, 372
Euxine Sea, 290. See also Black Sea
Evangelides, 134
Evans, Sir Arthur, 37, 82, 116, 117, 118, 125, 143, 144, 146, 149, 151, 155, 158, 159, 162, 174, 178, 180, 182, 183, 184, 187, 193, 195, 197, 198, 209, 211, 218, 222, 230, 239, 242, 246, 250, 253, 257, 265, 302, 303, 306, 339, 342, 357
Evans, John D., 59, 82
Eynan (Palestine), 59

Faience working, 214
farmsteads : Achladia, 186, Epano Zakros, 186, Hagios Konstantinos, 186, Metropolis, 186, Plate (in Lasithi), 186, Prophetes Elias, 186, Seteia, 186, Vathypetro, 186, Vitsilia, 186, Zou, 186
fauna : of Megalopolis, 25, 43
fibulae, 361, 362, 363, arched, 363, bronze, 361, 363, iron, 361, 363, violin-bow, 363
figurines, 50, 66, 72, 74, 81, 86, 91, 92, 93, 105, 111, 112, 113, 119, 123, 127, 132, 139, 180, 182, 185, 187, 214, 215, 233, 237, 263, 306, 308, 328, 329, 363, animal, 92, 127, 330, bronze, 232, clay, 92, 233, 347, faience, 214, female, 92, 93, 113, fiddle-shapped, 113, ivory, 214, kourotrophos, 72, 81, 330, marble, 92, 109, 132, 233, of worshippers (votaries), 127, 132, 214. See also idols, statuettes
fishing, 30, 53, 54, 57, 62, 68, 88, 105, 109, 110, 131
flake tools, 41, 44, 46, 49
flint, 41, 50, 65, 85
flute, 235, 335
formulas, poetic, 336, 337
fortification of acropolises : Mesolithic, 73, Neolithic, 80, Mycenaean, 316
fortification, 347, circuit walls, 79, 80, towers, 70, trenches, 70, walls, 62, 70
Fouqué, F., 220, 221
France, 365, 366
free-standing figures, ivory (Mycenaean), 331, 333
frescoes : at Hagia Triada, 192, 345, of Middle Cycladic period, 140, Mycenaean, 261, 308, 316, 322, 323, 324, 325, 326, of New-Palace period, 209, 210, 211, 216, of Old-Palace period, 165, at Palace of Knosos, 180, 182, 183, 184, 186, 265, 338, 339, 341, in royal apartments, 183, at Palace of Phaistos, 187, at Phylakope, 218, at Pylos, 338, at Thera, 224
friezes, stone, 338
Funerary customs. See burial customs
furnace, potter's, at Knosos, 183, - smelting, at Phaistos, 187

Gabrovo, Mt., 19
Galana Charakia (Crete), 120
gates : Lion Gate, 244, 282, 299, 312, 319, 330, 333, in Mycenaean walls, 312, 313, 318, at palace of Knosos, 180, 182, 185, at palace of Malia, 189
Gazi (Crete), 363
Gelb, I., 159
Geleontes (Ionian tribe), 376

405

LIST OF ILLUSTRATIONS

LIST OF MAPS AND DIAGRAMS

ACKNOWLEDGEMENTS

British Museum Photographic Service : pp. 348, 349, 351a, 351b.
David Harris (Israel Museum) : p. 103a.
D. Charisiadis : pp. 222b, 247, 314b.
The Cyprus Museum : pp. 352, 353a, 353b, 354a, 355, 356a, 356b, 358, 359a, 359b, 359c, 360.
Foto VAT-NIC (Nicosia) : pp. 84, 85.
G.K. Ioakeimidis : p. 220.
Ioannidis - Batziotis : p. 113.
N. Kontos : pp. 63, 64a, 70, 71a, 71b, 72, 73, 80a, 80b, 81, 90, 93, 98, 99, 100, 101a, 101b, 106, 107a, 107b, 108a, 108b, 109 110a, 110b, 111, 112, 114, 115, 136, 138, 139, 140, 141a, 141b, 141c, 142, 144, 147a, 178, 192, 194, 196a, 196b, 244, 251a, 251b, 251c, 254, 256, 257, 258a, 259, 262, 263a, 264, 265, 267, 274, 275, 277b, 278, 279a, 279b, 280, 287, 293, 296a, 296b, 297b, 309, 316, 323, 325b, 328, 330, 331b, 332b, 334, 336a, 336b. Aerial photographs: 142, 144, 147a, 178, 192, 193, 196a, 196b, 244, 316.
N. Mavrogenis : p. 222a.
A. Petrocheilou : pp. 44, 45.
Photographie Giraudon (Paris) : p. 295.
M. Skiadaresis : pp. 43b, 51, 52c, 53a, 53b, 55a, 61, 64b, 65, 67a, 67b, 74, 83, 88, 89, 103b, 104, 116, 117, 118, 119, 120, 121, 122, 123, 124, 125a, 125b, 126, 127a, 127b, 129a, 192b, 143, 145, 147b, 148-49, 150a, 150b, 151, 152, 153, 159b, 161a, 161b, 162, 163, 164a-d, 166, 181a, 181b, 182, 186, 188a, 188b, 189, 190, 191, 193a, 193b, 198a, 198b, 199, 202a, 202b, 203, 204a, 204b, 205a, 206-7, 208, 209, 210, 211a, 211b, 212-213, 214, 215a, 215b, 216, 217, 218, 230, 231, 232, 233, 234, 235a, 235b, 236-237, 238-239, 252a, 252b, 258b, 260a, 260b, 261, 263b, 282a, 282b, 285, 294, 303, 304, 307, 308a, 308b, 339, 340a, 340b, 341, 342a, 343b, 344.
M. Stournaras : Aerial photographs: pp. 24, 31, 32, 33.
D. Tloupas : pp. 43a, 46a, 46b, 47a, 47b, 52a, 52b, 60.
N. Tombazis : p. 255b.
Sp. Tsavdaroglou: pp. 54, 76, 77, 154, 155a, 155b, 158, 159a, 195a, 205b, 223, 224b, 225, 227a, 227b, 228a, 228b, 255a, 276, 277a, 281, 283, 292a, 292b, 297a, 311a, 311b, 312, 313, 314a, 314c, 317, 318, 319, 324, 325a, 326, 327, 329a, 329b, 331a, 332a, 335, 337.
U.S.I.S. : p. 26.
Special permission for reproduction of reconstructions by P. de Jong : 276, 277, 292, 310, 313, and 317, from "The Palace of Nestor at Pylos in Western Messenia", The University of Cincinnati, vol. I by Carl W. Blegen and Marion Rawson, vol. II by Mabel Lang (Copyright 1966 and 1969 Princeton University Press).

JOHN N. THEODORAKOPOULOS

Member of the Academy of Athens, Professor Emeritus. Born at Sparta in 1900. He studied at the Universities of Vienna and Heidelberg, and was Professor of Philosophy at the Universities of Thessalonike (1936 - 1939), Athens (1939 - 1968), and at the Panteios School of Political Sciences (1950 - 1964). Prof. Theodorakopoulos has been a member of the Academy of Athens since 1960, and was its President in 1963 - 1964. In 1945 and again in 1966 - 1967, he served as Minister of Education. He was awarded an honorary doctorate by Ohio University and was Visiting Professor at the Universities of Chicago (1954) and Heidelberg (1969); he has also taken part in many Philosophical Congresses in Europe and the United States. Prof. Theodorakopoulos is Vice-President of the Federation Internationale des Sociétés de Philosophie and a member of the committee of the International Institute of Philosophy and the Société Internationale pour l'Étude de Philosophie Mediévale. From 1929 to 1940, along with Panayotis Kanellopoulos and Constantine Tsatsos, he published the Greek jurnal "Archives of Philosophy and Scientific Theory", of which he was also the editor. His basic works are the following:

> Platons Dialektik des Seins. Tübingen, 1927
> Plotins Metaphysik des Seins. Bühl/Baden, 1928
> The Theory of Logos, or Epistemology. Athens, 1928. (Greek)
> The Principles of the Philosophy of History. Athens, 1928. (Greek)
> The Fundamental Ideas of Plotinus' Philosophy. Athens, 1928. (Greek)
> The Epistemology of Rickert: Introduction to Neo-Kantianism. Athens, 1929. (Greek)
> The Philosophy of Art. Athens, 1929. (Greek)
> The Spirit of Modern Hellenism and the Change of the Times. Athens, 1945. (Greek)
> System of Philosophic Ethics. Athens, 1947. (Greek)
> Philosophical and Christian Studies. Athens, 1949. (Greek)
> Philosophie und Religion. Munich, 1961.
> Goethe's Faust. (2nd ed.) Athens, 1963. (Greek)
> Philosophy and Life. (Essays) Athens, 1967. (Greek)
> Introduction to Plato. (5th ed.) Athens, 1970. (Greek)
> Plato's Phaedrus. (3rd ed.) Athens, 1971. (Greek)
> Die Hauptprobleme der Platonischen Philosophie. The Hague, 1972

Other Publications:

> The Spirit and its Life. 'Αρχεῖον Φιλοσοφίας καὶ Θεωρίας τῶν 'Επιστημῶν, 1932. (Greek)
> The Theory of Plato's Ideas. Πρακτικὰ τῆς 'Ακαδημίας 'Αθηνῶν, 1960. (Greek)
> The Philosophical View of our Times. Πρακτικὰ τῆς 'Ακαδημίας 'Αθηνῶν, 1961. (Greek)
> Philosophy and Science. L'Héritage vivant de l'antiquité grecque, The Hague, 1967
> The Philosophy of Religion. Πρακτικὰ τῆς 'Ακαδημίας 'Αθηνῶν, 1969. (Greek)
> Greece as a Universal Idea. Πρακτικὰ τῆς 'Ακαδημίας 'Αθηνῶν, 1970. (Greek)
> The Philosophy of Zeno. Πρακτικὰ Κυπρολογικοῦ Συνεδρίου, Nicosia, 1971. (Greek)
> Aristotle's Definition of Tragedy. Πρακτικὰ τῆς 'Ακαδημίας 'Αθηνῶν, 1972. (Greek)

CONSTANTINE D. TSATSOS

Member of the Academy of Athens, Professor Emeritus. Born in 1899. He studied at the Universities of Athens and Heidelberg, and was Professor of Law at the University of Athens from 1933 until 1946. In 1945 he began a successful political career. He was elected to Parliament and served as Minister of the Interior, Press, Education, and Social Welfare, Minister to the Prime Minister, and Deputy-Minister of Coordination. Since 1961, he has been a full member of the Academy. Prof. Tsatsos has published numerous studies on philosophical, social, and literary subjects, although he is mainly interested in Social Philosophy and Jurisprudence. His basic works are the following:

> Der Begriff des Positiven Rechts. Heidelberg, 1928
> The Problem of the Interpretation of Law. Athens, 1932. (Greek)
> The Problem of the Sources of Law. Athens, 1941. (Greek)
> Studies in Philosophy and Law. Athens, 1960. (Greek)
> Essays on Aesthetics and Education. Athens, 1960. (Greek)
> Essays on Aesthetics. Athens, 1961. (Greek)
> Politics. Athens, 1965. (Greek)
> Palamas. (3rd ed.) Athens, 1966. (Greek)
> The Progress of Hellenism. (2nd ed.) Athens, 1967. (Greek)
> Cicero. Athens, 1969. (Greek)
> Aphorisms and Meditations. 4 vols, Athens, 1965 - 1972. (Greek)

The Social Philosophy of the Ancient Greeks. (2nd ed.) Athens, 1970. *(Greek)*
Other Publications:
    The Contradictions of Practical Reason. Πρακτικὰ τῆς ᾿Ακαδημίας ᾿Αθηνῶν, 1962. *(Greek)*
    The Meaning of the Nation. Πρακτικὰ τῆς ᾿Ακαδημίας ᾿Αθηνῶν, 1963. *(Greek)*
    Plato's Politics. Πρακτικὰ τῆς ᾿Ακαδημίας ᾿Αθηνῶν, 1966. *(Greek)*
    The Mission of Greece in the Modern World. Πρακτικὰ τῆς ᾿Ακαδημίας ᾿Αθηνῶν, 1966.
    (Greek)
    Chateaubriand's Struggle for Greece. Πρακτικὰ τῆς ᾿Ακαδημίας ᾿Αθηνῶν, 1968. *(Greek)*

GEORGE E. MYLONAS

Member of the Academy of Athens, Professor Emeritus. Born in 1898. He studied at the University of Athens and Johns Hopkins University (Lld, University of Ohio; L.H.D., Wesleyan University; L.H.D., Southern Illinois University; Litt.D., Washington University, St. Louis). He is Professor of Archaeology at the University of Chicago, Washington University (St. Louis, Mo.) and the University of Athens. Prof. Mylonas has conducted excavations at Olynthos, Polygyros, Hagios Kosmas, Eleusis, and Mycenae. A specialist in the Early Helladic, Middle Helladic, and Mycenaean Periods, he is also interested in the religion and customs of these periods. He has written many articles in Greek and foreign journals and encyclopedias of Prehistoric and Classical Greece. He has given many lectures in various institutions of learning in the United States, Japan, New Zealand, and Australia. Prof. Mylonas has also taken part in many Archaeological Congresses both in the United States and Europe. The following are his basic works:
    The Neolithic Period in Greece. Athens, 1928. *(Greek)*
    The Neolithic Settlement of Olynthus. Baltimore, 1929
    Prehistoric Eleusis. ᾿Ελευσινιακὰ I, Athens, 1932. *(Greek)*
    The Balkan States: An Introduction to their History. St. Louis, 1946
    Ancient Mycenae: The Capital City of Agamemnon. Princeton, 1957
    The Proto-Attic Amphora of Eleusis. Athens, 1957. *(Greek)*
    Aghios Kosmas: An Early Bronze Age Settlement and Cemetery in Attica. Princeton, 1959
    Eleusis and the Eleusinian Mysteries. Princeton, 1961
    Mycenae and the Mycenaean Age. Princeton, 1966
    Mycenae: A Guide to its Ruins and its History. Athens, 1967. *(Both Greek and English)*
    Mycenae's Last Century of Greatness. Sydney, 1968
    The Grave Circle B of Mycenae. 2 vols, Athens, 1972, 1973. *(Greek)*
Other publications:
    The Prehistoric Inhabitants of Greece and the Greek Races of Historical Times. ᾿Αρχαιο-
        λογικὴ ᾿Εφημερίς, 1930. *(Greek)*
    The Early Helladic and Middle Helladic Periods. ᾿Αρχαιολογικὴ ᾿Εφημερίς, 1937. *(Greek)*
    Athens and Minoan Crete. Harvard Studies in Classical Philology, Supplement 1940
    Religion and Prehistoric Greece: Forgotten Religions, *New York,* 1949
    Homeric and Mycenaean Burial Customs. ᾿Επιστημονικὴ ᾿Επετηρὶς Φιλοσοφικῆς Σχολῆς
    Πανεπιστημίου ᾿Αθηνῶν, 1953 - 54. *(Greek)*
    The Acropolis of Mycenae. Part I: General. ᾿Αρχαιολογικὴ ᾿Εφημερίς, 1958. *(Greek)*
    The Acropolis of Mycenae. Part II: Enclosures, Gates, and Approaches. ᾿Αρχαιολογικὴ
    ᾿Εφημερίς, 1962. *(Greek)*
    Mycenaean Burial Customs: Postscript. ᾿Επιστημονικὴ ᾿Επετηρὶς Φιλοσοφικῆς Σχολῆς
    Πανεπιστημίου Θεσσαλονίκης, 1965. *(Greek)*
    The Wanax of the Tablets. ᾿Αρχαιολογικὴ ᾿Εφημερίς, 1966. *(Greek)*

APOSTOLOS E. VACALOPOULOS

University of Thessalonike. Born in 1909. He studied at the University of Thessalonike, where he has held the chair of Modern Greek History since 1951. He has taken part in many Historical Congresses in Europe and published many studies both in Greece and abroad. In 1970, he was awarded the Historical and Social Sciences Prize by the Academy of Athens. His basic works are the following:
    Refugees and the Refugee Question during the Revolution of 1821. Thessalonike, 1939.
        (Greek)
    Prisoners of War Held by the Greeks during the Greek Revolution of 1821. Thessalonike,
        1941. (Greek)
    Thasos, son histoire, son administration de 1453 à 1912. Paris, 1953
    Refugee Settlements in the Region of Thessalonike (with M. Maravelakis). Thessalonike,

1955. *(Greek)*
History of Modern Hellenism. 4 vols. Thessalonike, 1962 - 1973
A History of Thessalonike. Thessalonike, 1963
History of Macedonia, 1354 - 1833. Thessalonike, 1973
Sources for the History of Modern Hellenism. Vol. 1: 1204 - 1669. Thessalonike, 1965.
    (Greek)
The Greek Armies of 1821 (2nd ed.). Thessalonike, 1970. (Greek)
History of the Greek Revolution of 1821. Athens, 1971
The Fortresses of Platamon and Oria and the Teke of Hasan Baba. Thessalonike, 1972.
    (Greek)

Studies:
Modern Greek Tradition concerning the Privileges of the Inhabitants of the Dervenochoria
    (Corinthia) during the Turkish Occupation. Thessalonike, 1941. (Greek)
Unpublished Court Proceedings of the Turkish Occupation Period. Ἀρχεῖον Ἰδιωτικοῦ
    Δικαίου, *1946. (Greek)*
Thessalonike in 1430, 1821, and 1912 - 1918. Thessalonike, 1947. (Greek)
History of Thessalonike (315 B.C. - 1912). Thessalonike, 1947. (Greek)
Rumours Spread During the Greek Revolution of 1821. Ἐπιστημονικὴ Ἐπετηρὶς Φιλοσο-
    φικῆς Σχολῆς Πανεπιστημίου Θεσσαλονίκης, *1950. (Greek)*
The Dramatic Events of May 1876 in Thessalonike and their Influence on the Eastern
    Question. Μακεδονικά, *1947, 1952. (Greek)*
Aspects of the History and Organization of the Philike Hetaireia. Ἑλληνικά, *1951. (Greek)*
New Historical Information on the Revolutions of 1821 and 1854 in Macedonia. Ἐπι-
    στημονικὴ Ἐπετηρὶς Φιλοσοφικῆς Σχολῆς Πανεπιστημίου Θεσσαλονίκης, *1956.*
    (Greek)
New Information on the Greek Armatoles and the Revolution of Thymios Blachavas in
    Thessaly in 1808. Ἐπιστημονικὴ Ἐπετηρὶς Φιλοσοφικῆς Σχολῆς Πανεπιστημίου
    Θεσσαλονίκης, *1965. (Greek)*
Zur Datierung Zweier Griechischer Volkslieder. Zeitschrift für Balkanologie, 1965.

COSTIS J. BASTIAS

Writer and journalist (1901 - 1972). He studied Law at the University of Athens and Theatre at the school of Charles Dullin in Paris. From an early age, he was a journalist of distinction, contributing to many newspapers. He was correspondent of "Free Press" in Bulgaria, Rumania, and Yugoslavia, and later (1946 - 54) of "Vradyne" in New York and Washington. He was also publisher of the literary journal "Greek Letters" (1927 onwards) and of the daily "Echo of Greece" (from 1935). From 1930, when the National Theatre was founded, Bastias was the Secretary-General. In 1937, he was appointed Director-General of Letters and Fine Arts in the Ministry of Education, and Director-General of the National Theatre. Classical tragedies were presented for the first time at the ancient Theatre of Epidauros, while the presentation of tragedies at the Theatre of Herodes Atticus became regular. During this period also, and under the aegis of Bastias, successful performances were given by the National Theatre in London, Cambridge, Oxford, Frankfurt, and Berlin. At the same time, the touring theatre Chariot of Thespis was founded, giving performances throughout Greece. The crowning of his activities was the founding in 1939 of the National Opera. From 1945 to 1947, Bastias was cultural relations adviser at the Greek Embassy in Washington. In 1959, he was appointed Director-General and President of the Board of Governors of the National Opera, and in 1961 Director-General of the National Broadcasting Institute. The following are some of his main works (all in Greek):
Lands and Seas (prose pieces). Athens, 1932
Fishing. Athens, 1935
Menas Rebelos (novel). Academy of Athens Prize. (2nd ed.) Athens, 1968
Harbours (Short stories) Athens, 1939
Men and Beasts. Athens, 1939
Spider 44 (Chronicle of the Occupation). (2nd ed.) Athens, 1973
Papoulakos (Transl. into English). (5th ed.) Athens, 1973
Konstantinos Oikonomos ex Oikonomon. Athens, 1958
Neon Kyriakodromion. Athens, 1956
Christ Resurrected and Unresurrected Men. Athens, 1960
Papadiamantis (Essay). Athens, 1962
Aristophanes (Comedy). Athens, 1970
Captain Anghélis (novella). Translated into French. Athens, 1970

CONTRIBUTORS

STYLIANOS E. ALEXIOU

Director of the Herakleion Museum: Born in 1921. He studied at the University of Athens, the Archäologisches Institut Heidelberg, and the École Normale Supérieure in Paris. Dr. Alexiou is an authority on Minoan Civilization. Among his main works are the following:
> *The Minoan Goddess with Up-Raised Arms. Herakleion, 1958. (Greek)*
> *Minoan Civilization. Herakleion, 1969, 1973. (English)*
> *Late Minoan Graves at the Port of Knossos. Athens, 1967. (Greek)*
> *A Guide to the Palaces of Crete. Herakleion, 1973. (English)*

Dr. Alexiou also wrote a special chapter in Leonard von Matt, Ancient Crete, London, 1968
Other publications:
> *The Character of Erotokritos. Κρητικὰ Χρονικά, 1952. (Greek)*
> *Aspects of Prehistoric Life: Cretan and Mycenaean Trade. Ἀρχαιολογικὴ Ἐφημερίς, 1953 - 1954*
> *Minoan Art. Ἀρχιτεκτονική, 1966. (Greek)*

CHRISTOS G. DOUMAS

Director of Antiquities, Dodecanese. Born in 1933. He studied at the Universities of Athens and London. Dr. Doumas has conducted excavations on Naxos, Paros, Syros, Keos, Santorine and other Cycladic islands. He is a specialist in Cycladic Civilization. The following are some of his works:
> *The N. P. Goulandris Collection of Early Cycladic Art. Athens, 1968*
> *Korphe t'Aroniou. Ἀρχαιολογικὸν Δελτίον, 1965. (Greek)*
> *A Mycenaean Rhyton from Naxos. Archäolog. Anzeiger, 1968*
> *Zwei Jahre Archäologischer Forschung auf Santorini. Mannus, 1969*
> *Akrotiri: The Third Campaign of Excavations on Thera. Kadmos, 1970*
> *Notes on Early Cycladic Architecture. Archäolog. Anzeiger, 1972*

GEORGE C. HOURMOUZIADES

Archaeologist. Born in 1932. He studied at the University of Thessalonike. Hourmouziades has taken part in excavations in Thessaly. He is a specialist in Prehistoric Art and Religion, and has published the following studies:
> *A Clay Image of a Neolithic Dwelling from Krannon. Ἀρχαιολογικὰ Ἀνάλεκτα ἐξ Ἀθηνῶν, 1969. (Greek)*
> *Reports of excavations. Ἀρχαιολογικὸν Δελτίον καὶ Ἀρχαιολογικὰ Ἀνάλεκτα ἐξ Ἀθηνῶν.*

SPYRIDON E. IAKOVIDES

University of Athens. Born in 1923. He studied at the University of Athens. Prof. Iakovides has taken part in the excavations at Pylos, Eleusis, and Mycenae, and directed the excavations at Perate. He is a specialist in the Mycenaean Period. The following are his main works:
> *The Mycenaean Acropolis of Athens. Athens, 1962. (Greek)*
> *Perate. 3 vols, Athens, 1969, 1970. (Greek)*

Other publications:
> *Observations concerning the Threshold of the Lion Gate. Ἀρχαιολογικὴ Ἐφημερίς, 1961. (Greek)*
> *A Mycenaean Mourning Custom. American Journal of Archaeology, 1966*
> *Mycenaean Burial Customs. Ἀρχαιολογικὰ Ἀνάλεκτα ἐξ Ἀθηνῶν, 1969. (Greek)*
> *The Black Dye used on Ancient Vases. Ἀρχαιολογικὰ Ἀνάλεκτα ἐξ Ἀθηνῶν, 1969. (Greek)*
> *The Cyclopean Walls. Ἀρχαιολογικὰ Ἀνάλεκτα ἐξ Ἀθηνῶν, 1969. (Greek)*

VASSOS KARAGEORGHIS

Director of Antiquities, Cyprus. Born in 1929. He studied at University College and the Institute of Archaeology, London University. Dr. Karageorghis has conducted numerous excavations in Cyprus, the main ones being those at the Mycenaean cities of Kition and Salamis. He has given many lectures in the United States, Canada, and Europe, and has taken part in several Archaeological Congresses. The following are some of his basic works:
> *Treasures in the Cyprus Museum. Nicosia, 1962*
> *Corpus Vasorum Antiquorum. 2 vols, Nicosia, 1963, 1965*

Sculptures from Salamis. 2 vols, Nicosia, 1964, 1966
Nouveaux documents pour l'étude du Bronze récent à Chypre. Paris, 1965
Excavations in the Necropolis of Salamis. Nicosia, 1967
Mycenaean Art from Cyprus. Nicosia, 1968
Chypre. Editions Nagel, Geneva, 1968
Salamis in Cyprus. (New Aspects of Antiquity). London, 1969
Cypriote Antiquities. Athens, 1973

SPYRIDON N. MARINATOS

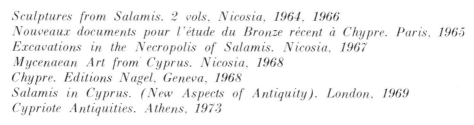

Member of the Academy of Athens, General Inspector of Antiquities, Professor Emeritus. Born in 1901. He studied at the Universities of Athens, Berlin, and Halle. Prof. Marinatos has conducted excavations in Crete and Kephallenia, and at Thermopylai, Pylos, Marathon, and Thera. His excavations at Thera in the last few years have brought to light marvellous finds representing the magnificent civilization of the island in prehistoric times. Prof. Marinatos has taught as a Visiting Professor at several foreign Universities, and has taken part in many Archaeological Congresses. The following are his chief works:

Ancient Cretan Civilization. Athens, 1927. (Greek)
Thermopylai: Historical and Archaeological Guide. Athens, 1951. (Greek)
Kephallenia. Athens, 1962. (Greek)
Crete and Mycenae. New York, 1960. (Also in German, Italian, and Greek)
Two Interplanetary Phenomena of 468 B.C. Πραγματεῖαι Ἀκαδημίας Ἀθηνῶν, v.24,4.1963. (Greek)
Some Words about the Legend of Atlantis. Athens, 1969
Thera. 5 vols, Athens, 1967 - 1972

In the series Archaeologica Homerica, Prof. Marinatos wrote the first two volumes, on Costume and Hair-style.

Founder of the journal Ἀρχαιολογικὰ Ἀνάλεκτα ἐξ Ἀθηνῶν (Athens Annals of Archaeology) produced in Greek and other languages.

He has published over 200 excavation reports, studies, and reviews in Greek and foreign archaeological journals. These include:

Homer, Mycenae, and the Orient. Ἀρχαιολογικὴ Ἐφημερίς, 1927 - 1928. (Greek)
La marine créto-mycénienne. Bulletin de Correspondance Hellénique, 1933
Crete and the Hittite and Asia Minor World during the Second Millennium B.C. Μικρασιατικὰ Χρονικά, 1939. (Greek)
The Volcanic Destruction of Minoan Crete. Antiquity, 1939
The Cult of the Cretan Caves. Review of Religion, 1941
Les legendes royales de la Crète minoenne. Revue Archéologique, 1949
The New Royal Tombs of Mycenae. Γέρας Κεραμοπούλλου, Athens, 1953. (Greek)
Royal Perfumeries at Mycenae. Πρακτικὰ Ἀκαδημίας Ἀθηνῶν, 1958. (Greek)
Delphi and the Spirit of the Pythia, Vice-Chancellor's Address, 1958. (Greek)
Helice: A Submerged Town. Archaeology, 1960
Alasia: A Greek Settlement in Cyprus. Πρακτικὰ Ἀκαδημίας Ἀθηνῶν, 1961. (Greek)
Minoan and Mycenaean Civilization on the Mediterranean and Europe. Proceedings of the Sixth Congress of Prehistoric Studies, 1962
Polidipsion Argos. Proceedings of the Cambridge Colloquium on Mycenaean Studies, Cambridge, 1966
X-Ray Presentations. Πρακτικὰ Ἀκαδημίας Ἀθηνῶν, 1966. (Greek)
The Volcano of Thera and the Civilizations of the Aegean. Πεπραγμένα τοῦ Β′ Διεθνοῦς Κρητολογικοῦ Συνεδρίου, vol. I, Athens, 1968. (Greek)
Aiora. Antichthon II, Sydney, 1968
La diaspora creto-mycénienne. Actes du Ier Congrès International del Études Balcaniques, II, Sofia, 1970
Mycenaean Elements within the Royal Houses of Macedonia. First International Symposium on Ancient Macedonia, 1970
On the «Pigs» (Choiroi) of Edessa. Athens Annals of Archaeology, 1970. (Greek)

JOHN K. MELENTIS

University of Thessalonike. Born in 1922. He studied at the Universities of Athens and Munich. Prof. Melentis is a Paleontologist, and his excavations in Greece, especially in Samos, have brought to light very interesting finds. The following are some of his works:

The Vertebrates of the Pleistocene in the Megalopolis Basin. Annales Géologiques des

Pays Helléniques, *1961, 1963, 1965, 1966. (Greek)*

The Geological Formation of the Island of Ankistri. Πρακτικὰ ᾿Ακαδημίας ᾿Αθηνῶν, *1963. (Greek)*

The Hydrogeological Conditions of the Plain of Marathon. Ann. Géol. P. Hell., *1963. (Greek)*

The Pikermian Fauna of Halmyropotamos. Ann. Géol. P. Hell., *1968, 1970. (Greek)*

The Mammals of the Pleistocene in the Haliakmon Valley. Ann. Géol. P. Hell., *1968, 1970. (Greek)*

Prof. Melentis has also written a series of articles on geology for the layman, and three hand-books for students: Mineralogy, The Palaeontology of Vertebrates, and Micropalaeontology.

NICHOLAS E. PLATON

University of Thessalonike. Born in 1909. He studied at the University of Athens, the Faculté des Lettres de l'Université de Paris, the École Pratique des Hautes Études, the Institut d'Art et d'Archéologie, and the École du Louvre. Prof. Platon is a specialist in Minoan Civilization, and has conducted excavations in Boiotia, Phtiotis, Euboia, the Sporades, and Crete. The discovery and excavation of the Minoan Palace at Kato Zakros from 1961 until today has been his most important work. The following are some of his basic works:

Guide to the Herakleion Museum. Athens, 1954. (Greek)

Corpus der Minoischen-Mykenischen Siegel Band II.I Herakleion Museum. Berlin, 1969

Crète. Editions Nagel, Geneva, 1965

Cretese-Miceneo. Enciclopedia dell'Arte

Zakros: The Discovery of a Lost Palace of Ancient Crete. New York, 1971

Prof. Platon also wrote a special chapter in Leonard von Matt, Ancient Crete, London, 1968 Other publications:

Contribution on the study of Minoan Wall-Paintings. I: The Saffron-Collecting Ape. Κρητικὰ Χρονικά, *1947.* II: The Wall-Painting of the Libation Offering. Κρητικὰ Χρονικά, *1959. (Greek)*

The Chronology of the Minoan Palace at Phaistos. Κρητικὰ Χρονικά, *1949. (Greek)*

The Tomb at Staphylos and the Minoan Colony at Peparethos. Κρητικὰ Χρονικά, *1949 (Greek)*

The Sanctuary of Maza and the Minoan Peak Sanctuaries. Κρητικὰ Χρονικά, *1951 (Greek)*

Minoan Thrones. Κρητικὰ Χρονικά, *1951. (Greek)*

Problèmes de consolidation et de restauration des ruines minoennes. Atti del VIIo Congresso di Archeologia Classica, *I,* Rome, *1961*

Chronologie de la Crète et des Cyclades à l'âge du Bronze. Bericht V. Internationaler Kongress Vor- und Frühgeschichte, *Berlin, 1961*

Minoan Lyre. Χαριστήριον εἰς Α. Κ. ᾿Ορλάνδον. *I vol., Athens, 1968. (Greek)*

Bathroom and Lustral Basins in Minoan Dwellings. Europa, *Berlin, 1967*

The Final Destruction of the Minoan Palaces. Πεπραγμένα τοῦ Β' Διεθνοῦς Κρητολογικοῦ Συνεδρίου. *I vol. Athens, 1968. (Greek)*

Mycenaean Archaeology: Basic Results and Future Plans. Atti del Io Congresso Internazionale di Micenologia, *Rome, 1968. (Greek)*

Problems of Chronology at the Minoan Palaces. Part I. ᾿Αρχαιολογικὴ ᾿Εφημερίς, *196 (Greek)*

JOHN A. SAKELLARAKIS

Curator of Prehistoric Collections, National Archaeological Museum, Athens. Born in 1936. He studied at the Universities of Athens, Heidelberg, and London. Since 1964, when he found the palace group of Archanes and the neighbouring Minoan cemetery, Dr. Sakellarakis has been excavating on this site. He gave lectures at foreign Universities and took part in many international congresses both in Greece and abroad. A specialist in Minoan religion and art, he wrote many articles in Greek and foreign journals. The following are his basic works:

Corpus der Minoischen und Mykenischen Siegel. Band IV. Die Metaxas Sammlung (with V.E.G. Kenna). Berlin, 1969

Das Kuppergrar a von Archanes und das Kretisch-Mykenische Tieropferritual. Prähistorische Zeitschrift, 1970

Ivory Ship from Mycenae. ᾿Αρχαιολογικὴ ᾿Εφημερίς, *1971. (Greek)*

Other publications:

    Late Minoan Cenotaph at Archanes. Ἀρχαιολογικὸν Δελτίον *1963. (Greek)*

    Die Newen Hieroglyphensiegel vom Phourni. Kadmos *1966. (Greek)*

    Mason's Marks from Archanes. Europa, Festschrift E. Grumach, *Berlin, 1967*

    Ivory Finds from Archanes. Atti e Memorie del Io Congresso Internazionale di Miceno-

    Über die Echtheit des Sogenannten Nestorringes. Πεπραγμένα τοῦ Γ΄ Κρητολογικοῦ Συνε-
δρίου.

    *Apothetes of the Pottery from the Last Phase of Pre-Palace Period at Archanes. (with
E. Sakellaraki).* Ἀρχαιολογικὴ Ἐφημερίς, *1972. (Greek)*

    The Mould Cast of the Seal CMS I 220 from Vapheio. Ἀρχαιολογικὴ Ἐφημερίς, *1972.
(Greek)*

    The Subject of the Annimal-carrying Woman in Creto-Minoan Seal-engraving. Ἀρχαιο-
λογικὴ Ἐφημερίς, *1972. (Greek)*

MICHAEL B. SAKELLARIOU

Professor of Ancient History at Université de Lyon II. Born in 1912. He studied at the University of Athens and at the Faculté des Lettres de l'Université de Paris (Sorbonne). Scholar of the British Council (1945 - 1946), Research-fellow of the Centre National de la Recherche Scientifique (1951 - 1954). Ph. D. (Thessalonike), docteur ès Lettres (Sorbonne). Professor of Ancient History at the University of Thessalonike (1960 - 1968). Dean of the Faculty of Letters of the same University (1964 - 1965). Prof. Sakellariou has taken part in several International Congresses. His chief works are the following:

    *The Peloponnesos during the Second Turkish Occupation 1715 - 1821, Athens, 1939.
(Greek)*

    The Government and Administration of Samos during the Greek Revolution 1821 - 1834.
Ἀθηνᾶ, *1940. (Greek)*

    Motive und Zielsetzung der herodoteischen Geschichtswerkes. Πρακτικὰ τῆς Ἀκαδημίας
Ἀθηνῶν, *1940*

    Herodotos's prooemium. Ἀθηνᾶ, *1941. (Greek)*

    Ἰάϝων, *fleuve, dieu fluvial et eponyme des Ioniens, in Mélanges, Octave et Melpo Merlier,
II, 1956*

    Contribution to the study of the Tribal System at Ephesos. Ἑλληνικά, *1957. (Greek)*

    La migration grecque en Ionie, Athens, 1958

    A Problem of Homeric Geography. Πελοποννησιακά, *1959. (Greek)*

    Les Achéens. Atti del VIo Congresso Internazionale delle Scienze Preistoriche e
Protoistoriche, *II, 1965*

    Les tribus ioniennes-attiques. Europa, Festschrift E. Grumach, *1967*

    Ἐφύρη μυχῷ Ἄργεος ἱπποβότοιο. Atti del Io Congresso Internazionale di Micenologia,
II, 1968. (French)

    L'origine des Doriens. Actes du VIIe Congrès International des Sciences Prehistoriques
et Protohistoriques, *II, 1971*

    In addition, Prof. Sakellariou is completing the following works,

    Pélasges et autres peuples indo-européens en Grèce à l'âge du Bronze

    Dialectes et ethne grecs à l'âge du Bronze, 3 vols.

DEMETRIOS R. THEOCHARIS

Inspector of Antiquities, Thessaly. Born in 1919. He studied at the University of Athens. Dr. Theocharis has taken part in the excavations at Mycenae, Pylos, and Brauron, and directed excavations of prehistoric sites in Attica, Thessaly, Euboia, Northern Sporades, and eastern Macedonia. He is a specialist in the Greek Stone Age. The following are his chief publications:

    The Dawn of Thessalian Prehistory: Origins and Early Evolution of the Neolithic. Volos,
1957. (Greek)

    Excavations at Araphen. Πρακτικὰ τῆς ἐν Ἀθήναις Ἀρχαιολογικῆς Ἑταιρείας, *1951 -
1955. (Greek)*

    Excavations at Palaia Kokkinia. Πρακτικὰ τῆς ἐν Ἀθήναις Ἀρχαιολογικῆς Ἑταιρείας,
1951. (Greek)

    Excavations at Iolkos. Πρακτικὰ τῆς ἐν Ἀθήναις Ἀρχαιολογικῆς Ἑταιρείας, *1956 - 1957,
1960 - 1961. (Greek)*

    Nea Makri: Eine grosse Neolithische Siedlung in der Nähe von Marathon. Athenische
Mitteilungen, *1956*

Iolkos. Archaeology, *1958*
Neolithic Finds from the Iolkos Region. Θεσσαλικά, *1958. (Greek)*
From Preceramic Thessaly. Θεσσαλικά, *1958. (Greek)*
From the Prehistory of Euboia and Skyros. 'Αρχεῖον Εὐβοϊκῶν Μελετῶν, *1959. (Greek)*
Asketario: An Early Helladic Acropolis near Raphena. 'Αρχαιολογικὴ 'Εφημερίς, *1953 -*
    1954, vol. III. (Greek)
Excavations at Sesklo. Πρακτικὰ τῆς ἐν 'Αθήναις 'Αρχαιολογικῆς 'Εταιρείας, *1962 - 1963*
    1965 - 1966, 1968. (Greek)
Prehistory of Eastern Macedonia and Thrace. 1972
Articles and excavation reports in: 'Αρχαιολογικὴ 'Εφημερίς, 'Αρχαιολογικὸν Δελτίον, 'Αρχαιο-
λογικὰ 'Ανάλεκτα ἐξ 'Αθηνῶν.

MARIA D. THEOCHARIS

*Archaeologist. Born in 1933. She studied at the University of Athens. Mrs. Theocharis is a spe-
cialist in the Mycenaean and Protogeometric Period in Thessaly. The following are some of her
works:*
Magoulitsa. Θεσσαλικά, *1958. (Greek)*
Prehistoric Finds from Trikke. Θεσσαλικά, *1959. (Greek)*
Mycenaean Finds from Larisa. Θεσσαλικά, *1960. (Greek)*
A Knossian Vase from Attica. Antiquity, *1960.*
Protogeometric Finds from Thessaly. Θεσσαλικά, *1966. (Greek)*
From the Mycenaean Cemetery of Iolkos. 'Αρχαιολογικὰ 'Ανάλεκτα ἐξ 'Αθηνῶν, *1970*
    (Greek)
Guide to the Volos Museum. Volos. 1972. (Greek)

ENGLISH EDITION

Associate Editor :   John Koliopoulos
Assistant Translators : Elizabeth Jeffreys, Sylvia Moody,
                        Timothy Cullen, Brian de Jongh